H. G. (Heinrich Gottfried) Ollendorff, Eleutario Felice Foresti

Ollendorff's new method of learning to read, write, and speak the Italian language

Adapted for the use of schools and private teachers

H. G. (Heinrich Gottfried) Ollendorff, Eleutario Felice Foresti

Ollendorff's new method of learning to read, write, and speak the Italian language
Adapted for the use of schools and private teachers

ISBN/EAN: 9783741157028

Manufactured in Europe, USA, Canada, Australia, Japa

Cover: Foto ©Andreas Hilbeck / pixelio.de

Manufactured and distributed by brebook publishing software (www.brebook.com)

H. G. (Heinrich Gottfried) Ollendorff, Eleutario Felice Foresti

Ollendorff's new method of learning to read, write, and speak the Italian language

D. Appleton & Company publish, uniform with the Grammar,

A PROGRESSIVE

ITALIAN READER.

Prepared with reference to the American edition of

OLLENDORFF'S ITALIAN GRAMMAR,

WITH NOTES AND A VOCABULARY,

By FELIX FORESTI,

Professor of the Italian Language and Literature in the University of the City of New-York and Columbia College.

OLLENDORFF'S

NEW METHOD

OF LEARNING TO

READ, WRITE, AND SPEAK

THE

ITALIAN LANGUAGE:

ADAPTED FOR

THE USE OF SCHOOLS AND PRIVATE TEACHERS.

WITH ADDITIONS AND CORRECTIONS

By FELIX FORESTI, LL. D.,

PROFESSOR OF THE ITALIAN LANGUAGE AND LITERATURE IN COLUMBIA COLLEGE
AND IN THE UNIVERSITY OF THE CITY OF NEW-YORK.

NEW-YORK:
D. APPLETON & COMPANY, 200 BROADWAY.
PHILADELPHIA:
GEO. S. APPLETON, 148 CHESNUT-STREET.
MDCCCXLVI.

Entered, according to Act of Congress, in the year 1846, by
D. APPLETON & COMPANY,
In the Clerk's Office of the District Court for the Southern District of New-York.

NOTICE.

A Key to the Exercises of this Grammar is published in a separate volume.

PREFACE.

My system of acquiring a living language is founded on the principle, that each question nearly contains the answer which one ought or which one wishes to make to it. The slight difference between the question and the answer is always explained before the question: so that the learner does not find it in the least difficult, either to answer it, or to make similar questions for himself. Again, the question containing the same words as the answer, as soon as the master pronounces it, it strikes the pupil's ear, and is therefore easily reproduced by his speaking organs. This principle is so evident, that it is impossible to open the book without being struck by it.

Neither the professor nor the pupils lose an instant of time. When the professor reads the lesson, the pupil answers; when he examines the lesson written by the pupil he speaks again, and the pupil answers; also when he examines the exercise which the pupil has translated, he speaks and the pupil answers: thus both are, as it were, continually kept in exercise.

The phrases are so arranged that, from the beginning to the end of the method, the pupil's curiosity is excited by the want of a word or an expression: this word or expression is always given in the following lesson, but in such a manner as to create a desire for others that render the phrase still more complete. Hence, from one end of the book to the other, the pupil's attention is continually kept alive, till at last he has acquired a thorough knowledge of the language which he studies.

The numerous and pressing demands for this, the English and Italian part of my Method, make me hope that my endeavours towards facilitating the study of foreign languages in England will on this, as on former occasions, be crowned with success; and should it meet with as extensive favour as all my other publications have found at the hands of the public, I shall be amply rewarded for the many years of labour it has cost me.

67, Rue de Richelieu, Paris.
July 25, 1846.

OSSERVAZIONE

PEL PROFESSORE ITALIANO.

L'AUTORE di questo metodo non ha il minimo dubbio di venir criticato nella scelta delle frasi e dei vocaboli di cui si servì nel corso dell' opera: la lingua italiana, ricca di tante bellezze fornitele da una letteratura di più di sei secoli, offre una scelta d' espressioni qualche volta imbarazzante per lo studioso; ma l' autore, attenendosi a solido appoggio, preferì il Manzoni, fra i moderni scrittori il più unanimemente stimato in fatto di precisione e di buon gusto.

EXPLANATION OF SOME SIGNS USED IN THIS BOOK.

Expressions which vary either in their construction or idiom from the English are marked thus: †

A hand (☞) denotes a rule of syntax or construction.

PREFACE TO THE AMERICAN EDITION.

THE thanks of all who are interested in the cultivation of the Italian language and literature in the United States are justly due to the enterprising publishers of this American edition of Ollendorff's NEW METHOD. Teachers and scholars are now, for the first time, provided with a clear, philosophical, and well-digested Grammar, by means of which a thorough and correct knowledge of Italian may be gained with comparatively little labour, and in a space of time that will be deemed incredibly short by those who have confined themselves to the tedious systems heretofore in use. My experience in teaching long since convinced me that a work of this description was needed in America; and, after a careful perusal of Ollendorff's Method, I do not hesitate to commend it to the public, as in every respect worthy of the great and well-deserved fame of its author.

Scarcely a week passes among us that is not marked by the advent of one or more new books to facilitate the acquisition of foreign languages. Grammars, Manuals, and Treatises, fall rapidly from the press, flutter for a moment, and disappear, like snow-flakes upon a river. Each claims to be superior, in its method of teaching, to all its predecessors, if not absolutely infallible in every important detail. Pedantic vanity and the desire of gain crowd the republic of letters with eager aspirants, the character of whose productions unerringly corresponds to the meanness of the motives that gave them birth. Hence the faint hope of any important improvement at the present day, particularly in those favoured countries where freedom of the press is enjoyed.

Now it will be found upon examination that all the details of these different modes of teaching languages are resolvable into the two following methods:—

1. The *classical, scholastic,* or *scientific* method. In this the practice is almost entirely subordinated to abstract, formal rules, which are prominently brought forward and hold the first place.

2. The *empirical* or *practical* method. Here a commencement is made with the concrete tongue: almost exclusive attention is given to the living practice, the grammatical principles of the language being either postponed or subordinated, or perhaps altogether neglected.

Of the first method I had harsh experience in the happy days of my youth, as did also, probably, all my cotemporaries. We studied, alas! in the old-fashioned colleges. In the beautiful land of my native Italy I applied myself to the Latin, Italian, and French; and oh, what days of vexation and toil; what slow and tedious progress! It could not be otherwise, for the method did violence to every process of nature. It had nothing in it to excite the attention or engage the sympathies of the pupils. In speaking a foreign language we enjoy the pleasing satisfaction of expressing our own thoughts and feelings in a form at once novel and attractive; but the method of which I am speaking can never afford this advantage but in the slightest degree, as a slowly-piled, granite-faced Cyclopean substructure of grammatical rules is considered an indispensable preliminary to any attempt at speaking. And while the student reluctantly submits his understanding and memory to the task of encountering these barren formulas and abstract rules, he is never called to make an attempt to connect the sound of his written, though rarely spoken words, with the objects to which they belong; but instead thereof is obliged to work out the connection in the slowest and most painful manner possible, by means of his mother tongue and a dictionary. To learn foreign languages by such a system in a pleasing, rapid, and practically useful manner, is obviously impossible. Question the hopeful youths in European colleges who are compelled to pursue by this method the study of Greek and Latin—the supposed principal foundations of human knowledge; question them, and you will find that after four or five years of tedious drilling they are unable, in every thing that constitutes a practical knowledge of these languages, to get beyond an awkward and painful crawl. Iron energy and vaulting ambition will now and then spur on a solitary individual; but the many flag, and flagging, in the study of languages, is equivalent to retrogression.

I came to the United States strongly impressed with the absurdity of this classical method. Exiled by long and sorrowful political misfortunes from my native land, and compelled to engage in the humble occupation of teaching my mother tongue, I felt awaken within me my ancient disgust for such a method, and immediately commenced, as my pupils well know, with an oral system resembling that of Professor Ollendorff.

The *empirical* or practical system is in accordance with nature. It may be that experimental philosophy, which, since the days of Bacon and Galileo, has for ever dethroned the ancient jargon of the schools of logic and metaphysics, has also contributed to the improvement of the method of teaching languages; or it may be that the two constant facts, that a child learns so easily its mother tongue, and an adult so readily a foreign language, by residence in a country where it is spoken, could not be forgotten. But whatever may have been the immediate cause of the improvement, it is certain that books of practical oral teaching have supplied a deficiency that was deeply and extensively felt in this country, as is evidenced by the welcome reception and rapid sale of Mr. Arnold's Latin Lessons, and the French and German Grammars of Professor Ollendorff.

Ollendorff's Method possesses the distinctive characteristic of commencing with the concrete practice on the simplest elements. The grammatical forms and syntactical rules are gradually developed by means of this practice, which consists mainly of common and familiar conversations on the most ordinary subjects. In a word, it is the grammar put into a conversational form: it thereby serves its purpose admirably—because,

1. There is a direct appeal to the ear, the natural organ by which a language is acquired.

2. This appeal is made under circumstances in which a direct relation is established between the sound and the thing signified: no painful series of steps is to be taken through the grammar,

dictionary, and the idiom of another language, before the connection is made.

3. The appeal is made with such familiar phrases as cannot fail to excite strongly the attention and engage the sympathies of the scholar.

It is, in short, a very close imitation of the method by which a child learns its mother tongue, or an adult the language of a foreign country in which he resides.

An English and Italian Grammar of this description has been hitherto unknown in this country. Teachers of Italian have been under the necessity of supplying, by their own ingenuity, the deficiency of a well-ordered method. By availing themselves of Ollendorff's Grammar they will therefore lighten their own labour, and at the same time cheer and encourage their pupils, and hasten their progress. By this means they will also pay a well-deserved compliment to those who, by their enterprise in this publication, have expressed a feeling of sympathy and veneration for the language and literature of our beloved Italy.

In order to increase the advantages to be derived from studying Italian by Ollendorff's Method, a Reading Book, with the title, *Crestomazia Italiana*, has also been issued by the publishers of this Grammar. Such a work, as every teacher of languages knows, is always needed by pupils. The *Crestomazia Italiana* contains interesting extracts selected from the best Italian professors of modern times. The most involved passages and the idioms are explained by means of a glossary at the end of each piece, so that the work may serve at the same time for exercises in reading, translating, and committing to memory.

F. F.

Columbia College, September, 1846.

FIRST LESSON.[1]

Lezione Prima.

DEFINITE ARTICLE.

MASCULINE SINGULAR.

(When the word begins with any consonant except *s*, followed by another consonant.)

Nominative,	the.		*Nominativo,*	il.
Genitive,	of the.		*Genitivo,*	del.
Dative,	to the.		*Dativo,*	al.
Accusative,	the.		*Accusativo,*	il.
Ablative,	from the.		*Ablativo,*	dal.

Have you ? | Avete ? Ha Ella ?[2]

---

[1] To Professors.—Each lesson should be dictated to the pupils, who should pronounce each word as soon as dictated. The professor should also exercise his pupils by putting the questions to them in various ways. Each lesson includes three operations: the teacher, in the first place, looks over the exercises of the most attentive of his pupils, putting to them the questions contained in the printed exercises; he then dictates to them the next lesson; and, lastly, puts fresh questions to them on all the preceding lessons. The teacher may divide one lesson into two, or two into three, or even make two into one, according to the degree of intelligence of his pupils.

[2] It is, perhaps through an abuse of civilization that the use of the second person plural *you* has been introduced into modern languages. The Italians, however, go still further, and use, as the pronoun of address, even in speaking to a man, the third person singular feminine, *Ella*, which they begin with a large letter, out of deference for the person they speak to, and to distinguish it from the third person feminine. It relates to *Vostra Signoria* (contracted: *Vossignoria*, abridged *V. S.*, your worship), which is understood.

There are, however, three ways of addressing a person, viz.:—
1. *Dar del tu,* to say thou.
2. *Dar del voi,* to say you.
3. *Dar del Lei,* (*Ella,* nominative,) to speak in the third person.

Well-educated persons use the second person singular *tu,* thou, only in

FIRST LESSON.

Yes, Sir, I have. — Sì, Signore,[2] l'ho.
The. — Il (before s, followed by a consonant lo; and before a vowel, l').
The hat. — Il cappello.
Have you the hat? — Ha Ella il cappello?
Yes, Sir, I have the hat. — Sì, Signore, ho il cappello.
The bread. — Il pane.
The salt. — Il sale.
The soap. — Il sapone.

DEFINITE ARTICLE, MASCULINE SINGULAR,

When the word begins with s, followed by a consonant (or with z).

Nom.	the.	Nom.	lo.
Gen.	of the.	Gen.	dello.
Dat.	to the.	Dat.	allo.
Acc.	the.	Acc.	lo.
Abl.	from the.	Abl.	dallo.

The looking-glass. — Lo specchio.
The boot. — Lo stivale.
The sugar. — Lo zucchero.

speaking to their intimate friends. It is also used in all sorts of poetry. The second person plural, voi, you, is used towards servants, but towards other persons it is a mark of familiarity. The third person, ella, she, is most generally used as the pronoun of address, and you may be sure never to give offence in using it, either towards your superiors or inferiors. But as we must know how to speak to our servants and intimate friends, as well as to other persons, we have in the course of our method made use sometimes of the one, sometimes of the other, and sometimes of both ways of expression, giving, however, always the preference to Ella.

In speaking in the third person singular, Ella is used for the subject or nominative; Lei, La, Le, for the other cases: and in speaking in the same manner to more than one person, the plural of those pronouns must be made use of, viz., Elle or Elleno, for the subject or nominative, and Loro, Le, for the other cases. These pronouns being feminine, the adjective must needs agree with them. Ex.: E' Ella contenta? or simply: è contenta? are you satisfied? (literally: is she satisfied?) Come sta Ella? or simply: Come sta? how do you do? (literally: how is she?) Le parlo, I speak to you (literally: I speak to her). Sono suo (or il di Lei) devotissimo servo, I am your most devoted servant (literally: I am her most devoted servant). Ho veduto il di Lei (or il suo) signor fratello, or else il fratello di V. S., I have seen your brother (literally: I have seen her Mr. brother), i. e. the brother of your worship.

[3] When Signor is followed by a noun, it has no e at the end, except when it begins with s, followed by a consonant. Ex.: il Signor Alessandro, Mr. Alexander; il Signor Conte, Count: il Signor Abate, Abbot; il Signore Stefano, Mr. Stephen.

FIRST LESSON.

Obs. A. When the word begins with a vowel the same article is made use of, with this difference only, that for the letter *o* an apostrophe (') is substituted, as:

Nom.	the.	Nom.	l'.
Gen.	of the.	Gen.	dell'.
Dat.	to the.	Dat.	all'.
Acc.	the.	Acc.	l'.
Abl.	from the.	Abl.	dall'.

| The coat. | L' abito, Il vestito. |
| The man. | L' uomo. |

| My hat. | Il mio cappello. |

Obs. B. In Italian the definite article precedes the possessive pronoun.

Your bread.	Il di Lei pane. Il suo pane.[1]
	Il vostro pane.
Have you my hat?	Ha Ella Il mio cappello?
	Avete Il mio cappello?
Yes, Sir, I have your hat.	Sì, Signore, ho il { di Lei / vostro } cappello.[3]
Have you your bread?	Ha Ella Il di Lei pane?
	Avete Il vostro pane?
Yes, Sir, I have my bread.	Sì, Signore, ho il mio pane.
Have you my sugar?	Ha Ella / Avete } Il mio zucchero?
Yes, Sir, I have your sugar.	Sì, Signore, ho il di Lei zucchero.

Obs. C. When the word beginning with *z*, or with *s*, followed by a consonant, is preceded by another word, the article is not *lo*, but *il*.

| *Which* or *what?* | *Quale?* or *Che?* |

Obs. D. Which or *what* is more generally rendered by *che*, when the noun follows immediately, and by *quale* (plural *quali*) when it is separated from it.[3] But *what* is preferably rendered by *che*, and *which* by *quale* (abridged *qual*).

| Which hat have you? | Qual cappello ha Ella? |
| I have my hat. | Ho il mio cappello. |

---

[1] The first of these expressions is generally used by well-educated persons.
[2] That is to say, *il cappello di V. S.*, the hat of your worship.
[3] Ex: *Ecco due spade: quale volete?* Here are two swords, which will you have? *Quali fra questi libri sono i miei?* Which of these books are mine?

FIRST LESSON.

Which bread have you?	Che pane ha Ella?
I have your bread.	Ho il di Lei pane.
Which soap have you?	Qual sapone ha Ella?
I have my soap.	Ho il mio sapone.
Which coat have you?	Che abito ha Ella?
I have your coat.	Ho il di Lei abito.

EXERCISE.

1.

Have you the bread?—Yes, Sir, I have the bread.—Have you your bread?—I have my bread.—Have you the salt?—I have the salt.—Have you my salt?—I have your salt.—Have you the soap.—Yes, Sir, I have the soap.—Have you your soap?—I have my soap.—Which soap have you?—I have your soap.—Have you the sugar?—I have the sugar.—Have you your sugar?—I have my sugar.—Which sugar have you?—I have your sugar?—Which boot have you?—I have my boot.—Have you my boot?—I have your boot.—Which bread have you?—I have my bread.—Which salt have you?—I have your salt.—Have you the looking-glass?—I have the looking-glass.—Which looking-glass have you?—I have my looking-glass.—Have you my looking-glass?—I have your looking-glass.—Have you the coat?—Yes, Sir, I have the coat.—Which coat have you?—I have my coat.—Have you my coat?—I have your coat.[1]

---

[1] Pupils desirous of making rapid progress may compose a great many phrases, in addition to those we have given them in the exercises; but they must pronounce them aloud, as they write them. They should also make separate lists of such substantives, adjectives, pronouns, and verbs, as they meet with in the course of the lessons, in order to be able to find those words more easily, when they require to refer to them in writing their lessons.

SECOND LESSON.

Lezione Seconda.

It.	Lo (sometimes il).
Have you my hat?	Ha Ella il mio cappello?
Yes, Sir, I have it.	Sì, Signore, l' ho.

Good.	Buono.[1]
Bad.	Cattivo.
Pretty.	Vezzoso, leggiadro, vago, grazioso, bellino.
Handsome, fine or beautiful.	Bello.[2]
Ugly.	Brutto.
Old.	Vecchio.

The cloth.	Il panno.
The wood.	Il legno.[3]
The thread.	Il refe.
The handkerchief.	Il fazzoletto, il moccichino.
The waistcoat.	Il giubbetto.
The cotton.	Il cotone.
The dog.	Il cane.
The horse.	Il cavallo.
Have you the fine dog?	Ha Ella il bel cane?
Yes, Sir, I have it.	Sì, Signore, l' ho.

Not.	Non.
I have not.	Non ho.
I have not the bread.	Non ho il pane.
No, Sir.	No, Signore.
Have you my old hat?	Avete il mio vecchio cappello?
No, Sir, I have it not.	No, Signore, non l' ho.

[1] Where two words happen to finish with the same vowel, we generally suppress, for the sake of euphony, that of the first word, as : *buon panno*, good cloth ; *buon giorno*, good morning ; instead of : *buono panno*, *buono giorno*. But the suppression does not take place when the second word begins with *s* followed by a consonant.

[2] Before a consonant (not before *s* followed by a consonant) *bel* is employed.

[3] Wood for fuel is feminine, and is rendered by *la legna*.

SECOND LESSON.

Which dog have you ?	Qual cane ha Ella ?
I have my pretty dog.	Ho il mio bel cane.
Which handkerchief have you?	Qual fazzoletto ha Ella ?
I have your pretty cotton handkerchief.	Ho il di Lei bel fazzoletto di cotone.

Of. — *Di.*

The cloth coat. { L' abito di panno.
{ Il vestito di panno.

Obs. A. The preposition *di* (like *de* in French) is always put between the name of the thing and the name of the matter of which it is made, and this is in Italian always the last.

The cotton handkerchief.	Il fazzoletto di cotone.
The gun.	Lo schioppo.
The leather.	Il cuoio.
The gold.	L' oro.
The lead.	Il piombo.[*]
The iron.	Il ferro.
The candlestick.	Il candeliere.
The wooden gun.	Lo schioppo di legno.
The leaden horse.	Il cavallo di piombo.
The golden candlestick.	Il candeliere d' oro.

Obs. B. The preposition *di* loses its *i* before a vowel, as may be seen from the example above.

Which gun have you ?	Che schioppo ha Ella ?
I have the iron gun.	Ho lo schioppo di ferro.
Which candlestick have you?	Che candeliere ha Ella ?
I have the fine golden candlestick.	Ho il bel candeliere d' oro.
Have you my fine wooden horse?	Ha Ella il mio bel cavallo di legno?
No, sir, I have it not.	No, Signore, non l' ho.

---

[*] It will not be amiss for those who are acquainted with the French and Latin languages to notice, that whenever the letter *l* is found in those languages after *b, f, p,* it is in Italian changed into *i*. Ex. :—

Lead,	French,	plomb;	Italian,	piombo.
Flower,	..	fleur,	..	fiore.
White,	..	{ blanc,	..	bianco,
		{ blanche,	..	bianca.
Full,	..	plein,	..	pieno.
Temple,	..	temple,	..	tempio.

THIRD LESSON.

EXERCISE.

2.

Have you my fine horse?—Yes, Sir, I have it.—Have you my old waistcoat?—No, Sir, I have it not. Which dog have you?—I have your pretty dog.—Have you my ugly handkerchief?—No, Sir, I have it not.—Have you the good cloth?—Yes, Sir, I have it.—Have you my ugly gun?—No, Sir, I have it not.—Which gun have you? I have your fine gun.—Which candlestick have you?—I have the golden candlestick.—Have you my golden candlestick?—I have not your golden candlestick.—Which boot have you?—I have the leathern boot.—Have you my wooden gun?—No, Sir, I have it not.—Have you the good bread?—I have not the good bread.—Which waistcoat have you?—I have my fine cotton waistcoat.—Which soap have you?—I have my old soap.—Which sugar have you?—I have your good sugar.—Which salt have you?—I have the bad salt.—Which coat have you?—I have my old cloth coat.—Have you my ugly wooden candlestick?—No, Sir, I have it not.—Have you my leaden gun?—No, Sir, I have it not.—Have you my pretty coat?—No, Sir, I have it not.—Which horse have you?—I have your iron horse.—Have you my fine hat? No, Sir, I have it not.

THIRD LESSON.

Lezione Terza.

Something, any thing. | { *Qualche cosa.*
  | { *Alcuna cosa.*
Have you any thing? | { Ha Ella qualche cosa?
  | { Ha Ella alcuna cosa?
I have something. | { Ho qualche cosa.
  | { Ho alcuna cosa.

THIRD LESSON.

Nothing, or not any thing.	{ Non——niente. { Non——nulla.
Nothing, not any thing.	Or simply: Nulla (before the verb).
I have nothing.	{ Non ho niente. { Non ho nulla. { Nulla ho.

Obs. A. Nulla may simply be used for *nothing, not any thing;* but then it stands before the verb.

The wine.	Il vino.
My money (cash).	Il mio denaro (*or* danaro).
The silver (metal).	L'argento.
Of silver.	D'argento
The silver candlestick.	Il candeliere d'argento.
The string.	Il cordone.
The ribbon, the tape.	Il nastro.
The golden ribbon.	Il nastro d'oro.
The button.	Il bottone.
The coffee.	Il caffè.
The cheese.	{ Il cacio. { Il formaggio.

Are you hungry?	{ † Ha Ella fame? { † Avete fame?
I am hungry.	† Ho fame.
I am not hungry.	† Non ho fame.
Are you thirsty?	{ † Ha Ella sete? { † Avete sete?
I am thirsty.	† Ho sete.
I am not thirsty.	† Non ho sete.
Are you sleepy?	{ † Ha Ella sonno? { † Avete sonno?
I am sleepy.	† Ho sonno.
I am not sleepy.	† Non ho sonno.

Something, or any thing good.	Qualche cosa di buono.
Have you any thing good?	{ Ha Ella } qualche cosa di buono? { Avete }
Nothing, or not any thing bad.	{ Non—niente di cattivo. { Non—nulla di cattivo.
	Or simply:
Nothing, or not any thing bad.	Nulla di cattivo (before the verb).
I have nothing good.	{ Non ho niente di buono. { Non ho nulla di buono. { Nulla ho di buono.

THIRD LESSON.

Obs. B. Qualche cosa, non—niente, non—nulla, niente or *nulla, require di* when they are before an adjective.

Have you any thing pretty?	{ Ha Ella } qualche cosa di vago? { Avete }
I have nothing pretty.	{ Non ho niente di vago. { Nulla ho di leggiadro.

What?	{ *Che?* { *Che cosa?* { *Cosa?*
What have you?	{ Che ha Ella? { Che cosa ha Ella? { Cosa ha Ella¹?
What have you good?	Che ha Ella di buono?
I have the good coffee.	Ho del (some) buon caffè.
Are you afraid?	{ † Ha Ella paura? { † Avete paura?
I am afraid.	† Ho paura.
I am not afraid.	† Non ho paura.
Are you warm?	{ Ha Ella caldo? { Avete caldo?
I am warm.	† Ho caldo.
I am not warm.	† Non ho caldo.
Are you cold?	† Ha Ella freddo?
I am not cold.	† Non ho freddo.

EXERCISE.

3.

Have you my good wine?—I have it.—Have you the good gold? —I have it not.—Have you the money?—I have it.—Have you the gold ribbon?—No, Sir, I have it not.—Have you your silver candlestick?—Yes, Sir, I have it.—What have you?—I have the good cheese. I have my cloth coat.—Have you my silver button? —I have it not. Which button have you?—I have your beautiful gold button.—Which string have you?—I have the gold string. —Have you any thing?—I have something.—What have you? —I have the good bread. I have the good sugar.—Have you any thing good?—I have nothing good.—Have you any thing handsome?—I have nothing handsome. I have something ugly. —What have you ugly? I have the ugly dog.—Have you any

¹ The third expression is the least correct, and used only in conversation.

thing pretty?—I have nothing pretty. I have something old.—What have you old?—I have the old cheese.—Are you hungry?—I am hungry.—Are you thirsty?—I am not thirsty.—Are you sleepy?—I am not sleepy.—What have you beautiful?—I have your beautiful dog.—What have you bad?—I have nothing bad.—Are you afraid?—I am not afraid.—Are you cold?—I am cold.—Are you warm?—I am not warm.—Which thread have you?—I have your good thread.—Have you the fine horse?—No, Sir, I have it not.—Which boot have you?—I have my old leather boot.—Which handkerchief have you?—I have your fine cotton handkerchief.—Which waistcoat have you?—I have my pretty cloth waistcoat.—Which gun have you?—I have your fine silver gun.—Have you any thing pretty?—I have nothing pretty.—Have you any thing?—I have nothing.

FOURTH LESSON.

Lezione Quarta.

That.
{ *Quel.*
  Quello.
  Quell'. }

Obs. Quel is used before a consonant, *quello* before *s* followed by a consonant, and *quell'* before a vowel. Ex.:—

That book.	Quel libro.
That looking-glass.	Quello specchio.
That coat.	Quell' abito.

Of the.
{ *Del* (genitive before a consonant).
  Dello (—— before *s*, followed by a consonant).
  Dell' (—— before a vowel). }

Of the dog.   Del cane

FOURTH LESSON.

Of the boot.	Dello stivale.
Of the coat.	Dell' abito.
Of the man.	Dell' uomo.

Of the tailor.	Del sartore.
Of the baker.	Del fornaio.
Of the neighbour.	Del vicino.

That or the one.   Quello.

The neighbour's, or that of the neighbour.	Quello del vicino.
The baker's, or that of the baker.	Quello del fornaio.
The man's, or that of the man.	Quello dell' uomo.

Or.   O.

Have you my book or the neighbour's?	{ Ha Ella } il mio libro, o quello del { Avete } vicino?
I have the neighbour's.	Ho quello del vicino.
Have you my bread or that of the baker?	{ Ha Ella } il mio pane, o quello del { Avete } fornaio?
I have yours.	Ho il di Lei. Ho il vostro. Ho il suo.
I have not the baker's.	Non ho quello del fornaio.

Mine or my own.	{ Nominative. Accusative. }	Il mio.
Of mine.	Genitive.	Del mio.
From mine.	Ablative.	Dal mio.

Yours.	{ Nom. Accus. }	Il vostro. Il suo. Il di Lei.
Of yours.	Gen.	Del vostro. Del suo. Del di Lei.
From yours.	Abl.	Dal vostro. Dal suo. Dal di Lei.

The friend.	L' amico.
Of the friend.	Dell' amico.
That of the friend.	Quello dell' amico.

The stick.	Il bastone.
The thimble.	Il ditale.
The coal.	Il carbone.
My brother.	Mio fratello.

Rule. There is no article before the possessive pronoun in the singular, when it is immediately followed by a noun of quality or kindred.

My dear brother.	Il mio caro fratello.
My brother's, or that of my brother.	Quello di mio fratello.
Your friend's, or that of your friend.	Quello del vostro (di Lei) amico.

FOURTH LESSON.

EXERCISES.

4.

Have you that book ?—No, Sir, I have not.—Which book have you ?—I have that of the neighbour.—Have you my stick, or that of my friend ?—I have that of your friend.—Have you my bread or the baker's ?—I have the baker's. I have not yours.—Have you the neighbour's horse.—No, Sir, I have it not.—Which horse have you ?—I have that of the baker.—Have you your thimble or the tailor's.—I have my own.—Have you the pretty gold string of my dog ?—I have it not.—Which string have you ?—I have my silver string.—Have you my gold button or the tailor's ?—I have not yours ; I have the tailor's.—Have you my brother's coat or yours ?—I have your brother's.—Which coffee have you ?—I have the neighbour's.—Have you your dog or the man's ?—I have the man's.—Have you your friend's money ?—I have it not.—Are you cold ?—I am cold.—Are you afraid ?—I am not afraid.—Are you warm ?—I am not warm.—Are you sleepy ?—I am not sleepy ; I am hungry.—Are you thirsty ?—I am not thirsty.

5.

Have you my coat or the tailor's ?—I have the tailor's.—Have you my gold candlestick or that of the neighbour ?—I have yours.—Have you your coal or mine ?—I have mine.—Have you your cheese or the baker's ?—I have my own.—Which cloth have you ?—I have that of the tailor.—Which boot have you ?—I have my own—Have you the old wood of my brother ?—I have it not.—Which soap have you ?—I have my brother's good soap.—Have you my wooden gun, or that of my brother ?—I have yours.—Which waistcoat have you ?—I have my friend's cloth waistcoat.—Have you your leather boot or mine ?—I have not yours ; I have my own.—What have you ?—I have nothing.—Have you any thing ?—I have nothing.—Have you any thing good ?—I have nothing good.—Have you any thing old ?—I have nothing old.—What have you pretty ?—I have my friend's pretty dog.—Have you my handsome or my ugly stick ?—I have your ugly stick.—Are you hungry or thirsty ?

FIFTH LESSON.

Lezione Quinta.

The merchant.	Il mercante.
Of the shoemaker.	Del calzolaio.
The boy.	Il ragazzo.
The knife.	Il coltello.
The spoon.	Il cucchiaio.

Have you the merchant's stick or yours.	Avete il bastone del mercante, o il vostro ?
Neither.	Non—nè.
Nor.	Nè.
I have neither the merchant's stick nor mine.	Non ho il bastone del mercante, nè il mio.
Are you hungry or thirsty ?	† Avete fame, o sete ?
I am neither hungry nor thirsty.	† Non ho fame, nè sete.
Are you warm or cold ?	† Avete caldo, o freddo ?
I am neither warm nor cold.	† Non ho caldo, nè freddo.
Have you the wine or the bread ?	Avete il vino, o il pane ?
I have neither the wine nor the bread.	Non ho il vino, nè il pane.
I have neither yours nor mine.	Non ho il vostro, nè il mio.
I have neither my thread nor the tailor's.	Non ho il mio refe, nè quello del sartore.

The cork.	Il turacciolo.
The corkscrew.	Il tiraturacciolo.
The umbrella.	L' ombrello, l' ombrella (masc. fem.)
The honey.	Il miele.
The nail.	Il chiodo.
The iron nail.	Il chiodo di ferro.
The hammer.	Il martello.
The carpenter.	Il legnaiuolo.
The Frenchman.	Il Francese.

What have you ? or, What is the matter with you ?	{ Che cosa avete ? { Cosa avete ? { Che avete ?

FIFTH LESSON.

Nothing.

I have nothing, or
Nothing is the matter with me.
Is any thing the matter with you?
Nothing is the matter with me.

Non—niente (niente).	
Non—nulla (nulla).	
† Non ho niente.	
† Non ho nulla.	
† Avete qualche cosa?	
† Non ho niente.	
Non ho nulla (nulla ho).	

EXERCISES.

6.

I am neither hungry nor thirsty.—Have you my boot or the shoemaker's?—I have neither yours nor the shoemaker's.—Have you your knife or the boy's?—I have neither mine nor the boy's.—Which knife have you?—I have that of the merchant.—Have you my spoon or the merchant's?—I have neither yours nor the merchant's; I have my own.—Have you the honey or the wine?—I have neither the honey nor the wine.—Have you your thimble or the tailor's?—I have neither mine nor the tailor's.—Have you your corkscrew or mine?—I have neither yours nor mine; I have the merchant's.—Which cork have you?—I have the neighbour's.—Have you the iron or the silver nail?—I have neither the iron nor the silver nail; I have the golden nail.—Are you warm or cold?—I am neither warm nor cold; I am sleepy.—Are you afraid?—I am not afraid.—Have you my hammer or the carpenter's?—I have neither yours nor the carpenter's.—Which nail have you?—I have the iron nail.—Which hammer have you?—I have the wooden hammer of the carpenter.—Have you any thing?—I have something.—What have you?—I have something fine.—What have you fine?—I have the Frenchman's fine umbrella.—Have you the cotton or the thread tape?—I have neither the cotton nor the thread tape.

7.

Have you your gun or mine?—I have neither yours nor mine.—Which gun have you?—I have my friend's.—Have you my cotton handkerchief or that of my brother?—I have neither yours nor your brother's.—Which string have you?—I have my neighbour's thread string.—Have you the book of the Frenchman or that of the merchant?—I have neither the Frenchman's nor the merchant's.—Which book have you?—I have my own.—What is the matter with you?—Nothing.—Is any thing the matter with you?—Nothing is the matter with me.—Are you cold?—I am not cold; I am warm.—Have you the cloth or the cotton?—I have neither the cloth nor the cotton.—Have you any thing good or bad? —I have neither any thing good nor bad.—What have you?—I have nothing.

SIXTH LESSON.

Lezione Sesta.

The beef, the ox.	Il manzo, il bue.
The biscuit.	Il biscotto.
Of the captain.	Del capitano.
Of the cook.	Del cuoco.

Have I?	Ho Io?
You have.	Avete. Ella ha.
You have not.	Non avete. Ella non ha.
Am I hungry?	† Ho fame Io?
You are hungry,	† Avete fame. Ella ha fame.
You are not hungry.	† Non avete fame. Ella non ha fame.
Am I afraid?	† Ho paura Io?
You are afraid.	† Avete paura. Ella ha paura.
You are not afraid.	† Non avete paura. Ella non ha paura.
Am I ashamed?	† Ho vergogna Io?
You are not ashamed.	† Non avete vergogna.
	† Ella non ha vergogna.
Are you ashamed?	† Ha Ella vergogna?
	† Avete vergogna.
I am ashamed.	† Ho vergogna.
Am I wrong?	† Ho torto Io?
You are wrong.	† Avete torto. Ella ha torto.
You are not wrong.	† Ella non ha torto.
	† Non avete torto.
Am I right?	† Ho Io ragione?
You are right.	† Ella ha ragione.
	† Avete ragione.
You are not right.	† Ella non ha ragione.
	† Non avete ragione.

16   SIXTH LESSON.

Have I the nail?	Ho io il chiodo?
You have it.	L' avete. Ella lo ha (lo ha or l' ha).
You have it not.	Non l' avete. Ella non lo ha (or non l' ha).

Have I any thing good?	Ho io qualche cosa di buono?
You have nothing good.	Ella non ha } niente (nulla) di buono. Non avete } no.
You have neither any thing good nor bad.	Ella non ha } niente di buono nè di Non avete } cattivo.

What have I?	Che ho io? Che cosa ho io?
Have I the carpenter's hammer?	Ho io il martello del legnaiuolo?
You have it not.	Non l' avete. Non l' ha.
Have you it?	L' avete voi? Lo ha Ella?
I have it not.	Non l' ho.
Have I it?	L' ho io?

The butter.	Il burro, il butirro.
The mutton.	Il castrato (montone).
The milk.	Il latte.
The penknife.	Il temperino.

Which one?	*Quale?*
That of the captain, or the captain's.	Quello del capitano.
That of the cook, or the cook's.	Quello del cuoco.
The fine one.	Il bello.
The ugly one.	Il brutto.

Am I right or wrong?	† Ho ragione, o torto?
You are neither right nor wrong.	† Ella non ha nè ragione, nè torto. † Non avete nè ragione, nè torto.
You are neither hungry nor thirsty.	† Ella non ha nè fame, nè sete. † Non avete nè fame, nè sete.
You are neither afraid nor ashamed.	† Ella non ha nè paura, nè vergogna. † Non avete nè paura, nè vergogna.

Have I your butter or mine?	Ho il vostro butirro, o il mio?
You have neither yours nor mine.	Ella non ha nè il di Lei, nè il mio. Non avete nè il vostro, nè il mio.

EXERCISES.

8.

I have neither the baker's dog nor that of my friend.—Are you ashamed?—I am not ashamed.—Are you afraid or ashamed?—I

am neither afraid nor ashamed.—Have you my knife?—Which?
—The fine one.—Have you my beef or the cook's?—I have
neither yours nor the cook's.—Which have you?—I have that of
the captain.—Have I your biscuit?—You have it not.—Am I
hungry or thirsty?—You are neither hungry nor thirsty.—Am I
warm or cold?—You are neither warm nor cold.—Am I afraid?
—You are not afraid. You are neither afraid nor ashamed.—
Have I any thing good?—You have nothing good.—What have
I?—You have nothing.—Which penknife have I?—You have that
of the Frenchman.—Have I your thimble or that of the tailor?—
You have neither mine nor that of the tailor.—Which one have I?
—You have your friend's.—Which umbrella have I?—You have
mine.—Have I the baker's good bread?—You have it not.—
Which money have I?—You have your own.—Have you my iron
gun?—I have it not.—Have I it?—You have it.—Have I your
mutton or the cook's?—You have neither mine nor the cook's.—
Have I your knife?—You have it not. Have you it?—I have it.
—Which biscuit have I?—You have that of the captain.—Which
cloth have I?—You have the merchant's.—Have you my coffee
or that of my boy?—I have that of your good boy.—Have you
your cork or mine?—I have neither yours nor mine.—What have
you?—I have my brother's good candlestick.

0.

Am I right?—You are right.—Am I wrong?—You are not
wrong.—Am I right or wrong?—You are neither right nor wrong;
you are afraid.—You are not sleepy.—You are neither warm nor
cold.—Have I the good coffee or the good sugar?—You have
neither the good coffee nor the good sugar.—Have I any thing
good or bad?—You have neither any thing good nor bad.—What
have I?—You have nothing.—What have I pretty?—You have my
friend's pretty dog.—Which butter have I?—You have that of
your cook.—Have I your corkscrew or the merchant's?—You
have neither mine nor the merchant's.—Which milk have you?
—I have that of the Frenchman.—Which penknife have you?—
I have the silver penknife of my neighbour.—Which have I?—
You have that of the old baker.—Which have you?—I have that
of my old tailor.—What is the matter with you?—I am afraid.—
Have I any thing?—You have nothing.

SEVENTH LESSON.

Lezione Settima.

Who?	*Chi?*
Who has?	Chi ha?
Who has the knife?	Chi ha il coltello?
The man has the knife.	L' uomo ha il coltello.
The man has not the knife.	L' uomo non ha il coltello.
Who has it?	Chi lo ha?
The boy has it.	Lo ha il ragazzo.
The boy has it not.	Il ragazzo non l' ha.

The chicken.	Il pollastro (il pollo).
The chest, the trunk.	Il baule (il forziere).
The bag, the sack.	Il sacco.
The ship.	Il bastimento.
The young man.	Il giovane (il giovine).
The youth.	L' adolescente (il giovinetto).

He.	*Egli* (for persons).
	Esso (for persons and for things).
	Ei or *e'* (also for persons).

Obs. A. Egli is used for persons, *esso* for persons and for things, and *ei* or *e'* for persons, but not generally before a vowel or before *s* followed by a consonant.

He has.	Egli ha (esso ha, egli à [1]).
He has the chest.	Egli ha il baule.
He has not the chest.	Ei (e') non ha il baule.
He has it.	Egli (esso) l' ha.
	Ei (e') l' ha.
He has it not.	Ei (e') non l' ha.

---

[1] The letter *h* is never pronounced in Italian. What proves this is, that it may be entirely omitted, and a grave accent be put in its stead on the three first persons singular and third person plural of the verb *avere*, to have; and instead of *ho*, I have; *hai*, thou hast; *ha*, he (she) has; *hanno*, they have, we may write: *à, ài, à, ànno.* This kind of orthography has been followed by *Metastasio*, but is not generally approved.

SEVENTH LESSON.

Has he?	{ Ha egli? } Ha esso? (Ha?
Has he the knife?	Ha egli il coltello?
Has the man?	Ha l' uomo?
Has the friend?	Ha l' amico?
Has the baker?	Ha il fornajo?
Has the young man?	Ha il giovane?

The Englishman.	L' Inglese.

Is the man hungry?	† Ha fame l' uomo?
He is hungry.	† Ha fame.
He is not hungry.	† Non ha fame.
He is neither hungry nor thirsty.	† Non ha nè fame, nè sete.
Is your brother warm or cold?	† Ha caldo o freddo il di Lei fratello?
Is the man afraid or ashamed?	† Ha paura o vergogna l' uomo?
Is the man right or wrong?	† Ha ragione o torto l' uomo?
Has the boy the hammer of the carpenter?	Ha il ragazzo il martello del legnaiuolo?
He has it.	L' ha.
He has it not.	Non l' ha.
Has the baker it?	L' ha il fornajo?
What has my friend?	Che ha il mio amico?

The rice.	Il riso.
The countryman, the peasant.	Il contadino, il paesano, il rustico.
The servant.	Il servitore, il servo, il domestico.

His or her penknife.	Il suo temperino.
His or her dog.	Il suo cane.
The bird.	L' uccello.
His or her foot.	Il suo piede (piè).
His or her eye.	Il suo occhio.
His money.	Il suo denaro.
The tea.	Il tè.

His, her, hers.	*Il suo.*
Has the servant his trunk or mine?	Ha il servitore il suo forziere, o il mio?
He has his own.	Ha il suo (ha il suo proprio).

Somebody or *any body,* *some one* or *any one* (indefinite pronouns).	*Qualcheduno, qualcuno,* or *alcuno, taluno.*
Has any body my book?	Ha qualcuno il mio libro?
Somebody has it.	Qualcheduno l' ha.
Who has my stick?	Chi ha il mio bastone?

SEVENTH LESSON.

No one, nobody, not any body.	*Nessuno, niuno, veruno.*
Nobody has your stick.	Nessuno ha il vostro bastone.
Nobody has it.	Nessuno l' ha. Niuno l' ha. Veruno l' ha.

Obs. B. In using *alcuno* for *no one, nobody, not any body*, it must always be accompanied by *non;* but *nessuno, niuno*, and *veruno*, require *non* only when they follow the verb.

Who has your gun?	Chi ha il di Lei schioppo?
	Alcuno non l' ha. Non l' ha nessuno.
Nobody has it.	Non l' ha niuno. Non l' ha veruno. Non l' ha alcuno. Nessuno l' ha.

EXERCISES.

10.

Who has my trunk?—The boy has it.—Is he thirsty or hungry?—He is neither thirsty nor hungry.—Has the man the chicken?—He has it.—Who has my waistcoat?—The young man has it.—Has the young man my ship?—The young man has it not.—Who has it?—The captain has it.—What has the youth?—He has the fine chicken.—Has he the knife?—He has it not.—Is he afraid?—He is not afraid.—Is he afraid or ashamed?—He is neither afraid nor ashamed.—Is the man right or wrong?—He is neither right nor wrong.—Is he warm or cold?—He is neither warm nor cold.—Who has the countryman's rice?—My servant has it.—Has your servant my penknife or his?—He has neither yours nor his.—Which penknife has he?—He has that of his neighbour?—Who has my old boot?—Your shoemaker has it.—What has your friend?—He has his good money.—Has he my gold?—He has it not.—Who has it?—The baker has it.—Has the baker my bird or his?—He has his.—Who has mine?—The carpenter has it.—Who is cold?—Nobody is cold.—Is any body warm?—Nobody is warm.—Has any body my chicken?—Nobody has it.—Has your servant your waistcoat or mine?—He has neither yours nor mine.—Which has he?—He has his own.

SEVENTH LESSON.

11.

Has any one my gun?—No one has it.—Has the youth my book?—He has it not.—What has he?—He has nothing.—Has he the hammer or the nail?—He has neither the hammer nor the nail.—Has he my umbrella or my stick?—He has neither your umbrella nor your stick.—Has he my coffee or my sugar?—He has neither your coffee nor your sugar; he has your honey.— Has the boy my brother's biscuit or that of the Frenchman?— He has neither that of your brother nor that of the Frenchman; he has his own.—Have I your bag or that of your friend?—You have neither mine nor my friend's; you have your own.—Who has the peasant's bag?—The good baker has it.—Who is afraid? —The tailor's boy is afraid.—Is he sleepy?—He is not sleepy.— Is he cold or hungry?—He is neither cold nor hungry.—What is the matter with him?—Nothing.—Has the peasant my money? —He has it not.—Has the captain (got) it?—He has it not?— Who has it?—Nobody has it.—Has your neighbour any thing good?—He has nothing good.—What has he ugly?—He has nothing ugly.—Has he any thing?—He has nothing.

12.

Has the merchant my cloth or his?—He has neither yours nor his.—Which cloth has he?—He has that of my brother.—Which thimble has the tailor?—He has his own.—Has your brother his wine or the neighbour's?—He has neither his nor the neighbour's. —Which wine has he?—He has his own.—Has any body my gold ribbon?—Nobody has it.—Who has my silver string?— Your good boy has it.—Has he my wooden or my leaden horse? —He has neither your wooden nor your leaden horse; he has his friend's leathern horse.—Is any body wrong?—Nobody is wrong. —Who has the Frenchman's good honey?—The merchant has it. —Has he it?—Yes, Sir, he has it.—Are you afraid or ashamed? —I am neither afraid nor ashamed.—Has your cook his mutton? —He has it.—Have you my bread or my cheese?—I have neither your bread nor your cheese.—Have I your salt or your butter?— You have neither my salt nor my butter.—What have I?—You have your mutton.—Has any body my gold button?—No one has it.—Who has the tea?—Which?—Mine.—Your servant has it. —Which tea has the Englishman?—He has his own.

EIGHTH LESSON.

Lezione Ottava.

The sailor.	Il marinaio.
The tree.	L' albero.
His looking-glass.	Il suo specchio.
His mattress.	Il suo materasso.
The stranger (the foreigner).	Lo straniero, lo straniere.
The foreigner.	Il forestiero.
The garden.	Il giardino.
The glove.	Il guanto.

This or that ox.	Questo, o quel bue.
This or that hay.	Questo, o quel fieno.
This or that boot.	Questo, o quello stivale.

This or that friend.	Questo, o quell' amico.
This or that man.	Questo, o quell' uomo.
This or that ass.	Questo, o quell' asino.

This book.	Questo libro (cotesto libro).
That book.	Quel libro.

Have you this or that book?	Ha Ella questo libro o quello?
I have this one, I have not that one.	Ho questo, non ho quello.

DECLENSION OF THE DEMONSTRATIVE PRONOUNS.

Questo (cotesto), quello.

MASCULINE SINGULAR.

Nom. Acc. }	Questo,	this.	Quello,	that.
Gen.	Di questo,	of this.	Di quello,	of that.
Dat.	A questo,	to this.	A quello,	to that.
Abl.	Da questo,	from this.	Da quello,	from that.

Obs. A. Demonstrative pronouns are never preceded by an article, prepositions being the words employed before them.

EIGHTH LESSON. 23

| This one. | Questo (cotesto). |
| That one. | Quello. |

Obs. B. **Questo** designates the object near the person who speaks, *cotesto* the object distant from the person who speaks, and near the person spoken to; but *quello* designates at the same time the object distant from both the person who speaks and that spoken to.

Have I this or that?	Ho io questo o quello?
You have this, you have not that.	Ella ha questo, non quello.
Has the man this hat or that?	Ha l' uomo questo cappello, o quello?

But.	*Ma.*
He has not this, but that.	Non ha questo, ma quello.
He has this, but not that.	Ha questo, ma non quello.

The note, the billet, or the ticket.	Il biglietto (viglietto).
The granary.	Il granajo.
The corn.	Il grano.

Have you this note or that?	Ha Ella questo biglietto, o quello?
I have not this, but that.	Non ho questo, ma ho quello.
I have this, but not that.	Ho questo, ma non ho quello.
Has the neighbour this looking-glass or that?	Ha il vicino questo specchio, o quello?
He has this, but not that.	Ha questo, ma non ha quello.

| The horse-shoe. | Il ferro da cavallo. |

Obs. C. The preposition *da* is made use of between two substantives, when the latter expresses the use of the former.

The wine-bottle.	Il fiasco* da vino.
The oil-bottle.	Il fiasco da olio.
The milk-pot.	Il vaso da latte.
The bottle of wine.	Il fiasco di vino.
The bottle, the oil.	Il fiasco, l' olio.

That or which (relative pronoun).	Che, Il quale.
Have you the note which my brother has?	Ha Ella il biglietto che ha mio fratello?
I have not the note which your brother has?	Non ho il biglietto che ha il di Lei fratello.
Have you the horse which I have?	Ha Ella il cavallo che io ho?
I have the horse which you have.	Ho il cavallo che ha V. S, o che voi avete.

[* N. B. The word *battiglia* is used also instead of *fiasco*.]

That which, the one which.	{ *Quel che,* { *Quello che.*
I have not that which you have.	Non ho quello che ha Ella.
I have not that which he has.	Non ho quello che egli ha.
Have I the glove which you have?	Ho io il guanto che ha Vossignoria?
You have not the one which I have.	Non avete quello che ho io.

EXERCISES.

13.

Which hay has the stranger?—He has that of the peasant.—Has the sailor my looking-glass?—He has it not.—Have you this glove or that?—I have this.—Have you the hay of my garden or that of yours?—I have neither that of your garden nor that of mine, but I have that of the stranger.—Which glove have you?—I have that of the sailor.—Have you his mattrass?—I have it.—Which thread has the sailor?—He has his own.—Who has my good note?—This man has it.—Who has that gun?—Your friend has it.—Have you the corn of your granary or that of mine?—I have neither that of your granary nor that of mine, but I have that of my merchant.—Who has my glove?—That servant has it.—What has your servant?—He has the tree of this garden.—Has he that man's book?—He has not the book of that man, but he has that of this boy.—Has the peasant this or that ox?—He has neither this nor that, but he has the one which his boy has.—Has this ass his hay or that of the horse?—He has neither his nor that of the horse.—Which horse has this peasant?—He has that of your neighbour.—Have I your note or his?—You have neither mine nor his, but you have that of your friend.—Have you this horse's hay?—I have not his hay, but his shoe.—Has your brother my note or his?—He has neither yours nor his own, but he has the sailor's.—Has the foreigner my bird or his own?—He has that of the captain.—Have you the tree of this garden?—I have it not.—Are you hungry or thirsty?—I am neither hungry nor thirsty, but I am sleepy.

14.

Has the sailor this bird or that?—He has not this but that.—Has your servant this stick or that?—He has this, but not that.—

Has your cook this chicken or that?—He has neither this nor that, but he has that of his neighbour.—Am I right or wrong?—You are neither right nor wrong, but your good boy is wrong.—Have I this knife or that?—You have neither this nor that.—What have I?—You have nothing good, but you have something bad.—Have you the chest which I have?—I have not that which you have.—Which horse have you?—I have the one which your brother has.—Have you the ass which my friend has?—I have not that which he has, but I have that which you have.—Has your friend the looking-glass which you have or that which I have?—He has neither that which you have nor that which I have, but he has his own.

15.

Which bag has the peasant?—He has the one which his boy has.—Have I your golden or your silver candlestick?—You have neither my golden nor my silver candlestick, but you have my iron candlestick.—Have you my waistcoat or that of the tailor?—I have neither yours nor that of the tailor.—Which have you?—I have that which my friend has.—Are you cold or warm?—I am neither cold nor warm, but I am thirsty.—Is your friend afraid or ashamed?—He is neither afraid nor ashamed, but he is sleepy.—Who is wrong?—Your friend is wrong.—Has any one my umbrella?—No one has it.—Is any one ashamed?—No one is ashamed, but my friend is hungry.—Has the captain the ship which you have or that which I have?—He has neither that which you have, nor that which I have.—Which has he?—He has that of his friend.—Is he right or wrong?—He is neither right nor wrong.—Has the Frenchman any thing good or bad?—He has neither any thing good nor bad, but he has something pretty.—What has he pretty?—He has the pretty looking-glass.—Has he the good biscuit?—He has it not, but his neighbour has it.—Has the Englishman the wine-bottle?—He has the wine-bottle, but he has not the bottle of wine.—Which shoe (*il ferro*) has your baker?—He has that of the horse.—Has he my oil-bottle?—He has not your oil bottle, but he has your milk-pot.

NINTH LESSON.

Lezione Nona.

DECLENSION OF THE DEFINITE ARTICLE MASCULINE IN THE PLURAL

(when the word begins with a consonant, except *s* followed by another consonant).

PLURAL.		PLURALE. *Mascolino.*	
Nom.	the.	Nom.	I.
Gen.	of the.	Gen.	Dei or de'.
Dat.	to the.	Dat.	Ai or a'.
Acc.	the.	Acc.	I.
Abl.	from the.	Abl.	Dai or da'.

THE FORMATION OF THE PLURAL.

Rule. Masculine nouns and adjectives, whatever may be their ending, change it in the plural into *i*. Ex.

The hats.	I cappelli.
The books.	I libri.
The good books.	I buoni libri.
Of the books.	Dei libri.
The sticks.	I bastoni.
Of the sticks.	Dei bastoni.
The thimbles.	I ditali.
The dogs.	I cani.
The brothers.	I fratelli.
The merchants.	I mercanti.
The horses.	I cavalli.
The neighbours.	I vicini.
The good neighbours.	I buoni vicini.
Of the neighbours.	Dei vicini.
The peasants.	I rustici, contadini.
The servants.	I domestici, i servi.

NINTH LESSON.

DECLENSION OF THE DEFINITE ARTICLE MASCULINE IN THE PLURAL
(when the word begins with s followed by a consonant, or with a vowel).

PLURAL.		PLURALE MASCOLINO.	
Nom.	the.	Nom.	gli
Gen.	of the.	Gen.	degli.
Dat.	to the.	Dat.	agli.
Acc.	the.	Acc.	gli.
Abl.	from the.	Abl.	dagli.

The guns.	Gli schioppi.
The boots.	Gli stivali.
The good boots.	I buoni stivali.
The friends.	Gli amici.
The umbrellas.	Gli ombrelli, le ombrelle.
The coats.	Gli abiti, i vestiti, le vestimenta.

Obs. A. When the word begins with *i*, an apostrophe is substituted in the article *gli*, for the letter *i*, thus:

Nom. } the Englishmen.	Nom. } Gl' Inglesi.
Acc. }	Acc. }
Gen. of the }	Gen. Degl' Inglesi.
Dat. to the } Englishmen.	Dat. Agl' Inglesi.
Abl. from the }	Abl. Dagl' Inglesi.

FIRST EXCEPTION.—All nouns ending in the singular in *e*, monosyllables, and nouns having the accent on the last vowel, as also words ending in *ie*, do not change their termination in the plural. Ex.

Sing.	Plur.	Singulare.	Plurale.
The king.	The kings.	Il re.	I re.
The foot.	The feet.	Il piè.	I piè.
The tea.	Teas.	Il tè.	I tè.
The coffee.	Coffees.	Il caffè.	I caffè.
The bailiff.	The bailiffs.	Il podestà.	I podestà.

SECOND EXCEPTION.—Nouns ending in *co* and *go*, generally insert in the plural the letter *h*. Ex.

The cook.	The cooks.	Il cuoco.	I cuochi.
The bag.	The bags.	Il sacco.	I sacchi.
The inn.	The inns.	L'albergo.	Gli alberghi.
The dialogue.	The dialogues.	Il dialogo.	I dialoghi.
The German.	The Germans.	Il Tedesco.	I Tedeschi.
The Pole.	The Poles.	Il Polacco.	I Polacchi.
The fire.	The fires.	Il fuoco.	I fuochi.

NINTH LESSON.

THIRD EXCEPTION.—Nouns ending in *io*, preceded by a vowel, lose the letter *o* in the plural, and those in which *io* is preceded by a consonant, change in the plural *io* into *ii*.[1] Ex.

The baker.	The bakers.	Il fornaio.	I fornai.
The spoon.	The spoons.	Il cucchiaio.	I cucchiai.
The shoemaker.	The shoemakers.	Il calzolaio.	I calzolai.
The bookseller.	The booksellers.	Il libraio.	I librai.
The uncle.	The uncles.	Lo zio.	Gli zii.
The temple.	The temples.	Il tempio.	I templi.
The principle.	The principles.	Il principio.	I principii.

Obs. B. When, however, the final syllable *io* is preceded by *c, ch, g, gl,* it may in the plural be changed merely into *i.* Ex.

The looking-glass.	The looking-glasses.	Lo specchio.	Gli specchi.
The eye.	The eyes.	L' occhio.	Gli occhi.
The cheese.	The cheeses.	Il formaggio.	I formaggi.
The son.	The sons.	Il figlio.	I figli.

FOURTH EXCEPTION.—The following few words form their plural quite irregularly, viz.

The man.	The men.	L' uomo.	Gli uomini.
God.	The gods.	Dio.	Gli[2] Dei.
The ox.	The oxen.	I bue.	I buoi.

Obs. There are some masculine nouns terminated in *o*, which in the plural take the feminine termination *a*, together with the feminine article,[3] and others also in *o*, which in the plural may take either the masculine article and termination, or the feminine; we shall speak of them hereafter.[4]

---

[1] Formerly these nouns took *j* in the plural, but the generality of modern authors have entirely rejected this letter from the alphabet. The reason is that it is pronounced like *i*, and whenever it occurs in the formation of the plural, two *i*'s are substituted for it.

[2] *Dio* is the only word in Italian beginning with a consonant, which in the plural takes the article *gli* instead of *i*.

[3] Nouns terminated in *a, i, u*, with a few exceptions (of which hereafter), and when they do not represent male individuals, or dignities, or professions belonging to male individuals, are feminine; all others are generally masculine.

[4] The principal are:—

Il centinaio,	the hundred.	*Plur.*	Le centinaia.
Il ciglio,	the eye-lid.		Le ciglia.
Il migliaio,	the thousand.		Le migliaia.
Il miglio,	the mile.		Le miglia.
Il moggio,	a measure.		Le moggia.
Lo staio,	the bushel.		Le staia.
Il paio,	the pair.		Le paia.
L' uovo,	the egg.		Le uova.

NINTH LESSON.

My looking-glasses.	I miei specchi.
Your looking-glasses.	I vostri specchi.
Have you my small looking-glasses?	Ha Ella i miei piccoli[a] specchi?
I have not your small looking-glasses, but I have your large looking-glasses.	Non ho i di Lei piccoli, ma i di Lei grandi specchi. Non ho i di Lei piccoli specchi, ma ho bensì, i grandi.

Great, large.	Grande.
Little, small.	Piccolo.

Obs. C. Grande, great, loses the syllable *de* before a consonant (not before *s* followed by a consonant), and for the letter *e* before a vowel an apostrophe is substituted. Before a noun in the plural, beginning with a vowel, *grandi* must be used.

The large hat.	Il gran cappello.
The large coat.	Il grand' abito.

Masculino.

	Singolare.	Plurale.
My or mine.	Il mio.	I miei.
Your—yours.	Il vostro.	I vostri.
His.	Il suo.	I suoi[b].
Our—ours.	Il nostro.	I nostri.
Your—yours.	Il vostro.	I vostri.
Their—theirs.	Il loro.	I loro.

His books, looking-glasses, coats.	I suoi libri, specchi, abiti.
Our books, looking-glasses, coats.	I nostri libri, specchi, abiti.
Their books, looking-glasses, coats.	I loro libri, specchi, abiti.
Which books, looking-glasses, coats?	Quali (qual, qua'), libri, specchi, abiti?
Which?	Quali (qual, qua')?
These or those books.	Quei (or que') libri.
These or those coats.	Quegli abiti.
These or those looking-glasses.	Quegli specchi.

[a] There is in Italian that particularity, that the signification of nouns can be augmented or diminished by the addition of certain syllables called augmentatives and diminutives (of which hereafter; see Lesson X.). But in the present instance we cannot make use of them, on account of the contradictory answer.

[b] To avoid ambiguity, we may, in the third person, *di lui,* instead of *il suo, i suoi.* Ex.: Paul loves Peter and his children, *Paolo ama Pietro e i di lui figliuoli,* or *i figliuoli di lui;* for in using *i suoi* it might convey the meaning that Paul loves his own children.

NINTH LESSON.

Which books have you?
I have the fine books of your good neighbours.
Have I his small boots?
You have not his small boots, but you have his large boots.
Which looking-glasses have I?
You have the pretty looking-glasses of your brothers.
Have you the large hammers of the carpenters?
I have not their large hammers, but their large nails.
Has your brother my wooden guns?

He has not your wooden guns.
Which has he?

Have you the Frenchmen's fine umbrellas?
I have not their fine umbrellas, but I have their fine sticks.

Qual libri avete voi? (ha Ella)?
Ho i bei libri dei vostri buoni vicini.
Ho lo i suoi piccoli stivali?
Ella non ha i suoi piccoli stivali, ma ha i suoi stivali grandi.
Quali specchi ho io?
Ella ha i leggiadri specchi dei di Lei fratelli.
Ha Ella i grandi martelli dei legnaiuoli?
Non ho i loro grandi martelli, ma ho i loro gran chiodi.
Ha il di Lei fratello i miei schioppi di legno?
Egli non ha i di Lei schioppi di legno.
Quali ha?

Ha Ella i begli ombrelli dei Francesi?
Non ho i loro begli ombrelli, ma ho i loro bei bastoni.

    My oxen.
    Their asses.
    His horses.
    Of my gardens.
    Of your horses.
Have you the trees of my gardens?
I have not the trees of your gardens.
    Of my pretty gardens.
    Of my fine horses.
I have not your cotton handkerchiefs, but I have your cloth coats.
    The bread, the loaves.

I miei buoi.
I loro asini.
I suoi cavalli.
Dei miei giardini.
Dei $\begin{Bmatrix} \text{di Lei} \\ \text{vostri} \end{Bmatrix}$ cavalli.
Ha Ella gli alberi dei miei giardini?
Non ho gli alberi dei di Lei giardini.
Dei miei leggiadri giardini.
De' miei bei cavalli.
Non ho i vostri fazzoletti di cotone, ma ho i vostri abiti di panno.
Il pane, i pani.

EXERCISES.
16.

Have you the gloves?—Yes, Sir, I have the gloves.—Have you my gloves?—No, Sir, I have not your gloves.—Have I your looking-glasses?—You have my looking-glasses.—Have I your pretty handkerchiefs?—You have not my pretty handkerchiefs.—Which handkerchiefs have I?—You have the pretty handkerchiefs of your friends.—Has the foreigner our good penknives?—He has not our good penknives, but our good ships.—Who has our fine horses?—Nobody has your fine horses, but somebody has your fine oxen.—Has your neighbour the trees of my gardens?—He has not the trees of my gardens, but he has your handsome notes.—Have you the horses' hay?—I have not their hay, but their shoes (*i loro ferri*).—Has your tailor my pretty golden buttons?—He has not your pretty golden buttons, but your pretty golden threads (*fili*).—What has the sailor?—He has his fine ships.—Has he my sticks or my guns?—He has neither your sticks nor your guns.—Who has the tailor's good waistcoats?—Nobody has his waistcoats, but somebody has his silver buttons.—Has the Frenchman's boy my good umbrellas?—He has not your good umbrellas, but your good knives.—Has the shoemaker my leathern boots?—He has your leathern boots.—What has the captain?—He has his good sailors.—What has our bookseller?—He has his good books.—Which books have you?—I have the fine books of our booksellers.

17.

Which mattrasses has the sailor?—He has the good mattrasses of his captain.—Which gardens has the Frenchman?—He has the gardens of the English.—Which servants has the Englishman?—He has the servants of the French.—What has your boy? He has his pretty birds.—What has the merchant?—He has our pretty chests.—What has the baker?—He has our fine asses.—Has he our nails or our hammers?—He has neither our nails nor our hammers, but he has our good loaves.—Has the carpenter his iron hammers?—He has not his iron hammers, but his iron nails.—Which biscuits has the baker?—He has the biscuits of his friends.—Has our friend our fine penknives?—He has not our fine penknives.—Which has he?—He has the small penknives of his merchants.—Which looking-glasses has your servant?—He has the looking-glasses of his good merchants.—Has your friend the small knives of our merchants?—He has not their small knives, but their golden candlesticks.—Have you these notes?—I have not these notes, but these silver knives.—Has the man this or that note?—He has neither this nor that.—Has he your book or your friend's?—He has neither mine nor my friend's; he has his own.—Has your brother the wine which I have, or that which you have?—He has neither that which you have nor that which I have.—Which wine has he?—He has that of his merchants.—Have you the bag which my servant has?—I have not the bag which your servant has.—Have you the chicken which my cook has, or that which the peasant has?—I have neither that which your cook has, nor that which the peasant has.—Is the peasant cold or warm?—He is neither cold nor warm.

TENTH LESSON.

Lezione Decima.

OF AUGMENTATIVES.

There are in Italian two sorts of augmentatives, viz.

1. In ONE, to express any thing great and large. Ex.

The hat	.. the large hat.	Il cappello	.. il cappellone.
The book	.. the large book.	Il libro	.. il librone.
The hall	.. the large hall.	La sala	.. il salone.
The house	.. the large house.	La casa	.. il casone.

Obs. A. The augmentatives in one are always masculine, though the radicals be feminine.

The door	.. the { large door. / gate. }	La porta	.. il portone.
The chamber	.. the large chamber.	La camera	.. il camerone.

2. In ACCIO for the masculine, and ACCIA for the feminine. These designate something bad or contemptible. Ex.

The hat	.. the large ugly hat.	Il cappello	.. il cappellaccio.
The table	.. the large ugly table.	La tavola	.. la tavolaccia.
The house	.. the ugly house.	La casa	.. la casaccia.

Obs. B. Nouns terminated in *ame* denote plenty or abundance, as: *Gentame*, abundance of people; *ossame*, abundance of bones.

Obs. There are nouns in all these terminations, without being augmentatives. Ex. *Il bastone*, the stick; *lo stame*, the carded wool; *il laccio*, the noose; *la faccia*, the face.

TENTH LESSON.

OF DIMINUTIVES.

There are also two sorts of diminutives, viz.

1. Of kindness and flattery in: *ino, etto, ello*, for the masculine, and *ina, etta, ella*, for the feminine. Ex.

From *povero*, poor, are derived:

| A poor little man. | Poverino, poveretto, poverello. |
| A poor little woman. | Poverina, poveretta, poverella. |

Of compassion in: *uccio, uzzo, icciuolo*, for the masculine, and in: *uccia, uzza, icciuola*, for the feminine. Ex.

From *l' uomo*, the man, are formed:

| The poor little man. | L' omuccio, l' omuzzo, l' omicciuolo, or l' omuccio—omicciuolo. |

Obs. C. The diminutives convey no bad meaning, like the augmentatives; and to express a little old man, you may use indifferently: *vecchietto, vecchino, vecchiettino, vecchierello, vecchierellino, vecchiuzzo*. From *la casa*, you may form: *la casina, la casetta, la casuzza, la casuccia, la casucciola*, to express the small house.

Obs. D. The diminutives in *ino* and *ina*, express something tender, flattering, and cajoling. Ex. The pretty little prince, *il principino* (from *principe*); the pretty little princess, *la principessina* (from *principessa*); the little table, *il tavolino* (from *tavola*); the pretty small house, *il casino* (from *casa*); the little chamber, *il camerino* (from *camera*); the little cap, *il berrettino* (from *berretta*); the pretty little dog, *il cagnolino* (from *cane*).

Obs. E. These examples show that many feminine nouns in *a* form their diminutives in *ino*, which termination is masculine.

Those.	Quelli, Quei or que'.
Have you my books or those of the man?	Ha Ella i miei libri, o quei (que') dell' uomo ?
I have not yours; I have those of the man.	Non ho i di Lei, ho quelli dell' uomo.

Those which.	Quelli, che (or cui). Quei (or que'), che.
Have you the books which I have ?	Ha Ella i libri che ho io ? Avete i libri che ho io ?
I have those which you have.	Ho quei che Ella ha. Ho quelli cheha Ella.
Has the Englishman the knives which you have, or those which I have ?	Ha l' Inglese i coltelli che avete voi, o quelli che ho io ?

TENTH LESSON.

He has neither those which you have, nor those which I have.	Non ha nè quelli che avete voi, nè quelli che ho io.
Which knives has he?	Quali coltelli ha egli?
He has his own.	Ha i suoi.

These books.	Questi libri.
Those books.	Quei (que') libri.
Those coats.	Quegli abiti.
Those looking-glasses.	Quegli specchi.

Have you these or those books?	Avete questi libri, o quelli?
These (Plur. of *this one*).	*Questi.*
Those (Plur. of *that one*).	*Quelli (quegli).*

Have I these or those?	Ho questi, o quelli?
You have these, you have not those.	Avete questi, non avete quelli.

Have I the looking-glasses of the French, or those of the English?	Ho io gli specchi del Francesi, o quelli degl' Inglesi?
You have neither the former nor the latter.	Non avete nè questi, nè quelli.

Obs. F. In Italian, as in French, *the former and the latter, the one and the other*, are expressed in an inverted order; *questo, questi*, referring to the latter, and *quello, quelli*, to the former.

Has the man these or those sticks?	Ha l' uomo questi bastoni, o quelli?
He has these, but not those.	Ha questi, non ha quelli.
Have you your guns or mine?	Ha Ella i di Lei schioppi, o i miei?
I have neither yours nor mine, but those of our good friends.	Non ho nè i di Lei, nè i miei, ma ho quelli dei nostri buoni amici.

One	.. one book.	Uno	.. Un libro.
Good	.. good bread.	Buono	.. Buon pane.
Fine	.. fine horse.	Bello	.. Bel cavallo.
Great	.. great courage.	Grande	.. Gran coraggio.
Saint	.. Saint Peter.	Santo	.. San Pietro.
That	.. that dog.	Quello	.. Quel cane.

Obs. G. These adjectives lose, the two first their last vowel, the others their last syllable, in the singular, when they precede a word beginning with a consonant (not *s* followed by a consonant).

But when they precede a word beginning with a vowel, all lose their last vowel. Ex.

The fine tree.	Il bell' albero.
The large tree.	Il grand' albero.

Obs. H. This suppression of a letter or a syllable never takes place before a feminine noun or before a masculine noun in the plural, except with respect to the word *grande*, for we say:

TENTH LESSON.

But we must say:
Large books. | Gran libri.
Great man. | Grand' uomo.
Great men. | Grandi uomini.

Obs. I. The word *bello* may be used in the plural as follows:

Fine. | Plur. { Belli.
       | Bei or be'.
       | Begli (before a followed by a consonant, and before a vowel).

EXERCISES.

18.

Have you these or those notes?—I have neither these nor those.—Have you the horses of the French or those of the English?—I have those of the English, but I have not those of the French.—Which oxen have you?—I have those of the foreigners.—Have you the chests which I have?—I have not those which you have, but those which your brother has.—Has your brother your biscuits or mine?—He has neither yours nor mine.—Which biscuits has he?—He has his own.—Which horses has your friend?—He has those which I have.—Has your friend my books or his?—He has neither yours nor his, but he has those of the captain.—Have I your waistcoats, or those of the tailors?—You have neither these nor those.—Have I our asses?—You have not ours, but those of our neighbours.—Have you the birds of the sailors?—I have not their birds, but their fine sticks.—Which glasses (*il bicchiere*) has your boy?—He has mine.—Have I my boots or those of the shoemakers?—You have not yours, but theirs.

19.

Which milk has the man?—He has ours.—Has he our coffee?—He has it not.—Have you our coats or those of the strangers?—I have not yours, but theirs.—Has your carpenter our hammers or those of our friends?—He has neither ours nor those of our friends.—Which nails has he?—He has his good iron nails.—Has any one the ships of the English?—No one has those of the English, but some one has those of the French.—Who has the cook's chickens?—Nobody has his chickens, but somebody has his butter.—Who has his cheese?—His boy has it.—Who has my old gun?—The sailor has it.—Have I the peasant's bag?—You have not his bag, but his corn.—Which guns has the Englishman?—He has those which you have.—Which umbrellas has the Frenchman?—He has those which his friend has.—Has he our books?—He has not ours, but those which his neighbour has.—Is the merchant's boy hungry?—He is not hungry, but thirsty.—Is your friend cold or warm?—He is neither cold nor warm.—Is he afraid?—He is not afraid, but ashamed.—Has the young man the birds of our servants?—He has not their birds, but their soap.—Which penknives has he?—He has those of his old merchants.—Have you any thing good or bad?—I have neither any thing good nor bad, but something fine.—What have you fine?—I have our cook's fine beef.—Have you not their fine mutton?—No, Sir, I have it not.

ELEVENTH LESSON.

Lezione Undecima.

The comb.	Il pettine.
The small comb.	{ Il pettinino.
	Il piccolo pettine.
The glass.	Il bicchiere.
Have you my small combs?	Ha Ella i miei piccoli pettini (pettinetti)?

The nose.	Il naso.
The wood or forest.	Il bosco; *plur.* I. boschi.
The work.	{ Il lavoro, l'opera.
	Il travaglio.
The jewel.	Il gioiello.

ELEVENTH LESSON.

Them.	Li, gli.
Has he my fine glasses?	Ha esso i miei begli bicchieri?
He has them.	Li ha. / Esso li ha.
Have I them?	Li ho io?
You have them.	Ella li ha. / Li avete.
You have them not.	Ella non li ha. / Non li avete.
Has the man my fine jewels?	Ha l' uomo i miei bei gioielli?
He has them not.	Non li ha.
Has the boy (got) them?	Li ha il ragazzo?
The men have them.	Gli uomini li hanno.
Have the men (got) them?	Li hanno gli uomini?

They.	Eglino, essi (ei, e').
They have them.	Eglino li hanno.
They have them not.	Essi non li hanno.
Who has them?	Chi li ha?

The German,	the Germans.	Il Tedesco,	i Tedeschi.
The Turk,	the Turks.	Il Turco,	i Turchi.
The Italian,	the Italians.	L' Italiano,	gl' Italiani.
The Spaniard,	the Spaniards.	Lo Spagnuolo,	gli Spagnuoli.
The Russian,	the Russians.	Il Russo,	i Russi.
The American,	the Americans.	L' Americano,	gli Americani.
The clothes.		I vestiti. / Gli abiti.	

Some or any.[1]	Sing. Del, dello, dell'. Plur. Dei, degli, degl'
Some or any wine.	Del vino.
Some or any bread.	Del pane.
Some or any butter.	Del butirro.
Some or any sugar.	Dello zucchero.
Some or any money.	Del denaro.
Some or any books.	Dei libri.
Some or any buttons.	Dei bottoni.

---

[1] *Some* or *any* is sometimes expressed in Italian, and sometimes not; nearly as in English. It is expressed when *a quantity* or *a little* may be understood, otherwise it is not expressed. Ex. Give me some bread, *datemi del pane;* I drink wine and you drink water, *io bevo vino, e voi berete acqua;* we have seen no soldiers, *or* we have not seen any soldiers, *non abbiamo veduto soldati;* wine and bread are sufficient for me, *pane ed acqua mi bastano;* to write well we must employ good paper and good ink, *per bene scrivere bisogna adoperare buona carta e buon inchiostro;* the poor are often reduced to bad meat, *i poveri sono spesso ridotti a cattiva carne.*

ELEVENTH LESSON.

Some or any gold.	Dell' oro.
Some or any silver (metal).	Dell' argento.
Some or any men.	Degli uomini.
Some or any friends.	Degli amici.
Some or any coats.	Degli abiti.
Have you any wine?	Avete del vino?
I have some wine.	Ho del vino.
Has this man any cloth?	Ha del panno quell' uomo?
He has some cloth.	Ha del panno.
Has he any books?	Ha egli dei libri?
He has some books.	Ha libri.
Have you any money?	Avete denaro?
I have some money.	Ho denaro.

No or *not any*, before a noun.	*Non*.
I have no wine.	Non ho vino.
He has no money.	Non ha danaro.
You have no books.	Ella non ha libri.
	Non avete libri.
They have no friends.	Non hanno amici.

Some or any good wine.	Del buon vino.
Some or any bad cheese.	Del cattivo formaggio.
Some or any excellent wine.	Del vino eccellente.
Some or any excellent coffee.	Dell eccellente caffè.
Some or any good books.	Dei buoni libri.
Some or any pretty glasses.	Dei leggiadri bicchieri.
Some or any fine coats.	Dè begli abiti.
Some or any old wine.	Del vino vecchio.

Have you any good butter?	Ha Ella buon burro?
	Avete buon burro?
I have no good butter, but some excellent cheese.	Non ho buon burro, ma ho eccellente formaggio.
Has this man any good books?	Ha buoni libri quell' uomo?
He has not any good books.	Non ha buoni libri.
Has the merchant any pretty gloves?	Ha leggiadri guanti il mercante?
He has no pretty gloves, but some pretty jewels.	Non ha leggiadri guanti, ma ha leggiadri gioielli.

What has the baker?	Che ha il fornaio?
He has some excellent bread.	Ha del pane eccellente.
The painter.	Il pittore.
Some coals.	Carbone.
The pencil (of a painter).	Il pennello.
The picture.	Il quadro.
The pencil.	Il lapis (*la matita*, a feminine noun).

EXERCISES.
20.

Have you my fine glasses?—I have them.—Have you the fine horses of the English?—I have them not.—Which sticks have you?—I have those of the foreigners.—Who has my small combs? —My boys have them.—Which knives have you?—I have those of your friends.—Have I your good guns?—You have them not, but your friends have them.—Have you my pretty birds, or those of my brothers?—I have neither yours nor your brothers', but my own.—Which ships have the Germans?—The Germans have no ships.—Have the sailors our fine mattrasses?—They have them not.—Have the cooks (got) them?—They have them.—Has the captain your pretty books?—He has them not.—Have I them? —You have them. You have them not.—Has the Italian (got) them?—He has them.—Have the Turks our fine guns?—They have them not.—Have the Spaniards them?—They have them. —Has the German the pretty umbrellas of the Spaniards?—He has them.—Has he them?—Yes, Sir, he has them.—Has the Italian our pretty gloves?—He has them not.—Who has them? —The Turk has them.—Has the tailor our waistcoats or those of our friends?—He has neither the latter nor the former.—Which coats has he?—He has those which the Turks have.—Which dogs have you?—I have those which my neighbours have.

21

Have you any wood?—I have some wood.—Has your brother any soap?—He has no soap.—Have I any mutton?—You have no mutton, but you have some beef.—Have your friends any money?—They have some money.—Have they any milk?— They have no milk, but they have some excellent butter.—Have I any fire?—You have no fire, but you have some coals (*in the sing. in Italian*).—Has the merchant any cloth?—He has no cloth, but some pretty garments.—Have the English any silver? —They have no silver, but they have some excellent iron.—Have you any good coffee?—I have no good coffee, but some excellent wine.—Has the merchant any good books?—He has some good books.—Has the young man any milk?—He has no milk, but some excellent tea.—Have the French any good gloves?—They have some excellent gloves.—Have they any birds?—They have no birds, but they have some pretty jewels.—Who has the fine pencils of the English?—Their friends have them.—Who has the good biscuits of the bakers?—The sailors of our captains have them.—Have they our clothes?—Yes, Sir, they have them.—What have the Italians?—They have some beautiful pictures.—What have the Spaniards?—They have some fine asses.—What have the Germans?—They have some excellent corn.

22.

Have you any friends?—I have some friends.—Have your friends any fire?—They have some fire.—Have the shoemakers any good boots?—They have no good boots, but some excellent leather.—Have the tailors any good waistcoats?—They have no good waistcoats, but some excellent cloth.—Has the painter any umbrellas?—He has no umbrellas, but he has some beautiful pictures.—Has he the pictures of the French or those of the Italians?—He has neither the latter nor the former.—Which has he?—He has those of his good friends.—Have the Russians any thing good?—They have something good.—What have they good? —They have some good oxen.—Has any one my small combs? —No one has them.—Who has the peasants' fine chickens?— Your cooks have them.—What have the bakers?—They have some excellent bread.—Have your friends any old wine?—They have no old wine, but some good milk.—Has any one your golden candlesticks?—No one has them.

TWELFTH LESSON.

Lezione Duodecima.

Some of it, any of it, of it.
Some of them, any of them, of them.

{ *Ne* (is always placed before the verb, except when this is in the infinitive, participle, or imperative).

TWELFTH LESSON.

Have you any wine?	Ha Ella vino? / Avete vino?
I have some.	Ne ho.
Have you any bread?	Avete pane?
I have not any, or none.	Non ne ho.
Have you any good wine?	Ha Ella buon vino? / Avete buon vino?
I have some good.	Ne ho di buono. / Ne ho del buono.
Have I any good cloth?	Ho io buon panno?
You have not any good.	Ella non ne ha di buono. / Non ne avete di buono.
Has the merchant any sugar?	Ha zucchero il mercante?
He has some sugar.	Ha zucchero.
He has some.	Ne ha.
He has not any.	Non ne ha.
Has he any good sugar?	Ha egli buon zucchero?
He has some good.	Ne ha di buono. / Ne ha del buono.
He has not any good.	Non ne ha di buono.
Have I any salt?	Ho sale?
You have some salt.	Avete sale.
You have no salt.	Non avete sale.
You have some.	Ne avete.
You have not any.	Non ne avete.
Have you any boots?	Avete stivali?
I have some boots.	Ho stivali.
I have no boots.	Non ho stivali.
I have some.	Ne ho.
I have not any.	Non ne ho.
Has the man any good horses?	Ha l' uomo buoni cavalli?
He has some good ones.	Ne ha dei buoni.
He has not any good ones.	Non ne ha di buoni.
Has he any pretty knives?	Ha egli leggiadri coltelli?
He has some pretty ones.	Ne ha dei leggiadri.
He has not any pretty ones.	Non ne ha di leggiadri.
Has he any money?	Ha egli danaro?
He has some.	Ne ha.
He has not any.	Non ne ha.
Have our friends any good butter?	Hanno buon burro i nostri amici?
They have some good.	Ne hanno di buono.
They have not any good.	Non ne hanno del buono.
Have you good or bad books?	Ha Ella buoni, o cattivi libri?
I have some good ones.	Ne ho dei buoni.
Have you good or bad bread?	Avete buono, o cattivo pane?
I have some good.	Ne ho del buono.
Who has some bad wine?	Chi ha cattivo vino?
Our merchant has some.	Ne ha il nostro mercante.

TWELFTH LESSON.

What bread has the baker?	Qual pane ha il fornaio?
He has some good.	Ne ha del buono.
What boots has the shoemaker?	Quali stivali ha il calzolaio?
He has some good ones.	Ne ha di buoni.
The hatter.	Il cappellaio.
The joiner.	Il falegname.

A or *one*.
{ *Un* (before a consonant or a vowel).
Uno (before *s* followed by a consonant, or when it stands alone). }

DECLENSION OF THE INDEFINITE ARTICLE.

				Masculine.
Nom.	a or an.		*Nom.*	uno.
Gen.	of a — an.		*Gen.*	d' uno.
Dat.	to a — an.		*Dat.*	ad uno.
Acc.	a — an.		*Acc.*	uno.
Abl.	from a — an.		*Abl.*	da uno.

A or one horse.	Un cavallo.
Have you a book?	{ Ha Ella / Avete } un libro?
I have a book.	Ho un libro.
Have you a glass?	{ Ha Ella / Avete } un bicchiere?
I have no glass.	Non ho bicchiere.
I have one.	Ne ho uno.
Have you a good horse?	Ha Ella un buon cavallo?
I have a good horse.	Ho un buon cavallo.
I have a good one.	Ne ho uno buono.
I have two good ones.	Ne ho due buoni.
I have two good horses.	Ho due buoni cavalli.
I have three good ones.	Ne ho tre buoni.
Have I a gun?	Ho uno schioppo?
You have a gun.	Ella ha uno schioppo.
You have one.	Ella ne ha uno.
You have a good one.	Ella ne ha uno buono.
You have two good ones.	Ella ne ha due buoni.
Has your brother a friend?	Ha un amico il di Lei fratello?
He has a friend.	Ha un amico.
He has one.	Ne ha uno.
He has a good one.	Ne ha uno buono.

TWELFTH LESSON. 43

He has two good ones.	Ne ha due buoni.
He has three good ones.	Ne ha tre buoni.
Four.	Quattro.
Five.	Cinque.
Has your friend a fine knife?	Ha il vostro amico un bel coltello?
He has one.	Ne ha uno.
He has none.	Non ne ha.
He has two of them.	Ne ha due.
He has three.	Ne ha tre.
He has four.	Ne ha quattro.
Have you five good horses?	Ha Ella / Avete } cinque buoni cavalli?
I have six.	Ne ho sei.
I have six good and seven bad ones.	Ne ho sei buoni e sette cattivi.
Who has a fine umbrella?	Chi ha un bell' ombrello? or una bella ombrello?
The merchant has one.	Il mercante ne ha uno.

EXERCISES.

23.

Have you any salt?—I have some.—Have you any coffee?—I have not any.—Have you any good wine?—I have some good (wine).—Have you any good cloth?—I have no good cloth, but I have some good money.—Have I any good sugar?—You have not any good.—Has the man any good honey?—He has some.—Has he any good cheese?—He has not any.—Has the American any money?—He has some.—Have the French any cheese?—They have not any.—Have the English any good milk?—They have no good milk, but they have some excellent butter.—Who has some good soap?—The merchant has some.—Who has some good bread?—The baker has some.—Has the foreigner any coals?—He has not any.—Has he any cloth?—He has some.—What rice have you?—I have some good (rice).—What hay has the horse?—He has some good (hay).—What leather has the shoemaker?—He has some excellent (leather).—Have you any jewels?—I have not any.—Who has some jewels?—The merchant has some.—Have I any boots?—You have some boots.—Have I any hats?—You have no hats.—Has your friend any good knives?—He has some good ones.—Has he any good oxen?—He has not any good ones.—Have the Italians any fine horses?

—They have not any fine ones.—Who has some fine asses?—The Spaniards have some.

24.

Has the captain any good sailors?—He has some good ones.—Have the sailors any good mattrasses?—They have not any good ones.—Who has some good biscuits?—The baker of our good neighbour has some.—Has he any bread?—He has not any.—Who has some beautiful ribbons?—The French have some.—Who has some excellent iron nails?—The carpenter has some.—Has he any hammers?—He has some.—What hammers has he?—He has some iron ones.—What is the matter with your brother?—Nothing is the matter with him.—Is he cold?—He is neither cold nor warm.—Is he afraid?—He is not afraid.—Is he ashamed?—He is not ashamed.—What is the matter with him?—He is hungry.—Who has some pretty gloves?—I have some.—Who has some fine pictures?—The Italians have some.—Have the painters any fine gardens?—They have some fine ones.—Has the hatter good or bad hats?—He has some good ones.—Has the joiner good or bad wood?—He has some good (wood).—Who has some pretty jewels?—The boys of our merchants have some.—Have they any birds?—They have not any.—Have you any tea?—I have not any.—Who has some?—My servant has some.—Has your servant any clothes?—He has not any.—Who has some?—The servants of my neighbour have some.

25.

Have you a pencil?—I have one.—Has your boy a good book?—He has a good one.—Has the German a good ship?—He has none.—Has your tailor a good coat?—He has a good one.—He has two good ones.—He has three good ones.—Who has some fine boots?—Our shoemaker has some.—Has the captain a fine dog?—He has two.—Have your friends two fine horses?—They have four.—Has the young man a good or bad gun?—He has no good one: he has a bad one.—Have you a cork?—I have none.—Has your friend a good corkscrew?—He has two.—Have I a friend?—You have a good one.—You have two good friends.—You have three good ones.—Your brother has four good ones.—

Has the carpenter an iron nail?—He has six iron nails.—He has six good ones, and seven bad ones.—Who has good beef?—Our cook has some.—Who has five good horses?—Our neighbour has six.—Has the peasant any corn?—He has some.—Has he any looking-glasses?—He has not any.—Who has some good friends? The Turks have some.—Have they any money?—They have not any.—Who has their money?—Their friends have it.—Are their friends thirsty?—They are not thirsty, but hungry.—Has the joiner any bread?—He has not any.—Has your servant a good coat?—He has one.—Has he this or that coat?—He has neither this nor that.—Which coat has he?—He has that which your servant has.—Have the peasants these or those bags?—They have neither these nor those.—Which bags have they?—They have their own.—Have you a good servant?—I have a good one.—Who has a good chest?—My brother has one.—Has he a leathern or a wooden chest?—He has a wooden one.

THIRTEENTH LESSON.

Lezione Decimaterza.

How much? How many?	*Quanto? Quanti?*
How much bread?	Quanto pane?
How much money?	Quanto denaro?
How many knives?	Quanti coltelli?
How many men?	Quanti uomini?
How many friends?	Quanti amici?

Only, but.	Soltanto. Solamente. Non—che. Non—se non.
I have but one friend. I have but one.	Ho soltanto un amico? Ne ho solamente uno.

THIRTEENTH LESSON.

I have but one good gun.	Ho soltanto un buono schioppo.
I have but one good one.	Ne ho solamente uno buono.
You have but one good one.	Ne avete solamente uno buono.
How many horses has your brother?	Quanti cavalli ha vostro fratello?
He has but one.	{ Non ne ha che uno. { Non ne ha se non uno.
He has but two good ones.	{ Non ne ha che due buoni. { Non ne ha se non due buoni.

Much, a good deal of, very much.	Molto } assai.
Many.	Molti }
Much bread.	Molto pane (assai pane).
A good deal of good bread.	Molto pane buono.
Many men.	Molti uomini (assai uomini).
Have you much money?	Avete molto denaro?
I have a good deal.	Ne ho molto.
Have you much good wine?	Ha Ella molto buon vino? Ha Ella del vino molto buono.
I have a good deal.	Ne ho molto.

Too much.	Troppo.
Too many.	Troppi.
You have too much wine.	Avete troppo vino.
They have too many books.	Hanno troppi libri.

Enough.	Abbastanza.
Enough money.	Abbastanza denaro.
Knives enough.	Abbastanza coltelli.

Little.	{ Poco. Sing. { Pochi. Plur.
A little.	Un poco di (alquanto).
A little cloth.	Un poco di panno.
A little salt.	Un poco di sale.
A few men.	Pochi uomini.
A few friends.	Pochi amici.

But little, only a little, not much.	{ Non—quasi. Non—che poco. { Non—molto. { Solamente poco. { Non—se non poco.

THIRTEENTH LESSON. 47

Not many, but few.   { Non—molti.
                    { Non—che pochi.
                    { Non—se non pochi.
I have but little money.   { Non ho che poco danaro.
                           { Non ho se non poco danaro.
He has few friends.   { Non ha molti amici.
                      { Ha pochi amici.
We have but little gold.   { Non abbiamo molto oro.
                           { Non abbiamo che poco oro.
                           { Non abbiamo se non poco oro.

Courage.   Coraggio, cuore.
You have not much courage.   Non avete quasi coraggio.
We have few friends.   Non abbiamo quasi amici.

Have we?   Abbiamo? abbiamo noi?
We have.   Abbiamo, noi abbiamo.
We have not.   Non abbiamo.

Some pepper.   Pepe.
Some vinegar.   Aceto.
Have we any vinegar? Abbiamo aceto?
We have some.   Ne abbiamo.
We have not any.   Non ne abbiamo.

Have you a good deal of money?   { Ha Ella molto danaro?
                                 { Avete molto denaro?
I have but little of it.   { Non ne ho se non poco.
                           { Non ne ho molto.
You have but little of it.   Non ne avete se non poco.
He has but little of it.   Non ne ha molto.
We have but little of it.   Non ne abbiamo che poco.
Have you enough wine?   Ha Ella abbastanza vino?
I have only a little, but enough.   Non ne ho molto, ma abbastanza.
Eight.   Otto.
Nine.   Nove.
Ten.   Dieci.
Eleven.   Undici.

And. | E.

EXERCISES.

26.

How many friends have you?—I have two good friends.—Have you eight good trunks?—I have nine.—Has your servant three coats?—He has only one good one.—Has the captain two good ships?—He has only one.—How many hammers has the carpenter?—He has but two good ones.—How many boots has the shoemaker?—He has ten.—Has the young man nine good books?—He has only five.—How many guns has your brother?—He has only four.—Have you much bread?—I have a good deal.—Have the Spaniards much money?—They have but little.—Has our neighbour much coffee?—He has only a little.—Has the foreigner much corn?—He has a good deal.—What has the American?—He has much sugar.—What has the Russian?—He has a great deal of salt.—Has the peasant much rice?—He has not any.—Has he much cheese?—He has but little.—What have we?—We have much bread, much wine, and many books. Have we much money?—We have only a little, but enough.—Have you many brothers?—I have only one.—Have the French many friends?—They have but few.—Has our friend much hay?—He has enough.—Has the Italian much cheese?—He has a good deal.—Has this man courage?—He has none.—Has the painter's boy any pencils?—He has some.

27.

Have you much pepper?—I have but little.—Has the cook much beef?—He has but little beef, but he has a good deal of mutton.—How many oxen has the German?—He has eight.—How many horses has he?—He has only four.—Who has a good many biscuits?—Our sailors have a good many.—Have we many notes?—We have only a few.—How many notes have we?—We have only three pretty ones.—Have you too much butter?—I have not enough.—Have our boys too many books?—They have too many.—Has our friend too much milk?—He has only a little, but enough.—Who has a good deal of money?—The peasants have a good deal.—Have they many gloves?—They have not any.—Has the cook enough butter?—He has not enough.—Has he enough vinegar?—He has enough.—Have you much soap?—I have only a little.—Has the merchant much cloth?—He has a good deal.—Who has a good deal of pepper?—Our neighbour has a good deal.—Has our tailor many buttons?—He has a good many.—Has the painter many gardens?—He has not many.—How many gardens has he?—He has but two.—How many knives has the German?—He has three.—Has the captain any fine horses?—He has some fine ones, but his brother has none.—Have we any jewels?—We have a good many.—What jewels have we?—We have gold jewels.—What candlesticks have our friends?—They have silver candlesticks.—Have they gold ribbons?—They have some.

28.

Has the youth any good sticks?—He has no good sticks, but some beautiful birds.—What chickens has our cook?—He has some pretty chickens.—How many has he?—He has six.—Has the hatter any hats?—He has a good many.—Has the joiner much wood?—He has not a great deal, but enough.—Have we the horses of the French or those of the Germans?—We have neither these nor those.—Which horses have we?—We have our own.—Has the Turk my small combs?—He has them not.—Who has them? Your son has them.—Have our friends much sugar?—They have little sugar, but much honey.—Who has our looking-glasses?—The Italians have them.—Has the Frenchman this or that spoon?—He has neither this nor that.—Has he the mattrasses which we have?—He has not those which we have, but those which his friends have.—Is he ashamed?—He is not ashamed but afraid.

3

FOURTEENTH LESSON.

Lezione Decimaquarta.

A few books.	{ Alcuni libri. { Qualche libro.

Obs. A. The noun following *qualche* is always used in the singular.

Have you a few books?	{ Ha Ella alcuni libri? { Avete qualche libro?
A few.	Alcuni (parecchi).
I have a few.	Ne ho alcuni (parecchi).
You have a few.	Ne avete parecchi.
He has a few.	Ne ha alcuni.
I have but a few books.	{ Non ho se non alcuni libri. { Non ho se non parecchi libri. { Ho soltanto alcuni libri.
You have but a few books.	Avete solamente alcuni libri.
He has but a few sous.	Non ha se non alcuni soldi.
I have but a few.	Ne ho soltanto alcuni.
You have but a few.	Ne avete solamente alcuni.
He has but a few.	Ne ha soltanto alcuni.

One or a sou.	*Plur.* sous.	Un soldo.	*Plur.* soldi.
One — a franc.	" francs.	Un franco.	" franchi.
One — a crown.	" crowns.	Uno scudo.	" scudi.

Other.	Altro.
Another sou.	Un altro soldo.
Some other sous.	Alcuni altri soldi.
Have you another horse?	Ha Ella un altro cavallo?
I have another.	Ne ho un altro.
No other horse.	Non—altro cavallo.
I have no other horse.	Non ho altro cavallo.
I have no other.	Non ne ho altro.
Have you any other horses?	Ha Ella alcuni altri cavalli?
I have some others.	Ne ho degli altri.
I have no others.	Non ne ho altri.

FOURTEENTH LESSON.

The arm.	Il braccio (*plur.* le braccia).
The heart.	Il cuore.
The month.	Il mese.
The volume.	Il volume.

What day of the month is it?	Quanti ne abbiamo del mese? / A quanti siamo del mese?
It is the first.	È il primo (Ne abbiamo uno). / Siamo al primo.
It is the second.	Ne abbiamo due. / Siamo ai (*or* al) due.
It is the third.	Ne abbiamo tre. / Siamo ai (*or* al) tre.

Obs. B. The cardinal numbers must be used in Italian when speaking of the days of the month, though the ordinal are used in English, except *il primo*, the first.[1]

It is the eleventh.	Ne abbiamo undici. / Siamo all' undici (*or* agli undici).
Which volume have you?	Qual volume ha Ella?
I have the fourth.	Ho il quarto.

	Singular.	Plural.
The first.	Il primo,	I primi.
— second.	Il secondo,	I secondi.
— third.	Il terzo,	I terzi.
— fourth.	Il quarto,	I quarti.
— fifth.	Il quinto,	I quinti.
— sixth.	Il sesto,	I sesti.
— seventh.	Il settimo,	I settimi.
— eighth.	L' ottavo,	gli ottavi.
— ninth.	Il nono,	i noni.
— tenth.	Il decimo,	I decimi.
— eleventh.	L' undecimo,	gli undecimi.
— twentieth.	Il ventesimo,	I ventesimi.
— twenty-first.	Il ventesimo-primo.	I ventesimi-primi.
— twenty-second.	Il ventesimo-secondo.	I ventesimi-secondi.
— thirtieth.	Il trentesimo,	I trentesimi.
— fortieth.	Il quarantesimo,	I quarantesimi.
&c.	&c.	
Have you the first or second book?	Ha Ella il primo, o il secondo libro?	
I have the third.	Ho il terzo.	
Which volume have you?	Qual volume ha Ella?	
I have the fifth.	Ho il quinto.	

[1] Henceforth the learners should write the date before their task. Ex. *Londra, al (il or a) quindici di Luglio mille otto cento quaranta quattro.* London, 15th July, 1844.

FOURTEENTH LESSON.

The remaining numerals are:—

		1. Cardinal Numbers.	2. Ordinal Numbers
Twelve,	twelfth.	Dodici.	Duodecimo.
Thirteen,	thirteenth.	Tredici.	Decimo terzo, or Tredicesimo.
Fourteen,	fourteenth.	Quattordici.	Decimo quarto, or Quattordicesimo.
Fifteen,	fifteenth.	Quindici.	Decimo quinto, or Quindicesimo.
Sixteen,	sixteenth.	Sedici.	Decimo sesto, or Sedicesimo.
Seventeen,	seventeenth.	Diciasette, or Diciasette.	Decimo settimo. Diciassettesimo.
Eighteen,	eighteenth.	Dieciotto, or Diciotto.	Decimottavo.
Nineteen,	nineteenth.	Diecinove, or Dicianove.	Decimo nono.
Twenty.		Venti, &c.	
Twenty-one.		Vent' uno, &c.	
Twenty-two.		Ventidue, &c.	
Twenty-three,	twenty-third.	Ventitre.	Ventesimo terzo. &c.
Thirty.		Trenta, &c.	
Forty.		Quaranta, &c.	
Fifty,	fiftieth.	Cinquanta,	Cinquantesimo
Sixty,	sixtieth.	Sessanta,	Sessantesimo.
Seventy,	seventieth.	Settanta,	Settantesimo.
Eighty,	eightieth.	Ottanta,	Ottantesimo.
Ninety,	ninetieth.	Novanta,	Novantesimo.
A or one hundred,	hundredth.	Cento,	Centesimo.
A or one thousand,	thousandth.	Mille,	Millesimo.
Two hundred,	two hundredth.	Ducento (dugento).	Ducentesimo.
Three hundred,	three hundredth.	Trecento,	Trecentesimo.
Two thousand,	two thousandth.	Due mila,	Due millesimo.
A million,	millionth.	Millione,	Millionesimo.
Two millions.		Due millioni.	
The last.		L' ultimo.	
A tenth.		Una decina or dicina.	
A dozen.		Una dozzina.	
A score.		Una ventina.	
A thirtieth.		Una trentina.	

Obs. C. From the above may be seen that *cento* is invariable in the plural, and *mille* is in the plural changed into *mila*.

FOURTEENTH LESSON.

EXERCISES.

29.

Have you many knives?—I have a few.—Have you many pencils?—I have only a few.—Has the painter's friend many looking-glasses?—He has only a few.—Has your son a few sous?—He has a few.—Have you a few francs?—We have a few.—How many francs have you?—I have ten.—How many sous has the Spaniard?—He has not many; he has only five.—Who has the beautiful glasses of the Italians?—We have them.—Have the English many ships?—They have a good many.—Have the Italians many horses?—They have not many horses, but a good many asses.—What have the Germans?—They have many crowns.—How many crowns have they?—They have eleven.—Have we the horses of the English or those of the Germans?—We have neither the former nor the latter.—Have we the umbrellas of the Spaniards?—We have them not, but the Americans have them.—Have you much butter?—I have only a little, but enough.—Have the sailors the mattrasses which we have?—They have not those which we have, but those which their captain has.—Has the Frenchman many francs?—He has only a few, but he has enough.—Has your servant many sous?—He has no sous, but francs enough.

30.

Have the Russians pepper?—They have but little pepper, but a good deal of salt.—Have the Turks much wine?—They have not much wine, but a good deal of coffee.—Who has a good deal of milk?—The Germans have a good deal.—Have you no other gun?—I have no other.—Have we any other cheese?—We have some other.—Have I no other picture?—You have another.—Has our neighbour no other horse?—He has no other.—Has your brother no other friends?—He has some others.—Have the shoemakers no other boots?—They have no others.—Have the tailors many coats?—They have only a few; they have only four.—How many gloves have you?—I have only two.—Have you any other biscuits?—I have no other.—How many corkscrews has the merchant?—He has nine.—How many arms has this man?

FOURTEENTH LESSON.

—He has only one; the other is of wood.—What heart has your son?—He has a good heart.—Have you no other servant?—I have another.—Has your friend no other birds?—He has some others.—How many other birds has he?—He has six others.—How many gardens have you?—I have only one, but my friend has two of them.

31.

Which volume have you?—I have the first.—Have you the second volume of my book?—I have it.—Have you the third or fourth book?—I have neither the former nor the latter.—Have we the fifth or sixth volumes?—We have the fifth, but we have not the sixth volumes.—Which volumes has your friend?—He has the seventh volumes.—What day of the month is it?—It is the eighth.—Is it not the eleventh?—No, Sir, it is the tenth.—Who has our crowns?—The Russians have them.—Have they our gold?—They have it not.—Has the youth much money?—He has not much money, but much courage.—Have you the nails of the carpenters or those of the joiners?—I have neither those of the carpenters nor those of the joiners, but those of my merchants.—Have you this or that glove?—I have neither this nor that.—Has your friend these or those notes?—He has these, but not those.—Has the Italian a few crowns?—He has a few.—Has he a few francs?—He has five.—Have you another stick? I have another.—What other stick have you?—I have another iron stick.—Have you a few good candlesticks?—We have a few.—Has your boy another hat?—He has another.—Have these men any vinegar?—These men have none, but their friends have some.—Have the peasants any other bags?—They have no others.—Have they any other bread?—They have some.

FIFTEENTH LESSON.

Lezione Decimaquinta.

The tome (the volume).	Il tomo (il volume).
Have you the first or second volume of my book?	Ha Ella il primo, o il secondo tomo del mio libro?
Both.	L' uno e l' altro (ambidue), or simply ambo.
I have both.	Ho l' uno e l' altro. Ho ambidue.
Have you my book or my stick?	Ha Ella il mio libro, o il mio bastone?
I have neither the one nor the other.	Non ho nè l' uno nè l' altro.
The one and the other (plural).	Gli uni e gli altri.
Has your brother my gloves or his own?	Ha il di Lei fratello i miei guanti, o i suoi?
He has both yours and his.	Egli ha gli uni e gli altri.
Has he my books or those of the Spaniards?	Ha egli i miei libri, o quelli degli Spagnuoli?
He has neither the one nor the other.	Non ha gli uni nè gli altri.
The Scotchman.	Lo Scozzese.
The Irishman.	L' Irlandese.
The Dutchman.	L' Olandese.
Still, yet, some or any more.	Ancora, Anche, più, di più. Anco (per anco).
Some more wine.	Ancora vino. Ancora del vino (see note 1, Lesson XI).
Some more money.	Ancoro danaro. Ancora del danaro.
Some more buttons.	Ancora bottoni. Ancora dei bottoni.
Have you any more wine?	Ha Ella ancora vino?
I have some more wine.	Ho ancora vino.
I have some more.	Ne ho ancora.
Has he any more money?	Ha egli ancora danaro?
He has some more.	Ne ha ancora.
Have I any more books?	Ho ancora libri?
You have some more.	Ella ne ha ancora.

FIFTEENTH LESSON.

Not any more, no more.	Non—più.
I have no more bread.	Non ho più pane.
He has no more money.	Non ha più danaro.
Have you any more butter?	Ha Ella ancora del burro?
I have no more.	Non ne ho più.
We have no more.	Non ne abbiamo più.
Has he any more vinegar?	Ha egli ancora aceto?
He has no more.	Non ne ha più.
We have no more books.	Non abbiamo più libri.
We have no more.	Non ne abbiamo più.
He has no more dogs.	Non ha più cani.
He has no more.	Non ne ha più.

Not much more, not many more.	Non—più molto. Non—più molti.
Have you much more wine?	Ha Ella ancora molto vino?
I have not much more.	Non ne ho più molto.
Have you many more books?	Ha Ella ancora molti libri?
I have not many more.	Non ne ho più molti.

One book more.	Ancora un libro.
One good book more.	Ancora un buon libro.
A few books more.	Ancora alcuni libri (qualche libro).
Have you a few francs more?	Ha Ella ancora alcuni franchi (qualche franco)?
I have a few more.	Ne ho ancora alcuni.
Have I a few more sous?	Ho ancora alcuni soldi?
You have a few more.	Ella ne ha ancora alcuni.
We have a few more.	Ne abbiamo ancora alcuni.
They have a few more.	Ne hanno ancora alcuni.

EXERCISES.

32.

Which volume of his book have you?—I have the first.—How many volumes has this book?—It has two.—Have you my book or my brother's?—I have both.—Has the foreigner my comb or my knife?—He has both.—Have you my bread or my cheese? I have neither the one nor the other.—Has the Dutchman my glass or that of my friend?—He has neither the one nor the other.—Has the Irishman our horses or our chests?—He has both.—Has the Scotchman our boots or our waistcoats?—He has neither the one nor the other.—What has he?—He has his good iron guns.—Have the Dutch our ships or those of the Spaniards?

FIFTEENTH LESSON.

—They have neither the one nor the other.—Which ships have they?—They have their own.—Have we any more hay?—We have some more.—Has our merchant any more pepper?—He has some more.—Has our friend any more money?—He has not any more.—Has he any more jewels?—He has some more.—Have you any more coffee?—We have no more coffee, but we have some more tea.—Has the Dutchman any more salt?—He has no more salt, but he has some more butter.—Has the painter any more pictures?—He has no more pictures, but he has some more pencils.—Have the sailors any more biscuits?—They have not any more.—Have your sons any more books?—They have not any more.—Has the young man any more friends?—He has no more.

33.

Has our cook much more beef?—He has not much more.—Has he many more chickens?—He has not many more.—Has the peasant much more milk?—He has not much more milk, but he has a great deal more butter.—Have the French many more horses?—They have not many more.—Have you much more oil?—I have much more.—Have we many more looking-glasses? We have many more.—Have you one book more?—I have one more.—Have our neighbours one more garden?—They have one more.—Has our friend one umbrella more?—He has no more.—Have the Scotch a few more books?—They have a few more.—Has the tailor a few more buttons?—He has not any more.—Has our carpenter a few more nails?—He has no more nails, but he has a few more sticks.—Have the Spaniards a few more sous?—They have a few more.—Has the German a few more oxen?—He has a few more.—Have you a few more francs?—I have no more francs, but I have a few more crowns.—What more have you?—We have a few more ships, and a few more good sailors.—Have I a little more money?—You have a little more.—Have you any more courage?—I have no more.—Have you much more vinegar?—I have not much more, but my brother has a great deal more.

34.

Has he sugar enough?—He has not enough.—Have we francs enough?—We have not enough.—Has the joiner wood enough?

—He has enough.—Has he hammers enough?—He has enough.
—What hammers has he?—He has iron and wooden hammers.
—Have you rice enough?—We have not rice enough, but we
have sugar enough.—Have you many more gloves?—I have not
many more.—Has the Russian another ship?—He has another.
—Has he another bag?—He has no other.—What day of the
month is it?—It is the sixth.—How many friends have you?—I
have but one good friend.—Has the peasant too much bread?—
He has not enough.—Has he much money?—He has but little
money, but enough hay.—Have we the cotton or the thread coats
of the Americans?—We have neither their cotton nor their thread
coats.—Have we the gardens which they have?—We have not
those which they have, but those which our neighbours have.—
Have you any more honey?—I have no more.—Have you any
more oxen?—I have not any more.

SIXTEENTH LESSON.

Lezione Decimasesta.

Several.	Diversi (molti, parecchi). Varii.
Several men.	Diversi uomini.
Several children.	Diversi fanciulli (bambini).
Several knives.	Varii coltelli.

The father.	Il padre.
The child.	Il fanciullo (il bambino).
The ink.	L' inchiostro.
The inkstand.	Il calamaio.
The cloak.	Il mantello (il pastrano).
The cake (the pastry, the pie).	Il pasticcio.
The small cake.	Il pasticcino.
The macaroni.	I maccheroni.
The pastry-cook.	Il pasticciere.
Petty-patties.	Pasticcini.

SIXTEENTH LESSON.

As much.	Tanto.
As many.	Tanti.
As much—as.	Tanto— $\begin{cases} quanto, \text{plur. } quanti.^1 \\ che. \\ come. \end{cases}$
As many—as.	Tanti—
As much bread as wine.	Tanto pane quanto vino (che or come vino).
As many men as children.	Tanti uomini quanti fanciulli (come or che fanciulli).

Have you as much gold as silver?	Ha Ella tanto oro quanto argento?
I have as much of this as of that.	
I have as much of the latter as of the former.	Ho tanto di questo quanto di quello.
I have as much of the one as of the other.	Ho tanto dell' uno quanto dell' altro.
Have you as many boots as handkerchiefs?	Ha Ella tanti stivali quanti fazzoletti?
I have as many of these as of those.	
I have as many of the former as of the latter.	Ho tanti di questi quanto di quelli.
I have as many of the one as of the other.	Ho tanti degli uni quanto degli altri.

Quite (or just), as much, as many.	Altrettanto, altrettanti.
I have quite as much of this as of that.	Ho altrettanto di questo quanti di quello.
Quite as much of the one as of the other.	Altrettanto dell' uno quanto dell' altro.
Quite as much of these as of those.	Altrettanto di questi quanto di quelli.
Quite as many of the one as of the other.	Altrettanto degli uni quanti degli altri.

An enemy, enemies.	Un nemico, nemici.
My dear friend.	Mio caro amico (vocative).
Dear.	Caro.
The heart.	Il cuore.

Obs. A. Words in the singular, having one of the liquid consonants, *l, m, n, r,* before their final vowel, may lose it (except before words beginning with

---

[1] Though *che* and *come* are sometimes used as the correlatives of *tanto*, it is only tolerated, and none of the great writers, or indeed no Italians who speak their language correctly, use any thing but *quanto, quanti*, as the correlatives of *tanto, tanti*.

SIXTEENTH LESSON.

s followed by a consonant). The vowels after *l* and *r*, however, are oftener dropped than those after *n* and *s*.

The linen thread.	Il fil di lino (instead of *filo*).
The faithful heart.	Il cuor (or cor) fedele (instead of *cuore* or *core*).
Your welfare.	Il ben vostro (instead of *bene*).
My opinion.	Il parer mio (instead of *parere*.[1])

More (a comparative adverb).   *Più.*

More bread.	Più pane.
More men.	Più uomini.

Than.   *Che.*

More bread than wine.	Più pane che vino.
More knives than sticks.	Più coltelli che bastoni.
More of this than of that.	Più di questo che di quello.
More of the one than of the other.	Più dell' uno che dell' altro.
More of these than of those.	Più di questi che di quelli.
More of the ones than of the others.	Più degli uni che degli altri.
I have more of your sugar than of mine.	Ho più del vostro zucchero che del mio.
He has more of our books than of his own.	Egli ha più dei nostri libri che dei suoi.

Obs. B. Quanto, che, and come, are employed for the comparative of equality, but che only for the comparative of superiority and minority.

Less, fewer.   *Meno.*

Less wine than bread.	Meno vino che pane.
Less knives than sticks.	Meno coltelli che bastoni.
Less than I.	Meno di me.

Obs. C. After *meno*, *than* is rendered by *di* before a pronoun. Ex.

Less than he.	Meno di lui.
Less than we.	Meno di noi.
Less than you.	Meno di voi (di Lei).
Less than they.	Meno di loro.

They.	Loro.
As they.	Quanto loro.
Than they.	Di loro. / Che loro.
As much as you.	Tanto quanto Lei, Ella, voi (Loro).
As much as he.	Tanto quanto lui.
As much as they.	Tanto quanto loro.

[1] But as soon as the word following begins with *s* followed by a consonant, there is no elision. We say: il sole splendente, the splendid sun; un bene straordinario, an extraordinary benefit; un parere strano, a strange opinion, and not il sol splendente, un ben straordinario, un parer strano.

EXERCISES.
35.

Have you a horse?—I have several.—Has he several coats?—He has only one.—Who has several looking-glasses?—My brother has several.—What looking-glasses has he?—He has beautiful looking-glasses.—Who has good petty-patties?—Several pastry-cooks have some.—Has your brother a child?—He has several.—Have you as much coffee as tea?—I have as much of the one as of the other.—Has this man a son?—He has several. —How many sons has he?—He has four.—How many children have our friends?—They have many; they have ten.—Have we as much bread as butter?—You have as much of the one as of the other.—Has this man as many friends as enemies?—He has as many of the one as of the other.—Have we as many spoons as knives?—We have as many of the one as of the other.—Has your father as much gold as silver?—He has more of the latter than of the former.—Has the captain as many sailors as ships? —He has more of the latter than of the former.—He has more of the one than of the other.

36.

Have you as many guns as I?—I have as many.—Has the foreigner as much courage as we?—He has quite as much.— Have we as much good as bad coffee?—We have as much of the one as of the other.—Have our neighbours as much cheese as milk?—They have more of the latter than of the former.—Have your sons as many petty-patties as books?—They have more of the latter than of the former; more of the one than of the other. —How many noses has the man?—He has but one.—How many feet has he?—He has several.—How many cloaks have you?— I have but one, but my father has more than I; he has five.— Have my children as much courage as yours?—Yours have more than mine.—Have I as much money as you?—You have less than I.—Have you as many books as I?—I have less than you.—Have I as many enemies as your father?—You have fewer than he.—Have the Russians as many children as we?—We have fewer than they.—Have the French as many ships as we?

They have fewer than we.—Have we as many jewels as they ?
—We have fewer than they.—Have we fewer clothes than the
children of our friends ?—We have fewer than they.

37.

Who has fewer friends than we ?—Nobody has fewer.—Have
you as much of your wine as of mine ?—I have as much of yours
as of mine.—Have I as many of your books as of mine ?—You
have fewer of mine than of yours.—Has the Turk as much of
your money as of his own ?—He has less of his own than of ours.
—Has your baker less bread than money ?—He has less of the
latter than of the former.—Has our merchant fewer dogs than
horses ?—He has fewer of the latter than of the former; fewer
of the one than of the other.—Have your servants more sticks
than spoons ?—They have more of the latter than of the former.
—Has our cook as much butter as beef ?—He has as much of the
one as of the other.—Has he as many chickens as birds ?—He
has more of the latter than of the former.

38.

Has the carpenter as many sticks as nails ?—He has as many
of these as of those.—Have you more biscuits than glasses ?—I
have more of the latter than of the former.—Has our friend more
sugar than money ?—He has not so much of the latter as of the
former.—Has he more gloves than umbrellas ?—He has not so
many of the latter as of the former.—Who has more soap than I ?
—My son has more.—Who has more pencils than he ?—The
painter has more.—Has he as many horses as I ?—He has not so
many horses as you, but he has more pictures.—Has the merchant fewer oxen than we ?—He has fewer oxen than we, and we
have less corn than he.—Have you another note ?—I have another.—Has your son one more inkstand ?—He has several more.
—Have the Dutch as many gardens as we ?—We have fewer
than they.—We have less bread and less butter than they.—We
have but little money, but enough bread, beef, cheese, and wine.
—Have you as much courage as our neighbour's son ?—I have
just as much.—Has the youth as many notes as we ?—He has
just as many.

SEVENTEENTH LESSON.

Lezione Decimasettima.

OF THE INFINITIVE.

There are in Italian three Conjugations, which are distinguished by the termination of the Present of the Infinitive, viz.

1. The first has its infinitive terminated in AAE, as:—
   parlare, to speak;
   comprare, to buy;
   tagliare, to cut.
2. The second . . . . in ERE, as:—
   *temere, to fear;
   perdere, to lose;
   credere, to believe.
3. The third . . . . in IRE, as:—
   sentire, to feel;
   finire, to finish;
   udire, to hear.

Each verb we shall give hereafter will have the number of the class to which it belongs marked after it. The verbs marked with an asterisk (*) are irregular.

Fear.	Paura, timore.	All these words require the preposition DI, of, after them, when followed by any infinitive verb. Ex.
Shame.	Vergogna.	
Wrong.	Torto.	
Right.	Ragione, diritto.	
Time.	Tempo.	
Courage.	Coraggio.	
A mind, a wish.	Desiderio *or* voglia.	

To work.	Lavorare 1.
To speak.	Parlare 1.
Have you a mind to work?	Ha Ella desiderio o voglia di lavorare?
I have a mind to work.	Ho desiderio o voglia di lavorare.
He has not the courage to speak.	Egli non ha coraggio di parlare.
Are you afraid to speak?	Ha Ella paura di parlare?
I am ashamed to speak.	Ho vergogna di parlare.
To cut.	Tagliare 1.
To cut it.	Tagliarla.

SEVENTEENTH LESSON.

Obs. In Italian, as in English, the accusative of the personal pronouns and the relative *ne* are placed after the Infinitive; but in Italian the pronoun is joined to the verb in the Infinitive (which loses its final vowel), the present participle, and in the Imperative (of which more hereafter). Ex.

To cut them.	Tagliarli.
To cut some.	Tagliarne.

Have you time to cut the bread?	Ha Ella tempo di tagliare il pane?
I have time to cut it.	Ho tempo di tagliarlo.
Has he a mind to cut trees?	Ha egli desiderio di tagliare alberi?
He has a mind to cut some.	Ha desiderio di tagliarne.

To buy.	*Comprare (comperare)* 1.
To buy some more.	Comprarne ancora.
To buy one.	Comprarne uno.
To buy two.	Comprarne due.

To buy one more.	Comprarne ancora uno.
To buy two more.	Comprarne ancora due.

To break.	Rompere* 2.
To pick up.	{ Raccorre* (raccogliere*) 2. { Raccattare 1.
To mend, to repair.	{ Accommodare 1. { Raccommodare 1. { Assettare 1.
To look for, to seek.	Cercare 1.

Have you a mind to buy one more horse?	Ha Ella desiderio di comprare ancora un cavallo?
I have a mind to buy one more.	Ho desiderio di comprarne ancora uno.
Have you a mind to buy some books?	Ha Ella desiderio di comprare libri?
I have a mind to buy some, but I have no money.	Ho desiderio di comprarne, ma non ho danaro.
Are you afraid to break the glasses?	Ha Ella paura di rompere i bicchieri?
I am afraid to break them.	Ho paura di romperli.
Has he time to work?	Ha egli tempo di lavorare?
He has time, but no mind to work.	Ha tempo, ma non ha voglia di lavorare.
Am I right in buying a horse?	Ho io ragione di comprare un cavallo?
You are not wrong in buying one.	Ella non ha torto di comprarne uno.

SEVENTEENTH LESSON.

EXERCISES.

39.

Have you still a mind to buy my friend's horse?—I have still a mind to buy it, but I have no more money.—Have you time to work?—I have time, but no mind to work.—Has your brother time to cut some sticks?—He has time to cut some.—Has he a mind to cut some bread?—He has a mind to cut some, but he has no knife.—Have you time to cut some cheese?—I have time to cut some.—Has he a desire to cut the tree?—He has a desire to cut it, but he has no time.—Has the tailor time to cut the cloth?—He has time to cut it.—Have I time to cut the trees?—You have time to cut them.—Has the painter a mind to buy a horse?—He has a mind to buy two.—Has your captain time to speak?—He has time, but no desire to speak.—Are you afraid to speak?—I am not afraid, but I am ashamed to speak.—Am I right in buying a gun?—You are right in buying one.—Is your friend right in buying a great ox?—He is wrong in buying one.—Am I right in buying little oxen?—You are right in buying some.

40.

Have you a desire to speak?—I have a desire, but I have not the courage to speak.—Have you the courage to cut your arm?—I have not the courage to cut it.—Am I right in speaking?—You are not wrong in speaking, but you are wrong in cutting my trees.—Has the son of your friend a desire to buy one more bird?—He has a desire to buy one more.—Have you a desire to buy a few more horses?—We have a desire to buy a few more, but we have no more money.—What has our tailor a mind to mend?—He has a mind to mend our old clothes.—Has the shoemaker time to mend our boots?—He has time, but he has no mind to mend them.—Who has a mind to mend our hats?—The hatter has a mind to mend them.—Are you afraid to look for my horse?—I am not afraid, but I have no time to look for it.—What have you a mind to buy?—We have a mind to buy something good, and our neighbours have a mind to buy something beautiful.—Are their children afraid to pick up some nails?—They are not

afraid to pick up some.—Have you a mind to break my jewel ?
—I have a mind to pick it up, but not to break it.—Am I wrong
in picking up your gloves?—You are not wrong in picking them
up, but you are wrong in cutting them.

41.

Have you the courage to break these glasses?—I have the
courage, but I have no mind to break them.—Who has a mind to
break our looking-glass?—Our enemy has a mind to break it.—
Have the foreigners a mind to break our guns?—They have a
mind, but they have not the courage to break them.—Have you
a mind to break the captain's ship?—I have a mind, but I am
afraid to break it.—Who has a mind to buy my beautiful dog?
—Nobody has a mind to buy it.—Have you a desire to buy my
beautiful trunks, or those of the Frenchman?—I have a desire to
buy yours, and not those of the Frenchman.—Which books has
the Englishman a mind to buy?—He has a mind to buy that
which you have, that which your son has, and that which mine
has.—Which gloves have you a mind to seek?—I have a mind
to seek yours, mine, and our children's.

42.

Which looking-glasses have the enemies a desire to break?—
They have a desire to break those which you have, those which
I have, and those which our children and our friends have.—Has
your father a desire to buy those or those pelly-patties?—He has
a mind to buy these.—Am I right in picking up your notes?—
You are right in picking them up.—Is the Italian right in seeking
your handkerchief?—He is wrong in seeking it.—Have you a
mind to buy another ship?—I have a mind to buy another.—Has
our enemy a mind to buy one ship more?—He has a mind to buy
several more, but he is afraid to buy some.—Have you two
horses?—I have only one, but I have a wish to buy one more.

EIGHTEENTH LESSON.

Lezione Decimaottava.

To make.
To do. } *Fare** 1.

To be willing.
To wish. } *Volere** 2. (*desiderare* 1.)

Will you?
Are you willing?
Do you wish? } Vuol Ella? (Volete?)

I will, I am willing, I wish. — Voglio (or vo').
Will he? Is he willing? does he wish? — Vuol egli?
He will, he is willing, he wishes. — Egli vuole.
We will, we are willing, we wish. — Vogliamo.
You will, you are willing, you wish. — Volete.
They will, they are willing, they wish. — Vogliono.

Thou wilt, thou art willing, thou wishest. | Vuoi.

Do you wish to make my fire? — Vuol Ella fare il mio fuoco?
I am willing to make it. — Voglio farlo.
I do not wish to make it. — Non voglio farlo.
Does he wish to buy your horse? — Vuol egli comprare il di Lei cavallo?
He wishes to buy it. — Egli vuol comprarlo.
He does not wish to buy it. — Egli non vuol comprarlo.

To burn. } Bruciare 1.
{ Abbruciare 1.
To warm. } Scaldare 1.
{ Riscaldare 1.
To tear. | Stracciare 1.

The broth. | Il brodo.
My bed. | Il mio letto.

EIGHTEENTH LESSON.

To go.	Andare* 1.
With or at the house of.	In casa di, or da.
To or to the house of.	
To be.	Essere* 2.
To be with the man or at the man's house.	Essere in casa dell' uomo. / Essere dall' uomo.
To go to the man or to the man's house.	Andare in casa dell' uomo. / Andare dall' uomo.
To be with his (one's) friend, or at his (one's) friend's house.	Essere in casa del suo amico. / Essere dal suo amico.
To go to my father, or to my father's house.	Andare da mio padre. / Andare in casa di mio padre.

At home.	In casa. / In casa sua.
To be at home.	Essere in casa.
To go home.	Andare a casa.

To be with me,	or at my house.	Essere in casa mia	da me.[1]
To go to me,	— to my house.	Andare a casa mia	
To be with him, her,	— at his house.	Essere in casa sua	da lui, da lei
To go to him, her,	— to his house.	Andare a casa sua	(fem.)
To be with us,	— at our house.	Essere in casa nostra	da noi.[2]
To go to us,	— to our house.	Andare a casa nostra	
To be with you,	— at your house.	Essere { in casa sua, di Lei / " " vostra, di voi }	da Lei.
To go to you,	— to your house.	Andare { a casa sua, di Lei / " " vostra, di voi }	da voi.
To be with them,	— at their house.	Essere in casa loro	da loro.
To go to them,	— to their house.	Andare a casa loro	
To be with some one,	— at some one's house.	Essere in casa	{ d' uno. / di qualcuno.
To go to some one,	— to some one's house.	Andare a casa	{ d' uno. / di qualcuno.
To be with no one,	— at no one's house.	Non essere	{ in casa di nessuno. / da nessuno. / in casa di alcuno. / da alcuno.
To go to no one,	— to no one's house.	Non andare	{ a casa di nessuno. / da alcuno. / a casa di alcuno.

[1] We cannot say in Italian *da me, da noi*, when we speak of ourselves.

[2] Ex. *Voglio andare a casa mia* (not *da me*), I wish to go home. But: *Mio fratello vuol venire da me*, My brother wishes to come to me; *Vogliamo andare a casa nostra* (not *da noi*), We will go home. But: *Vogliono, i Signori, venire da noi?* Gentlemen, will you come to us?

EIGHTEENTH LESSON. 69

At whose house? With whom?　　Da chi? in casa di chi?
To whose house? To whom?

To whom (or to whose house) do you　Da chi vuol Ella andare?
 wish to go?
I wish to go to no one (to no one's　Non voglio andare a casa di nessuno.
 house).
At whose house (with whom) is your　Da chi è il di Lei fratello?
 brother?
He is at ours (with us).　　Egli è in casa nostra.
Is he at home?　　È egli in casa?
He is not at home.　　Non è in casa.

Are you?　　È Ella? (Siete voi?)
Tired.　　Stanco, lasso.
Are you tired?　　È Ella stanca? (Siete lasso?)
I am tired.　　Sono stanco.
I am not tired.　　Non sono stanco.
Is he?　　È egli?
He is.　　Egli è.
We are.　　Noi siamo.
You are.　　Voi siete.
They are.　　Eglino o elleno sono.

Thou art.　　| Sei.

To drink.　　| Bere* or bevere* 2.
Where?　　| Dove? ove? onde? donde?

What do you wish to do?　　Che vuol Ella fare? o che volete voi
 　　　fare?
What does your brother wish to do?　Che vuol fare il di Lei o suo fratello?

Is your father at home?　　E in casa vostro padre?
What will the Germans buy?　　Che vogliono comprare i Tedeschi?
They will buy something good.　　Vogliono comprare qualche cosa di
　　　buono.
They will buy nothing.　　Non vogliono comprare niente.
Do they wish to buy a book?　　Vogliono eglino comprare un libro?
They wish to buy one.　　Vogliono comprarne uno.
Do you wish to drink any thing?　　Vuol Ella bere qualche cosa?
I do not wish to drink any thing.　　Non voglio bever niente.

EIGHTEENTH LESSON.

EXERCISES.

43.

Do you wish to work?—I am willing to work, but I am tired.—Do you wish to break my glasses?—I do not wish to break them—Are you willing to look for my son?—I am willing to look for him.—What do you wish to pick up?—I wish to pick up that crown and that franc.—Do you wish to pick up this or that sou?—I wish to pick up both.—Does your neighbour wish to buy these or those combs?—He wishes to buy both these and those.—Does that man wish to cut your foot?—He does not wish to cut mine, but his own.—Does the painter wish to burn some oil?—He wishes to burn some.—What does the shoemaker wish to mend?—He wishes to mend our old boots.—Does the tailor wish to mend any thing?—He wishes to mend some waistcoats.—Is our enemy willing to burn his ship?—He is not willing to burn his own, but ours.—Do you wish to do any thing?—I do not wish to do any thing.—What do you wish to do?—We wish to warm our tea and our father's coffee.—Do you wish to warm my brother's broth?—I am willing to warm it.—Is your servant willing to make my fire?—He is willing to make it, but he has no time.

44.

Do you wish to speak?—I do wish to speak.—Is your son willing to study?—He is not willing to study.—What does he wish to do?—He wishes to drink some wine.—Do you wish to buy any thing?—I wish to buy something.—What do you wish to buy?—I wish to buy some jewels.—Are you willing to mend my handkerchief?—I am willing to mend it.—Who will mend our son's clothes?—We will mend them.—Does the Russian wish to buy this or that picture?—He will buy neither this nor that.—What does he wish to buy?—He wishes to buy some ships.—Which looking-glasses does the Englishman wish to buy?—He wishes to buy those which the French have, and those which the Italians have.—Does your father wish to look for his umbrella or for his stick?—He wishes to look for both.—Do you wish to drink some wine?—I wish to drink some, but I have not any.—Does the sailor wish to drink some milk?—He does not wish to drink any;

he is not thirsty.—What does the captain wish to drink?—He does not wish to drink any thing.—What does the hatter wish to make?—He wishes to make some hats.—Does the carpenter wish to make any thing?—He wishes to make a large ship.—Do you wish to buy a bird?—I wish to buy several.

45.

Does the Turk wish to buy more guns than knives?—He wishes to buy more of the latter than of the former.—How many corkscrews does your servant wish to buy?—He wishes to buy three. —Do you wish to buy many corks?—We wish to buy only a few, but our children wish to buy a good many.—Will your children seek the gloves that we have?—They will not seek those that you have, but those which my father has.—Does any one wish to tear your coat?—No one wishes to tear it.—Who wishes to tear my books?—Your children wish to tear them.—With whom is our father?—He is at his friend's.—To whom do you wish to go?—I wish to go to you.—Will you go to my house?— I will not go to yours, but to my brother's.—Does your father wish to go to his friend's?—He does not wish to go to his friend's, but to his neighbour's.—At whose house is your son?—He is at our house.—Will you look for our hats, or for those of the Dutch? —I will look for neither yours, nor for those of the Dutch, but I will look for mine and for those of my good friends.

46.

Am I right in warming your broth?—You are right in warming it.—Is my servant right in warming your bed?—He is wrong in warming it.—Is he afraid to tear your coat?—He is not afraid to tear it, but to burn it.—Do your children wish to go to our friends?—They do not wish to go to your friends, but to ours.— Are your children at home?—They are not at home, but at their neighbours'.—Is the captain at home?—He is not at home, but at his brothers'.—Is the foreigner at our brother's?—He is not at our brother's, but at our father's.—At whose house is the Englishman?—He is at yours.—Is the American at our house?—He is not at our house, but at his friend's.—With whom is the Italian? —He is with nobody; he is at home.—Do you wish to go home? —I do not wish to go home; I wish to go to the son of my neighbour.—Is your father at home?—No, Sir, he is not at home.—With whom is he?—He is with the good friends of our old neighbour.—Will you go to any one's house?—I will go to no one's house.

47.

Where is your son?—He is at home.—What will he do at home?—He wishes to drink some good wine.—Is your brother at home?—He is not at home; he is at the foreigner's.—What do you wish to drink?—I wish to drink some milk.—What will the German do at home?—He will work, and drink some good wine.—What have you at home?—I have nothing at home.—Has the merchant a desire to buy as much sugar as tea?—He wishes to buy as much of the one as of the other.—Are you tired?—I am not tired.—Who is tired?—My brother is tired.—Has the Spaniard a mind to buy as many horses as asses?—He wishes to buy more of the latter than of the former.—Do you wish to drink any thing?—I do not wish to drink any thing.—How many chickens does the cook wish to buy?—He wishes to buy four.—Do the French wish to buy any thing?—They do not wish to buy any thing.—Does the Spaniard wish to buy any thing?—He wishes to buy something, but he has no money.—Do you wish to go (*venire*) to our brothers'?—I do not wish to go to their house, but to their children's.—Is the Scotchman at any body's house?—He is at nobody's.—Where is he?—He is at his own house.

NINETEENTH LESSON.

Lezione decimanona.

Where? Whither? Where to?	Ove? Dove? Onde? Donde?
There or thither, to it, at it, in it.	Vi or ci.[1]
To go thither.	Andarvi, andarci, o andare là.

[1] When not united to the verb, *there* is expressed by *ivi, là, fi.*

NINETEENTH LESSON. 73

Obs. The relative or local adverbs *ci* and *vi* are joined to the verb which loses its final vowel.

| To be there. | Esscrvi, esserci, od essere là. |

| It to it, it there or thither. | Ce lo, ve lo. |
| Them there, or thither. | Ce li, ve li. |

To take, to carry.	Portare 1.
To send.	Inviare 1. Mandare 1. Spedire 3.
To lead, to take.	Menare 1.
To conduct.	Condurre* 2.

| To take it there, or thither. | { Portarcelo.
 { Portarvelo. |

| Him (object of the verb). | Lo or l'. |
| Them (—). | Li or gli. |

Him there, or thither.	Ce lo, ve lo.
To send him thither.	{ Inviarcelo. { Inviarvelo.
To take him thither.	{ Menarvelo. { Condurvelo.

Them there, or thither.	Ce li (or gli). Ve li (or gli).
Some of it there, or thither.	Vene, cene.
To carry them thither.	Portarceli, portarveli.
To carry some thither.	Portarcene, portarvene.

| Will you send him to my father? | { Vuol Ella inviarlo a casa di mio padre?
 { Vuol Ella mandarlo da o a mio padre? |
| I will send him thither, or to him? | { Voglio inviarvelo.
 { Voglio inviarcelo.
 { Voglio mandarvelo.
 { Voglio mandarcelo. |

| The physician. | Il medico. |
| To come. | Venire* 3. |

4

NINETEENTH LESSON.

When?	Quando?
To-morrow.	Domani.
To-day.	Oggi.

Some where or *whither, any where* or *whither.*	*In qualche luogo.*
No where, not any where.	*In nessun luogo.*
Do you wish to go any where?	Vuol Ella andare in qualche luogo?
I wish to go some where.	Voglio andare in qualche luogo.
I do not wish to go any where.	Non voglio andare in nessun luogo.

To write.	*Scrivere* * 2.
At what o'clock?	A che ora?
At one o'clock.	Al tocco. A un' ora.
At two o'clock.	Alle due. A due ore.

Half.	Mezzo; *feminine,* Mezza.
The quarter.	Il quarto.
At half-past one.	{ Al tocco e mezzo. { All' una e mezzo.
At a quarter past one.	{ Al tocco e un quarto. { All' una e un quarto.
At a quarter past two.	Alle due e un quarto.
At a quarter to one.	{ Al tocco meno un quarto. { All' una meno un quarto.
At twelve o'clock.	A mezzo giorno. Al meriggio o mezzodì.
At twelve o'clock at night (midnight).	A mezza notte.
Less.	Meno.

EXERCISES.

48.

Do we wish to go home?—I wish to go thither.—Does your son wish to go to my house?—He wishes to go there.—Is your brother at home?—He is there (*Egli c' è* or *egli v' è*).—Whither do you wish to go?—I wish to go home.—Do your children wish to go to my house?—They do not wish to go there.—To whom will you take that note?—I will take it to my neighbour.—Will your servant take my note to your father's?—He will take it there.—Will your brother carry my guns to the Russian's?—He will carry them thither.—To whom do our enemies wish to carry our guns?—They wish to carry them to the Turks.—

NINETEENTH LESSON.

Whither will the shoemaker carry my boots?—He will carry them to your house.—Will he carry them home?—He will not carry them thither.—Will you come to me?—I will not come.—Whither do you wish to go?—I wish to go to the good English.—Will the good Italians go to our house?—They will not go thither.—Whither do they wish to go?—They will go no where.

49.

Will you take your son to my house?—I will not take him to your house, but to the captain's.—When will you take him to the captain's?—I will take him there to-morrow.—Do you wish to take my children to the physician?—I will take them thither.—When will you take them thither?—I will take them thither to-day.—At what o'clock will you take them thither?—At half-past two.—When will you send your servant to the physician?—I will send him there to-day.—At what o'clock?—At a quarter-past ten.—Will you go any where?—I will go some where.—Whither will you go?—I will go to the Scotchman.—Will the Irishman come to you?—He will come to me.—Will your son go to any one?—He will go to some one.—To whom does he wish to go?—He wishes to go to his friends.—Will the Spaniards go any where?—They will go no where.—Will our friend go to any one?—He will go to no one.

50.

When will you take your youth to the painter's?—I will take him thither to-day.—Whither will he carry these birds?—He will carry them no where.—Will you take the physician to this man?—I will take him there.—When will the physician go to your brother?—He will go there to-day.—Will you send a servant to me?—I will send one.—Will you send a child to the painter's?—I will send one thither.—With whom is the captain?—He is with nobody.—Has your brother time to come to my house?—He has no time to come there.—Will the Frenchman write one more note?—He will write one more.—Has your friend a mind to write as many notes as I?—He has a mind to write quite as many.—To whose house does he wish to send them?—He will send them to his friends.—Who wishes to write little notes?—The young man wishes to write some.—Do you wish to carry many books to my father's?—I will only carry a few.

51.

Will you send one more trunk to our friend's?—I will send several more there.—How many more hats does the hatter wish to send?—He wishes to send six more.—Will the tailor send as many boots as the shoemaker?—He will send less.—Has your son the courage to go to the captain's?—He has the courage to go there, but he has no time.—Do you wish to buy as many dogs as horses?—I will buy more of the latter than of the former.—At what o'clock do you wish to send your servant to the Dutchman's?—I will send him thither at a quarter to six.—At what o'clock is your father at home?—He is at home at twelve o'clock.—At what o'clock does your friend wish to write his notes?—He will write them at midnight.—Are you afraid to go to the captain's?—I am not afraid, but ashamed to go there.

TWENTIETH LESSON.

Lezione ventesima.

To, meaning *in order to*.	*Per.*
Have you money to buy bread?	Ha Ella danaro per comprare del pane?
I have some to buy some.	No ho per comprarne.
Will you go to your brother in order to see him?	Vuole Ella andare dal di Lei fratello per vederlo?
I have no time to go there to see him.	Non ho tempo di andarvi (d' andarvi) per vederlo.
Has your brother a knife to cut his bread?	Ha un coltello il di Lei fratello per tagliare il suo pane?
He has none to cut it.	Non ne ha per tagliarlo.

TWENTIETH LESSON.

To sweep.	Scopare 1. / Spazzare 1.
To eat.	Mangiare 1.
To kill.	Ammazzare 1. Uccidere* 2.
To salt.	Salare 1. (Mettere* in sale).

To be able (can).	Potere* 2.
Can you? or are you able?	Può Ella? (potete?)
I can, or I am able.	Posso.
I cannot, I am not able.	Non posso.
Can he? or is he able?	Può egli?
He can, or he is able.	Egli può.
He cannot, he is unable.	Non può.
We can, we are able.	Possiamo.
You can, you are able.	Potete (può).
They can, they are able.	Possono (ponno).

Thou canst, art able.	Puoi.

Me. (direct object or accusative).	Mi.
Him. (direct object or accusative).	Lo.

To see.	Vedere* 2.
To see me.	Vedermi.
To see him.	Vederlo.
To see the man.	Vedere l' uomo.
To kill him.	Ammazzarlo, ucciderlo.

To.	A.
To the or at the.	Sing. Al, allo, all'. (See Lesson IX.) Plur. Ai (a'), agli, agl'.

Singular.	Plural.	Singular.	Plural.
To the friend.	To the friends.	All' amico.	Agli amici.
To the man.	To the men.	All' uomo.	Agli uomini.
To the captain.	To the captains.	Al capitano.	Ai capitani.
To the coat.	To the coats.	All' abito.	Agli abiti.
To the book.	To the books.	Al libro.	Ai libri.
To the Englishman.	To the English.	All' Inglese.	Agl' Inglesi.
To the Italian.	To the Italians.	All' Italiano.	Agl' Italiani.

TWENTIETH LESSON.

To him—*a lui* (indirect object or dative).	*Gli.*
To me—*a me.*	*Mi.*

To speak to me.	Parlarmi.
To speak to him.	Parlargli.
To write to him.	Scrivergli.
To write to me.	Scrivermi.
To speak to the man.	Parlare all' uomo.
To speak to the captain.	Parlare al capitano.
To write to the captain.	Scrivere al capitano.

Can you write to me?	Può Ella scrivermi?
I can write to you.	Posso scriverlo (or scrivervi).
Can the man speak to you?	Può parlarle (parlarvi) l' uomo?
He can speak to me.	Può parlarmi.
Will you write to your brother?	Vuole scrivere al di Lei fratello?
I will write to him.	Voglio scrivergli.
The basket.	Il canestro, il paniere.
The carpet.	Il tappeto.
The floor.	Il pavimento.
The cat.	Il gatto.

Will you send the book to the man?	Vuole mandare il libro all' uomo?
I will send it to him.	Voglio mandarglielo.

Obs. A. When the pronoun *gli* precedes *lo* or *ne*, an *e* is inserted between the two pronouns.

When will you send it to him?	Quando vuole mandarglielo?
I will send it to him to-morrow.	Voglio mandarglielo domani.

SINGULAR.

			Indirect object, or Dative.	Direct object, or Accusative.
First person:	To me.	Me.	Mi, or *a me*.	Me, or mi.
Third person:	To him.	Him.	Gli, — *a lui*.	Lo, — lui.

PLURAL.

First person:	To us.	Us.	Ci, ne, or *a noi*.	Noi, or ci.
Second person:	To you.	You.	Vi, — *a voi*.	Vi, — voi.
Third person:	To them.	Them.	Loro, — *a loro*.	Loro — li, le (fem).

Does he wish to speak to you?	Vuol parlarle (parlarvi)?
He does not wish to speak to me, but to you.	Non vuol parlare a me, ma a Lei, a voi.

TWENTIETH LESSON.

Do you wish to write to him?	Vuole Ella scrivergli?
I do not wish to write to him, but to his brother.	Non voglio scrivere a lui, ma a suo fratello?

The following is the order in which the personal pronouns must be placed in the sentence:—

Singular.	Plural.	Singulars.	Plurals.
It to me.	Them to me.	† Me lo.	† Me li.
It to him.	Them to him.	† Glielo.	† Glieli.
It to us.	Them to us.	† Ce lo (ne lo).	† Ce li.
It to you.	Them to you.	† Ve lo.	† Ve li.
It to them.	Them to them.	Lo loro.	Li loro.

Obs. B. The pronouns: *mi, ti, ci, vi, si*, are changed into : *me, te, ce, ve, se*, when they are followed by one of the pronouns: *lo, la, li, gli, le, ne*.

When will you send me the basket?	Quando vuol Ella mandarmi il paniere?
I will send it you to-day.	Voglio mandarglielo (mandarvelo) oggi.

In the following manner the relative pronoun *ne*, some of it, is placed with regard to the personal pronoun:

Some to me.	† Me ne.
Some to him.	† Gliene.
Some to us.	† Ce ne.
Some to you.	† Ve ne.
Some to them.	Ne loro. [¹]

To give.	Dare * 1.
To lend.	Prestare 1.

Are you willing to give me some bread?	Vuole darmi del pane? *or*, Volete darmi del pane.
I am willing to give you some.	Voglio dargliene (darlene), *or*, Voglio darvene.
Will you lend my brother some money?	Vuole prestare del danaro a mio fratello?
I will lend him some.	Voglio prestargliene.

¹ N. B. The verb must be placed between *ne* and *loro*.

A TABLE
OF THE PERSONAL PRONOUNS.

SINGULAR.

	FIRST PERSON.		SECOND PERSON.		THIRD PERSON. Masculine.		THIRD PERSON. Feminine.	
Subject, or Nominative	Io,	I.	Tu,	thou.	Egli, esso, ei, e'	he.	Ella, essa,	she.
Object indirect in the Genitive	Di me,	of me.	Di te,	of thee.	Di lui,	of him,	Di lei,	of her.
Object indirect in the Dative	Me, mi, a me, to me.		Ti, ti, a te, to thee.		Gli, li, a lui,	to him.	Le, a lei,	to her.
Object direct, or Accusative	Me, mi,	me.	Te, ti,	thee.	Lui, lo, il,	him.	La, lei,	her.
Object indirect in the Ablative	Da me,	from me.	Da te,	from thee.	Da lui,	from him.	Da lei,	from her.

PLURAL.

Subject, or Nominative	Noi,	we.	Voi,	you.	Eglino, essi,	they.	Elleno, esse,	they.
Object indirect in the Genitive	Di noi,	of us.	Di voi,	of you.	Di loro,	of them.	Di loro,	of them.
Object indirect in the Dative	A noi, ci, ce, ne, to us.		Vi, ve, a voi, to you.		Loro, a loro,	to them.	Loro, a loro,	to them.
Object direct, or Accusative	Ci, ce, ne, noi,	us.	Vi, ve, voi,	you,	Loro, gli, li,	them.	La, loro,	them,
Object indirect in the Ablative	Da noi,	from us.	Da voi,	from you.	Da loro,	from them.	Da loro,	from them.

EXERCISES.

52.

Has the carpenter money enough to buy a hammer?—He has enough to buy one.—Has the captain money enough to buy a ship?—He has not enough to buy one.—Has the peasant a desire to buy some bread?—He has a desire to buy some, but he has not money enough to buy some.—Has your son ink to write a note? —He has not any to write one.—Have you time to see my brother?—I have no time to see him.—Does your father wish to see me?—He does not wish to see you.—Has your servant a broom (*unos copino*) to sweep the floor?—He has one to sweep it. —Is he willing to sweep it?—He is willing to sweep it.—Has the sailor money to buy some tea?—He has none to buy any.—Has your cook money to buy some beef?—He has some to buy some. —Has he money to buy some chickens?—He has some to buy some.—Have you salt enough to salt my beef?—I have enough to salt it.—Will your friend come to my house in order to see me?—He will neither come to your house, nor see you.—Has your neighbour a desire to kill his horse?—He has no desire to kill it.—Will you kill your friends?—I will only kill my enemies.

53.

Can you cut me some bread?—I can cut you some.—Have you a knife to cut me some?—I have one.—Can you mend my gloves?—I can mend them, but I have no wish to do it.—Can the tailor make me a coat?—He can make you one.—Will you speak to the physician?—I will speak to him.—Does your son wish to see me in order to speak to me?—He wishes to see you in order to give you a crown.—Does he wish to kill me?—He does not wish to kill you; he only wishes to see you.—Does the son of our old friend wish to kill an ox?—He wishes to kill two.—Who has a mind to kill our cat?—Our neighbour's child has a mind to kill it.—How much money can you send me?—I can send you twenty francs.—Will you send me my carpet?—I will send it you.—Will you send the shoemaker any thing?—I will send him my boots.—Will you send him your coats?—No, I will send them to my tailor.—Can the tailor send me my coat?—He cannot send it you.—Are your children able to write to me?—They are able to write to you.—Will you lend me your basket?—I will lend it you.

54.

Have you a glass to drink your wine?—I have one, but I have no wine; I have only tea.—Will you give me money to buy some? —I will give you some, but I have only a little.—Will you give me that which you have?—I will give it you.—Can you drink as much wine as milk?—I can drink as much of the one as of the other.—Has our neighbour any coals to make a fire?—He has some to make one, but he has no money to buy bread and butter. —Are you willing to lend him some?—I am willing to lend him some.—Do you wish to speak to the German?—I wish to speak to him.—Where is he?—He is with the son of the American.— Does the German wish to speak to me?—He wishes to speak to you.—Does he wish to speak to my brother or to yours?—He wishes to speak to both.—Can the children of our neighbour work?—They can work, but they will not.

55.

Do you wish to speak to the children of the Dutchman?—I wish to speak to them.—What will you give them?—I will give them good patty-patties.—Will you lend them any thing?—I am willing to lend them something.—Can you lend them any thing? —I cannot lend them any thing; I have nothing.—Has the cook some more salt to salt the beef?—He has a little more.—Has he some more rice?—He has a great deal more.—Will he give me some?—He will give you some.—Will he give some to my little children?—He will give them some.—Will he kill this or that chicken?—He will neither kill this nor that.—Which ox will he kill?—He will kill that of the good peasant.—Will he kill this or that ox?—He will kill both.—Who will send us biscuits?—The baker will send you some.—Have you any thing to do?—I have nothing to do.

56.

What has your son to do?—He has to write to his good friends and to the captain.—To whom do you wish to speak?—I wish to speak to the Italians and to the French.—Do you wish to give them some money?—I wish to give them some.—Do you wish to give this man some bread?—I wish to give him some.—Will you give him a coat?—I will give him one.—Will your friends give me some coffee?—They will give you some.—Will you lend me your books?—I will lend them you.—Will you lend your neighbours your mattress?—I will not lend it them.—Will you lend them the looking-glass?—I will lend it them.—To whom will you lend your umbrellas?—I will lend them to my friends.—To whom does your friend wish to lend his bed?—He will lend it to nobody.

TWENTY-FIRST LESSON.

Lezione ventesima prima.

To whom?	A chi? (a question followed by the object indirect in the dative).
Whom?	Chi? (for persons.)
What?	Che? (for things.)

DECLENSION OF THE INTERROGATIVE PRONOUNS.
Chi? Who?—Che? What?

	For persons.	For things.	For persons.	For things.
Subject, or Nominative.	Who?	What?	Chi?	Che?
Object indirect in the Genitive.	Of whom?	Of what?	Di chi?	Di che?
Object indirect in the Dative.	To whom? Whose?	To what?	A chi?	A che?

TWENTY-FIRST LESSON.

Object direct, or Accusative,	Whom?	What?	Chi?	Che?
Object indirect in the Ablative.	From whom?	From what?	Da chi?	Da che?

Chi? who? has no plural, and always refers to persons, without distinction of sex, as *who* in English.
Che? what? has no plural, and always relates to things.
Obs. A. In *che* the letter *e* may be substituted by an apostrophe before a vowel, but not the letter *i* in *chi*.

To answer.	Rispondere* 2.
To answer the man.	Rispondere all' uomo.
To answer the men.	Rispondere agli uomini.

Who is it?	Chi è?
Of whom do you wish to speak?	Di chi vuol parlare?
What do you wish to say?	Che vuol dire? / Che cosa vuol dire?
To whom do you wish to answer?	A chi vuole rispondere?
I wish to answer my brother.	Voglio rispondere a mio fratello.
To answer him.	Rispondergli.
To answer you.	Risponderle (the feminine *le* is here used out of politeness).
To answer them.	Risponder loro.

Obs. B. Loro, them or to them, is not joined to the verb like the other pronouns.

To answer the note.	Rispondere al biglietto.
To answer it.	Risponderci, rispondervi.
To answer the notes.	Rispondere ai biglietti.
To answer them.	Risponderci, rispondervi.
To it, to them.	Ci or vi.
Will you answer my note?	Vuol rispondere al mio biglietto?
I will answer it.	Voglio risponderci (rispondervi).
Will you answer the men?	Vuol rispondere agli uomini?
I will answer them.	Voglio risponder loro.
My father wishes to speak to them.	Mio padre vuol parlar loro.

The theatre.	Il teatro.	
The play.	Lo spettacolo.	
The ball.	Il ballo.	
	Singular.	Plural.
To or at the theatre.	Al teatro.	Ai teatri.
To — at the play.	Allo spettacolo.	Agli spettacoli.
To — at the ball.	Al ballo.	Ai balli.
To — at the garden.	Al giardino.	Ai giardini.

TWENTY-FIRST LESSON.

The magazine.	
The warehouse.	Il magazzino.
The storehouse.	
The counting-house.	Il banco (lo studio).
The market.	Il mercato.

There, thither.	*Ci* or *vi.*
To go there, thither.	Andarci or andarvi.
To be there.	Esserci or esservi.
Do you wish to go to the theatre?	Vuol Ella andare al teatro.
I wish to go there.	Voglio andarci (andarvi).
Is your brother at the theatre?	Il di Lei fratello è al teatro (or in teatro)?
He is there.	Vi è.
He is not there.	Non c' è (non vi è).
Where is he?	Ov' è egli?

In.	*Nel, nello, nei, negli, in.*
Is your father in his garden?	È nel suo giardino il di Lei padre?
He is there.	Egli c' è or egli v' è.
Where is the merchant?	Dov' è il mercante?
He is in his warehouse.	È nel suo magazzino.

What have you to do?	Che ha Ella da fare?

Obs. C. The preposition *to* is rendered by *da* when it precedes an infinitive depending on the verb *avere*, to have, or *essere*, to be.

I have nothing to do.	Non ho da far niente.
What has the man to drink?	Che ha da bere l' uomo?
He has nothing to drink.	Non ha da ber niente.
Have you any thing to do?	Ha Ella qualche cosa da fare?
I have to answer a note.	Ho da rispondere ad un biglietto.
I have to speak to your brother.	Ho da parlare al di Lei fratello.
Where is your brother?	Dov' è suo fratello?
The place.	Il luogo.
He is in that place.	È in questo luogo.
Whither does he wish to go?	Ove vuol egli andare?
He wishes to go into the garden.	Vuol andare al giardino.
Does he wish to go to the garden?	Vuol egli andare al giardino?
He wishes to go there.	Vuol andarci (or andarvi).

EXERCISES.

57.

Will you write to me?—I will write to you.—Will you write to the Italian?—I will write to him.—Will your brother write to the English?—He will write to them, but they have no mind to answer him.—Will you answer your friend?—I will answer him.—But whom will you answer?—I will answer my good father.—Will you not answer your good friends?—I will answer them.—Who will write to you?—The Russian wishes to write to me.—Will you answer him?—I will not answer him.—Who will write to our friends?—The children of our neighbour will write to them.—Will they answer them?—They will answer them.—To whom do you wish to write?—I wish to write to the Russian.—Will he answer you?—He wishes to answer me, but he cannot.—Can the Spaniards answer us?—They cannot answer us, but we can answer them.—To whom do you wish to send this note?—I wish to send it to the joiner.

58.

What have you to do?—I have to write.—What have you to write?—I have to write a note.—To whom?—To the carpenter.—What has your father to drink?—He has to drink some good wine.—Has your servant any thing to drink?—He has to drink some tea.—What has the shoemaker to do?—He has to mend my boots.—What have you to mend?—I have to mend my thread handkerchiefs.—To whom have you to speak?—I have to speak to the captain.—When will you speak to him?—To-day.—Where will you speak to him?—At his house.—To whom has your brother to speak?—He has to speak to your son.—What has the Englishman to do?—He has to answer a note.—Which note has he to answer?—He has to answer that of the good German.—Have I to answer the note of the Frenchman?—You have to answer it.—Which note have you to answer?—I have to answer that of my good friend.—Has your father to answer a note?—He has to answer one.—Who has to answer notes?—Our children have to answer a few.—Will you answer the notes of the merchants?—I will answer them.—Will your brother answer this or that note?—He will answer neither this nor that.—Will any one answer my note?—No one will answer it.

59.

Which notes will your father answer?—He will answer only those of his good friends.—Will he answer my note?—He will answer it.—Have you to answer any one?—I have to answer no one.—Who will answer my notes?—Your friends will answer them.—Have you a mind to go to the ball?—I have a mind to go there.—When will you go there?—To-day.—At what o'clock?—At half-past ten.—When will you take your child to the play?—I will take him there to-morrow.—At what o'clock will you take him there?—At a quarter to six.—Where is your son?—He is at the play.—Is your friend at the ball?—He is there.—Where is the merchant?—He is in his counting-house.—Where do you wish to take me to?—I wish to take you to my warehouse.—Where does your cook wish to go?—He wishes to go to the market.—Is your brother at the market?—He is not there.—Where is he?—He is in his warehouse.

60.

Where is the Dutchman?—He is in his granary.—Will you come to me in order to go to the play?—I will come to you, but I have no mind to go to the play.—Where is the Irishman?—He is at the market.—To which theatre do you wish to go?—I wish to go to that of the French.—Will you go to my garden or to that of the Scotchman?—I will go to neither yours nor to that of the Scotchman; I wish to go to that of the Italian.—Does the physician wish to go to our warehouses or to those of the Dutch?—He will go neither to yours nor to those of the Dutch, but to those of the French.—What do you wish to buy at the market?—I wish to buy a basket and some carpets.—Where do you wish to take them?—I will take them home.

61.

How many carpets do you wish to buy?—I wish to buy two.—To whom do you wish to give them?—I will give them to my servant.—Has he a mind to sweep the floor?—He has a mind to do it, but he has no time.—Have the English many warehouses?—They have many.—Have the French as many dogs as cats?—They have more of the latter than of the former.—Have you many guns in your warehouses?—We have many there, but we have but little corn.—Do you wish to see our guns?—I will go into your warehouses in order to see them.—Do you wish to buy any thing?—I wish to buy something.—What do you wish to buy?—I wish to buy a pocket-book (*un portafolio*), a looking-glass, and a gun.—Where will you buy your trunk?—I will buy it at the market.—Have you as much wine as tea in your storehouses?—We have as much of the one as of the other.—Who wishes to tear my coat?—No one wishes to tear it.

62.

Will the English give us some bread?—They will give you some.—Will they give us as much butter as bread?—They will give you more of the latter than of the former.—Will you give this man a franc?—I will give him several.—How many francs will you give him?—I will give him five.—What will the French lend us?—They will lend us many books.—Have you time to write to the merchant?—I wish to write to him, but I have no time to-day.—When will you answer the German?—I will answer him to-morrow.—At what o'clock?—At eight.—Where does the Spaniard wish to go?—He wishes to go no where.—Does your servant wish to warm my broth?—He wishes to warm it.—Is he willing to make my fire?—He is willing to make it.—Where does the baker wish to go to?—He wishes to go to the wood.—Where is the youth?—He is at the play.—Who is at the captain's ball?—Our children and our friends are there.

TWENTY-SECOND LESSON.

Lezione ventesima seconda.

	Singular.	Plural.
To *or* at the corner.	Nel / Al } canto.	Nei / Ai } canti.
To *or* at the hole.	Nel / Al } buco.	Nei / Ai } buchi [1].
In the hole, in the holes.	Nel buco.	Nei buchi.
Where is your cat?	Ove è il suo gatto?	
It is in the bag.	È nel sacco.	

[1] The *hole* is rendered by *il buco* (mas.), and : *la buca* (fem.); but the feminine,

TWENTY-SECOND LESSON.

To or at the bottom.	In fondo. / Al fondo.
To or at the bottom of the bag.	Nel fondo del sacco.
At the corner of the fire.	Nel canto del fuoco.
To or at the end.	Al fine.
To the end of the wood.	Al fine del bosco.
To the end of the woods.	Al fine dei boschi.

To send for.	*Mandare a cercare.*
To go for, to fetch.	*Andare a cercare.*
Will you send for some wine?	Vuol mandare a cercar del vino?
I will send for some.	Voglio mandare a cercarne.
Will your son go for some bread?	Il di Lei figlio vuol andare a cercar del pane?
He will not go for any.	Non vuol andare a cercarne.
I will send for the physician.	Voglio mandar a cercare il medico.
I will send for him.	Voglio mandarlo a cercare.
He will send for my brothers.	Vuol e mandar a cercare i miei fratelli.
He will send for them.	Vuol e mandarli a cercare.
Will you send for glasses?	Vuol Ella mandar a cercare dei bicchieri?
I will send for some.	Voglio mandarne a cercare.

What have you to do?	Che ha Ella da fare?
I have to go to the market.	Ho da andare al mercato (Devo andare al mercato).
What have you to drink?	Che hanno Elleno da bere?
We have to drink some good wine.	Abbiamo da bere del buon vino.
You have to mend your handkerchiefs.	Ha da raccommodare i di Lei fazzoletti.

They have.	Hanno.
What have the men to do?	Che hanno da fare gli uomini?
They have to go to the warehouse.	Hanno da andare al magazzino.

This evening (to-night).	Stasera.
In the evening.	La sera, or nella sera.
This morning.	Stamattina (stamane).
In the morning.	La mattina, il mattino. / Nella mattina, nel mattino.

la buca, is used to designate a rather large hole, whilst the masculine, *il buco*, is used to designate a rather small hole. Ex. *Il gatto, il cane è nella buca*, the cat, the dog is in the hole; *un buco nel vestito*, a hole in the coat; *gli uccelli hanno fatto il loro nido nella buca*, the birds have made their nest in the hole.

TWENTY-SECOND LESSON.

| Now, at present. | { Adesso, in questo punto.
{ Ora. |

Thou.	Tu.[a]
Thou hast—thou art.	Tu hai (ài)—tu sei.
John, art thou here?	Giovanni, sei tu là?
Yes, Sir, I am.	Sì, Signore, ci sono.

[a] We have already seen (Note *, Lesson I.) in what instances the Italians use the second person singular; let us, in addition, observe, that it is a mark of intimacy among friends, and is used by parents and children, brothers and sisters, husbands and wives, towards one another: in general it implies familiarity, founded on affection and fondness, or hatred and contempt. *Voi*, as we have seen in the above note, is used towards servants and persons with whom we are on a familiar footing, as: *Che dite voi?* What do you say? *Mi avete veduto?* Have you seen me? *No, non vi ho veduto;* No, I have not seen you. *Io vi dirò*, I will tell you. But the most polite way of addressing a person is with *Vossignoria* (*V. S.*), contracted and abridged from *Vostra Signoria*, your worship, and in speaking to persons of rank, *Vossignoria Illustrissima*, *Vostra Eccellenza*, and to persons of royal blood, *Vostra Altezza*, to monarchs, *Vostra Maestà*.

All these titles being expressed by feminine substantives in the singular, the word *Ella* is used to avoid a continual repetition of them. It must therefore always be considered as a relative to, or a substitute for, the above titles.

According to this principle the nominative should always be *Ella* (as it is the custom in Tuscany), and the accusative *Lei*, as: *Sta Ella bene?* Are you well? *Come ha Ella dormito?* How have you slept? In Rome, however, and the rest of Italy, they say in the nominative also *Lei* (generally considered as incorrect), as: *Sta bene Lei?* Are you well? *Come ha dormito Lei?* How have you slept? and it would sound affected, if, according to the Florentine manner, you were to use there *Ella*.

In addressing with *Ella* the participle or adjective agrees, according to the best authors, with the feminine noun, *Vossignoria*. Ex. *Si Ella si fosse compiaciuta*, If you had been so kind; *Quant' è già ch' Ella è arrivata?* How long is it since you arrived? (and not *compiaciuto, arrivato*).

The five cases are therefore used in the following manner:—

You.	N.	Vossignoria.	Ella, also Lei.
Your.	G.	di Vossignoria.	Di Lei (suo, sua).
To you.	D.	a Vossignoria.	A Lei, La.
You.	Acc.	Vossignoria.	Lei, La.
From you.	Abl.	da Vossignoria.	Da Lei.

Obs. If a particular stress is to be put on the person addressed to, a *Lei* is used in the dative, and *Lei* in the accusative, if not *Le* in the dative and *La* in the accusative. If *Le* happens to meet with one of the pronouns, *lo, la, li, le, ne*, it is changed into *gli*, as: *glielo, gliela*, it to you; *glieli, gliele*, them to you; *gliene*, some to you.

TWENTY-SECOND LESSON.

Art thou fatigued?	Sei stanco?
I am not fatigued.	Non sono stanco.
Are the men tired?	Sono stanchi gli uomini?

EXAMPLES.

NOMINATIVE.

Where are you going?	Dove va Vossignoria? (or Ella? or Lei?)
Have you always been well?	È Ella stata sempre bene?
You look very well.	Ella (Lei) ha buonissima cera.

GENITIVE.

Your observation is right.	Il riflesso di V. S. (or di V. Ecc.) è giusto, or il di Lei riflesso, or il suo riflesso è giusto.
Where are your gloves?	Dove sono i di Lei guanti? or i suoi guanti?
Which is your room?	Qual è la di Lei camera? or la sua camera?
I sit down here near you.	Io seggo qui presso di Lei.

DATIVE.

Let us take a walk, if it pleases you (i. e. if you please).	Andiamo a spasso, se Le piace.
That will neither please you nor him.	Questo non piacerà nè a Lei, nè a lui.
I thank you very humbly.	Le rendo devotissime grazie.
I thank you and your uncle very much.	Rendo a Lei e al Signor zio le dovute grazie.
Listen then, I will tell it you directly.	Ascolti dunque, glielo dirò subito.
He is not willing to tell it either you or me.	Non lo vuol dire nè a Lei, nè a me.
To you alone I will say it.	Lo dirò a Lei solo.
I shall be eternally grateful to you for it.	Gliene sarò eternamente obbligato.
I will let you see them.	Glieli farò vedere.
I will show them you and your sister.	Li farò vedere a Lei e alla sorella.
I will show it to you to-morrow.	Gliela (fem.) mostrerò domani.
Well! to you I can refuse nothing.	Alla buon' ora! a Lei non posso dar un rifiuto.

ACCUSATIVE.

Do not trouble yourself, I pray.	Non s' incomodi, La prego.
I begged you and not your brother.	Ho pregato Lei e non il fratello.
Pardon me, if I interrupt you.	Scusi, se La interrompo.
He has interrupted you and us.	Egli ha interrotto Lei e noi.
I thank you for it.	Ne La ringrazio.
Do not refuse me that favour, I entreat you.	Via, non mi rifiuti questo favore, ne La scongiuro.
To-morrow I shall go with you to my cousin's.	Domani andrò con Lei dal cugino.

TWENTY-SECOND LESSON.

Obs. A. The adjective in Italian, the same as in French, when it is preceded by a noun or pronoun, must agree with it in number; that is, if the noun or pronoun is in the plural, the adjective must be put in the same number, as may be seen from the example in the question above, and in the answer below.

| They are not tired. | Non sono stanchi. |

Obs. B. It will moreover be noticed, that the adjectives in Italian form their plural number exactly in the same manner as the nouns or substantives.

Thou wilt (wishest)—thou art able (canst).	Vuoi—Puoi.
Art thou willing to make my fire?	Vuoi fare il mio fuoco?
I am willing to make it, but I cannot.	Voglio farlo, ma non posso.

Art thou afraid?	† Hai paura?
I am not afraid; I am cold.	† Non ho paura; ho freddo.
Art thou hungry?	† Hai fame?

To sell.	Vendere 2.
To tell, to say.	Dire* 3.
To tell some one, to say to some one.	Dire a qualcuno.
The word, the jest, device, motto.	Il vocabolo (la parola, *a fem. noun*). Il motto.
Will you tell the servant to make the fire?	Vuol dire al servitore di fare il fuoco?
I will tell him to make it.	Voglio dirgli di farlo. Gli voglio dire di farlo, o Glielo dirò.

	Sing.	Plur.
Thy.	Tuo.	Tuoi.
Thine.	Il tuo.	I tuoi.
Thy book—thy books.	Il tuo libro.	I tuoi libri.

With me, with thee, with him.	Meco, teco, seco (con lui), also con me, con te.
With her.	Con lei.
With us, with you, with them.	Con noi, con voi, con loro.

| Wilt thou go with me? | Vuoi venir meco? con me? |

Obs. C. When a person is spoken to, the verb *to go* is rendered by *venire, to come.*

| I will not go with thee, but with him. | Non voglio venir teco, ma con lui. Non voglio venir con te, ma con lui. |

ABLATIVE.

This depends upon you.	Questo dipende da Lei.
That comes from you.	Questo proviene da Lei.
He was already twice at your house.	Ei fu già due volte da Lei.

| With our friends. | Coi (plur. of col) nostri amici. |
| I will go with our good friends. | Voglio andare coi nostri buoni amici. |

EXERCISES.

63.

Will you send for some sugar?—I will send for some.—Son (*figlio mio*), wilt thou go for some petty-patties?—Yes, father (*padre mio*), I will go for some.—Whither wilt thou go?—I will go into the garden.—Who is in the garden?—The children of our friends are there.—Will you send for the physician?—I will send for him.—Who will go for my brother?—My servant will go for him.—Where is he?—He is in his counting-house.—Will you give me my broth?—I will give it you.—Where is it?—It is at the corner of the fire.—Will you give me some money to (*per*) fetch some milk?—I will give you some to fetch some.—Where is your money?—It is in my counting-house; will you go for it?—I will go for it.—Will you buy my horse?—I cannot buy it; I have no money.—Where is your cat?—It is in the bag.—In which bag is it?—In the bag of the granary.—Where is this man's (*di costui*) dog?—It is in a corner of the ship.—Where has the peasant (got) his corn?—He has it in his bag.—Has he a cat?—He has one.—Where is it?—It is at the bottom of the bag.—Is your cat in this bag?—It is in it.

64.

Have you any thing to do?—I have something to do.—What have you to do?—I have to mend my gloves, and to go to the garden.—Who is in the garden?—My father is there.—Has your cook any thing to drink?—He has to drink some wine and some good broth.—Can you give me as much butter as bread?—I can give you more of the latter than of the former.—Can our friend drink as much wine as coffee?—He cannot drink so much of the latter as of the former.—Have you to speak to any one?—I have to speak to several men.—To how many men have you to speak?—I have to speak to four.—When have you to speak to them?—This evening.—At what o'clock?—At a quarter to nine.—When can you go to the market?—I can go thither in the morning.—

TWENTY-SECOND LESSON.

At what o'clock?—At half-past seven.—When will you go to the Frenchman?—I will go to him to night.—Will you go to the physician in the morning or in the evening?—I will go to him in the morning.—At what o'clock?—At a quarter past ten.

66.

Have you to write as many notes as the Englishman?—I have to write less than he.—Will you speak to the German?—I will speak to him.—When will you speak to him?—Now.—Where is he?—He is at the other end of the wood.—Will you go to the market?—I will go thither to (*per*) buy some cloth.—Do not your neighbours wish to go to the market?—They cannot go thither; they are fatigued.—Hast thou the courage to go to the wood in the evening?—I have the courage to go thither, but not in the evening.—Are your children able to answer my notes?—They are able to answer them.—What do you wish to say to the servant?—I wish to tell him to make the fire, and to sweep the warehouse.—Will you tell your brother to sell me his horse?—I will tell him to sell it you.—What do you wish to tell me?—I wish to tell you something.—Whom do you wish to see?—I wish to see the Scotchman.—Have you any thing to tell him?—I have a motto to tell him.—Which books does my brother wish to sell?—He wishes to sell thine and his own.—Will you come with me?—I cannot go with you.—Who will come with me?—Nobody.—Will your friend come with us?—He will go with you.—With whom wilt thou go?—I will not go with any one.—Will you go with my friend?—I will not go with him, but with thee.—Wilt thou go with me to the warehouse?—I will go with you, but not to the warehouse.—Whither wilt thou go?—I will go with our good friends into the garden of the captain.

TWENTY-THIRD LESSON.

Lezione ventesima terza.

To go out.	Uscire* 3.[1]
To remain, to stay.	Rimanere* 2. Restare 1.
	Stare* 1.
When do you wish to go out?	Quando vuol Ella uscire?
I wish to go out now.	Voglio uscire adesso.
To remain (to stay) at home.	Rimanere in casa.
	Stare in casa.
Here.	Quà, qui, in questo luogo (ci, vi).
To remain here.	Rimaner quà, rimaner qui.
	Stare quà, star qui.
There.	Là, lì (ci, vi).
Will you stay here?	Vuol Ella rimaner quà?
	Vuol Ella stare in questo luogo?
I will stay here.	Voglio starvi (rimanervi).
Will your friend remain there?	Vuol rimaner là il di Lei amico?
	Il di Lei amico vuol star lì?
He will not stay there.	Non vuole rimaner là (star là).
Will you go to your brother?	Vuol andare dal di Lei fratello?
I will go to him.	Voglio andarci.
The pleasure, the favour.	Il piacere, il favore.
To give pleasure.	Far piacere.
To do a favour.	Far un piacere.
	Rendere* un servizio (servigio).
Are you going?	Va Ella (andate)?
I am going.	Vado.
I am not going.	Non vado.
Thou art going.	Vai.
Is he going?	Va egli?
He goes, or is going.	Egli va.
He is not going.	Non va.

[1] Many Italians make use of sortire instead of uscire; but this is done erroneously, for sortire means, to select, to draw lots, and not, to go out.

TWENTY-THIRD LESSON.

Are we going?	Andiamo?
We go, *or* are going.	Andiamo.
They go, *or* are going.	Eglino vanno.
Are you going to your brother?	Va Ella dal di Lei fratello?
I am going there.	Ci vado, vi vado (vadovi, vadoci, little used).
Where is he going?	Dove va egli?
He is going to his father.	Va da suo padre.
All, every.	SING. *Tutto* } ogni, qual- PLUR. *Tutti* } *lunque.*
Every day.	Tutti i giorni. Ogni giorno.
Every morning.	Tutte le mattine. Ogni mattino (mattina).
Every evening.	Tutte le sere. Ogni sera.
It is.	È.
Late.	Tardi.
What o'clock is it?	Che ora è?
It is three o'clock.	Sono le tre.
It is twelve o'clock.	È mezzodì (è mezzo giorno). Sono le dodici.
It is a quarter past twelve.	È mezzodì e un quarto. Sono le dodici e un quarto.
It wants a quarter to six.	Sono le sei meno un quarto. Sono le cinque e tre quarti.
It is half-past one.	È un' ora e mezzo.
To be acquainted with (to know).	Conoscere * 2.
To be acquainted with (to know) a man.	Conoscere un uomo.
Need. *To want.* *To be in want of.* }	*Bisogno.* Aver bisogno di. Abbisognare.
I want it. I am in want of it. }	Ne ho bisogno.
Are you in want of this knife?	Ha Ella bisogno di questo coltello?
I am in want of it.	Ne ho bisogno.
Are you in want of these knives?	Ha Ella bisogno di questi coltelli?

TWENTY-THIRD LESSON.

I am in want of them.	Ne ho bisogno.
I am not in want of them.	Non ne ho bisogno.
I am not in want of any thing.	Non ho bisogno di nulla. / Non ho bisogno di niente.
Is he in want of money?	Ha egli bisogno di danaro?
He is not in want of any.	Non ne ha bisogno.

Of what?	Di che cosa? / Di qual cosa? / Di che?
What are you in want of?	
What do you want?	Di che ha Ella bisogno?
Of whom?	Di chi?

OBJECT INDIRECT IN THE GENITVE OF THE PERSONAL PRONOUNS.

Of me, of thee, of him, of her.	Di me, di te, di lui, di lei (ne).
Of us, of you, of them.	Di noi, di voi, di loro (ne).

Is your father in want of me?	Il di Lei padre ha bisogno di me?
He is in want of you.	Ha bisogno di Lei (di voi).
Are you in want of these books?	Ha Ella bisogno di questi libri?
I am in want of them.	Ne ho bisogno.
Is he in want of my brothers?	Ha egli bisogno dei miei fratelli?
He is in want of them.	Non ha bisogno. / Ha bisogno di loro.

To read.	Leggere.*

EXERCISES.

66.

Will you do me a favour?—Yes, Sir, which?—Will you tell my servant to make the fire?—I will tell him to make it.—Will you tell him to sweep the warehouses?—I will tell him to sweep them.—What will you tell your father?—I will tell him to sell you his horse.—Will you tell your son to go to my father?—I will tell him to go to him.—Have you any thing to tell me?—I have nothing to tell you.—Have you any thing to say to my father?—I have a word to say to him.—Do these men wish to sell their carpets?—They do not wish to sell them.—John, art thou here (*là*)?—Yes, Sir, I am here.—What art thou going to do?—I am going to your hatter to (*per*) tell him to mend your hat.—Wilt thou go to the tailor to tell him to mend my coats?—I will go to him.—Are you willing to go to the market?—I am willing to go thither.—What has your merchant to sell?—He has to sell some beautiful leather gloves (*guanti di pelle*), combs, good cloth, and fine wooden baskets.—Has he any iron guns to sell?—He has some to sell.—Does he wish to sell me his horses?—He wishes to sell them you.—Have you any thing to sell?—I have nothing to sell.

67.

Is it late?—It is not late.—What o'clock is it?—It is a quarter past twelve.—At what o'clock does the captain wish to go out?—He wishes to go out at a quarter to eight?—What will you do?—I wish to read.—What have you to read?—I have a good book to read.—Will you lend it me?—I will lend it you.—When will you lend it me?—I will lend it you to-morrow.—Have you a mind to go out?—I have no mind to go out.—Are you willing to stay here, my dear friend?—I cannot remain here.—Whither have you to go?—I have to go to the counting-house.—When will you go to the ball?—To-night.—At what o'clock?—At midnight.—Do you go to the Scotchman in the evening or in the morning?—I go to him (both) in the evening and in the morning.—Where are you going now?—I am going to the theatre.—Where is your son going?—He is going no where; he is going to stay at home to (*per*) write his notes.—Where is your brother?—He is at his warehouse.—Does he not wish to go out?—No, Sir, he does not wish to go out.—What does he wish to do?—He wishes to write to his friends.—Will you stay here or there?—I will stay there.—Where will your father stay?—He will stay there.—Has our friend a mind to stay in the garden?—He has a mind to stay there.

68.

At what o'clock is the Dutchman at home?—He is at home every evening at a quarter past nine.—When does your cook go to the market?—He goes thither every morning at half-past five.—When does our neighbour go to the Irishmen?—He goes to them every day.—At what o'clock?—At eight o'clock in the morning.—What do you wish to buy?—I do not wish to buy any thing; but my father wishes to buy an ox.—Does he wish to buy

TWENTY-THIRD LESSON.

this or that ox?—He wishes to buy neither.—Which does he wish to buy?—He wishes to buy your friend's.—Has the merchant one more coat to sell?—He has one more, but he does not wish to sell it.—Has this man one knife more to sell?—He has not one knife more to sell, but he has a few more guns to sell.—When will he sell them?—He will sell them to-day.—Where?—At his warehouse.—Do you wish to see my friend?—I wish to see him in order to know him.—Do you wish to know my children?—I do wish to know them.—How many children have you?—I have only two, but my brother has more than I: he has six.—Does that man wish to drink too much wine?—He wishes to drink too much.—Have you wine enough to drink?—I have only a little, but enough.—Does your brother wish to buy too many petty-patties?—He wishes to buy a great many, but not too many.

69.

Can you lend me a knife?—I can lend you one.—Can your father lend me a book?—He can lend you several.—What are you in want of?—I am in want of a good gun.—Are you in want of this picture?—I am in want of it.—Does your brother want money?—He does not want any.—Does he want some boots?—He does not want any.—What does he want?—He wants nothing.—Are you in want of these sticks?—I am in want of them.—Who wants some sugar?—Nobody wants any.—Does any body want pepper?—Nobody wants any.—What do I want?—You want nothing.—Does your father want these pictures or those?—He wants neither these nor those.—Are you in want of me?—I am in want of you.—When do you want me?—At present.—What have you to say to me?—I have something to say to you.—Is your son in want of us?—He is in want of you and your brothers.—Are you in want of my servants?—I am in want of them.—Does any one want my brother?—No one wants him.—Does your father want any thing?—He does not want any thing.—What does the Englishman want?—He wants some corn.—Does he not want some jewels?—He does not want any.—What does the sailor want?—He wants some biscuits, milk, cheese, and butter.—Will you give me any thing?—I will give you some bread and wine.

TWENTY-FOURTH LESSON.

Lezione ventesima quarta.

THE PRESENT.

In regular verbs[1] the present tense is formed from the infinitive, whose termination is changed into *o*.

The first and second persons singular, and the first person plural, are for all the three conjugations terminated in the same manner, viz.

The first person singular in *o*. Ex.
- I speak. Parlo.
- I sell. Vendo.
- I serve. Servo.

The second person singular in *i*. Ex.
- Thou speakest. Parli.
- Thou sellest. Vendi.
- Thou servest. Servi.

The first person plural in iamo. Ex.
- We speak. Parliamo.
- We sell. Vendiamo.
- We serve. Serviamo.

As for the third person singular, it is for the first conjugation terminated in *a* (from *are*, as *parlare*), and for the second and third conjugations in *e*. The second person plural terminates for the first conjugation in *ate* (from *are*, as *parlare*), for the second in *ete* (from *ere*, as *vendere*), and for the third in *ite* (from *ire*, as *servire*). The third person plural ends for the first conjugation in *ano* (from *are*, as *parlare*), and for the second and third conjugations in *ono*.

EXAMPLES.

INFINITIVE.

1. Parlare, to speak.
2. Vendere, to sell.
3. Servire, to serve.

PRESENT TENSE.

First Conjugation.		Second Conjugation.		Third Conjugation.	
Parlo,	I speak.	Vendo,	I sell.	Servo,	I serve.
Parli,	thou speakest.	Vendi,	thou sellest.	Servi,	thou servest.
Parla,	he speaks.	Vende,	he sells.	Serve,	he serves.
Parliamo,	we speak.	Vendiamo,	we sell.	Serviamo,	we serve.
Parlate,	you speak.	Vendete,	you sell.	Servite,	you serve.
Parlano,	they speak.	Vendono,	they sell.	Servono,	they serve.

[1] As for the irregular verbs, it is impossible to give, as for the present, any fixed rules concerning them. The learner must mark them in his list of irregular verbs as he meets with them in proceeding.

TWENTY-FOURTH LESSON.

Obs. A. As the rules which I give above, on the formation of the present tense, are applicable only to regular verbs, it remains now to point out the irregularities in the present tense of all those irregular verbs which we have employed already to enable the learner to use them in his exercises. They are as follows:—

Those that are not given here are, of course, regular in the present tense.

To give.

I give,	thou givest,	he gives,
We give,	you give,	they give.

To make, to do.

I make or do,	thou makest or dost,	he makes or does.
We do,	you do,	they do.

To stay, to remain.

I stay,	thou stayest,	he stays.
We stay,	you stay,	they stay.

To drink.

I drink,	thou drinkest,	he drinks.
We drink,	you drink,	they drink.

To see.

I see,	thou seest,	he sees.
We see,	you see,	they see.

To remain.

I remain,	thou remainest,	he remains.
We remain,	you remain,	they remain.

Dare* 1.

First Person.	Second Person.	Third Person.
Io do,	tu dai,	egli dà.
Noi diamo,	voi date,	eglino danno.

Fare* 1 (formerly *facere*).

Io faccio or fo,	tu fai,	egli fa.
Noi facciamo,	voi fate,	eglino fanno.

Stare* 1 ².

Io sto,	tu stai,	egli sta.
Noi stiamo,	voi state,	eglino stanno.

Bere or bevere* 2.

Bevo,	bevi,	beve.
Beviamo,	bevete,	bevono (or beono).

Vedere* 2.

Vedo, veggo, or veggio,	vedi,	vede.
Vediamo or veggiamo,	vedete,	vedono or veggono.

Rimanere* 2.

1st Pers.	2nd Pers.	3rd Pers.
Rimango,	rimani,	rimane.
Rimaniamo,	rimanete,	rimangono.

¹ These three verbs, viz., *dare,* *fare,* *stare,* together with *andare* (which see in the foregoing Lesson), are the only irregular verbs of the first conjugation, all the others being regular.

TWENTY-FOURTH LESSON.

To pick up.			Raccorre * 2 (abridged from raccogliere).		
I pick up,	thou pickest up,	he picks up.	Raccolgo,	raccogli,	raccoglie,
We pick up,	you pick up,	they pick up.	Raccogliamo,	raccogliete,	raccolgono.

To say, to tell.			Dire * 3 (formerly dicere).		
I say,	thou sayest,	he says.	Dico,	dici (or di'),	dice.
We say,	you say,	they say.	Diciamo,	dite,	dicono.

To conduct, to take.			Condurre * 2 (formerly conducere).		
I conduct,	thou conductest,	he conducts.	Conduco,	conduci,	conduce,
We conduct,	you conduct,	they conduct.	Conduciamo,	conducete,	conducono.

To come.			Venire * 3.		
I come,	thou comest.	he comes.	Vengo,	vieni,	viene
We come,	you come,	they come.	Veniamo,	venite,	vengono.

To go out.			Uscire * 3.		
I go out,	thou goest out,	he goes out.	Esco,	esci,	esce.
We go out,	you go out,	they go out.	Usciamo, or esciamo,	uscite, or escite.	escono.

Obs. B. There is no distinction in Italian between I love, do love, and am loving. All these present tenses are expressed by *amo*, I love. Ex.

To love.			Amare 1.	
I { love. do love. am loving.	He { loves. does love. is loving.		Amo,	ama.
Thou { lovest. dost love. art loving.	You { love. do love. are loving.		Ami,	amate.
We { love. do love. are loving.	They { love. do love. are loving.		Amiamo,	amano.

TWENTY-FOURTH LESSON.

To love, to like, to be fond of.	Amare 1.
To arrange, to set in order.	{ Ordinare 1. Mettere * (2) in ordine. Assestare 1.
Do you like him?	L' ama Ella? (L' amate?) Voi?
I do like him.	L' amo.
I do not like him.	Non l' amo.

☞ Personal pronouns, not standing in the nominative, take their place before the verb, except when this is in the Infinitive, the present participle, or the Imperative, for then the pronoun is joined to the verb, which loses its final e, as we have seen in Obs. Lesson XVII.

Do you sell your horse?	{ Vende Ella il di Lei cavallo? Vendete il vostro cavallo?
I do sell it.	Lo vendo.
Do you sell it?	{ Lo vende Ella? Lo vendete?
Does he send you the note?	Le manda egli il biglietto?
He does send it me.	Egli me lo manda.
Does the servant sweep the floor?	Spazza il pavimento il servitore? or better, il servitore spazza egli il pavimento?
He does sweep it.	Egli lo spazza.

To want, to miss.	Mancare 1.
To pay.	Pagare 1.

Obs. C. Verbs ending in *care* or *gare* take the letter *h* after *c* or *g*, in all tenses and persons where *c* or *g* meets with one of the vowels, *e*, *i*, Ex.

Art thou in want of any thing?	{ Manchi tu di qualche cosa? Ti manca qualche cosa?
I am in want of nothing.	{ Non manco di niente. Non mi manca niente.
Dost thou pay for thy boots?	† Paghi tu i tuoi stivali?
I pay for them.	† Li pago.

Obs. D. *To want, to be in want of,* may be rendered in Italian in various manners; amongst others, also in the following:—

To want, to be in want of.	{ Essere d' uopo, Essere uopo, Essere mestieri,	{ Aver d' uopo di, Aver mestieri di.
Are you in want of this knife?	Le è d' uopo cotesto coltello? (Le è mestieri cotesto coltello?) very little used.	
I am in want of it.	Mi è d' uopo. (Mi è mestieri.)	

TWENTY-FOURTH LESSON.

Are you in want of these knives? | Ha son d' uopo questi coltelli? avete
 | d' uopo di questi coltelli?
I am in want of them. | Mi son d' uopo. Ne ho d' uopo.
I am not in want of them. | Non mi son d' uopo. Non ne ho d'
 | uopo.
I am not in want of any thing. | Non mi è d' uopo niente. Non ho
 | d' uopo di niente.
Is he in want of money? | Gli è d' uopo danaro?
He does not want any. | Non gliene è d' uopo.

To open.

I open, thou openest, he opens. | Apro, apri, apre.
We open, you open, they open. | Apriamo, aprite, aprono.
Do you open his note? | Apre Ella (aprite,) voi il suo biglietto?
I do not open it. | Non l' apro.
Does he open his eyes? | Apre egli gli occhi?
He opens them. | Egli li apre.
Whom do you love? | Chi ama Ella (amate) voi?
I love my father. | Amo mio padre
Does your father love his son? | Il di Lei padre ama suo figlio?
He does love him. | Egli l' ama.
Do you love your children? | Ama Ella i di Lei fanciulli?
I do love them. | Li amo.

Aprire 3 (regular in Present).

To like.
To be fond of. } Piacere.*

I like, thou likest, he likes. | Piaccio, piaci, piace.
We like, you like, they like. | Piacciamo, piacete, piacciono.

Obs. E. This verb, the same as *dolere** (see next Lesson), is in Italian employed impersonally with the dative of the personal pronoun. Ex.

Are you fond of wine? | Le piace il vino?
I am fond of it. | Mi piace.
What are you fond of? | Che Le piace? (Che vi piace?)
 Cider. | Del cidro.
I am fond of cider. | Il cidro mi piace.
What is the American fond of? | Che piace all' Americano?
He is fond of coffee | Gli piace il caffè?
 The ugly man. | L' uomaccio.

To receive.
To finish.

I finish, thou finishest, he finishes. | Finisco, finisci, finisce.
We finish, you finish, they finish. | Finiamo, finite, finiscono.

Ricevere 2.
*Finire** 3.

This instant.	*All' instante.*
Now.	*Ora.*
At once.	*Subito.*
What are you going to do?	† Che fa ora Ella?
	† Che fate ora?
I am going to read.	† Ora leggo (sto per leggere).
What is he going to do?	† Che fa egli all' istante?
He is going to write a note.	† All' istante scrive un biglietto.
Are you going to give me any thing?	† Mi dà Ella subito qualcosa?
I am going to give you some bread and wine.	† Le do subito pane e vino.

Obs. F. Instead of saying *questo uomo*, this man; *cotesto uomo*, that man, the Italians often use the plural of the pronouns, *questo*, *cotesto*, and translate as follows:

This man.	*Questi.*
That man.	*Cotesti.*

Otherwise:

This man.	*Costui* (Plur. *costoro*, these men).
That man.	*Colui* (Plur. *coloro*, those men).

Obs. G. As for *cotestui*, that man, it is grown obsolete.

Do you know this man?	Conosce Ella questi?
I know neither this nor that one.	Non conosco né questi né quello.
Do you see this man?	Vede Ella costui?
I do not see this man, but that one.	Non vedo costui, ma colui.
Do you hear these men?	Sente Ella costoro?
I do not hear these men, but those.	Non sento costoro, ma coloro.

To know.	*Sapere* 2.
I know, thou knowest, he knows.	So, sai, sa.
We know, you know, they know.	Sappiamo, sapete, sanno.

EXERCISES.

70.

Do you love your brother?—I do love him.—Does your brother love you?—He does not love me.—My good child, dost thou love me?—Yes, I do love thee.—Dost thou love this ugly man (*quell' uomaccio*) I do not love him.—Whom do you love?—I love my children.—Whom do we love?—We love our friends.—Do we like any one?—We like no one.—Does any body like us?—The Ame-

ricans like us.—Do you want any thing?—I want nothing.—
Whom is your father in want of?—He is in want of his servant.
—What do you want?—I want the note.—Do you want this or
that note?—I want this.—What do you wish to do with it (*farne*)?
—I wish to open it, in order to read it.—Does your son read our
notes?—He does read them.—When does he read them?—He
reads them when he receives them.—Does he receive as many
notes as I?—He receives more than you.—What do you give
me?—I do not give thee any thing.—Do you give this book to
my brother?—I do give it him.—Do you give him a bird?—I do
give him one.—To whom do you lend your books?—I lend them
to my friends.—Does your friend lend me a coat?—He lends you
one.—To whom do you lend your clothes?—I do not lend them
to any body.

71.

Do we arrange any thing?—We do not arrange any thing.—
What does your brother set in order?—He sets his books in order.
—Do you sell your ship?—I do not sell it.—Does the captain sell
his?—He does sell it.—What does the American sell?—He sells
his oxen.—Does the Englishman finish his note?—He does finish
it.—Which notes do you finish?—I finish those which I write to
my friends.—Dost thou see any thing?—I see nothing.—Do you
see my large garden?—I do see it.—Does your father see our
ships?—He does not see them, but we see them.—How many
soldiers do you see?—We see a good many; we see more than
thirty.—Do you drink any thing?—I drink some wine.—What
does the sailor drink?—He drinks some cider.—Do we drink wine
or cider?—We drink wine and cider.—What do the Italians
drink?—They drink some coffee.—Do we drink wine?—We do
drink some.—What art thou writing?—I am writing a note.—To
whom?—To my neighbour.—Does your friend write?—He does
write.—To whom does he write?—He writes to his tailor.—What
are you going to do?—I am going to write.—What is your father
going to do?—He is going to read.—What is he going to read?—
He is going to read a book.—What are you going to give me?—
I am not going to give you any thing.—What is our friend going
to give you?—He is going to give me something good.—Do you
know my friend?—I do know him.

TWENTY-FOURTH LESSON.

72.

Do you write your notes in the evening?—We write them in the morning.—What dost thou say?—I say nothing.—Does your brother say any thing?—He says something.—What does he say?—I do not know.—What do you say to my servant?—I tell him to sweep the floor, and to go for some wine, bread, and cheese.—Do we say any thing?—We say nothing.—What does your friend say to the shoemaker?—He tells him to mend his boots.—What do you tell the tailors?—I tell them to make my clothes.—Dost thou go out?—I do not go out.—Who goes out?—My brother goes out.—Where is he going?—He is going to the garden.—To whom are you going?—We are going to the good English.—What art thou reading?—I am reading a note from my friend.—What is your father reading?—He is reading a book.—What are you doing?—We are reading.—Are your children reading?—They are not reading; they have no time to read.—Do you read the books which I read?—I do not read those which you read, but those which your father reads.—Do you know this man?—I do not know him.—Does your friend know him?—He does know him.—What is your friend going to do?—He is not going to do any thing.

73.

Do you know my children?—We do know them.—Do they know you?—They do not know us.—With whom are you acquainted?—I am acquainted with nobody.—Is any body acquainted with you?—Somebody is acquainted with me.—Who is acquainted with you?—The good captain knows me.—What dost thou eat?—I eat some bread.—Does not your son eat some cheese?—He does not eat any.—Do you cut any thing?—We cut some wood.—What do the merchants cut?—They cut some cloth.—Do you send me any thing?—I send you a good gun.—Does your father send you money?—He does send me some.—Does he send you more than I?—He sends me more than you.—How much does he send you?—He sends me more than fifty crowns.—When do you receive your notes?—I receive them every morning.—At what o'clock?—At half-past ten.—Is your son coming?—He is coming.—To whom is he coming?—He is coming to me.—Do you come to me?—I do not come to you, but to your children.—Where is our friend going?—He is going no where; he remains at home.—Are you going home?—We are not going home, but to our friends.—Where are your friends?—They are in their garden.—Are the Scotchmen in their gardens?—They are there.

74.

What do you buy?—I buy some knives.—Do you buy more knives than glasses?—I buy more of the latter than of the former.—How many horses does the German buy?—He buys a good many; he buys more than twenty of them.—What does your servant carry?—He carries a large trunk.—Where is he carrying it?—He is carrying it home.—To whom do you speak?—I speak to the Irishman.—Do you speak to him every day?—I speak to him every morning and every evening.—Does he come to you?—He does not come to me, but I go to him.—What has your servant to do?—He has to sweep my floor and to set my books in order.—Does my father answer your notes?—He answers them.—What does your son break?—He breaks nothing, but your children break my glasses.—Do they tear any thing?—They tear nothing.—Who burns my hat?—Nobody burns it.—Are you looking for any body?—I am not looking for any body.—What is my son looking for?—He is looking for his pocket-book.—What does your cook kill?—He kills a chicken.

75.

Are you killing a bird?—I am killing one.—How many chickens does your cook kill?—He kills three of them.—To whom do you take my boy?—I take him to the painter.—When is the painter at home?—He is at home every evening at seven o'clock.—What o'clock is it now?—It is not yet six o'clock.—Do you go out in the evening?—I go out in the morning.—Are you afraid to go out in the evening?—I am not afraid, but I have no time to go out in the evening.—Do you work as much as your son?—I do not work as much as he.—Does he eat as much as you?—He eats less than I.—Can your children write as many notes as my children?—They can write just as many.—Can the Russian drink as much wine as cider?—He can drink more of the latter than of the former.—When do our neighbours go out?—They go out every morning at a quarter to five.—Which note do you send to your father?—I am sending him my own.—Do you not send mine?—I am sending it also.—To whom do you send your clothes?—I send them to nobody; I want them.—To whom do your sons send their boots?—They send them to no one; they want them.

₊ We should fill volumes were we to give all the exercises that are applicable to our lessons, and which the pupils may very easily compose by themselves. We shall, therefore, merely repeat what we have already mentioned at the commencement:—Pupils who wish to improve rapidly ought to compose a great many sentences in addition to those given; but they must pronounce them aloud. This is the only way by which they will acquire the habit of speaking fluently.

TWENTY-FIFTH LESSON.

Lezione ventesima quinta.

To go to the play.	Andare* allo spettacolo.
To be at the play.	Essere* allo spettacolo.

To bring.	{ Recare 1. { Portare 1.
To find.	Trovare 1.
The butcher.	Il macellaio.
The sheep.	Il montone.

What, or *the thing which.*	{ Ciò che. { Quel che. { Quanto.
Do you find what you look for (or what you are looking for)?	Trova Ella ciò che cerca? o trovate voi quel che cercate?
I find what I look for. I find what I am looking for.	Trovo ciò che cerco.

He does not find what he is looking for. Egli non trova ciò che cerca.
We find what we look for. Troviamo ciò che cerchiamo.
They find what they look for. Eglino trovano ciò che cercano.
I mend what you mend. Assetto ciò che assetti Ella, assetto od accomodo ciò che Ella assetta.
I buy what you buy. Compro quello che compra Ella (comprate voi).
I pay what you pay. Pago quanto paga Ella.
Are you in want of money? Manca Ella di danaro?
I am not in want of any. Non ne manco.
Do you take him to the play? Lo conduce Ella allo spettacolo?
I do take him thither. Ve lo conduco.

To study. Studiare 1.

Instead of. { In luogo di.
              { Invece di.

Obs. Instead of is in English followed by the present participle, whilst in Italian it is followed by the infinitive.

To play. Giuocare 1.
To listen. Ascoltare 1.
To hear. Sentire 3.

Instead of listening. { Invece d' ascoltare.
                       { In luogo d' ascoltare.

Instead of playing. { In luogo di giuocare.
                     { Invece di giuocare.

Do you play instead of studying? Giuoca Ella invece di studiare?
I study instead of playing. Studio invece di giuocare.
That man speaks instead of listening. Quest! parla invece d' ascoltare.

To ache. Dolere.*
To complain. Dolersi.*
The finger. Il dito (plur. le dita, fem.).
I complain — thou complainest. Mi dolgo or doglio — ti duoli.
We complain — they complain. Ci dogliamo — si dolgono.
You complain — he complains. Vi dolete — si duole.
Have you a sore finger? † Le duole il dito?
Have you the headache? † Le duole il capo (la testa)?
I have a sore finger. † Il dito mi duole.
I have the headache. † Il capo (la testa) mi duole. Ho mal di testa.
Has your brother a sore foot? † Duole il piede al di Lei fratello?
He has a sore eye. † Gli duole l' occhio.
We have sore eyes. † Ci dolgono gli occhi.

The study (a closet).	Lo scrittoio. Lo studio.
The desk.	Lo scrittoio.
The elbow.	Il gomito.
The back.	Il dorso.
The arm.	Il braccio (plur. le braccia).
The knee.	Il ginocchio (plur. le ginocchia).
I have a sore elbow.	Mi duole il gomito.
Thou hast a pain in thy back.	Ti duole il dorso.
He has a sore arm.	Gli duole il braccio.
You have a sore knee.	Vi duole il ginocchio.

Do you read instead of writing?	Leggo Ella invece di scrivere?
Does your brother read instead of speaking?	Legge li di Lei fratello invece di parlare?
Does the servant make the bed?	Fa il letto il servitore?
He makes the fire instead of making the bed.	Egli fa il fuoco invece di fare il letto.

To learn.	Imparare I.
To learn to read.	Imparare a leggere.
I learn to read.	Imparo a leggere.
He learns to write.	Egli impara a scrivere.

EXERCISES.

76.

Do you go to the play this evening?—I do not go to the play.—What have you to do?—I have to study.—At what o'clock do you go out?—I do not go out in the evening.—Does your father go out?—He does not go out.—What does he do?—He writes.—Does he write a book?—He does write one.—When does he write it?—He writes it in the morning and in the evening.—Is he at home now?—He is at home (He is).—Does he not go out?—He cannot go out; he has a sore foot.—Does the shoemaker bring our boots?—He does not bring them.—Is he not able to work?—He is not able to work; he has a sore knee.—Has any body a sore elbow?—My tailor has a sore elbow.—Who has a sore arm?—I have a sore arm.—Do you cut me some bread?—I cannot cut you any; I have sore fingers (*mi dogliono le dita*).—Do you read your book?—I cannot read it; I have sore eyes (*mi dogliono gli occhi*).—Who has sore eyes?—The French have

sore eyes.—Do they read too much ?—They do not read enough.
—What day of the month is it to-day ?—It is the third.—What day
of the month is it to-morrow ?—To-morrow is the fourth.—Are you
looking for any one ?—I am not looking for any one.—What is
the painter looking for ?—He is not looking for any thing.—
Whom are you looking for ?—I am looking for your son.—Have
you any thing to tell him ?—I have something to tell him.—What
have you to tell him ?—I have to tell him to go to the play this
evening.

77.

Who is looking for me ?—Your father is looking for you.—Is
any body looking for my brother?—Nobody is looking for him.
Dost thou find what thou art looking for ?—I do find what I am
looking for.—Does the captain find what he is looking for ?—He
finds what he is looking for, but his children do not find what
they are looking for.—What are they looking for ?—They are
looking for their books.—Where dost thou take me to ?—I take
you to the theatre.—Do you not take me to the market ?—I do
not take you thither.—Do the Spaniards find the umbrellas which
they are looking for ?—They do not find them.—Does the tailor
find his thimble ?—He does not find it.—Do the merchants find
the cloth which they are looking for ?—They do find it.—What
do the butchers find ?—They find the oxen and sheep which they
are looking for.—What does your cook find ?—He finds the chickens which he is looking for.—What is the physician doing ?—
He is doing what you are doing.—What is he doing in his study ?
—He is reading.—What is he reading ?—He is reading your
father's book.—Whom is the Englishman looking for ?—He is
looking for his friend, in order to take him to the garden.—What
is the German doing in his study ?—He is learning to read.—
Does he not learn to write ?—He does not learn it (*l' impara*).—
Does your son learn to write ?—He learns to write and to read.

78.

Does the Dutchman speak instead of listening ?—He speaks
instead of listening.—Do you go out instead of remaining at
home ?—I remain at home instead of going out.—Does your son
play instead of studying ?—He studies instead of playing.—When

does he study?—He studies every day.—In the morning or in the evening?—In the morning and in the evening.—Do you buy an umbrella instead of buying a book?—I buy neither the one nor the other.—Does our neighbour break his sticks instead of breaking his glasses?—He breaks neither.—What does he break?—He breaks his guns.—Do the children of our neighbour read?—They read instead of writing.—What is our cook doing?—He makes a fire instead of going to the market.—Does the captain give you any thing?—He does give me something.—What does he give you?—He gives me a great deal of money.—Does he give you money instead of giving you bread?—He gives me money and bread.—Does he give you more cheese than bread?—He gives me less of the latter than of the former.

79.

Do you give my friend less knives than gloves?—I give him more of the latter than of the former.—What does he give you?—He gives me many books instead of giving me money.—Does your servant make your bed?—He does not make it.—What is he doing instead of making your bed?—He sweeps the study instead of making my bed.—Does he drink instead of working?—He works instead of drinking.—Do the physicians go out?—They remain at home instead of going out.—Does your servant make coffee?—He makes tea instead of making coffee.—Does any one lend you a gun?—Nobody lends me one.—What does your friend lend me?—He lends you many books and many jewels.—Do you read the books which I read?—I do not read the one which you read, but the one which the great captain reads.—Are you ashamed to read the books which I read?—I am not ashamed, but I have no wish to read them.

SECOND MONTH.

Secondo mese.

TWENTY-SIXTH LESSON.

Lezione ventesima sesta.

Do you learn French?	Impara Ella il francese? Impara Ella l' idioma francese (or la lingua francese)?
I do learn it.	L' imparo.
I do not learn it.	Non l' imparo.
French.	Il francese.
English.	L' inglese.
German.	Il tedesco.
Italian.	L' italiano.
Spanish.	Lo spagnuolo.
Polish.	Il polonese.
Russian.	Il russo.
Latin.	Il latino.
Greek.	Il greco.
Arabian, Arabic.	L' arabo.
Syrian, Syriac.	Il siriaco.
I learn Italian.	Imparo l' italiano.
My brother learns German.	Mio fratello impara il tedesco.
The Pole.	Il Polacco.
The Roman.	Il Romano.
The Greek.	Il Greco.
The Arab, the Arabian.	L' Arabo.
The Syrian.	Il Siriaco.
Are you an Englishman?	È Ella Inglese?
No, Sir, I am a Frenchman.	No, Signore, sono Francese.

Obs. A. When the indefinite article is used in English to denote qualities, the Italians make use of no article.

TWENTY-SIXTH LESSON. 115

He is a German.	Egli è Tedesco.
Is he a tailor?	È egli sarto?
No, he is a shoemaker.	No, egli è calzolaio.

The fool.	Il pazzo.
He is a fool.	Egli è pazzo.

The morning.	Il mattino, la mattina.
The evening.	La sera.
The day.	Il giorno (il dì).

To wish.	Desiderare 1. Dare* (conjugated Lesson XXIV). Augurare 1.
I wish you a good morning.	Le do (auguro) il buon giorno.

Obs. B. Often the indefinite article in English answers to the definite article in Italian.

Does he wish me a good evening?	Mi dà (augura) egli la buona sera?
He wishes you a good morning.	Egli Le dà (augura) il buon giorno.
He has a large nose.	Egli ha il naso grande.
He has blue eyes.	Egli ha gli occhi azzurri.
Blue.	Azzurro, turchino.
Black.	Nero, negro.
Long.	Lungo.

A large knife.	Un coltellone.
A large man.	Un uomone.
A French book.	Un libro francese.
An English book.	Un libro inglese.
French money.	Danaro francese.
English soap.	Sapone inglese.

Do you read a German book?	Legge Ella un libro tedesco?
I read an Italian book.	Leggo un libro italiano.

To listen to some one.	† Ascoltare { qualcuno. uno. alcuno.

To listen to something.	† Ascoltare { qualcosa. qualche cosa. alcuna cosa.

What or the thing which.	Ciò che, quel che, quanto.
Do you listen to what the man tells you?	† Ascolta Ella ciò che l' uomo Le dice?

TWENTY-SIXTH LESSON.

I listen *to* it.	† L' ascolto.
He listens *to* what I tell him.	† Egli ascolta ciò che gli dico.
Do you listen *to* what I tell you?	† Ascolta Ella quel che Le dico?
Do you listen *to* me?	† Mi ascolta (*or* m' ascolta) Ella? mi ascoltate voi?
I do listen *to* you.	† La ascolto (*or* L' ascolto).
Do you listen *to* my brother?	† Ascolta Ella mio fratello?
I do not listen *to* him.	† Non l' ascolto.
Do you listen *to* the men?	† Ascolta Ella quegli uomini?
I listen *to* them.	† Li ascolto.

To take away. *Portar via (levare)* 1.
To take off. *Levarsi* 1.

Do you take your hat off?	† Si leva Ella il cappello?
I take it off.	† Me lo levo.
Does he take off his coat?	† Levasi egli l' abito?
He does take it off.	† Se lo leva.
He does not take it off.	† Non se lo leva.
Do your children take off their boots?	† Si levano gli stivali i di Lei fanciulli?
They do take them off.	† Se li levano.
You take your gloves off.	Ella si leva i guanti. / Vi levate i guanti.
We take off our gloves.	† Ci leviamo i guanti.
We take them off.	† Ce li leviamo.

To correct. *Correggere*† 2.

Does your father correct your exercises?	Corregge i di Lei temi suo padre?
The exercise.	Il tema.

Obs. C. There are in Italian many nouns terminated in *a*, for the most part derived from the Greek, which are masculine.

The exercises.	I temi.
He corrects them.	Egli li corregge.

To speak French.	Parlare francese.
To speak English.	Parlare inglese.
Do you speak French?	Parla Ella francese?
No, Sir, I speak English.	No, Signore, parlo inglese.

To take. *Prendere** (regular in the present).

To drink coffee.	† Prendere il caffè. / † Prendere del caffè (*or* simply prendere caffè).

TWENTY-SIXTH LESSON. 117

To drink tea.	† Prendere il tè.
	† Prendere del tè (prendere ul).
Do you drink tea ?	† Prende Ella del tè ?
I do drink some.	† Ne prendo.
Do you drink tea every day ?	† Prende Ella il tè ogni giorno ?
I drink some every day.	† Lo prendo ogni giorno.
My father drinks coffee.	† Mio padre prende del caffè.
He drinks coffee every morning.	† Prende il caffè ogni mattina.
My brother drinks tea.	† Mio fratello prende del tè.
He drinks tea every morning.	† Prende il tè ogni mattina.

To take away.	Portar via.
Who takes away the book ?	Chi porta via il libro ?
The Frenchman takes it away.	Lo porta via il Francese.
Does any one take away the glasses ?	Qualcuno porta via i bicchieri ? Porta via qualcuno i bicchieri ?
No one takes them away.	Nessuno li porta via.
What do you take away ?	Che cosa portate via ?
I take away your boots and your brother's clothes.	Porto via i di Lei stivali ed i vestiti dei di Lei fratello.

EXERCISES.

80.

Do you go for any thing ?—I do go for something.—What do you go for ?—I go for some cider.—Does your father send for any thing ?—He sends for some wine.—Does your servant go for some bread ?—He goes for some.—For whom does your neighbour send ?—He sends for the physician.—Does your servant take off his coat in order to make the fire ?—He does take it off in order to make it.—Do you take off your gloves in order to give me some money ?—I do take them off in order to give you some. —Do you learn French ?—I do learn it.—Who learns English ? —The Frenchman learns it.—Does your brother learn German ? —He does learn it.—Do we learn Italian ?—You do learn it.— What do the English learn ?—They learn French and German. —Do you speak Spanish ?—No, Sir, I speak Italian.—Who speaks Polish ?—My brother speaks Polish.—Do our neighbours speak Russian ?—They do not speak Russian, but Arabic.—Do you speak Arabic ?—No, I speak Greek and Latin.—What knife have you ?—I have an English knife.—What money have you there ?

Is it Italian or Spanish money?—It is Russian money.—Have you an Italian hat?—No, I have a Spanish hat.—Are you an Englishman?—No, I am a Frenchman.—Are you a Greek?—No, I am a Spaniard.

81.

Are these men Germans?—No, they are Russians.—Do the Russians speak Polish?—They do not speak Polish, but Latin, Greek, and Arabic.—Is your brother a merchant?—No, he is a joiner.—Are these men merchants?—No, they are carpenters.—Are you a cook?—No, I am a baker.—Are we tailors?—No, we are shoemakers. Art thou a fool?—I am not a fool.—What is that man?—He is a physician.—Do you wish me any thing?—I wish you a good morning.—What does the young man wish me?—He wishes you a good evening.—Do your children come to me in order to wish me a good evening?—They come to you in order to wish you a good morning.—Has the German black eyes?—No, he has blue eyes.—Has this man large feet?—He has little feet and a large nose.—Have you time to read my book?—I have no time to read it, but much courage to study Italian.—What dost thou do instead of playing?—I study instead of playing.—Dost thou learn instead of writing?—I write instead of learning.—What does the son of our friend do?—He goes into the garden instead of doing his exercises.—Do the children of our neighbours read?—They write instead of reading.—What does our cook?—He makes a fire instead of going to the market.—Does your father sell his ox?—He sells his horse instead of selling his ox.

82.

Does the son of the painter study English?—He studies Greek instead of studying English. Does the butcher kill oxen?—He kills sheep instead of killing oxen.—Do you listen to me?—I do listen to you.—Does your brother listen to me?—He speaks instead of listening to you.—Do you listen to what I am telling you?—I do listen to what you are telling me.—Dost thou listen to what thy brother tells thee?—I do listen to it.—Do the children of the physician listen to what we tell them?—They do not listen to it.—Do you go to the theatre?—I am going to the warehouse instead of going to the theatre.—Are you willing to read my book?—I am willing to read it, but not now; I have sore eyes.—Does your father correct my exercises or those of my brother?—He corrects neither yours nor those of your brother.—Which exercises does he correct?—He corrects mine.—Do you take off your hat in order to speak to my father?—I do not take it off in order to speak to him.—Do you take off your boots?—I do not take them off.—Who takes off his hat?—My friend takes it off.—Does he take off his gloves?—He does not take them off.—What do these boys take off?—They take off their boots and their clothes.—Who takes away the glasses?—Your servant takes them away.—What do your children take away?—They take away the books and my notes.—What do you take away?—I take away nothing.—Do we take away any thing?—We take away our father's penknife and our brothers' trunks.—Do you give me English or German cloth?—I give you neither English nor German cloth; I give you French cloth.—Do you read Spanish?—I do not read Spanish, but German.—What book is your brother reading?—He is reading a French book.—Do you drink tea or coffee in the morning?—I drink tea.—Do you drink tea every morning?—I drink some every morning.—What do you drink?—I drink coffee.—What does your brother drink?—He drinks tea.—Does he drink some every morning?—He drinks some every morning.—Do your children drink tea?—They drink coffee instead of drinking tea.—What do we drink?—We drink tea or coffee.

TWENTY-SEVENTH LESSON.

Lezione ventesima settima.

To wet, to moisten.	Bagnare 1.
To show.	Mostrare 1.
	Far vedere.
I show.	Faccio vedere. Mostro.

TWENTY-SEVENTH LESSON.

Thou showest.	Fai vedere. Mostri.
He shows.	Fa vedere. Mostra.
To show some one.	{ Mostrare } a qualcuno. { Far vedere }
Do you show me your gun?	Mi fa Ella vedere { il di Lei schioppo? o volete Mi mostra Ella { mostrarmi il vostro schioppo?
I do show it you.	Glielo faccio vedere.
What do you show the man?	Che mostra Ella all' uomo?
I show him my fine clothes.	Gli mostro i miei begli abiti.
The tobacco.	Il tabacco.
Tobacco (for smoking).	Del tabacco da fumare.
Snuff.	{ Del tabacco in polvere. { Del tabacco da naso.
To smoke.	Fumare 1.
The gardener.	Il giardiniere.
The valet.	Il cameriere.
The concert.	Il concerto.
To intend.	{ Pensare 1, } do not take a preposition before the { Intendere* 2, } infinitive.
The ball.	{ Il ballo. { La festa da ballo.
Do you intend to go to the ball this evening?	Pensa Ella andare alla festa da ballo stassera (or questa sera)?
I intend to go thither.	Penso andarci.
To know.	Sapere* 2. (Lesson XXIV).
To swim.	Nuotare 1.
Do you know *how* to swim?	Sa Ella nuotare?

Obs. To *know* is in English followed by *how to* before the infinitive, whilst in Italian the infinitive joined to the verb *sapere* is not preceded by any particle.

Do you know how to write?	Sa Ella scrivere?
Does he know how to read?	Sa egli leggere?
To extinguish.	Spegnere* 2 (or spengere* 2).
Do you extinguish the fire?	Spegne Ella il fuoco?
I do extinguish it.	Non lo spengo.
He extinguishes it.	Egli lo spegne.
Thou extinguishest it.	Tu lo spegni.

To light, to kindle.	Accendere* 2.
Often.	Spesso (spesse volte, sovente).
Do you often go to the ball?	Va Ella spesso alla festa da ballo?
As often as you.	Così spesso che Lei, o tanto spesso quanto voi.
	Così spesso come Lei.
	Spesso quanto Lei.
As often as I.	Così spesso che me.
As often as he.	Così spesso come lui.
As often as they.	Così spesso come loro.
	Spesso come loro.
Do you often see my father?	Vede Ella spesso mio padre?
Oftener.	Più spesso.
I see him oftener than you.	Lo vedo più spesso di Lei.
Not so often.	Meno spesso.
	Non tanto spesso.
Not so often as you.	Meno sovente di Lei.
Not so often as I.	Meno spesso di me.
Not so often as they.	Meno spesso di loro.

EXERCISES.

83.

What does your father want?—He wants some tobacco.—Will you go for some?—I will go for some.—What tobacco does he want?—He wants some snuff.—Do you want tobacco (for smoking)?—I do not want any; I do not smoke.—Do you show me any thing?—I show you gold ribbons (*dei nastri d' oro*).—Does your father show his gun to my brother?—He does show it him.—Does he show him his beautiful birds?—He does show them to him.—Does the Frenchman smoke?—He does not smoke. Do you go to the ball?—I go to the theatre, instead of going to the ball.—Does the gardener go into the garden?—He goes to the market instead of going into the garden.—Do you send your valet (*il cameriere*) to the tailor?—I send him to the shoemaker instead of sending him to the tailor.—Does your brother intend to go to the ball this evening?—He does not intend to go to the ball, but

TWENTY-SEVENTH LESSON.

to the concert.—When do you intend to go to the concert?—I intend to go there this evening.—At what o'clock?—At a quarter past ten.—Do you go for my son?—I do go for him.—Where is he?—He is in the counting-house.—Do you find the man whom you are looking for?—I do find him.—Do your sons find the friends whom they are looking for?—They do not find them.

84.

Do your friends intend to go to the theatre?—They do intend to go thither.—When do they intend to go thither?—They intend to go thither to-morrow.—At what o'clock?—At half past seven.—What does the merchant wish to sell you?—He wishes to sell me some pocket-books.—Do you intend to buy some?—I will not buy any.—Dost thou know any thing?—I do not know any thing.—What does your little brother know?—He knows how to write and to read?—Does he know French?—He does not know it.—Do you know German?—I do know it.—Do your brothers know Greek?—They do not know it, but they intend to study it.—Do you know English?—I do not know it, but I intend to learn it.—Do my children know how to read Italian?—They know how to read, but not how to speak it.—Do you know how to swim?—I do not know how to swim, but how to play.—Does your son know how to make coats?—He does not know how to make any; he is no tailor.—Is he a merchant?—He is not (non l' è).—What is he?—He is a physician.—Do you intend to study Arabic?—I do intend to study Arabic and Syriac.—Does the Frenchman know Russian?—He does not know it, but he intends learning it.—Whither are you going?—I am going into the garden in order to speak to my gardener.—Does he listen to you?—He does listen to me.

85.

Do you wish to drink some cider?—I wish to drink some wine; have you any?—I have none; but I will send for some.—When will you send for some?—Now.—Do you know how to make tea? I know how to make some.—Where is your father going?—He goes no where; he remains at home.—Do you know how to write a note?—I know how to write one.—Can you write exercises?—I can write some.—Dost thou conduct any body?—I conduct nobody.—Whom do you conduct?—I conduct my son. —Where do you conduct him?—I conduct him to my friends to (per) wish them a good morning.—Does your servant conduct your child?—He conducts him.—Whither does he conduct it?— He conducts it into the garden.—Do we conduct any one?—We conduct our children.—Whither are our friends conducting their sons?—They are conducting them home.

86.

Do you extinguish the fire?—I do not extinguish it.—Does your servant light the fire?—He does light it.—Where does he light it?—He lights it in your warehouse.—Do you often go to the Spaniard?—I go often to him.—Do you go oftener to him than I?—I go oftener to him than you.—Do the Spaniards often come to you?—They do come often to me.—Do your children oftener go to the ball than we?—They do go thither oftener than you.—Do we go out as often as our neighbours?—We do go out oftener than they.—Does your servant go to the market as often as my cook?—He does go thither as often as he.—Do you see my father as often as I?—I do not see him as often as you.— When do you see him?—I see him every morning at a quarter to five.

TWENTY-EIGHTH LESSON.

Lezione ventesima ottava.

We have seen in many of the foregoing lessons and exercises that the Italians have no particular way to construe interrogative sentences; all depends on the tone with which the sentence is pronounced. The English interrogative auxiliaries, *do* and *am*, therefore, are not generally rendered in Italian. Sometimes they may be rendered by *forse*, which signifies *perhaps*, *why*, as will be seen by the following examples:—

TWENTY-EIGHTH LESSON.

Do I wish?	Voglio? / Voglio forse?
Am I able?	Posso? / Posso forse?
Am I doing?	Faccio (or fo)? / Faccio forse?

What am I doing?	Come faccio? / Che cosa faccio?
What do I say?	Come dico? / Che dico?
Where am I going to?	Ove vado?
To whom do I speak?	A chi parlo?

Am I going?	Vado? Vado forse?
Am I coming?	Vengo? Vengo forse?
You are coming.	Ella viene.
Do you tell or say?	Dice Ella?
I do say or tell.	Dico.
He says or tells.	Egli dice.
What does he say?	Che dice egli?
We say.	Diciamo.
Do I speak?	Parlo? Parlo forse?
Do I love or like?	Amo? Amo forse?

Are you acquainted with that man?	Conosce Ella colui? o quell' uomo?
I am not acquainted with him.	Non lo conosco.
Is your brother acquainted with him?	Lo conosce il di Lei fratello?
He is acquainted with him.	Egli lo conosce.
Do you drink cider?	Beve Ella del cidro?
I do drink cider, but my brother drinks wine.	Bevo del cidro, ma mio fratello beve del vino.
Do you receive a note to-day?	Riceve Ella oggi un biglietto?
I do receive one.	Ne ricevo uno. / Lo ricevo.[1]
What do we receive?	Che riceviamo?
What do our children receive?	Che ricevono i nostri fanciulli?
They receive some books.	Essi ricevono dei libri.

To begin, to commence.	*Principiare* 1. / *Cominciare* 1 (*incominciare*).
I begin to speak.	Principio (incomincio) a parlare.

---

[1] *Uno*, in the sense of an indefinite article, can in Italian never stand at the end of a sentence; in its stead the pronoun is used before the verb, or joined to it.

TWENTY-EIGHTH LESSON.

Before.	Prima di. Innanzi di (che). Avanti di.
Do you speak before you listen?	Parla Ella prima d' ascoltare?
Does he go to the market before he breakfasts?	Va egli al mercato prima di far colazione.

To breakfast.	Far colazione.
He goes thither before he writes.	Egli ci va prima di scrivere.
Do you take off your gloves before you take off your boots?	Si leva Ella i guanti prima di levarsi gli stivali?

To depart, to set out.	Partire* 3 (regular in Present).
When do you intend to depart?	Quando pensa Ella partire?
I intend to depart to-morrow.	Penso partire domani.

Well.	Bene.
Badly.	Male.
Do I speak well?	Parlo bene?
You do not speak badly	Ella non parla male.

| Does your brother know Italian? | Sa l' Italiano il di Lei fratello? |

Obs. When a tense of a verb is a monosyllable, or when it has the accent on the last syllable, the pronoun may follow it, but the consonant must be doubled. This applies more generally to poetry than prose. Ex.

He knows it.	Egli sallo (instead of lo sa).
Who knows English?	Chi sa l' Inglese?
My father knows it.	Mio padre sallo (lo sa is more elegant).

EXERCISES.

87.

Do I read well?—You do read well.—Do I speak well?—You do not speak well.—Does my brother speak French well?—He speaks it well.—Does he speak German well?—He speaks it badly.—Do we speak well?—You speak badly.—Do I drink too much?—You do not drink enough.—Am I able to make hats?—You are not able to make any; you are not a hatter.—Am I able to write a note?—You are able to write one.—Am I doing my exercise well?—You are doing it well.—What am I doing?—You

TWENTY-EIGHTH LESSON.

are doing exercises.—What is my brother doing?—He is doing nothing.—What do I say?—You say nothing.—Do I begin to speak?—You do begin to speak.—Do I begin to speak well?—You do not begin to speak well (*a parlar bene*), but to read well (*ma a legger bene*).—Where am I going?—You are going to your friend.—Is he at home?—Do I know?—Am I able to speak as often as the son of our neighbour?—He is able to speak oftener than you.—Can I work as much as he?—You cannot work as much as he.—Do I read as often as you?—You do not read as often as I, but you speak oftener than I.—Do I speak as well (*cosi bene*) as you?—You do not speak so well as I.—Do I go (*vengo*) to you, or do you come to me?—You come to me, and I go (*vengo*) to you.—When do you come to me?—Every morning at half past six.

88.

Do you know the Russian whom I know?—I do not know the one you know, but I know another.—Do you drink as much cider as wine?—I drink less of the latter than of the former.—Does the Pole drink as much as the Russian?—He drinks just as much.—Do the Germans drink as much as the Poles?—The latter drink more than the former.—Dost thou receive any thing?—I do receive something.—What dost thou receive?—I receive some money.—Does your friend receive books?—He does receive some.—What do we receive?—We receive some cider.—Do the Poles receive tobacco?—They do receive some.—From whom (*da chi*) do the Spaniards receive money?—They receive some from the (*degl'*) English, and from the (*dai*) French.—Do you receive as many friends as enemies?—I receive less of the latter than of the former.—From whom (*da chi*) do your children receive books?—They receive some from me and from their friends.—Do I receive as much cheese as bread?—You receive more of the latter than of the former.—Do our servants receive as many waistcoats as coats?—They receive less of the latter than of the former.—Do you receive one more gun?—I do receive one more.—How many more books does our neighbour receive?—He receives three more.

89.

When does the foreigner intend to depart?—He intends to depart to-day.—At what o'clock?—At half past one.—Do you intend to depart this evening?—I intend to depart to-morrow.—Does the Frenchman depart to-day?—He departs now. Where is he going to?—He is going to his friends.—Is he going to the English?—He is going to them (*ci va*).—Dost thou set out to-morrow?—I set out this evening.—When do you intend to write to your friends?—I intend to write to them to-day.—Do your friends answer you?—They do answer me.—Does your father answer your note?—He answers it.—Do you answer my brothers' notes?—I do answer them.—Does your brother begin to learn Italian?—He begins to learn it.—Can you speak French?—I can speak it a little.—Do our friends begin to speak German?—They do begin to speak it.—Are they able to write it?—They are able to write it.—Does the merchant begin to sell?—He does begin.—Do you speak before you listen?—I listen before I speak.—Does your brother listen to you before he speaks?—He speaks before he listens to me.—Do your children read before they write?—They write before they read.

90.

Does your servant sweep the warehouse before he goes to the market?—He goes to the market before he sweeps the warehouse.—Dost thou drink before thou goest out?—I go out before I drink.—Do you intend to go out before you breakfast?—I intend to breakfast before I go out.—Does your son take off his boots before he takes off his coat?—He neither takes off his boots nor his coat.—Do I take off my gloves before I take off my hat?—You take off your hat before you take off your gloves.—Can I take off my boots before I take off my gloves?—You cannot take off your boots before you take off your gloves.—At what o'clock do you breakfast?—I breakfast at half past eight.—At what o'clock does the American breakfast?—He breakfasts every day at nine o'clock.—At what o'clock do your children breakfast?—They breakfast at seven o'clock.—Do you go to my father before you breakfast?—I go to him before I breakfast.

TWENTY-NINTH LESSON.

Lezione ventesima nona.

We have seen (Lessons XVI and XXVII.) that the comparative of equality is formed by *come, tanto, quanto, altrettanto, così*; the comparative of superiority by *più*, and that of minority by *meno*. As for the superlative, it is formed by changing the last vowel of the adjective for the masculine into *issimo*, and for the feminine into *issima*. Ex.

			Positive.	Comparative.	Superlative.
Learned,	more learned,	most learned.	Dotto,	più dotto,	dottissimo.
Poor,	poorer,	poorest.	Povero,	più povero,	poverissimo.
Wise,	wiser,	wisest.	Savio,	più savio,	savissimo.[1]
Pious,	more pious,	most pious.	Pio,	più pio,	piissimo.
Rich,	richer,	richest.	Ricco,	più ricco,	ricchissimo.
Cool,	cooler,	coolest.	Fresco,	più fresco,	freschissimo.
Broad,	broader,	broadest.	Largo,	più largo,	larghissimo.
Often,	oftener,	most often.	Spesso,	più spesso,	spessissimo.

Obs. A. From these examples it may be seen that the superlative is always formed by joining to the adjective in the plural the syllable *ssimo*.

Obs. B. The relative superlative, i. e. when the article *the* is joined to *most* or *least*, is expressed by *il più*, *il meno*, for the masculine, and by *la più*, *la meno*, for the feminine. Ex.

The greatest.	Il più grande.
The smallest.	Il meno grande.
The finest.	Il più bello.
The least fine.	Il meno bello.

This book is small, that is smaller, and this is the smallest of all.	Questo libro è piccolo, quello è più piccolo e cotesto è il più piccolo di tutti.
This hat is large, but that is larger.	Questo cappello è grande, ma quello è più grande.
Is your hat as large as mine?	Il di Lei cappello è così grande come il mio?
It is larger than yours.	È più grande del di Lei.
It is not so large as yours.	È meno grande del di Lei.
Are our neighbour's children as good as ours?	I fanciulli del nostro vicino sono così savi come i nostri?

[1] Many grammarians form the plural of *savio* into *savi*, instead of *savii*. According to this formation the superlative would be *savissimo*, instead of *saviissimo*.

TWENTY-NINTH LESSON.

They are better than ours.	Sono più savi dei nostri.
They are not so good as ours.	Sono meno savi dei nostri.
He is the happiest man in the world.	Egli è il più felice degli uomini (or fra gli uomini).

A very fine book.	Un bellissimo libro.
Very fine books.	Dei bellissimi libri.
A very pretty knife.	Un leggiadrissimo coltello.
Very well.	Benissimo.

That man is extremely learned.	Questi è dottissimo.
This bird is very pretty.	Questo uccello è vezzosissimo.

Obs. C. *Molto* and *assai* serve also to form absolute superlatives. Ex.

Very wise.	Molto savio.
Very large.	Assai grande.

Obs. D. The prefix *arci* also serves to form an absolute superlative. Ex.

Very handsome.	Arcibello.
Extremely long.	Arcilunghissimo.

Obs. E. To some words the particle *stra* may be prefixed to form an absolute superlative. Ex.

Over rich.	Straricco.
Over done (cooked).	Stracotto.

Obs. F. The following adjectives are irregular in the formation of their comparatives and superlatives:—

			Positive.	Comparative.	Superlative.
Good,	better,	best.	Buono,	migliore,	ottimo.
Bad,	worse,	the worst.	Cattivo,	peggiore,	pessimo.
Great,	greater,	greatest.	Grande,	maggiore,	massimo.
Little,	less,	the least.	Piccolo,	minore,	minimo.

ADVERBS.

Well,	better,	the best.	Bene,	meglio,	ottimamente.
Bad,	worse,	the worst.	Male,	peggio,	pessimamente.

The least noise hurts me.	Il minimo strepito mi fa male.
The least thing hurts him.	La minima cosa gli fa male.

Obs. G. In Italian the repetition of the positive forms a superlative. Ex.

A very learned man.	Un uomo dotto dotto.
The weather is very cold.	Il tempo è freddo freddo.
This seems to me most ugly.	Questo mi sembra brutto brutto.
She is the finest woman in the world.	È la bella delle belle.

Obs. H. Superlative adverbs are formed by joining to the adjective in the plural the termination *ssimamente*. Ex.

6*

TWENTY-NINTH LESSON.

Learned — most learnedly.	Dotto — dottissimamente.
Prudent — most prudently.	Prudente — prudentissimamente.
Rich — most richly.	Ricco — ricchissimamente.

Whose?	**Di chi?**
Whose hat is this?	Di chi è questo cappello?
It is.	*È.*
It is my brother's hat.	
It is the hat of my brother.	È il cappello di mio fratello.
It is my brother's.	
Who has the finest hat?	Chi ha il più bel cappello?
Whose hat is the finest?	
That of my father is the finest.	Quello di mio padre è il più bello.
Whose ribbon is the handsomer, yours or mine?	Qual è il più bel nastro, il di Lei, il vostro o il mio?

Do you read as often as I?	Legge Ella così spesso come io?
I read oftener than you.	Leggo più spesso di Lei.
Does he read as often as I?	Legge egli così spesso come io?
He reads and writes as often as you.	Egli legge e scrive così spesso come Ella (or legge e scrive spesso al pari di Lei).
Do your children write as much as we?	Scrivono quanto noi i di Lei fanciulli?
They write more than you.	Eglino scrivono più di Loro, or più di Voi.
We read more than the children of our friends.	Noi leggiamo più dei fanciulli dei nostri amici.
To whom do you write.	A chi scrivete Voi?
We write to our friends.	Scriviamo ai nostri amici.
We read good books.	Leggiamo dei buoni libri.

EXERCISES.

91.

Whose book is this?—It is mine.—Whose hat is that?—It is my father's.—Are you taller than I?—I am taller than you.—Is your brother as tall as you?—He is as tall as I.—Is thy hat as bad as that of my father?—It is better, but not so black as his.—Are the clothes of the Italians as fine as those of the Irish?—They are finer, but not so good.—Who have the finest gloves?—The French have them.—Who has the finest horses?—Mine are fine, yours are finer than mine; but those of our friends are the finest of all.—Is your horse good?—It is good, but yours is better, and that of the Englishman is the best of all the horses which we know.—Have you pretty boots?—I have very pretty ones, but my brother has prettier than I.—From whom (*da chi*) does he receive them?—He receives them from his best friend.

92.

Is your wine as good as mine?—It is better.—Does your merchant sell good knives?—He sells the best knives that I know (*che conosca*, subjunctive).—Do we read more books than the French?—We read more than they; but the English read more than we, and the Germans read the most (*i più*).—Hast thou a finer garden than that of our physician?—I have a finer one than he (*del suo*).—Has the American a finer stick than thou?—He has a finer one.—Have we as fine children as our neighbours?—We have finer ones.—Is your coat as pretty as mine?—It is not so pretty, but better than yours.—Do you depart to-day?—I do not depart to-day.—When does your father set out?—He sets out this evening at a quarter to nine.—Which of these two children is the better (*savio*)?—The one who studies is better than the one who plays.—Does your servant sweep as well as mine?—He sweeps better than yours.—Does the Englishman read as many bad books as good ones?—He reads more good than bad ones.

93.

Do the merchants sell more sugar than coffee?—They sell more of the latter than of the former.—Does your shoemaker make as many boots as mine?—He makes more than yours.—Can you swim as well (*così bene*) as my son?—I can swim better than he; but he can speak French better than I.—Does he read as well as you?—He reads better than I.—Does the son of your neighbour go to market?—No, he remains at home; he has sore feet.—Do you learn as well as the son of our gardener?—I learn better than he, but he studies better than I.—Whose gun is the finest?—Yours *is* very fine, but that of the captain is still finer, and ours is the finest of all.—Has any one finer children than you?—No one has finer ones.—Does your son read as often as I?—He reads oftener than you.—Does my brother speak

French as often as you?—He speaks and reads it as often as I.
—Do I write as much as you?—You write more than I.—Do
our neighbours' children read German as often as we?—We do
not read it as often as they.—Do we write as often as they?—
They write oftener than we.—To whom do they write?—They
write to their friends.—Do you read English books?—We read
French books instead of reading English books.

THIRTIETH LESSON.

Lezione trentesima.

To believe.
To put on.

I put on my hat.

He puts on his gloves.
Do you put on your boots?
We do put them on.
What do your brothers put on?
They put on their clothes.
Whither do you conduct me?
I conduct you to my father.

Credere 2.
Mettere,* mettersi.

{ Metto il mio cappello.
{ Mi metto il cappello.
{ Si mette i guanti.
{ Mette i suoi guanti.
Si mettono gli stivali?
Ce li mettiamo.
Che si mettono i di Lei fratelli?
Si mettono i loro vestiti.
Ove mi conduce Ella?
La conduco dal padre mio, (or vi conduco da mio padre.

Do you go out.
I do go out.
Do we go out?
We do go out.
When does your father go out?

Esce Ella? or Usidte Voi?
Esco.
Usciamo Noi?
Usciamo.
Quando esce il di Lei padre?

Early.

{ Per tempo.
{ Di buon' ora.
{ A buon' ora.
{ Presto.

As early as you.

{ Così per tempo come Ella.
{ Così di buon' ora come Ella.

THIRTIETH LESSON.

He goes out as early as you.	Egli esce così per tempo come Ella, or che Voi.

Late.	*Tardi.*
Too.	*Troppo.*
Too late.	Troppo tardi.
Too soon, too early.	Troppo di buon' ora (troppo a buon' ora).
	Troppo per tempo. Troppo presto.
Too large, too great.	Troppo grande.
Too little.	Troppo piccolo.
Too much.	*Troppo.*
Do you speak too much?	Parla Ella troppo?
I do not speak enough.	Non parlo abbastanza.

Later than you.	*Più tardi* di Lei.
I go out later than you.	Esco più tardi di Lei.
Do you go to the play as early as I?	Va Ella allo spettacolo così di buon' ora come Io?
I go thither earlier than you.	Ci vado più di buon' ora di Lei (più presto di Lei).
Sooner.	*Più presto (più tosto).*
Earlier.	*Più per tempo.*
	Più di buon' ora.
Does your father go thither earlier than I?	Ci va il di { più presto di me? Lei padre { più per tempo di me?
He goes thither too early.	Ci va { troppo di buon' ora. { troppo presto.

Already.	*Già di già.*
Do you speak already?	Parla Ella di già?
Not—yet.	{ *Non—ancora.* { *Non—per anco.*
I do not speak yet.	Non parlo ancora (per anco).
Do you finish your note?	Finisce Ella il di Lei biglietto?
I do not finish it yet.	Non lo finisco ancora.
Do you breakfast already?	Fa Ella già colazione?
Do you come to see me?	Viene Ella a vedermi? Venite voi a vedermi?

Obs. A. Verbs of motion always require the preposition *a* (*ad* before a vowel), and verbs of rest the preposition *in*. Ex.

THIRTIETH LESSON.

I go to see my children.	Vado a vedere i miei fanciulli.
I send for some wine.	Mando a cercare del vino.
I am sending for the physician.	Mando a cercare il medico.
I am going to the theatre.	Vado al teatro.
I stay in the garden (in the room).	Resto in giardino (in camera), or me ne sto in camera.

Obs. B. But as we have seen in the foregoing lessons, the infinitive is in Italian sometimes preceded by *di* (Lesson XVII.), sometimes by *a* or *ad* (Lessons XXV., XXVIII., and this), sometimes by *per* (Lesson XX.), and sometimes it is simply used without any of these prepositions before it. The latter is the case when it is joined to one of the following verbs, some of which have already been exemplified in some of the preceding lessons, such as: *volere,** to wish, to be willing (Lesson XVIII.); *potere,** to be able, can (Lesson XX.); *far vedere,* to show (Lesson XVXII.); *pensare, intendere,* to intend to (Lessons XXVII. and XXVIII.).

Bisognare,	to be requisite.		Negare,	to deny.
Calcolare,	to intend to.		Osare, ardire,*	to dare.
Credere,	to believe.		Parere,*	to appear.
Degnare o degnarsi,	to deign.		Pensare,	to think.
			Potere,*	to be able (can).
Desiderare,	to wish.		Pretendere,*	to pretend.
Dichiarare,	to declare.		Sapere,*	to know.
Dovere,*	to owe.		Sembrare,	to appear.
Fare,*	to do.		Sostenere,*	to maintain.
Intendere,*	to hear, to intend.		Vedere,*	to see.
Lasciare,	to let.		Volere,*	to be willing, to want.

EXAMPLES.

It is necessary to do that.	Bisogna far ciò.
I intend going to the play.	Calcolo andare allo spettacolo.
He thinks he is able to do it.	Egli crede poterlo fare.
He deigns to give it me.	Ei si degna darmelo.
He wishes to speak to the king.	Egli desidera parlare al re.
I declare I cannot do that.	Dichiaro non potere far ciò.
I ought to go there.	Devo andarci.
He sends me word.	Egli mi fa dire, *or* Egli mi manda a dire.
I intend to speak to him.	Intendo parlargli.
He lets me do it.	Egli me lo lascia fare.
He says he cannot do it.	Egli nega poterlo fare.
I dare to go there; I dare to do it.	Oso andarci; ardisco farlo.
They seem to say.	Eglino paiono dire, *or* sembra che essi dicono.
I intend to make a journey.	Penso far un viaggio.
Can you give me a franc?	Può Ella darmi un franco?
He pretends he can do it.	Egli pretende poterlo fare.
I can do it; I know how to do it.	So farlo.

He seems to have a wish to do it. | Egli sembra volerlo fare.
I maintain I can do it. | Sostengo saperlo fare.
We see him come. | Lo vediamo venire.
Will you do me a favour? | Vuol Ella farmi un piacere?

Obs. C. Further, there is no preposition before the infinitive when it is used in an absolute sense. Ex.

To eat too much is dangerous. | *Mangiare* troppo è pericoloso.
To speak too much is foolish. | *Parlar* troppo è imprudente.
To do good to those that have offended us, is a commendable action. | *Far* del bene a quelli chi ci hanno offeso, è un' azione lodevole.

EXERCISES.

94.

Do you put on another coat in order to go to the play?—I do put on another.—Do you put on your gloves before you put on your boots?—I put on my boots before I put on my gloves.—Does your brother put on his hat instead of putting on his coat?—He puts on his coat before he puts on his hat.—Do our children put on their boots in order to go to our friends?—They put them on in order to go to them.—What do our sons put on?—They put on their clothes and their gloves.—Do you already speak French?—I do not speak it yet, but I begin to learn.—Does your father go out already?—He does not yet go out.—At what o'clock does he go out?—He goes out at ten o'clock.—Does he breakfast before he goes out?—He breakfasts and writes his notes before he goes out.—Does he go out earlier than you?—I go out earlier than he.—Do you go to the play as often as I?—I go thither as often as you.—Do you begin to know that man?—I do begin to know him.—Do you breakfast early?—We do not breakfast late.—Does the Englishman go to the concert earlier than you?—He goes there later than I.—At what o'clock does he go thither?—He goes thither at half-past eleven.

95.

Do you not go too early to the concert?—I go thither too late.—Do I write too much?—You do not write too much, but you speak too much.—Do I speak more than you?—You speak more than I and my brother.—Is my hat too large?—It is neither too

large nor too small.—Do you speak French oftener than English?
—I speak English oftener than French.—Do your friends buy
much corn?—They buy but little.—Have you bread enough?
—I have only a little, but enough.—Is it late?—It is not late.—
What o'clock is it?—It is one o'clock.—Is it too late to go to
your father?—It is too late to go to him.—Do you conduct me to
him?—I do conduct you to him.—Where is he?—He is in his
counting-house.—Does the Spaniard buy a horse?—He cannot
buy one.—Is he poor?—He is not poor; he is richer than you.
—Is your brother as learned as you?—He is more learned than
I, but you are more learned than he and I.

96.

Do you know that man?—I do know him.—Is he learned?—
He is the most learned of all the men that I know (*conosca*, subjunctive).—Is your horse worse than mine?—It is not so bad as
yours.—Is mine worse than the Spaniard's?—It is worse; it is
the worst horse that I know (*conosca*, subjunctive).—Do you give
those men less bread than cheese?—I give them less of the latter
than of the former.—Do you receive as much money as your
neighbours?—I receive much more than they.—Who receives
the most money?—The French receive the most.—Can your son
already write a note?—He cannot write one yet, but he begins
to read a little.—Do you read as much as the Russians?—We
read more than they, but the French read the most (*più di tutti*).
—Do the Americans write more than we?—They write less than
we, but the Italians write the least (*meno di tutti*).—Are they as
rich as the Americans?—They are less rich than they.—Are
your birds as fine as those of the Irish?—They are less fine than
theirs, but those of the Spaniards are the least fine.—Do you sell
your bird?—I do not sell it; I like it too much to sell it.

THIRTY-FIRST LESSON.
Lezione trentesima prima.

THE PAST PARTICIPLE.

The past participle, when it is regular,[1] always terminates in *to*. It is formed from the infinitive, whose termination is for the first conjugation changed into *ato*, thus: *parlare—parlato*; for the second into *uto*, thus: *vendere—venduto*; and for the third into *ito*, thus: *servire—servito*. Examples:—

FIRST CONJUGATION.

Inf.		P. P.
Parlare,	to speak,	parlato.
Comprare,	to buy,	comprato.
Studiare,	to study,	studiato.

SECOND CONJUGATION.

Inf.		P. P.
Vendere,	to sell,	venduto.
Credere,	to believe,	creduto.
Ricevere,	to receive,	ricevuto.

THIRD CONJUGATION.

Inf.		P. P.
Servire,	to serve,	servito.
Sentire,	to hear,	sentito.
Dormire,	to sleep,	dormito.

To be—been.	Essere*—stato.[2]
Have you been to market?	È Ella stata al mercato?

Obs. In Italian the auxiliary verb *essere** is conjugated in its compound tenses with the help of the same auxiliary, and not as in English.[3]

I have been there.	Vi sono stato.
I have not been there.	Non vi sono stato.
Have I been there?	Vi sono stato?
You have been there.	Vi siete stato. Ella vi è stata.
You have not been there.	Ella non vi è stata. Non vi siete stato.
Has he been there?	Vi è stato egli?
He has been there.	Egli vi è stato.
He has not been there.	Egli non vi è stato.

---

[1] When it is irregular it will be separately noted.

[2] The pupils, in repeating the irregular verbs already given, must not fail to mark in their lists the past participles of those verbs.

[3] The same is the case in German. Ex.: Ich bin da gewesen, I have been there. (See German Method, Lesson XLIII.)

THIRTY-FIRST LESSON.

Ever.	Mai.
Never.	Non—mai.

Have you been at the ball?	Siete stato al ballo (alla festa da ballo)?
	È Ella stata al ballo (alla festa da ballo)?
Have you ever been at the ball?	Siete mai stato al ballo?
	È Ella stata mai alla festa da ballo?
I have never been there.	Non vi sono mai stato.
Thou hast never been there.	Tu non vi sei mai stato.
He has never been there.	Non vi è mai stato.
You have never been there.	Non vi siete mai stato.
	Ella non vi è mai stata.

Already or yet.	Già, di già.
Have you already been at the play?	È Ella già stata allo spettacolo?
I have already been there.	Vi sono già stato.
You have already been there.	Ella vi è già stata.
	Vi siete già stato.

Not yet.	Non—ancora (non per anco).
I have not yet been there.	Non vi sono stato ancora.
Thou hast not yet been there.	Non vi sei per anco stato.
He has not yet been there.	Egli non vi è ancora stato.
You have not yet been there.	Non vi siete stato ancora.
	Ella non vi è per anco stata.
We have not yet been there.	Non vi siamo per anco stati.

Have you already been at my father's?	È Ella già stata da mio padre?
I have not yet been there.	Non vi sono per anco stato.

Where have you been this morning?	Ove è Ella stata stamane?
I have been in the garden.	Sono stato nel giardino.
Where has thy brother been?	Ove è stato tuo fratello?
He has been in the warehouse.	Egli è stato nel magazzino.
Has he been there as early as I?	Vi è stato così presto come io?
He has been there earlier than you.	Vi è stato più presto di Lei.

EXERCISES.
97.

Where have you been?—I have been at the market.—Have you been at the ball?—I have been there.—Have I been to the play?—You have been there.—Hast thou been there?—I have not been there.—Has your son ever been at the theatre?—He has never been there.—Hast thou already been in my warehouse?—I have never been there.—Do you intend to go thither?—I intend to go thither?—When will you go thither?—I will go thither to-morrow.—At what o'clock?—At twelve o'clock.—Has your brother already been in my large garden?—He has not yet been there.—Does he intend to see it?—He does intend to see it.—When will he go thither?—He will go thither to-day.—Does he intend to go to the ball this evening?—He intends to go thither.—Have you already been at the ball?—I have not yet been there.—When do you intend to go thither?—I intend to go thither to-morrow.—Have you already been in the Frenchman's garden?—I have not yet been in it.—Have you been in my warehouses?—I have been there.—When did you go there?—I went there this morning.—Have I been in your counting-house or in that of your friend?—You have neither been in mine nor in that of my friend, but in that of the Englishman.

96.

Has the Italian been in our warehouses or in those of the Dutch?—He has neither been in ours nor in those of the Dutch, but in those of the Germans.—Hast thou already been at the market?—I have not yet been there, but I intend to go thither.—Has our neighbour's son been there?—He has been there.—When has he been there?—He has been there to-day.—Does the son of our gardener intend to go to the market?—He intends to go thither.—What does he wish to buy there?—He wishes to buy there some chickens, oxen, corn, wine, cheese, and cider.—Have you already been at my brother's?—I have already been there.—Has your friend already been there?—He has not yet been there.—Have we already been at our friends'?—We have not yet been there.—Have our friends ever been at our house?—They have never been there.—Have you ever been at the theatre?—I have never been there.—Have you a mind to write an exercise?—I have a mind to write one.—To whom do you wish to write a note?—I wish to write one to my son.—Has your father already been at the concert?—He has not yet been there, but he intends to go there.—Does he intend to go there to-day?—He intends to go there to-morrow.—At what o'clock will he set out?—He will set out at half-past six.—Does he intend to leave (*partire*) before he breakfasts?—He intends to breakfast before he leaves.

99.

Have you been to the play as early as I?—I have been there earlier than you.—Have you often been at the concert?—I have often been there.—Has our neighbour been at the theatre as often as we?—He has been there oftener than we.—Do our friends go to their counting-house too early?—They go thither too late.—Do they go thither as late as we?—They go thither later than we.—Do the English go to their warehouses too early?—They go thither too early.—Is your friend as often in the counting-house as you?—He is there oftener than I.—What does he do there?—He writes.—Does he write as much as you?—He writes more than I.—Where does your friend remain?—He remains in his counting-house.—Does he not go out?—He does not go out.—Do you remain in the garden?—I remain there.—Do you go to your friend every day?—I go to him every day.—When does he come to you?—He comes to me every evening.—Do you go any where in the evening?—I go no where; I stay at home.—Do you send for any one?—I send for my physician.—Does your servant go for any thing?—He goes for some wine.—Have you been any where this morning?—I have been no where.—Where has your father been?—He has been no where.—When do you drink tea?—I drink some every morning.—Does your son drink coffee?—He drinks tea.—Have you been to drink some coffee?—I have been to drink some.

THIRTY-SECOND LESSON.

Lezione trentesima seconda.

To have—had.	Avere*—avuto.
Have you had my book?	Ha Ella avuto il mio libro?
I have not had it.	Non l' ho avuto.
Have I had it?	L' ho avuto io?
You have had it.	L' ha avuto.
You have not had it.	Non l' ha avuto.
Thou hast not had it.	Non l' hai avuto.
Has he had it?	L' ha egli avuto?
He has had it.	Egli l' ha avuto.
He has not had it.	Egli non l' ha avuto.
Hast thou had the coat?	Hai avuto l' abito?
I have not had it.	Non l' ho avuto.
Have you had the books?	Ha Ella avuto i libri?

☞ The past participle in Italian (the same as the adjective, Obs. A. Lesson XXII), when it is preceded by its object, must agree with it in number; that is, if the object is in the plural, the past participle must be put in the same number. It may, however, also agree when followed by its object; but the past participle of *essere*, to be, must always agree in number and gender with its subject. Ex.

I have had them.	Li ho avuti.
I have not had them.	Non li ho avuti.
Have I had them?	Li ho io avuti?
You have had them.	Li ha avuti.
You have not had them.	Ella Non li ha avuti. Voi non li avete avuti.
Has he had them?	Li ha egli avuti?
He has had them.	Egli li ha avuti.
He has not had them.	Non li ha avuti.
Have you had any bread?	Ha Ella avuto del pane?
I have had some.	Ne ho avuto.
I have not had any.	Non ne ho avuto.
Have I had any?	Ne ho avuto io?
You have had some.	Ella Ne ha avuto, or Voi ne avete avuto.
You have not had any.	Ella Non ne ha avuto. Voi non ne avete avuto
Has he had any?	Ne Ne ha egli avuto?
He has not had any.	Egli non ne ha avuto.

THIRTY-SECOND LESSON.

Have you had any knives?	Ha Ella avuto dei coltelli?
I have had some.	No ho avuti.
I have not had any.	Non ne ho avuti.
What has he had?	Che ha egli avuto?
He has had nothing.	Egli non ha avuto niente.
Have you been hungry?	† Ha Ella avuto fame?
I have been afraid.	† Ho avuto paura.
He has never been either right or wrong.	† Egli non ha mai avuto torto nè ragione.
To take place.	† Aver luogo.
That (meaning that thing).	Ciò, quello.
Does the ball take place this evening?	† Ha luogo stassera la festa da ballo?
It does take place.	† Ha luogo.
It takes place this evening.	† Essa ha luogo questa sera.
It does not take place to-day.	† Non ha luogo quest' oggi.
When did the ball take place?	† Quando ha avuto luogo la festa da ballo?
It took place yesterday.	† Ha avuto luogo ieri.
Yesterday.	Ieri.
The day before yesterday.	L' altro ieri.
How many times (how often)?	Quante volte? Quante fiate? (not much used.)
Once.	Una volta.
Twice.	Due volte (fiate).
Thrice (three times).	Tre volte.
Many times.	Molte volte.
Several times.	Varie volte (diverse volte).
Formerly.	Altre volte (altra volta). Altre fiate.
Sometimes.	Qualche volta. Talvolta. Talora.
Do you go sometimes to the ball?	Va Ella qualche volta alla festa da ballo? or andate voi alla festa da ballo?
I go sometimes.	Vi vado qualche volta.

THIRTY-SECOND LESSON.

Gone.	Andato.
Gone thither.	Andatoci (andatovi).
Have you gone thither sometimes?	Vi è Ella andata qualche volta?
I have gone thither often.	Ci sono andato spesso.
Oftener than you.	Più spesso di Lei.

Have the men had my trunk?	Hanno avuto il mio baule gli uomini?
They have not had it.	Non lo hanno avuto.
Who has had it?	Chi l' ha avuto?
Have they had my knives?	Hanno avuto i miei coltelli?
They have not had them.	Non li hanno avuti.

Have I been wrong in buying books?	Ho avuto lo torto di comprar libri?
You have not been wrong in buying some.	Non ha avuto torto di comprarne.
Singing rejoices.	Il cantare rallegra.

Obs. The infinitives and adverbs are sometimes used in Italian substantively, and preceded by the article.

Jesting is permitted.	Lo scherzare è permesso.
Flattery is despicable.	L' adulare è cosa vile.
I do not know either when or how.	Io non so nè il quando, nè il come.

EXERCISES.

100.

Have you had my pocket-book?—I have had it.—Have you had my glove?—I have not had it.—Hast thou had my umbrella?—I have not had it.—Have I had your knife?—You have had it.—When have I had it?—You have had it yesterday.—Have I had your gloves?—You have had them.—Has your brother had my wooden hammer?—He has had it.—Has he had my golden ribbon?—He has not had it.—Have the English had my beautiful ship?—They have had it.—Who has had my linen (*di lino*) handkerchiefs?—Your servants have had them.—Have we had the iron trunk of our good neighbour?—We have had it.—Have we had his fine gun?—We have not had it.—Have we had the mattresses of the foreigners?—We have not had them.—Has the American had my good book?—He has had it.—Has he had my silver knife?—He has not had it.—Has the young man had the first volume of my work?—He has not had the first, but the second.—Has he had it ?—Yes, Sir, he has had it.—When has he had it ?—He has had it this morning.—Have you had any sugar ?—I have had some.—Have I had any pepper ?—You have not had any.—Has the cook of the Russian captain had any chickens ?—He has had some. He has not had any.

101.

Has the Frenchman had good wine ?—He has had some, and he has still (*ancora*) some.—Hast thou had large books ?—I have had some.—Has thy brother had any ?—He has not had any.—Has the son of our gardener had any butter ?—He has had some.—Have the Poles had good tobacco ?—They have had some.—What tobacco have they had ?—They have had tobacco and snuff.—Have the English had as much sugar as tea ?—They have had as much of the one as of the other.—Has the physician been right ?—He has been wrong.—Has the Dutchman been right or wrong ?—He has never been either right or wrong.—Have I been wrong in buying honey ?—You have been wrong in buying some.—What has the painter had ?—He has had fine pictures.—Has he had fine gardens ?—He has not had any.—Has your servant had my boots ?—He has not had them.—What has the Spaniard had ?—He has had nothing.—Who has had courage ?—The English sailors have had some.—Have the Germans had many friends ?—They have had many.—Have we had more friends than enemies ?—We have had more of the latter than of the former.—Has your son had more wine than cider ?—He has had more of the latter than of the former.—Has the Turk had more pepper than corn ?—He has had less of the latter than of the former.—Has the Italian painter had any thing ?—He has had nothing.

102.

Have I been right in writing to my brother ?—You have not been wrong in writing to him.—Have you had a sore foot ?—I have had a sore eye.—Have you had any thing good ?—I have had nothing bad.—Did the ball take place yesterday ?—It did not take place.—Does it take place to-day ?—It takes place to-morrow.—When does the ball take place ?—It takes place this evening.—Did it take place the day before yesterday?—It did take place.—At what o'clock did it take place?—It took place (*ha avuto luogo*) at eleven o'clock.—Did you go to my brother's?—I went thither.—How many times have you been at my friend's house?—I have been there twice.—Do you go sometimes to the theatre?—I go thither sometimes (*talvolta*).—How many times have you been at the theatre?—I have been there only once.—Have you sometimes been at the ball?—I have often been there.—Has your brother ever gone to the ball?—He has never gone thither.—Has your father sometimes gone to the ball?—He went thither formerly.—Has he gone thither as often as you?—He has gone thither oftener than I.—Dost thou go sometimes into the garden?—I go thither sometimes.—Hast thou often been there?—I have often been there?—Does your old cook often go to the market?—He goes thither often.—Does he go thither as often as my gardener?—He goes thither oftener than he.—Did that take place?—It did take place.—When did that take place?

103.

Did you formerly go to the ball?—I went thither sometimes.—When hast thou been at the concert?—I was there (*vi sono stato*) the day before yesterday.—Didst thou find any body there?—I found (*non vi ho trovato*) nobody there.—Hast thou gone to the ball oftener than thy brothers?—I have not gone thither so often as they.—Has your friend often been at the play?—He has been there many times.—Have you sometimes been hungry?—I have often been hungry.—Has your valet (*il cameriere*) often been thirsty?—He has never been either hungry or thirsty.—Did you go to the play early?—I went thither late.—Did I go to the ball as early as you?—You went thither earlier than I.—Did your brother go thither too late?—He went thither too early.—Have your brothers had any thing?—They have had nothing.—Who has had my sticks and gloves?—Your servant has had both.—Has he had my hat and my gun?—He has had both.—Hast thou had my horse or my brother's?—I have had neither yours nor your brother's.—Have I had your note or the physician's?—You have had neither the one nor the other.—What has the physician had?—He has had nothing.—Has any body had my gold candlestick?—Nobody has had it.—Has any body had my silver knives?—Nobody has had them.

THIRTY-THIRD LESSON.

Lezione trentesima terza.

OF THE PRETERITE INDEFINITE.
(PASSATO PROSSIMO.)

This tense is formed as the perfect tense is in English, viz. from the present of the auxiliary and the past participle of the verb you conjugate. Examples:—

I have studied this morning.	Ho studiato questa mattina.
I studied yesterday.	Ho studiato ieri.
I studied last month.	Ho studiato il mese passato (scorso).
I have studied this month.	Questo mese ho studiato.
Last month.	{ Il mese passato. { Il mese scorso.

To make, to do—made, done.	*Fare°—fatto.*
What have you done?	Che ha Ella fatto? or Che avete fatto Voi?
I have done nothing.	Non ho fatto niente.

Has that shoemaker made my boots?	Ha fatto i miei stivali cotesto calzolaio? (or quel calzolaio).
He has made them.	Li ha fatti.
He has not made them.	Non li ha fatti.

To put—put.	*Mettere°—messo.*
To put on—put on.	*Mettersi°—messosi.*
Have you put on your boots?	† Si è Ella messi gli stivali?
I have put them on.	† Me li sono messi.

To lift—lifted.	*Levare—levato.*
To take off—taken off.	*Levarsi—levatosi.*
Have you taken off your gloves?	† Si è Ella levati i guanti?
I have taken them off.	† Me li sono levati.

THIRTY-THIRD LESSON. 147

To tell, to say—told, said.	Dire*—detto.
Have you said the devices?	Ha Ella detto i motti?
I have said them.	Li ho detti.
Have you told me the devices?	Mi ha Ella detto li motto?
I have told you the device.	Le ho detto il motto.
I have told it you.	Gliel' ho detto, or Ve l' ho detto.
The device, the motto.	Il motto.
That (meaning that thing).	Ciò.
This (meaning this thing).	Questo.
Has he told you that?	Le ha detto ciò?
He has told me that.	Mi ha detto ciò.
Have I told you that?	Le ho detto io questo?
You have told me that.	Ella mi ha detto questo.
It.	Lo, l'.
Have you told it me?	Me l' ha Ella detto?

Obs. A. Whenever the pronouns, mi, ci, ti, vi, si, are followed by lo, la, li, gli, le, ne, the letter i is changed into o; and instead of saying mi lo, mi la, mi li, &c., we must say me lo, me la, me li, ce lo, &c. These pronouns are separated when used before the verb, but joined together when they stand after it. Examples:

I imagine it.	Me lo figuro.
I promise it thee.	Te lo prometto.
You may assure yourself of it.	Potete assicurarvene.
I have told it you.	Glief ho detto.
I have not told it you.	Non gliel' ho detto.
Has he told it you?	Glief ha egli detto?
He has told it me.	Egli me l' ha detto.
He has not told it me.	Egli non me l' ha detto.
Have you told him that?	Gli ha detto ella ciò o questo?
I have told it him.	Glief ho detto.

Obs. B. When the pronoun gli is followed by lo, la, li, le, ne, it takes an e, and forms but one word with the pronoun that follows it. Gli always precedes lo, la, li, le, ne, thus: glielo, gliela, it to him; glieli, gliele, them to him; gliene, some to him; and not lo gli, &c.

I beg of you to speak to him of it.	Vi prego di parlargliene.
Have you told it them?	L' ha Ella detto loro?
I have told it them.	L' ho detto loro.
Have you spoken to the men?	Ha Ella parlato agli uomini?
I have spoken to them.	Ho parlato loro.
To whom did you speak?	A chi ha Ella parlato?

THIRTY-THIRD LESSON.

Are you the brother of my friend? | È Ella fratello del mio amico?

So.   Lo.

Obs. C. The pronoun *lo*, which is sometimes expressed in English by *so*, and more elegantly omitted, may in Italian relate to a substantive, an adjective, or even a whole sentence. It alters neither gender nor number, when it relates to an adjective or a whole sentence. Sometimes *il* is used instead of *lo*, as; *il so*, I know it, instead of *lo so*. Ex.

I am.	Lo sono (il sono).
Are you rich?	È Ella ricca? Siete voi ricco?
I am not.	Non lo sono.
Is he learned?	È egli dotto?
He is.	Egli l' è (or lo è).
He is not.	Egli non l' è (or non lo è).
Are our neighbours as poor as they say?	Sono così poveri i nostri vicini come lo dicono (or, il dicono)?
They are so.	Lo sono.
Did your brother go to the ball the day before yesterday?	È stato alla festa da ballo il di Lei fratello l' altro ieri?
I do not know.	Non lo so.

To write—written.	Scrivere*—scritto.
Which notes have you written?	Quai biglietti ha Ella scritti?
I have written these.	Ho scritto questi.
Which devices has he written?	Quai motti ha egli scritti?
He has written those which you see.	Egli ha scritto quelli ch' Ella vede.

To drink,	— drunk.	Bere* (bevere),	— bevuto.
To see,	— seen.	Vedere*,	— veduto (visto).
To read,	— read (past part.).	Leggere*,	— letto.
To be acquainted with.	— been acquainted with.	Conoscere*,	— conosciuto.

Which men have you seen?	Che uomini ha Ella veduti (visti)?
I have seen those.	Ho veduto (visto) quelli.
Which books have you read?	Quai libri ha Ella letti?
I have read those which you have lent me.	Ho letto quei ch' Ella mi ha prestati.
Have you been acquainted with those men?	Ha Ella conosciuto quegli uomini?
I have not been acquainted with them.	Non li ho conosciuti.

Have you seen any sailors?	Ha Ella veduto dei marinai?
I have seen some.	Ne ho veduti (visti).
I have not seen any.	Non ne ho veduti.

To call.	Chiamare 1.
To throw.	Gettare 1.
To throw away.	Gettar via.
Who calls me?	Chi mi chiama?
Your father calls you.	La chiama il di Lei padre.
Have you called the men?	Ha Ella chiamato gli uomini?
I have called them.	Li ho chiamati.

Do you throw your money away?	Getta Ella via il di Lei danaro?
I do not throw it away.	Non lo getto via.
Who throws away his books?	Chi getta via i propri libri?
Have you thrown away any thing?	Ha Ella gettato via qualcosa?
I have thrown away my gloves.	Ho gettato via i miei guanti.
Have you thrown them away?	Li ha Ella gettati via?
I have thrown them away.	Li ho gettati via.

EXERCISES.

104.

Have you any thing to do?—I have nothing to do.—What hast thou done?—I have done nothing.—Have I done any thing?—You have done something.—What have I done?—You have torn my books.—What have your children done?—They have torn their clothes.—What have we done?—You have done nothing; but your brothers have burnt my fine books.—Has the tailor already made your coat?—He has not yet made it.—Has your shoemaker already made your boots?—He has already made them.—Have you sometimes made a hat?—I have never made one.—Have our neighbours ever written books?—They wrote some formerly.—How many coats has your tailor made?—He has made twenty or thirty.—Has he made good or bad coats?—He has made (both) good and bad.—Has your father put on his coat?—He has not yet put it on, but he is going to put it on.—Has your brother put his boots on?—He has put them on.—Have our neighbours put on their boots and their gloves?—They have put on neither (questi nè quelli).—What has the physician taken away?—He has taken nothing away.—What have you taken off?—I have taken off my large hat.—Have your children taken off their gloves?—They have taken them off.—When did the ball take place?—It took place the day before yesterday.—Who has told you that?—My servant has told it me.—What has your brother told you?—He has told me nothing.—Did I tell you that? —You did not tell it me.—Has he told it you?—He has told it me.—Who has told it your neighbour?—The English have told it him.—Have they told it to the French?—They have told it them. —Who has told it you?—Your son has told it me.—Has he told it you?—He has told it me.—Are you willing to tell your friends that?—I am willing to tell it them.

105.

Are you the brother of that young man?—I am.—Is that young man your son?—He is.—Are your friends as rich as they say?—They are so.—Are these men as learned as they say?— They are not so.—Do you often sweep the warehouse?—I sweep it as often as I can.—Has our neighbour money enough to buy some coals?—I do not know.—Did your brother go to the ball yesterday?—I do not know.—Has your cook gone to the market?—He has not gone thither.—Is he ill (*malato*)?—He is.— Am I ill?—You are not.—Are you as tall as I?—I am.—Are you as fatigued as your brother?—I am more so than he.—Have you written a note?—I have not written a note, but an exercise. —What have your brothers written?—They have written their exercises.—When did they write them?—They wrote them yesterday.—Have you written your exercises?—I have written them.—Has your friend written his?—He has not written them yet.—Which exercises has your little brother written?—He has written his own.—Have you spoken to my father?—I have spoken to him.—When did you speak to him?—I spoke to him the day before yesterday.—How many times have you spoken to the captain?—I have spoken to him many times.—Have you often spoken to his son?—I have often spoken to him.—To which men has your friend spoken?—He has spoken to these and to those.

106.

Have you spoken to the Russians?—I have spoken to them.—Have the English ever spoken to you?—They have often spoken to me.—What has the German told you?—He told me the words.—Which words has he told you?—He has told me these words.—What have you to tell me?—I have a few words to tell you.—Which exercises has your friend written?—He has written those.—Which men have you seen at the market?—I have seen these.—Which books have your children read?—They have read those which you have lent them.—Have you seen these men or those?—I have seen neither these nor those.—Which men have you seen?—I have seen those to whom (*a cui*) you have spoken.—Have you been acquainted with those men?—I have been acquainted with them.—With which boys has your brother been acquainted?—He has been acquainted with those of our merchant.—Have I been acquainted with these Frenchmen?—You have not been acquainted with them.—Which wine has your servant drunk?—He has drunk mine.—Have you seen my brothers?—I have seen them.—Where have you seen them?—I have seen them at their own house (*in casa loro*).—Have you ever seen Greeks?—I have never seen any.—Has your brother seen any?—He has sometimes seen some.—Do you call me?—I do call you.—Who calls your father?—My brother calls him.—Dost thou call any one?—I call no one. Have you thrown away your hat?—I have not thrown it away.—Does your father throw away any thing?—He throws away the notes which he receives.—Have you thrown away your nails?—I have not thrown them away.—Dost thou throw away thy book?—I do not throw it away; I want it to study Italian.

THIRTY-FOURTH LESSON.
Lezione trentesima quarta.

To light (kindle)	— lighted or lit.	Accendere *	— acceso.
To extinguish,	— extinguished.	Spegnere *	— spento.
To open,	— opened.	Aprire *	— aperto.
To conduct,	— conducted.	Condurre *	— condotto.
To pick up (gather),	— picked up (gathered).	Raccorre *	— raccolto.
To answer,	— answered.	Rispondere *	— risposto.
To take,	— taken.	Prendere *	— preso.
To break,	— broken.	Rompere *	— rotto.
To know,	— known.	Sapere *	— saputo.
To be able (can),	— been able (could).	Potere *	— potuto.
To be willing,	— been willing.	Volere *	— voluto.
To give,	— given.	Dare *	— dato.

NEUTER VERBS.

In neuter verbs the action is intransitive; that is, it remains in the agent. They are conjugated like the active. The latter, however, always form their past tenses with the auxiliary *avere*, to have; the neuter verbs, on the contrary, take *essere*, to be; and their past participle must agree in gender and number with the subject. (See ☞ Lesson XXXII.) Those neuter verbs, which are conjugated with the auxiliary *to have* in English, and *essere* in Italian, will always be marked.

To go,	— gone.	Andare *	— andato.
To stay,	— stood.	Stare *	— stato.
To remain,	— remained.	Rimanere *	— rimaso, or rimasto.
To set out,	— set out (past part.).	Partire	— partito.
To go out,	— gone out.	Uscire *	— uscito.
To come,	— come (past part.).	Venire *	— venuto.

Did you stay long in that country?   È Ella stata molto tempo in questo paese?

When did you go to the ball?   Quando è Ella andata alla festa da ballo?

I went thither at midnight.   Vi sono andato a mezza notte.
Did he remain long in Paris?   È egli rimasto molto in Parigi?
He remained there a year.   Ci è rimasto un anno.
Has your father set out?   È partito il di Lei padre?
Have your friends set out?   Sono partiti i di Lei amici?
They have not set out.   Non sono partiti.

THIRTY-FOURTH LESSON. 153

When did your brothers go out? | Quando sono usciti i di Lei fratelli?
They went out at ten o'clock. | Sono usciti alle dieci.
Did the men come to your father? | Sono venuti dal di Lei padre gli uomini? (better) gli uomini sono venuti dal di Lei padre?
They did come to him. | Ci sono venuti.

Which fires have you extinguished? | Quai fuochi ha Ella spenti?
Which warehouses have you opened? | Che magazzini ha Ella aperti?
Have you conducted them to the storehouse? | Li ha Ella condotti al magazzino?
I have conducted them thither. | Ce li ho condotti.
Which books have you taken? | Quai libri ha Ella presi?
How many notes have you received? | Quanti biglietti ha Ella ricevuti?
I have received but one. | Ne ho ricevuto solamente uno.
Which fires has he lighted? | Quai fuochi ha egli accesi?
Have you opened the trunks? | Ha Ella aperto i bauli?
I have opened them. | Li ho aperti.
Which nails has the carpenter picked up? | Quai chiodi ha raccattati il legnaiuolo?
   To pick up — picked up. | Raccattare — raccattato.
Which notes have you answered? | † A quai biglietti ha Ella risposto?
   To answer a note. | † Rispondere • ad un biglietto.
Which books has he taken? | Quai libri ha egli presi?
Have they broken the glasses? | Hanno eglino rotto i bicchieri?
They have not broken them. | Non li hanno rotti.
Have you the gloves which I gave you? | Ha Ella i guanti che Le ho dati? or avete voi i guanti che vi ho dati?
I have had them, but have them no longer. | Li ho avuti, ma non li ho più.

    Upon. | Su, Sopra, Sovra.
The bench. | Il banco (lo scanno).
Upon the bench. | Sopra il banco. Sul banco.
Upon it. | Sopra (disopra).

    Under. | Sotto.
Under the bench. | Sotto il banco.
Under it (underneath). | Sotto (disotto).
Where is my hat? | Ove è il mio cappello?
It is upon the bench. | È sopra il banco.
Are my gloves on the bench? | Sono sopra il banco (or sul banco) i miei guanti?
They are under it. | Sono sotto (disotto).

7*

THIRTY-FOURTH LESSON.

Do you learn to read?	Impara Ella a leggere?
I do (learn it).	Imparo.
I learn to write.	Imparo a scrivere.
Have you learnt to speak?	Ha Ella imparato a parlare?
I have (learnt it).	Ho imparato.

In the storehouse.	Nel magazzino.
The stove.	Il fornello (la stufa).
In the stove.	Nel fornello (nella stufa).
In it or within.	Dentro (al di dentro).

To wash.	Lavare 1.
To get or to have — got or had mended,	† Far rassettare, — fatto rassettare.
	† Far raccomodare, — fatto raccomodare.
To get or to have — got or had washed,	† Far lavare, — fatto lavare.
To get or to have — got or had made,	† Far fare, — fatto fare.
To get or to have — got or had swept,	† Far spazzare, — fatto spazzare.
To get or to have — got or had sold,	† Far vendere, — fatto vendere.

To get the coat mended.	† Far raccomodare l' abito.
To have it mended.	† Farlo raccomodare.
To get them mended.	† Farli raccomodare.
To get some mended.	† Farne raccomodare.

Are you getting a coat made (do you order a coat)?	† Si fa ella fare un abito?
I am getting one made (I order one).	† Me lo faccio fare.
I have had one made.	† Me ne son fatto fare uno.
Have you had your coat mended?	† Ha Ella fatto raccomodare il di Lei abito?
I have had it mended.	† L' ho fatto raccomodare.
I have not had it mended.	† Non l' ho fatto raccomodare.
I have had my boots mended.	† Ho fatto raccomodare i miei stivali.
I have had them mended.	† Li ho fatti raccomodare.

To wipe.	Asciugare 1.
Have you not seen my book?	Non ha Ella veduto il mio libro?
I have seen it.	L' ho veduto (visto).

* Learners ought now to use in their exercises the adverbs of time, place, and number, mentioned in Lessons XIX., XXII., XXIII., and XXXII.

When ?—Where ?	Quando ? { Dove ? / Ove' ?
When did you see my brother ?	Quando ha Ella veduto mio fratello ?
I saw him the day before yesterday.	L' ho veduto l' altro ieri.
Where did you see him ?	Dove l' ha Ella veduto ?
I saw him at the theatre.	L' ho veduto al teatro.

EXERCISES.

107.

Where are your brothers gone ?—They are gone to the theatre.—Have your friends left (*partire*) ?—They have not yet left.—When do they set out ?—This evening.—At what o'clock ?—At half-past nine.—When did the French boys come to your brother ?—They came to him yesterday.—Did their friends come also ?—They came also.—Has any one come to us ?—The good Germans have come to us.—Who has come to the English ?—The French have come to them.—When did you drink some wine ?—I drank some yesterday, and to-day.—Has the servant carried my note ?—He has carried it.—Where has he carried it ?—He has carried it to your friend.—Which notes have you carried ?—I have carried those which you have given me to carry.—To whom have you carried them ?—I have carried them to your father.—Which books has your servant taken ?—He has taken those which you do not read.—Have your merchants opened their warehouses ?—They have opened them.—Which warehouses have they opened ?—They have opened those which you have seen.—When have they opened them ?—They have opened them to-day.—Have you conducted the foreigners to the storehouses ?—I have conducted them thither.—Which fires have the men extinguished ?—They have extinguished those which you have perceived (*scorti*).—Have you received any notes ?—We have received some.—How many notes have you received ?—I have received only one ; but my brother has received more than I : he has received six.

108.

Where is my coat ?—It is on the bench.—Are my boots upon the bench ?—They are under it.—Are the coals under the bench ?

—They are in the stove.—Have you put some coals into the stove?
—I have put some into it.—Are you cold?—I am not cold.—Are
the coals which I have seen in the stove?—They are in it.—Are
my notes upon the stove?—They are in it (within).—Have you
not been afraid to burn my notes?—I have not been afraid to burn
them.—Have you sent your little boy to the market?—I have
sent him thither.—When did you send him thither?—This morning.—Have you written to your father?—I have written to him.
—Has he answered you?—He has not yet answered me.—Are
you getting your floor swept?—I am getting it swept.—Have
you had your counting-house swept?—I have not had it swept
yet, but I intend to have it swept to-day.—Have you wiped your
feet?—I have wiped them.—Where did you wipe them?—I
wiped them upon the carpet.—Have you had your benches
wiped?—I have had them wiped.—What does your servant wipe?
—He wipes the knives.—Have you ever written to the physician?
I have never written to him.—Has he sometimes written to you?
—He has often written to me.—What has he written to you?—
He has written something to me.—How many times have your
friends written to you?—They have written to me more than
twenty times.—Have you seen my sons?—I have never seen
them.

109.

Have you ever seen any Greeks?—I have never seen any.—
Have you already seen a Syrian?— I have already seen one.—
Where have you seen one?—At the theatre.—Have you given
the book to my brother?—I have given it to him.—Have you
given money to the merchant?—I have given him some.—How
much have you given to him?—I have given him fourteen
crowns.—Have you given any gold ribbons to the children of our
neighbours?—I have given them some.—Wilt thou give me some
wine?—I have given you some already.—When didst thou give
me some?—I gave you some formerly.—Wilt thou give me some
now?—I cannot give you any; I have none.—Has the American
lent you money?—He has lent me some.—Has he often lent you
some?—He has sometimes lent me some.—Has the Italian ever
lent you money?—He has never lent me any.—Is he poor?—

He is not poor; he is richer than you.—Will you lend me a crown?—I will lend you two.—Has your boy come to mine?—He has come to him.—When?—This morning.—At what o'clock?—Early.—Has he come earlier than I?—At what o'clock did you come?—I came at half-past five.—He came earlier than you.

110.

Has the concert taken place?—It has taken place.—Did it take place late?—It took place early.—At what o'clock?—At twelve.—At what o'clock did the ball take place?—It took place at midnight.—Does your brother learn to write?—He does learn.—Does he know how to read?—He does not know how yet.—Do you know the Frenchman whom I know?—I do not know the one whom you know, but I know another.—Does your friend know the same (*i medesimi*) merchants as I know?—He does not know the same (*i medesimi*), but he knows others.—Have you ever had your coat mended?—I have sometimes had it mended.—Hast thou already had thy boots mended?—I have not yet had them mended.—Has your brother sometimes had his waistcoats mended?—He has had them mended several times (*alcune volte*).—Hast thou had thy hat or thy waistcoat mended?—I have neither had the one nor the other mended.—Have you had your gloves or your handkerchiefs mended?—I have had neither the one nor the other mended.—Has your father had any thing made?—He has not had any thing made.—Have you looked for my gloves?—I have looked for them.—Where have you looked for them?—I have looked for them upon the bed, and have found them under it.—Have you found my notes in the stove?—I have found them in it.—Have you found my boots under the bed?—I have found them upon it.—How long did you stay in that country?—I stayed there two years.—Did your father remain long at the ball?—He remained there only a few minutes.

THIRTY-FIFTH LESSON.
Lezione trentesima quinta.

To promise	— promised.	*Promettere*°	— promesso.
To understand	— understood.	*Comprendere*°	— compreso.
		Intendere°	— inteso.
		Capire°	— capito.
To wait	— waited.	*Attendere*°	— atteso.
		Aspettare°	— aspettato.
To intend (to hear).	— intended (heard).	*Intendere*°	— inteso.

Obs. Compound and derivative verbs are generally conjugated like their primitives: thus the verb *promettere*° is conjugated like *mettere*°, to put (Lesson XXXIII), *comprendere*°, like *prendere*°, to take (Lesson XXXIV), *attendere*° and *intendere*°, like *tendere*°, to tend.

Do you promise me to come?	Mi promette Ella di venire?
I do promise you.	Glielo prometto.
What have you promised the man?	Che ha Ella promesso all' uomo?
I have promised him nothing.	Non gli ho promesso nulla.

To lose — lost.	*Perdere*° — *perduto.*
How much has your brother lost?	Quanto danaro ha perduto il di Lei fratello?
He has lost about a crown.	Ha perduto circa uno scudo.
About.	Circa, incirca.
I have lost more than he.	Ho perduto più di lui.

Have you ever learnt Italian?	Ha Ella imparato mai l' italiano?
I have learnt it formerly.	L' ho imparato altre volte.

To wear, to use.	Usare.
To wear out.	Logorare 1.
This coat is worn out.	Questo abito è logorato.
The worn-out coat.	L' abito logoro.

To refuse.	Rifiutare (ricusare).
To spell.	Compitare.

THIRTY-FIFTH LESSON.

How?	Come?
Well.	Bene.
Badly.	Male.

So, thus.	Così, in questo modo.
So so.	Così così.
In this manner.	In questa maniera.
How has your brother written his exercise?	Come ha scritto il suo tema il di Lei fratello?
He has written it well.	L' ha scritto bene.

To dry.	Asciugare (seccare).
Do you put your coat to dry?	Mette Ella ad asciugare il suo abito?
I do put it to dry.	Lo metto ad asciugare.

How old are you?	† Che età ha Ella?
	† Quanti anni ha Ella?
I am twelve years old.	† Ho dodici anni.
How old is your brother?	† Quanti anni ha il di Lei fratello?
	† Che età ha il di Lei fratello?
He is thirteen years old.	† Egli ha tredici anni.

Almost.	Quasi, incirca (all' incirca).
He is almost fourteen years old.	† Egli ha incirca quattordici anni.
About.	Circa, incirca (all' incirca).
I am about fifteen years old.	† Ho circa quindici anni.
Nearly.	Press' a poco, quasi, incirca.
He is nearly fifteen years old.	† Ha quasi quindici anni.
	† Si avvicina ai quindici anni.

To draw near.	Avvicinare, avvicinarsi.
Hardly.	Appena.
You are hardly seventeen years old.	† Ella ha appena diciassette anni.

Not quite.	Non intieramente.
	Non del tutto.
	Non tutt' affatto.
I am not quite sixteen years old.	† Non ho tutt' affatto sedici anni.
	† Non ho ancor compito il sedicesimo anno.

To complete.	Compire 3.

THIRTY-FIFTH LESSON.

Art thou older than thy brother?	† Sei tu maggiore di tuo fratello?
I am younger than he.	{ Sono più giovane di lui. { Sono minore di lui.
Old (in years).	Vecchio.
Aged.	{ Attempato. { Avanzato in età.
Young.	Giovane.

There is.	*C' è, vi è (vi ha, avvi).*
There are.	*Ci sono or vi sono.*

How many francs are there in a crown?	† Quanti franchi ci vogliono per fare uno scudo?
Three.	Tre.
There are twenty sous, or a hundred centimes, in one franc.	† Venti soldi, o cento centesimi fanno un franco.
There are five centimes in a sou.	† Cinque centesimi fanno un soldo.
A sr one hundred.	Cento.
The centime.	Il centesimo.

The gold sequin.	Lo zecchino d' oro.
The livre (a coin).	La lira (*a feminine noun*).
The crown.	Lo scudo.
The sou.	Il soldo.
A sequin has four crowns.	Quattro scudi fanno uno zecchino d' oro.
There are seven livres (or francs) in a crown.	Sette lire fanno uno scudo.
There are twenty sous in a livre.	Venti soldi fanno una lira.

To understand — understood.	Capire — capito.
I understand, thou understandest, he understands.	Capisco, capisci, capisce.
We, you, they understand.	Capiamo, capite, capiscono.

The noise.	Lo strepito, il rumore.
The wind.	Il vento.
The noise (roaring) of the wind.	Lo strepito del vento.
Do you hear the roaring of the wind?	Intende Ella lo strepito del vento?
I do hear it.	L' intendo.

To bark.	*Latrare, abbaiare* 1.
The barking.	Il latrato.
Have you heard the barking of the dogs?	Ha Ella inteso il latrato dei cani?
I have heard it.	L' ho inteso.

To wait for some one or something.	Aspettare qualcuno o qualche cosa.
To expect some one or something.	
Are you waiting for my brother?	Aspetta Ella mio fratello?
I am waiting for him.	Lo aspetto.
Do you expect some friends?	Aspetta Ella degli amici?
I do expect some.	Ne aspetto alcuni.

The nobleman.	Il gentiluomo (il nobile).
Noblemen.	I gentiluomini (i nobili).
Gentle, pretty.	Gentile, grazioso.
Where has the nobleman remained?	Ove è rimasto il gentiluomo?
He has remained at home.	E rimasto in casa.
Have you remained with him?	E Ella rimasta con lui (seco)?
With.	Con.
With him.	Seco, con lui.

EXERCISES.

111.

Do you promise me to come to the ball?—I promise you.—Have I promised you any thing?—You have promised me nothing.—What has my brother promised you?—He has promised me a fine book.—Have you received it?—Not yet.—Do you give me what you have promised me?—I give it you.—Has your friend received much money?—He has received but little.—How much has he received?—He has received but one crown.—How much money have you given to my son?—I have given him thirty francs.—Did you not promise him more?—I have given him what I promised him.—Have you Italian money?—I have some.—What money have you?—I have some sequins, crowns, livres, and sous.—How many crowns are there in a gold sequin?—There are four crowns in a gold sequin.—Have you any French money?—I have some; I have French and Italian money.—What kind of (che) French money have you?—I have some francs, sous, and centimes.—How many sous are there in a franc?—There are twenty sous in a franc.—Have you any centimes?—I have several.—How many centimes are there in a sou?—There are five.—And how many centimes are there in a franc?—One hundred (*cento*).—Will you lend me your coat?—I will lend it you, but it is worn out.—Are your boots worn out?—They are not worn out.—Will you lend them to my brother?—I will lend them to him.—To whom have you lent your hat?—I have not lent it; I have given it to somebody.—To whom have you given it?—I have given it to a pauper (*un povero*).

112.

Does your little brother already know how to spell?—He does know.—Does he spell well?—He spells well.—How has your little brother spelt?—He has spelt so so.—How have your children written their exercises?—They have written them badly.—Has my neighbour lent you his gloves?—He has refused to lend them to me.—Do you know Spanish?—I know it.—Does your son speak Italian?—He speaks it well.—How do your friends speak?—They do not speak badly.—Do they listen to what you tell them?—They listen to it.—How hast thou learnt English? —I have learnt it in this manner.—Did you call me?—I have not called you, but I have called your brother.—Is he come?— Not yet.—Where did you wet your clothes?—I wetted them in the garden.—Will you put them to dry?—I have already put them to dry.—Does the nobleman wish to give me any thing to do?—He wishes to give you something to do.—How old are you? —I am hardly eighteen years old.—How old is your brother?— He is twenty years old.—Are you as old as he?—I am not so old.—How old art thou?—I am about twelve years old.—Am I younger than you?—I do not know.—How old is our neighbour? He is not quite thirty years old.—Are our friends as young as we?—They are older than we.—How old are they?—The one is nineteen, and the other twenty years old.—Is your father as old as mine?—He is older than yours.

113.

Have you read my book?—I have not quite read it yet.—Has your friend finished his books?—He has almost finished them.— Do you understand me?—I understand you.—Does the Frenchman understand us?—He understands us.—Do you understand what we are telling you?—We understand it.—Dost thou understand Italian?—I do not understand it yet, but I am learning it.—Do we understand the English?—We do not understand them.—Do the English understand us?—They understand us.—Do we understand them?—We hardly understand them.—Do you hear any noise?—I hear nothing.—Have you heard the roaring of the wind?—I have heard it.—What do you hear?—I hear the barking of the dogs.—Whose dog is this?—It is the dog of the Scotchman.—Have you lost your stick?—I have not lost it.—Has your servant lost my notes?—He has lost them.—Did you go to the ball?—I did not go.—Where did you remain?—I remained at home.—Where did the noblemen remain?—They remained in the garden.—Has your father lost as much money as I?—He has lost more than you.—How much have I lost?—You have hardly lost one crown.—Did your friends remain at the ball?—They remained there.—Do you know as much as the English physician?—I do not know as much as he.—How many books have you read?—I have read hardly two.—Do you wait for any one?—I wait for no one.—Do you wait for the man whom I saw this morning?—I wait for him.—Art thou waiting for thy book?—I am waiting for it.—Do you expect your father this evening?—I do expect him.—Do you expect some friends?—I do expect some.—Where is your little brother?—He is gone with the nobleman (*col signore*).—Is he gone to the play with him?—He is gone there with him.

THIRTY-SIXTH LESSON.

Lezione trentesima sesta.

To bite—bitten. | Mordere*—morso.
To beat. | Battere 2.
Why do you beat the dog? | Perchè batte Ella il cane?

Why? | Perchè?
Because. | Poichè, perchè.
I beat it because it has bitten me. | Lo batto perchè mi ha morso.

To owe — owed. | *Dovere* — dovuto.*
How much do you owe me? | Quanto mi deve Ella?
I owe you fifty crowns. | Le devo cinquanta scudi.
How much does the man owe you? | Quanto Le deve l' uomo?
He owes me sixty francs. | Mi deve sessanta franchi.
Do our neighbours owe as much as we? | Debbono i nostri vicini quanto noi?
We owe more than they. | Dobbiamo più di loro.
How much dost thou owe? | Quanto devi?
Two hundred crowns. | Due cento scudi.
Eighty francs. | Ottanto franchi.
Two hundred and fifty sequins. | Due cento cinquanta secchini.

Are you to....? | † Deve Ella..?
I am to...... | † Devo.....
Where are you to go to this morning? | † Ove deve Ella andare stamane?
I am to go to the warehouse. | † Devo (debbo) andare al magazzino.
Is your brother to come hither to-day? | † Il di Lei fratello deve venire qui oggi?

Soon, shortly. | { *Quanto prima, fra poco, ben-tosto.*
 | { *Presto, subito.*
He is to come hither soon. | † Deve venire qui quanto prima.

To return (to come back). | *Ritornare 1.*
At what o'clock do you return from the market? | A che ora ritorna Ella dal mercato?
I return from it at twelve o'clock. | Ne ritorno { alle dodici.
 | { a mezzodì.
 | { a mezzo giorno.

From it, from there, thence. | *Ne.*
Does the servant return early from the warehouse? | Il servitore ritorna per tempo dal magazzino?
He returns from it at ten o'clock in the morning. | { Ne ritorna alle dieci antimeridiane.
 | { Ne ritorna alle dieci del mattino.
 | { Ne ritorna alle dieci della mattina.
At nine o'clock in the morning. | † Alle nove antimeridiane.
At five o'clock in the evening. | † Alle cinque della sera (pomeridiane).
At eleven o'clock at night. | † Alle undici della sera (o della notte).

THIRTY-SIXTH LESSON.

How long?	*Quanto tempo?*
During, for.	*Durante, per lo spazio di.*[1]
How long has he remained there?	Quanto tempo vi è egli restato (rimasto)?
A minute.	Durante un minuto.
An hour.	Per lo spazio di un' ora.
A day.	Durante un giorno.
A month.	Per lo spazio di un mese.
A year.	Durante un anno.

The summer.	L' estate (*fem.*) La state (*fem.*)
The winter.	L' inverno.
During the summer.	Durante la state.

To dwell, to live, to reside, to remain.	*Stare di casa; dimorare. Stare.*
To lodge.	*Alloggiare, abitare.*
Where do you live?	Dove sta Ella di casa? (Ove alloggia?)
I live in William-street, number twenty-five.	Alloggio nella contrada Guglielmo (or via Guglielmo) numero venti cinque.
Where did your brother live?	Dove ha alloggiato il di Lei fratello?
He lived in Rivoli-street, number forty-nine.	Ha alloggiato nella contrada (or via) di Rivoli, numero quaranta nove.
Dost thou live at thy brother's house?	Stai da tuo fratello?
I do not live at his, but at my father's house.	Non isto da lui, ma in casa di mio padre.
Does your friend still live where I lived?	Il di Lei amico sta (alloggia) ancora ove ho alloggiato (sono stato) io?
He lives no longer where you lived.	Non ista più dove Ella ha alloggiato.

No longer.	*Non più.*
The number.	Il numero.
How long were you speaking to the man?	Quanto tempo ha Ella parlato all' uomo?
I spoke to him for two hours.	Gli ho parlato per il corso di due ore.
Did you remain long with my father?	È Ella restata molto tempo con mio padre (col padre mio)?
I remained with him an hour.	Vi son restato un' ora.
Long.	Molto tempo.

---

[1] *Durante*, or *per lo spazio di*, when it signifies *for*, may be left out in Italian as in English, but it is then understood.

THIRTY-SIXTH LESSON.

EXERCISES.

114.

Why do you not drink?—I do not drink, because I am not thirsty.—Why do you pick up this ribbon?—I pick it up, because I want it.—Why do you lend money to this man?—I lend him some, because he wants some.—Why does your brother study?—He studies, because he wishes to learn French.—Has your cousin drunk already?—He has not drunk yet, because he has not yet been thirsty.—Does the servant show you the floor which he sweeps?—He does not show me that which he sweeps now, but that which he swept yesterday.—Why do you love that man?—I love him because he is good.—Why does your neighbour beat his dog?—Because it has bitten his boy.—Why do our friends love us?—They love us because we are good.—Why do you bring me wine?—I bring you some, because you are thirsty.—Why does the sailor drink?—He drinks, because he is thirsty.—Do you see the sailor who is in the (*sul*, upon the) ship?—I do not see the one who is in the ship, but the one who is in the (*al*) market.—Do you read the books which my father has given you?—I read them.—Do you understand them?—I understand them so so.—Do you know the Italians whom we know?—We do not know those whom you know, but we know others.—Does the shoemaker mend the boots which you have sent him?—He does not mend them, because they are worn out (*non sono più buoni*).

115.

Is your servant returned from the market?—He has not returned yet from it.—At what o'clock did your brother return from the ball?—He returned from it at one o'clock in the morning (*al tocco dopo mezza notte*).—At what o'clock didst thou come back from thy friend?—I came back at eleven o'clock in the morning.—Didst thou remain long with him?—I remained with him about an hour.—How long do you intend to remain at the ball?—I intend to remain there a few minutes.—How long did the Frenchman remain with you?—He remained with me for two hours.—How long did your brothers remain in town (*nella città*)?—They remained there during the winter.—Do you intend to remain long with us?—I intend to remain with you during the summer.—How much do I owe you?—You do not owe me much.—How much do you owe your tailor?—I owe him eighty sequins.—How much dost thou owe thy shoemaker?—I owe him already eighty-five sequins.—Do I owe you any thing?—You do not owe me any thing.—How much does the Englishman owe you?—He owes me more than you.—Do the English owe as much as the Spaniards?—Not quite so much.—Do I owe you as much as my brother?—You owe me more than he.—Do our friends owe you as much as we?—They owe me less than you.—How much do they owe you?—They owe me two hundred and fifty sequins.—How much do we owe you?—You owe me three hundred sequins.

116.

Why do you give money to the merchant?—I give him some, because he has sold me something.—Whither are you to go?—I am to go to the market.—Is your friend to come hither to-day?—He is to come hither.—When is he to come hither?—He is to come hither soon.—When are our sons to go to the play?—They are to go thither to-night (*stassera*.)—When are they to return from it?—They are to return from it at half-past ten.—When are you to go to the physician?—I am to go to him at ten o'clock at night.—When is your son to return from the painter's?—He is to return from him at five o'clock in the evening.—Where do you live?—I live in Rivoli-street, number forty-seven.—Where does your father live?—He lives in his friend's house.—Where do your brothers live?—They live in William-street, number one hundred and twenty.—Dost thou live at thy brother's?—I live in his house.—Do you still live where you lived (*dove è stata dapprima*)?—I still live there.—Does your friend still live where he did (*dove è stato altre volte*)?—He no longer lives where he did.—Where does he live at present?—He lives in his father's house.

THIRTY-SEVENTH LESSON.
Lezione trentesima settima.

How long ?	Fino a quando ? Fin quando ? / Insino a quando ?
Till, until.	Fino, insino.
Till twelve o'clock (till noon).	Fino a mezzo giorno. / Fino a mezzodì.
Till to-morrow.	Fino a domani.
Till the day after to-morrow.	Fino a { domani l' altro. / posdomani.
Till Sunday.	Fino a domenica.
Till Monday.	Fino a lunedì.
Till this evening.	Fino a stasera.
Till evening.	Fino alla sera. / Fino a sera.
Until morning.	Fino al mattino. / Fino alla mattina.
Until the next day.	Fino all' indomani.
Until that day.	Fino a questo giorno.
Until that moment.	Fino a questo momento.
Till now—hitherto.	Fino adesso—fin qui.
Until then.	Fino allora.
Then.	Allora.
Tuesday, Wednesday.	Martedì, mercoledì.
Thursday, Friday.	Giovedì, venerdì.
Saturday.	Sabato.

Obs. A. The names of the days and months are masculine, except *la domenica*, Sunday, which is feminine. Of the seasons, *la Primavera*, Spring, and *l' Estate*, Summer, are feminine; *l' Autunno*, Autumn, and *l' Inverno*, Winter, are masculine.

Till I return (till my return).	Fino al mio ritorno.
Till my brother returns (till my brother's return).	Fino al ritorno di mio fratello.
Till four o'clock in the morning.	Fino alle quattro del mattino. / Fino alle quattro mattutine.
Till midnight (till twelve o'clock at night).	Fino a mezza notte (fino alle dodici di notte.)
The return or coming back.	Il ritorno.
How long did you remain at my father's house ?	Fino a quando è Ella restata da mio padre ?
I remained at his house till eleven o'clock at night.	Ci sono restato fino all' undici di notte.

THIRTY-SEVENTH LESSON.

They, the people, any one, or one.	Si.
It is said, that is, people say.	Si dice, dicono.
They are known, that is, people or they know them.	Si conoscono.
I am told, that is, they tell me.	† Mi si dice (mi vien detto, mi dicono).
It is not said—people do not say.	Non si dice. Non dicono.
I am not told—they do not tell me.	† Non mi si dice (non mi vien detto).
They do not speak of it.	Non se¹ ne parla.
A great many people are seen there (that is, one sees there a great many people).	Vi si vede molta gente.

Obs. B. They, the people, any one, or one, are generally not expressed in the compound tenses, or even in simple tenses, when they are followed by a personal pronoun. Ex.

I am expected (that is, they expect me).	Sono aspettato (Mi aspettano).
Here are the books which he was asked for (that is, which they asked him for).	Ecco i libri che gli sono stati domandati.
It has been said (that is, people said).	È stato detto (Hanno detto).
It has been written (that is, people wrote).	È stato scritto (Hanno scritto), or Si scrive.
I was told (that is, they told me).	† Mi è stato detto (Mi hanno detto).
They wrote to me.	† Mi è stato scritto (Mi hanno scritto).

Have they brought my boots?	{ † Sono stati portati i miei stivali? { † Hanno portato i miei stivali?
They have brought them.	{ † Sono stati portati. { † Li hanno portati.
They have not brought them yet.	{ † Non sono ancora stati portati. { Non li hanno per anco portati.
What have they said?	† Che è stato detto? (Che hanno detto?)
They have said nothing.	{ † Non è stato detto niente. { † Non hanno detto niente.
What have they done?	† Che è stato fatto? (Che hanno fatto?)
They have done nothing.	{ † Non è stato fatto niente. { † Non hanno fatto niente.

To be willing (wish) — been willing (wished).	Volere*—voluto.
Have they been willing to mend my coat?	† Hanno essi voluto raccomodare il mio abito?

---

¹ *Si* is here changed into *se*, because it is followed by *ne*. (See Lesson XXXIII. *Obs. A.*)

THIRTY-SEVENTH LESSON.

They have not been willing to mend | † Non hanno voluto raccomodarlo.
it.
Have they been willing to mend my | † Hanno voluto raccomodare i miei
coats? | abiti?
They have not been willing to mend | † Non hanno voluto raccomodarli.
them.

To be able (can) — been able (could). *Potere—potuto.*

Have they been able to find the books? | † Hanno eglino potuto trovare i libri?
They could not find them. | {† Non li hanno potuto trovare.
                          | † Non si son potuti trovare.
Can they find them now? | † Si possono trovare adesso?
They cannot find them. | † Non si possono trovare.

Can they do what they wish? | † Possono eglino fare ciò che vogliono?
They do what they can, but they do | † Si fa ciò che si può, ma non si fa
not what they wish. | ciò che si vuole.

What do they say? | {† Che si dice?
                  | † Che dicono?
What do they say now? | {† Che si dice di nuovo?
                      | † Che dicono di nuovo?
They say nothing new. | {† Non si dice niente di nuovo.
                      | † Non dicono niente di nuovo.
Something or any thing new. | Qualcosa di nuovo.
Nothing or not any thing new. | Niente di nuovo.

New. | Nuovo.
My new coat. | Il mio abito nuovo.
My new horse. | Il mio nuovo cavallo.
My fine horse. | Il mio bel cavallo.
My new friend. | Il mio nuovo amico.
My handsome coat. | Il mio bell' abito.

To brush. | *Spazzare, spazzolare* 1.
This fine man. | Questo bell' uomo.
These fine men. | Questi begli uomini.
This fine tree. | Questo bell' albero.
My new friends. | I miei nuovi amici.
These fine trees. | Quei, or questi begli alberi.

THIRTY-SEVENTH LESSON. 171

Do they believe that? { Si crede ciò?
                     { Credono ciò?

They do not believe it. { Non si crede.
                        { Non lo credono.

Do they speak of that? { Si parla di ciò?
                       { Parlano di ciò?

They do speak of it. { Se ne parla (see Lesson XXXIII.
                     {   Obs. A.).
                     { Ne parlano.

They do not speak of it. { Non se ne parla.
                         { Non ne parlano.

EXERCISES.

117.

How long have you been writing?—I have been writing until midnight.—How long did I work?—You worked till four o'clock in the morning.—How long did my brother remain with you?—He remained with me until evening.—How long hast thou been working?—I have been working till now.—Hast thou still long to write?—I have to write till the day after to-morrow.—Has the physician still long to work?—He has to work till to-morrow.—Am I to remain here long?—You are to remain here till Sunday.—Is my brother to remain long with you?—He is to remain with us till Monday.—How long are we to work?—You are to work till the day after to-morrow.—Have you still long to speak? I have still an hour to speak.—Did you speak long?—I spoke till the next day.—Did you remain long in my counting-house?—I remained in it till this moment.—Have you still long to live at the Frenchman's house?—I have still long to live at his house.—How long have you to remain at his house?—Till Tuesday.—Has the servant brushed my clothes?—He has brushed them.—Has he swept the floor?—He has swept it.—How long did he remain here?—Till noon (*mezzo giorno*).—Does your friend still live with you?—He lives with me no longer.—How long did he live with you?—He lived with me only a year.—How long did you remain at the ball?—I remained there till midnight.—How long did you remain in the ship?—I remained an hour in it.—Have you remained in the garden till now?—I have remained there till now (*fino ad ora*).

118.

What do you do in the morning?—I read.—And what do you do then?—I breakfast and study.—Do you breakfast before you read?—No, Sir, I read before I breakfast.—Dost thou play instead of studying?—I study instead of playing.—Does thy brother go to the play instead of going into the garden?—He goes neither to the play nor into the garden.—What do you do in the evening?—I study.—What hast thou done this evening?—I have brushed your clothes, and have gone to the theatre.—Didst thou remain long at the theatre?—I remained there but a few minutes.—Are you willing to wait here?—How long am I to wait?—You are to wait till my father returns.—Has any body come?—Somebody has come.—What did they want?—They wanted to speak to you.—Would they not wait?—They would not wait.—Have you waited for me long?—I have waited for you two hours.—Have you been able to read my note?—I have been able to read it.—Have you understood it?—I have understood it.—Have you shown it to any body?—I have shown it to nobody.—Have they brought my fine clothes?—They have not brought them yet.—Have they swept my floor and brushed my clothes?—They have done both.—What have they said?—They have said nothing.—What have they done?—They have done nothing.—Has your little brother been spelling?—He has not been willing to spell.—Has the merchant's boy been willing to work?—He has not been willing.—What has he been willing to do?—He has not been willing to do any thing.

119.

Has the shoemaker been able to mend my boots?—He has not been able to mend them.—Why has he not been able to mend them?—Because he has had no time.—Have they been able to find my gold buttons?—They have not been able to find them.—Why has the tailor not mended my coat?—Because he has no good thread.—Why have you beaten the dog?—Because it has bitten me.—Why do you drink?—Because I am thirsty.—What have they wished to say?—They have not wished to say any thing.—Have they said any thing new?—They have not said any thing new.—What do they say new in the market?—They say nothing new (there).—Did they wish to kill a man?—They wished to kill one.—Do they believe that?—They do not believe it.—Do they speak of that?—They speak of it.—Do they speak of the man that has been killed?—They do not speak of him.—Can they do what they wish?—They do what they can, but they do not do what they wish.—What have they brought?—They have brought your new coat.—Has my servant brushed my fine carpets?—He has not brushed them yet.—Have you bought a new horse?—I have bought two new horses.—How many fine trees have you seen?—I have seen but one fine tree.—Have you seen a fine man?—I have seen several fine men.—Have you a new friend?—I have several.—Do you like your new friends?—I like them.

THIRTY-EIGHTH LESSON.

Lezione trentesima ottava.

How far?	Fin dove?
	Fin donde?
Up to, as far as.	Fino, sino.
As far as my brother's.	Fin da mio fratello.
	Fino a casa di mio fratello.
As far as here, hither.	Fin qui (or quà).
As far as there, thither.	Fin là.
As far as London.	Fino a (or in) Londra.
As far as Paris.	Fino a Parigi.
To, at, or in Paris.	A Parigi, in Parigi.
To, " " Berlin.	A Berlino, — Berlino.
To, " " London.	A Londra, — Londra.
To, " " Rome.	A Roma, — Roma.
To, at, or in France.	In Francia.
To, " " Italy.	In Italia.
To, " " England.	In Inghilterra.

THIRTY-EIGHTH LESSON.

As far as England.	Fino in Inghilterra.
As far as Italy.	Fino in Italia.
As far as Germany.	Fino in Germania (Alemagna).
As far as France.	Fino in Francia.
As far as Spain.	Fino in Ispagna.

As far as my house.	Fino a casa mia (or in casa mia). Fino da me.
As far as the warehouse.	Fino al magazzino.
As far as the corner.	Fino al canto (all' angolo).
As far as the end of the road.	Fino in fondo alla strada (a capo della strada).
As far as the middle of the road.	Fino alla metà della via. Fino in mezzo della via.

Above or *up stairs*.	*Sopra, in alto, dissopra*.
Below — down stairs.	*Giù, abbasso*.
As far as above.	Fino dissopra, fino in alto.
As far as below.	Fin giù, fin' abbasso.
As far as the other side of the road.	Fino all' altra parte della via.

This side.	Da questo lato. Da questa parte (da questo canto).
That side.	Da quella (cotesta) parte.
On this side of the road.	Di quà della via. Al di quà della via.
On that side of the road.	Al di là della via. Di là della via.

Germany.	L' Alemagna, la Germania.
America.	L' America.
Holland.	L' Olanda.
Italy.	L' Italia.
England.	L' Inghilterra.
France.	La Francia.
Spain.	La Spagna.

The middle.	Il mezzo (la metà, a fem. noun).
The well.	Il pozzo.
The cask.	La botte (a fem. noun).
The river.	Il fiume.
The lake.	Il lago.
The castle.	Il castello.
The corner.	Il canto, l' angolo.

THIRTY-EIGHTH LESSON.

To travel.	*Viaggiare* 1.
Do you go to Paris?	Va Ella a Parigi?
Do you travel to Paris?	Va Ella a Parigi?
Do you go to Florence?	Va Ella a Firenze?
Do you go to Rome?	Va Ella a Roma?
I do travel (or go) thither.	Ci vado.
Is he gone to England?	È egli andato in Inghilterra?
He is gone thither.	Ci è andato.
How far is he gone?	Fin dove è egli andato?
How far has he travelled?	Fino dove ha egli viaggiato?
He is gone as far as America.	Egli è andato fino in America.
He is gone as far as Italy.	Egli è andato fino in Italia.

To steal.	*Rubare* 1.
To steal something from some one.	{ Rubare qualcosa ad uno. { Portar via qualcosa ad uno.
Have they stolen your hat from you?	{ Le è stato rubato il cappello? { Le hanno portato via il cappello?
They have stolen it from me.	{ Mi è stato rubato. { Me l' hanno portato via.
Has the man stolen the books from thee?	{ T' ha rubato i tuoi libri l' uomo? { Ha portato via i tuoi libri l' uomo?
He has stolen them from me.	Me li ha portati via.
What have they stolen from you?	Che Le è stato rubato?
What have they stolen from your friend?	Che è stato rubato al di Lei amico?
They have stolen all his good wine from him.	Gli è stato rubato tutto il suo buon vino.

All.	*Tutto.*
All the wine.	Tutto il vino.
All the good wine.	Tutto il buon vino.
All his good wine.	Tutto il suo buon vino.
All the books.	Tutti i libri.
All his good books.	Tutti i suoi buoni libri.
All the men.	{ Tutti gli uomini. { Ogni uomo.

How do you spell this word?	{ Come si scrive questo vocabolo (questa parola)?
How is this word written?	{ Come scrivesi questa parola?
It is written thus.	{ Si scrive in questo modo (or così). { Si scrive in questa maniera.

THIRTY-EIGHTH LESSON.

To dye (to colour)—dyed.	Tignere* or tingere*—tinto.
I dye, thou dyest, he dyes.	Tingo, tingi, tinge or tinge.
We dye, you dye, they dye.	Tigniamo, tignete, tingono.
To dye black.	Tignere nero.
To dye red.	Tignere rosso.
To dye green.	Tignere verde.
To dye blue.	Tignere azzurro (turchino).
To dye yellow.	Tignere giallo.

My blue coat.	Il mio abito turchino.
This white hat.	Questo cappello bianco.
His round hat.	Il suo cappello tondo.
His yellow waistcoat.	I suo giubbettino giallo.
I have a three-cornered hat.	Ho un cappello a tre corni (a tre punte).

Do you dye your coat blue?	Tigne il di Lei abito turchino?
I dye it green.	Lo tingo verde.
What colour will you dye your cloth?	Come vuole tingere il di Lei panno?
I will dye it red.	Voglio tingerlo rosso.
The dyer.	Il tintore.

To get dyed—got dyed.	Far tingere—fatto tingere.
What colour do you get your coat dyed?	Come fa Ella tingere il di Lei vestito?
I get it dyed green.	Lo faccio tingere verde.
What colour have you had your hat dyed?	Come ha fatto tingere il di Lei cappello?
I have had it dyed black.	L' ho fatto tingere nero.
Red.	Rosso.
Brown.	Bruno.
Grey.	Grigio (bigio).
I have had my waistcoat dyed yellow.	Ho fatto tingere giallo il mio giubbettino.

EXERCISES.

120.

How far have you travelled?—I have travelled as far as Germany.—Has he travelled as far as Italy?—He has travelled as far as America.—How far have the Spaniards gone?—They have gone as far as London.—How far has that poor man come?—He has come as far as here.—Has he come as far as your house?—

He has come as far as my father's.—Have they stolen any thing from you?—They have stolen all the good wine from me.—Have they stolen any thing from your father?—They have stolen all his good books.—Dost thou steal any thing?—I steal nothing.—Hast thou ever stolen any thing?—I have never stolen any thing.—Have they stolen your good clothes from you?—They have stolen them from me.—What have they stolen from me?—They have stolen all the good books from you.—When did they steal the money from you?—They stole it from me the day before yesterday.—Have they ever stolen any thing from us?—They have never stolen any thing from us.—How far did you wish to go?—I wished to go as far as the wood.—Have you gone as far as there?—I have not gone as far as there.—How far does your brother wish to go?—He wishes to go as far as the end of that road.—How far does the wine go (*arriva*)?—It goes (*arriva*) as far as the bottom of the cask (*della botte*).—Whither art thou going?—I am going to the market.—How far are we going?—We are going as far as the theatre.—Art thou going as far as the well?—I am going as far as the castle.—Has the carpenter drunk all the wine?—He has drunk it all.—Has his little boy torn all his books?—He has torn them all.—Why has he torn them?—Because he does not wish to study.

121.

How much have you lost?—I have lost all my money.—Do you know where my father is?—I do not know.—Have you not seen my book?—I have not seen it.—Do you know how this word is written?—It is written thus.—Do you dye any thing?—I dye my hat.—What colour do you dye it?—I dye it black.—What colour do you dye your clothes?—I dye them yellow.—Do you get your trunk dyed?—I get it dyed.—What colour do you get it dyed?—I get it dyed green.—What colour dost thou get thy gloves dyed?—I get them dyed blue.—Does your boy get his ribbon dyed?—He gets it dyed.—Does he get it dyed red?—He gets it dyed grey.—What colour have your friends got their clothes dyed?—They have got them dyed green.—What colour have the Italians had their hats dyed?—They have had them dyed brown.—Have you a white hat?—I have a black one.—

THIRTY-EIGHTH LESSON.

What hat has the nobleman?—He has two hats; a white one and a black one.—What hat has the American?—He has a round hat.—Have I a white hat?—You have several white and black hats.—Has your dyer already dyed your cloth?—He has dyed it.—What colour has he dyed it?—He has dyed it green.—Do you travel sometimes?—I travel often.—Where do you intend to go this summer (*quest' estate*)?—I intend to go to Paris.—Do you not go to Italy?—I do go thither.—Hast thou sometimes travelled?—I have never travelled.—Have your friends a mind to go to Holland?—They have a mind to go thither.—When do they intend to depart?—They intend to depart the day after to-morrow.

122.

Has your brother already gone to Spain?—He has not yet gone thither.—Have you travelled in Spain?—I have travelled there.—When do you depart?—I depart to-morrow.—At what o'clock?—At five o'clock in the morning.—Have you worn out all your boots?—I have worn them all out.—What have the Spaniards done?—They have burnt all our good ships.—Have you finished all your exercises?—I have finished them all.—How far is the Frenchman come?—He has come as far as the middle of the road.—Where does your friend live?—He lives on this side of the road.—Where is your warehouse?—It is on that side of the road.—Where is the counting-house of our friend?—It is on that side of the theatre.—Is your friend's garden on this or that side of the wood?—It is on that side.—Is not our warehouse on this side of the road?—It is on this side.—Where have you been this morning?—I have been at the castle.—How long did you remain at the castle?—I remained there an hour.—Is your brother above or below?—He is above.—How far has your servant carried my trunk?—He has carried it as far as my warehouse.—Has he come as far as my house?—He has come as far as there.—How far does the green carpet go?—It goes as far as the corner of the counting-house.—Have you been in France?—I have been there several times.—Have your children already been in Germany?—They have not yet been there, but I intend to send them thither in the spring.—Will you go on this or that side of the road?—I will go neither on this nor on that side; I will go in the middle of the road.—How far does this road lead?—It leads as far as London.

THIRTY-NINTH LESSON.
Lezione trentesima nona.

To be necessary (must) — been necessary.	*Esser* d' uopo—*stato* d' uopo. *Bisognare* —*bisognato.* *Abbisognare* —*abbisognato.*
Is it necessary? Must I, he, we, you, they, or she? It is necessary.	Bisogna? E d' uopo? È d' uopo. Bisogna.

Obs. A. All verbs expressing necessity, obligation, or want, as, *to be obliged, to want, to be necessary, must,* are generally rendered in Italian by *esser* • *d' uopo* or *bisognare.*

Is it necessary to go to the market?	Bisogna andare al mercato? È d' uopo andare al mercato?
It is not necessary to go thither.	Non bisogna andarci. Non è d' uopo andarci.
What must one do to learn Italian?	Ch' è d' uopo (che bisogna) fare per imparare l' Italiano?
It is necessary to study a great deal.	È d' uopo (bisogna) studiar molto.
What must *I* do?	Che m' è (mi è) d' uopo fare? Che debbo fare?

Obs. B. The English nominative, or subject of the verb *must,* is rendered in Italian by the indirect cases in the dative: *mi, ti, gli, le, ci, vi, loro* (see the Personal Pronouns, Lesson XX.), according to number and person.

You must stay still.	Le è d' uopo restar quieta.
Whither must *he* go?	Ove gli è d' uopo andare? Ove gli bisogna andare?
He must go for his book.	Gli è d' uopo andare in cerca del suo libro.
What must *they* buy? *They* must buy some beef.	Che è *loro* d' uopo comprare? È *loro* d' uopo comprar del manzo.
What must we read?	Che ci è d' uopo leggere? Che ci bisogna leggere? † Che ci conviene leggere?

THIRTY-NINTH LESSON.

What must you have?	Che *Le* è d' uopo? / Che vi è d' uopo? / Che *Le* bisogna?
I must have some money.	Mi è d' uopo danaro.
Must you have a sou?	Le è d' uopo un soldo?
Must you have a great deal?	Gliene è d' uopo molto?
I must have a great deal.	Me n' è d' uopo molto.
I only want one sou.	Mi è d' uopo solamente un soldo.
Is that all you want?	Non *Le* bisogna che questo?
That is all I want.	Non mi bisogna che questo.
How much must thou have? / How much dost thou want?	Quanto ti è d' uopo?
I only want a livre.	Non mi è d' uopo che una lira. / Non mi bisogna che una lira. / Mi è d' uopo solamente una lira.
How much must *your brother* have?	Quanto bisogna al di Lei fratello?
He only wants two livres.	Non gli bisognano che due lire. / Non *gli* è d' uopo che due lire. / Gli è d' uopo solamente due lire.

Have you what you want?	Ha Ella ciò che *Le* bisogna? / che *La* è d' uopo?
I have what I want.	Ho ciò che m' è d' uopo.
He has what *he* wants.	Ha ciò che gli è d' uopo.
They have what *they* want.	Hanno ciò che loro è d' uopo.

More.	*Di più* (*più*).
No—more.	*Non—di più* (*non—più*).
Do you not want more?	Non *Le* abbisogna di più?
I do not want more.	Non *mi* abbisogna di più.
He does not want more.	Non *gli* abbisogna di più.

Have you been obliged to work much to learn Italian?	Le è stato d' uopo studiar molto per imparare l' italiano?
I have been obliged to work much.	Mi è stato d' uopo studiar molto.

What am *I* to do?	Che debbo fare?
You must work.	Devo lavorare, *or* Dovete lavorare.
Am *I* to go thither?	Devo andarvi?
You may go thither.	Può andarvi.

To be worth—been worth.	*Valere*—valuto* (*valso*).
How much may that horse be worth?	Quanto può valere questo cavallo?
It may be worth a hundred sequins.	Può valere cento zecchini.
Are you worth?	Vale Ella (valete)? (not much used.)

THIRTY-NINTH LESSON.

I am worth.	Valgo.
Thou art worth.	Vali.
He is worth.	Vale.
We are worth—they are worth.	Vagliamo—vagliono or valgono.

How much is that gun worth?	Quanto vale questo fucile?
It is worth but one sequin.	Vale solamente uno zecchino.
How much is that worth?	Quanto val ciò?
That is not worth much.	Ciò non val molto. Ciò non val gran cosa.
That is not worth any thing.	Ciò non val niente.

This is worth more than that.	Questo val più di quello.
The one is not worth so much as the other.	L' uno non vale quanto l' altro.

To be better.	Valer* più. Costar più.
Am I not as good as my brother?	Non valgo quanto mio fratello?
You are better than he.	Ella val più di lui.
I am not so good as you.	Non valgo quanto Ella.

To give back, to restore. Given back, restored.	Rendere*—reso.
Does he restore you your book?	Le rende li di Lei libro?
He restores it to me.	Me lo rende.
Has he given you back your gloves?	Le ha reso i di Lei guanti?
He has given them me back.	Me li ha resi.

Has your brother already commenced his exercises?	Il di Lei fratello ha già cominciato i suoi temi?
Not yet.	Non—ancora; non—per anco.
He has not yet commenced them.	Non li ha ancora incominciati.
The present.	Il regalo.
Have you received a present?	Ha ricevuto un regalo?
I have received several.	Ne ho ricevuti parecchi.
Have you received the books?	Ha Ella ricevuto i libri?
I have received them.	Li ho ricevuti.

From whom?	Da chi?
From whom have you received presents?	Da chi ha ricevuto dei regali?
From my friends.	Dai miei amici.

THIRTY-NINTH LESSON.

Whence ? Where from ?	{ *Da dove ?* { *D' onde ?*
Where do you come from ?	D' onde (da dove) viene ?
I come from the garden.	Vengo dal giardino.
Where is he come from ?	Da dove è venuto ?
He is come from the theatre.	È venuto dal teatro.
Where did they come from ?	Da dove son venuti ?
They are come from home.	Son venuti da casa loro.

EXERCISES.

123.

Is it necessary to go to the market ?—It is not necessary to go thither.—What must you buy ?—I must buy some beef.—Must I go for some wine ?—You must go for some.—Am I to go to the ball ?—You must go there.—When must I go there ?—You must go there this evening.—Must I go for the carpenter ?—You must go for him.—What must be done to learn Russian ?—It is necessary to study a great deal.—Is it necessary to study a great deal to learn German ?—It is necessary to study a great deal.—What must I do ?—You must buy a good book.—What is he to do ?—He must sit still.—What are we to do ?—You must work.—Must you work much in order to learn the Arabic ?—I must work much to learn it.—Why must I go to the market ?—You must go thither to buy some beef and wine.—Must I go any where ?—Thou must go into the garden.—Must I send for any thing ?—Thou must send for some wine.—What must I do ?—You must write an exercise.—To whom must I write a note ?—You must write one to your friend.—What do you want, Sir ?—I want some cloth.—How much is that hat worth ?—It is worth four crowns.—Do you want any boots ?—I want some.—How much are these boots worth ?—They are worth twenty livres.—Is that all you want ?—That is all I want.—Do you not want any gloves ?—I do not want any.—Dost thou want much money ?—I want much.—How much must thou have ?—I must have five sequins.—How much does your brother want ?—He wants but six francs.—Does he not want more ?—He does not want more.—Does your friend want more ?—He does not want so much as I.—What do you want ?—

I want money and clothes.—Have you now what you want?—I have what I want.—Has your father what he wants?—He has what he wants.

124.

Have the neighbour's children given you back your books?—They have given them me back.—When did they give them you back?—They gave them me back yesterday.—Has your little boy received a present?—He has received several.—From whom has he received any?—He has received some from my father and from yours.—Have you received any presents?—I have received some.—What presents have you received?—I have received fine presents.—Do you come from the garden?—I do not come from the garden, but from the warehouse.—Where are you going to?—I am going to the garden.—Whence does the Irishman come?—He comes from the garden.—Does he come from the garden from which (*dal quale*) you come?—He does not come from the same (*dal medesimo*).—From which (*da qual*) garden does he come?—He comes from that of our old friend.—Whence comes our boy?—He comes from the play.—How much may that horse be worth?—It may be worth five hundred crowns.—Is this book worth as much as that?—It is worth more.—How much is my gun worth?—It is worth as much as that of your friend.—Are your horses worth as much as those of the English?—They are not worth so much.—How much is that knife worth?—It is worth nothing.

125.

Is your servant as good as mine?—He is better than yours.—Are you as good as your brother?—He is better than I.—Art thou as good as thy friend?—I am as good as he.—Are we as good as our neighbours?—We are better than they.—Is your umbrella worth as much as mine?—It is not worth so much.—Why is it not worth so much as mine?—Because it is not so fine as yours.—How much is that gun worth?—It is not worth much.—Do you wish to sell your horse?—I wish to sell it.—How much is it worth?—It is worth two hundred crowns.—Do you wish to buy it?—I have bought one already.—Does your father intend to buy a horse?—He intends to buy one, but not (*ma non*) yours (*il di*

Lei).—Have your brothers commenced (*incominciato*) their exercises?—They have commenced them.—Have you received your notes?—We have not yet received them.—Have we what we want?—We have not what we want.—What do we want?—We want fine horses, several servants, and much money.—Is that all we want?—That is all we want.—What must I do?—You must write.—To whom must I write?—You must write to your friend.—Where is he?—He is in America.—Whither am I to (*debbo*) go?—You may go to France.—How far must I (*mi è d' uopo*) go?—You may go as far as Paris.—Which (*a quai*) notes has your brother answered?—He has answered those of his friends.—Which (*quai*) dogs have your servants beaten?—They have beaten those that have made much noise.

FORTIETH LESSON.

Lezione quarantesima.

To eat—eaten.	Mangiare 1 — *mangiato.*
To dine (eat dinner).	Desinare 1 — *desinato.* Pranzare 1 — *pranzato.*
The dinner.	Il pranzo.
The breakfast.	La colazione (a fem. noun).
To eat supper (to sup).	Cenare 1 — *cenato.*
The supper.	La cena (a fem. noun).

After.	*Dopo.*
After me.	Dopo di me.
After him.	Dopo di lui.
After you.	Dopo di Lei (di voi).
After my brother.	Dopo mio fratello.

Obs. The preposition *dopo* requires the genitive before a personal pronoun, otherwise it governs the accusative.

After *having* spoken.	† Dopo *aver* parlato.

☞ When the present participle is used in English after a preposition, it is rendered in Italian by the infinitive.

FORTIETH LESSON. 185

After having sold his horse.	† Dopo aver venduto il suo cavallo.
After having been there.	† Dopo esservi stato.
I broke your knife after cutting the beef.	† Ho rotto il di Lei coltello dopo aver tagliato il manzo.
I have dined earlier than you.	Ho desinato più per tempo di Lei.
You have supped late.	Ella ha cenato tardi.

To pay for.   Pagare 1 — pagato.

To pay a man for a horse.	† Pagare un cavallo ad un uomo.
To pay the tailor for the coat.	† Pagare l'abito al sarto.
Do you pay the shoemaker for the boots?	† Paga Ella gli stivali al calzolaio?
I pay him for them.	† Glieli pago.
Does he pay you for the knife?	Le paga egli il coltello?
He does pay me for it.	† Me lo paga.
I pay what I owe.	Pago ciò che debbo.

To ask for.   Domandare 1 — domandato (Chiedere* — chiesto).

☞ The English verbs *to pay* and *to ask* require the preposition *for*; but in Italian, as in French, they require the person in the dative and the object in the accusative. When the verb *pagare*, however, has no object in the accusative, it requires the person in that case.

I have paid the tailor.	Ho pagato il sarto.
I have paid him.	L' ho pagato.
Have you paid the shoemaker?	Ha Ella pagato il calzolaio?
I have paid him.	L' ho pagato.
To ask a man for some money.	† Domandare del danaro ad un uomo?
I ask my father for some money.	† Domando danaro a mio padre.
Do you ask me for your hat?	† Mi domanda Ella il di Lei cappello?
I ask you for it.	† Glielo domando (chiedo).

To ask for—asked for.   Chiedere*—chiesto.

I ask for,	thou askest for,	he asks for.	Chiedo, chiedi, chiede.
We ask for,	you ask for,	they ask for.	Chiediamo, chiedete, chiedono.

To ask him for it.
{ † Chiederglielo.
{ † Domandarglielo.

To ask him for them.
{ † Chiederglieli.
{ † Domandarglieli.

What do you ask me for?	† Che mi chiede Ella?
I ask you for nothing.	† Non Le chiedo niente.

186 FORTIETH LESSON.

To try.	*Provare (provarsi) 1 — provato.*
Will you try to do that?	Vuol Ella provare a far ciò?
I have tried to do it.	Ho provato a farlo.
You must try to do better.	Bisogna provare a far meglio.

To hold—held.	*Tenere*—tenuto.*
I hold, thou holdest, he holds.	Tengo, tieni, tiene.
Do you hold my stick?	Tiene Ella il mio bastone?
I hold it.	Lo tengo.
We hold.	Teniamo.
You hold.	Tenete.
They hold.	Tengono.

Are you looking *for* any one?	† Cerca Ella qualcuno?
Whom are you looking *for*?	† Chi cerca Ella?
I am looking *for* a brother of mine.	† Cerco un mio fratello.

My uncle.	Mio zio.
My cousin.	Mio cugino.
My relation.	Il mio parente; pl. i miei parenti.
The parents (father and mother).	I genitori (padre e madre).

A brother of mine.	† Un mio fratello.
A cousin of yours.	† Un di Lei cugino.
A relation of his (or hers).	† Un suo parente.
A friend of ours.	† Un nostro amico.
A neighbour of theirs.	† Un loro vicino.

He tries to see you.	Cerca vederla.
Does he try to see me?	Cerca vedermi?
He tries to see an uncle of his.	Cerca vedere un suo zio.

To inquire after some one.	*Domandare di qualcuno.* / *Chiedere di qualcuno.*
After whom do you inquire?	Di chi domanda Ella?
I inquire after a friend of mine.	Domando di un mio amico.
They inquire after you.	Domandano di Lei. / † Si domanda di Lei.
Do they inquire after me?	Domandano di me? / † Si domanda di me?

FORTIETH LESSON.

Properly.	{ Benissimo. { A perfezione.
You write properly.	Ella scrive benissimo (a perfezione).
These men do their duty properly.	Questi uomini fanno il dover loro a maraviglia.
The duty.	Il dovere.
The task.	Il dovere (il lavoro).
Have you done your task?	Ha Ella fatto il di Lei dovere?
I have done it.	L' ho fatto.
Have ye done your task?	Hanno fatto il loro dovere?
We have done it.	L' abbiamo fatto.
A glass of wine.	Un bicchier di vino.
A piece of bread.	{ Un pezzo } di pane. { Un tozzo }

EXERCISES.

126.

Have you paid for the gun?—I have paid for it.—Has your uncle paid for the books?—He has paid for them.—Have I paid the tailor for the clothes?—You have paid him for them.—Hast thou paid the merchant for the horse?—I have not yet paid him for it. —Have we paid for our gloves?—We have paid for them.—Has your cousin already paid for his boots?—He has not yet paid for them.—Does my brother pay you what he owes you?—He pays it me.—Do you pay what you owe?—I pay what I owe.— Have you paid the baker?—I have paid him.—Has your uncle paid the butcher for the beef?—He has paid him for it.—Who has broken my knife?—I have broken it after cutting the bread. —Has your son broken my glasses?—He has broken them after drinking the wine.—When has your cousin broken my penknife? —He has broken it after writing his notes.—Have you paid the merchant for the wine after drinking it?—I have paid for it after drinking it.—What did you do after finishing your exercises?— I went to my cousin, in order to conduct him to the play.—How do I speak?—You speak properly (*benissimo*).—How has my cousin written his exercises?—He has written them properly (*a perfezione*).—How have my children done their task?—They

FORTIETH LESSON.

have done it well.—Does this man do his duty?—He always does it.—Do these men do their duty?—They always do it.—Do you do your duty?—I do what I can.—What do you ask this man for?—I ask him for some money.—What does this boy ask me for?—He asks you for some money.—Do you ask me for any thing?—I ask you for a crown.—Do you ask me for the bread? I ask you for it.—Which man do you ask for money?—I ask him whom you ask for some.—Which merchants do you ask for gloves?—I ask those for some who live in William-street.—What do you ask the baker for?—I ask him for some bread.

127.

Do you ask the butchers for some meat?—I ask them for some. —Dost thou ask me for the stick?—I ask thee for it.—Does he ask thee for the book?—He asks me for it.—What have you asked the Englishman for?—I have asked him for my leather trunk.—Has he given it you?—He has given it me.—Whom have you asked for some sugar?—I have asked the merchant for some.—Whom does your brother pay for his boots?—He pays the shoemaker for them.—Whom have we paid for the bread?— We have paid our bakers for it.—How old art thou?—I am not quite ten years old.—Dost thou already learn French?—I do already learn it.—Does thy brother know German?—He does not know it.—Why does he not know it?—Because he has not had time to learn it.—Is your father at home?—No, Sir, he is gone (*partito*), but my brother is at home.—Where is your father gone to?—He is gone to England.—Have you sometimes been there? —I have never been there.—Do you intend going to France this summer?—I do intend going thither.—Do you intend to stay there long?—I intend to stay there during the summer.—How long does your brother remain at home?—Till twelve o'clock.—Have you had your gloves dyed?—I have had them dyed.—What have you had them dyed?—I have had them dyed yellow.—Have you already dined?—Not yet.—At what o'clock do you dine?—I dine at six o'clock.—At whose house (*da chi,* or *in casa di chi*) do you dine? —I dine at the house of a friend of mine.—With whom did you dine yesterday?—I dined with a relation of mine.—What did you eat?—We eat good bread, good beef, and petty-patties.—What

did you drink?—We drank good wine and excellent cider.—
Where does your uncle dine to-day?—He dines with us.—At
what o'clock does your father sup?—He sups at nine o'clock?—
Do you sup earlier than he?—I sup later than he.

129.

Where are you going to?—I am going to a relation of mine, in
order to dine with him.—Art thou willing to hold my gloves?—I
am willing to hold them.—Who holds my hat?—Your son holds it.
—Dost thou hold my stick?—I do hold it.—Do you hold any
thing?—I hold your gun.—Who has held my book?—Your servant has held it.—Will you try to speak?—I will try.—Has your
little brother ever tried to do exercises?—He has tried.—Have
you ever tried to make a hat?—I have never tried to make one.
—Whom are you looking for?—I am looking for the man who
has sold a horse to me.—Is your relation looking for any body?
—He is looking for a friend of his.—Are we looking for any
body?—We are looking for a neighbour of ours.—Whom dost
thou look for?—I look for a friend of ours.—Are you looking for
a servant of mine?—No, I am looking for one of mine.—Have
you tried to speak to your uncle?—I have tried to speak to him.
—Have you tried to see my father?—I have tried to see him.—
Has he received you?—He has not received me.—Has he received your brothers?—He has received them.—Have you been
able to see your relation?—I have not been able to see him.—
What did you do after writing your exercises?—I wrote my note
after writing my exercises.—After whom (*di chi*) do you inquire
(*domandare*)?—I inquire after the tailor.—Does this man inquire
after any one?—He inquires after you (*di Lei*).—Do they inquire (*si domanda*) after you?—They inquire after me.—Do they
inquire after me?—They do not inquire after you, but after a
friend of yours (*di un di Lei amico*).—Do you inquire after the
physician?—I inquire after him.—What does your little brother
ask for?—He asks for a small piece of bread.—Has he not yet
breakfasted?—He has breakfasted, but he is still hungry.—What
does your uncle ask for?—He asks for a glass of wine.—Has he
not already drunk?—He has already drunk, but he is still
hungry.

FORTY-FIRST LESSON.

Lezione quarantesima prima.

To perceive (*to discover*).	*Scorgere*—*scorto*.
Him who.	Quello, il quale (or *che*) Colui, il quale (or *che*).
Those who.	Quelli, i quali (or *che*). Coloro, i quali (or *che*).

Obs. Colui and coloro relate only to persons, quello and quelli to persons and things.

Do you perceive the man who is coming?	Scorge Ella l' uomo che viene?
I perceive him who is coming.	Scorgo quello che viene.
Do you perceive the men who are going into the warehouse?	Scorge Ella gli uomini che vanno al magazzino?
I perceive those who are going into it.	Scorgo coloro (quelli) che vi vanno.

How is the weather? What kind of weather is it?	† Che tempo fa?
It is fine weather at present.	† Adesso fa bel tempo.
How was the weather yesterday? What kind of weather was it yesterday?	† Che tempo ha fatto ieri?
Was it fine weather yesterday?	† Ha fatto bel tempo ieri?
It was bad weather yesterday.	† Ieri ha fatto cattivo tempo.
It is fine weather this morning.	† Stamane fa bel tempo.

Is it warm?	† Fa caldo?
It is warm.	† Fa caldo.
Very.	*Molto.*
It is very warm.	† Fa molto caldo (*or* fa caldissimo).
It is cold.	† Fa freddo.
It is very cold.	† Fa freddissimo (*or* fa molto freddo).
It is neither warm nor cold.	† Non fa caldo nè freddo.

FORTY-FIRST LESSON.

Dark.	Nuvoloso, oscuro.
Obscure.	Oscuro, fosco.
Dusky, gloomy.	Buio, opaco.
Clear, light.	Chiaro.
It is dark in your warehouse.	† Fa oscuro nel di Lei magazzino.
Is it dark in his granary?	† Fa oscuro nel suo granajo?
It is dark there.	† Vi fa oscuro.

Wet, damp.	Umido.
Dry.	Asciutto.

Is the weather damp?	È umido il tempo?
It is not damp.	Non è umido.
It is dry weather.	È asciutto.
The weather is too dry.	È troppo asciutto.
The moonlight, moonshine.	Il chiaro di luna.
The sun.	Il sole.
It is moonlight.	C' è chiaro di luna (splende la luna).
We have too much sun.	† Fa troppo sole.

To taste.	{ Gustare 1. { Assaggiare 1.
Have you tasted that wine?	Ha Ella assaggiato questo vino?
I have tasted it.	L' ho assaggiato.
How do you like it?	{ Come lo trova? { Come Le piace? { Come Le pare?
I like it well.	{ Lo trovo buono. { Mi piace. { Mi par buono.
I do not like it.	{ Non mi par buono. { Non mi piace. { Non lo trovo buono.

To appear—appeared.	Parere*—paruto (or parso) (an impersonal verb governing the dative).
I appear, thou appearest, he appears.	Pajo, pari, pare.
We, you, they appear.	Pariamo, parete, pajono.

To like—liked.	Piacere*—piacciuto (an impersonal verb governing the dative).
I like, thou likest, he likes.	Mi, ti, gli, piace.
We, you, they like.	Ci, vi piace, piace loro.[1]

[1] *Piacere*, in the signification of *to please*, is conjugated thus: *Piaccio, piaci, piace; piacciamo, piacete, piacciono.*

FORTY-FIRST LESSON.

I like fish.	† Mi piace il pesce.
He likes fowl.	† Gli piace il pollastro.
Do you like cider?	† Le piace il cidro?
No, I like wine.	† No, mi piace il vino.
The fish.	† Il pesce; pl. i pesci.

Do you like to see my brother?	Le piace vedere mio fratello?
I like to see him.	Mi piace vederlo.
I like to do it.	† Mi piace farlo.
He likes to study.	† Gli piace studiare.

To learn by heart.	*Imparare a memoria.*
The scholar.	Lo scolaro.
The pupil.	L' allievo.
The master (teacher).	Il maestro.
The professor.	Il professore.
Do your scholars like to learn by heart?	I di Lei scolari imparano volontieri a memoria?
They do not like learning by heart.	Non imparano volontieri a memoria.
Have you learnt your exercises by heart?	Hanno imparato i loro temi a memoria?
We have learnt them.	Li abbiamo imparati.

Once a day.	† Una volta al giorno.
Thrice, or three times a month.	† Tre volte al mese.
So much a year.	† Tanto all' anno.
So much a head.	† Tanto a testa.
So much a soldier.	† Tanto per soldato.
Six times a year.	† Sei volte all' anno. / † Sei volte l' anno.

Early in the morning.	† *Di buon mattino* or *di buon' ora*
We go out early in the morning.	Usciamo di buon mattino.
When did your father go out?	Quando è uscito il di Lei padre?
To speak of some one or something.	*Parlare di uno o di qualcosà.*
Of whom do you speak?	Di chi parla Ella?
We speak of the man whom you know.	Parliamo dell' uomo che Ella conosce.
Of what are they speaking?	Di che parlano (di che si parla)?
They are speaking of the weather.	Parlano del tempo (si parla del tempo).

FORTY-FIRST LESSON.

The weather. | Il tempo.
The soldier. | Il soldato.
Also. | Anche (ancora).

To be content (satisfied) with some one or something. | Essere contento (soddisfatto) di uno o di qualcosa.
Are you satisfied with this man? | È Ella contenta (soddisfatta) di costui?
I am satisfied with him. | Ne son contento (soddisfatto).
Are you content with your new coat? | È Ella soddisfatta del di Lei nuovo abito?
I am contented with it. | Ne son soddisfatto.
With what are you contented? | Di che cosa è Ella contenta (soddisfatta)?

Discontented. | Scontento, malcontento.
I am discontented with him or it. | Ne sono scontento.

They speak of your friend. | Si parla del di Lei amico.
 | Parlano del di Lei amico.
They speak of him. | Se ne parla.
 | Ne parlano.
They are speaking of your book. | Si parla del di Lei libro.
 | Parlano del di Lei libro.
They are speaking of it. | Se ne parla.
 | Ne parlano.

If. | *Se.*
I intend paying you, if I receive my money. | Intendo pagarla, se ricevo il mio danaro.
Do you intend to buy coals? | Intende comprar del carbone?
I intend to buy some, if they pay me what they owe me. | Intendo comprarne, se mi pagano ciò che mi debbono.

How was the weather yesterday? | † Che tempo ha fatto ieri?
Was it fine weather yesterday? | † Ha fatto bel tempo ieri?
It was bad weather. | † Ha fatto cattivo tempo.
I intend to take a walk, if the weather is fair. | † Penso passeggiare se fa bel tempo.
If the weather is fine, I intend to go to the country. | † Se fa bel tempo intendo andare alla campagna.

To take a walk (go a walking). | Passeggiare 1.

EXERCISES.

129.

Do you perceive the man who is coming?—I do not perceive him.—Do you perceive the soldier's children?—I perceive them.—Do you perceive the men who are going into the garden?—I do not perceive those who are going into the garden, but those who are going to the market.—Does your brother perceive the man who has lent him money?—He does not perceive the one who has lent him, but the one to whom he has lent some.—Dost thou see the children who are studying?—I do not see those who are studying, but those who are playing.—Dost thou perceive any thing?—I perceive nothing.—Have you perceived my parents' warehouses?—I have perceived them.—Where have you perceived them?—I have perceived them on that side of the road.—Do you like a large hat?—I do not like a large hat, but a large umbrella.—What do you like to do?—I like to write.—Do you like to see these litttle boys?—I like to see them.—Do you like wine?—I like it.—Does your brother like cider?—He does not like it.—What do the soldiers like?—They like wine.—Dost thou like tea or coffee?—I like both.—Do these children like to study?—They like to study and to play.—Do you like to read and to write?—I like to read and to write.—How many times a day do you eat?—Four times.—How often do your children drink a day?—They drink several times a day?—Do you drink as often as they?—I drink oftener.—Do you often go to the theatre?—I go thither sometimes.—How often in a month do you go thither?—I go thither but once a month.—How many times a year does your cousin go to the ball?—He goes thither twice a year.—Do you go thither as often as he?—I never go thither.—Does your cook often go to the market?—He goes thither every morning (*ogni mattina*).

130.

Do you often go to my uncle?—I go to him six times a year.—Do you like fowl?—I like fowl, but I do not like fish.—What do you like?—I like a piece of bread and a glass of wine.—Do you learn by heart?—I do not like learning by heart.—Do your pupils like learning by heart?—They like to study, but they do not like learning by heart.—How many exercises do they do a day?—They only do two, but they do them properly.—Were you able to read the note which I wrote to you?—I was able to read it.—Did you understand it?—I did understand it.—Do you understand the man who is speaking to you?—I do not understand him.—Why do you not understand him?—Because he speaks too badly.—Does this man know French?—He knows it, but I do not know it.—Why do you not learn it?—I have no time to learn it.—Do you intend going to the theatre this evening?—I intend going thither, if you go.—Does your father intend to buy that horse?—He intends buying it, if he receives his money.—Does your friend intend to go to England?—He intends going thither, if they pay him what they owe him.—Do you intend going to the concert?—I intend going thither, if my friend goes.—Does you brother intend to study Italian?—He intends studying it, if he finds a good master.

131.

How is the weather to-day?—It is very fine weather.—Was it fine weather yesterday?—It was bad weather yesterday.—How was the weather this morning?—It was bad weather, but now it is fine weather.—Is it warm?—It is very warm.—Is it not cold?—It is not cold.—Is it warm or cold?—It is neither warm nor cold.—Did you go to the garden the day before yesterday?—I did not go thither.—Why did you not go thither?—I did not go thither, because it was bad weather.—Do you intend going thither to-morrow?—I intend going thither, if the weather is fine.—Is it light in your counting-house?—It is not light in it.—Do you wish to study in mine?—I wish to study in it.—Is it light there?—It is very light there.—Why cannot your brother work in his warehouse?—He cannot work there, because it is too dark (*perchè ci fa troppo buio*).—Where is it too dark?—In his warehouse.—Is it light in that hole?—It is dark there.—Is the weather dry?—It is very dry.—Is it damp?—It is not damp. It is too dry.—Is it moonlight?—It is not moonlight; it is very damp.—Of what does your uncle speak?—He speaks of the fine weather.—Of what do those men speak?—They speak of fair and bad weather.—Do they not speak of the wind?—They also speak of it.—Dost thou speak of my uncle?—I do not speak of him.—Of whom dost thou speak?—I speak of thee and thy parents.—Do you inquire after any one?—I inquire after your cousin; is he at home?—No, he is at his best friend's.

132.

Have you tasted that wine?—I have tasted it.—How do you like it?—I like it well.—How does your cousin like that cider?—He does not like it.—Which wine do you wish to taste?—I wish to taste that which you have tasted.—Will you taste (*sentire*) this tobacco?—I have tasted (*sentito*) it already.—How do you like it (*come Le pare*)?—I like it (*mi pare*) well.—Why do you not taste that cider?—Because I am not thirsty.—Why does your friend not taste this beef?—Because he is not hungry.—Of whom have they spoken (*si è parlato*)?—They have spoken of your friend.—Have they not spoken of the physicians?—They have not spoken of them.—Do they not speak of the man of whom we have spoken?—They speak of him.—Have they spoken of the noblemen?—They have spoken of them.—Have they spoken of those of whom we speak?—They have not spoken of those of whom we speak, but they have spoken of others.—Have they spoken of our children or of those of our neighbours?—They have neither spoken of ours, nor of those of our neighbours. Which children have been spoken of?—Those of our master have been spoken of.—Do they speak of my book?—They speak of it.—Are you satisfied with your pupils?—I am satisfied with them.—How does my brother study?—He studies well.—How many exercises have you studied?—I have already studied forty-one.—Is your master satisfied with his scholar?—He is satisfied with him.—Is your master satisfied with the presents which he has received?—He is satisfied with them.—Have you received a note?—I have received one.—Will you answer it?—I am going to answer it (*ora ci rispondo*).—When did you receive it?—I received it early this morning.—Are you satisfied with it?—I am not satisfied with it.—Does your friend ask you for money?—He asks me for some.

FORTY-SECOND LESSON.

Lezione quarantesima seconda.

OF PASSIVE VERBS.

Passive verbs represent the subject as receiving or suffering from others the action expressed by the verb. They are conjugated by means of the auxiliary verb *essere*, to be, joined to the past participle of the active verb, in Italian as well as in French and English.[1] Thus any active verb may be changed into the passive voice.

		Active voice.	*Passive voice.*
I love.	I am loved.	Amo.	Sono amato.
Thou praisest.	Thou art praised.	Lodi.	Sei lodato.
He believes.	He is believed.	Crede.	È creduto.
We beat.	We are beaten.	Battiamo.	Siamo battuti.
You punish.	You are punished.	Punite.	Siete puniti.
They serve.	They are served.	Servono.	Sono serviti.

To praise.	Lodare 1.
To blame.	Biasimare 1.
To punish.	Punire 3.
To serve.	Servire 3.

By.		*Da.*	
By me,	— by us.	Da me,	— da noi.
By thee,	— by you.	Da te,	— da voi.
By him,	— by them.	Da lui,	— da { loro. coloro. essi. }

I am loved by him.	Sono amato da lui.
Who is punished?	Chi è punito?
The naughty boy is punished.	Il cattivo fanciullo è punito.
By whom is he punished?	Da chi è egli punito?
He is punished by his father.	È punito da suo padre.
Which man is praised, and which is blamed?	Qual uomo è lodato e quale è biasimato?

---

[1] With this difference only, that in English and French we say: I have been esteemed, *J'ai été estimé*; and in Italian: *Sono stato stimato* (I am been esteemed, *Je suis été estimé*), for the compound tenses of *essere* are formed by means of the same verb.

FORTY-SECOND LESSON.

	A DIMINUTIVE
	of tenderness, of contempt.
Naughty.	Cattivo, cattivello, cattivaccio.
Skilful, diligent, clever.	Abile, destro.
Awkward.	Inabile, incapace.
Assiduous, industrious, studious.	Assiduo, diligente, studioso.
Idle.	Pigro, poltrone.
Ignorant.	Ignorante.

The idler, the lazy fellow.	Il pigro, il poltrone.

To reward.	*Ricompensare* 1.
To esteem.	*Stimare* 1.
To despise.	*Disprezzare* 1. *Sprezzare* 1.
To hate.	*Odiare* 1.

Good (wise).	Buono (savio).
These children are loved, because they are studious and good.	Questi fanciulli sono amati, perchè sono diligenti e buoni.

To travel to a place.	† *Andare* 1.
Where has he travelled to?	† Dove è andato?
He has travelled to Vienna.	† E andato a Vienna.

Is it good travelling?	† Si viaggia bene?
It is good travelling.	† Si viaggia bene.
It is bad travelling.	† Si viaggia male.

In the winter.	Nell' inverno.
In the summer.	Nella state.
In the spring.	Nella (*or* in) primavera.
In the autumn.	Nell' autunno.
It is bad travelling in the winter.	† Si viaggia male in inverno.

To drive, to ride in a carriage.	Andare in carrozza (in vettura, in legno).
To ride (on horseback).	Andare a cavallo, *or* cavalcare. Montare a cavallo.
To go on foot.	Andare a piedi.
Do you like to ride?	Le piace andare a cavallo?
I like to drive.	Mi piace andare in legno.

FORTY-SECOND LESSON.

To live—lived. | Vivere *—vissuto.
Is it good living in Paris? | † Si vive bene a Parigi?
Is the living good in Paris? |
It is good living there. | † Ci si vive bene.
The living is good there. |

Dear. | Caro.
Is the living dear in London? | Si vive a caro prezzo in Londra?
Is it dear living in London? | E caro il vivere in Londra?
The living is dear there. | Ci si vive a caro prezzo.
 | Il vivere vi è caro.

Thunder. | Il tuono, il fulmine.
The storm. | Il temporale, la tempesta (fem.)
The fog. | La nebbia (fem.)
Is it windy? Does the wind blow? | † Fa vento? Tira vento?
It is windy. The wind blows. | † Fa vento. Tira vento.
It is not windy. | † Non fa vento.
It is very windy. | † Fa molto vento.
Does it thunder? | Tuona?

To thunder. | Tuonare 1. Fulminare 1.
Is it foggy? | † Fa nebbia?
It is stormy. | † Fa burrasca. Fa temporale.
It is not stormy. | † Non fa burrasca (temporale).
Does the sun shine? | C' è sole?
It thunders very much. | Tuona molto.

Afterwards. | Poi, di poi.
As soon as. | Subito che, appena.
As soon as I have eaten, I drink. | Subito che ho mangiato, bevo.
As soon as I have taken off my boots, I take off my coat. | Subito che ho levato i miei stivali, mi levo l' abito.
What do you do in the evening? | Che fa Ella la sera?

To sleep. | Dormire 3.
Does your father still sleep? | Dorme ancora il di Lei padre?
He still sleeps. | Dorme ancora.

Without. | Senza.
Without money. | Senza danaro.
Without speaking. | Senza parlare.

Obs. *Without* requires in English the present participle; in Italian *senza* is followed by the infinitive.

Without saying any thing. | Senza dir niente.

FORTY-SECOND LESSON.

At last.	*Alfine, finalmente.*
To arrive.	*Arrivare* 1. *Ritornare* 1.
Has he arrived at last?	È arrivato alfine?
He has not arrived yet.	Non è ancor arrivato.
Is he coming at last?	Viene finalmente?
He is coming.	Viene.

And then.	*Poi, di poi, indi.*
And then he sleeps.	Poi dorme.
As soon as he has supped he reads, and then he sleeps.	Subito che ha cenato, legge; poi dorme.
He comes in at ten o'clock, sups, reads a little, takes tea, and then he goes to bed.	Entra alle dieci, cena, legge un poco, prende il tè; indi si corica.
To enter.	*Entrare* 1.
To go to bed—gone to bed.	*Coricarsi—coricatosi.*

EXERCISES.

133.

Are you loved?—I am loved.—By whom are you loved?—I am loved by my uncle.—By whom am I loved?—Thou art loved by thy parents.—By whom are we loved?—You are loved by your friends.—By whom are those children loved?—They are loved by their friends.—By whom is this man conducted?—He is conducted by me.—Where do you conduct him to?—I conduct him home.—By whom are we blamed?—We are blamed by our enemies.—Why are we blamed by them?—Because they do not love us.—Are you punished by your master?—I am not punished by him, because I am good and studious.—Are we heard? We are.—By whom are we heard?—We are heard by our neighbours.—Is thy master heard by his pupils?—He is heard by them.—Which children are praised?—Those that are good.—Which are punished?—Those that are idle and naughty.—Are we praised or blamed?—We are neither praised nor blamed.—Is our friend loved by his masters?—He is loved and praised by

FORTY-SECOND LESSON. 201

them, because he is studious and good; but his brother is despised by his, because he is naughty and idle.—Is he sometimes punished?—He is (*L' è*) every morning and every evening.—Are you sometimes punished?—I never am (*non lo sono mai*); I am loved and rewarded by my good masters.—Are these children never punished?—They never are (*non lo sono mai*), because they are industrious and good; but those are so (*lo sono*) very often, because they are idle and naughty.—Who is praised and rewarded?—Skilful children (*i fanciulli abili*) are praised, esteemed, and rewarded; but the ignorant are blamed, despised, and punished.—Who is loved, and who is hated?—He who is studious and good is loved, and he who is idle and naughty is hated.—Must one be (*è mestieri esser*) good in order to be loved? —One must be so (*é d'uopo esserlo*).—What must one do (*che bisogna fare*) in order to be loved?—One must be good and industrious.—What must one do in order to be rewarded?—One must be (*bisogna esser*) skilful, and study much.

134.

Why are those children loved?—They are loved because they are good.—Are they better than we?—They are not better, but more studious than you.—Is your brother as assiduous as mine? —He is as assiduous as he, but your brother is better than mine. —Do you like to drive?—I like to ride.—Has your brother ever been on horseback?—He has never been on horseback.—Does your brother ride on horseback as often as you?—He rides on horseback oftener than I.—Did you go on horseback the day before yesterday?—I went on horseback to-day.—Do you like travelling?—I like travelling.—Do you like travelling in the winter?—I do not like travelling in the winter; I like travelling in the spring and in autumn.—Is it good travelling in the spring? —It is good travelling in spring and in autumn, but it is bad travelling in the summer and in the winter.—Have you sometimes travelled in the winter?—I have often travelled in the winter and in the summer.—Does your brother often travel?—He travels no longer; he formerly travelled much.—When do you like to ride?—I like to ride in the morning.—Have you been in London?—I have been there.—Is the living good there?—The

9*

living is good there, but dear.—Is it dear living in Paris?—It is good living there, and not dear.—Do you like travelling in France?—I like travelling there, because one finds (*ci si trova*) good people there.—Does your friend like travelling in Holland?—He does not like travelling there, because the living is bad there.—Do you like travelling in Italy?—I like travelling there, because the living is good, and one finds (*e vi si trova*) good people; but the roads are not very good there.—Do the English like to travel in Spain (*in Ispagna*)?—They like to travel there; but they find the roads too bad.—How is the weather?—The weather is very bad.—Is it windy?—It is very windy.—Was it stormy yesterday?—It was very stormy.

135.

Do you go to the market this morning?—I do go thither, if it is not stormy.—Do you intend going to France this year?—I intend going thither, if the weather is not too bad.—Do you like to go on foot?—I do not like to go on foot, but I like going in a carriage when I am travelling.—Will you go on foot?—I cannot go on foot, because I am tired.—What sort of weather is it?—It thunders.—Does the sun shine?—The sun does not shine; it is foggy.—Do you hear the thunder?—I hear it.—Is it fine weather?—The wind blows hard, and it thunders much.—Of whom have you spoken?—We have spoken of you.—Have you praised me?—We have not praised you; we have blamed you.—Why have you blamed me?—Because you don't study (*non istudia*) well.—Of what has your brother spoken?—He has spoken of his books, his horses, and his dogs.—What do you do in the evening?—I work as soon as I have supped.—And what do you do afterwards?—Afterwards I sleep.—When do you drink?—I drink as soon as I have eaten.—When do you sleep? I sleep as soon as I have supped.—Have you spoken to the merchant?—I have spoken to him,—What has he said?—He has left (*è partito*) without saying any thing.—Can you work without speaking?—I can work, but not study French without speaking.—Wilt thou go for some wine?—I cannot go for wine without money.—Have you bought any horses?—I do not buy without money.—Has your father arrived at last?—He has arrived.—

When did he arrive ?—This morning at four o'clock.—Has your cousin set out at last ?—He has not set out yet.—Have you at last found a good master ?—I have at last found one.—Are you at last learning Italian ?—I am at last learning it.—Why have you not already learnt it ?—Because I have not been able to find a good master.

FORTY-THIRD LESSON.

Lezione quarantesima terza.

OF REFLECTIVE VERBS.

When the action falls upon the agent, and the objective case refers to the same person as the nominative, the verb is called reflective. In reflective verbs, therefore, the pronoun of the object is of the same person as that of the subject.

In such verbs each person is conjugated with a double pronoun, thus:

I,	myself.	Io,	mi.
Thou,	thyself.	Tu,	ti.
He,	himself.	Egli,	
She,	herself.	Ella,	si.
It,	itself.	Esso,	
One,	one's self.	Uno, Taluno, Alcuno,	si.
They, The people,	themselves.	Altri, Alcuni,	si.
We,	ourselves.	Noi,	ci.
You, Ye,	yourself. yourselves.	Voi,	vi.
They,	themselves.	Eglino, Essi, Esse, Elleno,	si.

Obs. A. It will be remarked that the third person is always *si*, whatever may be its number or gender.

To cut yourself.	Tagliarvi.
To cut myself.	Tagliarmi.
To cut ourselves.	Tagliarci.
To cut { himself, herself, itself, one's self. }	Tagliarsi.

Do you burn yourself?	Si brucia Ella (vi bruciate)?

Obs. B. In Italian, however, the first pronoun is often not expressed, but understood.

I do not burn myself.	Non mi brucio.
You do not burn yourself.	Non si brucia (non vi bruciate).
I see myself.	Mi vedo.
Do I see myself?	Mi vedo io?
He sees himself.	Si vede.
We see ourselves.	Ci vediamo (*or* veggiamo).
They see themselves.	Eglino si vedono (*or* veggono).

Do you wish to warm yourself?	Si vuol Ella scaldare (volete scaldarvi)?
I do wish to warm myself.	Voglio scaldarmi.
Does he wish to warm himself?	{ Si vuol egli scaldare? Vuol egli scaldarsi? }
He does wish to warm himself.	Egli vuol scaldarsi (*or* Egli si vuol scaldare).
They wish to warm themselves.	Si vogliono scaldare (*or* Vogliono scaldarsi).

To enjoy, to divert, to amuse one's self.	{ Divertirsi — divertitosi. Dilettarsi — dilettatosi. }
In what do you amuse yourself?	† A che si diletta (si diverte) Ella?
I amuse myself *in reading.*	† Mi diletto *a leggere.*
He diverts himself *in playing.*	† Si diverte *a giuocare.*

Each.	Qualunque, ogni.
Each one.	Ciascuno, ognuno.
Each man.	Qualunque uomo.
Each man amuses himself as he likes.	Ciascuno si diverte come gli piace.
Each one amuses himself in the best way he can.	{ Ciascuno si diverte alla meglio. Ciascuno si diverte a modo suo. }
The taste.	Il piacere, il gusto.
Each man has his taste.	Ognuno ha il suo gusto.
Each of you.	Ciascuno di voi (di Loro).
The world, the people.	La gente.
Every one, every body.	Tutta la gente, tutti.

FORTY-THIRD LESSON.

Every body speaks of it.   Tutti ne parlano.
Every one is liable to error.   Ciascuno ne parla.
   Ognuno è soggetto ad ingannarsi.

To mistake, to be mistaken.   *Ingannarsi.*
You are mistaken.   Ella s' inganna (v' ingannate).
He is mistaken.   S' inganna.

To deceive, to cheat.   *Ingannare* 1.
He has cheated me.   M' ha ingannato.
He has cheated me of a hundred sequins.   Mi ha ingannato di cento zecchini.

You cut your finger.   Ella si taglia il dito (vi tagliate il dito).

Obs. C. When an agent performs an act upon one part of himself, the verb is made reflective.

I cut my nails.   Mi taglio le unghie (a fem. noun, the sing. of which is l' unghia).
A hair.   Un capello.

To pull out.   *Strappare* 1.
He pulls out his hair.   Egli si strappa i capelli.
He cuts his hair.   Egli si taglia i capelli.
   The piece.   Il pezzo.
A piece of bread.   Un pezzo di pane.

To go away.   *Andarsene* *.
Are you going away?   Se ne va (ve ne andate)?
I am going away.   Me ne vado.
Is he going away?   Se ne va egli?
He is going away.   Egli se ne va.
Are we going away?   Ce ne andiamo noi?
We are going away.   Ce ne andiamo.
Are these men going away?   Se ne vanno questi uomini?
They are not going away.   Non se ne vanno.

To feel sleepy.   *Aver voglia di dormire.*
Do you feel sleepy?   Ha Ella voglia di dormire?
I feel sleepy.   Ho voglia di dormire.

To soil.   { *Insudiciare* 1.
              { *Sporcare* 1.
To fear, to dread.   *Aver paura, temere,* 2.

He fears to soil his fingers	Ha paura d' insudiciarsi le dita.
Do you dread to go out?	Ha Ella paura d' uscire?
I dread to go out.	Ho paura d' uscire.
He is afraid to go thither.	Ha paura d' andarci.

To fear some one.	*Temere uno.* *Aver paura d' uno.*
I do not fear him.	Non lo temo.
Do you fear that man?	Teme costui (temete quesii)?
What do you fear?	Che teme Ella? Di che cosa ha Ella paura?
Whom do you fear?	Chi teme Ella? Di chi ha Ella paura?
I fear nobody.	Non temo nessuno.
I fear nothing.	Non temo niente.

EXERCISES.

136.

Do you see yourself?—I see myself.—Do you see yourself in that small looking-glass (*nello specchietto*)?—I see myself in it.—Can your friends see themselves in that large looking-glass (*nello specchione*)?—They can see themselves therein (*vedervisi*).—Why does your brother not light the fire?—He does not light it, because he is afraid of burning himself.—Why do you not cut your bread?—I do not cut it, because I fear to cut my finger.—Have you a sore finger (*Le duole il dito*)?—I have a sore finger and a sore foot (*e anche il piede*).—Do you wish to warm yourself?—I wish to warm myself, because I am very cold.—Why does that man not warm himself?—Because he is not cold.—Do your neighbours warm themselves?—They warm themselves, because they are cold.—Do you cut your hair?—I cut my hair. —Does your friend cut his nails?—He cuts his nails and his hair.—What does that man do (*costui*)?—He pulls out his hair. —In what (*a che cosa*) do you amuse yourself?—I amuse myself in the best way I can (*alla meglio*).—In what do your children amuse themselves?—They amuse themselves in studying, writing, and playing.—In what does your cousin amuse himself? —He amuses himself in reading good books, and in writing to his friends.—In what do you amuse yourself when you have nothing to do at home?—I go to the play, and to the concert. I often say: Every one (*ciascuno*) amuses himself as he likes. Every man (*ciascuno*) has his taste; which is yours?—Mine is to study (*lo studiare*), to read a good book (*il leggere*, &c.), to go to the theatre, the concert (*indi al concerto*), and the ball, and to ride.

137.

Why does your cousin not brush his coat?—He does not brush it, because he is afraid of soiling his fingers (*le dita*).—What does my neighbour tell you?—He tells me that you wish to buy his horse; but I know that he is mistaken, because you have no money to buy it.—What do they say (*che si dice*, or *che dicono*) at the market?—They say that the enemy is beaten.—Do you believe that (*lo*)?—I believe it, because every one says so.—Why have you bought that book?—I have bought it, because I want it (*perchè ne ho bisogno*) to learn Italian, and because every one speaks of it.—Are your friends going away?—They are going away.—When are they going away?—They are going away tomorrow.—When are you going away (*se ne vanno Loro*)?—We are going away to-day.—Am I going away?—You are going away, if you like.—What do our neighbours say?—They are going away without saying any thing.—How do you like this wine?—I do not like it.—What is the matter with you?—I feel sleepy.—Does your friend feel sleepy?—He does not feel sleepy, but he is cold.—Why does he not warm himself?—He has no coals to make a fire.—Why does he not buy some coals?—He has no money to buy any.—Will you lend him some?—If he has none I will lend him some.—Are you thirsty?—I am not thirsty, but very hungry.—Is your servant sleepy?—He is sleepy.—Is he hungry?—He is hungry.—Why does he not eat?—Because he has nothing to eat.—Are your children hungry?—They are hungry, but they have nothing to eat.—Have they any thing to drink?—They have nothing to drink.—Why do you not eat?—I do not eat when I am not hungry.—Why does the Russian not drink?—He does not drink when he is not thirsty.—Did your brother eat any thing yesterday evening?—He ate a piece of beef, a small bit (*un pezzetto*) of fowl, and a piece of bread.—Did he not drink?—He also (*anche*) drank.—What did he drink?—He drank a glass of wine. (See end of Lesson XXIV).

FORTY-FOURTH LESSON.

Lezione quarantesima quarta.

PERFECT OF REFLECTIVE VERBS.

In Italian, all reflective verbs, without exception, take in their compound tenses the auxiliary *essere*, whilst in English they take *to have*.

Have you cut yourself?	Si è Ella tagliata?
I have cut myself.	Mi son tagliata?
Have I cut myself?	Mi son tagliato?
You have cut yourself.	Si è tagliata.
You have not cut yourself.	Ella non s' è tagliata.
Hast thou cut thyself?	Ti sei tagliato?
I have not cut myself.	Non my son tagliato.
Has your brother cut himself?	Il di Lei fratello s' è tagliato?
He has cut himself.	Egli s' è tagliato.
Have we cut ourselves?	Ci siamo tagliati?
We have not cut ourselves.	Noi non ci siamo tagliati.
Have these men cut themselves?	Si sono tagliati questi uomini?
They have not cut themselves.	Essi non si sono tagliati.

To take a walk.	Passeggiare 1.
To go a walking.	Andare * a passeggiare.
To take an airing in a carriage.	Andare * in { carrozza. / legno. / vettura. }
	Fare una trottata.
To take a ride.	Andare * a cavallo.
The coach.	La carrozza, la vettura (*fem. nomes*). Il legno.
Do you take a walk?	Passeggia Ella?
I take a walk.	Passeggio.
He takes a walk.	Passeggia.
We take a walk.	Passeggiamo.
Thou wishest to take an airing.	Vuol fare una trottata. Vuol andare in carrozza.
They wish to take a ride.	Vogliono andar a cavallo.

FORTY-FOURTH LESSON.

To take a child a walking.	Condurre a spasso un fanciullo.
Do you take your children a walking?	Conduce Ella a spasso i di Lei fanciulli?
I take them a walking every morning.	Li conduco a spasso ogni mattina.

To go to bed, to lie down.	Coricarsi—coricato.
To go to bed.	{ *Porsi* * in *letto*. { *Andare* * a *letto*.
To put (to place, to fix).	*Porre* * (anciently *ponere*)— *posto*.
I put, thou puttest, he puts.	Pongo, poni, pone.
We put, you put.	Poniamo *or* ponghiamo, ponete.
They put.	Pongono.

To get up, to rise.	Levarsi, alzarsi.
Do you rise early?	Si alza presto (di buon mattino)?
I rise at sunrise.	Mi alzo (mi levo) allo spuntar del sole.
I go to bed at sunset.	Mi corico al tramontar del sole.
The sunrise.	Lo spuntar del sole.
The sunset.	Il tramontar del sole.
At what time did you go to bed?	A che ora s' è Ella coricata?
At three o'clock in the morning.	Alle tre del mattino.
At what o'clock did he go to bed yesterday?	A che ora s' è coricato ieri?
He went to bed late.	S' è coricato tardi.

To rejoice at something.	{ † *Rallegrarsi per qualcosa.* { † *Rallegrarsi di qualche cosa.*
I rejoice at your happiness.	Mi rallegro per la di Loi felicità (o della vostra).
At what does your uncle rejoice?	Per che cosa (perchè) si rallegra il di Lei zio?
I have rejoiced.	Mi son rallegrato.
They have rejoiced.	Si sono rallegrati.
You have mistaken.	† Ella s' è ingannata.
We have mistaken.	† Ci siamo ingannati.

At what did your uncle rejoice? What was your uncle delighted with?	Per che cosa s' è rallegrato il di Lei zio?
For the.	{ Sing. *Pel* (contraction of *per il*). { Plur. *Pei* (contraction of *per i*).

FORTY-FOURTH LESSON.

He rejoiced at (was delighted with) the horse which you have sent him.	† S' è rallegrato pel cavallo che Ella gli ha mandato.
At what did your children rejoice? (What were your children delighted with?)	† Per che cosa si sono rallegrati i di Lei fanciulli?
They rejoiced at (they were delighted with) the fine clothes which I had made for them.	† Si son rallegrati pei bei vestiti che ho fatti far loro.

The rapidity of pronouncing has led to a contraction of the definite article with certain prepositions which precede it; thus *pel* is used instead of *per il*, *pei* instead of *per i*, &c.

According to this contraction we say and write:

Singular.			Plural.		
Del, of the,	for	*di il*.	*Dei* or *de'*,	for	*di i*.
Al, to the,	—	*a il*.	*Ai* or *a'*,	—	*a i*.
Dal, from the,	—	*da il*.	*Dai* or *da'*,	—	*da i*.
Nel, in the,	—	*in il*.	*Nei* or *ne'*,	—	*in i*.
Col, with the,	—	*con il*.	*Coi* or *co'*,	—	*con i*.
Pel, for the,	—	*per il*.	*Pei* or *pe'*,	—	*per i*.
Sul, upon the,	—	*su il*.	*Sui* or *su'*,	—	*su i*.

Singular.			Plural.		
Dello, of the,	for	*di lo*.	*Degli*, for		*di gli*.
Allo, to the,	—	*a lo*.	*Agli*, —		*a gli*.
Dallo, from the,	—	*da lo*.	*Dagli*, —		*da gli*.
Nello, in the,	—	*in lo*.	*Negli*, —		*in gli*.
Collo, with the,	—	*con lo*.	*Cogli*, —		*con gli*.
Pello, for the,	—	*per lo*.	*Pegli*, —		*per gli*.
Sullo, upon the,	—	*su lo*.	*Sugli*, —		*su gli*.

To hurt somebody.	{ *Apportar male ad uno*. { *Far del male ad uno*.
The evil, the pain, the harm.	*Il male, il danno*.
Have you hurt that man?	{ *Ha Ella apportato danno a costui?* { *Ha Ella fatto male a questi?* o a quest' uomo?
I have hurt that man.	{ *Ho apportato danno a costui*. { *Ho fatto male a costui*.
Why did you hurt that man?	*Perchè ha apportato danno a quest' uomo?*
I have not hurt him.	{ *Non gli ho apportato danno alcuno*. { *Non gli ho fatto alcun male*.
Does that hurt you?	{ *Ciò Le fa male?* { *Ciò Lo apporta danno?*
That hurts me.	{ *Ciò m' apporta danno*. { *Ciò mi fa male*.

FORTY-FOURTH LESSON.

To do good to any body.	Far bene ad uno.
Have I ever done you any harm?	Le ho giammai apportato danno?
On the contrary.	Al contrario.
No, on the contrary, you have done me good.	No, al contrario, Ella mi ha fatto del bene,
I have never done harm to any one.	Non ho giammai apportato danno a nessuno.

Have I hurt you?	Le ho fatto male? o Vi ho io fatto male?
You have not hurt me.	Ella non mi ha fatto male.

That does me good.	Ciò mi fa bene.

To do with, to dispose of.	Far di.
What does the tailor make with the cloth?	Che fa il sarto del panno?
He makes coats with it.	Ne fa degli abiti.
What does the painter do with his brush?	Che fa il pittore col suo pennello
He makes a picture with it.	Fa un quadro.
What does he wish to make of this wood?	Che vuol far di questo legno?
He does not wish to make any thing of it.	Non vuol farne niente.

He is flattered, but he is not beloved.	† Lo adulano, ma non l' amano. È adulato, ma non è amato.
That (conjunction).	Che.
I am told that he is arrived.	Mi si dice (mi dicono) ch' è arrivato.
A knife was given to him to cut his bread, and he cut his finger.	Gli hanno dato (gli è stato dato) un coltello per tagliare il suo pane e si è tagliato il dito.
To flatter some one.	Adulare qualcuno.
To flatter one's self.	Adularsi, lusingarsi di.
He flatters himself that he knows French.	† Si lusinga di sapere il francese.
Nothing but.	Non—che.
He has nothing but enemies.	Non ha che nemici.

FORTY-FOURTH LESSON.

To become.	{ *Diventare — diventato.* { *Divenire* * — divenuto.*
He has turned a soldier.	† S' è fatto soldato.
Have you turned a merchant?	† È diventato mercante?
I have turned (become) a lawyer.	† Son diventato avvocato.
What has become of your brother?	{ † Che n' è stato del di Lei fratello? { † Che cosa è stato del di Lei fratello?
What has become of him?	† Che ne è stato?
I do not know what has become of him.	† Non so che sia divenuto (*subjunctive*, of which hereafter).
To enlist, to enrol.	{ *Ingaggiarsi.* { *Farsi soldato, arruolarsi.*
He has enlisted.	{ Si è fatto soldato. { S' è ingaggiato (si è arruolato).
For (meaning *because*).	*Perchè, poichè.*
I cannot pay you, for I have no money.	Non posso pagarla perchè non ho danaro.
He cannot give you any bread, for he has none.	Non può darle pane poichè non ne ha.
To believe some one.	{ *Credere qualcuno.* { † *Credere a qualcuno.*
Do you believe that man?	† Crede a costui?
I do not believe him.	† Non gli credo.
I believe what that man says.	† Credo a quest' uomo ciò che dice.
To believe in God.	*Credere in Dio.*
I believe in God.	Credo in Dio.
To utter a falsehood, to lie.	*Mentire * — mentito.*
The story-teller, the liar.	Il bugiardo, il mentitore.
I do not believe that man, for I know him to be a story-teller.	Non credo a questi perchè so che è un bugiardo.

EXERCISES.

138.

Why has that child been praised?—It has been praised because it has studied well.—Hast thou ever been praised?—I have often been praised.—Why has that other child been punished?—It has been punished because it has been naughty and idle.—Has this child been rewarded?—It has been rewarded because it has studied well.—What must one do (*che è bisogno fare*) in order not to be despised?—One must be studious and good.—What has become of your friend?—He has become a lawyer.—What has become of your cousin?—He has enlisted.—Has your neighbour enlisted?—He has not enlisted.—What has become of him?—He has turned a merchant.—What has become of his children?—His children have become men.—What has become of your son?—He has become a great man.—Has he become learned?—He has become learned.—What has become of my book?—I do not know what has become of it.—Have you torn it?—I have not torn it.—What has become of our friend's son?—I do not know what has (*che sia*, subj.) become of him.—What have you done with your money?—I have bought a book with it (*con quello*).—What has the joiner done with his wood?—He has made a bench of it.—What has the tailor done with the cloth which you gave him?—He has made clothes of it for your children and mine.—Has that man hurt you?—No, Sir, he has not hurt me.—What must one do (*ch' è d' uopo fare*) in order to (*per*) be loved?—One must do good to those that have done us harm.—Have we ever done you harm?—No; you have, on the contrary, done us good.—Do you do harm to any one?—I do no one any harm.—Why have you hurt these children?—I have not hurt them.—Have I hurt you?—You have not hurt me, but your children have (*me ne hanno fatto*).—What have they done to you?—They have beaten me.—Is it (*è*) your brother who has hurt my son?—No, Sir, it is not (*non è*) my brother, for he has never hurt any one.

139.

Have you drunk that wine?—I have drunk it.—How did you like it?—I liked it very well.—Has it done you good?—It has done me good.—Have you hurt yourself?—I have not hurt myself.—Who has hurt himself?—My brother has hurt himself, for he has cut his finger.—Is he still ill (*malato*)?—He is better (*star meglio*).—I rejoice to hear (*me rallegra l' intendere*) that he is no longer ill, for I love him.—Why does your cousin pull out his hair?—Because he cannot pay what he owes.—Have you cut your hair?—I have not cut it (myself), but I have had it cut (*me li son fatti tagliare*).—What has this child done?—He has cut his foot.—Why was a knife given to him?—A knife was given him to (*per*) cut his nails, and he has cut his finger and his foot.—Do you go to bed early?—I go to bed late, for I cannot sleep when I go to bed early.—At what o'clock did you go to bed yesterday?—Yesterday I went to bed at a quarter past eleven.—At what o'clock do your children go to bed?—They go to bed at sunset.—Do they rise early?—They rise at sunrise.—At what o'clock did you rise to-day?—To-day I rose late, because I went to bed late yesterday evening (*ieri sera*).—Does your son rise late?—He rises early, for he never goes to bed late.—What does he do when he gets up?—He studies, and then he breakfasts.—Does he go out before he breakfasts?—No, Sir, he studies and breakfasts before he goes out.—What does he do after breakfasting?—As soon as he has breakfasted he comes to me, and we take a ride.—Didst thou rise this morning as early as I?—I rose earlier than you, for I rose before sunrise.

140.

Do you often go a walking?—I go a walking when I have nothing to do at home.—Do you wish to take a walk?—I cannot take a walk, for I have too much to do.—Has your brother taken a ride?—He has taken an airing in a carriage.—Do your children often go a walking?—They go a walking every morning after breakfast (*dopo la colazione*).—Do you take a walk after dinner (*dopo il pranzo*)?—After dinner I drink tea, and then I take a walk.—Do you often take your children a walking?—I take them a walking every morning and every evening.—Can you go (*venire*) with me?—I cannot go (*venire*) with you, for I am to take my little brother a walking.—Where do you walk?—We walk in our uncle's garden.—Did your father rejoice to see you?—He did rejoice to see me.—What did you rejoice at?—I rejoiced at seeing my good friends.—What was your uncle delighted with?—He was delighted with the horse which you have sent him.—What were your children delighted with?—They were delighted with the fine clothes which I had made for them (*che lor ho fatti fare*).—Why does this man rejoice so much (*tanto*)?—Because he flatters himself he has good friends.—Is he not right in rejoicing (*di rallegrarsi*)?—He is wrong, for he has nothing but enemies.—Is he not loved?—He is flattered, but he is not loved.—Do you flatter yourself that you know Italian?—I flatter myself that I know it, for I can speak, read, and write it. —Has the physician done any harm to your son?—He has cut his finger (*gli ha tagliato il dito*), but he has not done him any harm; so (*r*) you are mistaken, if you believe that he has (*che gli abbia*) done him any harm.—Why do you listen to that man? —I listen to him, but I do not believe him; for I know that he is a story-teller (*un bugiardo*).—How do you know that he is (*che sia*, subj.) a story-teller?—He does not believe in God; and all those (*e tutti quelli*) who do not believe in God are story-tellers. —Are we story-tellers?—You are no story-tellers, for you believe in God (*in Dio*) our Lord (*nostro Signore*).

FORTY-FIFTH LESSON.

Lezione quarantesima quinta.

OF IMPERSONAL VERBS.

We have already seen (Lessons XLI. and XLII.) some expressions belonging to the impersonal verbs. These verbs, having no determinate subject, are only conjugated in the third person singular.

To rain,—It rains.	Piovere * 2,—piove.
It has rained.	È piovuto (or ha piovuto).
To snow,—It snows.	Nevicare 1,—nevica.
It has snowed.	È nevicato (or ha nevicato).
To hail,—It hails.	Grandinare 1 (tempestare), — grandina (tempesta).
It has hailed.	È grandinato (tempestato), or ha tempestato [1].

---

[1] From these examples it may be seen, that in Italian impersonal verbs relating to the weather may take either *essere* or *avere* in their compound tenses.

FORTY-FIFTH LESSON.

The three substantives belonging to these verbs are feminine, and will be seen when we come to such nouns; but as in Italian any infinitive may be used as a masculine noun, we may say also: *il piovere*, the rain; *il nevicare*, the snow; *il grandinare*, the hail.

To lighten.	Lampeggiare 1.
Does it lighten?	Lampeggia?
It lightens.	Lampeggia.
The lightning.	Il lampo, il baleno.
The parasol.	Il parasole, l' ombrellino.
It rains very hard.	Piove dirottamente diluvia.
It lightens much.	Lampeggia molto.
Does it snow?	Nevica?
It snows much.	Nevica molto.
It hails much.	Grandina molto.
The sun does not shine.	† Non c' è sole.
The sun is in my eyes.	† Il sole mi dà agli occhi.
To thunder,—it thunders.	Tuonare 1,—tuona.
It has thundered.	È tuonato *or* ha tuonato.
To shine, to glitter,—shone.	{ Riverberare 1,—riverberato. Risplendere 2, risplenduto.

To shut.	Chiudere *, past part. *chiuso*.
Shut the door.	Chiudete la porta.

Have you done?	† Ha Ella finito? avete voi finito?

Is the walking good?	† Si cammina bene?
In that country.	In questo paese.
The country.	Il paese.
He has made many friends in that country.	Si è fatto molti amici in questo paese.
To walk, to travel.	Camminare 1, passeggiare 1.

Of which, of whom, whose.	{ Di cui (onde). Del quale (plur. *dei quali*).
I see the man of whom you speak.	Vedo l' uomo di cui (del quale) Ella parla.
I have bought the horse of which you spoke to me.	Ho comprato il cavallo di cui (del quale) Ella mi ha parlato.
I see the man whose brother has killed my dog.	Veggo (vedo) l' uomo *il* di cui fratello ha ammazzato il mio cane.
I see the man whose dog you have killed.	Veggo l' uomo di cui Ella ha ammazzato il cane.
Do you see the child whose father set out yesterday?	† Vede Ella il fanciullo *il* di cui padre è partito ieri?
I see it.	Lo vedo.

FORTY-FIFTH LESSON.

Whom have you seen?	Chi ha Ella visto?
I have seen the merchant whose warehouse you have taken.	Ho visto il mercante di cui Ella ha preso il magazzino.
I have spoken to the man whose warehouse has been burnt.	Ho parlato all' uomo il di cui magazzino è stato bruciato.

That of which.	*Ciò di che, quanto.*
	Quello di che.
That, or *the one of which.*	*Quello di cui.*
Those, or *the ones of which.*	*Quelli di cui.*
I have that of which I have need.	Ho quanto mi abbisogna.
	Ho ciò di che ho bisogno.
I have what I want.	Ho ciò che mi è d' uopo.
He has what he wants.	Egli ha ciò di che ha bisogno.
	Egli ha ciò che gli è d' uopo.

Have you the book of which you are in need?	Ha Ella il libro di cui ha bisogno?
I have that of which I am in need.	Ho quello di cui ho bisogno.

Has the man the nails of which he is in need?	L' uomo ha i chiodi di cui egli ha bisogno?
He has those of which he is in need.	Ha quelli di cui ha bisogno.

To need, to want.	*Aver bisogno di.*
To have need of.	
To be in want of something.	*Aver bisogno di qualche cosa.*
I am in want of this book.	Ho bisogno di questo libro.
Did you find the book which you want?	Ha Ella trovato il libro di cui ha bisogno?

Which man do you see?	Quali uomini vede Ella? or vedete voi?
I see those of whom you have spoken to me.	Vedo quelli di cui Ella mi ha parlato.
Do you see the pupils of whom I have spoken to you?	Vede Ella gli scolari di cui Le ho parlato?
I see them.	Li vedo.

FORTY-FIFTH LESSON.

	Masc. and Fem.	
	Sing. and Plur.	Masc. Plur.
To whom.	A chi.	Ai quali.
I see the children to whom you have given some petty-patties.	Veggo i fanciulli ai quali Ella ha dato dei pasticcini.	
To which men do you speak?	A quali uomini parla Ella?	
I speak to those to whom you have applied.	Parlo a quelli ai quali si è indirizzata Lei.	

To apply to.	Indirizzarsi a—indirizzato a.
	Dirigersi " a—diretto a.
To meet with some one.	Incontrare uno.
	Rincontrare uno.
I have met with the men to whom you have applied.	Ho incontrato gli uomini ai quali Ella si è diretta (vi siete diretto).
Of which men do you speak?	Di quali uomini parla Ella?
I speak of those whose children have been studious and obedient.	Parlo di quelli i di cui fanciulli sono stati studiosi ed obbedienti.
Obedient, disobedient.	Obbediente, disobbediente.
	L'obbidiente, disubbidiente.

	In guisa che—sicché.
So that.	Di modo che, per cui.
	Di maniera che.
I have lost my money, so that I cannot pay you.	Ho perduto il mio danaro, in guisa che non posso pagarla.
Ill.	Malato, ammalato.
I am ill, so that I cannot go out.	Sono malato, in guisa che non posso uscire.

EXERCISES.

141.

Have you at last learnt Italian?—I was ill, so that I could not learn it.—Has your brother learnt it?—He has not learnt it, because he has not yet been able to find a good master.—Do you go to the ball this evening?—I have sore feet, so that I cannot go to it.—Did you understand that German?—I do not know German, so that (per cui) I could not understand him.—Have you bought the horse of which you spoke to me?—I have no money, so that (*di modo che*) I could not buy it.—Have you seen the man from whom I received a present?—I have not seen him.—Have you seen the fine gun of which I spoke to you?—I have seen it.—Has your uncle seen the books of which you spoke to him?—He has seen them.—Hast thou seen the man whose children have been punished?—I have not seen him.—To whom have you been speaking at the theatre?—I have been speaking to the man whose brother (*il di cui fratello*) has killed my fine dog.—Have you seen the little boy whose father has become a lawyer?—I have seen him.—Whom have you seen at the ball?—I have seen there the men whose horses, and those whose coach you have bought (*e quelli dei quali ha comprato la carrozza*).—Whom do you see now?—I see the man whose servant has broken my looking-glass.—Have you heard the man whose friend has lent me money?—I have not heard him.—Whom have you heard?—I have heard the French captain, whose son is my friend.—Hast thou brushed the coat of which I spake to thee?—I have not yet brushed it.—Have you received the money which you were wanting?—I have received it.—Have I the sugar of which I have need?—You have it.—Has your brother the books which he is wanting?—He has them.—Have you spoken to the merchants whose warehouse we have taken?—We have spoken to them.—Have you spoken to the physician whose son has studied German?—I have spoken to him.—Hast thou seen the poor men whose warehouses have been burnt?—I have seen them.—Have you read the books which we have lent you?—We have read them.—What do you say of them (*ne*)?—We say that they are very fine.—Have your children what they want (*che loro abbisogna*)?—They have what they want.

142.

Of which man do you speak?—I speak of the one (*di guello*) whose brother has turned soldier.—Of which children have you spoken?—I have spoken of those whose parents are learned.—Which book have you read?—I have read that of which I spoke to you yesterday.—Which book has your cousin?—He has that of which he is in need.—Which fishes has he eaten?—He has eaten those which you do not like.—Of which books are you in want?—I am in want of those of which you have spoken to me. —Are you not in want of those which I am reading?—I am not in want of them.—Do you see the children to whom I have given petty-patties?—I do not see those to whom you have given petty-patties, but those whom you have punished. —To whom have you given some money?—I have given some to those who have been skilful.—To which children must one give (*è mestieri dare*) books?—One must give some to those who are good and obedient.—To whom do you give to eat and to drink?—To those that are hungry and thirsty.—Do you give any thing to the children who are idle?—I give them nothing.—Did it snow yesterday?—It did snow, hail, and lighten.—Did it rain? —It did rain.—Did you go out?—I never go out, when it is bad weather.—Have the captains at last listened to the man?—They have refused to listen to him; all those to whom he applied (*si è indirizzato*) have refused to hear him.—With whom have you met this morning (*questa mane*)?—I have met with the man by whom I am esteemed.—Have you given petty-patties to your pupils?— They have not studied well, so that I have given them nothing.

FORTY-SIXTH LESSON.

Lezione quarantesima sesta.

OF THE FUTURE.

Rule.—The first or simple future is formed, in all Italian verbs, from the infinitive, by changing for the second and third conjugations *re* into :—

Singular.			Plural.		
1	2	3	1	2	3
rò,	rai,	rà,	remo,	rete,	ranno.

And for the first *are* into :—

| erò, | erai, | erà. | eremo, | erete, | eranno. |

FORTY-SIXTH LESSON. 221

EXAMPLES.

			Inf. Amare 1.	
To love.		Future.	Amerò, amerai,	amerà.
I shall or will love, &c.			Ameremo, amerete,	ameranno.
To speak.			Parlare 1.	
I shall or will speak, &c.		,,	Parlerò, parlerai,	parlerà,
			Parleremo, parlerete,	parleranno.
To receive.			Ricevere 2.	
I shall or will receive, &c.		,,	Riceverò, riceverai,	riceverà,
			Riceveremo, riceverete,	riceveranno.
To believe.			Credere 2.	
I shall or will believe, &c.		,,	Crederò, crederai,	crederà,
			Crederemo, crederete,	crederanno.
To punish.			Punire 3.	
I shall or will punish, &c.		,,	Punirò, punirai,	punirà.
			Puniremo, punirete,	puniranno.
To serve.			Servire 3.	
I shall or will serve.		,,	Servirò, servirai,	servirà.
			Serviremo, servirete,	serviranno.

Obs. A. It will be remarked, that in all Italian verbs the first and third persons singular of the future have the grave accent (`).

EXCEPTIONS.

		Infinitive.	Future.
To have.	I shall or will have, &c.	Avere *	Avrò, avrai, avrà.
			Avremo, avrete, avranno.
To be.	I shall or will be, &c.	Essere *	Sarò, sarai, sarà.
			Saremo, sarete, saranno.

Obs. B. The following eighteen verbs, besides the auxiliaries *avere* and *essere*, form all the exceptions to our rule on the formation of the future. We need not give all the persons, as the first person singular of the exceptions being once known, all the others are, being, as may be seen from the above, the same in all verbs of the Italian language.

		Infinitive.	Future.
To go.	I shall or will go.	Andare * 1.	Andrò (also regular).
To fall.	I shall or will fall.	Cadere * 2.	Cadrò.
To gather.	I shall or will gather.	Cogliere * 2.	Corrò.
To give.	I shall or will give.	Dare * 1.	Darò.
To complain.	I shall or will complain.	Dolere * 2.	Dorrò.
To owe.	I shall or will owe.	Dovere * 2.	Dovrò.

FORTY-SIXTH LESSON.

To do.	I shall or will do.	Fare • 1.	Farò.
To die.	I shall or will die.	Morire • 3.	Morrò or morirò.
To appear.	I shall or will appear.	Parere • 2.	Parrò.
To put.	I shall or will put.	Porre • 2.	Porrò (regular).
To be able.	I shall or will be able.	Potere • 2.	Potrò.
To rest.	I shall or will rest.	Rimanere • 2.	Rimarrò.
To know.	I shall or will know.	Sapere • 2.	Saprò.
To hold.	I shall or will hold.	Tenere • 2.	Terrò.
To be worth.	I shall or will be worth.	Valere • 2.	Varrò.
To see.	I shall or will see.	Vedere • 2.	Vedrò.
To come.	I shall or will come.	Venire • 3.	Verrò.
To be willing.	I shall or will be willing.	Volere • 2.	Vorrò.

Shall or will he have money ? — Avrà egli danaro?
He will have some. — Ne avrà.
He will not have any. — Non ne avrà.
Shall you soon have done writing ? — † Quanto prima avrà (avrete) finito di scrivere ?
I shall soon have done. — † Quanto prima avrò finito.
He will soon have done his exercise. — Quanto prima avrà finito il suo tema.

Soon (ere long).   *Quanto prima, fra poco.*

When shall you do your exercises ? — Quando farà Ella i di Lei temi ?
I will do them soon (ere long). — Quanto prima li farò.
My brother will do his exercises tomorrow. — Mio fratello farà i suoi temi domani.

Next Monday. — Lunedì venturo.
Last Monday. — Lunedì passato.
Next month. — † Il mese venturo.
This month. — Questo mese.
This country. — Questo paese.

When will your cousin go to the concert ? — Quando andrà al concerto il di Lei cugino ?
He will go next Tuesday. — Egli vi andrà martedì venturo.
Shall you go any where ? — { Andrà Ella } In qualche luogo ? { Andranno }
We shall go no where. — Non andremo in verun luogo.

Will he send me the book ? — Mi manderà egli il libro ?
He will send it you, if he has done with it. — { Glielo manderà, se l' ha finito. { Se l' ha finito glielo manderà.

FORTY-SIXTH LESSON. 223

Shall you be at home this evening?	Sarà Ella in casa questa sera? Questa sera sarà Ella in casa?
I shall be there.	Vi sarò.
Will your father be at home?	Sarà in casa il di Lei padre?
He will be there.	Vi sarà.
Will your cousins be there?	I di Lei cugini vi saranno?
They will be there.	Vi saranno.

Will he send me the books?	Mi manderà egli i libri?
He will send them you.	Glieli manderà.
Will he send some ink to my counting-house?	Manderà dell' inchiostro al mio banco (studio)?
He will send some thither.	Ce ne manderà.

Shall you be able to pay your shoe-maker?	Potrà pagare il di Lei calzolaio? (o potrete voi pagare il vostro).
I have lost my money, so that I shall not be able to pay him.	Ho perduto il danaro, di modo che non potrò pagarlo.
My friend has lost his pocket-book, so that he will not be able to pay for his boots.	Il mio amico ha perduto il porta-foglio, in guisa che non potrà pagare i suoi stivali.

Will you hold any thing?	Terrà Ella una cosa? (o qualche cosa)?
I shall hold your umbrella.	Terrò il di Lei ombrello.
Will your friend come to my concert?	Il di Lei amico verrà al mio con-certo?
He will come.	Verrà.
Shall you come?	Verrà Ella? Verrete voi?
I shall come.	Verrò.
Will it be necessary to go to the market?	Sarà d' uopo andar al mercato? Bisognerà andare al mercato?
It will be necessary to go thither to-morrow morning.	Sarà d' uopo andarci domani mattina (domani mattina) do-mattina.
It will not be necessary to go thither.	Non sarà d' uopo andarci.
Shall you see my father to-day?	Vedranno oggi le vostre signorie mio padre?
We shall see him.	Vedrete voi mio padre oggi?

To foresee—foreseen.	Prevedere * 2	preveduto. previsto.
To restore—restored.	Rendere *—reso.	

EXERCISES.

143.

Shall you have any books?—I shall have some.—Who will give you any?—My uncle will give me some.—When will your cousin have money?—He will have some next month.—How much money shall you have?—I shall have thirty-five sequins. —Who will have good friends?—The English will have some. —Will your father be at home this-evening?—He will be at home (*ci sarà*).—Will you be there?—I shall also be there (*anch' io*).—Will your uncle go out to-day?—He will go out, if it is fine weather.—Shall you go out?—I shall go out, if it does not rain.—Will you love my son?—I shall love him, if he is good.— Will you pay your shoemaker?—I shall pay him, if I receive my money.—Will you love my children?—If they are good and assiduous, I shall love them; but if they are idle and naughty, I shall despise and punish them.—Am I right in speaking (*di parlare*) thus?—You are not wrong.—Is your friend still writing? —He is still writing.—Have you not done speaking?—I shall soon have done.—Have your friends done reading?—They will soon have done.—Has the tailor made my coat?—He has not made it yet; but he will soon make it.—When will he make it? —When he shall have time.—When will you do your exercises? —I shall do them when I shall have time.—When will your brother do his?—He will do them next Saturday.—Wilt thou come to me?—I shall come.—When wilt thou come?—I shall come next Friday.—When have you seen my uncle?—I saw him last Sunday.—Will your cousins go to the ball next Tuesday?—They will go.—Will you come to my concert?—I shall come, if I am not ill.

144.

When will you send me the money which you owe me?—I shall send it you soon.—Will your brothers send me the books which I have lent them?—They will send them you.—When will they send them to me?—They will send them to you next month.—Will you be able to pay me what you owe me?—I shall not be able to pay it you, for I have lost all my money.—Will the American be able to pay for his boots?—He has lost his pocket-book, so that he will not be able to pay for them.—Will it be necessary (*bisognerà*) to send for the physician?—Nobody is ill, so that (*per cui*) it will not be necessary to send for him.—Will it be necessary to go to the market to-morrow?—It will be necessary to go thither, for we want (*c' è d' uopo*) some beef, some bread, and some wine.—Shall you see your father to-day?—I shall see him.—Where will he be?—He will be at his counting-house.—Will you go to the ball to-night (*questa sera*)?—I shall not go, for I am too ill to go to it.—Will your friend go?—He will go, if you go.—Where will your neighbours go?—They will go no where; they will remain at home, for they have a good deal to do.

FORTY-SEVENTH LESSON.

Lezione quarantesima settima.

To belong.	Appartenere * (is conjugated like its primitive *tenere* *, Lesson XL.)
Do you belong?	Appartiene Ella?
I do belong.	Appartengo.
Does that horse belong to your brother?	Questo cavallo appartiene al di Lei fratello? (o al vostro.)
It belongs to him.	Gli appartiene.
To whom do these gloves belong?	A chi appartengono questi guanti? Di chi son questi guanti?
They belong to the captains.	Appartengono ai capitani. Sono dei capitani.
Do these horses belong to the captains?	Questi cavalli appartengono ai capitani?
They belong to them.	Appartengono loro.

FORTY-SEVENTH LESSON.

To suit.	*Piacere* * (*esser* * *di gusto*).
Does that cloth suit your brother?	Piace questo panno al di Lei fratello?
	Questo panno è di gusto del di Lei fratello?
It suits him.	Gli piace (è di suo gusto).
Do these boots suit your brothers?	Piacciono questi stivali al di Lei fratelli?
	Questi stivali sono di gusto del di Lei fratelli?
They suit them.	Piaccion loro (sono di lor gusto).

To suit.	*Convenire* *, *addirsi* *, *esser convenevole* or *dicevole*.
Does it suit you to do that?	Le piace di far ciò?
It suits me to do it.	Mi piace di farlo.
Does it suit your cousin to come with us?	Piace al di Lei cugino di venire con noi?
It does not suit him to go out.	Non gli piace d' uscire.
It does not suit me to go to him, for I cannot pay him what I owe him.	Non mi è convenevole d' andare da lui, poichè non posso pagargli ciò che gli debbo.

To succeed.	*Riuscire* *, *riuscito* (conjugated like *uscire* *).
	Pervenire *, *pervenuto* (conjugated like its primitive *venire* *).
Do you succeed in learning Italian?	Riesce Ella ad imparar l' italiano?
I succeed in it.	Vi riesco.
I do succeed in learning it.	Pervengo ad impararlo.
To succeed.	*Riuscire* *—*riuscito*.
I succeed, thou succeedest, he succeeds.	Riesco, riesci, riesce.
We, you, they succeed.	Riusciamo, riuscite, riescono.
Do these men succeed in selling their horses?	Riescono cotesti uomini a rendere i loro cavalli?
They do succeed therein.	Vi riescono.
Do you succeed in doing that?	Riesce Ella a far ciò? o questo?
I succeed in it.	Vi riesco.

FORTY-SEVENTH LESSON.   227

To forget.	Dimenticare 1 (takes di before the infinitive).
I forgot to do it.	Ho dimenticato di farlo (or ho dimenticato farlo).
To clean.	Pulire 3—pulito. Ripulire 3—ripulito. Nettare 1—nettato.
The Inkstand.	Il calamaio.
Immediately, directly. This instant, instantly. Presently. I am going to do it. I will do it immediately. I am going to work.	Subito. Immantinente, all' istante. A momenti, fra poco. Lo faccio subito. Sto per farlo. Lo faccio immantinente subito. Lavorerò fra poco.
Is there? Are there? There is not. There are not. Will there be? There will be. Was there or has there been? Were there or have there been? There has been. There have been. Is there any wine? There is some. There is not any. Are there any men? There are some. There are not any.	C' è? V' è? Havvi? Ci sono? Vi sono? Sonvi? Non c' è or non v' è. Non ci sono or vi sono. Vi sarà or ci sarà. Ci sarà or vi sarà? C' è stato or v' è stato? Ci sono stati or vi sono stati? C' è stato or v' è stato. Ci sono stati or vi sono stati. C' è del vino? Ce n' è. Non ce n' è. Sonvi degli nomini? Ve ne sono. Non ve ne sono.
There are men who will not study.	Vi sono degli uomini che non hanno voglia di studiare (or che non vogliono studiare).
Is there any one? There is no one. Are there to be many people at the ball? There are to be a great many people there.	V' è qualcuno? Non v' è nessuno. Ci deve essere molta[1] gente alla festa da ballo? Ce ne deve essere molta.

---

[1] *Molta* here agrees with *gente*, people, which is feminine.

FORTY-SEVENTH LESSON.

On credit.	*A credenza, a credito.*
To sell on credit.	Vendere a credenza (a credito).
The credit.	Il credito.
Ready money.	Danaro in contante (danaro contante).
To buy for cash.	Comprare per contanti (comprar contante).
To sell for cash.	Vendere per contanti (vender contante).
To pay down.	Pagare in contanti (pagar contante).
Will you buy for cash?	Vuole Ella comprare per contanti?
Does it suit you to sell to me on credit?	Le conviene vendermi a credenza?

To fit.	*Star * bene.*
Does that coat fit me?	Mi sta bene questo abito?
It fits you.	Le sta bene.
That hat does not fit your brother.	Cotesto cappello non istà bene al di Lei fratello.
It does not fit him.	Non gli sta bene.
Do these boots fit you?	Le stanno bene cotesti stivali?
They fit me.	Mi stanno bene.
That fits you very well.	Ciò (questa cosa) Le sta benissimo (a maraviglia).

To keep.	*Tenere *, ritenere *,—tenuto.*
You had better.	† Ella farà meglio (di).
I had better.	† Farò meglio (di).
He had better.	† Egli farà meglio (di).
Instead of keeping your horse you had better sell it.	† In vece di tenere il di Lei cavallo, farà meglio di venderlo.
Instead of selling his hat he had better keep it.	† In vece di vendere il suo cappello, farà meglio di tenerlo.
Will you keep the horse?	Terrà Ella il cavallo?
I shall keep it.	Lo terrò.
You must not keep my money.	Non è d' uopo ritenere il mio danaro.
	Non dovete tenervi il mio danaro.

To please, to e pleased.	*Piacere* (Lesson XLI.).*
To please some one.	*Piacere * a qualcuno.*
Does that book please you?	Le piace questo libro?
It pleases me much.	Mi piace molto.
I will do what you please.	† Farò ciò che vorrà, o che vorrete.

FORTY-SEVENTH LESSON. 229

You are pleased to say so.	† Ciò I.e piace di dire (a familiar expression).
What is your pleasure?	Che desidera, Signore?
What do you want?	Che vuole, Signore?
What do you say?	Che dice?

To please one's self.	{ *Piacersi* *—piaciutosi.* { *Trovarsi* *—trovatosi.*
How do you please yourself here?	Come vi godete qui.
I please myself very well here.	Mi ci godo benissimo.

Whose book is this?	Di chi è questo libro?
It is his.	È il suo.
Whose boots are these?	Di chi sono questi stivali?
They are ours.	Sono i nostri.
It is they who have seen him.	Sono essi che l' hanno veduto.
It is your friends who are in the right.	Sono i di Lei amici che hanno ragione.
It is we who have done it.	Siamo noi che l' abbiamo fatto.
It is you who say so.	È Lei che lo dice. Siete voi che lo dite.
It is of you that I speak.	È di Lei che parlo. Si è di voi che parlo.

EXERCISES.

145.

To whom does that horse belong?—It belongs to the English captain whose son has written a note to you.—Does this money belong to you?—It belongs to me.—From whom have you received it?—I have received it from the men whose children you have seen.—Whose horses are those?—They are ours.—Have you told your brother that I am waiting for him here?—I have forgotten to tell him so (*dirglielo*).—Is it your father or mine who is gone to Berlin?—It is mine.—Is it your baker, or that of our friend, who has sold you bread on credit?—It is ours.—Is that your son?—He is not mine; he is my friend's.—Where is yours?—He is at Paris.—Have you brought me the book which you promised me?—I have forgotten it.—Has your uncle brought you the pocket-books which he promised you?—He has forgotten to bring them to me.—Have you already written to your friend?

—I have not yet (*per anco*) had time to write to him.—Have you forgotten to write to your relative?—I have not forgotten to write to him.—Does this cloth suit you?—It does not suit me; have you no other?—I have some other; but it is dearer than this.—Will you show it me?—I will show it you.—Do these boots suit your uncle?—They do not suit him, because they are too dear.—Are these the boots of which you have spoken to us? —They are the same (*i medesimi*, or *gli stessi*).—Whose books are these?—They belong to the gentleman whom you have seen this morning in my warehouse.—Does it suit you to come with us?—It does not suit me.—Does it suit you to go to the market? —It does not suit me to go thither.—Did you go on foot to Germany?—It does not suit me to go on foot, so that (*per cui*) I went thither in a coach.

140.

What is your pleasure (*che desidera*), Sir?—I am inquiring after your father.—Is he at home?—No, Sir, he is gone out.— What do you say?—I tell you that he is gone out.—Will you wait till he comes back?—I have no time to wait.—Does that merchant sell on credit?—He does not sell on credit.—Does it suit you to buy for cash?—It does not suit me.—Where did you buy these pretty knives (*coltellini*)?—I bought them at the merchant's (*dal mercante*), whose warehouse you saw yesterday.— Has he sold them you on credit?—He has sold them to me for cash.—Do you often buy for cash?—Not so often as you.—Have you forgotten any thing here?—I have forgotten nothing.—Does it suit you to learn this (*ciò*) by heart?—I have not much time to study, so that (*di modo che*) it does not suit me to learn it by heart.—Has that man tried to speak to your father?—He has tried to speak to him, but he has not succeeded in it.—Have you succeeded in writing an exercise?—I have succeeded in it.— Have those merchants succeeded in selling their horses?—They have not succeeded therein.—Have you tried to clean my inkstand?—I have tried, but I have not succeeded in it.—Do your children succeed in learning English?—They do succeed in it. —Is there any wine in this cask (*in questo barile*)?—There is some in it.—Is there any vinegar in this glass?—There is none in it.—Is there wine or cider in it?—There is neither wine nor cider in it.—What is there in it?—There is some vinegar in it.

147.

Are there any men in your warehouse?—There are some there.—Is there any one in the warehouse?—There is no one there.—Were there many people in the theatre?—There were many there.—Will there be many people at your ball (*alla di Lei festa da ballo*)?—There will be many there.—Are there many children that will not play?—There are many that will not study, but all will play.—Hast thou cleaned my trunk?—I have tried to do it, but I have not succeeded.—Do you intend buying an umbrella?—I intend buying one, if the merchant sells it me on credit.—Do you intend to keep mine?—I intend to give it you back (*o restituir glielo*), if I buy one.—Have you returned the books to my brother?—I have not returned them to him yet.—How long do you intend to keep them?—I intend to keep them till next Saturday.—How long do you intend keeping my horse?—I intend keeping it till my father returns.—Have you cleaned my knife?—I have not had time yet, but I will do it this instant.—Have you made a fire?—Not yet, but I will make one presently.—Why have you not worked?—I have not yet been able.—What had you to do?—I had to clean your carpet, and to mend your linen handkerchiefs.—Do you intend to sell your coat?—I intend keeping it, for I want it.—Instead of keeping it you had better sell it.—Do you sell your horses?—I do not sell them.—Instead of keeping them you had better sell them.—Does your friend keep his parasol?—He keeps it; but instead of keeping it he had better sell it, for it is worn out.—Does your son tear his book?—He tears it; but he is wrong in doing so; instead of tearing it he had better read it.

FORTY-EIGHTH LESSON.

Lezione quarantesima ottava.

To go away.	*Andarsene* * (Less. XLIII.).
When will you go away?	Quando se ne andrà Ella? (o ve ne andrete voi?)
I will go soon.	Me ne andrò quanto prima.
By and by.	Fra poco.
He will go away soon (by and by).	Se ne andrà fra poco.
We will go away to-morrow.	Ce ne andremo domani.
They will go away to-morrow.	Se ne andranno domani.
Thou wilt go away immediately.	Te ne andrai immantinente.

When.	*Quando (allorchè, allorquando).*

To become.	† *Esser* * *mai (diventare, divenire* *, Lesson XLIV.).*
What will become of you if you lose your money?	† Che sarà mai di voi se perdate il vostro?
I do not know what will become of me.	† Non so che sarà di me.
What will become of him?	† Che sarà mai di lui?
What will become of us?	† Che sarà mai di noi?
What will become of them?	† Che sarà mai di loro?
I do not know what will become of them.	† Non so cosa sarà di loro.

The turn.	*La volta.*
My turn.	† La mia volta.
In my turn.	† Alla mia volta (tocca a me *or* spetta a me).
In his turn.	† Alla sua volta (spetta a lui *or* tocca a lui).
In my brother's turn.	† Alla volta di mio fratello (tocca (spetta) a mio fratello).
Each in his turn.	† Ciascuno alla sua volta.

FORTY-EIGHTH LESSON. 233

When it comes to your turn.
Our turn will come.

Quando verrà la di Lei volta (quando toccherà a Lei *or* quando spetterà a Lei) o a voi.
Avremo la nostra volta (spetterà a noi *or* toccherà a noi).

A turn, a tour, a walk.
To take a turn.
To take a walk.
He is gone to take a walk.
To walk round the garden.

Un giro.
Far un giro.
Far una passeggiata.
{ È andato a fare un giro.
{ È andato a fare una passeggiata.
Far un giro interno del giardino.

To run — run (past part.).
Do you run?
I do run.
Shall or will you run?
I shall or will run.

Correre * — corso.
Corre Ella? Correte voi?
Corro.
Correrà Ella? Correrete voi?
Correrò.

Behind.
Behind him.
Behind the castle.

Dietro (or di dietro).
Dietro a lui.
Dietro al castello.

A blow, a stroke, a clap.

Have you given that man a blow?
I have given him one.
A blow with a stick.

A kick (with the foot).
A blow with the fist.
A stab of a knife.

A shot (or the report of a gun).

A shot of a pistol.

A glance of the eye.
A clap of thunder.

Un colpo, una botta (a fem. noun).

Ha Ella dato un colpo a costui?
Glial' ho dato.
Una bastonata, un colpo di bastone.
Un calcio, una pedata.
Un pugno.
Una coltellata, un colpo di coltello.
{ Una schioppettata (una fucilata).
{ Un colpo di fucile.
Una pistolettata, un colpo di pistola.
Un' occhiata, un colpo d' occhio.
Un colpo di fulmine.

To give a cut with a knife.
To give a man a blow with a stick.
To give a man a kick.
To give a man a blow with the fist.

Dare una coltellata.
Dare una bastonata ad un uomo.
Dare un calcio ad un uomo.
Dare un pugno ad un uomo.

FORTY-EIGHTH LESSON.

To pull, to draw.	*Tirare* 1. *Sparare* 1. *Far fuoco.*
To shoot, to fire.	
To fire a gun.	Sparare un fucile.
	Tirare una fucilata.
To fire a pistol.	Tirare un colpo di pistola.
To fire at some one.	Tirare un colpo di fucile a qualcuno.
I have fired at that bird.	Ho tirato una schioppettata a quell' uccello.
I have fired twice.	Ho fatto fuoco due volte.
I have fired three times.	Ho sparato tre colpi.
I have fired several times.	Ho sparato varie volte.
How many times have you fired?	Quanti colpi di fucile ha tirati?
I have fired six times.	Ne ho tirati sei.
How many times have you fired at that bird?	Quante volte ha tirato a quell' uccello?
I have fired at it several times.	Ho tirato parecchie volte sopra di lui.
I have heard a shot.	Ho inteso un colpo di fucile.
He has heard the report of a pistol.	Ha inteso una pistolettata.
We have heard a clap of thunder.	Abbiamo inteso un colpo di fulmine (o scoppio di fulmine).
The fist.	Il pugno.

To cast an eye upon some one or something.	*Gettare un' occhiata sopra uno, o qualcosa.*
Have you cast an eye upon that book?	Ho Ella gettato un' occhiata su questo libro? (o dato un' occhiata).
I have cast an eye upon it.	Vi ho gettato un' occhiata.

Has that man gone away?	Se n' è andato costui?
He has gone away.	Egli se n' è andato.
Have your brothers gone away?	I di Lei fratelli se ne sono andati?
They have gone away.	Se ne sono andati.
They have not gone away.	Non se ne sono andati.
Have they gone away?	Se ne sono eglino andati?
They were not willing to go away.	Non hanno voluto andarsene.

To ask some one, that is, to question, to interrogate him.	*Interrogare qualcuno.*

EXERCISES.

149.

Are you going away already?—I am not going yet.—When will that man go away?—He will go away presently.—Will you go away soon?—I shall go away next Thursday.—When will your friends go away?—They will go away next month.—When wilt thou go away?—I will go away instantly.—Why has your father gone away so soon (*così tosto*)?—He has promised his friend to be at his house at a quarter to nine, so that (*di modo che*) he went away early in order to keep (*per mantenere*) what he has promised.—When shall we go away?—We shall go away to-morrow.—Shall we start early?—We shall start at five o'clock in the morning.—When will you go away?—I shall go away as soon as I have done writing.—When will your children go away?—They will go as soon as they have done their exercises.—Will you go when I go?—I shall go away when you go. —Will our neighbours soon go away?—They will go away when they have done speaking.—What will become of your son if he does not study?—If he does not study he will learn nothing. —What will become of you if you lose your money?—I do not know what will become of me.—What will become of your friend if he loses his pocket-book?—If he loses it I do not know what will become of him.—What has become of your son?—I do not know what has become of him.—Has he enlisted?—He has not enlisted.—What will become of us if our friends go away? —If they go away I do not know what will become of us.—What has become of your relations?—They have gone away.

140.

Do you intend buying a horse?—I cannot buy one, for I have not yet received my money.—Must I go (*Mi è duopo andare Devo io andare al teatso'*) to the theatre?—You must not go thither, for it is very bad weather.—Why do you not go to my brother?—It does not suit me to go to him, for I cannot yet pay him what I owe him.—Why does your servant give that man a cut with his knife?—He gives him a cut, because the man has given him a blow with his fist.—Which of these two pupils begins to speak?—The one who is studious begins to speak.—What does the other who is not so?—He also (*anch' egli*) begins to speak, but he knows neither how to write nor to read.—Does he listen to what you tell him?—He does not listen to it, if I do not give him a beating (*se non lo batto dei colpi*).—Why do those children not study?—Their master has given them blows, so that (*di maniera che*) they will not study. Why has he given them blows with his fist?—Because they have been disobedient.—Have you fired a gun?—I have fired three times.—At what did you fire?—I fired at a bird.—Have you fired a gun at that man?—I have fired a pistol at him.—Why have you fired a pistol at him?—Because he has given me a stab with his knife.—How many times have you fired at that bird?—I have fired at it twice.—Have you killed it?—I have killed it at the second shot (*al secondo colpo*).—Have you killed that bird at the first shot?—I have killed it at the fourth (*al quarto colpo*).—Do you fire at the birds which you see upon the trees, or at those which you see in the gardens?—I fire neither at those which I see upon the trees nor at those which I see in the gardens, but at those which I perceive on the castle behind the wood.

130.

How many times have the enemies fired at us (*sù di noi*)?—They have fired at us several times.—Have they killed any body?—They have killed nobody.—Have you a wish to fire at that bird?—I have a wish to fire at it.—Why do you not fire at those birds?—I cannot, for I have a sore finger.—When did the captain fire?—He fired when his soldiers fired.—How many birds have you shot at?—I have shot at all that I have perceived, but I have killed none, because my gun is good for nothing.—Have you cast an eye upon that man?—I have cast an eye upon him.—Has he seen you?—He has not seen me, for he has sore eyes.—Have you drunk of that wine?—I have drunk of it, and it has done me good.—What have you done with my book?—I have put it upon your trunk.—Am I (*debbo*) to answer you?—You will answer me when it comes to your turn (*quando verrà*

la di Lei volta).—Is it my brother's turn (*tocca a mio fratello*) ?—
When it comes to his turn I shall ask him (*lo interrogherò*), for
each in his turn.—Have you taken a walk this morning ?—I have
taken a walk round the garden.—Where is your uncle gone to?
—He is gone to take a walk.—Why do you run ?—I run because
I see my best friend.—Who runs behind us (*dietro a noi*) ?—Our
dog runs behind us.—Do you perceive that bird ?—I perceive it
behind the tree.—Why have your brothers gone away ?—They
have gone away, because they did not wish to be seen by the
man whose dog they have killed. (See end of XXIVth Lesson.)

FORTY-NINTH LESSON.

Lezione quarantesima nona.

To hear—heard.	Udire * 3—udito.		
I hear, thou hearest, he hears.	Odo,	odi,	ode.
We hear, you hear, they hear.	Udiamo,	udite,	odono.

| To hear of. | † *Udire * parlare.* |
	† *Sentir parlare.*
Have you heard of your brother ?	Ha Ella udito parlare del di Lei fratello ?
I have heard of him.	Ne ho udito parlare.
Is it long since you breakfasted ?	È molto tempo che Ella ha fatto colazione ?
How long is it since you breakfasted ?	Quanto è che Ella ha fatto colazione ?
It is not long since I breakfasted.	Non è molto tempo che ho fatto colazione.
It is a great while since.	È moltissimo tempo che.
It is a short time since.	È poco tempo che.
How long is it since you heard of your brother ?	Quanto tempo è che ha udito parlare del di Lei fratello ?

FORTY-NINTH LESSON.

It is a year since I heard of him.	È un anno che ho udito parlar di lui.
	È un anno che non ho udito parlare.

It is only a year since.	È solamente un anno che.
It is more than a year since.	È più d' un anno che.

Obs. A. Than, when before a number, is rendered by *di*.

More than nine.	Più di nove.
More than twenty times.	Più di venti volte.
It is hardly six months since.	Sono appena sei mesi che.
A few hours ago.	È qualche ora (sono alcune ore).
Half an hour ago.	È una mezz' ora (mezz' ora fa).
Two years ago.	Sono due anni.

Obs. B. The word *fa*, third person singular of the verb *fare*, is used in Italian whenever there is in English *ago*, relating to the singular.

I have seen him a month ago.	L' ho veduto un mese *fa*.
Two hours and a half ago.	Sono due ore e mezzo.
Three centuries ago.	Tre secoli sono.
A fortnight ago.	† Sono quindici giorni.
Ten years ago.	Dieci anni sono.
A fortnight.	Quindici giorni.[1]

Have you long been in France?	† È molto tempo ch' Ella è in Francia?

Obs. C. In English the state of existence or of action, when in its duration, is always expressed in the preterperfect tense; whilst in Italian, as well as in French, it is expressed by the present tense.

He has been in Paris these three years.	† Son tre anni ch' è in Parigi.
I have been living here these two years.	Son due anni che sto qui.
How long have you had that horse?	Quanto tempo è ch' Ella ha cotesto cavallo?
I have had it these five years.	Sono cinque anni che l' ho.

How long (since when)?	Da quando in quà?
	Da quanto tempo?
How long has he been here?	Da quanto tempo è qui?
Since.	Dacchè (che).
	Da.

---

[1] In Italian, as well as in French, we say fifteen days for a *fortnight*.

FORTY-NINTH LESSON.

These three days.	Da tre giorni.
This month.	Da un mese.
I have seen him more than twenty times.	L' ho veduto più di venti volte.
It is six months since I spoke to him.	Sono sei mesi che non gli ho parlato.

Obs. D. The negative *non* in this and similar expressions is necessary in Italian, though the English use no negative in such instances.

It is more than a year since I heard of him.	È più d' un anno che non ne ho udito parlare.
Since I saw you it has rained very often.	Da che l' ho veduta ha piovuto spessissimo.

Just.	{ *Poco fa, poc' anzi, testè.* { *Ora, or ora, in questo punto.* { *Appunto.*
I have just seen your brother.	Ho visto il di Lei fratello poco fa.
He has just done writing.	Ha finito di scrivere poc' anzi.
The men have just arrived.	Gli uomini sono appunto arrivati.
Has that man been waiting long?	È molto tempo che questi aspetta?
He has but just come.	È arrivato in questo punto.
I have just seen him.	L' ho veduto testè.
I have just received it.	L' ho ricevuto or ora.
I have just written to him.	Gli ho scritto poc' anzi.

To do one's best.	† *Fare il possibile.*
I will do my best.	† Farò il possibile (ciò che potrò).
He will do his best.	† Farà il possibile (ciò che potrà).

To spend money — spent.	*Spendere* * 2. — *speso.*
How much have you spent to-day?	Quanto ha Ella speso oggi?
He has fifty sequins a month to live upon.	Egli ha cinquanta zecchini al mese da spendere.

Have the horses been found?	Sono stati trovati i cavalli?

☞ The passive participle agrees with the nominative in number; that is, when the nominative is plural, the participle must also be in the plural.

They have been found.	Sono stati trovati.
Where? When?	Ove *or* Dove? Quando?
The men have been seen.	Gli uomini sono stati veduti.
Our children have been praised and rewarded, because they have been good and studious.	I nostri fanciulli sono stati lodati e ricompensati, poiché sono stati savi e studiosi.

FORTY-NINTH LESSON.

By whom have they been rewarded? | Da chi sono stati ricompensati?
By whom have we been blamed? | Da chi siamo stati biasimati?

To pass.	Passare 1.
Before.	Davanti.
	Innanzi.

Obs. E. Before is expressed in Italian by *prima*, when it denotes priority (Lesson XXVIII.), and by *davanti, innanzi*, when it signifies in presence of. Ex.

To pass before some one.	Passar davanti a qualcuno.
To pass before a place.	Passar davanti un luogo.
A place.	Un luogo.
I have passed before the theatre.	Son passato davanti al teatro.
He passed before me.	È passato innanzi a me (or davanti me).

| I breakfasted before you. | Ho fatto colazione prima di Lei. |

To spend time in something.	Passare il tempo a qualche cosa.

What do you spend your time in?	† Come passa il tempo?
I spend my time in studying.	† Passo il tempo a studiare.
What has he spent his time in?	† Come ha egli passato il tempo?
What shall we spend our time in?	† Come passeremo il tempo?

To miss, to fail.	Mancare 1.

The merchant has failed to bring the money.	Il mercante ha mancato di portare il danaro.
You have missed your turn.	Ella ha mancato alla di Lei volta.
You have failed to come to me this morning.	Ella ha mancato di venire da me questa mane (o questa mattina).

To be good for something.	Esser * buono a qualcosa.

Of what use is that?	† A che serve ciò?
It is good for nothing.	† Ciò non serve a niente (Non val niente).
The good-for-nothing fellow.	Il discolo, lo sfaccendato.
Is the gun which you have bought a good one?	Il fucile ch' Ella ha comprato è buono?
No, it is worth nothing.	No, Signore, non è buono a niente.

FORTY-NINTH LESSON.

To throw away.
Have you thrown away any thing?
I have not thrown away any thing.
Have you used the books which you have bought?
I have not used them; I have examined them, and found them very bad, so that I have thrown them away.

To examine.

Gettar via.
Ha Ella gettato via qualche cosa?
Non ho gettato via niente.
Si è Ella servita dei libri che ha comprati?
Non me ne son servito; li ho esaminati e li ho trovati cattivissimi, di maniera che li ho gettati via.

Esaminare.

EXERCISES.

151.

Have you heard of any one?—I have not heard of any one, for I have not gone out this morning.—Have you not heard of the man who has killed a soldier?—I have not heard of him.—Have you heard of my brothers?—I have not heard of them.—Of whom has your cousin heard?—He has heard of his friend who is gone to America.—Is it long since he heard of him?—It is not long since he heard of him.—How long is it?—It is only a month.—Have you been long in Paris?—These three years.—Has your brother been long in London?—He has been there these ten years.—How long is it since you dined?—It is long since I dined, but it is not long since I supped.—How long is it since you supped?—It is half an hour.—How long have you had these books?—I have had them these three months.—How long is it since your cousin set out?—It is more than a year since he set out.—What has become of the man who has lent you money?—I do not know what has become of him, for it is a great while since I saw him.—Is it long since you heard of the soldier who gave your friend a cut with the knife?—It is more than a year since I heard of him.—How long have you been learning French?—I have been learning it only these two months.—Do you know already how to speak it?—You see (*Ella sente*) that I am beginning to speak it.—Have the children of the English noblemen been learning it long?—They have been learning it these three years, and they do not yet begin to speak.—Why do they not know how to speak it?—They do not know how to speak it, because they are learning it badly.—Why do they not learn it well?—They have not a good master, so that they do not learn it well.

152.

Is it long since you saw the young man who learnt German with the (*dal*) master with whom (*presso il quale*) we learnt it?—I have not seen him for nearly a year.—How long is it since the child ate?—It ate a few minutes ago.—How long is it since those children drank?—They drank a quarter of an hour ago.—How long has your friend been in Spain?—He has been there this month.—How often have you seen the king?—I saw him more than ten times when I was in Paris.—When did you meet my brother?—I met him a fortnight ago.—Where did you meet him?—I met him before the theatre.—Did he do you any harm?—He did me no harm, for he is a good boy.—Where are my gloves?—They have thrown them away.—Have the horses been found?—They have been found.—Where have they been found?—They have been found behind the wood, on this side of the road.—Have you been seen by any one?—I have been seen by no one.—Do you expect any one?—I expect my cousin the captain.—Have you not seen him?—I have seen him this morning; he has passed before my warehouse.—What does this young man wait for?—He waits for money.—Art thou waiting for any thing?—I am waiting for my book.—Is this young man waiting for his money?—He is waiting for it.—Has the king passed here?—He has not passed here, but before the theatre.—Has he not passed before the castle?—He has passed there, but I have not seen him.

153.

What do you spend your time in?—I spend my time in studying.—What does your brother spend his time in?—He spends his time in reading and playing.—Does this man spend his time in working?—He is a good-for-nothing fellow; he spends his time in drinking and playing.—What do your children spend

FORTY-NINTH LESSON.   248

their time in ?—They spend their time in learning.—Can you pay me what you owe me ?—I cannot pay it you, for the merchant has failed to bring me my money.—Why have you breakfasted without me ?—You failed to come at nine o'clock, so that we have breakfasted without you.—Has the merchant brought you the gloves which you bought at his house (*da lui*)?—He has failed to bring them to me.—Has he sold them you on credit ?—He has sold them me, on the contrary, for cash.—Do you know those men ?—I do not know them; but I believe that they are (*che siano*, subjunctive) good-for-nothing fellows, for they spend their time in playing.—Why did you fail to come to my father this morning ?—The tailor did not bring me the coat which he promised me, so that I could not go to him.—Who is the man who has just spoken to you ?—He is a merchant.—What has the shoemaker just brought ?—He has brought the boots which he has made us.—Who are the men who have just arrived ?—They are Russians.—Where did your uncle dine yesterday ?—He dined at home.—How much did he spend ?—He spent five francs.—How much has he a month to live upon ?—He has a hundred sequins a month to live upon.—Do you throw your hat away ?—I do not throw it away, for it fits me very well.—How much have you spent to-day ?—I have not spent much: I have only spent one sequin.—Do you spend every day as much ?—I sometimes spend more than that.—Has that man been waiting long ?—He has but just come.—What does he wish ?—He wishes to speak to you.—Are you willing to do that ?—I am willing to do it.—Shall you be able to do it well ?—I will do my best.—Will this man be able to do that ?—He will be able to do it, for he will do his best.

FIFTIETH LESSON.

Lezione cinquantesima.

Far.	Lontano, lungi.
How far (meaning What distance)?	Qual distanza? Quanto è lontano?
How far is it from here to Paris?	Qual distanza v'è da qui a Parigi? Qual distanza corre da qui a Parigi?
Is it far from here to Paris?	C'è molto da qui a Parigi?
It is far.	C'è molto. È lontano.
It is not far.	Non c'è molto. Non è lontano.
A mile.	Un miglio.¹
How many miles is it?	Quante miglia vi sono?
It is twenty miles.	Vi sono venti miglia.
It is almost two hundred miles from here to Paris.	Vi son circa due cento miglia da qui a Parigi.
It is nearly five hundred miles from Paris to Vienna.	Vi son circa cinque cento miglia da Parigi a Vienna.

From.	Da.
From Venice.	Da Venezia.
From London.	Da Londra.
From Rome.	Da Roma.
From Florence.	Da Firenze.
What countryman are you?	† Di qual paese è Ella? o siete voi?
Are you from France?	† È Ella di Francia? Siete voi francese?
I am.	Lo sono.
The Parisian.	Il Parigino.
He is a Parisian (from Paris).	È Parigino.
The king.	Il re.
The philosopher.	Il filosofo.²
The preceptor, the tutor.	Il precettore,³ l'aio.
The actor.	L'attore.⁴
The professor.	Il professore.
The landlord, the innkeeper.	L'oste, il locandiere, l'albergatore.

---

¹ *Miglio* is one of the nouns in *o*, which, though masculine in the singular, take in the plural the form of the feminine singular, as *le miglia*, miles. We shall see hereafter a list of such nouns.

² Whenever *ph* occurs in English, it is in Italian changed into *f*.

³,⁴ In Italian *c* or *p* is never put before *t*, but they are changed into *t*.

FIFTIETH LESSON. 245

Are you an Englishman?	È Ella Inglese? } Siete voi.
Are you an Italian?	È Ella Italiano?
Whence?	*Da dove? D' onde?*
Whence do you come?	Da dove viene? D' onde viene? o venite?
I come from Rome.	Vengo da Roma.
I come from Paris.	Vengo da Parigi.

To fly, to run away.	*Fuggire* 3. *Fuggirsene,*
To run away.	*Scappare* 1.
I run away, thou runnest away, he runs away.	Fuggo, fuggi, fugge.
We run away, you run away, they run away.	Fuggiamo, fuggite, fuggono.
Why do you fly?	Perchè fugge? fuggite?
I fly, because I am afraid.	Fuggo, perchè ho paura.

To assure.	*Assicurare* 1.
I assure you that he is arrived.	L' assicuro ch' è arrivato.
To arrive.	*Arrivare* 1.

To hear — heard.	*Intendere * — inteso.*
Have you heard nothing new?	Non ha Ella inteso niente di nuovo?
I have heard nothing new.	Non ho inteso niente di nuovo.
What do they say of our prince?	Che si dice (che dicono) del nostro principe?
They say he is wise and generous.	† Lo dicono saggio e magnanimo. (better, Si dice che è saggio.)

To happen — happened.	*Accadere * — accaduto.* *Sopraggiungere* — sopraggiunto.* *Succedere *, — successo.* *Arrivare* 1.
The happiness, fortune.	La felicità (a *fem. noun*).
The unhappiness, misfortune.	La disgrazia (a *fem. noun*).
A great misfortune has happened.	È sopraggiunta una gran disgrazia.
He has met with a great misfortune.	Gli è sopraggiunta una gran disgrazia, o sventura.

FIFTIETH LESSON.

What has happened to you?	Che Le è sopraggiunto?
Nothing has happened to me.	Non mi è sopraggiunto niente.
I have met with your brother.	Ho incontrato il di Lei fratello

The poor man.	Il povero.
I have cut his finger.	† Gli ho tagliato il dito.
You have broken the man's neck.	† Ella ha rotto il collo all' uomo.
He broke his leg.	† Si è rotta la gamba.
The leg.	La gamba (a *fem. noun*).

To pity—pitied.	*Compiangere* * — *compianto*.
	Compatire (a) — *compatito*.
	Aver compassione (di)—*avuto compassione*.
I pity, thou pitiest, he pities.	Compatisco, compatisci, compatisce.
We, you, they pity.	Compatiamo, compatite, compatiscono.

Obs. Most verbs of the third conjugation terminate in the three first persons of the present indicative in: *isco, isci, isce*, and in the third person plural in *iscono*, just as *compatire*. As there are a great many of them (some grammarians make their number amount to nearly four hundred), we shall content ourselves with marking them thus: (*isco,*) as they will occur in the course of the Method.

Do you pity that man?	Compiange Ella costui?
I pity him with all my heart.	Lo compiango di tutto cuore.
With all my heart.	Di tutto cuore.

To complain.	† *Lamentarsi, lagnarsi*.
Do you complain?	† Si lamenta?
I do not complain.	† Non mi lamento.
Do you complain of my friend?	† Si lagna del mio amico?
I complain of him.	† Me ne lagno.
I do not complain of him.	† Non me ne lagno.

To dare—dared or durst.	*Osare* — *osato*.
	Ardire — *ardito*.
I dare, thou darest, he dares.	Ardisco, ardisci, ardisce.
We, you, they dare.	Osiamo,[5] ardite, ardiscono.

---

⁴ The first person plural of *osare* is substituted for the first person plural of *ardire*, not to confound this with the first person plural of *ardere*, to burn.

FIFTIETH LESSON. 247

To spoil.	Guastare 1.
You have spoiled my knife.	Ha guastato il mio coltello. (Avete guastato).
To serve, to wait upon.	Servire 3.
To serve some one, to wait upon some one.	Servire qualcuno. Essere * al servizio di qualcuno.
Has he been in your service? Has he served you?	È egli stato al di Lei servizio? L' ha servita? Vi ha egli servito?
How long has he been in your service?	† Quanto tempo è che La servo? (o servo Lei.) † Quanto tempo è che trovasi al di Lei servizio? (al servizio di Lei.) † Da quanto tempo è al di Lei servizio? (o al servigio di voi.)
The service.	Il servizio.

To offer.	Offrire * — offerto.
Do you offer?	Offre Ella? Offrite voi?
I offer.	Offro.
Thou offerest.	Offri.
He offers.	Offre.

To confide, to trust with, to intrust.	Dare * in custodia. Confidare 1.
Do you trust me with your money?	Mi confida Ella il di Lei danaro?
I trust you with it.	Glielo confido.
I have intrusted that man with a secret.	Ho confidato un segreto a costui.
The secret.	Il segreto.
To keep any thing secret.	Tenere qualche cosa segreta. Osservare il segreto su qualche cosa.
I have kept it secret.	L' ho tenuto segreto.

To take care of something.	Aver cura di qualcosa.
Do you take care of your clothes?	Ha Ella cura dei di Lei abiti?
I take care of them.	Ne ho cura.
Will you take care of my horse?	Vuole aver cura del mio cavallo?
I will take care of it.	Voglio averne cura, or Ne voglio aver cura.

To leave — left.	*Lasciare* 1 *— lasciato.*
To squander, to dissipate.	*Dissipare* 1 *— dissipato.*
He has squandered all his wealth.	Ha dissipato ogni suo avere.
He has left nothing to his children.	Non ha lasciato niente ai suoi figliuoli.

To hinder, to keep from.	*Impedire* * *—impedito.*
I hinder, thou hinderest, he hinders.	Impedisco, impedisci, impedisce.
We, you, they hinder.	Impediamo, impedite, impediscono.
You hinder me from sleeping.	Ella mi impedisce di dormire.
He has hindered me from writing.	Mi ha impedito di scrivere.

To purchase, to spend.	*Far spesa, far compera* (*la spesa, la compera,* the expense, fem. nouns). *Far delle spese.* *Far delle compere.*
What have you purchased to-day?	Cosa ha comprato oggi?
I have purchased two handkerchiefs.	Ho comprato due fazzoletti.
Have you purchased any thing to-day?	Ha fatto delle spese (delle compere) oggi?
I have.	Ne ho fatto.

Most lovely, charming.	Grazioso, leggiadro, vago.
Admirably.	A meraviglia.'
That hat fits you admirably.	Questo cappello Le sta a meraviglia.
That coat fits him very well.	Quest' abito gli sta benissimo.
It is charming.	È grazioso.

EXERCISES.

154.

How far is it from Paris to London?—It is nearly three hundred miles from Paris to London.—Is it far from here to Berlin?—It is far.—Is it far from here to Vienna?—It is nearly five hundred miles from here to Vienna.—Is it further from Paris to Blois than from Orleans to Paris?—It is further from Orleans to Paris than from Paris to Blois.—How far is it from Paris to Berlin?—It is almost five hundred and thirty miles from Paris to Berlin.—Do you intend to go to Paris soon?—I intend to go thither soon.—Why do you wish to go this time (*questa volta*)?—In order to buy good books and good gloves, and to see my good friends.—Is it long since you were there?—It is nearly a year since I was there.—Do you not go to Italy this year (*quest' anno*)?—I do not go thither, for it is too far from here to Italy.—Who are the men that have just arrived?—They are philosophers.—Of what country are they?—They are from London.—Who is the man who has just left?—He is an Englishman who has squandered away (*dissipato*) all his fortune (*ogni suo avere*) in France.—What countryman are you?—I am a Spaniard, and my friend is an Italian.—Are you from Tours?—No, I am a Parisian.—How much money have your children spent to-day?—They have spent but little; they have spent but one crown.—Where did you dine yesterday?—I dined at the inn-keeper's.—Did you spend a great deal?—I spent a crown and a half.—Has the king passed here (*di qui*)?—He has not passed here (*di qui*), but before the theatre.—Have you seen him?—I have seen him.—Is it the first time (*è la prima volta*) you have seen him?—It is not the first time, for I have seen him more than twenty times.

155.

Why does that man run away?—He runs away because he is afraid.—Why do you run away?—I run away because I am afraid.—Of whom are you afraid?—I am afraid of the man who does not love me.—Is he your enemy?—I do not know whether he is (*s' è*) my enemy; but I fear all those who do not love me, for if they do me no harm they will do me no good.—Do you fear my cousin?—I do not fear him, for he has never done any body harm.—You are wrong to run away before that man, for I assure you that he is (*l' assicuro esser egli*) a very good man (*un bravo uomo*), who has never done harm to any one.—Of whom has your brother heard?—He has heard of a man to whom (*al quale*) a misfortune has happened (*è accaduta una disgrazia*).—Why have your scholars not done their exercises?—I assure you that they have done them, and you are mistaken if you believe that they have (*abbiano*, subj.) not done them.—What have you done with my book?—I assure you that I have not seen it.—Has your son had my knives?—He assures me that he has not had them.—Is your uncle arrived already?—He is not arrived yet (*per anco*).—Will you wait till he returns?—I cannot wait, for I have a good deal (*molto*) to do.—Have you not heard any thing new?—I have heard nothing new.—Is the king arrived?—They say he is (*che sia*) arrived.—What has happened to you?—A great misfortune (*una gran disgrazia*) has happened to me.—What (*quale*)?—I have met with my greatest enemy, who has given me a blow with a stick.—Then I pity you with all my heart (*di tutto cuore*).—Why do you pity that man (*a costui*)?—I pity him because you have broken his neck.—Why do you complain of my friend? I complain of him because he has cut my finger.—Does that man (*costui*) serve you well?—He serves me well, but he spends too much.—Are you willing to take this servant?—I am willing to take him, if he will serve me.—Can I take that servant?—You can take him, for he has served me very well.—How long is it since he has left your service (*che ha lasciato il di Lei servizio*)?—It is but two months since.—Has he served you long?—He has served me for (*durante*) six years.

156.

Do you offer me any thing?—I have nothing to offer you.—What does my friend offer you?—He offers me a book.—Have the Parisians offered you any thing?—They have offered me wine, bread, and good beef.—Why do you pity our neighbour? I pity him, because he has trusted (*perchè ha dato in custodia*) a merchant of Paris with his money, and the man (*e questi*) will not return it to him.—Do you trust this man with any thing?—I do not trust him with any thing.—Has he already kept any thing from you?—I have never trusted him with any thing, so that he has never kept any thing from me.—Will you trust my father with your money?—I will trust him with it.—With what secret has my son intrusted you?—I cannot intrust you with that with which he has intrusted me, for he has desired me (*m' ha pregato*) to keep it secret.—Whom do you intrust with your secrets?—I intrust nobody with them, so that nobody knows them.—Has your brother been rewarded?—He has, on the contrary, been punished; but I beg of you to keep it secret, for nobody knows it.—What has happened to him?—I will tell you what has happened to him, if you promise me to keep it secret (*di osservarne il segreto*).—Do you promise me to keep it secret? —I promise you, for I pity him with all my heart.—Will you take care of my clothes?—I will take care of them.—Are you taking care of the book which I lent you?—I am taking care of it.—Who will take care of my servant?—The landlord will take care of him.—Do you throw away your hat?—I do not throw it away, for it fits me admirably (*a meraviglia*).—Does your friend sell his coat?—He does not sell it, for it fits him most beautifully.—Who has spoiled my book?—No one has spoiled it, because no one has dared to touch it.—Do you hinder any one from studying?—I hinder no one from studying, but I hinder you from doing harm to this boy.

THIRD MONTH.
Terzo mese.

FIFTY-FIRST LESSON.
Lezione cinquantesima prima.

The people.	La gente (*a fem. noun*).
Will the people come soon?	Verrà la gente quanto prima?
They will come soon.	Verrà quanto prima.
Soon, *very soon*.	*Tosto, per tempo, quanto prima.*
A violin.	Un violino.
The flute.	Il flauto.
The horn.	Il corno.
To play upon the violin.	Suonare il violino.
To play the violin.	

Obs. The verb *to play* is rendered by *suonare* with the accusative, when a musical instrument is spoken of, and by *giuocare* with the dative, when a game is spoken of. Ex. To play at cards, *giuocare alle carte;* to play at chess, *giuocare agli scacchi.*

The harpsichord.	Il cembalo.
The piano-forte.	Il pianoforte.
To play the harpsichord.	Suonare il cembalo.
To play upon the harpsichord.	
To play the, or upon the, flute.	Suonare il flauto.
What instrument do you play?	Che strumento suona Ella? o suonate voi?

To touch.	*Toccare* 1.
I play upon the piano.	† Tocco il pianoforte. (o suono il.)

Near.	*Vicino a, presso a.*
Near me.	Vicino a me.
Near them.	Vicino a loro.

Near the fire. | Vicino al fuoco, presso al fuoco.
Near the trees. | Vicino agli alberi.
Near going. | Vicino ad andare. Star per andare.
Where do you live? | Ove sta Ella?
I live near the castle. | Sto vicino al castello.
What are you doing near the fire? | Che fa Ella vicino al fuoco?

To dance. | *Ballare* 1.
To fall. | *Cadere* * — *caduto.*
To drop (to let fall). | *Lasciar cadere.*
Has he dropt any thing? | † Gli è caduto qualche cosa?
He has not dropt any thing. | † Non gli è caduto niente.
I dropt my gloves. | † Mi son caduti i guanti.

To retain, to hold back. | *Ritenere* * (is conjugated like its primitive *tenere* *, Lesson XL.).

To approach, to draw near. | *Avvicinarsi* (gov. the dative, *acctarossi.*
Do you approach the fire? | S' avvicina ella al fuoco? (vi avvicinate voi al.)
I do approach it. | Me ne avvicino (or merely m' avvicino).

To approach, to have access to. | { *Accostarsi ad uno.*
 { *Avvicinare uno.*
He is a man difficult of access. | { È un uomo che non si può avvicinare.
 { È un uomo che nessuno può accostare.

I go away (withdraw) from the fire. | M' allontano dal fuoco.
To withdraw from. } *Allontanarsi da* (gov. the ablative).
To go away from. }
Why does that man go away from the fire? | Perchè e' allontana costui dal fuoco?
He goes away from it, because he is not cold. | Se ne allontana perchè non ha freddo.
I go away from it. | Me ne allontano.

FIFTY-FIRST LESSON.

To recollect.

Do you recollect that?
I recollect it.
Does your brother recollect that?
He recollects it.
Do you recollect the devices?
I recollect them.
Have you recollected the devices?
I have recollected them.
I have not recollected them.
Have you recollected them?
You have recollected them.
Has he recollected them?
He has recollected them.
We have recollected them.
They have recollected them.

{ *Ricordarsi* 1 (gov. the genitive).
Rammentarsi.[1]

Si rammenta di ciò?
Me ne rammento.
Si rammenta di ciò il di Lei fratello?
Se ne rammenta.
Si rammenta dei motti?
Me no rammento. Me ne ricordo.
Si è Ella rammentata dei motti?
Me ne son rammentato.
Non me ne son rammentato.
Si è Ella rammentata di quelli?
Ella se n' è ricordata.
Se n' è egli rammentato?
Se n' è rammentato.
Ce ne siamo rammentati.
Se ne sono rammentati.

To remember, to recollect.

Do you remember that man?
I remember him.
Do you remember that?
I remember it.
What do you remember?
I remember nothing.

Ricordarsi 1 (gov. the genitive).

Si ricorda ella di costui? (o vi ricordate voi di.)
Me no ricordo, *or* lo ricordo.
Si ricorda di ciò?
Me ne ricordo.
Di che si ricorda Ella?
Non mi ricordo di niente.

To sit down.

I sit down, thou sittest down, he sits down.
We, you, they sit down.
Do you sit down?

I do sit down.
Thou art sitting down.
He is sitting down.
I shall or will sit down.
He sits near the fire.

{ *Sedere* * — *seduto.*
Mettersi a sedere.
Porsi a sedere.

Seggo, siedi, siede.

Sediamo, sedete, seggono.
Siede Ella (Si mette Ella a sedere)?
(Vi mettere voi a.)
Seggo (mi metto a sedere).
Siedi (ti metti a sedere).
Siede (si mette a sedere).
Sederò (mi metterò a sedere).
È seduto vicino al fuoco.

---

[1] *Ricordare, rammentare,* when they are not reflective, govern the accusative.

FIFTY-FIRST LESSON.

He sat down near the fire.
S' è messo a sedere vicino al fuoco.
S' è posto a sedere vicino al fuoco.

To like better, to prefer.
Piacer meglio (più), preferire (isco).
Aver più caro.
Amar meglio (più).

Do you like to stay here better than going out?
Le piace meglio restar qui che uscire?

I like staying here better than going out.
Mi piace meglio restar qui che uscire.

He likes to play better than to study.
Ama meglio giuocare che studiare.

Do you like to write better than to speak?
Le piace più scrivere che parlare?

I like to speak better than to write.
Preferisco parlare a scrivere.
Il parlar mi piace più che lo scrivere.

Better than.
Meglio che.
Più che.

I like beef better than mutton.
Mi piace più il manzo che il montone.

Do you like bread better than cheese?
Le piace più il pane che il cacio?

He likes to do both.
Gli piace fare l' uno e l' altro.

I like neither the one nor the other.
Non mi piace nè l' uno nè l' altro.

I like tea as much as coffee.
Mi piace altrettanto il tè quanto il caffè.

Just as much.
Altrettanto.

Some veal.
Del vitello.

A calf, calves.
Un vitello, dei vitelli.

Quick, fast.
Presto.

Slow, slowly.
Lentamente, adagio.

Aloud.
Forte, ad alta voce.

Does your master speak aloud?
Il di Lei maestro parla forte?

He speaks aloud.
Parla forte.

In order to learn Italian one must speak aloud.
Per imparar l' italiano bisogna parlar forte.

Quicker, faster.
Più presto.

Not so quick, less quick.
Non così presto, meno presto, più adagio.

As fast as you.
Così presto come Lei.

He eats quicker than I.
Mangia più presto di me.

FIFTY-FIRST LESSON.

Do you learn as fast as I?	Impara presto come io (al pari di me)?
I learn faster than you.	Imparo più presto di Lei.
I do not understand you, because you speak too fast.	Non La capisco, perchè parla troppo presto.

To sell cheap. — *Vendere a buon mercato.*
To sell dear. — *Vender caro.*

Does he sell cheap?	Vende a buon mercato?
He does not sell dear.	Non vende caro.
He has sold me very dear.	M' ha venduto carissimo.

So. — *Così.*

This man sells every thing so dear that one cannot buy any thing of him.	Questi vende tutto così caro che non si può comprar niente da lui.
You speak so fast that I cannot understand you.	Ella parla così presto che non posso comprenderla.

To buy something from some one. — *Comprar qualche cosa da qualcuno.*

I have bought it of him.	L' ho comprato da lui.
I have bought that horse of your brother.	Ho comprato questo cavallo dal di Lei fratello.
I have bought a cake for my child.	Ho comprato un pasticcino a mio figlio.
I have bought it for him.	Glielo ho comprato.

So much; plur. *so many.* — *Tanto;* plur. *tanti.*

I have written so many notes that I cannot write any more.	Ho scritto tanti biglietti che non posso scriver più.

Do you fear to go out?	Teme Ella d' uscire?
I fear to go out.	Temo d' uscire.

To run away, to fly. — *Salvarsi* 1. *Scappare* 1.

Did you run away?	È Ella scappata?
I did not run away.	Non sono scappato.
Why did that man run away?	Perchè è scappato costui? (o corso, o fuggito via.)
He ran away because he was afraid.	È scappato, perchè ha avuto paura.
Who has run away?	Chi è scappato? / Chi s' è salvato?
He has run away.	Egli è scappato. / Egli è fuggito.

EXERCISES.

157.

Do you play the violin?—I do not play the violin, but the harpsichord.—Shall we have a ball to-night?—We shall have one.—At what o'clock?—At a quarter to eleven.—What o'clock is it now?—It is almost eleven, and the people will soon come.—What instrument will you play?—I shall play the violin.—If you play the violin, I shall play the harpsichord.—Are there to be a great many people at our ball?—There are to be a great many.—Will you dance?—I shall dance.—Will your children dance?—They will dance if they please (*se piace loro*).—In what do you spend your time in this country?—I spend my time in playing on the harpsichord, and in reading.—In what does your cousin divert himself?—He diverts himself in playing upon the violin.—Does any one dance when you play?—A great many people dance when I play.—Who?—At first (*in primo luogo*) our children, then our cousins, at last (*in fine*) our neighbours.—Do you amuse yourself?—I assure you that we amuse ourselves very much.—Whom do you pity?—I pity your friend.—Why do you pity him?—I pity him because he is ill.—Has any one pitied you?—Nobody has pitied me, because I have not been ill.—Do you offer me any thing?—I offer you a fine gun.—What has my father offered you?—He has offered me a fine book.—To whom have you offered your fine horses?—I have offered them to the English captain.—Dost thou offer thy pretty little dog to these children?—I offer it to them, for I love them with all my heart.—Why have you given that boy a blow with your fist?—Because he has hindered me from sleeping.—Has any body hindered you from writing?—Nobody has hindered me from writing, but I have hindered somebody from hurting your cousin.

158.

Have you dropt any thing?—I have dropt nothing, but my cousin dropt some money.—Who has picked it up?—Some men have picked it up.—Was it returned to him (*Gli è stato reso*)?—It was returned to him, for those who picked it up did not wish to keep it.—Is it cold to day ?—It is very cold.—Will you draw near the fire ?—I cannot draw near it, for I am afraid of burning myself.—Why does your friend go away from the fire ?—He goes away from it, because he is afraid of burning himself.—Art thou coming near the fire ?—I am coming near it, because I am very cold.—Do you go away from the fire ?—I go away from it. —Why do you go away from it ?—Because I am not cold.—Are you cold or warm ?—I am neither cold nor warm.—Why do your children approach the fire ?—They approach it because they are cold.—Is any body cold ?—Somebody is cold.—Who is cold ?— The little boy, whose father has lent you a horse, is cold.—Why does he not warm himself ?—Because his father has no money to buy coals.—Will you tell him to come to me to warm himself ? —I will tell him so (*dirglielo*).—Do you remember any thing ?— I remember nothing.—What does your uncle recollect ?—He recollects what you have promised him.—What have I promised him ?—You have promised him to go to Italy with him next winter.—I intend to do so, if it is not too cold.—Why do you withdraw from the fire ?—I have been sitting near the fire this hour and a half, so that I am no longer cold.—Does not your friend like to sit near the fire ?—He likes, on the contrary, much (*molto*) to sit near the fire, but only when he is cold.—May one (*ci può*) approach your uncle ?—One may approach him, for he receives every body (*tutti*).—Will you sit down ?—I will sit down.—Where does your father sit down ?—He sits down near me.—Where shall I sit down ?—You may (*può*) sit near me.— Do you sit down near the fire ?—I do not sit down near the fire, for I am afraid of being too warm.—Do you recollect my brother ? —I recollect him.

159.

Do your parents recollect their old friends ?—They recollect them.—Do you recollect these devices ?—I do not recollect them. —Have you recollected that ?—I have recollected it.—Has your uncle recollected those devices ?—He has recollected them.— Have I recollected my exercise ?—You have recollected it.— Have you recollected your exercises ?—I have recollected them, for I have learnt them by heart; and my brothers have recollected theirs, because they have learnt them by heart.—Is it long since you saw your friend from Paris?—I saw him a fortnight ago.—Do your scholars like to learn by heart?—They do not like to learn by heart; they like reading and writing better than learning by heart.—Do you like cider better than wine?—I like wine better than cider.—Does your brother like to play?—He likes to study better than to play.—Do you like veal better than mutton?—I like the latter better than the former.—Do you like to drink better than to eat?—I like to eat better than to drink; but my uncle likes to drink better than to eat.—Does the Frenchman like fowl better than fish?—He likes fish better than fowl. —Do you like to speak better than to write?—I like to do both. —Do you like honey better than sugar?—I like neither.—Does your father like coffee better than tea?—He likes neither.—Can you understand me?—No, Sir, for you speak too fast.—Will you be kind enough (*aver la bontà*) not to speak so fast?—I will not speak so fast, if you will listen to me.

160.

Can you understand what my brother tells you?—He speaks so fast that I cannot understand him.—Can your pupils understand you?—They understand me when I speak slowly; for, in order to be understood, one must speak slowly.—Is it necessary to speak aloud (*forte* or *ad alta voce*) to learn Italian?—It is necessary to speak aloud.—Does your master speak aloud?—He speaks aloud and slow.—Why do you not buy any thing of that merchant?—He sells so dear that I cannot buy any thing of him. —Will you take me to another?—I will take you to the son of the one whom you bought of last year.—Does he sell as dear as this?—He sells cheaper (*a miglior mercato*).—Do your children like to learn Italian better than Spanish?—They do not like to learn either; they only like to learn German.—Do you like mutton?—I like beef better than mutton.—Do your children like cake better than bread?—They like both.—Has he read all the books which he bought?—He bought so many (*tanti*) that he cannot read them all.—Do you wish to write some exercises?— I have written so many that I cannot write any more.—Why does that man run away?—He runs away because he is afraid.

—Will any one do him harm?—No one will do him harm; but he dares not stay, because he has not done his task, and is afraid of being punished.—Will any one touch him?—No one will touch him, but he will be punished by his master for not having (*per non aver*) done his task. (See end of Lesson XXIV.)

FIFTY-SECOND LESSON.

Lezione cinquantesima seconda.

By the side of.	† *Accanto a.* † *Allato a.*
To pass by the side of some one.	† Passare accanto ad uno.
I have passed by the side of you.	† Son passato accanto a Lei.
Have you passed by the side of my brother?	† È Ella passata accanto a mio fratello?
I have passed by the side of him.	† Son passato accanto a lui.

To pass by a place.	† *Passare accanto ad un luogo.* † *Passare vicino ad un luogo.*
I have passed by the theatre.	† Son passato vicino al teatro.
He has passed by the castle.	† È passato vicino al castello.
You have passed before my warehouse.	† Ella è passata davanti al mio magazzino.

To dare.	Ardire (see Lesson L).
I dare not go thither.	Non ardisco andarci.
He dares not do it.	Non ardisce farlo.
I did not dare to tell him so.	Non ho ardito dirglielo.

FIFTY-SECOND LESSON.

To make use of, to use.	Servirsi di, adoperare 1.
Do you use my horse?	† Si serve Ella del mio cavallo? (Vi servite voi.)
I use it.	† Me ne servo.
Does your father use it?	† Se ne serve il di Lei padre?
He uses it.	† Se ne serva.
Have you used my gun?	† S' è Ella servita del mio schioppo?
I have used it.	† Me ne son servito.
They have used your books.	† Hanno adoperato i di Lei libri.
They have used them.	† Li hanno adoperati.

To instruct.	Ammaestrare—ammaestrato. Istruire, or istruire (isco)—istruito, or istruito.
I instruct, thou instructest, he instructs.	Istruisco, istruisci, istruisce.
We, you, they instruct.	Istruiamo, istruite, istruiscono.

To teach.	Insegnare 1.
To teach some one something.	Insegnare qualcosa a qualcuno.
He teaches me arithmetic.	M' insegna l' aritmetica (a fem. noun).
I teach you Italian.	Le insegno l' italiano. O vi insegno.
I have taught him Italian.	Gli ho insegnato l' italiano.

To teach some one to do something.	Insegnar a qualcuno a far qualche cosa.
He teaches me to read.	M' insegna a leggere.
I teach him to write.	Gli insegno a scrivere.

The French master (meaning the master of the French language).	Il maestro di francese.
The French master (meaning that the master is a Frenchman, whatever he teaches).	Il maestro francese.

To shave.	{† Sbarbarsi. † Farsi la barba.
To get shaved.	{† Farsi far la barba. † Farsi sbarbare.

FIFTY-SECOND LESSON.

To dress.	Vestire — vestito.
To undress.	Spogliare — spogliato.
To dress one's self.	Vestirsi.
To undress one's self.	Spogliarsi.
Have you dressed yourself?	S' è Ella vestita? Vi siete vestito?
I have not yet dressed myself.	Non mi sono ancor vestito.
Have you dressed the child?	Avete vestito il bambino?
I have dressed it.	L' ho vestito.

To undo.	Disfare.
To get rid of.	Disfarsi di.
Are you getting rid of your damaged sugar?	Si disfà Ella del di Lei zucchero avariato?
I am getting rid of it.	Me ne disfaccio.
Did you get rid of your old ship?	S' è Ella disfatta del di Lei vecchio bastimento?
I did get rid of it.	Me ne son disfatto.

To part with.	Disfarsi.
The design, the intention.	L' intenzione (a *fem. noun*), il disegno.
To intend, or to have the intention.	Designare, o aver intenzione di.
I intend to go thither.	Ho intenzione di andarci.
We have the intention to do it.	Abbiamo intenzione di farlo.
Do you intend to part with your horses?	Ha Ella intenzione di disfarsi del di Lei cavalli?
I have already parted with them.	Me ne sono già disfatto.
He has parted with his gun.	S' è disfatto del suo schioppo.

To discharge.	{ Licenziare 1. { Mandar via.
Have you discharged your servant?	Ha Ella licenziato il di Lei servitore?
I have discharged him.	L' ho licenziato.

To get rid of some one.	{ † Sbarazzarsi di qualcuno. { † Sbrogliarsi di qualcuno.
I did get rid of him.	Mi sono sbrogliato di lui.
Did your father get rid of that man?	Il di Lei padre s' è sbrogliato di costui?
He did get rid of him.	Se n' è sbrogliato.

FIFTY-SECOND LESSON.

To wake.	Svegliare 1. Risvegliare 1.
To awake.	Svegliarsi 1. Risvegliarsi 1.
I generally awake at six o'clock in the morning.	Ordinariamente mi sveglio alle sei del mattino.
My servant generally wakes me at six o'clock in the morning.	Il mio servitore ordinariamente (di solito) mi sveglia alle sei del mattino.
The least noise wakes me.	Il minimo strepito mi risveglia.
A dream has waked me.	Un sogno m' ha risvegliato.
I do not make a noise in order not to wake him.	Non faccio strepito per non risvegliarlo.

A dream.	Un sogno.
Generally.	Di solito, ordinariamente.

To come down.	Scendere * 2 ; past part. sceso. Discendere calare.
To alight from one's horse, to dismount.	Smontare da cavallo.

To conduct one's self.	Condursi *. (Less. XXXIV.)
To behave.	Comportarsi 1.
I conduct myself well.	Mi conduco bene.
How does he conduct himself?	Come si conduce?

Towards.	Verso, or inverso di.
He behaves ill towards that man.	Si comporta male verso costui.
He has behaved ill towards me.	S' è comportato male verso di me.

To be worth while.	Valer la pena. Meritare il conto.
Is it worth while?	Val la pena?
It is worth while.	Ciò val la pena.
It is not worth while.	Ciò non val la pena.
Is it worth while to do that?	Val la pena di farlo?
Is it worth while to write to him?	Val la pena di scrivergli?
It is worth nothing.	Ciò non val niente. Non val niente.

Is it better?	È meglio?
It is better.	È meglio.
Will it be better?	Sarà meglio?

It will not be better.	Non sarà meglio.
It is better to do this than that.	È meglio far questo che quello.
It is better to stay here than go a walking.	È meglio restar qui che passeggiare.
It is better to read a good book than go to the theatre.	È meglio legger un buon libro che andare al teatro.

EXERCISES.

161.

Have your books been found?—They have been found.—Where?—Under the bed.—Is my coat on the bed?—It is under it.—Are your brother's clothes under the bed?—They are upon it.—Have I been seen by any body.—You have been seen by nobody.—Have you passed by any body?—I passed by the side of you, and you did not see me.—Has any body passed by the side of you?—Nobody has passed by the side of me.—Where has your son passed?—He has passed by the theatre.—Shall you pass by the castle?—I shall pass there.—Why have you not cleaned my trunk?—I was afraid to soil my fingers.—Has my brother's servant cleaned his master's (*il padrone*) guns?—He has cleaned them.—Has he not been afraid to soil his fingers?—He has not been afraid to soil them, because his fingers are never clean (*pulite*).—Do you use the books which I have lent you?—I use them.—May I (*posso*) use your knife?—Thou mayest use it, but thou must not (*non devi*) cut thyself.—May my brothers use your books?—They may use them.—May we use your gun?—You may use it, but you must not spoil it (*non dovete guastarlo*).—What have you done with my coals?—I have used them to warm myself.—Has your brother used my horse?—He has used it.—Have our neighbours used our clothes?—They have not used them, because they did not want them.—Who has used my hat?—Nobody has used it.—Have you told your brother to come down?—I did not dare to tell him.—Why have you not dared to tell him?—Because I did not wish to wake him.—Has he told you not to wake him?—He has told me not to wake him when he sleeps.

102.

Have you shaved to-day?—I have shaved.—Has your brother shaved?—He has not shaved himself, but he got shaved.—Do you shave often?—I shave every morning, and sometimes also in the evening.—When do you shave in the evening?—When I do not dine at home.—How many times a day does your father shave?—He shaves only once a day, but my uncle shaves twice a day.—Does your cousin shave often?—He shaves only every other day (*ogni due giorni*).—At what o'clock do you dress in the morning?—I dress as soon as I have breakfasted, and I breakfast every day at eight o'clock, or a quarter past eight.—Does your neighbour dress before he breakfasts?—He breakfasts before he dresses.—At what o'clock in the evening dost thou undress?—I undress as soon as I return from the theatre.—Dost thou go every evening to the theatre?—I do not go every evening, for it is better to study than to go to the theatre.—At what o'clock dost thou undress when thou dost not go to the theatre?—Then I undress as soon as I have supped, and go to bed at ten o'clock.—Have you already dressed the child (*il bambino*)?—I have not dressed it yet, for it is still asleep (*dorme ancora*).—At what o'clock does it get up?—It gets up as soon as it is waked.—Do you rise as early as I?—I do not know at what o'clock you rise (*si levi*, subj.), but I rise as soon as I awake.—Will you tell my servant to wake me to-morrow at four o'clock?—I will tell him.—Why have you risen so early?—My children have made such a noise (*tanto strepito*) that they awakened me.—Have you slept well?—I have not slept well, for you made too much noise.—At what o'clock did the good captain awake?—He awoke at a quarter past five in the morning.

103.

How did my child behave?—He behaved very well.—How did my brother behave towards you?—He behaved very well towards me, for he behaves well towards every body.—Is it worth while to write to that man?—It is not worth while to write to him.—Is it worth while to dismount from my horse in order to buy a cake?—It is not worth while, for it is not long since you ate.—Is it worth while to dismount from my horse in order to give something to that poor man (*a questo povero*)?—Yes, for he seems (*pare*) to want it; but you can give him something without dismounting from your horse.—Is it better to go to the theatre than to study?—It is better to do the latter than the former.—Is it better to learn to read French than to speak it?—It is not worth while to learn to read it without learning to speak it.—Is it better to go to bed than to go a walking?—It is better to do the latter than the former.—Is it better to go to France than to Germany?—It is not worth while to go to France or to Germany when one has no wish to travel.—Did you at last get rid of that man?—I did get rid of him.—Why has your father parted with his horses?—Because he did not want them any more.—Has your merchant succeeded at last to get rid of his damaged sugar?—He has succeeded in getting rid of it.—Has he sold it on credit?—He was able to sell it for cash, so that he did not sell it on credit.—Who has taught you to read?—I have learnt it with (*da*) a French master.—Has he taught you to write?—He has taught me to read and to write.—Who has taught your brother arithmetic (*l' aritmetica*)?—A French master has taught it him (*insegnata*).—Do you call me?—I call you.—What do you wish (*desiderare*)?—Why do you not rise? do you not know that it is already late?—What do you want me for (*che vuol Ella*)?—I have lost all my money, and I came to beg you to lend me some.—What o'clock is it?—It is already a quarter past six, and you have slept long enough (*dormito abbastanza*).—Is it long since you rose?—It is an hour and a half since I rose.—Do you wish to take a walk with me?—I cannot go a walking, for I am waiting for my Italian master.

FIFTY-THIRD LESSON.

Lezione cinquantesima terza.

To change.	*Cambiare, far cambio di.*
To change one thing for another.	Cambiare qualche cosa con qualche cosa.
	Far cambio di qualche cosa con qualche cosa.
I change my hat for his.	Faccio cambio del mio cappello col suo.
	Cambio il mio cappello col suo.
The change (exchange).	Il cambio (concambio).
To change (meaning *to put on other things*).	*Mutare* 1.
Do you change your hat?	Muta Ella il cappello?
I do change it.	Lo muto.
He changes his boots.	Egli muta gli stivali.
They change their clothes.	Eglino mutano i vestiti.

To mix.	† *Mischiarsi* 1.
I mix among the men.	† Mi mischio fra gli uomini.
He mixes among the soldiers.	† Si mischia fra i soldati.
Among.	Fra, tra.

To recognize, or to acknowledge.	*Riconoscere* * (is conjugated like its primitive *conoscere* *, Lessons XXVIII. and XXXIII.).
Do you recognize that man?	Riconosce Ella quest' uomo?
It is so long since I saw him that I do not recollect him.	È sì lungo tempo che non l' ho visto che non lo riconosco più.

Obs. A. When there is a comparison between two sentences, *than* is rendered by *di quello che*, followed by *non*. Ex.

FIFTY-THIRD LESSON.

I have more bread than I shall eat.	† Ho più pane di quello che non mangerò.
That man has more money than he will spend.	† Quest' uomo ha più danaro di quello che non ispenderà.
There is more wine than will be necessary.	† Vi è più vino di quello che non farà d' uopo (or non sarà bisogno).
You have more money than you will want.	† Ella ha più danaro di quello che non le abbisognerà.
We have more clothes than we want.	† Abbiamo più vestiti di quello che non ce ne abbisognerà.
That man has fewer friends than he imagines.	† Quest' uomo ha meno amici di quello che egli non pensi (subjunctive, of which hereafter).

To fancy.	Imaginare or immaginare.
	Imaginarsi, credersi.
To think.	Pensare 1.

To hope, to expect.	Sperare 1. Aspettarsi.
Do you expect to find him there?	Spera Ella trovarcelo?
I do expect it.	Lo spero.

To earn, to gain, to get.	Guadagnare 1.
How much have you gained?	Quanto ha Ella guadagnato?

Has your father already started (departed)?	È già partito il di Lei padre?
He is ready to depart.	È pronto a partire.
Ready.	Pronto (takes a before the Infinitive).
To make ready.	Preparare, allestire (isco).
To make one's self ready.	Prepararsi, allestirsi a.
To keep one's self ready.	Tenersi pronto a.
I am ready to set out.	Mi tengo pronto a partire.
	Son pronto a partire.

To rend, to split.	Squarciare 1.
To break some one's heart.	Squarciare il cuore ad uno.
You break that man's heart.	Ella squarcia il cuore a quest' uomo?
Whose heart do I break?	A chi squarcio io il cuore?

FIFTY-THIRD LESSON.

To spill.	*Spargere* * ; past part. *sparso*.
To spill ink upon the book.	Spargere dell' inchiostro sul libro. Spandere versare.
To spread, extend.	*Stendere* * ; past part. *steso*.
To expatiate, to lay stress upon.	*Estendersi* * *sopra*.
That man is always expatiating upon that subject.	Quest' uomo si estende sempre su questo soggetto. (O si diffonde.)
The subject.	Il soggetto.
Always.	Sempre.
To stretch one's self.	{ *Sdraiarsi*. { *Stendersi*.
To stretch one's self along the floor.	Sdraiarsi (stendersi) sul pavimento.
The sofa, the bed.	Il sofà, il canapè, il letto.
He stretches himself upon the sofa.	Si stende (si sdraia) sul canapè.
To hang on or *upon*.	{ *Appendere* * *a*; past part. *appeso*. { *Appiccare* 1.
The wall.	Il muro.
I hang my coat on the wall.	Appendo il mio abito al muro.
He hangs his hat upon the tree.	Egli appende il suo cappello all' albero.
We hang our clothes upon the nails.	Appendiamo i nostri vestiti ai chiodi.
The thief has been hanged.	Il ladro è stato appiccato.
The thief.	Il ladro.
The robber, the highwayman.	Il ladro da strada, il masnadiero.
You have always been studious, and will always be so.	Ella è sempre stata studiosa e lo sarà sempre. (Voi siete stato sempre studioso e lo sarete sempre).
Your brother is, and will always be good.	Il di Lei fratello è sempre savio e lo sarà sempre.
A well-educated son never gives his father any grief; he loves, honours, and respects him.	Un figlio ben educato non dà mai dolore a suo padre; l'ama, l'onora e lo rispetta.

If I can, I will receive him willingly. | † Se potrò, lo riceverò volontieri.

Obs. B. The conditional conjunction *se*, if, may in Italian be followed by the future.

If you go there, we shall see each other.	Se andrà, ci vedremo. O se voi vi andrete.
If our affairs permit us, we shall take a short journey.	Se i nostri affari ce lo permetteranno, andremo a fare un piccolo viaggio.
Willingly.	Volontieri *or* volentieri.
The affair, the occupation.	L' affare.
To allow, to permit.	Permettere * (is conjugated like its primitive *mettere* *, Lessons XXIV. and XXXIII.)
The voyage, the journey.	Il viaggio.

EXERCISES.

164.

Do you hope to receive a note to-day ?—I hope to receive one. —From whom ?—From a friend of mine.—What dost thou hope ? —I hope to see my parents to-day, for my tutor has promised me to take me to them.—Does your friend hope to receive any thing ? —He hopes to receive something, for he has studied well.—Do you hope to arrive early in Paris ?—We hope to arrive there at a quarter past eight, for our father is waiting for us this evening. —Do you expect to find him at home ?—We expect it.—For what have you changed your coach, of which you have spoken to me ? —I have changed it for a fine Arabian horse.—Do you wish to exchange your book for mine ?—I cannot, for I want it to study Italian.—Why do you take your hat off ?—I take it off because I see my old master coming (*vedo venire*).—Do you put on another (*mutare*) hat to go to the market ?—I do not put on another to go to the market, but to go to the concert.—When will the concert take place ?—It will take place the day after to-morrow.—Why do you go away ?—Do you not amuse yourself here ?—You are mistaken, Sir, when you say that I do not amuse myself here ; for I assure you that I find a great deal of pleasure in conversing (*a conversare*) with you ; but I am going, because I am expected at my relation's ball.—Have you promised to go ?—I have promised.—Have you changed your hat in order to go to the English captain's ?—I have changed my hat, but I have not changed my coat or my boots.—How many times a day dost thou change thy clothes?—I change them to dine and to go to the theatre.

165.

Why do you mix among these men?—I mix among them in order to know what they say of me.—What will become of you if you always mix among the soldiers?—I do not know what will become of me, but I assure you that they will do me no harm, for they do not hurt any body.—Have you recognized your father? —It was so long since I saw him, that I did not recognize him.— Did he recognize you?—He recognized me instantly.—How long have you had this coat?—It is a long time since I have had it.— How long has your brother had that gun?—He has had it a great while.—Do you still speak French?—It is so long since I spoke it, that I have nearly forgotten it all.—How long is it since your cousin has been learning French?—It is only three months since. —Does he know as much as you?—He knows more than I, for he has been learning it longer.—Do you know why that man does not eat?—I believe he is not (*che non abbia*, subj.) hungry, for he has more bread than he can (*possa*, subj.) eat.—Have you given your son any money?—I have given him more than he will spend (*che non ispenderà*).—Will you give me a glass of cider? —You need not drink cider, for there is more wine than will be necessary.—Am I to (*debbo io*) sell my gun in order to buy a new hat?—You need not sell it, for you have more money than you will want.—Do you wish to speak to the shoemaker?—I do not wish to speak to him, for we have more boots than we shall want. —Why do the French rejoice?—They rejoice because they flatter themselves they have many good friends.—Are they not right in rejoicing (*di rallegrarsi*)?—They are wrong, for they have fewer friends than they imagine (*che pensino*, subj.).

166.

Are you ready to depart with me?—I am so.—Does your uncle depart with us?—He departs with us, if he pleases (*se vuole*).— Will you tell him to be ready (*di tenersi pronto*) to start to-morrow at six o'clock in the evening?—I will tell him so.—Is

this young man ready to go out?—Not yet, but he will soon be
ready.—Why have they hanged that man?—They have hanged
him, because he has killed somebody.—Have they hanged the
man who stole the horse from your brother?—They have
punished him, but they have not hanged him; they only hang
highwaymen in our country (*nel nostro paese*).—What have you
done with my coat?—I have hanged (*appeso*) it on the wall.—
Will you hang my hat upon the tree?—I will hang it thereon
(*appendervelo*).—Have you not seen my gloves?—I found them
under your bed, and have hanged them upon the rails.—Has the
thief who stole your gun been hanged?—He has been punished,
but he has not been hanged.—Why do you expatiate so much
upon that subject?—Because it is necessary to speak on all subjects.—If it is necessary to listen to you, and to answer you when
you expatiate upon that subject, I will hang my hat upon the
nail, stretch myself along the floor, listen to you, and answer you
as well as I can (*alla meglio*).—You will do well.—Shall you go
to Italy this year?—If I prosper (*se farò buoni affari*) I shall go
there.—Shall you go to the captain?—I will go if you go.—Will
you lend me a book?—If I can (*se potrò*) I will lend you one.—
Will your son receive a present?—If he is (*se sarà*) good and industrious, he will receive one; but if he is idle, he will receive
nothing.—Shall you go out?—If it is (*sarà*) fine weather, I shall
go out; but if it rains I shall remain at home.

FIFTY-FOURTH LESSON.

Lezione cinquantesima quarta.

To be well.	Star bene.
How do you do?	Come sta?
I am well.	Sto bene (or simply bene).

FIFTY-FOURTH LESSON. 273

Obs. A. The verbs *to be*, and *to do*, are both expressed in Italian by the verb *stare**, when they are used in English to inquire after, or to speak of a person's health.

To serve you.	Per ubbidirla. Per servirla (an expression commonly used in Italian, in answer to an inquiry after one's health).
How is your father?	Come sta il di Lei signor padre?

Obs. B. The qualifications of *Signore*, Mr., *Signora*, Mrs., *Signorina*, Miss, usually follow the possessive pronouns in Italian, when we speak to a person respecting his parents, relations, or friends, and we mean to pay them some respect.

He is ill.	Sta male.
Your father.	† Il di Lei signor padre.
Your brother.	† Il di Lei signor fratello.
Your cousin.	† Il di Lei signor cugino.
Your cousins.	† I di Lei signori cugini.
Your uncles.	† I di Lei signori zii.

To doubt a thing. To question any thing.	Dubitare di qualche cosa.
Do you doubt that?	Dubita Ella pi ciò?
I doubt it.	
I do not doubt it.	Ne dubito.
I make no question, have no doubt of it.	Non ne dubito.
What do you doubt?	Di che dubita Ella?
I doubt what that man has told me.	Dubito di ciò che m' ha detto quest' uomo.
The doubt.	Il dubbio.
Without doubt, no doubt.	Senza dubbio.
There is no doubt about it.	Non v' ha dubbio.

To agree to a thing.	Convenire* di qualche cosa (conjugated like its primitive *venire*: Lessons XXIV., XXXIV., and XLVI.).
Do you agree to that?	Conviene Ella di ciò?
I agree to it.	Ne convengo.

How much have you paid for that hat?	† Quanto ha Ella pagato questo cappello?
I have paid three crowns for it.	† L' ho pagato tre scudi.

12*

FIFTY-FOURTH LESSON.

I have bought this horse *for* five hundred francs.	Ho comprato questo cavallo per cinque cento franchi.
The price.	Il prezzo.
Have you agreed about the price?	Sono Elleno convenute del prezzo? (O siete voi convenuto.)
We have agreed about it.	Ne siamo convenuti.
About what have you agreed?	Di che sono Elleno convenute?
About the price.	Del prezzo.

To agree, to compose a difference.	*Accordarsi.*
To feel (to perceive).	*Sentire* 3.
To consent.	{ *Consentire (di* before Infin.). { *Acconsentire (di* before Inf.).
I consent to go thither.	Acconsento d' andarvi.
He consents to pay it me.	Acconsente di pagarmelo.
However.	Pure, però.

To wear (meaning to wear garments).	*Portare* 1.
What garments does he wear?	Che vestimenti porta egli?
He wears beautiful garments.	Porta bei vestimenti.
The garment.	{ Il vestimento. { *Plur.* I vestimenti & le vestimenta.

Against my custom.	Contro il mio solito (costume).
As customary.	Come al solito.
My partner.	Il mio socio.

To observe something. } To take notice of something. }	*Accorgersi* * 2; *di qualche cosa.* Past part. *accortosi.*
Do you take notice of that?	Si accorge Ella di questo? Vi accorgete voi di.
I do take notice of it.	Me ne accorgo.
Did you observe that?	Si è Ella accorta di questo?
Did you notice what he did?	Si è Ella accorta di ciò che ha fatto?
I did notice it.	Me ne son accorto.

FIFTY-FOURTH LESSON. 275

To expect (to hope).	† Attendersi * 2 ; past part. attesosi. (Aspettare o aspettarsi.)
Do you expect to receive a note from your uncle?	S' attende Ella a ricevere un biglietto dal di Lei zio?
I expect it.	Mi vi attendo. Lo aspetto.
He expects it.	Vi si attende. Vi s' attende.
We expect it.	Vi ci attendiamo. Ce lo aspettiamo.
Have we expected it?	Vi ci siamo attesi?
We have expected it.	Vi ci siamo attesi. L' abbiamo atteso.

To get (meaning to procure).	† Procurarsi.
I cannot procure any money.	Non posso procurarmi danaro. Non posso procurarmi del danaro.
He cannot procure any thing to eat.	Non può procurarsi di che mangiare.

To make fun of some one, to laugh at some one. To laugh at something.	† Beffarsi (1) di qualcuno. Burlarsi di. Ridersi * (2) di qualche cosa, p. past. risosi.
He laughs at every body. He criticises every body. Do you laugh at that man? I do not laugh at him.	Ei si beffa di tutti. Si beffa Ella di quest' uomo? Non me ne beffo.

To stop, to stay.	Fermarsi 1.
Have you stayed long at Berlin?	La si è fermata molto tempo a Berlino? (Si è ella fermata.) È rimasta Ella longo tempo a Berlino? (Siete voi rimasto.)
I stayed there only three days.	Non mi vi son fermato che tre giorni.

To sojourn, to stay.	Soggiornare 1. Stare *.
Where does your brother stay at present?	Ove soggiorna attualmente li di Lei signor fratello?
At present, actually.	Attualmente.
He stays at Florence.	Soggiorna a Firenze.
The residence, stay, abode.	Il soggiorno.
Paris is a fine place to live in.	† Parigi è un bel soggiorno.

After reading. | † Dopo aver letto.
After cutting myself. | † Dopo essermi tagliato.

Obs. C. See ☞ Lesson XL.

After dressing yourself. | † Dopo essersi vestita. (O essersi vestito.)
After dressing himself. | † Dopo essersi vestito.
After shaving ourselves. | † Dopo esserci sbarbati.
After warming themselves. | † Dopo essersi scaldati (riscaldati).
I returned the book after reading it. | † Ho restituito il libro dopo averlo letto.
I threw the knife away after cutting myself. | † Ho gettato il coltello dopo essermi tagliato.
You went to the concert after dressing yourself. | † Ella è andata al concerto dopo essersi vestita.
He went to the theatre after dressing himself. | † Egli è andato a teatro ¹ dopo essersi vestito.
We breakfasted after shaving ourselves. | † Abbiamo fatto colazione dopo esserci sbarbati.
They went out after warming themselves. | † Sono usciti dopo essersi scaldati.

To return (*to restore*). | Restituire 3.

The sick person (the patient). | Il malato. L'infermo.
Tolerably well. | Mediocremente (abbastanza bene).
It is rather late. | È molto tardi.
It is rather far. | È molto lontano.

EXERCISES.

167.

How is your father (*il di Lei signor padre*) ?—He is (only) so-so (*così così*).—How is your patient ?—He is a little better to-day than yesterday (*d' ieri*).—Is it long since you saw your brothers (*i di Lei signori fratelli*) ?—I saw them two days ago.—How art thou ?—I am tolerably well (*abbastanza bene*).—How long has your cousin been learning French ?—He has been learning

¹ There is a difference between *andare al teatro*, and *andare a teatro*. The former determines the theatre we are going to, whilst the latter implies to go to the play merely. Ex. *Vado al teatro reale*, I am going to the royal theatre.

it only these three months.—Does he already speak it?—He already speaks, reads, and writes it better than your brother, who has been learning it these two years.—Is it long since you heard of my uncle?—It is hardly a fortnight (*quindici giorni*) since I heard of him.—Where is he staying now?—He is staying at Berlin, but my father is in London.—Did you stay long at Vienna?—I stayed there a fortnight.—How long did your cousin stay at Paris?—He stayed there only a month.—Do you like to speak to my uncle?—I like much to speak to him, but I do not like him to laugh (*che si beffi*, subj.) at me.—Why does he laugh at you?—He laughs at me, because I speak badly.—Why has your brother no friends?—He has none, because he criticises every body.—Why are you laughing at that man?—I do not intend (*non ho intenzione*) to laugh at him.—I beg (*pregare*) you not to do it, for you will break his heart if you laugh at him.—Do you doubt what I am telling you?—I do not doubt it.—Do you doubt what that man has told you?—I doubt it, for he has often told stories (*mentire*).—Have you at last bought the horse which you wished (*che voleva*) to buy last month?—I have not bought it, for I have not been able to procure money.

168.

Has your uncle at last bought the garden?—He has not bought it, for he could not agree about the price (*nel prezzo*).—Have you at last agreed about the price of that picture?—We have agreed about it.—How much have you paid for it?—I have paid fifteen hundred (*mille cinque cento*) francs for it.—What hast thou bought to-day?—I have bought two fine horses, three beautiful pictures, and a fine gun.—For how much hast thou bought the pictures? —I have bought them for seven hundred francs.—Do you find them dear?—I do not find them dear.—Have you agreed with your partner?—I have agreed with him (*con lui*).—Does he consent to pay you the price of the ship?—He consents to pay it me. —Do you consent to go to France?—I consent to go there.—Have you seen your old friend again (*rivedere* *)?—I have seen him again.—Did you recognize him?—I could hardly (*non l' ho quasi più*) recognize him, for, contrary to his custom, he wears a large hat.—How is he?—He is very well.—What garments does he wear?—He wears beautiful new garments.—Have you taken notice of what your boy has done?—I have taken notice of it.—Have you punished him for it?—I have punished him for it.—Has your father already written to you?—Not yet; but I expect to receive (*mi attendo*) a note from him to-day.—Of what do you complain?—I complain of not being able to procure some money.—Why do these poor men complain?—They complain because they cannot procure any thing to eat.—How are your parents?—They are as usual (*come al solito*) very well.—Is your uncle well?—He is better than he usually is (*del solito*).—Have you already heard of your friend who is in Germany?—I have already written to him several times (*parecchie volte*); however (*ma*), he has not answered me yet.

100.

What have you done with the books which the English captain has lent you?—I have returned them to him, after reading them.—Have you thrown away your knife?—I have thrown it away after cutting myself.—When did I go to the concert?—You went thither after dressing yourself.—When did your brother go to the ball?—He went thither after dressing himself.—When did you breakfast?—We breakfasted after shaving ourselves.—When did our neighbours go out?—They went out after warming themselves.—Why have you punished your boy?—I have punished him because he has broken my finest glass.—I gave him some wine, and instead of drinking it, he spilt it on the new carpet, and broke (*e ha rotto*) the glass.—What did you do this morning?—I shaved after rising, and went out after breakfasting.—What did your father do last night (*ieri sera*)?—He supped after going to the play, and went to bed after supping.—Did he rise early?—He rose at sunrise. (See end of Lesson XXIV.)

FIFTY-FIFTH LESSON.

Lezione cinquantesima quinta.

FEMININE SUBSTANTIVES AND ADJECTIVES.

DECLENSION OF THE ARTICLE FEMININE.

		Nom.	Gen.	Dat.	Acc.	Abl.
The	Singular,	La,	della,	alla,	la,	dalla.
	Plural,	Le,	delle,	alle,	le,	dalle.

EXAMPLE.

			Sing.		Plur.
The house	,,	the houses.	Nom. La casa	,,	Le case.
Of the house	,,	of the houses.	Gen. Della casa	,,	Delle case.
To the house	,,	to the houses.	Dat. Alla casa	,,	Alle case.
The house	,,	the houses.	Acc. La casa	,,	Le case.
From the house	,,	from the houses.	Abl. Dalla casa	,,	Dalle case.

The contraction of the feminine article with certain prepositions is as follows: (See Lesson XLIV.)

Singular.			Plural.		
Della, of the,	for	di la.	Delle,	for	di le.
Alla, to the,	—	a la.	Alle,	—	a le.
Dalla, from the,	—	da la.	Dalle,	—	da le.
Nella, in the,	—	in la.	Nelle,	—	in le.
Colla, with the,	—	con la.	Colle,	—	con le.
Pella, for the,	—	per la.	Pelle,	—	per le.
Sulla, upon the,	—	su la.	Sulle,	—	su le.

Obs. A. When the definite article stands before a vowel, it is in the singular alike for both genders, and in the plural the feminine article does not vary, as:

		Nom.	Gen.	Dat.	Acc.	Abl.
The	Singular,	L',	dell',	all',	l',	dall'.
	Plural,	Le,	delle,	alle,	le,	dalle.

Obs. B. The plural of the article le is never abridged, except, however, when the noun begins with an e, as:

FIFTY-FIFTH LESSON.

	Sing.	Plur.
The eloquence.	L' eloquenza,	l' eloquenze.
The eminence.	L' eminenza,	l' eminenze.
The execution.	L' esecuzione,	l' esecuzioni.
Of the eminences, of the executions.	Dell' eminenze,	dell' esecuzioni.

Obs. C. When, however, the noun beginning with *e* has in the plural the same termination as in the singular, the article cannot be abridged. Ex.

	Sing.	Plur.
The image.	L' effigie,	Le effigie.
The emphasis.	L' enfasi,	Le enfasi.
Ecstasy.	L' estasi,	Le estasi.
The age.	L' età,	Le età.
The extremity.	L' estremità,	Le estremità.

RULE 1.—Nouns and adjectives ending in *a* are feminine [1], and form their plural in changing *a* into *e*. Ex.

	Sing.	Plur.
The woman—women.	La donna,	le donne.
The table.	La tavola,	le tavole.
The shoe.	La scarpa,	le scarpe.
The stocking.	La calza,	le calze.
The pencil.	La matita,	le matite.
The stone.	La pietra,	le pietre.
The brush.	La spazzola,	le spazzole.
The broom.	La scopa,	le scope.
The pistol.	La pistola,	le pistole.
The daughter.	La figlia,	le figlie.
The sister.	La sorella,	le sorelle.
The candle.	La candela,	le candele.
The bottle.	La bottiglia,	le bottiglie.

[1] From this rule must be excepted some nouns of dignity and of professions belonging to men, and some nouns derived from the Greek, such as

Sing.		Plur.
Il papa,	the pope,	i papi.
Il clima,	the climate,	i climi.
Il diadema,	the diadem,	i diademi.
Il diploma,	the diploma,	i diplomi.
Il dogma (or domma),	the doctrine,	i dogmi (or dommi).
Il dramma,	the drama,	i drammi.
L' enigma (or enimma),	the enigma,	gl' enigmi (or enimmi).
L' idioma,	the idiom,	gl' idiomi.
Il poema,	the poem,	i poemi.
Il tema,	the exercise,	i temi, &c.

FIFTY-FIFTH LESSON.

	Sing.	Plur.
The shirt.	La camicia,	le camicie.
The amiable woman.	La donna amabile,	le donne amabili.
The straight stocking.	La scarpa stretta,	le scarpe strette.
The barbarous law.	La legge barbara,	le leggi barbare.
The soul.	L' anima,	le anime.
The island.	L' isola,	le isole.
The shade.	L' ombra,	le ombre.

Rule 2.—All nouns and adjectives, masculine and feminine, terminated in a form their plural in i. Ex.

	Sing.	Plur.
The mother.	La madre,	le madri.
The key.	La chiave,	le chiavi.
The invention.	L' invenzione,	le invenzioni.
The nut.	La noce,	le noci.

Rule 3.—Nouns ending in i, ie, an accented vowel, and monosyllables, have in the plural the same termination as in the singular. Ex.

	Sing.	Plur.
The metropolis.	La metropoli,	le metropoli.
The crisis.	La crisi,	le crisi.
The foot—feet.	Il pié (or piede),	i piè (or piedi).
The king.	Il re,	i re.
The crane (a bird).	La gru,	le gru.
The town.	La città,	le città.
Virtue.	La virtù,	le virtù.
Order—series.	La serie,	le serie.
Sort—species.	La specie,	le specie.

Obs. D. La moglie, the wife, is in the plural le mogli, wives.

Rule 4. Nouns and adjectives, masculine and feminine, terminated in ca, ga, co or go, generally take an h in the plural to keep the hard sound. Ex.

	Sing.	Plur.
The sleeve.	La manica,	le maniche.
The witch.	La strega,	le streghe.
The monarch.	Il monarca,	i monarchi.
The wood or forest.	Il bosco,	i boschi.
The lake.	Il lago,	i laghi.
The inn.	L' albergo,	gli alberghi.
The refreshment.	Il rinfresco,	i rinfreschi.
Rich.	Ricco,	ricchi.

FIFTY-FIFTH LESSON.

Ancient.	Antico,	antichi.
The parish-priest.	Il parroco,	i parrochi.
The obligation.	L' obbligo,	gli obblighi.
The punishment.	Il castigo,	i castighi.

Obs. E. All feminine nouns terminated in *co* and *ga* take, without exception, an *h* in the plural. Ex.

	Sing.	Plur.
The female friend.	L' amica,	le amiche.
The league.	La lega,	le leghe, &c.

The following masculine nouns are a few of the exceptions to the above rule :—

The physician.	Il medico,	i medici.
The friend.	L' amico,	gli amici.
The monk.	Il monaco,	i monaci.
The hog.	Il porco,	i porci.
The Greek.	Il Greco,	i Greci.
Asparagus.	L' asparago,	gli asparagi.

RULE 5.—Some masculine nouns form their plural in *a*, and become feminine; others have a masculine plural in *i*, and a feminine plural in *a*, of which the latter is most in use.

a) The following masculine nouns always form their plural in *a* :—

	Sing.	Plur.
A thousand.	Un migliaio,	le migliaia.
A hundred.	Un centinaio,	le centinaia.
An egg.	Un uovo,	le uova.
A mile.	Un miglio,	le miglia.
A pair.	Un paio,	le paia.
A bushel.	Uno staio,	le staia.
A sort of measure.	Un moggio,	le moggia.

b) The following have a masculine and a feminine plural, but the latter is used in preference :—

	Sing.	Plur.
The ring.	L' anello,	le anella.
The arm.	Il braccio,	le braccia.
The gut.	Il budello,	le budella.
The heel.	Il calcagno,	le calcagna.
The castle.	Il castello,	le castella.
The eye-brow.	Il ciglio,	le ciglia.
The horn.	Il corno,	le corna.
The finger.	Il dito,	le dita.
The thread.	Il filo,	le fila.
The basis.	Il fondamento,	le fondamenta.
The fruit [a].	Il frutto,	le frutta.

---

[a] *Il frutto* is employed for fruit in general, but *la frutta* and *le frutta* for dessert fruit only.

	Sing.	Plur.
The spindle.	Il fuso,	le fusa.
The action[3].	Il gesto,	le gesta.
The knee.	Il ginocchio,	le ginocchia.
The elbow[4].	Il gomito,	le gomita.
The cry.	Il grido,	le grida.
The lip.	Il labbro,	le labbra.
The wood[5].	Il legno,	le legna.
The sheet.	Il lenzuolo,	le lenzuola.
The limb[6].	Il membro,	le membra.
The wall[7].	Il muro,	le mura.
The bone.	L' osso,	le ossa.
The apple.	Il pomo,	le poma.
The arrow.	Il quadrello,	le quadrella.
The laughter.	Il riso,	le risa.
The rack.	Il sacco,	le sacca.
The shriek.	Lo strido,	le strida.

CONTINUATION OF THE FIFTY-FIFTH LESSON.

Continuazione della Lezione cinquantesima quinta.

	Sing.	Plur.
She — they.	Ella —	elle or elleno.
	Essa —	esse.
	Dessa —	desse (See Table of the Personal Pronouns, Lesson XX.).

Obs. A. In the plural, *elleno, esse,* and *desse,* are more frequently used than *elle.*

Has she?	Ha dessa?
She has.	Essa ha.
She has not.	Essa non ha.

---

[3] *Il gesto* means also gesture, and then its plural is *gesti.*
[4] *Il gomito* is also a measure, and its plural is then *i gomiti.*
[5] *Il legno* means wood for timber, or any thing else: but wood for fuel is *la legna* and *le legna.*
[6] *Membro,* a member of an assembly, is in the plural *i membri.*
[7] *Muro,* a rampart, is in the plural *i muri.*

Have they (*feminine*)?	Hanno desse?	
They have. "	Esse hanno.	
They have not. "	Esse non hanno.	

		Nom.	Gen.	Dat.	Acc.	Abl.
My, mine.	Fem. Sing.	La mia,	della mia,	alla mia,	la mia,	dalla mia
Thy, thine.	"	La tua,	della tua,	alla tua,	la tua,	dalla tua.
Her, hers.	"	La sua,	della sua,	alla sua,	la sua,	dalla sua.
My, mine.	Fem. Plur.	Le mie,	delle mie,	alle mie,	le mie,	dalle mie.

The father and *his* son, or *his* daughter.	Il padre e *suo* figlio, o *sua* figlia.
The mother and *her* son, or *her* daughter.	La madre e *suo* figlio, o *sua* figlia.
The child and *its* brother, or *its* sister.	Il fanciullo e *suo* fratello, o *sua* sorella.

Obs. B. See Rule, Lesson IV., about the possessive pronoun taking no article in the singular, when it is immediately followed by a name of quality or kindred.

RULE 1.—The English possessive adjectives or pronouns are in the *gender of the possessor*; in Italian and French they must be in the gender of the *thing possessed*. My, thy, his, her, its, must be expressed by *il mio, il tuo, il suo*, when the thing possessed is masculine, and by *la mia, la tua, la sua*, when it is feminine, without considering in the least the gender of the possessor, as may be seen from the above examples.

		Sing.	Plur.
My pen,	my pens.	La mia penna,	le mie penne.
Thy letter,	thy letters.	La tua lettera,	le tue lettere.
His or her fork,	his or her forks.	La sua forchetta,	le sue forchette.
Our nut,	our nuts.	La nostra noce,	le nostre noci.
Your mouth,	your mouths.	La vostra bocca,	le vostre bocche.
Their door,	their doors.	La loro porta, Il loro uscio,	le loro porte. I loro usci.
Their hand,	their hands.	La loro mano,	le loro mani.

RULE 2.—All nouns terminated in *o* are masculine, except *la mano*, the hand. As for the poetical words *Imago* and *Cartago*, they are abridged from *imagine*, image, *Cartagine*, Carthage, and are of course feminine.

		Sing.	Plur.
The pretty woman,	the pretty women.	La vezzosa donna,	le vezzose donne.
The small candle,	the small candles.	La piccola candela. La candeletta.	le piccole candele. le candelette.
The large bottle,	the large bottles.	La gran bottiglia.	le grandi bottiglie.

FIFTY-FIFTH LESSON.

		Sing.	*Plur.*
Which woman?	which women?	Che donna?	che donne?
Which daughter?	which daughters?	Che figlia?	che figlie?
		or	
		Quale, *Sing.*	Quali, *Plur.*

This or that woman,	these or those women.	Questa donna,	queste donne.
This young lady,	these young ladies.	Questa signorina,	queste signorine.
That young lady,	those young ladies.	Quella signorina,	quelle signorine.

The right hand.	La mano destra (dritta *or* diritta).
The left hand.	La mano manca (mancina).
I have a sore hand.	Ho la mano malata.
My hand hurts me.	} Mi fa male la mano.
My hand aches.	
The tooth, the teeth.	Il dente, i denti.
Have you the toothache?	{ Le fanno male i denti?
	{ Le dolgono i denti?
	† Ho male al capo. Mi duole la testa.
I have the headache.	† Mi fa male il capo. Mi fa male la testa.
I feel a pain in my side.	Ho male a un lato.
His feet are sore.	Egli ha male ai piedi.
His feet ache.	Ha i piedi che gli fan male.

The face.	La faccia, il viso, le facce, i visi, il volto, i volti.
The cheek.	La guancia, le guance*,
The tongue, the language.	La lingua, le lingue.
The window.	La finestra, le finestre.
The street.	La contrada, le contrade.
The town.	La città, le città.
The linen.	La tela, le tele.
The old woman, the little old woman.	{ La vecchia donna, le vecchie donne. La vecchietta le vecchiette (vecchierella). (vecchierette).

Obs. C. From what precedes, it may be seen that Italian adjectives terminate either in o or a. The adjectives in a, which form their masculine plural

---

* Feminine words, ending in cia, gia, scia, reject in the plural the letter i, as: la guancia, plur. le guance; la spiaggia, the coast; plur. le spiagge; la coscia, the thigh; plur. le cosce: except, however, where i has the accent. Ex. la bugia, the lie; plur. le bugie.

FIFTY-FIFTH LESSON.

In i, are made feminine by changing their termination into a for the singular, and into e for the plural. Those terminated in e are of both genders, and form their plural in changing e into i. Ex.

An industrious boy,	industrious boys.	Un ragazzo attivo,	dei ragazzi attivi.
An industrious young woman,	industrious young women.	Una ragazza attiva,	delle ragazze attive.
An amiable man,	amiable men.	Un uomo amabile,	degli uomini amabili.
An amiable woman,	amiable women.	Una donna amabile,	delle donne amabili.

The room.	La stanza, la camera.
The front room.	† La camera verso strada.
The back room.	† La camera verso corte.
The upper room.	† La camera in alto (la camera al piano superiore).

Obs. D. Adjectives terminated in *ore*, which are generally also substantives, change for the feminine *ore* into *trice*. Ex.

	Mas.	*Fem.*
Traitorous.	Traditore,	traditrice.
Enchanting.	Incantatore,	incantatrice.
Deceitful.	Ingannatore,	ingannatrice,
Avenging.	Vendicatore,	vendicatrice.

PARTITIVE ARTICLE FEMININE.

		Sing.	*Plur.*
Some.	*Nom.*	Della, dell',	Delle.
Of some.	*Gen.*	Di.	Di.
To some.	*Dat.*	A della, a dell',	A delle.
Some.	*Acc.*	Della, dell'.	Delle.

	Sing.	*Plur.*
Some silk.	Della seta,	delle sete.
Some meat.	Della carne,	delle carni.
Some good soup.	Della buona zuppa,	delle buone zuppe.

Bring lights.	Portate dei lumi.
Strike a light.	Fatemi lume.

INDEFINITE ARTICLE FEMININE.

A, one.	*Nom. Acc.*	} Una.	*Gen.*	D' una.
	Dat.	Ad una.	*Abl.*	Da una.

FIFTY-FIFTH LESSON.

A virtuous woman.	Una donna virtuosa.
An active young woman.	Una ragazza attiva.
A happy young lady.	Una signorina felice.
A new gown.	Una gonna (veste) nuova.
An ingenious proposal.	Una proposizione spontanea.
A dumb woman.	Una donna muta.
A good truth.	Una buona verità.
A cruel certainty.	Una crudele certezza.
Such a promise.	Una simile promessa.
An old acquaintance.	Una antica conoscenza.

Have you my pen?	Ha Ella la mia penna?
No, Madam, I have it not.	No, Signora, non l' ho.
Which bottles have you broken?	Che (quali) bottiglie ha Ella rotte?
Which door have you opened?	Che (qual) porta ha Ella aperta.
Which water have you drunk?	Che (quale) acqua ha Ella bevuto or bevuta?

Obs. E. With the auxiliary *avere* the past participle may or may not agree with the noun in gender and number, but it must always with the auxiliary *essere*.

Which letters have you written?	Che (or quali) lettere ha Ella scritte (or scritto)?
Which windows have you opened?	Che (quali) finestre ha Ella aperte?
Which young ladies have you conducted to the ball?	Che (quali) signorine ha Ella condotte al ballo?

These.	Questi or questi qui.
Those.	Quelli or quelli là.

Have you this pen or that?	Ha Ella questa penna, o quella?
I have neither this nor that.	Non ho nè questa nè quella.

It or *her* — *them*.	*La* — *le*.
Do you see that woman?	Vede Ella questa donna?
I see her.	La vedo.
Have you seen my sisters?	Ha Ella vedute le mie sorelle?
No, my lady, I have not seen them.	No, signorina, non le ho vedute.

To her — *to them*.	*Le* — *loro*.
Do you speak to my sisters?	Parla Ella alle mie sorelle?
I speak to them.	Parlo loro.
Some coarse linen.	Della grossa tela.
Some good water.	Della buon' acqua.
A napkin, a towel.	Una salvietta (un tovagliolo).

Some beautiful linen shirts.	Delle belle camicie* di tela.
Some fine silk stockings.	Delle belle calze di seta.
The Christian.	Il Cristiano. Fem. la Cristiana.
The Jew.	L' Ebreo, " l' Ebrea.
The negro.	Il nero, il negro, " la nera, la negra.
A companion.	Un compagno, " una compagna.
A friend.	Un amico, " un' amica.
To celebrate, to feast.	Celebrare 1. Festeggiare 1.
Do you wish to go to Spain?	Vuol Ella andar in Ispagna?
Have you paper to write a letter?	Ha Ella della carta per iscrivere una lettera?

Obs. F. Of two words, the first of which ends in *n* or *r*, and the second begins with *s*, followed by a consonant, the letter *i* is prefixed to the second.

I have some to write one.	Ne ho per iscriverne una.
Who does not study does not learn.	Chi non istudia non impara.
What have you found in the street?	Che ha Ella trovato per istrada?
A book to study Italian.	Un libro per istudiare l' Italiano.

EXERCISES.

170.

How are your brothers?—They have been very well for these few days.—Where do they reside?—They reside in Paris.—Which day of the week do the Turks celebrate?—They celebrate Friday (*il venerdì*), but the Christians celebrate Sunday (*la domenica*), the Jews Saturday, and the negroes their birthday (*il giorno della loro nascita*).—"Amongst you country people (*Fra voi altre genti della campagna*) there are many fools, are there not (*non è vero*)?" asked (*domandò*) a philosopher lately (*l' altro giorno*) of a peasant (*ad un contadino*).—The latter answered (*rispose*): "Sir, they are to be found (*se ne trovano*) in all stations (*gli stati*)."—"Fools sometimes tell the truth (*la verità*)," said (*disse*) the philosopher.—Has your sister my gold ribbon?—She has it not.—What has she?—She has nothing.—Has your mother any thing?—She has a fine gold fork.—Who has my large bot-

* In *camicia* the letter *i* is not suppressed in the plural, to prevent mistaking it for *camice*, a priest's garment. (See note *, p. 225.)

tle?—Your sister has it.—Do you see sometimes my mother?—
I see her often.—When did you see your sister?—I saw her a
fortnight ago.—Who has my fine nuts?—Your good sister has
them.—Has she also my silver forks?—She has them not.—Who
has them?—Your mother has them.—What fork have you?—I
have my iron fork.—Have your sisters had my pens?—They
have not had them, but I believe that their children have (*abbiano*,
subj.) had them.—Why does your brother complain?—He complains because his right hand aches.—Why do you complain?—
I complain because my left hand aches.

171.

Is your sister as old (*così attempata*) as my mother?—She is
not so old, but she is taller.—Has your brother purchased any
thing (*fare delle compre*)?—He has purchased something (*ne ha
fatto*).—What has he bought?—He has bought fine linen and
good pens.—Has he not bought some silk stockings?—He has
bought some.—Is your sister writing?—No, Madam, she is not
writing (*non iscrive*).—Why does she not write?—Because she
has a sore hand.—Why does not the daughter of your neighbour
go out?—She does not go out because she has sore feet.—Why
does not my sister speak?—Because she has a sore mouth.—Hast
thou not seen my silver pen?—I have not seen it.—Hast thou a
front room?—I have one behind, but my brother has one in the
front.—Is it an upper room?—It is one (*n' è una*).—Does the
wife of our shoemaker go out already?—No, my lady (*signora,
no*), she does not go out yet, for she is still very ill (*essendo essa
ancor molto ammalata*).—Which bottle has your little sister broken?
—She broke the one (*quella*) which my mother bought yesterday.
—Have you eaten of my soup or of my mother's?—I have eaten
neither of yours nor your mother's (*nè di quella di sua madre*),
but of that of my good sister.—Have you seen the woman who
was with me this morning?—I have not seen her.—Has your
mother hurt herself?—She has not hurt herself.—Have you paper to write a letter?—I have some, but to whom must I write?
—You must write to your mother's friend.—What has your sister to do?—She has to write to her friend.—Why does she not

write to her?—Because she has no pen to write to her.—Can she not write with her pencil?—She can write with it (*con quello*), but does not wish to do so (*non vuole*).

172.

Have you a sore nose?—I have not a sore nose, but I have the tooth-ache.—Have you cut your finger?—No, my lady, I have cut my hand.—Will you give me a pen?—I will give you one.—Will you have this or that?—I will have neither.—Which (*quale*) do you wish to have?—I wish to have that which your sister has.—Do you wish to have my mother's good black silk (*la buona seta nera*), or my sister's?—I wish to have neither your mother's nor your sister's, but that which you have.—Can you write with this pen?—I can write with it.—Each woman (*ogni donna*) thinks herself amiable, and each (*ciascuna*) is conceited (*ha dell' amor proprio*).—The same as (*del pari che*) men, my dear friend. Many a one (*tal*) thinks himself (*si crede*) learned who is not so (*non l' è*), and many men surpass women in vanity.—What is the matter with you?—Nothing is the matter with me.—Why does your sister complain?—Because she has a pain in her cheek.—Has your brother a sore hand?—No, but he feels a pain in his side.—Do you open the window?—I open it, because it is too warm.—Which windows has your sister opened?—She has opened those of the front room.—Have you been at the ball of my old acquaintance?—I have been there.—Which young ladies did you take to the ball?—I took my sister's friends there.—Did they dance?—They danced a good deal.—Did they amuse themselves?—They amused themselves.—Did they remain long at the ball?—They remained there two hours.—Is this young lady a Turk?—No, she is a Greek.—Does she speak French?—She speaks it.—Does she not speak English?—She speaks it, but she speaks French better.—Has your sister a companion?—She has one.—Does she like her?—She likes her very much, for she is very amiable.

FIFTY-SIXTH LESSON.
Lezione cinquantesima sesta.

To go to the country.	Andare in *or* alla campagna.
To be in the country.	Essere in — alla campagna.
To go to church.	Andare in — alla chiesa.
To be at church.	Essere in chiesa.
To go to school.	Andare in iscuola *or* alla scuola.
To be at school.	Essere in iscuola.
To go to the Italian school.	Andare alla scuola d' Italiano.
To be at the Italian school.	Essere nella *or* alla scuola d' Italiano.
To go to the dancing school.	Andare alla scuola di ballo.
To be at the dancing school.	Essere nella scuola di ballo.
To *or* at the bank.	Alla banca.
To *or* at the exchange.	Alla borsa.
To *or* in the kitchen.	In cucina.
To *or* in the cellar.	In cantina.
The play (the comedy).	La comedia.
The opera.	L' opera.
The river.	Il fiume.
The hunt.	La caccia.
The fishing.	La pesca.
To go a hunting.	Andar a (*or* alla) caccia.
To be a hunting.	Esser a (*or* alla) caccia.
To go a fishing.	Andar a (*or* alla) pesca.
To be a fishing.	Esser a (*or* alla) pesca.
To hunt.	Cacciare 1.
To fish.	Pescare 1.
The whole day, all the day.	Tutto il giorno (tutta la giornata).
The whole morning.	Tutto il mattino (tutta la mattina).
The whole evening.	Tutta la sera.
The whole night, all the night.	Tutta la notte (tutta notte).
The whole year.	Tutto l' anno.
The whole week.	Tutta la settimana.
The whole society.	Tutta la società.
All at once.	{ Tutto ad un tratto. { Tutto in una volta.
Suddenly, all of a sudden.	Repentinamente (repente).

¹ When the hunting is determined the article must be made use of, Ex. *Andar o esser alla caccia del cervo*, to go or be a stag-hunting; *andar o esser alla pesca delle perle, del corallo*, to go or be a pearl or coral-fishing.

FIFTY-SIXTH LESSON.

This week.	Questa settimana.
This year.	Quest' anno.
Last week.	La settimana scorsa (passata).
Next week.	La settimana ventura (prossima).
Every woman.	Tutte le donne, ogni donna.
Every time.	Tutte le volte, ogni volta.
Every week.	Tutte le settimane, ogni settimana.

Your mother.	La di Lei signora madre.
Your sister.	La di Lei signora sorella.
Your sisters.	Le di Lei signore sorelle.
A person.	Una persona.
A word.	Una parola.

The ear-ache.	Il male agli orecchi.
The nausea.	La nausea.
The belly-ache.	Il mal di ventre.
The stomach-ache.	Il mal di stomaco.

She has the stomach-ache.	† Ella ha un dolore allo stomaco.
His sister has a violent head-ache.	† Sua sorella ha un mal di testa violento.
I have the stomach-ache.	† Ho male di stomaco.

Our or ours, your or yours, their or theirs,	(*fem. sing.*)	La nostra, la vostra, la loro.
Thy or thine, his, her, or hers, its,	(*fem. plur.*)	La tua, la sua.
Our or ours, your or yours, their or theirs,	" "	Le nostre, le vostre, le loro.

Have you my pen or hers?	Ha Ella la mia penna, o la sua?
I have hers.	Ho la sua.
What do you wish to send to your aunt?	Che vuol Ella mandare alla di Lei zia?
I wish to send her a tart.	Voglio mandarle una torta.
Will you send her some fruit also?	Vuol mandarle anche delle frutta?
I will send her some.	Voglio mandargliene (inviargliene).
Have you sent the books to my sisters?	Ha Ella inviato i libri alle mie sorelle?
I have sent them to them.	Li ho inviati loro.

The ache.	Il dolore.
The tart.	La torta.
The peach.	La pesca.

FIFTY-SIXTH LESSON. 293

The strawberry.	La fragola.
The cherry.	La ciliegia.
The newspaper.	Il giornale.
The gazette.	La gazzetta.
The merchandise.	} La mercanzia.
The goods.	
The maid-servant.	La cameriera.

Obs. A. Some substantives have the same termination for both genders, and are only distinguished by the article, such as:

The husband.	Il consorte, *or,* il marito.
The wife.	La consorte, *or,* la moglie.
The heir.	L' erede.
The heiress.	L' erede.
The nephew.	Il nipote.
The niece.	La nipote.
The relation.	Il parente.
The female relation.	La parente, &c.

Obs. B. Others change their masculine ending *o* into *a*, such as:

		Masculine.	Feminine.
The uncle,	the aunt,	Lo zio,	la zia.
The cousin,		Il cugino,	la cugina.
The brother-in-law,	the sister-in-law.	Il cognato,	la cognata.
The cook,	the female-cook.	Il cuoco,	la cuoca.
The neighbour,	the female-neighbour.	Il vicino,	la vicina.
The lad,	the lass.	Il giovinetto,	la giovinetta.
The heathen,		Il pagano,	la pagana.
A peasant,	a country-woman.	{ Un contadino,	una contadina.
		{ Un paesano,	una paesana, &c.

Ob. C. Substantives (the same as adjectives, preceding Lesson) terminated in *tore*, are generally made feminine by changing *tore* into *trice*. Ex.

	Masculine.	Feminine.
The accuser.	L' accusatore,	l' accusatrice.
The actor.	L' attore,	l' attrice.
The ambassador.	L' ambasciatore,	l' ambasciatrice.
The benefactor.	Il benefattore,	la benefattrice.
The hunter.	Il cacciatore,	la cacciatrice.
The elector.	L' elettore,	l' elettrice.
The emperor.	L' imperatore,	l' imperatrice.
The founder.	Il fondatore,	la fondatrice.
The protector.	Il protettore,	la protettrice.
The painter.	Il pittore,	la pittrice.
The author.	L' autore,	l' autrice.
The victor.	Il vincitore.	la vincitrice.
The conqueror.	Il conquistatore, &c.	la conquistatrice, &c.

FIFTY-SIXTH LESSON.

Obs. D. Some have a distinct form for individuals of the female sex, such as :

	Masculine.	Feminine.
The abbot.	L' abate.	abbadessa (la badessa).
The baron.	Il barone,	la baronessa.
The shepherd.	Il pastore,	la pastorella.
The canon.	Il canonico,	la canonichessa.
The singer.	Il cantante,	la cantatrice.
The count.	Il conte,	la contessa.
God.	Dio *or* Iddio.	
The god.	Il dio,	la dea.
The duke.	Il duca,	la duchessa.
The lion.	Il leone,	la leonessa.
The marquis.	Il marchese, *Plur.* I marchesi,	la marchesa. *Plur.* Le marchese.
The prince.	Il principe,	la principessa.
The peacock.	Il pavone,	la pagonessa.
The prior.	Il priore,	la priora.
The king.	Il re,	la regina,
The poet.	Il poeta,	la poetessa.
The philosopher.	Il filosofo,	la filosofessa.
The merchant.	Il mercante,	la mercantessa.
The landlord.	L' oste,	l' ostessa.
The cock.	Il gallo,	la gallina.
The elephant.	L' elefante,	l' elefantessa.
The dog.	Il cane,	la cagna.
The prophet.	Il profeta,	la profetessa.
The lord mayor.	Il podestà,	la podesteressa (obs).
The doctor.	Il dottore,	la dottoressa.
The manager.	Il fattore,	la fattoressa.
The master.	Il padrone,	la padrona.

Obs. E. The names of trees are commonly masculine, and the same words with the feminine termination in *a* designate the fruits of the same trees. Ex.

The chestnut-tree,	the chestnut.	Il castagno,	la castagna.
The cherry-tree,	the cherry.	Il ciliegio, *or* ciriegio,	la ciliegia, *or* ciriegia.
The pear-tree,	the pear.	Il pero,	la pera.
The plum-tree,	the plum.	Il prugno,	la prugna.
The walnut-tree,	the walnut.	Il noce,	la noce.

The following, however, are always masculine, and designate the tree as well as the fruit : *il fico*, the fig-tree, and the fig ; *il cedro*, the citron-tree, and citron ; *il dattero*, the date-tree, and the date ; *il pomo*, the apple-tree, and the apple.

Obs. F. Of the names of animals several become feminine by changing *o* into *a*, as : *il cavallo*, the horse ; *la cavalla*, the mare ; *il gatto*, the cat ; *la gatta*, the she-cat, &c.

FIFTY-SIXTH LESSON.

Others have for each gender particular denominations, as: *il bue*, the ox; *la vacca*, the cow; *il becco*, the buck; *la capra*, the goat; *il montone*, the ram; *la pecora*, the sheep, &c.

Others again, though they are used for both genders, are always masculine, as: *il tordo*, the thrush; *il corvo*, the raven; *lo scarafaggio*, the beetle, &c. Others again are always feminine, as: *la rondine*, the swallow; *la pantera*, the panther; *la vipera*, the viper; *l' anguilla*, the eel. Finally, there are some which it is indifferent to make masculine or feminine, such as: *il* or *la lepra*, the hare; *il* or *la serpe*, the serpent, &c.

To hire.	Prendere in affitto (or a pigione). Prendere a nolo.
To let.	Affittare 1, or dar in affitto (or a pigione). Dare a nolo.
Have you already hired a room?	Ha Ella già preso a pigione una camera?

To admit or grant a thing. To confess a thing.	Convenire* di qualche cosa.
Do you grant that?	Conviene Ella di ciò (or in ciò)?
I do grant it.	Ne convengo.
Do you confess your fault?	Conviene Ella del di Lei errore?
I confess it.	Ne convengo.
I confess it to be a fault.	Convengo ch' è un errore.
To confess, avow, own, acknowledge.	Confessare 1.

So much.	Tanto.
She has so many candles that she cannot burn them all.	Ella ha tante candele che non può consumarle tutte.

To catch a cold. To make sick.	Raffreddarsi 1. Infreddarsi 1. Rendere malato.
If you eat so much it will make you sick.	Se Ella mangia troppo ciò La renderà malata.
Does it suit you to lend your gun?	Le conviene di prestare il di Lei schioppo?
It does not suit me to lend it.	Non mi conviene prestarlo.
It does not suit me.	Non mi conviene.
Where did you catch a cold?	Ove si è Ella raffreddata?
I caught a cold in going from the opera.	Mi son raffreddato nel sortire dal teatro dell' opera.

To have a cold.	Esser raffreddato (or infreddato).
The cold.	Il raffreddore (l' infreddatura).
The cough.	La tosse.
I have a cold.	Ho un infreddatura di testa.
You have a cough.	Ella ha la tosse.
The brain.	Il cervello.
The chest.	Il petto.

EXERCISES.

173.

Where is your cousin ?—He is in the kitchen.—Has your cook (fem.) already made the soup ?—She has made it, for it is already upon the table.—Where is your mother ?—She is at church.—Is your sister gone to school ?—She is gone thither.—Does your mother often go to church ?—She goes thither every morning and every evening.—At what o'clock in the morning does she go to church ?—She goes thither as soon as she gets up.—At what o'clock does she get up ?—She gets up at sunrise.—Dost thou go to school to-day ?—I do go thither.—What dost thou learn at school ?—I learn to read, write, and speak there.—Where is your aunt ?—She is gone to the play with my little sister.—Do your sisters go this evening to the opera ?—No, Madam, they go to the dancing-school.—Do they go to the French school ?—They go thither in the morning, but not in the evening.—Is your father gone a hunting ?—He has not been able to go a hunting, for he has a cold.—Do you like to go a hunting ?—I like to go a fishing better than a hunting (che non a caccia).—Is your father still in the country ?—Yes, Madam, he is still there.—What is he doing there ?—He goes a hunting and a fishing.—Did you hunt in the country ?—I hunted the whole day.—How long did you stay with my mother ?—I stayed with her the whole evening.—Is it long since you were at the castle ?—I was there last week.—Did you find many people there ?—I found only three persons there ; the count, the countess, and their daughter.

174.

Are these girls as good (savio) as their brothers ?—They are better than they.—Can your sisters speak German ?—They cannot, but they are learning it.—Have you brought any thing to your mother?—I have brought her some fine fruit and a fine tart.—What has your niece brought you?—She has brought us good cherries, excellent strawberries, and very good peaches.—Do you like peaches?—I like them much.—How many peaches has your neighbour (fem.) given you?—She has given me more than twenty.—Have you eaten many cherries this year?—I have eaten many.—Did you give any to your little sister?—I gave her so many that she cannot eat them all.—Why have you not given any to your good neighbour (fem.)?—I wished to give her some, but she would not take any, because she does not like cherries.—Were there many pears last year?—There were not many.—Has your cousin (fem.) many strawberries?—She has so many that she cannot eat them all.

175.

Why do your sisters not go to the play?—They cannot go thither because they have a cold, and that makes them very ill.—Where did they catch a cold?—They caught a cold in going from the opera (*nell' uscire dal teatro dell' opera*) last night.—Does it suit your sister to eat some peaches?—It does not suit her to eat any, for she has already eaten a good many, and if she eats so much it will make her ill.—Did you sleep well last night?—I did not sleep well, for my children made too much noise (*il rumore*) in my room.—Where were you last night?—I was at my brother-in-law's—Did you see your sister-in-law?—I saw her.—How is she?—She is better than usual (*meglio del solito*).—Did you play?—We did not play, but we read some good books; for my sister-in-law likes to read better than to play.—Have you read the gazette to-day?—I have read it.—Is there any thing new in it?—I have not read any thing new in it.—Where have you been since I saw you?—I have been at Vienna, Paris, and Berlin.—Did you speak to my aunt?—I did speak to her.—What does she say?—She says that she wishes to see you.—Where have you put my pen?—I have put it upon the bench.—Do you intend to see your niece to-day?—I intend to see her, for she has promised me to dine with us.—I admire (*ammirare*) that family (*la famiglia*), for the father is the king and the mother is the queen of it. The children and the servants are the subjects (*il suddito*) of the state (*lo stato*). The tutors of the children are the ministers (*il ministro*) who share (*dividere**) with the king and the queen the care (*la cura*) of the government (*il governo*). The good education (*l' educazione*) which is given to children is the crown (*la corona*) of monarchs (*il monarca*, plur. i).

176.

Have you already hired a room?—I have already hired one.—Where have you hired it?—I have hired it in William-street (*nella contrada Guglielmo*), number one hundred and fifty-two.—At whose house (*da chi*) have you hired it?—At the house of the man whose son has sold you a horse.—For whom has your father hired a room?—He has hired one for his son, who has just arrived from France.—Why have you not kept your promise (*la promessa*)?—I do not remember what I promised you.—Did you not promise us to take us to the concert last Tuesday?—I confess that I was wrong in promising you; the concert, however (*pure*), has not taken place.—Does your brother confess his fault?—He confesses it.—What does your uncle say to (*di*) that note?—He says that it is written very well, but he admits that he has been wrong in sending it to the captain.—Do you confess your fault now?—I confess it to be a fault.—Where have you found my coat?—I have found it in the blue room.—Will you hang my hat on the tree?—I will hang it thereon (*appendervelo*).—How are you to-day?—I am not (*son isto*) very well.—What is the matter with you?—I have a violent headache and a cold (*una infreddatura di testa*).—Where did you catch a cold?—I caught it last night in coming (*nell' uscire*) from the play.

FIFTY-SEVENTH LESSON.

Lezione cinquantesima settima.

OF THE PRESENT PARTICIPLE.

The present participle is in Italian formed from the infinitive by changing, for the first conjugation, *are* into *ando*, and for the two others *ere* and *ire* into *endo*.[1] Ex.

To speak, — speaking.	1. Parlare, — parlando.
To sell, — selling.	2. Vendere, — vendendo.
To serve, — serving.	3. Servire, — servendo.

To have, — having.	Avere, — avendo.
To be, — being.	Essere, — essendo.

Obs. A. This form of the verb is not so often used in Italian as in English, for whenever it is used in English after a preposition it is rendered in Italian by the infinitive. (See ☞ Lessons XL. and XLIV.) Moreover, it is often substituted by the infinitive with one of the prepositions *a*, *con*, *in*, *nel*, as: *col comprare*, in buying; *nel rendere*, in selling; *nel servire*, in serving. Ex.

In teaching one learns.	Coll' insegnare s' impara.
He was drowned in passing the river.	Egli si è annegato nel valicare il fiume.
In seeing him I judged that he was not satisfied.	Al vederlo argomentai che non era contento.
Having come too late he found no more room.	Per esser venuto tardi non trovò più posto.
To be drowned. To pass the river.	Annegarsi. Valicare il fiume.
To infer.	Argomentare (*argomentai* is its preterite definite).
Found.	Trovai (is the preterite definite of *trovare*).

---

[1] There is another present participle, which is also formed from the infinitive, and terminates for the first conjugation in *ante*, and for the two others in *ente*, as: *parlante*, speaking; *vendente*, selling; *servente*, serving. It is not much used in Italian, and in its stead the present or imperfect of the indicative is often employed.

300   FIFTY-SEVENTH LESSON.

I tremble only in thinking of it.	Tremo solamente in pensarvi.
I perceived it in reading the letter.	Me ne accorsi nel legger la lettera.
She gets a livelihood by spinning and weaving.	Ella si guadagna il vitto col filare e col tessere.
In going out of the church.	All' uscir dalla chiesa.

Obs. B. Yet the present participle is used when an agent performs two actions at the same time.

The man eats while running.	L' uomo mangia correndo.
I correct while reading.	Correggo leggendo.
I question while speaking.	Interrogo parlando.
You speak while answering me.	Ella parla rispondendomi.

Obs. C. The personal pronouns, the relative *ne*, and the local adverbs *ci* and *vi*, are joined to the present participle in the same manner as to the infinitive. (*Obs.* Lesson XVII.)

I read your exercises while correcting them.	Leggo i di Lei temi correggendoli.
I question you while speaking to you.	La interrogo parlandole.
You ride while fighting.	Ella cavalca battendosi.
He fights while retiring.	Egli si batte ritirandosi.
You speak while dancing.	Ella parla danzando.
I extemporate while eating.	Improvviso mangiando.
He walks while reading.	Passeggia leggendo.

Obs. D. When a certain continuation or succession of time is to be expressed, the present participle is made use of with the verbs *andare*, *mandare*, *stare*, *venire*. Ex.

I am writing.	Io sto scrivendo.
Thou art reading.	Tu vai (or stai) leggendo.
He is telling me.	Egli vien raccontandomi.
He is telling me his misfortunes.	Egli sta raccontandomi le sue sventure [3].
I am gathering flowers in my garden.	Vo cogliendo fiori nel mio giardino [3].
He was crying all day and all night.	Andò gridando [4] tutto il giorno e tutta la notte.
I was thinking of the things that had just happened.	Io andava pensando alle cose accadute [5].
Her grief is consuming her by degrees.	Il suo dolore la va struggendo lentamente [6].

[3] *Raccontare*, to tell, to relate; *la sventura*, the misfortune.
[3] *Cogliere fiori*, to gather flowers; *il fiore*, the flower.
[4] *Andò* is the third person singular of the preterite definite of the verb *andare*, to go: *gridare*, to cry.
[5] *Andava* is the first person singular of the imperfect indicative of the verb *andare*; *accadute* is the past participle in the plural feminine of the verb *accadere*, to happen.
[6] *Struggendo* is the present participle of *struggere*, to consume, to kill, to destroy.

FIFTY-SEVENTH LESSON. 301

They were descending slowly the hill.	Venivano scendendo lentamente il colle.⁷
I am beginning to perceive that I was mistaken.	Vado vedendo che mi sono ingannato.
What I am doing now, thou wilt know when it is time.	Quello che ora sto facendo, lo saprai a suo tempo.
They were conversing together for an hour, when....	Se la stavano discorrendo insieme da un' ora, quando.....⁸

You are thinking.	Voi state pensando.
I was perceiving.	Io andava accorgendomi.
He is saying.	Egli va dicendo.⁹
What were you doing when I arrived?	Che andavate (or stavate) facendo, quando son giunto.¹⁰
I was dining.	Io pranzava (Io stava pranzando).

To question.	*Interrogare* 1.
The cravat.	La cravatta.
The carriage.	La carrozza.
The family.	La famiglia.
The promise.	La promessa.
The leg.	La gamba.
The sore throat.	Il mal di gola.
The throat.	La gola.
I have a sore throat.	Mi fa mal la gola, or ho mal di gola.
The meat.	La carne.
Salt meat.	Carne salata.
Fresh meat.	Carne fresca.
Fresh beef.	Manzo fresco.
Cool water.	Acqua fresca.
The food (victuals).	L' alimento.
The dish (mess).	La vivanda, il cibo.
Salt meats.	Vivande salate.
Milk-food.	{ Il latticinio / Un latticinio } *Plur.* Dei latticinii.

The traveller.	Il viaggiatore; *fem.* la viaggiatrice.
To march, to walk, to step.	*Camminare* 1.
I have walked a good deal to-day.	Ho camminato molto oggi.

⁷ *Venivano* is the third person plural of the imperfect indicative of *venire*.
⁸ *Discorrere*, to converse.
⁹ *Dicendo* is the present participle of *dire*, to say.
¹⁰ *Andavate* is the second person plural of the imperfect indicative of *andare*, and *stavate* is the same of *stare*. *Giunto* is the past participle of *giungere*, to arrive.

FIFTY-SEVENTH LESSON.

Obs. E. Camminare must not be mistaken for passeggiare. The former means to walk, and the latter to walk for pleasure. (Lesson XLIV.)

I have been walking in the garden with my mother.	Ho passeggiato nel giardino con mia madre.
To walk or travel a mile — two miles.	† Far un miglio — due miglia.
To walk or travel a league — two leagues.	† Far una lega — due leghe.
To walk a step.	† Far un passo.
To take a step.	† Far un passo (presso di).
To go on a journey.	† Far un viaggio.
To make a speech.	Far un discorso.
A piece of business, an affair.	Un affare; plur. i: una faccenda.
To transact business.	Far degli affari.

To meddle with something.	*Mischiarsi di qualche cosa.* *Immischiarsi di qualche cosa.*
What are you meddling with?	Di che si mischia Ella?
I am meddling with my own business.	Mi mischio de' miei propri affari.
That man always meddles with other people's business.	Quest' uomo s' immischia sempre negli affari degli altri.
I do not meddle with other people's business.	Non m' immischio negli affari altrui.
Others, other people.	*Altrui.*

He employs himself in painting.	Si occupa di pittura.
The art of painting.	La pittura.
Chemistry.	La chimica.
The chemist.	Il chimico.
The art.	L' arte.
Strange.	Strano.
Surprising.	Sorprendente.
It is strange.	E strano.
To employ one's self in.	† *Occuparsi di qualche cosa.*
To concern some one.	*Concernere, riguardare qualcuno.*
To look at some one.	*Riguardare qualcuno.*
I do not like to meddle with things that do not concern me.	Non mi piace immischiarmi di ciò che non mi concerne.
That concerns nobody.	Ciò non riguarda nessuno.
To concern one's self about something. *To trouble one's head about something.*	*Curarsi di qualche cosa,* or *Prendersi cura di qualche cosa.*

FIFTY-SEVENTH LESSON.

To attract.	Attrarre * 2 Attraere * 2 } p. part attratto. Attirare 1, " attirato.
I attract, thou attractest, he attracts.	Attraggo, attrai, attrae.
We, you, they attract.	Attraiamo, attraete, attraggono.
Loadstone attracts iron.	La calamita attrae (attira) il ferro.
Her singing attracts me.	Il suo canto m' attrae.
To charm.	Incantare.
To enchant.	Dilettare.
I am charmed with it.	Ne sono felice, ne sono incantato.
The beauty.	La bellezza.
The harmony.	L' armonia.
The voice.	La voce.
The power.	La potenza, il potere.

To repeat.	Ripetere 2.
The repetition.	La ripetizione.
The commencement, beginning.	Il principio.
The wisdom.	La savìezza.
Study.	Lo studio.
The lord.	Il signore.
A good memory.	Una buona memoria.
A memorandum.	Un memoriale, un promemoria, una memoria.
The nightingale.	Il rosignuolo, l' usignuolo.
All beginnings are difficult.	Tutti i principii sono difficili.

To create.	Creare 1.
Creation.	La creazione.
The Creator.	Il Creatore.
The benefit, the benefactor.	Il benefizio, il benefattore; fem. trice.
The fear of the Lord.	Il timore di Dio.
Heaven.	Il cielo.
The earth.	La terra.
The solitude.	La solitudine.
The lesson.	La lezione.
The goodness.	La bontà.
Flour, meal.	La farina.
The mill.	Il molino.

Obs. F. We have seen (Lesson XLIV.) that all reflective verbs are, in Italian as well as in French, conjugated with the auxiliary *essere*, to be, in their compound tenses. There are besides some other verbs, which, in Italian, are likewise compounded with the auxiliary *essere*, to be, though they are not

FIFTY-SEVENTH LESSON.

reflective, and generally take *to have* for their auxiliary in English. The principal are the following:

To go.	Andare* 1.
To stop.	Arrestarsi 1, fermarsi 1.
To arrive.	Arrivare 1.
To decay.	Decadere* 2.
To die.	Morire* 3, trapassare 1.
To come in.	Entrare 1.
To be born.	Nascere* 2.
To set out.	Partire 3.
To go out.	Uscire* 3.
To fall.	Cadere* 2.
To come.	Venire* 3.
To become.	Divenire* 3. / Diventare 1.
To disagree.	Non convenire* 3.
To intervene.	Intervenire* 3.
To attain.	Pervenire* 3
To come back.	Ritornare 1, rinvenire* 3.
To happen.	Sopraggiugnere* 2.

Has your mother come? | È venuta la di Lei madre?

☞ The past participle of these verbs must agree in gender and number with the nominative of the verb *essere*, to be.

She has not come yet. | Non è ancor venuta.
Have the women already come? | Sono già arrivate le donne?
They have not come yet. | Non sono ancor arrivate.
Has your sister arrived? | È arrivata la di Lei sorella?

EXERCISES.

177.

Will you dine with us to-day?—With much pleasure.—What have you for dinner (*che ha Ella da pranzo*)?—We have good soup, some fresh and salt meat, and some milk food.—Do you like milk food?—I like it better than (*Li preferisco a*) all other food.—Are you ready to dine?—I am ready.—Do you intend to set out soon?—I intend setting out next week.—Do you travel alone (*sola*)?—No, Madam, I travel with my uncle.—Do you travel on foot or in a carriage?—We travel in a carriage.—Did you meet any one in your last journey (*nel di Lei ultimo viaggio*) to Berlin?—We met many travellers.—What do you intend to spend your time in this summer?—I intend to take a short (*piccolo*) journey.—Did you walk much in your last journey?—I like much to walk, but my uncle likes to go in a carriage.—Did he not wish to walk?—He wished to walk at first (*da principio*), but he wished to get into the coach after having taken a few steps (*poi fatti appena alcuni passi volle montar in legno*), so that I did not walk much.—What have you been doing at school to-day?—We have been listening to our professor.—What did he say?—He made a long speech on the goodness of God. After saying: "Repetition is the mother of studies, and a good memory is a great benefit of God," he said (*egli disse*), "God is the creator of heaven and earth; the fear of the Lord is the beginning of all wisdom."—What are you doing all day in this garden?—I am walking in it.—What is there in it that attracts you (*che mai L' attira colà*)?—The singing of the birds attracts me (*mi vi attrae*).—Are there nightingales in it?—There are some in it, and the harmony of their singing enchants me (*mi rapisce*).—Have those nightingales (*forse gli usignuoli hanno*) more power over you (*sopra di Lei*) than painting, or the voice of your tender (*tenero*) mother, who loves you so much?—I confess the harmony of the singing of those little birds (*di questi augellini*) has more power over me than the most tender words of my dearest friends.

178.

What does your niece amuse herself with in her solitude?—She reads a good deal, and writes letters to her mother.—What does your uncle amuse himself with in his solitude?—He employs himself in painting and chemistry.—Does he no longer do any business?—He no longer does any, for he is too old to do any.—Why does he meddle with your business?—He does not generally (*ordinariamente*) meddle with other people's business, but he meddles with mine, because he loves me.—Has your master made you repeat your lesson to-day?—He has made me repeat it.—Did you know it?—I knew it pretty well (*discretamente*).—Have you also done some exercises?—I have done some, but, pray, what is that to you (*ma che Le fa questo, ne La prego*)?—I do not generally meddle with things that do not concern me, but I love you so much that I concern myself much about (*che io m' interesso molto a*) what you are doing.—Does any one trouble his head (*havvi alcuno che si cora*) about you?—No one troubles his head about me, for I am not worth the trouble (*non ne valgo la pena*).—Who corrects your exercises?—My master corrects them.—How (*come*) does he correct them?—He corrects them in reading them; and in reading them he speaks to me.—How many things (*quante cose*) does your master at the same time (*in una volta*)?—He does four things at the same time.—How so (*come ciò*)?—He reads and corrects my exercises, speaks to me and questions me all at once (*al tempo stesso*).—Does your sister sing (*cantare*) while dancing?—She sings while working, but she cannot sing while dancing.—Has your mother left?—She has not left yet.—When will she set out?—She will set out to-morrow evening.—At what o'clock?—At a quarter to seven.—Have your sisters arrived?—They have not arrived yet, but we expect them this evening.—Will they spend (*passare*) the evening with us?—They will spend it with us, for they have promised me to do so.—Where have you spent the morning?—I have spent it in the country.—Do you go every morning to the country?—I do not go every morning, but twice a week.—Why has your niece not called upon me (*venir a vedere qualcuno*)?—She is very ill, and has spent the whole day in her room.

FIFTY-EIGHTH LESSON.

Lezione cinquantesima ottava.

OF THE PAST FUTURE.

The past or compound future is formed from the future of the auxiliary, and the past participle of the verb you conjugate. Ex.

I shall have loved.	Avrò amato.
Thou wilt have loved.	Avrai amato.

FIFTY-EIGHTH LESSON.

He will have loved.	Egli avrà amato.
She will have loved.	Ella avrà amato.
We shall have loved.	Avremo amato.
You will have loved.	Avrete amato.
They will have loved.	{ *Mas.* Eglino } avranno amato. { *Fem.* Elleno }

I shall have come.	Sarò venuto. *Fem.* venuta.
Thou wilt have come.	Sarai venuto. " venuta.
He will have come.	Sarà venuto.
She will have come.	Sarà venuta.
We shall have come.	Saremo venuti. *Fem.* venute.
You will have come.	Sarete venuti. " venute.
They will have come.	{ Saranno venuti. { Saranno venute.

I shall have been praised.	Sarò stato lodato. *Fem.* stata lodata.
Thou wilt have been praised.	Sarai stato lodato. " stata lodata.
He will have been praised.	Sarà stato lodato.
She will have been praised.	Sarà stata lodata.
We shall have been praised.	Saremo stati lodati. *Fem.* state lodate.
You will have been praised.	Sarete stati lodati. " state lodate.
They will have been praised.	{ Saranno stati lodati. { Saranno state lodate.

To have left.	† Rimanere * 2.
When I have paid for the horse I shall have only ten crowns left.	Quando avrò pagato il cavallo non mi rimarranno che dieci scudi.
How much money have you left?	Quanto danaro Le rimane?
I have one crown left.	Mi rimane uno scudo.
I have only one crown left.	{ Non mi rimane che uno scudo. { Mi rimane solamente uno scudo.
How much has your brother left?	Quanto rimane al di Lei fratello?
He has one crown left.	Gli rimane uno scudo.
How much has your sister left?	Quanto rimane alla di Lei sorella?
She has only three sous left.	Non le rimangono che tre soldi.
How much have your brothers left?	Quanto rimane ai di Lei fratelli?
They have one gold sequin left.	Rimane Loro uno zecchino d' oro.
When they have paid the tailor, they will have a hundred Italian livres left.	Quando avranno pagato il sartore, resteranno loro cento lire italiane.

FIFTY-EIGHTH LESSON.

Obs. In English the present, or the compound of the present, is used after the conjunctions: *when, as soon as*, or *after*, when futurity is to be expressed; but in Italian, as well as in French, the future must in such instances always be employed. Ex.

When I am at my aunt's, will you come to see me?	Quando sarò da mia zia, verrà Ella a vedermi?
After you have done writing, will you take a turn with me?	Quando avrà finito di scrivere, verrà Ella meco a far un passeggio? or una passeggiata.
You will play when you have finished your exercise.	Ella giuocherà quando avrà finito il di Lei tema (esercizio).
What will you do when you have dined?	Che farà Ella quando avrà pranzato?
When I have dined, I will take a turn with my sister in the garden of the marchioness.	Quando avrò pranzato, andrò a far una passeggiata con mia sorella nel giardino della marchesa.
When I have spoken to your brother, I shall know what I have to do.	Quando avrò parlato al di Lei fratello, saprò ciò che ho da fare.

Does it rain?	Piove?
It rains.	Piove.
Does it snow?	Nevica?
It snows.	Nevica.
Is it muddy?	† Vi è del fango? † V' è fango?
It is muddy.	† C' è del fango.
Is it muddy out of doors?	† C' è del fango in istrada?
It is very muddy.	† È cattivo andare.
Is it dusty?	V' ha della polvere?
It is very dusty.	Fa molta polvere. V' ha molta polvere.
Is it smoky?	V' è del fumo? V' è fumo?
It is too smoky.	V' è troppo fumo.
Out of doors.	Fuori. In istrada.

To enter, to go in, to come in.	*Entrare 1, in.*
Will you go into my room?	Vuol Ella entrar nella mia camera?
I will go in.	Voglio entrarvi.
Will you go in?	Vi entrerà Ella?
I shall go in.	Vi entrerò.

To sit down.	Sea dro*, mettersi a sedere (Lesson LI.).
To sit, to be seated.	*Essere seduto; fem. seduta.*
He is seated upon the large chair.	Egli è seduto sulla gran sedia.
She is seated upon the bench.	Essa è seduta sulla panca.
I sit down near you.	Seggo presso di Lei. Mi metto a sedere vicino a Lei.

FIFTY-EIGHTH LESSON. 309

To fill with.	Empire or riempire (isco) 3. Empiere or riempiere 2.
To fill the bottle with wine.	Riempire di vino la bottiglia.
Do you fill that bottle with water?	Riemple Ella d' acqua questa bottiglia?
I fill my purse with money.	Riempio di danaro la mia borsa.
He fills his belly with meat.	S' emple il ventre di carne (a vulgar expression).
The pocket.	La tasca.

Have you come quite alone?	È Ella venuta del tutto sola?
No, I have brought all my men along with me.	No, ho condotto meco tutta la mia gente.
He has brought all his men along with him.	Egli ha condotto seco tutta la sua gente.
Have you brought your brother along with you?	Ha Ella condotto seco il di Lei fratello? (or vostro.)
I have brought him along with me.	L' ho condotto meco.
Have you told the groom to bring me the horse?	Avete detto al palafreniere di condurmi il cavallo?
The groom.	Il palafreniere.
I have brought you a fine horse from Germany.	Le ho condotto d' Alemagna un bel cavallo.
Are you bringing me my books?	Mi porta Ella i miei libri?
I am bringing them to you.	Glieli porto.

To take, to carry.	Menare 1.
Will you take that dog to the stable?	Volete menare questo cane alla stalla?
I will take it thither.	Voglio menarvelo.
Are you carrying this gun to my father?	Porta Ella a mio padre questo schioppo?
I carry it to him.	Glielo porto.
The cane, stick.	La canna, or il bastone.
The stable.	La stalla.

To come down, to go down.	Scendere * 2—sceso. Discendere * 2; past part. disceso.
To go down into the well.	Discendere nel pozzo.
To go or come down the hill.	Scendere la montagna.
To go down the river.	Discendere il fiume.
To alight from one's horse, to dismount.	Smontare da cavallo (Lesson LII.).
To alight, to get out.	Scendere, or discendere dal legno.

FIFTY-EIGHTH LESSON.

To go up, to mount, to ascend.	Montare, salire *, ascendere *.
To go up the mountain.	Salire il monte, Salire il colle. Montare sulla collina.
Where is your brother gone to?	Ove è andato il di Lei fratello?
He has ascended the hill.	È montato sulla collina.
To mount the horse.	Montare a cavallo.
To get into the coach.	Montare in legno (in carrozza).
To get on board the ship.	Entrar nella nave. Ascendere il naviglio.

To desire, to beg, to pray, to request.	Pregare 1 (di before Inf.).
Will you desire your brother to come down?	Vuol Ella pregare il di Lei fratello di scendere?
I beg of you to call on me to-day.	La prego di venirmi a vedere oggi.
The beard.	La barba.
The river.	Il fiume, la riviera.
The stream, torrent.	Il torrente.
To go or come up the river.	Andar contro la corrente del fiume.
The stream.	La corrente.
To go or come down the river.	Discendere il fiume.

EXERCISES.

179.

Will your parents go to the country to-morrow?—They will not go, for it is too dusty.—Shall we take a walk to-day?—We will not take a walk, for it is too muddy out of doors (*perchè c'è troppo fango in istrada*, or *perchè le strade sono troppo fangose*).—Do you see the castle of my relation behind (*dietro*) yonder mountain (*quella montagna*)?—I see it.—Shall we go in?—We will go in if you like.—Will you go into that room?—I shall not go into it, for it is smoky.—I wish you a good morning, Madam.—Will you not come in?—Will you not sit down?—I will sit down upon that large chair.—Will you tell me what has become of your brother?—I will tell you.—Where is your sister?—Do you not see her?—She is sitting upon the bench.—Is your father seated upon the bench?—No, he sits upon the chair.—Hast thou spent all thy money?—I have not spent all.—How much hast thou left ?—I have not much left. I have but five Italian livres (*la lira italiana*) left.—How much money have thy sisters left ?—They have but three crowns left.—Have you money enough left to pay your tailor ?—I have enough left to pay him; but if I pay him I shall have but little left.—How much money will your brothers have left ?—They will have a hundred sequins left.—When shall you go to Italy ?—I shall go as soon as (*subito che*) I have learnt Italian.—When will your brothers go to France ?—They will go thither as soon as they know French ?—When will they learn it ?—They will learn it when they have found a good master.—How much money shall we have left when we have paid for our horses ?—When we have paid for them we shall have only a hundred crowns left.

180.

Do you gain (*guadagnare*) any thing by (*in*) that business ?—I do not gain much by it (*gran che*), but my brother gains a good deal by it. He fills his purse with money.—How much money have you gained ?—I have gained only a little, but my cousin has gained much by it. He has filled his pocket with money.—Why does not that man work ?—He is a good-for-nothing fellow (*disutilaccio*), for he does nothing but eat all the day long. He continually fills (*si riempie mai sempre*) his belly with meat, so that he will make himself (*diverrà*) ill, if he continues (*continuare*) to eat so much.—With what have you filled that bottle ? —I have filled it with wine.—Will this man take care of my horse ?—He will take care of it.—Who will take care of my servant ?—The landlord will take care of him, for he will give him to eat and to drink; he will also give him a good bed to sleep in (*per coricarsi*).—Does your servant take care of your horses ?—He takes care of them.—Is he taking care of your clothes ?—He is taking care of them, for he brushes them every morning.—Have you ever drunk French wine ?—I have never drunk any. —Is it long since you ate Italian bread ?—It is almost three years since I ate any.—Have you hurt my brother-in-law ?—I have not hurt him, but he has cut my finger.—What has he cut your finger with ?—With the knife which you have lent him.

181.

Is your father arrived at last?—Every body says that he is arrived, but I have not seen him yet.—Has the physician hurt your son?—He has hurt him, for he has cut his finger.—Have they cut off (*tagliare*) that man's leg?—They have cut it off.—Are you pleased (*soddisfatto*) with your servant?—I am much pleased with him, for he is fit for any thing (*buono a tutto*).—What does he know?—He knows every thing (*tutto*).—Can he ride (*andar a cavallo*)?—He can.—Has your brother returned at last from England?—He has returned thence, and has brought you a fine horse.—Has he told his groom to bring it to me (*di condurmelo quà*)?—He has told him to bring it you.—What do you think (*che dice Ella*) of that horse?—I think (*dico*) that it is a fine and good one (*ch' è bello e buono*), and beg you to lead it into the stable (*in istalla*).—In what did you spend your time yesterday?—I went to the concert, and afterwards (*e poi*) to the play.—When did that man go down into the well?—He went down this morning.—Has he come up again yet (*già risalito*)?—He came up an hour ago.—Where is your brother?—He is in his room.—Will you tell him to come down?—I will tell him so, but he is not dressed yet.—Is your friend still on the mountain?—He has already come down.—Did you go up or down the river?—We went down it.—Did my cousin speak to you before he started?—He spoke to me before he got into the coach.—Have you seen my brother?—I saw him before I went on board the ship.—Is it better to get into a coach than to go on board the ship (*o salir la nave*)?—It is not worth while to get into a coach, or to go on board the ship, when one has no wish to travel.

FIFTY-NINTH LESSON.

Lezione cinquantesima nona.

OF THE IMPERFECT.
(*Imperfetto.*)

The imperfect of the indicative is formed in all Italian verbs by changing the termination *re* of the infinitive into *va*.[1] Ex.

Infinitives.		Imperfects.		
To speak—I spoke, &c.	1. Parlare.	Parlava,	parlavi,	parlava.
		Parlavamo,	parlavate,	parlavano.
To believe—I believed, &c.	2. Credere.	Credeva,	credevi,	credeva.
		Credevamo,	credevate,	credevano.
To hear—I heard, &c.	3. Sentire.	Sentiva,	sentivi,	sentiva.
		Sentivamo,	sentivate,	sentivano.
To have—I had, &c.	2. Avere.	Aveva,	avevi,	aveva.
		Avevamo,	avevate,	avevano.

Obs. A. There is but one exception to this rule; it is the verb *essere*, to be:

To be—I was, &c.	Essere.	Era,	eri,	era.
		Eravamo,	eravate,	erano.

Obs. B. The imperfect is a past tense, which was still present at the time spoken of, and may always be recognised by using the two terms, "WAS DOING," or "USED TO DO." Ex.

When I was at Berlino, I often went to see my friends.	Quando io era a Berlino, andava spesso a vedere i miei amici.
When you were in Paris, you often went to the Champs-Elysées.	Quando Ella era (voi eravate) in Parigi, Ella andava (voi andavate) spesso ai Campi Elisi.
Rome was at first governed by kings.	Roma era da principio governata dai re.
Cæsar was a great man.	Cesare era un grand' uomo.
Cicero was a great orator.	Cicerone era un grand oratore.
Our ancestors went a hunting every day.	I nostri antenati andavano tutti i giorni a caccia.

---

[1] The termination of the first person of the imperfect indicative in *a* has grown obsolete. Besides, the best authors, and the Academy della Crusca, have rejected it, as being contrary to its Latin origin: *eram, amabam, legebam, audiebam*, &c.

The Romans cultivated the arts and sciences, and rewarded merit.	I Romani coltivavano le arti e le scienze, e ricompensavano il merito.
Were you walking?	Passeggiava Ella (passeggiavate voi)?
I was not walking.	Non passeggiava.
Were you in Paris when the king was there?	Era Ella (eravate voi) a Parigi quando vi era il re?
I was there when he was there.	V' era quando v' era lui.
Where were you when I was in London?	Ove era (eravate voi) quando io era a Londra?
At what time did you breakfast when you were in Germany?	Quando faceva Ella (facevate voi) colazione allorchè Ella era (eravate) in Alemagna?
I breakfasted when my father breakfasted.	Faceva colazione quando la faceva mio padre.
Did you work when he was working?	Lavorava Ella (lavoravate voi) quando lavorava lui?
I studied when he was working.	Io studiava quando egli lavorava.
Some fish.	Del pesce.
Some game.	Della cacciagione.
To live.	Dimorare 1.
When I lived at my father's, I rose earlier than I do now.	Quando io dimorava da mio padre, mi alzava più presto che noi¹ faccio adesso.
When we lived in that country we went a fishing often.	Quando stavamo (dimoravamo) in quel paese, andavamo spesso a pesca.
When I was ill, I kept in bed all day.	Quando era malato, stava a letto tutto il giorno.
Last summer, when I was in the country, there was a great deal of fruit.	L' estate (or nell' estate) scorsa, essendo io alla campagna, v' era gran copia di frutti.

A thing.	Una cosa.
The same thing.	La medesima cosa (la stessa cosa).
The same man.	Il medesimo uomo (lo stesso uomo).
It is all one (the same).	{ ¹ E lo stesso. { E tutt' uno.

Such.	Tale, simile.
Such a man.	Un tal uomo.
Such men.	Tali uomini.
Such a woman.	Una tal donna.
Such things.	Tali cose.
Such men merit esteem.	Tali uomini meritano della stima.

---

* Nol is a contraction of non lo.

FIFTY-NINTH LESSON.   315

Out of.	*Fuori di.*
Out of the city (the town).	Fuori della città.
Without, or out doors.	Fuori.
The church stands outside the town.	La chiesa è fuori della città.
I shall wait for you before the town gate.	L'aspetterò innanzi alla porta della città.
The town or city gate.	La porta della città.
The barrier, the turnpike.	La barriera, la porta, il dazio.
Seldom (rarely).	Raramente, or di rado.
Some brandy.	Dell' acquavite.
The life, the livelihood.	La vita, il vitto.
To get one's livelihood—by.	*Guadagnarsi il vitto (il pane) —col.*
I get my livelihood by working.	Mi guadagno il vitto lavorando.
He gets his living by writing.	Egli si guadagna il vitto collo scrivere.
I gain my money by working.	Guadagno il mio danaro col lavorare.
By what does that man get his livelihood?	Con che si guadagna quest' uomo il vitto?
To continue, to proceed, to go on.	*Continuare 1, proseguire 3, seguitare 1.*
I continue to write.	Continuo a scrivere.
He continues his speech.	Egli continua il suo discorso.
A good appetite.	Un buon appetito.
The narrative, the tale.	Il racconto, la novella.
The edge, the border, the shore.	La riva.
The edge of the brook.	La riva del ruscello.
The sea-shore.	La spiaggia del mare.
On the sea-shore.	Sulla spiaggia del mare.
The shore, the water-side, the coast, the bank.	La ripa, il lido, la sponda, l' argine.
People or folks.	La gente.
They are good people.	Sono buona gente.
They are wicked people.	Sono cattiva gente.

EXERCISES.

182.

Were you loved when you were at Dresden (*Dresda*)?—I was not hated.—Was your brother esteemed when he was in London?

—He was loved and esteemed.—When were you in Spain (*in Ispagna*)?—I was there when you were there.—Who was loved and who was hated?—Those that were good, assiduous, and obedient, were loved, and those who were naughty, idle, and disobedient, were punished, hated, and despised.—Were you in Berlin when the king was there?—I was there when he was there.—Was your uncle in London when I was there?—He was there when you were there.—Where were you when I was at Dresden?—I was in Paris.—Where was your father when you were in Vienna?—He was in England.—At what o'clock did you breakfast when you were in England?—I breakfasted when my uncle breakfasted.—Did you work when he was working?—I studied when he was working.—Did your brother work when you were working?—He played when I was working.—On what (*di che*) lived our ancestors?—They lived on nothing but fish and game, for they went a hunting and a fishing every day.—What sort of people were the Romans?—They were very good people, for they cultivated the arts and sciences, and rewarded merit.—Did you often go to see your friends when you were at Berlin?—I went to see them often.—Did you sometimes go to the Champs-Elysées when you were at Paris?—I often went thither.

183.

What did you do when you lived in that country?—When we lived there we often went a hunting.—Did you not go out a walking (*passeggiare*)?—I went out a walking sometimes.—Do you rise early?—Not so early as you; but when I lived at my uncle's I rose earlier than I do now.—Did you sometimes keep in bed when you stayed at your uncle's?—When I was ill I kept in bed all day.—Is there much fruit (*Avvi gran copia di frutti*) this year?—I do not know, but last summer (*nella scorsa estate*), when I was in the country, there was a great deal of fruit.—What do you get your livelihood by?—I get my livelihood by working.—Does your friend get his livelihood by writing?—He gets it by speaking and writing.—Do these gentlemen get their livelihood by working?—They get it by doing nothing (*facendo niente*), for they are too idle to work.—By what has your friend gained that money ?—He has gained it by working.—By what did you get your livelihood when you were in England ?—I got it by writing. —Did your cousin get his livelihood by writing ?—He got it by working.—Have you ever seen such a person ?—I have never seen such a one (*una simile*).—Have you already seen our church ? —I have not seen it yet.—Where does it stand (*essere*) ?—It stands outside the town.—If you wish to see it, I will go with you in order to show it you.—Upon what do the people live that inhabit the sea-shore ?—They live on fish alone.—Why will you not go a hunting any more ?—I hunted yesterday the whole day, and I killed nothing but an ugly bird, so that I shall not go a hunting any more.—Why do you not eat ?—Because I have not a good appetite.—Why does your brother eat so much ?—Because he has a good appetite.

184.

Whom are you looking for ?—I am looking for my little brother.—If you wish to find him you must go (*bisogna andar*) into the garden, for he is there.—The garden is large, and I shall not be able to find him, if you do not tell me in which part (*in qual parte*) of the garden he is (*sia*, subj.)—He is sitting under the large tree under which we were sitting yesterday.—Now I shall find him.—Why did you not bring me my clothes ?—They were not made, so that I could not bring them, but I bring them you now.—You have learnt your lesson : why has not your sister learnt hers ?—She has taken a walk with my mother, so that she could not learn it, but she will learn it to-morrow.—When will you correct my exercises ?—I will correct them when you bring me (*mi porter*, future) those of your sister.—Do you think you have made faults in them ?—I do not know.—If you have made faults you have not studied your lessons well ; for the lessons must be learnt well (*bisogna imparar bene*) to make no faults in the exercises.—It is all the same : if you do not correct them today, I shall not learn them before to-morrow (*non li imparerò se non domani*).—You must not (*Ella non deve*) make any faults in your exercises, for you have all that is necessary to prevent you from making any.

SIXTIETH LESSON.

Lezione sessantesima.

OF THE PRETERITE DEFINITE.

(*Passato remoto.*)

This past tense is formed from the infinitive by changing the terminations *are, ere, ire,* into *ai, ei, ii.* Ex.

		Preterite Definites.		
To speak—I spoke, &c.	1. Parlare.	Parlai,	parlasti,	parlò.
		Parlammo,	parlaste,	parlarono.
To believe—I believed, &c.	2. Credere.	Credei,	credesti,	credè
		Credemmo,	credeste,	crederono.[1]
To hear—I heard, &c.	3. Sentire.	Sentii,	sentisti,	sentì.
		Sentimmo,	sentiste,	sentirono.

Obs. A. The third person singular of the preterite definite has in the regular verbs always the grave accent (`).

To have—I had, &c.	Avere*.	Ebbi,	avesti,	ebbe.
		Avemmo,	aveste,	ebbero.
To be—I was, &c.	Essere*.	Fui,	fosti,	fu.
		Fummo,	foste,	furono.

Obs. B. The irregularity of an Italian verb almost always falls on the preterite definite. This is irregular only in the first and third persons singular, and

---

[1] Almost all the verbs of the second conjugation have a double form for the first and third persons singular, and third person plural, and instead of *ei, è, erono,* they end in *etti, ette, ettero,* as: *credere,* to believe.

    Credei, *or* credetti,
    Credesti,
    Credè *or* credette;
    Credemmo,
    Credeste,
    Crederono, *or* credettero.

Practice alone can teach which form is to be preferred. We have, however, ascertained that when the verb ends in *tere* the preference is to be given to the first form, as:

    Potere, to be able (can) — potei, I was able.
    Battere, to beat   " — battei, I did beat.
    Esistere, to exist   " — esistei, I existed, &c.

SIXTIETH LESSON. 319

the third person plural, which almost invariably end the first person singular in *i*, the third person singular in *e*, and the third person plural in *ero*. Ex.

To please—pleased (past part.).	Piacere—piaciuto.
	Preterite Definite
I pleased, &c.	Piacqui, piacesti, piacque.
	Piacemmo, piaceste, piacquero.[a]
To know—known.	Conoscere—conosciuto.
I knew, &c.	Conobbi, conoscesti, conobbe.
	Conoscemmo, conosceste, conobbero.
To hold—held.	Tenere—tenuto.
I held, &c.	Tenni, tenesti, tenne.
	Tenemmo, teneste, tennero.
To wish—wished.	Volere—voluto.
I wished, &c.	Volli, volesti, volle.
	Volemmo, voleste, vollero.[b]
To read—read.	Leggere—letto.
I read, &c.	Lessi, leggesti, lesse.
	Leggemmo, leggeste, lessero.[c]
To take—took.	Prendere—preso.
I took, &c.	Presi, prendesti, prese.
	Prendemmo, prendeste, presero.[d]

[a] All verbs having *c* before the termination *ere* of the infinitive are conjugated in the same manner, as: *nascere*, to be born; *tacere*, to be silent; *giacere*, to lie, to be situate; *nuocere*, to hurt; except *cuocere*, to cook, bake; and *conoscere*, to know; which have in the pret. def. *cossi* and *conobbi*.

[b] The principal verbs which, besides the above three, double in the preterite definite the consonant in the first and third persons singular and third person plural are: *avere*, to have; *ebbi*, I had: *rompere*, to break; *ruppi*, I broke: *cadere*, to fall; *caddi*, I fell: *sapere*, to know; *seppi*, I knew; *piovere*, to rain; *piovve*, it rained.

[c] All verbs whose first person singular of the indicative terminates in *ggo*, *co*, *vo*, *primo*, *cuoto*, have their preterite definite terminated in *ssi*, as: *Dico*, I say; *dissi*, I said: *scrivo*, I write; *scrissi*, I wrote: *esprimo*, I express; *espressi*, I expressed: *scuoto*, I shake; *scossi*, I shook: *percuoto*, I strike; *percossi*, I struck.

[d] All verbs whose first person singular of the indicative ends in *do* have their preterite definite either in *si*, *esi*, *isi*, *osi*, or *usi*, according to the letters that precede this termination, as: *persuado*, I persuade; *persuasi*, I persuaded;

SIXTIETH LESSON.

To choose—chosen.	Scegliere—scelto.
I chose, &c.	Scelsi, scegliesti, scelse.
	Scegliemmo, sceglieste, scelsero.*

Obs. C. The learner has only to make himself acquainted with the irregularity of the first person singular of this tense; this once known, all the others are. For, in addition to the first person singular, the irregular persons of this tense are the third person singular and third person plural, all the other persons are always regular. The first person singular, therefore, ending in *i*, the third person singular changes *i* into *e*, and the third person plural into *ero*, as may be seen from the above examples. This rule holds good throughout the Italian language. All the other rules that can be given on the formation of this tense in irregular verbs are contained in the above five notes.

ON THE USE OF THE PRETERITE DEFINITE.

This tense is so called, because it always expresses an action completed at a time specified, either by an adverb or some other circumstance. Ex.

I had done reading *when he entered*.	Aveva finito di leggere, *quando egli entrò*.
You had lost your purse, *when I found mine*.	Ella aveva (voi avevate) perduto la di Lei (la vostra) borsa, *quando trovai la mia*.

Obs. D. These examples show that the pluperfect is formed in Italian, as in English, with the imperfect of the auxiliary, and the past participle of the verb you conjugate.

We had dined, when he arrived.	Avevamo pranzato, quando egli arrivò (or giunse).
The king had named an admiral, when he heard of you.	Il re aveva fatto un ammiraglio, quando gli si parlò di Lei (or quando gli parlarono di Lei).
After having spoken, you *went away*.	Dopo aver parlato, Ella se ne andò.
After shaving, I *washed* my face.	Dopo essermi sbarbato, mi lavai la faccia.
After having warmed themselves, *they went* into the garden.	Dopo essersi scaldati, andarono in giardino.

---

chiedo, I ask; *chiesi*, I asked: *rodo*, I gnaw; *rosi*, I gnawed: *chiudo*, I shut; *chiusi*, I did shut: *fondo*, I melt; *fusi*, I melted.

* Verbs whose termination *o* of the first person singular indicative is preceded by a consonant, which in its turn is preceded by one of the liquids *l, n, r,* with which they form the syllables *lgo, nco, rdo,* have their preterite definite in *lsi, nsi,* or *rsi,* as : *vinco,* I vanquish; *vinsi,* I vanquished: *mordo,* I bite; *morsi,* I bit, &c.

SIXTIETH LESSON. 321

As soon as the bell rang, you awoke.	Tosto che la campana suonò, Ella si risvegliò (voi vi risvegliaste).
As soon as they called me, I got up.	Tosto che mi chiamarono, mi levai.
As soon as he was ready, he came to see me.	Tosto che fu pronto, venne a vedermi.
As soon as we had our money, we agreed to that.	Tosto che noi avemmo il nostro danaro, convenimmo di ciò.
As soon as he had his horse, he came to show it me.	Tosto che ebbe il suo cavallo, venne a mostrarmelo.
After having tried several times, they succeeded in doing it.	Dopo aver provato parecchie volte, pervennero a farlo.
As soon as I saw him, I obtained what I wanted.	Tosto che lo vidi, ottenni ciò di cui aveva bisogno.
As soon as I spoke to him, he did what I told him.	Tosto che gli parlai, fece ciò che gli dissi.
The business was soon over.	L'affare fu ben tosto fatto.

OF THE PRETERITE ANTERIOR.

(Passato anteriore.)

This tense is compounded of the preterite definitive of the auxiliary, and the past participle of the verb you conjugate. It is used (from its name *anteriore*, anterior,) to express an action past before another which is likewise past, and is hardly ever used except after one of the conjunctions:

As soon as.	Tosto che. / Subito che.
After.	Dopo che.
When.	Allorchè. / Quando.
No sooner.	Non tosto.
Scarcely.	Appena.

It also expresses an action as quickly done.

EXAMPLES.

As soon as I had finished my work, I carried it to him.	Tosto che ebbi finito il mio lavoro, glielo portai.
As soon as I had dressed myself, I went out.	Tosto che mi fui vestito, uscii.
When they had done playing, they began singing.	Quand' ebbero finito di giuocare, si misero a cantare.
When I had dined, it struck twelve.	Quando ebbi pranzato, suonò mezzodì.
As soon as the guests were assembled, the repast commenced.	Tosto che i convitati si furono radunati, il banchetto cominciò.

14*

SIXTIETH LESSON.

I had soon done eating.	Ebbi ben presto finito di mangiare.
After the soldiers had pillaged the town, they slaughtered without pity the women and children.	Dopo che i soldati ebbero saccheggiata la città, trucidarono spietatamente le donne e i fanciulli.
Scarcely had we arrived, when we were conducted to the king.	Appena fummo giunti, che ci si condusse (or che ci condussero) dal re.
He had no sooner perceived us, than he advanced towards us.	Non tosto egli ci ebbe scorti, che si avanzò verso noi.
When he had done reading, he exclaimed.	Quand' ebbe finito di leggere, esclamò.
When he had well understood, he left.	Quand' ebbe capito bene, partì.

To die (to lose life).

Morire; past part. morto.

I die, thou diest, he or she dies.
We, you, they die.

Muoio, muori, muore.
Moriamo, morite, muoiono.

Preterite definite.

I died, &c.

{ Morii, moristi, morì.
{ Morimmo, moriste, morirono.

Shall or will you die?
I shall die.
The man died this morning, and his wife died also.
The man is dead.
The woman died this morning.

Morrà Ella (morrete voi)?
Morrò.
L' uomo è morto questa mattina e sua moglie pure è morta.
L' uomo è morto.
La donna è morta questa mane.

To kill.

Uccidere*; past part. ucciso.

Preterite definite.

I killed, &c.

{ Uccisi, uccidesti, uccise.
{ Uccidemmo, uccideste, uccisero.

To tell, to relate.

Raccontare 1.

The spectacles.
The optician.
The accident.

Gli occhiali.
L' ottico.
L' accidente.

To write.

Scrivere 2—scritto.

Preterite definite.

I wrote, &c.

{ Scrissi, scrivesti, scrisse.
{ Scrivemmo, scriveste, scrissero.

EXERCISES.
185.

What did you do when you had finished your letter?—I went to my brother, who took me to the theatre, where I had the pleasure to find one of my friends whom I had not seen for ten years (*da dieci anni*).—What didst thou do after getting up this morning?—When I had read the letter of the Polish (*polacco*) count, I went to see (*uscii per vedere*) the theatre of the prince, which I had not seen before (*non—ancora*).—What did your father do when he had breakfasted?—He shaved and went out.—What did your friend do after he had been a walking?—He went to the baron (*il barone*).—Did the baron cut the meat after he had cut the bread?—He cut the bread after he had cut the meat.—When do you set out?—I do not set out till (*non parto che*) to-morrow; for before I leave I will once more see my good friends.—What did your children do when they had breakfasted?—They went a walking with their dear preceptor (*precettore*).—Where did your uncle go to after he had warmed himself?—He went nowhere. After he had warmed himself, he undressed and went to bed.—At what o'clock did he get up?—He got up at sunrise.—Did you wake him?—I had no need to wake him, for he had got up before me.—What did your cousin do when he heard of (*quando apprese*) the death (*la morte*) of his best friend?—He was much afflicted, and went to bed without saying a word (*senza dir motto*).—Did you shave before you breakfasted?—I shaved when I had breakfasted.—Did you go to bed when you had eaten supper?—When I had eaten supper I wrote my letters, and when I had written them I went to bed.—At what (*di che*) are you distressed (*afflitta*)? —I am distressed at that accident.—Are you afflicted at the death (*della morte*) of your relation?—I am much afflicted at it (*ne*).—When did your relation die?—He died last month.—Of whom do you complain?—I complain of your boy.—Why do you complain of him?—Because he has killed the pretty dog (*il cagnolino*) which I received from one of my friends.—Of what has your uncle complained?—He has complained of what you have done.—Has he complained of the letter which I wrote to him the day before yesterday?—He has complained of it.

166.

Why did you not stay longer in Holland?—When I was there the living was dear, and I had not money enough to stay there longer.—What sort of weather was it when you were on the way to Vienna?—It was very bad weather, for it was stormy (*temporale*), and snowed and rained very heavily (*dirottamente*).— Where have you been since I saw you?—We sojourned long on the sea-shore, until a ship arrived (*fino all' arrivo d' un—*) which brought us to France.—Will you continue your narrative?— Scarcely had we arrived in France when we were taken (*condurre* *) to the king, who received us very well, and sent us back to our country.—A peasant having seen that old men (*il vecchio*) used (*servirsi di*) spectacles (*occhiali*) to read, went to an optician (*un ottico*) and asked for a pair (*e ne domandò*). The peasant then took a book, and having opened it, said the spectacles were not good. The optician put another pair (*un altro paio*) of the best which he could find in his shop (*la bottega*) upon his nose; but the peasant being still unable to read, the merchant said to him: "My friend, perhaps you cannot read at all?" "If I could (*se sapessi leggere*)," said the peasant, "I should not (*non avrei bisogno di*) want your spectacles."—Henry (*Enrico*) the Fourth, meeting one day in his palace (*il palazzo*) a man whom he did not know (*che gli era sconosciuto*), asked him to whom he belonged (*appartenesse*, imp. subj.). "I belong to myself," replied the man. "My friend," said the king, "you have a stupid (*stolido*) master (*padrone*)." Tell us (*La ci racconti*) what has happened to you lately (*l' altro giorno*).—Very willingly (*benvolentieri*): but on condition (*colla condizione*) that you will listen to me without interrupting (*interrompere* *) me.—We will not interrupt you: you may be (*può esserne*) sure of it.—Being lately at the theatre, I saw the Speaking Picture and the Weeping (*piangere* *) Woman performed (*vedere* * *rappresentare*). As I did not find this latter play (*quest' ultima commedia*) very amusing (*troppo allegra per me*), I went to the concert, where the music (*la musica*) caused me (*cagionare*) a violent head-ache (*un violento mal di testa*). I then left (*lasciare*) the concert, cursing it (*maledicendo*), and went straight (*e me ne andai difilato*) to the madhouse (*lo spedale dei pazzi*), in order to see my cousin. On entering (*entrando*) the hospital of my cousin, I was struck with horror (*fui preso d' orrore*) at seeing (*vedendo*) several madmen (*il pazzo*), who came up to me (*avvicinarsi ad uno*), jumping (*saltare*) and howling (urlare).—What did you do then ?—I did the same (altrettanto), and they set up a laugh (mettersi* a ridere) as they withdrew (ritirarsi).

SIXTY-FIRST LESSON.

Lezione sessantesima prima.

To employ.	Impiegare 1.
When we received some money, we employed it in purchasing good books.	Quando ricevevamo del danaro, l' impiegavamo a comprare dei buoni libri.
When you bought of that merchant, you did not always pay in cash.	Quando Ella comprava da questo mercante, non pagava sempre in contanti.

Has your sister succeeded in mending your cravat ?	Sua sorella ha dessa potuto raccomodare la di Lei cravatta ?
She has succeeded in it.	L' ha potuto.
Has the woman returned from the market ?	La donna è dessa ritornata dal mercato ?
She has not yet returned.	Non n' è peranco ritornata.
Did the women agree to that ?	Sono convenute di ciò le donne ?
They agreed to it.	Ne son convenute.
Where is your sister gone ?	Ov' è andata la di Lei sorella ?
She is gone to church.	È andata in chiesa.

Here is, here are. There is, there are.	Ecco.
There is my book. Behold my book.	Ecco il mio libro.
There is my pen. Behold my pen.	Ecco la mia penna.
There it is.	Eccolo. *Fem.* eccola.
There they are.	Eccoli. " eccole.
Here I am.	Eccomi.

Obs. A. The pronouns are joined to the word ecco in the following manner :

SIXTY-FIRST LESSON.

	Sing.	Plur.
There or Here I am. There or here we are.	Eccomi.	Eccoci.
" " thou art. " " you are.	Eccoti.	Eccovi.
" " he is. " " they are.	Eccolo.	Eccoli.
" " she is. " " they are.	Eccola.	Eccole.

| I am there. | Eccomici, *or* eccomivi. |
| There is some. | Eccone. |

There is the man.	Ecco l' uomo.
There is the woman.	Ecco la donna.
That is the reason why.	Ecco perchè.
Therefore I say so.	Ecco perchè lo dico.

My feet are cold.	† Ho freddo ai piedi.
His feet are cold.	† Egli ha freddo ai piedi.
Her hands are cold.	† Essa ha freddo alle mani.
My body is cold.	† Ho freddo a tutto il corpo.
My head hurts me.	† Mi duole la testa (mi fa male la testa).
His leg hurts him.	† Gli fa male la gamba.
Her leg hurts her.	† Le fa male la gamba.
He has a pain in his side.	† Ha male ad un lato.
Her tongue hurts her very much.	† Le duole molto la lingua.

A plate.	Un tondo.
A clean plate.	Un tondo pulito.
Clean plates.	Dei tondi puliti.

The son-in-law.	Il genero.
The step-son.	Il figliastro.
The daughter-in-law.	La nuora.
The step-daughter.	La figliastra.
The father-in-law.	Il suocero.
The step-father.	Il patrigno.
The mother-in-law.	La suocera.
The step-mother.	La matrigna.

The progress.	Il progresso.
To improve.	† Far dei progressi.
To improve in learning.	† Far dei progressi negli studii, nelle scienze.
The progress of a malady.	Il progresso (*or* i progressi) d' una malattia.

SIXTY-FIRST LESSON. 327

What has become of your aunt?	Ch' è avvenuto della di Lei zia?
	Che n' è della di Lei zia?
I do not know what has become of her.	Non so che ne sia avvenuto (*subj.*).
What has become of your sisters?	Ch' è avvenuto delle di Lei sorelle?
I cannot tell you what has become of them.	Non posso dirle che sia avvenuto di loro (*subj.*).

Wine sells well.	† Il vino ha grande smercio.[1]
	† Vi ha molta ricerca di vino.
Wine will sell well next year.	† Il vino avrà grande smercio l' anno venturo.
	† L' anno venturo il vino si renderà benissimo.
That door shuts easily.	† Questa porta si chiude agevolmente.
That window does not open easily.	† Questa finestra non s' apre facilmente.
That picture is seen far off.	† Questo quadro si vede da lontano.
Winter clothes are not worn in summer.	† I vestiti del verno non si portano nella state.
That is not said.	† Ciò non si dice.
That cannot be comprehended.	† Questo non si capisce
	Questo non si concepisce.

To conceive, to comprehend.	*Concepire (concepisco); past part. concepito;* preterite def. *concepii.*
It is clear.	È chiaro.

According to circumstances.	† Secondo le occorrenze.
The circumstance.	L' occorrenza (or la circostanza).
That is according to circumstances.	Secondo le circostanze.
It depends.	Dipende (dalle circostanze).

Glad.	Contento (di before inf.).
Pleased.	Soddisfatto (di before inf.).
Sorry, displeased.	Malcontento, incresciozo.

To scold.	*Sgridare 1.*
To be angry with somebody.	*Essere in collera con qualcuno.*
	Essere indispettito contro qualcuno.
	Nutrire mal animo contro qualcuno.

---

[1] *Smercio*, though in constant use, has not been sanctioned yet by *la Crusca*.

SIXTY-FIRST LESSON.

To be angry about something.	Essere indispettito per qualche cosa.
What are you angry about?	† Qual è l' oggetto che La indispettisce?
Are you sorry for having done it?	† Le rincresce d' averlo fatto?
I am sorry for it.	Me ne rincresce.

Are you rich?	È Ella ricca?
I am.	Lo sono.
Are the women handsome?	Sono belle le donne?
They are; they are rich and handsome.	Lo sono; sono ricche e belle.
Are you from France?	† È Ella Francese? È Ella di Francia?
I am.	Lo sono.
What countrywoman is she?	† Di qual paese è dessa?
She is from Italy.	Essa è d' Italia.

Honest.	Onesto.
Polite.	Civile.
Uncivil.	Incivile.
Impolite.	Scortese (impulito).
Happy, lucky.	Felice.
Unhappy, unlucky.	Infelice.
Easy.	Facile.
Difficult.	Difficile.
Useful.	Utile.
Useless.	Inutile.
Is it useful to write a good deal?	È egli utile di scriver molto?
It is useful.	È utile.
Is it well (right) to take the property of others?	È egli lecito di prendere l' avere degli altri? (o la roba degl' altri).
It is wrong (bad).	Non va bene (sta male).
It is not well (wrong).	Non è lecito.
Well, right.	Bene.
Bad, wrong.	Male.

Of what use is that?	{ † A che serve ciò? { † A che giova?
That is of no use.	{ † Ciò non è buono a niente. { † Ciò non serve a niente.
What is that?	Che è questo?
I do not know what that is.	Non so che sia (*present subj.*).
What is it?	Che è?
I do not know what it is.	{ Non so che sia (*subj.*). { Non so che cosa sia (*pres. subj.*).

SIXTY-FIRST LESSON.

What is your name?	Come si chiama? / Qual è il di Lei nome? / Che nome ha Ella?
My name is Charles.	Mi chiamo Carlo. / Ho nome Carlo.
What do you call this in Italian?	Come si chiama ciò in Italiano?
How do you express this in Italian?	Come si dice questo in Italiano?
What is that called?	Come si chiama ciò?
That flower is called anemone.	Questo fiore ha nome anemone.

George the Third.	Giorgio terzo.

Obs. B. After the Christian names of sovereigns the Italians employ the ordinal numbers, as in English, but without using the article.

Lewis the Fourteenth.	Luigi decimo quarto.
Henry the Fourth.	Enrico quarto.
Henry the First.	Enrico primo.
Henry the Second.	Enrico secondo.
Charles the Fifth spoke several European languages fluently.	Carlo Quinto parlava speditamente parecchie lingue europee.
Europe, European.	Europa, europeo.
Fluently.	Speditamente.

Rather.	Piuttosto.
Rather—than.	Piuttosto che (di).
Rather than squander my money, I will keep it.	Piuttosto che dissipare il mio danaro, lo conserverò.
I will rather pay him than go thither.	Lo pagherò piuttosto che andarvi.
I will rather burn the coat than wear it.	Abbrucierò l' abito piuttosto che portarlo.
He has arrived sooner than I.	Egli è arrivato prima di me.
A half-worn coat.	Un abito mezzo logoro.
To do things imperfectly (by halves).	Far le cose a metà (a mezzo).

EXERCISES.

187.

Did your mother pray for any one when she went to church?—She prayed for her children.—For whom did we pray?—You prayed for your parents.—For whom did our parents pray?—They prayed for their children.—When you received your money what did you do with it (*che ne facevano*)?—We employed it in purchasing (*a comprare*) some good books.—Did you employ yours also (*pure*) in purchasing books?—No; I employed it in assisting (*a soccorrere*) the poor (*i poveri*).—Did you not pay your tailor?—We did pay him.—Did you always pay in cash when you bought of that merchant?—We always paid in cash, for we never bought on credit.—Has your sister succeeded in mending (*ha potuto raccomodare*) your stockings?—She has succeeded in it (*l' ha potuto*).—Has your mother returned from church?—She has not yet returned.—Whither is your aunt gone?—She is gone to church.—Whither are our cousins (*fem.*) gone?—They are gone to the concert.—Have they not yet returned from it?—They have not yet returned.—Did you forget any thing when you went to school?—We often forgot our books.—Where did you forget them?—We forgot them at the school.—Did we forget any thing?—You forgot nothing.

188.

Who is there?—It is I (*son io*).—Who are those men?—They are foreigners who wish to speak to you.—Of what country are they?—They are Americans.—Where is my book?—There it is.—And my pen?—Here it is.—Where is your sister?—There she is.—Where are our cousins (*fem.*)?—There they are.—Where art thou, John (*Giovanni*)?—Here I am.—Why do your children live in France?—They wish to learn French; that is the reason why they live in France.—Why do you sit near the fire?—My feet and hands are cold; that is the reason why I sit near the fire.—Are your sister's hands cold?—No; but her feet are cold.—What is the matter with your aunt?—Her leg hurts her.—Is any thing the matter with you?—My head hurts me.—What is the matter with that woman?—Her tongue hurts her very much.—Why do you not eat?—I shall not eat before I have a (*prima d' aver*) good appetite.—Has your sister a good appetite?—She has a very good appetite; that is the reason why she eats so much.—If you have read the books which I lent you, why do you not return them to me?—I intend reading them once more (*ancor una volta*); that is the reason why I have not yet returned them to you; but I will return them to you as soon as I have read them a second time (*per la seconda volta*).—Why have you not brought my shoes?—They were not made, therefore I did not bring them; but I bring them you now: here they are.—Why has your daughter not learnt her exercises?—She has taken a walk with her companion; that is the reason why she has not learnt them: but she promises to learn them to-morrow, if you do not scold (*sgridare*) her.

189.

A French officer (*uffiziale*) having arrived (*essendo arrivato*) at the court (*la corte*) of Vienna, the empress Theresa (*Teresa*) asked (*domandare*) him, if he believed that the princess of N., whom he had seen the day before (*la vigilia*), was (*fosse*, subj.) really the handsomest woman in the (*del*) world, as was said. "Madam," replied (*rispondere* *) the officer, "I thought so yesterday."—How do you like that meat?—I like it very well.—May I ask you for (*Oserei domandarle*) a piece of that fish?—If you will have the goodness (*la bontà*) to pass (*porgere*) me your plate, I will give you some.—Would you have the goodness to pour me out some drink (*di versarmi da bere*, or *di mescermi*)?—With much pleasure.—Cicero (*Cicerone*) seeing his son-in-law, who was very short (*piccolissimo*), arrive (*venire*) with a long sword (*con una lunga spada*) at his side (*al lato*), said, "Who has fastened (*attaccare*) my son-in-law to this sword?"

190.

What has become of your uncle?—I will tell you what has become of him. Here is the chair (*la sedia*) upon which he often sat (*essere seduto*).—Is he dead?—He is dead.—When did he die?—He died two years ago.—I am very much grieved at it.—Why do you not sit down?—If you will stay with me, I will sit down; but if you go I shall go along with you.—What has become of your aunt?—I do not know what has become of her.—Will you tell me what has become of your sister?—I will tell you what has become of her.—Is she dead?—She is not dead.—What has become of her?—She is gone to Vienna.—What has become of your sisters?—I cannot tell you what has become of them, for I have not seen them these two years.—Are your parents still alive?—They are dead.—How long is it since your cousin (*fem.*) died?—It is six months since she died.—Did the wine sell well last year?—It did not sell very well; but it will sell better next year, for there will be a great deal, and it will not be dear.—Why do you open the door?—Do you not see how it smokes here ?—I see it ; but you must (*bisogna*) open the window instead of opening the door.—The window does not open easily ; that is the reason why I open the door.—When will you shut it ?—I will shut it as soon as there is no (*che non vi sarà*) more smoke.—Did you often go a fishing when you were in that country ?—We often went a fishing and a hunting.—If you will go with us into the country you will see my father's castle.—You are very polite, Sir ; but I have seen that castle already.

191.

When did you see my father's castle ?—I saw it when I was travelling (*viaggiando*) last year.—It is a very fine castle, and is seen far off.—How is that said ?—That is not said.—That cannot be comprehended (*non si concepisce*) ; cannot every thing be expressed in your language ?—Every thing can be expressed, but not as in yours.—Will you rise early to-morrow ?—It will depend upon circumstances (*secondo*) ; if I go to bed early I shall rise early, but if I go to bed late I shall rise late.—Will you love my children ?—If they are good I shall love them.—Will you dine with us to-morrow ?—If you get ready (*far preparare*) the food I like I shall dine with you.—Have you already read the letter which you received this morning ?—I have not opened it yet.—When will you read it ?—I shall read it as soon as I have time (*che ne avrò il tempo*).—Of what use is that ?—It is of no use.—Why have you picked it up ?—I have picked it up in order to show it you.—Can you tell me what it is ?—I cannot tell you, for I do not know; but I will ask (*domandare a*) my brother, who will tell you.—Where did you find it ?—I found it on the shore of the river, near the wood.—Did you perceive it from afar ?—I had no need to perceive it from afar, for I passed by the side of the river.—Have you ever seen such a thing ?—Never.—Is it useful to speak much ?—It is, according to circumstances : if one wishes to learn a foreign (*straniero*) language, it is useful to speak a great deal.—Is it as useful to write as to speak ?—It is more useful to speak than to write ; but, in order to learn a foreign language, one must (*bisogna*) do both (*l' uno e l' altro*).—Is it useful to write all that one says ?—That is useless.

SIXTY-SECOND LESSON.

Lezione sessantesima seconda.

As to (as for).	In quanto a, or quanto a.
As to me.	Quanto a me. / In quanto a me.
As to that I do not know what to say.	Quanto a ciò, non so che dire.
I do not know what to do.	Non so che fare.
I do not know where to go.	Non so dove andare.
He does not know what to answer.	Non sa che rispondere.
We do not know what to buy.	Non sappiamo che comprare.

To die of a disease.	Morire* d' una malattia.
She died of the small-pox.	Essa è morta del vaiuolo.
The small-pox.	Il vaiuolo.
The fever.	La febbre.
The intermittent fever.	La febbre intermittente.
The apoplexy.	L' attacco d' apoplessia. / Il colpo apoplectico, l' apoplessia.
He had a cold fit.	Egli aveva un accesso di febbre.
He has an ague.	È preso dalla febbre.
His fever has returned.	Gli è ritornata la febbre.
He has been struck with apoplexy.	Egli è stato colpito d' apoplessia.

To strike.	Colpire (colpisco, &c.)

Sure.	Sicuro, certo (fem. sicura, certa).
To be sure of a thing.	Esser sicuro (certo) di qualche cosa.
I am sure of that.	Ne sono sicuro (certo). / Sono certo (sicuro) di ciò.
I am sure that she has arrived.	Sono certo ch' essa è arrivata.
I am sure of it.	Ne sono certo (sicuro).

To happen.	Accadere*; p. part. accaduto. (Conjugated like cadere, Less. LI.) *Preterite Definite.* Accaddi, accadesti, accadde. Accademmo, accadeste, accaddero. [Used only in the 3d pers.]
Something has happened.	È accaduto qualche cosa.

Nothing has happened.	Non è accaduto niente.
What has happened?	Ch' è accaduto?
What has happened to her?	Che le è accaduto?
She has had an accident.	Essa ha avuto un accidente.

To shed.	*Spargere* 2; p. part. *sparso*. *Preterite Definite*. Sparsi, spargesti, sparse. Spargemmo, spargeste, sparsero.
To pour out.	Versare 1.
A tear.	Una lagrima.
To shed tears.	Spargere lagrime.
To pour out some drink.	Versar da bere (mescere).
I pour out some drink for that man.	Verso da bere a quest' uomo.
With tears in his, her, our, or my eyes.	Colle lagrime agli occhi.

Sweet, mild.	Dolce.
Sour, acid.	Acido, acida.
Some sweet wine.	Del vino dolce.
A mild air.	Un' aria dolce.
A mild zephyr.	Un dolce zeffiro.
A soft sleep.	Un dolce sonno.
Nothing makes life more agreeable than the society of, and intercourse with, our friends.	Non avvi cosa che *renda* la vita così dolce quanto la società e il commercio dei nostri amici.

Obs. A. There is, in the above signification, may be rendered in seven different manners, viz. *avvi, evvi, vi ha, vi è, v' ha, v' è, c' è*.

To repair to.	Rendersi a (pret. def. *resi, rendesti, rese*, &c.)
To repair to the army, to one's regiment.	Rendersi all' esercito, al suo reggimento.
An army, a regiment.	Un esercito, un reggimento.
I repaired to that place.	Mi sono reso a questo luogo.
He repaired thither.	Vi si è reso.

To cry, to scream, to shriek.	Gridare 1.
To help.	Aiutare 1 (governs the accus. and takes *a* before the inf.).
I help him to do it.	L' aiuto a farlo.
I help you to write.	L' aiuto a scrivere.
I will help you to work.	Voglio aiutarla a lavorare.

SIXTY-SECOND LESSON. 335

To cry for help.	Chiamare aiuto.
	Domandar soccorso.
The help.	L' aiuto, il soccorso.

To inquire after some one.	*Informarsi di qualcuno.*
Will you have the goodness to pass me that plate?	Vuol Ella aver la bontà di porgermi quel piatto?
Will you pass me that plate, if you please?	† Favorisca di porgermi quel piatto?
To reach, offer, present.	*Porgere* * 2, past part. *porto* (pret. def. *porsi, porgesti, porse,* &c.).
To favour.	*Favorire* 3 (*favorisco*).

Obs. B. If you please is often rendered in Italian by the imperative *favorisca*.

Please to sit down.	Favorisca di sedersi.
As you please.	
At your pleasure.	Come Le piace.
As you like.	Come Le aggrada.
To please.	*Aggradire* 3 (*isco*).
To knock at the door.	Bussare alla porta.
	Picchiare alla porta.

To trust some one.	† *Affidarsi a qualcuno.*
To distrust one.	Non fidarsi di qualcuno.
	Diffidare di qualcuno.
Do you trust that man?	Si fida Ella di quest' uomo?
I trust him.	Me gli affido. Mi fido di Lui.
He trusts me.	Egli s' affida in me (or a me).
We must not trust every body.	Non bisogna fidarsi di tutti.

To laugh at something.	*Ridere* * *di qualche cosa* (Lessons LIV. and LX.)
	Preterite Definite
	Risi, ridesti, rise.
	Ridemmo, rideste, risero.
Do you laugh at that?	Ride Ella di ciò? Ridete voi di?
I laugh at it.	Ne rido.
At what do they laugh?	Di che ridono?
To laugh in a person's face.	Ridersi di qualcuno.

SIXTY-SECOND LESSON.

We laughed in his face.	Noi ci siamo risi di lui.
To laugh at, to deride some one.	Ridersi </br> Beffarsi } di qualcuno. </br> Farsi beffe
I laugh at (deride) you.	Mi rido di voi (di Lei). </br> Mi beffo di voi (di Lei).
Did you laugh at us?	Si beffava Ella di noi?
We did not laugh at you.	Non ci ridevamo di Lei (di voi). </br> Non ci beffavamo di Lei (di voi.)
We never laugh at any body.	Non ci beffiamo mal di nessuno. </br> Non ci facciamo mal beffe di nessuno.

Full.	Pieno.
A book full of errors.	Un libro pieno d' errori.

To afford.	† *Aver di che. Aver con che*
Can you afford to buy that horse?	Ha Ella di che comprare quel cavallo?
I can afford it.	Ho di che comprarlo.
I cannot afford it.	Non ho di che comprarlo.

Who is there?	Chi è là?
It is I.	Sono io.

Obs. C. The impersonal pronoun *it* is not rendered in Italian.

It is not I.	Non sono io.
Is it he?	È desso?
It is not he.	Non è desso.
Are they your brothers?	Sono i di Lei fratelli (or i suoi, or i vostri fratelli)?
It is they.	Sono essi.
It is not they.	Non sono essi.
Is it she?	È dessa?
It is she.	È dessa.
It is not she.	Non è dessa.
Are they your sisters?	Sono le di Lei sorelle (or le sue, or le vostre sorelle)?
It is they.	Sono esse.
It is not they.	Non sono esse.
It is I who speak.	Son io che parlo.
Is it they who laugh?	Son essi (*fem.* esse) che ridono?
It is you who laugh.	È Lei che ride (siete voi che ridete).
Is it thou who hast done it?	Sei tu che l' hai fatto?
It is you, gentlemen, who have said that.	Siete voi, signori, che avete detto ciò. </br> Sono loro signori che hanno detto ciò.

SIXTY-SECOND LESSON.

We learn Italian, my brother and I.	Mio fratello ed io impariamo l' Italiano.
You and I will go into the country.	Ella (voi) ed io andremo in campagna.
You and he will stay at home.	Ella (voi) ed esso resteranno a casa.
You will go to the country, and I will return to town.	Voi andrete (t-lla andrà) in campagna ed io ritornerò in città.
A lady. A lady of the court.	Una signora. Una dama di corte.
What were you doing when your tutor was here?	Che faceva (facevate) quando il di Lei (il vostro) precettore era qui?
I was doing nothing.	Io non faceva niente (nulla).
What did you say?	Che diceva Ella?
I said nothing.	Io non diceva niente.

EXERCISES.

192.

Where did you take this book from?—I took it out of the room (*nella camera*) of your friend (*fem.*).—Is it right (*permesso*) to take the books of other people?—It is not right, I know; but I wanted it, and I hope that your friend will not be displeased (*non ne sarà incresciosa*), for I will return it to her as soon as I have read it.—What is your name?—My name is William (*Guglielmo*).—What is your sister's name?—Her name is Eleanor (*Eleonora*).—Why does Charles complain of his sister?—Because she has taken his pens.—Of whom are these children complaining?—Francis (*Francesco*) complains of Eleanor, and Eleanor of Francis.—Who is right?—They are both (*tutti e due*) wrong; for Eleanor wishes to take Francis's books, and Francis Eleanor's.—To whom have you lent Dante's works (*le opere di Dante*)? —I have lent the first volume to William and the second to Louisa (*Luigia*).—How is that said in Italian?—It is said thus.—How is that said in French?—That is not said in French.—Has the tailor brought you your new coat?—He has brought it me, but it does not fit me.—Will he make you another?—He will make me another; for, rather than wear it, I will give it away (*dar via*).—Will you use that horse?—I shall not use it.—Why will you not use it?—Because it does not suit me.—Will you pay for it?—I will rather pay for it than use it.—To whom do those fine books belong (*appartengono*)?—They belong to William.—Who has given them to him ?—His father.—Will he read them ?—He will tear them rather than read them.—Who has told you that ? —He has told me so himself (*egli stesso*).

193.

What countrywoman is that lady (*la signora*) ?—She is from France.—Are you from France ?—No, I am from Germany.— Why do you not give your clothes to mend ?—It is not worth while, for I must have (*mi abbisognano*) new clothes.—Is the coat which you wear not a good one ?—It is a half-worn coat, and is good for nothing.—Are you angry with any one (*essere in collera con qualcuno*) ?—I am angry with Louisa, who went to the Opera without telling me a word of it.—Where were you when she went out ?—I was in my room.—I assure you that she did not know it.—Charles the Fifth, who spoke fluently (*speditamente*) several European languages, used to say (*aveva costume di dire*), that we should speak (*che bisognava parlare*) Spanish with the gods, Italian with our friend (*fem.*), French with our friend (*mas.*), German with soldiers, English with geese (*colle oche*), Hungarian (*ungherese*) with horses, and Bohemian (*boemo*) with the devil.

194.

Of what illness did your sister die ?—She died of fever.—How is your brother ?—My brother is no longer alive.—He died three months ago.—I am surprised (*maravigliato*) at it, for he was very well last summer when I was in the country.—Of what did he die ?—He died of apoplexy.—How is the mother of your friend ? —She is not (*non ista*) well; she had an attack of ague the day before yesterday, and this morning the fever has returned (*le è ritornata*).—Has she the intermittent fever ?—I do not know, but she has often cold fits.—What is become of the woman whom I saw at your mother's ?—She died this morning of apoplexy.—Do your scholars learn their exercises by heart ?—They will tear them rather than learn them by heart.—What does this man ask me for ?—He asks you for the money which you owe him.—If he will repair to-morrow morning (*domani mattina*) to my house, I will pay him what I owe him.—He will rather lose his money than repair thither (*rendervisi*).—Why does the mother of our old servant shed tears?—What has happened to her?—She sheds tears because the old clergyman (*il vecchio ecclesiastico*), her friend, who was so very good to her (*che le faceva tanto bene*), died a few days ago.—Of what illness did he die?—He has been struck with apoplexy.—Have you helped your father to write his letters?—I have helped him.—Will you help me to work when we go (*quando noi andremo*) to town?—I will help you to work, if you help me to get a livelihood.

195.

Have you inquired after the merchant who sells so cheap?—I have inquired after him, but nobody could tell me what has become of him.—Where did he live when you were here three years ago?—He lived then (*allora*) in Charles-street (*nella contrada Carlo*, or *via Carlo*), number fifty-seven.—How do you like this wine?—I like it very well, but it is a little sour.—How does your sister like those apples (*la mela*)?—She likes them very well, but she says that they are a little too sweet.—Will you have the goodness to pass me that plate?—With much pleasure. —Shall I (*devo*) pass you these fishes?—I will thank you to (*prego di*) pass them to me.—Shall I (*devo*) pass the bread to your sister?—You will oblige her (*Le farà piacere*) by passing it to her (*nel porgerglielo*).—How does your mother like our food? —She likes it very well, but she says that she has eaten enough. —What dost thou ask me for?—Will you be kind enough to (*La prego di*) give me a little bit (*un pezzetto*) of that mutton?—Will you pass me the bottle, if you please (*favorisca*)?—Have you not drunk enough?—Not yet, for I am still thirsty.—Shall I (*devo io*) give you (*versarle*) some wine?—No; I like cider better.— Why do you not eat?—I do not know what to eat.—Who knocks at the door?—It is a foreigner.—Why does he cry?—He cries because a great misfortune has happened to him.—What has happened to you?—Nothing has happened to me.—Where will you go this evening?—I do not know where to go.—Where will your brothers go?—I do not know where they will go; as for me, I shall go to the theatre.—Why do you go to town?—I go thither in order to purchase some books.—Will you go thither with me? —I will go with you, but I do not know what to do there.

SIXTY-THIRD LESSON.

Lezione sessantesima terza.

To get into a scrape.	† *Attirarsi cattivi affari.*
To get out of a scrape.	† *Cavarsi d' impiccio.*
I got out of the scrape.	Mi son cavato d' impiccio.
That man always gets into scrapes, but he always gets out of them again.	Quest' uomo s' attira mai sempre cattivi affari, ma n' esce sempre facilmente.

Between.	
Amongst or *amidst.*	*Fra* or *tra.*

To make some one's acquaintance.	
To become acquainted with somebody.	*Far conoscenza con qualcuno.*
I have made his or her acquaintance.	
I have become acquainted with him or her.	Ho fatto la sua conoscenza.
Are you acquainted with him (her)?	
Do you know him (her)?	Lo (la) conosce Ella?
I am acquainted with him (her).	
I know him (her).	Lo (la) conosco.
He or she is an acquaintance of mine.	
She or he is my acquaintance.	È di mia conoscenza, or È una mia conoscenza.
He is not a friend, he is but an acquaintance.	Non è un amico, è solamente una conoscenza.

To enjoy.	*Godere 2, di.*
Do you enjoy good health?	Gode Ella buona salute?
	Gode Ella d' una buona salute?
To be well.	*Star bene.*
	Essere in buona salute.
She is well.	Sta bene.
	È in buona salute.
To imagine.	*Immaginare.*
	† *Immaginarsi.*

SIXTY-THIRD LESSON.

Our fellow-creatures.	I nostri simili.
He has not his equal, or his match.	Egli non ha l' uguale.

To resemble some one, to look like some one.	*Rassomigliare a qualcuno.*
That man resembles my brother.	Quest' uomo rassomiglia a mio fratello.
That beer looks like water.	Questa birra è come acqua.
Each other.	L' un l' altro.
We resemble each other.	Noi ci rassomigliamo.
They do not resemble each other.	Eglino (*fem.* elleno) non si rassomigliano.
The brother and the sister love each other, but do not resemble each other.	Il fratello e la sorella s' amano, ma non si rassomigliano.
Are you pleased with each other?	Siete (sono) contenti l' un dell' altro?
We are.	Lo siamo.
So, thus.	Così.
As, or as well as.	Siccome, come. Egualmente che. In quel modo che.

The appearance, the countenance.	*La ciera (l' aspetto, la sembianza, la vista, la mostra).*
To show a disposition to.	*Far vista, far mostra di.*
That man whom you see shows a desire to approach us.	Quell' uomo che vede fa vista d' avvicinarsi a noi.
To look pleased with some one.	{ *Far buona cera a qualcuno.* { *Accoglier bene qualcuno.*
To look cross at some one.	{ *Far cattiva cera a qualcuno.* { *Accoglier male qualcuno.*
When I go to see that man, instead of receiving me with pleasure, he looks displeased.	Quando vado da quell' uomo, in vece di farmi (mostrarmi) buona cera, egli mi fa (mi mostra) cattiva cera. Quando vado da quell' uomo, in vece d' accogliermi bene, egli m' accoglie male.
A good-looking man.	Un uomo di buon aspetto.
A bad-looking man.	Un uomo di cattivo aspetto.
Bad-looking people, or folks.	Della gente di cattivo aspetto.
To go to see some one.	Visitare qualcuno, *or* far visita a qualcuno.

To pay some one a visit.	Restituire la visita a qualcuno, or render la visita a qualcuno.
To frequent a place.	Frequentare un luogo, or andar spesso in un luogo.
To frequent societies.	Frequentare delle società.
To associate with some one.	Frequentare qualcuno.

To look like, to appear.	*Aver l' aspetto (aver l' aria).*
How does he look?	Che cera ha?
He looks gay (sad, contented).	Ha la cera lieta (trista, contenta).
You appear very well.	Ella ha l' aspetto di star bene.
You look like a doctor.	Ella ha l' aspetto d' un medico.
She looks angry, appears to be angry.	Essa ha il semblante indispettito.
They look contented, appear to be contented.	Eglino hanno l' aspetto contento.
To look good, to appear to be good.	Aver l' aspetto buono.

To drink some one's health.	† Bere alla salute di qualcuno.
I drink your health.	† Devo alla di Lei salute.
It is all over with me.	† Sono perduto (*fem.* perduta).
	† Sono ito (*fem.* ita).
It is all over.	È finita.

To hurt some one's feelings.	Far dispiacere a qualcuno.
You have hurt that man's feelings.	Ha fatto dispiacere a quell' uomo.

A place.	Un luogo.
I know a good place to swim in.	† Conosco un buon luogo per nuotare.

To experience, to undergo.	*Sperimentare 1.*
I have experienced a great many misfortunes.	Ho sperimentato molte disgrazie.
	Son passato per molte disgrazie.

To suffer.	*Soffrire * 3; p. part. sofferto.*
To open.	Aprire * 3; " " aperto.
To offer.	Offrire * 3; " " offerto.
To cover.	Coprire * 3; " " coperto.
To cover again.	Ricoprire * 3; " " ricoperto.
To discover.	Scoprire * 3; " " scoperto.
To feel a pain in one's head or foot.	Soffrir dolori al capo, al piede.
I felt a pain in my eye.	Ho sofferto all' occhio.

SIXTY-THIRD LESSON. 343

To neglect.	Trascurare 1, negligere * 2, non badare 1; past part. negletto.
	Preterite Definite.
	Neglessi, negligesti, neglesse. Negligemmo, negligeste, neglessero.
He has neglected his duty.	Ha trascurato il suo dovere.
He neglects to call upon me.	Egli bada poco a visitarmi.
To yield.	Cedere 2; pret. def. regular, or cessi, or cedetti.
We must yield to necessity.	Bisogna cedere alla necessità.
To spring forward.	Lanciarsi 1, or slanciarsi 1.
The cat springs upon the rat.	Il gatto si slancia sul sorcio.
To leap on horseback.	Lanciarsi a cavallo.
An increase, an augmentation.	Un aumento (un' aggiunta, un accrescimento).
For more bad luck.	Per colmo di aventura (d' infelicità).
For more good luck.	Per colmo di felicità.
The fulness.	Il colmo.
For more bad luck (to complete my bad luck) I have lost my purse.	Per colmo di aventura ho perduto la mia borsa.
To lose one's wits.	Perdere la testa.
That man has lost his wits, and he does not know what to do.	Quell' uomo ha perduto la testa e non sa che fare.
Obstinately, by all means.	Ad ogni patto.
That man wishes by all means to lend me his money.	Quest' uomo vuole ad ogni patto prestarmi il suo danaro.
To follow.	Seguitare 1, seguire * 3.
I follow, thou followest, he follows, &c.	Seguo or siegue, segui or siegui, segue or siegue, &c.
To pursue.	Perseguitare 1, inseguire * 8 (is conj. like seguire *).
To preserve, to save.	Conservare 1.

EXERCISES.
196.

Must I sell to that man on credit?—You may sell to him, but not on credit; you must not trust him, for he will not pay you.

—Has he already deceived (*ingannare*) any body ?—He has already deceived several merchants who have trusted him.—Must I trust those ladies ?—You may trust them; but as to me I shall not trust them, for I have often been deceived by (*dalle*) women, and that is the reason why I say : We must not trust every body. —Do those merchants trust you ?—They trust me, and I trust them.—Whom do those gentlemen laugh at ?—They laugh at those ladies who wear red gowns (*la veste*) with yellow ribbons. —Why do these people laugh at us ?—They laugh at us because we speak badly.—Ought we (*dobbiamo*) to laugh at persons who speak badly ?—We ought not to laugh at them; we ought, on the contrary (*devesi al contrario*), to listen to them, and if they make blunders (*errori*), we ought to correct them.—What are you laughing at ?—I am laughing at your hat; how long (*da quando in quà*) have you worn it so large ?—Since (*da che*) I returned from Germany.—Can you afford to (*ha Ella di che*) buy a horse and a carriage ?—I can afford it.—Can your brother afford to buy that large house ?—He cannot afford it.—Will your cousin buy that horse ?—He will buy it, if it pleases (*convenire* *) him.—Have you received my letter ?—I have received it with much pleasure. I have shown it to my Italian master, who was surprised (*che è rimasto maravigliato*), for there was not a single fault in it.—Have you already received Petrarca's and Boccaccio's works (*le opere del Petrarca e del Boccaccio*) ?—I have received those of Boccaccio; as to those of Petrarca, I hope to receive them next week.

197.

Is it thou, Charles, who hast soiled my book ?—It is not I ; it is your little sister who has soiled it.—Who has broken my fine inkstand ?—It is I who have broken it.—Is it you who have spoken of me ?—It is we who have spoken of you, but we have said of you nothing but good (*se non del bene*).—Who knocks at the door ?—It is I; will you open ?—What do you want (*desiderare*) ?—I come to ask you for the money which you owe me, and the books which I lent you.—If you will have the goodness to come to-morrow I will return both to you.—Is it your sister who is playing on the harpsichord ?—It is not she.—Who is it ?

—It is my cousin (*fem.*).—Are they your sisters who are coming?—It is they.—Are they your neighbours (*fem.*) who were laughing at you?—They are not our neighbours.—Who are they?—They are the daughters of the countess whose brother has bought your house.—Are they the ladies of whom you have spoken to me?—They are.—Shall you learn German?—My brother and I will learn it.—Shall we go to the country tomorrow?—I shall go to the country, and you will remain in town.—Shall I and my sister go to the opera?—You and she will remain at home, and your brother will go to the opera.—What did you say when your tutor was scolding you (*La riprendeva*)?—I said nothing, because I had nothing to say, for I had not (*non avendo io*) done my task, and he was in the right to scold me (*di rampognarmi*).—What were you doing whilst (*quando*) he was out (*fuori*)?—I was playing on the violin, instead of doing what he had given me to do.—What has my brother told you?—He has told me that he will be the happiest man when he knows how (*quando saprà*) to speak Italian well.

199.

Why do you associate with those people?—I associate with them (*la frequento*) because they are useful to me.—If you continue to associate with them you will get into bad scrapes, for they have many enemies.—How does your cousin conduct himself?—He does not conduct himself very well, for he is always getting into some scrape (or other).—Do you not sometimes get into scrapes?—It is true (*vero*) that I sometimes get into them, but I always get out of them again (*ma n' esco sempre felicemente*).—Do you see those men who seem desirous (*che fanno vista*) of approaching us?—I see them, but I do not fear them; for they hurt nobody.—We must go away (*bisogna allontanarci*), for I do not like to mix with people whom I do not know.—I beg of you not to be afraid of them (*averne paura*), for I perceive my uncle among them.—Do you know a good place to swim in?—I know one.—Where is it?—On that side of the river, behind the wood, near the high road (*vicino alla via maestra*).—When shall we go to swim?—This evening, if you like.—Will you wait for me before the city gate?—I shall wait for you there; but I beg of

you not to forget it.—You know that I never forget my promises.
—Where did you become acquainted with that lady?—I became
acquainted with her at the house of one of my relations.—Why
does your cousin ask me for money and books?—He is a fool (*un
pazzo*); for of me (*a me*), who am his nearest relation (*il suo più
prossimo parente*) and his best friend, he asks nothing.—Why did
you not come to dinner (*venir a pranzare*)?—I have been
hindered, but you have been able to dine without me (*senza di
me*).—Do you think (*credere*) that we shall not dine, if you cannot come?—How long (*sino a quando*) did you wait for me?—
We waited for you till a quarter past seven, and as you did not
come, we dined without you.—Have you drunk my health?—
We have drunk your health, and that of your parents.

SIXTY-FOURTH LESSON.
Lezione sessantesima quarta.

How good you are!	Quanto Ella è buona! *or simply:* Quanto è buono! Quanta bontà!
How foolish he is!	Quanto è sciocco!
How foolish she is!	Quanto è sciocca!
How rich that man is!	Quanto è ricco quell' uomo!
How handsome that woman is!	Quanto è bella quella donna!
How much kindness you have for me!	Quanta bontà Ella ha per me!
How many obligations I am under to you!	Quante obbligazioni Le debbo! Quanto vi son debitore!

To be under obligations to some one.	Aver (dovere) delle obbliga-zioni verso qualcuno.
I am under many obligations to him.	Gli debbo molte obbligazioni.
How many people!	Quanta gente!
How happy you are!	Quanto Ella è felice!
How much wealth that man has!	Quante ricchezze ha quell' uomo!
How much money that man has spent in his life!	Quanto danaro ha speso quell' uomo nella sua vita!

SIXTY-FOURTH LESSON.   347

To be obliged to some one for something.	Esser obbligato verso qualcuno per qualche cosa.
To be indebted to some one for something.	Esser debitore verso (or a) qualcuno di qualche cosa.
I am indebted to him (to her) for it.	Gliene sono debitore.

To thank.	*Ringraziare* (governs the accusative of the person, and the preposition *per* of the object, as in English).
To thank some one for something.	*Ringraziare qualcuno per qualche cosa.*
I thank you for the trouble you have taken for me.	La ringrazio per la pena ch' Ella si è data per me. (or, Vi ringrazio per l' incomodo è).
You have no reason for it.	Non ne vale il prezzo. / Non ne vale la pena.

Is there any thing more great?	Che v' è di più grande?
Is there any thing more cruel?	Che v' è di più crudele?
Is there any thing more wicked?	Che v' è di più cattivo?
Can any thing be more handsome?	V' è qualche cosa di più bello?

How large?	Of what size?	Di che grandezza?
How high?	Of what height?	Quanto è alto (alta)?
How deep?	Of what depth?	Quanto è profondo (profonda)?

Of what height is his or her house?	Quanto è alta la sua casa?
It is nearly fifty feet high.	È alta cinquanta piedi incirca.
Our house is thirty feet broad.	La nostra casa è larga trenta piedi.
That table is six feet long.	Quella tavola è lunga sei piedi.
That river is twenty feet deep.	Questo fiume è profondo venti piedi.

The size.	*La statura, grandezza, forma.*
Of what size is that man?	Di quale statura è quell' uomo?

How was that child dressed?	Come era vestito quel fanciullo?
It was dressed in green.	† Egli era vestito di verde.
The man with the blue coat.	† L' uomo dall' abito turchino.
The woman with the red gown.	† La donna dalla veste rossa.

SIXTY-FOURTH LESSON.

True.	Vero.
Is it true that his house is burnt?	E vero che la sua casa è abbruciata?
It is true.	È vero.
Is it not?	Non è vero?
Is it not true?	Non è egli vero?

Perhaps.	Forse.
I shall perhaps go thither.	V' andrò forse.
To share, to divide.	Dividere * 2; p. part. diviso; pret. def. divisi.

| Whose? | Di chi? (See Lessons XXI. and XXIX.) |

Obs. The absolute possessive pronoun, *mine, thine,* &c., when it is preceded by the verb *to be, essere,* is in Italian rendered merely by the possessive pronoun. Ex.

Whose horse is this?	Di chi è questo cavallo?
It is mine.	È mio.
Whose horses are those?	Di chi son questi cavalli?
They are mine.	Sono miei.
Whose house is this?	Di chi è questa casa?
It is mine.	È mia.
Whose houses are those?	Di chi son queste case?
They are mine.	Sono mie.

To run up.	Accorrere * 2; past part. accorso; pret. def. accorsi.
Many men had run up; but instead of extinguishing the fire, they set to plundering.	Molti uomini erano accorsi, ma in vece d' estinguere il fuoco, s' erano messi a predare.
To run to the assistance of some one.	Accorrere al soccorso di qualcuno.

To extinguish.	Estinguere *; p. part. estinto; pret. def. estinsi.
The miscreant.	Lo scellerato.

To save, to deliver.	Salvare 1. Liberare 1.
To save any body's life.	Salvare la vita a qualcuno.
To plunder (to rob).	Predare 1.
To set about something.	† Mettersi a qualche cosa.
Have they succeeded in extinguishing the fire?	Sono pervenuti ad estinguere il fuoco?
They have succeeded in it.	Vi sono pervenuti.

SIXTY-FOURTH LESSON.

The watch.	L' oriuolo.
The watch indicates the hours.	L' oriuolo indica le ore.
To indicate, to mark.	Indicare 1.
To quarrel.	Querellarsi 1.
To quarrel with some one.	Rimproverare qualcuno.
To dispute (to contend) about something.	Disputare sopra qualche cosa.
About what are these people disputing?	Sopra che cosa disputano quegli uomini?
They are disputing about who shall go first.	Disputano a chi tocca andare il primo.
Thus or so.	Cosi, in questa guisa.
To be ignorant of.	Ignorare 1.
Not to know.	Non sapere.
The day before.	La vigilia.
The day before that day was Saturday.	La vigilia di quel giorno era un sabato.
The day before Sunday is Saturday.	La vigilia di domenica è sabato.

EXERCISES.

109.

How does your uncle look (che cera ha—)?—He looks (ha la cera) very gay (lietissima), for he is much pleased with his children.—Do his friends look as gay (hanno la cera cosi lieta) as he?—They, on the contrary, look sad, because they are discontented. My uncle has no money, and is always contented; and his friends, who have a good deal of it, are scarcely ever so.—Do you like your sister?—I like her much, and as she is (ed essendo) very good-natured (compiacentissima) to me, I am so to her; but how do you like your sister?—We love each other, because we are pleased with each other.—A certain (certo) man liked much wine, but he found in it (gli) two bad qualities (la qualità). "If I put water to it," said he, "I spoil it, and if I do not put any to it, it spoils me (mi guasta me)."—Does your cousin resemble you?—He resembles me.—Do your sisters resemble each other?—They do not resemble each other; for the elder (*la primogenita*) is idle and naughty, and the younger (*la cadetta*) assiduous and good-natured towards every body.—How is your aunt?—She is very well.—Does your mother enjoy good health?—She imagines she enjoys (*essa s' immagina di godere*) good health, but I believe she is mistaken (*ch' essa s' inganni*, subj.), for she has had a bad cough (*la tosse*) these six months, of which (*della quale*) she cannot get rid.—Is that man angry with you?—I think he is angry with me because I do not go to see him; but I do not like to go to his house, for when I go to him, instead of receiving me with pleasure, he looks displeased.—You must not believe that; he is not angry with you, for he is not so bad as he looks (*come ne ha l' aspetto*).—He is the best man in the (*del*) world; but one must know him in order to appreciate him (*per poterlo apprezzare*).—There is a great difference (*la differenza*) between you and him; you look pleased with all those who come to see you, and he looks cross with them.

200.

Is it right (*sta bene*) to laugh thus at every body?—If I laugh (*quando mi beffo*) at your coat, I do not laugh at every body.—Does your son resemble any one?—He resembles no one.—Why do you not drink?—I do not know what to drink, for I like good wine, and yours looks like vinegar (*è come aceto*).—If you wish to have some other I shall go down (*discenderò*) into the cellar to fetch you some.—You are too polite, Sir; I shall drink no more to-day.—Have you known my father long?—I have known him long, for I made his acquaintance when I was yet at school.—We often worked for one another, and we loved each other like brothers.—I believe it, for you resemble each other.—When I had not done my exercises he did them for me, and when he had not done his I did them for him.—Why does your father send for the physician?—He is ill; and as the physician does not come (*non venendo*), he sends for him.—Ah (*Ah*), it is all over with me!—But, bless me (*Dio mio*), why do you cry thus?—I have been robbed of my gold rings, my best clothes, and all my money; that is the reason why I cry.—Do not make (*non faccia*) so much noise, for it is we who have taken them all (*tutto ciò*), in order to teach you (*per apprenderle*) to take better care (*ad aver più cura*) of your things (*effetti*), and to shut the door of your room when you go out.—Why do you look so sad ?—I have experienced great misfortunes.—After having lost all my money, I was beaten by bad-looking men; and, to my still greater ill luck, I hear that my good uncle, whom I love so much, has been struck with apoplexy.—You must not afflict yourself (*affligersi*) so much, for you know that we must yield to necessity (*necessità non ha legge*).

201.

Can you not get rid of that man ?—I cannot get rid of him, for he will absolutely (*ad ogni patto*) follow me.—Has he not lost his wits ?—It may be (*può darsi*).—What does he ask you for ?—He wishes to sell me a horse which I do not want.—Whose houses are those ?—They are mine.—Do these pens belong to you ?—No, they belong to my sister.—Are those (*sono quelle*) the pens with which she writes so well ?—They are the same (*le medesime*).—Whose gun is this ?—It is my father's.—Are these books your sister's ?—They are hers.—Whose carriage is this ?—It is mine.—Which is the man of whom you complain ?—It is he (*quello*) who wears (*che indossa*) a red coat.—" What is the difference (*che differenza c' è*) between a watch and me ?" inquired (*domandò*) a lady of a young officer. " My lady," replied he (*questi le rispose*), " a watch marks the hours, and near you (*e presso di Lei*) one forgets them."—A Russian peasant, who had never seen asses (*un asino*), seeing several (*vedendone alcuni*) in France, said (*disse*): " Lord (*Dio mio*), what large hares (*la lepre*) there are in this country !"—How many obligations I am under to you, my dear friend ! you have saved my life ! without you I had been lost (*io era ito*).—Have those miserable men hurt you ?—They have beaten and robbed me ; and when you ran to my assistance they were about (*erano sul punto*) to strip (*spogliare*) and kill me.—I am happy to have delivered you from the hands of those robbers (*il briccone*).—How good you are !

SIXTY-FIFTH LESSON.

Lezione sessantesima quinta.

To propose.	*Proporsi* * (is conjugated like *porre*, Lesson XLIV.).
I propose, &c.	Mi propongo, ti proponi, si propone. Ci proponiamo, vi proponete, si propongono.
	P. part. propostosi ; *Fut.* proporrò ; *Pret. def.* proposi, proponesti, &c.
I propose going on that journey.	Mi propongo di far questo viaggio.
He proposes joining a hunting party.	Si propone d' andare ad una partita di caccia.
A game at chess.	Una partita agli scacchi (or a scacchi).
A game at billiards.	Una partita al bigliardo.
A game at cards.	Una partita alle carte.

To succeed.	*Riuscire* * (*a* before Inf.).
I succeed, &c.	Riesco, riesci, riesce. Riusciamo, riuscite, riescono.
Do you succeed in doing that ?	Riesce, Ella a far ciò ?
I do succeed in it.	Vi riesco.

To endeavour.	*Sforzarsi* (di before Inf.)
I endeavour to do it.	Mi sforzo di farlo.
I endeavour to succeed in it.	Mi sforzo di riuscirvi.
Endeavour to do better.	La si sforzi di far meglio.
	Sforzatevi di far meglio.

Since, considering.	*Giacchè* (*poichè, dacchè, da che*).
Since you are happy, why do you complain ?	Giacchè Ella è felice, perchè La si lagna ? or Poichè siete felice perchè vi lagnate ?

SIXTY-FIFTH LESSON.

To be thoroughly acquainted with a thing.	† Essere in istato di far qualche cosa.
	† Conoscere qualche cosa a fondo.
To make one's self thoroughly acquainted with a thing.	† Informarsi (istruirsi) di qualche cosa.
That man understands that business perfectly.	Quest' uomo è istruito di quell' affare.
I understand that well.	Sono istruito di ciò.

Since or from.	Da poi (or simply da).
From that time.	Da quel momento.
From my childhood.	Dalla mia giovinezza (infanzia).
From morning until evening.	Dal mattino fino alla sera.
	Da mane a sera.
From the beginning to the end.	Dal principio sino alla fine.
From here to there.	Da qui fino là.
I have had that book these two years.	Ho questo libro da due anni in poi.
	Ho questo libro da due anni.
I have lived in Paris these three years.	Dimoro a Parigi da tre anni.
	Dimoro a Parigi da tre anni in poi.

To blow, to blow out.	Soffiare 1.

To allege (to bring).	Addurre * 2; formerly adducere.
	Pres. Adduco; P. part. addotto; Pret. def. addussi; Fut. addurrò.
I allege, &c.	Adduco, adduci, adduce.
We allege, &c.	Adduciamo, adducete, adducono.

In the same manner are conjugated:

To conduct.	Condurre * 2, formerly conducere.
To infer.	Dedurre * 2, " deducere.
To introduce.	Introdurre * 2, " introducere.
To produce.	Produrre * 2, " producere.
To reconduct.	Ricondurre * 2, " riconducere.
To reduce, to subdue.	Ridurre * 2, " riducere.
To produce again.	Riprodurre * 2, " riproducere.
To seduce.	Sedurre * 2, " seducere.
To translate.	Tradurre * 2, " traducere.

Obs. A. Verbs ending in **surre, gliere, nere, arre**, have been contracted, so that they have two infinitives; the ancient Latin one, as *adducere*, to allege; *cogliere*, to gather (to catch); *ponere*, to put; *traere*, to draw; and the new

SIXTY-FIFTH LESSON.

contracted one, as: *addurre, corre, porre, trarre*. The second contracted one is always used in the infinitive from which *the future* and the present of the *conditional* (of which hereafter) are formed, as: *addurrò*, I shall allege; *corrò*, I shall gather; *porrò*, I shall put; *trarrò*, I shall draw, &c. (See Lesson XLVI) But all the other tenses are in such verbs formed from the ancient Latin infinitive.

To put, to place.	Porre * ; formerly ponere [1].
I put, &c.	Pongo, poni, pone.
We put, &c.	Poniamo, ponete, pongono.
	Past part. posto; Pret. def. posi; Fut. porrò.

To draw.	Trarre * 2 ; formerly traere.
I draw, &c.	Traggo, traggi, tragge or trae.
We draw, &c.	Traggiamo, traete, traggono.
	Past part. tratto; Pret. def. trassi; Fut. trarrò.

In the same manner are conjugated :

Astrarre,	to abstract.	Detrarre,	to detract.
Attrarre,	to attract.	Estrarre,	to extract.
Contrarre,	to contract.	Sottrarre,	to draw away.

To gather.	Corre * 2, or cogliere [2].
I gather, &c.	Colgo, cogli, coglie.
We gather, &c.	Cogliamo, cogliete, colgono.
	Past part. colto; Pret. def. colsi; Fut. corrò or coglierò.

In the same manner are conjugated :

To choose. Scerre * or scegliere 2 (*scelto, scelsi, scerrò or sceglierò*).

To untie, to loose. Sciorre * or sciogliere 2 (*sciolto, sciolsi, sciorrò or scioglierò*).

To take. Torre * or togliere 2 (*tolto, tolsi, torrò or toglierò*).

---

[1] And all its compounds, such as :

Anteporre,	to prefer.	Imporre,	to impose.
Apporre,	to add.	Opporre,	to oppose.
Comporre,	to compound.	Posporre,	to postpone.
Contrapporre,	to oppose.	Preporre,	to prefer.
Deporre,	to depose.	Proporre,	to propose.
Disporre,	to dispose.	Soprapporre,	to put over.
Esporre,	to expose.	Sottoporre,	to subdue.
Frapporre,	to interpose.	Supporre,	to suppose.

[2] In verbs in *gliere* the contracted are more generally used in poetry.

SIXTY-FIFTH LESSON.

To drink.	Bere * or bevere.
I drink, &c.	Bevo, bevi, beve.
We drink, &c.	Beviamo, bevete, bevono.
	Past part. beuto or bevuto; Pret. def. bevvi; Fut. berò.

Obs. B. Besides the above there are a few other verbs terminated in *ere* long, *i. e.* with the accent on the last syllable but one, which are not contracted in the infinitive, but only in the future (and consequently in the conditional, hereafter), when they reject the letter *e* of the last syllable but one (Lesson XLVI.). They are:

To have.	Avère *	Fut.	avrò.
To be obliged (owe).	Dovère	"	dovrò.
To be able (can).	Potère *	"	potrò.
To know.	Sapère *	"	saprò.
To see.	Vedère *	"	vedrò.
To appear.	Parère *	"	parrò.

Obs. C. When the verbs in *ere* long have *l* or *n* before that termination, those letters are in the contracted form of the future and conditional, for the sake of euphony, changed into *r*, as:

To remain.	Rimanere.	Fut.	rimarrò.
To hold.	Tenere	"	terrò.
To ache.	Dolere	"	dorrò.
To be worth.	Valere	"	varrò.
To be willing.	Volere	"	vorrò.

To destroy.	Distruggere *.
	P. part. distrutto; pret. def. distrussi.
To construct.	Costruire * (isco).
	P. part. costruito and costrutto; Pret. def. costrussi, costruisti, &c.

To reduce the price.	Ridurre * il prezzo.
To reduce the price to a crown.	Ridurre il prezzo ad uno scudo.
To translate into Italian.	Tradurre in italiano.
To translate from Italian into English.	Tradurre dall' italiano in inglese.
To translate from one language into another.	Tradurre da una lingua in un' altra.
I introduce him to you.	L' introduco da Lei.
I present him to you.	Glielo presento.
To present.	Presentare 1.

Self.	Stesso or medesimo; fem. stessa or medesima.
Selves.	PLUR. Stessi or medesimi; fem. stesse or medesime.
Myself.	Io stesso, or Io medesimo.
Thyself.	Tu stesso, or tu medesimo.
Himself.	Egli stesso, or egli medesimo.
Herself.	Ella stessa, or Ella medesima.
Ourselves.	Noi stessi, or noi medesimi.
Yourselves.	Voi stessi, or voi medesimi.
Themselves.	Eglino stessi, or eglino medesimi. Elleno stesse, or elleno medesime.
One's self.	Se stesso, or se medesimo.
He himself has told it me.	Me l' ha detto egli stesso (egli medesimo).
He has told me, myself (not to another person).	L' ha detto a me stesso (a me medesimo).
I also told him the same.	Gli ho detto anch' io lo stesso.
In the same manner.	Nello stesso modo.
It is all the same.	È tutto lo stesso (è tutt' uno).
One does not like to flatter one's self.	Non piace lusingar se stesso (or se medesimo).
Even.	Anche.
Even not.	Nemmeno.
He has not even money enough to buy some bread.	Non ha nemmeno abbastanza danaro per comprar del pane.
We must love every body, even our enemies.	Bisogna amar tutti, anche i nostri nemici.
Again (once more).	Di nuovo, un' altra volta.
He speaks again (anew).	Parla di nuovo.
To fall.	{ Abbassare 1. { Ribassare 1.
The price of the merchandise falls.	† La mercanzia ribassa di prezzo.
To deduct, to lower.	{ Diminuire (isco). { Dedurre* (formerly deducere).
To overcharge, to ask too much.	† Domandar più che la cosa non vale.
Not having overcharged you, I cannot deduct any thing.	Non avendo domandato troppo (più che la cosa non vale), non posso diminuir niente.
An ell, a yard.	Un braccio; pl. braccia; un' auna
A metre (measure).	Un metro.

SIXTY-FIFTH LESSON.   357

To produce (to yield, to profit, to bring in).	Riportare 1. Rendere * (p. part. reso; pret. def. resi). Dare * (p. part. dato; pret. def. diedi and detti).
How much does that employment yield you a year? An employment.	Quanto Le rende quest' impiego all' anno? Un impiego (un offizio)
To make one's escape. To run away (to flee). To take to one's heels.	Prender la fuga, fuggirsene.
To desert. He deserted the battle. He deserted his colours.	Disertare, scappare 1. Egli ha abbandonato la battaglia. Egli ha disertato la bandiera.
To run away. The thief has run away.	Evadersi, fuggirsene. Il ladro se n' è fuggito.
By no means. Not at all.	Non mica, in nessun modo. Niente affatto.

EXERCISES.

202.

Will you go to Mr. Vimerati to-night?—I shall perhaps go.—And will your sisters go?—They will, perhaps.—Had you any pleasure (*divertirsi*) yesterday at the concert?—I had no pleasure there; for there was such a multitude of people (*tanta gente*) that we could hardly get in.—I bring you a pretty present with which you will be much pleased.—What is it?—It is a silk cravat.—Where is it?—I have it in my pocket (*nella mia tasca*).—Does it please you?—It pleases me much, and I thank you for it with all my heart. I hope that you will at last (*finalmente*) accept (*accettare*) something of (*da*) me.—What do you intend to give me?—I will not tell you; for if I tell you, you will have no pleasure when I give it you (*glielo darò*).—Have you seen any one at the market?—I have seen a good many people there.—How were they dressed?—Some were dressed in blue, some in green, some in yellow, and several (*diversi altri*) in red.—Who are those men?—The one who is dressed in gray is my neighbour, and the man with the black coat the physician, whose son has given my neighbour a blow with a stick.—Who is the man with the green coat?—He is one of my relations.—Are there many philosophers in your country?—There are as many there as in yours.—How does this hat fit me?—It fits you very well.—How does that coat fit your brother?—It fits him admirably.—Is your brother as tall (*grande*) as you?—He is taller than I, but I am older than he.—Of what size (*di quale statura*) is that man?—He is five feet and four inches (*il pollice*) high.—How high is the house of our landlord?—It is sixty feet high.—Is your well deep?—Yes, Sir, for it is fifty feet deep. "There are many learned men (*il dotto*) in Rome, are there not (*n' è vero*)?" Milton asked a Roman. "Not so many as when you were there," answered (*rispose*) the Roman.

203.

Is it true that your uncle is arrived?—I assure you that he is arrived.—Is it true that the king has assured you of his assistance (*l' assistenza*)?—I assure you that it is true.—Is it true that the six thousand (*mila*, plur.) men whom we were expecting have arrived?—I have heard so.—Will you dine with us?—I cannot dine with you, for I have just eaten.—Will your brother drink a glass of wine?—He cannot drink, for I assure you that he has just drunk.—Why are these men quarrelling?—They are quarrelling because they do not know what to do.—Have they succeeded in extinguishing the fire?—They have at last succeeded in it; but it is said that several houses have been (*sinno state*, subj.) burnt.—Have they not been able to save any thing?—They have not been able to save any thing; for, instead of extinguishing the fire, the miserable wretches (*lo scellerato*), who had come up, set to plundering.—What has happened?—A great misfortune has happened.—Why did my friends set out without me?—They waited for you till twelve o'clock, and seeing that you did not come they set out.—What is the day before Monday called?—The day before Monday is Sunday.—Why did you not run to the assistance (*in aiuto*) of your neighbour whose house has been burnt?—I was quite ignorant (*ignorare interamente*) of his house being on fire (*che l' incendio fosse nella di lui casa*).

204.

Well (*Ebbene*)! does your sister make any progress?—She makes some, but you make more than she.—You flatter me.—Not at all; I assure you I am more satisfied with you than with all my other pupils.—Do you already know what has happened?—I have not heard any thing.—The house of our neighbour has been burnt down (*abbruciata*).—Have they not been able to save any thing?—They were very fortunate (*felicissimi*) in saving the persons who were in it; but out of the things (*delle cose*) that were there (*trovarsi*), they could save nothing.—Who told you that?—Our neighbour himself (*istesso*) has told it me.—Why are you without a light (*senza lume*)?—The wind blew it out (*l' ha spento*) when you came in.—What is the price of this cloth?—I sell it at three crowns and a half the ell.—I think (*trovare*) it very dear. Has the price of cloth not fallen (*diminuito*)?—It has not fallen; the price of all goods (*la mercanzia*) has fallen, except that of cloth (*eccettuato quello del panno*).—I will give you three crowns for it.—I cannot let you have (*dare**) it for that price (*a questo prezzo*), for it costs me more (*costa più a me*).—Will you have the goodness to show me some pieces (*la pezza*) of English cloth?—With much pleasure.—Does this cloth suit you?—It does not suit me.—Why does it not suit you?—Because it is too dear; if you will lower the price, I shall buy twenty yards of it.—Not having asked too much, I cannot take off any thing.

SIXTY-SIXTH LESSON.
Lezione sessantesima sesta.

A kind, sort (a species).	Una sorta.
What kind of fruit is that ?	Che sorta di frutto è questo ?
A stone (of a fruit).	Un nocciolo.
A stone of a peach, an apricot, a plum.	Un nocciolo di pesca, di albicocco, di prugna.
Stone-fruit.	Frutto da nocciolo.
One must break the stone before one comes at the kernel.	Bisogna rompere il nocciolo per aver la mandola.
A kernel.	Un acino, una mandola.
An almond.	Una mandola.
Kernel-fruit.	Frutto da acino.
It is a kernel-fruit.	È un frutto da acino.
To gather.	Corre* or cogliere.
To gather fruit.	Cogliere frutti.
To serve up the soup.	Portar in tavola la zuppa.
To bring in the dessert.	Portar in tavola la frutta.
The fruit.	Il frutto.
An apricot.	Un albicocco.
A peach.	Una pesca.
A plum.	Una prugna.
An anecdote.	Un aneddoto.
Roast-meat.	Dell' arrosto.
The last.	L' ultimo, l' ultima.
Last week.	La settimana scorsa. La settimana passata.
Last year.	L' anno scorso (passato).
To cease, to leave off.	Cessare 1.
I leave off reading.	Cesso di (or dal) leggere.
She leaves off speaking.	Cessa di (or dal) parlare.
To avoid.	Evitare 1.
To escape.	Scampare 1, scappare 1.
To escape a misfortune.	Scampare da una disgrazia.

SIXTY-SIXTH LESSON. 361

He ran away to avoid death.	Ha preso la fuga per iscampare dalla morte. Scappò per fuggir la morte.
To do without a thing.	*Privarsi di qualche cosa.* *Far a meno di qualche cosa.*
Can you do without bread?	Può Ella privarsi di pane? Può Ella far a meno del pane?
I can do without it.	Posso farne a meno.
There are many things which we must do without.	Vi sono moltissime cose di cui è necessario fare a meno.
To execute a commission. *To acquit one's self of a commission.*	*Far una commissione.*
I have executed your commission.	Ho fatto la di Lei commissione.
Have you executed my commission?	Ha Ella fatto la mia commissione?
I have executed it.	L' ho fatta.
To do one's duty.	*Far il suo dovere.*
To discharge, to do, or to fulfil one's duty.	*Adempiere il suo dovere.*
That man always does his duty.	Quest' uomo fa sempre il suo dovere.
That man always fulfils his duty.	Quest' uomo adempie sempre il suo dovere.
To rely, to depend upon something.	*Contare su qualche cosa.* *Far capitale di qualche cosa.*
He depends upon it.	Ci conta.
I rely upon you.	Fo capitale di Lei. Mi fido di Lei.
You may rely upon him.	Può fidarsi a (or di) lui. Può fidarsene. Può far capitale di lui.
To suffice, to be sufficient.	*Bastare.*
Is that bread sufficient for you?	Le basta questo pane?
It is sufficient for me.	Mi basta.
It is sufficient for me, for thee, &c.	† Mi basta, ti basta, &c.
Will that money be sufficient for that man?	Questo danaro basterà a quell' uomo?
It will be sufficient for him.	Gli basterà.
Little wealth suffices for the wise.	Poca fortuna basta al savio.
Was that man contented with that sum?	Quest' uomo si è egli contentato di quella somma?

16

Has that sum been sufficient for that man?	Quella somma è bastata a quest' uomo?
It has been sufficient for him.	Gli è bastata. Gli bastò.
He has been contented with it.	Se n' è contentato.
To be contented with something.	Contentarsi di qualche cosa.
It will be sufficient for him, if you will only add a few crowns.	Gli basterà se vuol aggiognervi solamente qualche scudo.
He will be contented, if you will only add a few crowns.	Se ne contenterà se vuol aggiugnervi appena pochi scudi.
To add.	*Aggiungere* * 2 (p. part. *aggiunto*; pret. def. *aggiunsi*).
To build.	*Costruire* * 2, *isco* (past. part. *costruito* or *costrutto* (p. d. *construssi*). *Fabbricare* 1.
To embark, to go on board.	*Imbarcarsi. Entrar nella nave.*
A sail.	Una vela.
To set sail.	† Mettere alla vela.
	† Spiegare le vele.
To set sail for.	† Far vela per.
To sail for America.	Far vela per l' America.
	Andare in America.
To sail.	Andare a vela.
Under full sail.	A piene vele.
	A gonfie vele.
To sail under full sail.	Spiegar tutte le vele.
He embarked on the sixteenth of last month.	S' è imbarcato il sedici del mese scorso.
	È entrato nella nave il sedici del mese passato.
He sailed on the third instant.	Ha fatto vela il tre del corrente.
The instant, the present month.	Il corrente.
The fourth or fifth instant.	Il quattro, o il cinque del corrente.
The letter is dated the sixth instant.	La lettera è del sei corrente.
That is to say (i. e.).	*Cioè, vale a dire.*
Et cætera (etc.).	*Eccetera, e simili.*
My pen (quill) is better than yours.	La mia penna è migliore della di Lei.
I write better than you.	Scrivo meglio di Lei.
They will warm the soup.	Si farà scaldare la zuppa.
Dinner (or supper) is on the table (is served up).	È in tavola.

Do you choose some soup ?	Desidera Ella della zuppa ?
Shall I help you to some soup ?	Desidera Ella che io Le serva della zuppa ?
I will trouble you for a little.	† Gliene domando un poco.
	† Me ne favorisca un poco.
To serve up, to attend.	Servire, presentare, offrire.

EXERCISES.

205.

You are learning Italian; does your master let you translate ?—He lets me read, write, and translate.—Is it useful to translate in learning a foreign language ?—It is useful to translate when you nearly know (*quando già si sa*) the language you are learning; but while (*quando*) you do not yet know any thing (*non se ne sa niente*) it is entirely (*affatto*) useless.—What does your Italian master make you do ?—He makes me read a lesson; afterwards he makes me translate English exercises into Italian on the lesson which he has made me read; and from the beginning to the end of the lesson he speaks Italian to me, and I have to (*devo*) answer him in the very language (*nella lingua stessa*) which he is teaching me.—Have you already learnt much in that manner ?—You see that I have already learnt something, for I have hardly been learning it three months, and I already understand you when you speak to me, and can answer you.—Can you read (it) as well (*del pari*) ?—I can read and write as well as speak (it).—Does your master also teach German ?—He teaches it.—Wishing to make (*desiderando fare*) his acquaintance, I must beg of you (*La prego*) to introduce me to him.—It will give me (*Mi farò un*) pleasure to introduce you to him.—When do you wish to go to him ?—To-morrow in the afternoon (*dopo mezzo giorno*), if you please (*se Le aggrada*).

206.

How many exercises do you translate a day ?—If the exercises are not difficult, I translate from three to four every day (*da tre a quattro al giorno*); and when they are so, I translate but one (*uno solo*).—How many have you already done to-day ?—It is the

SIXTY-SIXTH LESSON.

third which I am translating (*sto traducendo*); but to-morrow I hope to be able to do one more (*uno di più*), for I shall be alone (*solo*).—Have you paid a visit to my aunt?—I went to see her two months ago (*or fan due mesi*), and as she looked displeased I have not gone to her any more since that time (*da quel tempo*). —How do you do to-day?—I am very unwell (*molto male*).— How do you like that soup?—I think (*La trovo*) it is very bad; since I have lost my appetite (*l' appetito*), I do not like any thing (*non mi piace più niente*).—How much does that employment bring in (*rendere**) to your father?—It brings him in (*gli rende*, or *gli dà*) more than four thousand (*mila*, plur. of *mille*) crowns. —What news is there (*dire**)?—They say nothing new.—What do you intend to do to-morrow?—I propose joining a hunting party.—Does your brother purpose (*divisa egli*) playing (*far*) a game at billiards?—He proposes playing a game at chess.—Why do some people (*perchè mai sonvi persone*) laugh when I speak? —Those are unpolite people; you have only to laugh also (*Ella pure*), and they will no longer laugh at you.—If you will do as I do, you will speak well.—You must study a little (*Le abbisogna studiare qualche poco*) every day, and you will soon be no longer afraid to speak.—I will endeavour to follow your advice, for I have resolved (*mi son proposto*) to rise every morning at six o'clock, to study till ten o'clock, and to go to bed early.—Why does your sister complain?—I do not know; since (*quando*) she succeeds in every thing, and since she is (*e ch' è*) happy, even happier than you and I, why does she complain?—Perhaps she complains because she is not thoroughly acquainted (*non è istruita*) with that business (*in tale facenda*).—That may be (*può darsi*).

207.

Have they served up the soup?—They have served it up some minutes ago.—Then (*allora*) it must be (*dev' essere*) cold, and I only like soup hot (*la zuppa calda*).—They will warm it for you. —You will oblige me.—Shall I help you to some (*desidera Ella*) of this roast meat?—I will trouble you for a little.— Will you eat some of this mutton?—I thank you; I like fowl better.—May I offer you (*desidera Ella che Le serva*) some wine?—I will trouble you for a little (*me ne favorisca un poco*).

—Have they already brought in (*portato in tavola*) the dessert?—They have brought it in.—Do you like fruit?—I like fruit, but I have no more appetite.—Will you eat a little cheese?—I will eat a little.—Shall I help you to English or Dutch cheese?—I will eat a little Dutch cheese.—What kind of fruit is that?—It is a stone-fruit.—What is it called?—It is called thus.—Will you wash your hands?—I will wash them, but I have no towel to (*per*) wipe them (with).—I will let you have (*Le farò dare*) a towel, some soap, and some water.—I shall be much obliged to you.—May I ask you for (*oso domandarle*) a little water?—Here is some (*eccone*).—Can you do without soap?—As for soap I can do without it, but I must have a towel to wipe my hands (with). —Do you often do without soap?—There are many things which we must do without (*di cui è necessario privarsi*).—Why has that man run away?—Because he had no other means of escaping the punishment (*dalla punizione*) which he had deserved (*meritare*).—Why did your brothers not get (*procurarsi*) a better horse?—When they get rid of (*quando avranno alienato*) their old horse, they will get a better.—Has your father arrived already?—Not yet; but we hope that he will arrive this very day (*oggi stesso*).—Has your friend set out in time?—I do not know, but I hope he has (*che sarà*) set out in time.

SIXTY-SEVENTH LESSON.

Lezione sessantesima settima.

To be a judge of something.	Intendersi di qualche cosa. Conoscersi di (or in) qualche cosa.
Are you a good judge of cloth?	Si conosce Ella di panno?
I am a judge of it.	Mi vi conosco (me ne intendo).

SIXTY-SEVENTH LESSON.

I am not a judge of it.	Non mi vi conosco (non me ne intendo).
I am a good judge of it.	Mi vi conosco benissimo.
I am not a good judge of it.	Non mi vi conosco molto.

To draw.	*Disegnare* 1.
To chalk, to trace.	*Calcare* 1, *ricalcare* 1.
To draw a landscape.	Disegnare una vista di paese.
To draw after life.	Disegnare dal naturale (dal vero).
The drawing.	Il disegno.
The designer.	Il disegnatore.
Nature.	La natura.

To manage, or *to go about a thing.*	† *Prendersi.*
How do you manage to make a fire without tongs?	Come si prende Ella per far del fuoco senza molle? *or* Come fa ella a far.
I go about it so.	Mi vi prendo così, *or* Faccio così.
You go about it the wrong way.	Ella vi si prende male.
I go about it the right way.	Mi vi prendo bene.
How does your brother manage to do that?	Come si prende il di Lei fratello per far ciò.
Skilfully, handily, dexterously, cleverly.	Destramente.
Awkwardly, unhandily, badly.	Senza giudizio.

To forbid.	*Proibire* 3 (*isco*).
I forbid you to do that.	Le (vi) proibisco di far ciò.

To lower.	*Abbassare* 1.
To cast down one's eyes.	Abbassare gli occhi.
The curtain.	La tela, il sipario.
The curtain rises.	Si alza il sipario.
The curtain falls.	Cala il sipario.

To rise.	*Alzarsi* 1.
To fall, to descend.	*Calare* 1.
The stocks have fallen.	Il cambio ha bassato (è calato).
The day falls.	Declina il giorno.
Night comes on.	La notte s'avvicina.
It grows towards night.	† Si fa notte.
It grows dark.	† Si fa oscuro.
It grows late.	† Si fa tardi.

To stoop.	*Abbassarsi* 1.

SIXTY-SEVENTH LESSON.

To smell, to feel.	Sentire 3.
He smells of garlic.	Ha un cattivo odor d' aglio.
	Puzza d' aglio.
To feel some one's pulse.	Toccar il polso a qualcuno.
To consent.	Consentire 3. Acconsentire 3.
I consent to it.	V' acconsento
Who says nothing consents.	Chi tace consente.

To hide, to conceal.	Nascondere* 2 (past part. nascoso or nascosto; pret. def. nascosi).
The mind.	La mente, lo spirito.
In deed.	In verità.
In fact.	† In fatti, † in vero.
The truth.	La verità.
The fact.	Il fatto.
The effect.	L' effetto.
True.	Vero.
A true man.	Un uomo verace.
This is the right place for that picture.	Ecco il vero luogo per questo quadro.

To think much of one (to esteem one).	† Far conto di qualcuno.
	Aver in istima qualcuno.
To esteem some one.	Stimare qualcuno.
I do not think much of that man.	Non fo gran conto di quest' uomo.
I think much of him (I esteem him much).	Fo gran conto di lui (lo stimo molto).

The flower, the bloom, the blossom.	Il fiore.
That man has his eyes on a level with his head.	Quest' uomo ha gli occhi al piano della testa.
On a level with, even with.	Al piano, a livello.
To blossom (to flourish).	Fiorire 3 (isco).
To grow.	Crescere* 2 (past part. cresciuto; pret. def. crebbi).
To grow rapidly (fast).	Crescere rapidamente.
To grow tall or big.	Ingrandire 3 (isco).
That child grows so fast that we may even see it.	Questo fanciullo ingrandisce a vista.

SIXTY-SEVENTH LESSON.

That child has grown very fast in a short time.	Questo fanciullo ha molto ingrandito in poco tempo.
That rain has made the corn grow.	Questa pioggia ha fatto ingrandire il grano.
Corn.	Grano.

A cover.	Un alloggio.
A shelter.	Un ricovero, un rifugio.
A cottage, a hut.	Una capanna.
To shelter one's self from something.	Mettersi al ricovero di qualche cosa.
To take shelter from something.	
Let us shelter ourselves from the rain, the wind.	Mettiamoci al ricovero della pioggia del vento.
Let us enter that cottage, in order to be sheltered from the storm (the rain).	Entriamo in questa capanna per essere a coperto dalla tempesta, or per essere a ricovero delle ingiurie del tempo.

Every where, all over, throughout.	*Dappertutto.*
All over (throughout) the town.	Per tutta la città.
A shade.	Un' ombra.
Under the shade.	*All' ombra.*
Let us sit down under the shade of that tree.	Andiamo a sederci all' ombra di quest' albero.

To pretend.	*Fingere* di* (p. part. *finto*; pret. def. *finsi*).
That man pretends to sleep.	Quest' uomo finge di dormire. / Quest' uomo fa sembiante di dormire.
That young lady pretends to know Italian.	Questa signorina finge di sapere l' italiano.
They pretend to come near us.	Fanno sembiante d' avvicinarsi a noi.

Now.	*Ora, al presente, adesso.*
From, since.	*Da, fin da, dal.*
From morning.	Dalla mattina.
From morning till night.	Da mattina a sera.
From the break of day.	Dallo spuntar del giorno.

SIXTY-SEVENTH LESSON.

From the cradle. From a child. From this time forward.	Fin dalla culla. Fin dall' infanzia. Da ora in poi.
As soon as.	*Tosto che, appena.*
As soon as I see him, I shall speak to him.	Tosto ch' Io lo vedrò, gli parlerò.

For fear of.	{ *Per timore (per tema).* { *Sul timore.*
To catch a cold.	{ *Infreddarsi.* { *Pigliar un' infreddatura.*
I will not go out for fear of catching a cold.	Non voglio uscire per timore d' infreddarmi.
He does not wish to go to town for fear of meeting with one of his creditors.	Non vuol andar in città sul timore d' incontrar un suo creditore.
He does not wish to open his purse for fear of losing his money.	Non vuol aprire la borsa per timore di perdere il suo danaro.

To copy, to transcribe.	*Copiare* 1.
To decline.	*Declinare* 1.
To transcribe fairly.	Mettere in netto.
A substantive, an adjective, a pronoun.	Un sostantivo, un aggettivo (addittivo), un pronome.
A verb, a preposition, a grammar, a dictionary.	Un verbo, una preposizione, una grammatica, un dizionario.

EXERCISES.
208.

Have you executed my commission?—I have executed it.—Has your brother executed the commission which I gave him?—He has executed it.—Will you execute a commission for me?—I am under so many obligations to you that I shall always execute your commissions when it shall please you to give me any.—Will you ask the merchant whether (*se*) he can let me have (*darmi*) the horse at the price (*al prezzo*) which I have offered him?—I will ask him, but I know that he will be satisfied, if you will but add a few crowns.—Good morning, children (*ragazzi*)!—Have you done your task?—You well know that we always do it when we are not ill.—What do you give us to do to-day?—I

16*

give you the sixty-seventh lesson to study, and to do the exercises belonging to it (*che ne dipendono*); that is to say, the two hundred and eighth and two hundred and ninth.—Will you endeavour (*si studieranno*) to commit no errors (*far errori*)?—We shall endeavour (*ci studieremo*) to make none.—Is this bread sufficient for you?—It is sufficient for me, for I am not very hungry.—When did your brother embark for America?—He sailed on the thirtieth (*il trenta*) of last month.—Will you ask your brother whether he is satisfied with the (*del*) money which I have sent him?—As to my brother, he is satisfied with it, but I am not so; for having suffered shipwreck (*far naufragio*), I am in want of the money which you owe me.—Do you promise me to speak to your brother?—I promise you, you may depend upon it.—I rely upon you.—Will you work (*studiare*) harder (*meglio*) for the next lesson than you have done (*che non ha studiato*) for this?—I will work harder.—May I rely upon it?—You may.

209.

Are you a judge of cloth?—I am a judge of it.—Will you buy some yards for me?—If you will give me the money I will buy you some.—You will oblige me (*Ella mi farà piacere*, or *Gliene sarò tenuto*).—Is that man a judge of cloth?—He is not a good judge of it.—How do you manage to do that?—I manage it so.—Will you show me how you manage it?—Very willingly (*molto volentieri*).—What must I do (*che debbo fare*) for my lesson of to-morrow?—You will transcribe your exercises fairly (*mettere in netto*), do three others, and study the next lesson (*la lezione seguente*).—How do you manage to get goods (*delle mercanzie*) without money?—I buy on credit.—How does your sister manage to learn Italian without a dictionary?—She manages it thus.—She manages it very dexterously. But how does your brother manage it?—He manages it very awkwardly (*senza alcun giudizio*): he reads, and looks for the words in the dictionary.—He may (*può*) learn (*studiare*) in this manner twenty years without knowing how to make a single sentence (*una sola frase*).—Why does your sister cast down her eyes?—She casts them down because she is ashamed of not having done her task.—Shall we breakfast in the garden to-day?—The weather is so fine that we should take advantage of it (*che bisogna approfittarne*).—How do you like that coffee?—I like it very much.—Why do you stoop? —I stoop to pick up (*per prendere*) the handkerchief which I have dropped.—Why do your sisters hide themselves?—They hide themselves for fear of being seen.—Of whom are they afraid? —They are afraid of their governess (*la maestra*), who scolded (*rampognare* or *sgridare*) them yesterday because they had not done their tasks (*il lor dovere*, in the sing.).

SIXTY-EIGHTH LESSON.
Lezione sessantesima ottava.

To get beaten (whipped).	† Farsi battere.
To get paid.	† Farsi pagare.
To get one's self invited to dine.	† Farsi invitare a pranzo.
At first.	Da principio, a prima vista.
Firstly.	Primieramente, in primo luogo.
Secondly.	Secondariamente, in secondo luogo.
Thirdly, &c.	In terzo luogo, ecc.
Is your mother at home?	È in casa la di Lei madre?
She is.	Vi è.
I am going to her house.	Vado da essa.
A cause.	{ Un motivo, una causa, una cagione. { Un soggetto.
A cause of complaint.	Un soggetto di dispiacere.
A cause of sadness.	Un soggetto di tristezza.
She has reason to be sad.	Ha un motivo di tristezza.
Grief, sorrow, sadness.	Il dispiacere, la tristezza.
Is that woman ready to go out?	Questa donna è dessa pronta ad uscire?
She is.	Lo è.

SIXTY-EIGHTH LESSON.

Notwithstanding, in spite of. { *Malgrado.*
                                  { *A dispetto, ad onta.*

Notwithstanding that.   Malgrado ciò.
In spite of him.   Malgrado lui or suo malgrado.
In spite of her.   Malgrado essa or suo malgrado.
In spite of them.   Malgrado loro or loro malgrado.
In spite of me.   Mio malgrado.

To manage.   { † *Far in modo, di.*
                { *Procurare di.*

Do you manage to finish your work every Saturday night?   † Fa Ella in modo di finire il di Lei lavoro ogni sabato sera?
Do you manage to have your work done every Saturday night?   † Fa Ella in modo d' aver finito il di Lei lavoro ogni sabato sera?
Try to do that to oblige me.   Faccia in modo di far ciò *per* compiacermi.

Obs. Whenever *in order to* can be substituted for the preposition *to*, the latter is rendered in Italian by *per*, to express the end, the design, or the cause, for which a thing is done.

I will do every thing *to* oblige you.   Farò tutto *per* compiacerle.

To look upon.   { *Dar su.*
                  { *Sporgere su.*
                  { *Guardare su.*

The window looks into the street.   La finestra dà (sporge) sulla strada.
The window looks out upon the river.   La finestra sporge (dà) sul fiume.
That apartment looks upon the street.   Quest' appartamento dà (sporge) sulla strada.
The back-door looks into the garden.   La porta di dietro dà sul giardino.

To drown.   *Annegare (affogare).*
To drown a dog.   Annegare un cane.
To drown one's self, to get drowned. }   Annegarsi (affogarsi).
To be drowned, to be drowning.   }
To leap through the window.   Saltare dalla finestra.
To throw out of the window.   Gettare dalla finestra.
I am drowning.   Mi annego.
He jumped out of the window.   Saltò dalla finestra.

To fasten.   *Attaccare.*
He was fastened to a tree.   L' attaccarono ad un albero.

The cattle.	Il bestiame.
To keep warm.	† Tenersi caldo.
To keep cool.	† Tenersi fresco.
To keep clean.	† Tenersi pulito.
To keep on one's guard against some one.	† Star all' erta contro qualcuno. † Mettersi (porsi) in guardia contro qualcuno.
Keep on your guard against that man.	Stia all' erta contro quest' uomo.

To take care (to beware) of somebody.	*Guardarsi di (da) qualcuno.*
To take care (to beware) of something.	*Badare a qualche cosa.*
If you do not take care of that horse, it will kick you.	Se non bada a quel cavallo, Le darà un calcio.
Take care that you do not fall.	† Badi a non cadere!
To beware of somebody or something.	Guardarsi di qualcuno o di qualche cosa.
Keep on your guard against that man.	Le si guardi da quest' uomo.
Take care!	Badi! (La badi!)

A thought.	Un pensiere, un pensiero.
An idea.	Un' idea.
A sally.	Un impeto.
To be struck with a thought.	† Venir in pensiero. † Cader nell' animo.
A thought strikes me.	Mi viene un pensiero. Mi viene in mente.
A thought has struck me.	M' è venuto un pensiero. M' è venuto in mente.
That never crossed my mind.	Questo non m' è mai caduto nell' animo. Questo non m' è mai passato per la testa.

To take into one's head.	† *Immaginare* 1.
He took it into his head lately to rob me.	† Egli immaginò l' altro giorno di rubarmi.
What is in your head?	† Che immagina Ella?

In my place.	A (in) mio luogo. In mia vece.
In your, his, her place.	A (in) vostro, di Lei, suo, luogo.
We must put every thing in its place.	Bisogna mettere ogni cosa a suo luogo.

Around, round.
All around.
We sailed around England.

They went about the town to look at the curiosities.

To go round the house.
To go about the house.

To cost.
How much does that cost you?
How much does this book cost you?
It costs me three crowns and a half.
That table costs him seven crowns.

Intorno (a preposition).
Intorno intorno. Tutto intorno.
Navigammo intorno all' Inghilterra.
Andarono quà e là per la città per vederne le cose notabili.
{ Andare intorno alla casa.
{ Far il giro della casa.
Andar quà e là nella casa.

Costare 1.
Quanto Le costa?
Quanto Le costa questo libro?
Mi costa tre scudi e mezzo.
Questa tavola gli costa sette scudi.

Alone, by one's self.
I was alone.
One woman only.
One God.
God alone can do that.
The very thought of it is criminal.
A single reading is not sufficient to satisfy a mind that has a true taste.

Solo; fem. *sola.*
Io era solo.
Una sola donna.
Un solo Dio.
Dio solo può far questo.
Il pensiero solo di ciò è criminoso.
Una sola lettura non basta per contentare un uomo che ha buon gusto.

To kill by shooting.

To blow out some one's brains.

To shoot one's self with a pistol.
He has blown out his brains.
He has blown out his brains with a pistol.
He has shot him with a pistol.

Uccidere con arma da fuoco.
{ Far saltare le cervella a qualcuno.
{ Bruciare le cervella a qualcuno.
{ Mandar a qualcuno le cervella all' aria.
Uccidersi con una pistolettata.
Si è fatto saltare le cervella.
Si è fatto saltare le cervella con una pistolettata.
Gli ha mandato all' aria le cervella con una pistolettata.

He served for a long time, acquired honours, and died contented.
He arrived poor, grew rich in a short time, and lost all in a still shorter time.

Servì gran tempo, giunse agli onori, e morì contento.
Arrivò povero, diventò ricco in poco tempo, e perdè tutto in meno tempo ancora.

EXERCISES.

210.

What is the matter with you?—Why do you look so melancholy (*così melancolico*)?—I should not look so melancholy, if I had no reason to be sad. I have heard just now that one of my friends has shot himself with a pistol, and that one of my wife's best friends has drowned herself.—Where did she drown herself?—She drowned herself in the river which is behind her house.—Yesterday, at four o'clock in the morning, she rose (*si leva*) without saying a word to any one (*ad alcuno*), leaped out of the window which looks into the garden, and threw herself into the river, where she was drowned.—I have a great mind (*gran voglia*) to bathe (*bagnarsi*) to-day.—Where will you bathe?—In the river.—Are you not afraid of being drowned?—Oh, no! I can swim.—Who taught you?—Last summer I took a few lessons in the swimming-school (*alla scuola del* (or *di*) *nuoto*).

When had you finished your task?—I had finished it when you came in.—Those who had contributed (*contribuire*) most (*più*) to his elevation to the throne (*alla sua elevazione sul trono*) of his ancestors, were those who laboured (*lavorare*) with the greatest eagerness (*con più animosità*) to precipitate him from it (*per precipitarnelo*). As soon as (*Dacchè*) Cæsar (*Cesare*) had crossed (*passare*) the Rubicon (*il Rubicone*), he had no longer to deliberate (*deliberare*): he was obliged (*dovette*) to conquer (*vincere*) or to die.—An emperor (*un imperatore*), who was irritated at (*irritato contro*) an astrologer (*un astrologo*), asked him: "Wretch (*miserabile*)! what death (*di che sorta di morte*) dost thou believe thou wilt die?"—"I shall die of fever," replied the astrologer. "Thou liest," said the emperor, "thou wilt die this instant of a violent death (*di morte violenta*)." As he was going to be seized (*stavano per prenderlo*), he said to the emperor, "Sire (*Sire*), order some one (*ordinate*) to feel (*che mi si tocchi*, subj.) my pulse, and it will be found that I have a fever." This sally (*questo detto*) saved his life.

211.

Do you perceive yonder house (*quella casa laggiù*)?—I perceive it; what house is it?—It is an inn (*una locanda*); if you like we will go into it to drink a glass of wine, for I am very thirsty.—You are always thirsty when you see an inn.—If we enter I shall drink your health.—Rather than go into an inn I will not drink.—When will you pay me what you owe me ?—When I have (*avrò*) money ; it is useless to ask me for some to-day ; for you know very well that there is nothing to be had of him who has nothing.—When do you think you will have money ?—I think I shall have some next year.—Will you do what I am going to tell you ?—I will do it if it is not too difficult.—Why do you laugh at me ?—I do not laugh at you, but at your coat.—Does it not look like yours ?—It does not look like it, for mine is short (*corto*), and yours is too long (*lungo*) ; mine is black and yours is green.—Why do you associate with that man ?—I would not associate with him (*non lo frequenterei*, cond.) if he had not rendered me (*se non m' avesse reso*, subj.) great services (*gran servigi*).—Do not trust him (*non se ne fidi*), for if you are not on your guard he will cheat (*ingannare*) you.—Why do you work so much (*tanto*) ?—I work in order to be one day useful to my country.—When I was yet (*essendo ancor*) little I once (*un giorno*) said to my father, " I do not understand (*intendere* *) commerce (*il commercio*), and I do not know how to sell ; let me (*permettetemi*) play." My father answered me, smiling (*sorridendo*) : " By dealing (*mercantando*) one learns to deal, and by selling to sell." " But, my dear father," replied I, " by playing one learns also to play." " You are right," said he to me, " but you must first (*prima*) learn what is necessary (*necessario*) and useful."—Judge not (*non giudicate voi*) that you may not (*che non volete essere*) be judged! Why do you perceive (*scoprire*) the mote (*una paglia*) in your brother's eye, you who do not perceive (*vedere* *) the beam (*la trave*) which is in your eye ?

SIXTY-NINTH LESSON.

Lezione sessantesima nona.

PRESENT OF THE SUBJUNCTIVE.

That I may have, that thou mayest have.	Ch' io abbia, che tu abbia (abbi).
That he or she may have.	Ch' { egli (esso) / ella (essa) } abbia.
That we may have, that you may have.	Che noi abbiamo, che voi abbiate.
That they may have.	Ch' { eglino (essi) / elleno (esse) } abbiano.
That I may be, that thou mayest be.	Ch' io sia, che tu sia (sii).
That he or she may be.	Ch' { egli (esso) / ella (essa) } sia.
That we may be, that you may be.	Che noi siamo, che voi siate.
That they may be.	Ch' { eglino (essi) / elleno (esse) } siano (sieno).
That I may speak, that thou mayest speak.	Ch' io parli, che tu parli.
That he or she may speak.	Ch' { egli (esso) / ella (essa) } parli.
That we may speak, that you may speak.	Che noi parliamo, che voi parliate.
That they may speak.	Ch' { eglino (essi) / elleno (esse) } parlino.
That I may believe, &c.	Ch' io creda, che tu creda, ch' egli creda.
That we may believe, &c.	Che noi crediamo, che voi crediate, ch' eglino credano.
That I may hear, &c.	Ch' io senta, che tu senta, ch' egli senta.
That we may hear, &c.	Che noi sentiamo, che voi sentiate, ch' eglino sentano.

Obs. It will be remarked, firstly, that in the first conjugation the three persons singular terminate in *i*; in the two others, and in the two auxiliaries, in *a*-

The second person singular of the auxiliaries may also terminate in i. Secondly, that all the three conjugations have the first and second persons plural terminated alike, and the third person plural terminates in the second and third conjugations in *ono*, whilst in the first conjugation it ends in *ino*.

REMARKS ON THE USE OF THE SUBJUNCTIVE IN ITALIAN.

A. The subjunctive in Italian is made use of to express doubt or uncertainty.[1] It is governed by one of the following conjunctions, which generally precedes the verb which is put in the subjunctive mood.

Che, that.		*Avvegnachè*, whereas, though.	
Acciocchè	} to the end that.	*Finchè*, till.	
Affinchè,		*Sintantochè*, until.	
Benchè,	} although.	*Quansiunque*, though, although.	
Ancorchè,		*Purchè*, provided, that.	

B. The conjunction *che* makes all the words to which it is joined become conjunctions. The following conjunctive expressions, therefore, also require the subjunctive:

Dato che,	} suppose that.	*Bisogna che*, it is necessary that.	
Posto che,		*Dio faccia che,*	} would to God
In caso che, in case that.		*Voglia Iddio che,*	that.
Avanti che,	} before that.		
Prima che,			

C. Verbs expressing *will, desire, command, permission,* and *fear,* followed by the conjunction *che,* require the subjunctive, as: I will, I desire, I command, I permit my brother to study, to speak, to see, to go out, &c., *voglio, desidero, comando, permetto, che mio fratello studii, parli, veda, esca,* &c. I fear he may not sing, he may not say, &c., *temo che non canti, che non dica,* &c.

EXAMPLES.

I wish you may do it soon.	*Desidero che lo facciate presto.*
I fear it will rain to-night.	*Temo che piova questa sera.*
I hope to succeed in it.	† *Spero che la cosa mi riesca*
I must go there myself.	*Bisogna ch' io stesso ci vada.*
He says so, to the end that you may not attribute the fault to me, and that you may know what is to be expected from him.	*Lo dice, acciocchè non diate a me la colpa, ed affinchè sappiate, quanto si possa sperar da lui.*
Though it be difficult to subdue our passions, we must, notwithstanding, vanquish ourselves.	*Benchè sia difficile vincer le nostre passioni, bisogna però vincere se stesso.*
The count, though much frightened, had the boldness.	*Il conte avvegnachè (ancorchè) fosse molto spaventato, ebbe l' ardire.*
Wait till I return.	*Aspettate finchè lo torni.*
So long as I have not finished my work.	*Sintantochè io non abbia finito il mio lavoro.*
I will come, provided it does not rain.	*Verrò purchè non piova.*

[1] Hence the verb *credere,* to believe, always governs the subjunctive in Italian. Ex. *Mio fratello crede ch' io parli,* My brother thinks I speak.

SIXTY-NINTH LESSON. 379

Suppose that he were to die.	Posto che egli muoia.
In case he should not be in his apartment.	In caso che non fosse nel suo appartamento.
Suppose it to be so.	Dato che sia così.
Would to God that all were going well.	Dio faccia che tutto vada bene.
However wise the counsel that you have taken may be.	Comunque savio sia il consiglio che avete preso.
It is sufficient for me to know.	Basta ch' io sappia.
I must do.	Bisogna ch' io faccia.

D. The conjunction *che* does not require the subjunctive when it relates to verbs expressing certainty. Ex.

I know that thou hast not been at my house.	Io so che tu non sei stato da me.
He assured me that the work was by a master-hand.	M' assicurava che l' opera era di mano maestra.
I am sure that he is wrong.	Sono persuaso ch' egli ha torto.
I swear to thee that I have told him nothing.	Ti giuro che non gli ho detto niente.
I am convinced that he does not betray me.	Sono convinto che non mi tradisca.

E. The indicative is also employed after conjunctions expressing an action with certainty, such as :

Allorchè,	when.	*Frattanto,*	meanwhile.
Come,	as.	*Giacchè,*	since.
Così,	thus.	*Intantochè,*	so that.
Dacchè,	since.	*Mentrechè,*	whilst.
Dimodochè,	so that.	*Non pertanto,*	notwithstanding.
Dopo che,	after.	*Onde,*	therefore.
Perchè,	because, why.	*Se,*	if, since.
Perciò,	therefore.	*Sicchè,*	so that.
Però,	{ therefore. { nevertheless.	*Siccome,*	as.
		Stantechè,	since.
Poichè,	because.	*Tostochè,*	as soon as.
Quando,	when.	*Tuttavia,*	yet, nevertheless.

EXAMPLES.

Whilst he was at dinner, two horses were stolen from him.	Intanto ch' egli stava a pranzo, gli furono rubati due cavalli.
Whilst fortune came to his aid, it happened that the King of France died.	Mentrechè la fortuna veniva ad aiutarlo, avvenne che il Re di Francia morì.
Whilst I am speaking, time is passing.	Mentre ch' io parlo, il tempo passa.
It seemed to him he was ill, but he was nevertheless contented.	Gli pareva di star male, ma *non per tanto* era contento.
I should like to know why you do not call upon me any more.	Vorrei sapere, *perchè* non venite più da me.

I cannot come, because I am busy.	Non posso venire, perchè ho da fare.
He is an honest man, therefore I believe all he tells me.	Egli è galantuomo, perciò credo quanto mi dice.
Every thing lost may be recovered, but not life; therefore every one ought to take good care of it.	Ogni cosa perduta si può ricuperare, ma non la vita: epperò ciascuno deve esser di quella buon guardiano.
Though every body says it, I nevertheless do not believe it.	Benchè tutti lo dicano, io però non lo credo.
Now, as God has granted me so much grace, I shall die happy.	Ora, poichè Dio mi ha fatto tanta grazia, io morrò contento.
Though I have been advised by many physicians to use certain baths, I have nevertheless not been willing to do it.	Quantunque da molti medici mi sia stato consigliato d' usar certi bagni, pure non l' ho voluto fare.
If I do not mistake, I saw him the other night.	Se non m' inganno, lo vidi l' altra sera.
Though the smell of that juice offends, it is not for all that injurious to health.	Sebbene l' odore di questo sugo offenda, non perciò nuoce alla salute.
As soon as I am able, I will come.	Tostochè lo potrò, verrò.

F. The subjunctive is further made use of after the relative pronoun *che*, when it follows a superlative; and after the relative pronouns *che*, *il quale*, *chi*, *cui*, when the action which they present is doubtful or uncertain.

EXAMPLES.

The finest picture that is in Rome.	Il più bel quadro che sia in Roma.
The bravest man that I have ever known.	Il più brav' uomo ch' io abbia mai conosciuto.
The most ridiculous figure that one can see.	La figura la più ridicola che si possa vedere.
For that a man of some knowledge is required.	A ciò si vuole un uomo che abbia delle cognizioni.
You will not find any body who would do it.	Non troverete chi lo faccia.
I have nobody on whom I could rely.	Non ho nessuno in cui possa fidarmi.
Show me any one who has never committed a fault.	Mostratemi uno che non abbia mai commesso un fallo.
I want a horse that must be taller than this.	Ho bisogno di un cavallo che sia più alto di questo.
It is assured that peace is made.	Si dà per sicuro che la pace sia fatta.
They say that there has been a great battle near the Rhine.	Si dice che al Reno sia stata data una gran battaglia.
Whatever may happen.	Ne succeda quel che vuole.
However handsome she may be, she does not please me.	Per bella che sia non mi piace.
Let him be awake or asleep, I must speak to him.	Vegli o dorma, bisogna ch' io gli parli.

There is no one, however learned he may be, that knows all.	Non v' è uomo, per dotto che sia, che sappia tutto.
I do not see which is his intention.	Non vedo qual sia l' intenzione sua.
I do not know which are your books.	Non so quali siano i vostri libri.

G. When of two verbs the first is preceded by *non*, the second by *che*, the latter requires to be in the subjunctive. Ex.

I do not believe he studies.	Non credo che studii.
I do not think he walks.	Non penso che cammini.

EXERCISES.

212.

M. de Turenne would never buy (*non comprava mai*) any thing on credit of tradesmen (*il mercante*), for fear, said he, they should lose a great part of it, if he happened to be killed (*se gli accadesse di restar morto in guerra*). All the workmen (*gli operai*) who were employed about his house had orders to bring in the bills (*di presentare i loro conti*), before he set out for the campaign (*mettersi in campagna*), and they were regularly paid.

You will never be respected (*rispettare*) unless you forsake (*se non lasciando*) the bad company you keep.—You cannot finish your work to-night unless (*a meno che*) I help you. I will explain (*spiegare*) every difficulty to you, that you may not be disheartened (*scoraggiare*) in your undertaking (*l' impresa*).—Suppose you should lose your friends, what would become of you?—In case you want my assistance, call me; I shall help you.—A wise and prudent man (*un uomo savio e prudente*) lives with economy when young, in order that he may enjoy the (*per godere del*) fruit of his labour when he is old.—Carry (*portate*) this money to Mr. N., in order that he may be able to pay his debts (*il debito*).—Will you lend me that money?—I will not lend it you unless you promise to return (*rendere**) it to me as soon as you can.—Did the general arrive?—He arrived yesterday morning at the camp (*il campo*), weary and tired (*stanco ed abbattuto*), but very seasonably (*molto a proposito*); he immediately gave his orders to begin the action (*la battaglia* or *il combattimento*), though he had not (*non avesse*) yet all his troops.—Are your sisters happy?—They are not, though they are rich, because they are not contented.—Although they have a good memory, that is not enough to learn any language whatever (*qualunque siasi lingua*); they must make use of their judgment (*il giudizio*).—Behold (*Guardi*) how amiable that lady is; for all that she has no fortune (*quantunque sen sia agiata*), I do not love her the less (*l' amo istessamente*).—Will you lend me your violin?—I will lend it you, provided you return it me to-night.—Will your mother call upon me?—She will, provided you will promise to take her to the concert.—I shall not cease to importune (*importunare*) her till she has forgiven me.—Give me (*mi dia*) that penknife (*il temperino*).—I will give it you, provided you will not make a bad use of it.—Shall you go to London?—I will go, provided you accompany (*accompagnare*) me; and I will write again (*di nuovo*) to your brother, in case he should not have received my letter.

213.

Where were you during the engagement (*il fatto d' armi*)?—I was in bed to have my wounds (*la ferita*) dressed (*medicare*).—Would to God (*così fosse piaciuto a Dio che*) I had been there (*ch' io vi fossi stato*)! I would have (*avrei voluto*, cond.) conquered (*vincere*) or perished (*perire*).—We avoided (*si evitò*) an engagement for fear we should be (*che non fossimo*) taken, their force being superior (*superiore*) to ours.—God forbid (*Dio non voglia*) I should blame your conduct; but your business will never be done properly (*a dovere*), unless you do it yourself.—Will you set out soon?—I shall not set out till I have dined.—Why did you tell me that my father was arrived, though you knew (*mentre ch' Ella sapeva*) the contrary?—You are so hasty (*iracondo*), that however little you are contradicted (*ch' uno La contrarii*) you fly into a passion (*mettersi in collera*) in an instant.—If your father does not arrive to-day, and if you want money, I will lend you some.—I am much obliged (*tenutissimo*) to you.—Have you done your task?—Not quite; if I had had (*se avessi avuto*) time, and if I had not been (*fossi stato*) so uneasy about (*per*) the arrival of my father, I should have (*l' avrei*) done it.—If you study and are (*sia*) attentive, I assure you that you will learn the Italian language in a very short time. He who wishes to teach an art must know it thoroughly (*a fondo*); he must give none but clear (*preciso*) and well-digested (*digerire*) notions (*la nozione*); he must instil (*far entrare*) them one by one into the minds (*nello spirito*) of his pupils; and above all (*sopra tutto*), he must not overburthen (*sopraccaricare*) their memory with useless and unimportant (*vano*) rules.

My dear friend, lend me (*prestatemi*) a sequin.—Here are (*eccone*) two instead of one.—How much obliged I am to you (*quanto Le sono tenuto*)! I am always glad when I see you, and I find my happiness in yours.—Is this house to be sold?—Do you wish to buy it?—Why not?—Why does not your sister speak?—She would speak (*parlerebbe*, cond.) if she were not (*se non fosse*) always so absent (*disattenta*).—I like pretty anecdotes: they season (*condire*) conversation (*la conversazione*), and amuse every body. Pray relate me some.—Look, if you please, at page (*pagina*) one hundred and forty-eight of the book which I lent you, and you will find some.

214.

You must have patience, though you have no desire to have it, for I must also (*pure*) wait till I receive my money.—Should I (*nel caso ch' io*) receive it to-day, I will pay you all that I owe you.—Do not believe that I have forgotten it, for I think of it every day. Do you believe, perhaps (*crede Ella forse*) that I have already received it?—I do not believe that you have already received it; but I fear that your other creditors (*che gli altri di Lei creditori*) may already have received it.—You wish you had (*vorrebbe aver*, cond.) more time to study, and your brothers wish they did not need (*vorrebbero non aver bisogno*) to learn.—Would to God (*volesse Iddio*) you had (*avesse*) what I wish you, and that I had (*avessi*) what I wish.—Though we have not had what we wish (yet) we have almost always been contented; and Messieurs B. have almost always been discontented, though they have had every thing a reasonable man (*un uomo ragionevole*) can be contented with.—Do not believe, Madam, that I have had your fan (*il ventaglio*).—Who tells you that I believe it?—My brother-in-law wishes he had not had (*vorrebbe non aver avuto*) what he has had.—Wherefore?—He has always had many creditors, and no money.—I wish you would always speak Italian to me; and you must obey, if you wish to learn that language, and if you do not wish to lose your time (*inutilmente*).—I wish you were (*vorrei che foste*) more industrious and more attentive when I speak to you. If I were not (*non fossi*) your friend, and if you were not (*non foste*) mine, I should not speak (*parlerei*) thus to you.—Do not trust Mr. N. (*non vi fidate del Signor N.*), for he flatters you. —Do you believe a flatterer (*un adulatore*) can be a friend ?—You do not know him so well as I, though you see him every day.— Do not think that I am angry with him, because his father has offended me.—Oh! here he is coming (*eccolo che viene*); you may tell him all yourself.

SEVENTIETH LESSON.

Lezione settantesima.

THE SUBJUNCTIVE CONTINUED.

IMPERFECT OF THE SUBJUNCTIVE.

If I had, if thou hadst, if he had.	S' io avessi, se tu avessi, s' egli avesse.
If we had, if you had, if they had.	Se noi avessimo, se voi aveste, s' eglino avessero.
If I were, if thou wert, if he were.	S' io fossi, se tu fossi, s' egli fosse.
If we were, if you were, if they were.	Se noi fossimo, se voi foste, s' eglino fossero.
If I spoke, if thou spokest, if he spoke.	S' io parlassi, se tu parlassi, s' egli parlasse.
If we spoke, if you spoke, if they spoke.	Se noi parlassimo, se voi parlaste, s' eglino parlassero.
If I believed, if thou believedst, if he believed.	S' io credessi, se tu credessi, s' egli credesse.
If we believed, if you believed, if they believed.	Se noi credessimo, se voi credeste, s' eglino credessero.

If I heard, if thou heardest, if he heard. | S' io sentissi, se tu sentissi, s' egli sentisse.
If we heard, if you heard, if they heard. | Se noi sentissimo, se voi sentiste, s' eglino sentissero.

Obs. A. The imperfect of the subjunctive is formed from the *passato remoto* (Lesson LX.), by changing, for the first conjugation, *ai* into *assi*, for the second *ei* into *essi*, and for the third *ii* into *issi*. The second person plural is in all alike the second person plural of the *passato remoto*. (See Lesson LX.)

Obs. B. As to the formation of the preterite, or preterperfect and pluperfect of the subjunctive, it is exactly the same as in the indicative; the former being compounded of the present subjunctive of the auxiliary, and the past participle of another verb, the latter of the imperfect subjunctive of the auxiliary, and the past participle of another verb. *Ex.*

That I may have loved. | Ch' io abbia amato.
That he may have come. | Ch' egli sia venuto.
If I had loved. | S' io avessi amato.
If I were come. | S' io fossi venuto.

REMARK H.—ON THE USE OF THE SUBJUNCTIVE.

The imperfect of the subjunctive is employed after the conditional conjunction *se*, If, expressed or understood [1].

EXAMPLES.

If I had money. | Se io avessi danaro.
If he had time. | Se avesse tempo.
If you were rich. | S' Ella fosse ricca.
If he were a little more amiable. | S' egli fosse un po' più cortese.
If he loved me. | Se mi amasse.
If I lost my money. | Se io perdessi il mio danaro.
If he were to beat his dog. | Se battesse il suo cane.
If she heard me. | Se essa mi sentisse.
If the child slept. | Se il fanciullo dormisse.

OF THE CONDITIONAL OR POTENTIAL TENSES.

CONDITIONAL PRESENT.

This is formed from the present future (Lesson XLVI.) by changing

	Sing.	1	2	3	Plur.	1	2	3
into		à,	ai,	à,		remo,	rete,	ranno,
	"	ei,	resti,	rebbe,	"	remmo,	reste,	rebbero.

[1] Except when futurity is to be expressed, for then the future must be made use of. *Ex.*

If he comes, we shall see him. | Se verrà, lo vedremo.
I will go to see him to-morrow, if I have time. | Andrò a vederlo domani, se avrò tempo.

SEVENTIETH LESSON.

I should have, thou wouldst have, he would have.	Avrei, avresti, avrebbe.
We should have, you would have, they would have.	Avremmo, avreste, avrebbero.
I should be, thou wouldst be, he would be.	Sarei, saresti, sarebbe.
We should be, you would be, they would be.	Saremmo, sareste, sarebbero.

I should love, thou wouldst love, he would love.	Amerei, ameresti, amerebbe.
We should love, you would love, they would love.	Ameremmo, amereste, amerebbero.

I should believe, thou wouldst believe, he would believe.	Crederei, crederesti, crederebbe.
We should believe, you would believe, they would believe.	Crederemmo, credereste, crederebbero.

I should hear, thou wouldst hear, he would hear.	Sentirei, sentiresti, sentirebbe.
We should hear, you would hear, they would hear.	Sentiremmo, sentireste, sentirebbero.

J. Whenever there is a condition to be expressed, the imperfect of the subjunctive is used, and the conditional present answers to it. It is indifferent to begin the sentence by the imperfect of the subjunctive or the conditional, and vice versa.

EXAMPLES.

If I had money, I would buy some books.	Se avessi danaro, comprerei de' libri.
I would buy some books, if I had money.	Comprerei de' libri, se avessi danaro.
If he were a little more amiable, he would have many friends.	S' egli fosse un po' più cortese, avrebbe molti amici.
He would have many friends, if he were a little more amiable.	Avrebbe molti amici, s' egli fosse un po' più cortese.
I would do it, if I could.	Lo farei, se potessi.
If I could, I would do it.	Se potessi, lo farei.
If I had money, I would have a new coat.	Se avessi danaro, avrei un' abito nuovo.
I would have a new coat, if I had money.	Avrei un' abito nuovo, se avessi danaro.
If thou couldst do this, thou wouldst do that.	Se tu sapessi far questo, vorresti far quello.

SEVENTIETH LESSON. 387

Thou wouldst do that, if thou couldst do this.
If he could, he would.
He would, if he could.
I would go there, if I had time.
If I had time, I would go there.
If he knew what you have done, he would scold you.
He would scold you, if he knew what you have done.
To scold.
If there were any wood, he would make a fire.
He would make a fire, if there were any wood.

Should the men come, it would be necessary to give them something to drink.

Should we receive our letters, we would not read them until to-morrow.

Vorresti far quello, se tu sapessi far questo.
Se potesse, vorrebbe.
Vorrebbe, se potesse.
V' andrei, se avessi tempo.
Se avessi tempo, v' andrei.
Se sapesse ciò che avete fatto, vi rampognerebbe.
Vi rampognerebbe se sapesse ciò ch' avete fatto.
Rampognare (sgridare).
Se ci fosse legna, farebbe fuoco.

Farebbe fuoco, se ci fosse legna.

{ Se gli uomini venissero, bisognerebbe dar loro qualche cosa da bere.
Bisognerebbe dar loro qualche cosa da bere, se gli uomini venissero.

Se ricevessimo le nostre lettere, non le leggeremmo prima di domani.

CONDITIONAL PAST.

It is formed from the present conditional of the auxiliary and the past participle of the verb you conjugate.

I should have had, &c.	Avrei avuto, &c.
I should have been, &c.	Sarei stato. Fem. stata, &c.
We should have been, &c.	Saremmo stati. Fem. state, &c.

I should have, thou wouldst have, he would have,
We should have, you would have, they would have,
} spoken. believed. heard.

Avrei, avresti, avrebbe,
Avremmo, avreste, avrebbero,
} parlato. creduto. sentito.

I should have, thou wouldst have, he (she) would have,
We should have, you would have, they would have,
} set out.

Sarei, saresti, sarebbe,
Saremmo, sareste, sarebbero,
} partito; Fem. partita. partiti; Fem. partite.

EXAMPLES.

They would have been more cautious, if they had been warned.
He would have been freed, if he had requested it.

Sarebbero stati più cauti, se fossero stati avvertiti.
Sarebbe stato dispensato se l' avesse richiesto.

If I had received my money, I would have bought new shoes.	S' io avessi ricevuto il mio danaro, avrei comprato delle scarpe nuove.
If he had had a pen, he would have recollected the word.	S' avesse avuto una penna, si sarebbe ricordato della parola.
If you had risen early, you would not have caught a cold.	Se si fosse levata (alzata) di buon' ora, non si sarebbe infreddata.
If they had got rid of their old horse, they would have procured a better one.	Se avessero venduto il lor vecchio cavallo, se ne sarebbero procurato uno migliore.
If he had washed his hands, he would have wiped them.	S' avesse lavato le sue mani, se le sarebbe asciugate.
If I knew that, I would behave differently.	Se sapessi ciò, mi condurrei differentemente.
If I had known that, I would have behaved differently.	Se avessi saputo ciò, mi sarei condotto altrimenti.
If thou hadst taken notice of that, thou wouldst not have been mistaken.	Se ti fossi accorto di ciò, non ti saresti ingannato.

K. The pluperfect of the subjunctive and the past conditional meeting with each other, may sometimes be substituted by the imperfect of the indicative. Ex.

Had I known it yesterday, I would certainly have come.	Se lo sapeva ieri, lo veniva sicuramente. Instead of: Se l' avessi saputo ieri, sarei venuto sicuramente.
I would have given it you, if I had had it.	Io ve lo dava, se l' aveva. Instead of: Ve l' avrei dato, se l' avessi avuto.

L. As soon as *se* is not conditional it requires the indicative mood. Ex.

If at that time I had Italian books, they were not mine.	Se allora io aveva libri italiani, non erano miei.
If he is not ill, why does he send for the physician?	Se non è ammalato, perchè fa venir il medico?

M. The imperfect of the subjunctive is further used to express a wish in an exclamatory form. Ex.

O could I but know your sentiments!	Oh potessi sapere i vostri sentimenti!
O could I also come!	Oh potessi venir anch' io!
O had I but money!	Oh avessi danaro!

And when there is another verb following, it is also put in the imperfect of the subjunctive. Ex.

SEVENTIETH LESSON. 389

Would to God he never returned any more!	*Volesse* Iddio che non *ritornasse* mai più!

N. But when the wish is not exclamatory, the present of the conditional must be employed. Ex.

I should like to see him.	*Vorrei* vederlo.
I should willingly accompany you to Florence.	L' *accompagnerei* volentieri a Firenze.
I could not say so.	Non *saprei* dirlo.
I would lay any thing that it will not succeed.	*Scommetterei* tutto, che la cosa non andrà bene.¹

O. The past conditional alone is made use of to represent as doubtful an event that is to follow a preceding event. Ex.

He has promised to send me the goods, as soon as he would have received them.	Ha promesso di mandarmi le mercanzie subito che le avrebbe ricevute.
He has promised to write to me, as soon as he should be arrived in London.	Ha promesso di scrivermi subito che sarebbe arrivato in Londra.

Would you learn Italian, if I learnt it?	Imparerebbe Ella l' Italiano, se io l' imparassi?
I would learn it, if you learnt it.	L' imparerei, s' Ella l' imparasse.
Would you have learnt German, if I had learnt it?	Avrebbe Ella imparato il tedesco, se io l' avessi imparato?
I would have learnt it, if you had learnt it.	L' avrei imparato, se ella l' avesse imparato.
Would you go to Italy, if I went thither with you?	Andrebbe Ella in Italia, s' io v' andassi con Lei?
I would go thither, if you went thither with me.	V' andrei s' Ella ci venisse meco.
Would you have gone to Germany, if I had gone thither with you?	Sarebbe Ella andata in Alemagna, se io vi fossi andato con Lei?
Would you go out, if I remained at home?	Uscirebbe Ella, se io stessi in casa?
Would you have written a letter, if I had written a note?	Avrebbe Ella scritto una lettera, se io avessi scritto un biglietto?

---

¹ Such expressions are, in fact, elliptical, for they should be: *Vorrei vederla, se potessi,* I would see him, if I could; *l' accompagnerei volentieri a Firenze, se avessi tempo,* I should willingly accompany you to Florence, if I had time; *non saprei dirla, se dovessi,* I could not say so, if I were obliged. Hence it comes that when such expressions are followed by another verb, this must stand in the imperfect of the subjunctive. Ex. *Vorrei trovare uno che m' accompagnasse,* I should like to find one who would accompany me; *Vorrei un segretario che sapesse la lingua italiana,* I should like to have a secretary who knew the Italian language.

SEVENTIETH LESSON.

P. The imperfect of the subjunctive is often substituted for the imperfect of the indicative in speaking emphatically. Ex.

How much I relied on your promise, you know; how much I loved you, is not unknown to you; how little I deserved your forgetfulness, let your heart tell it you for me.	Quanto io mi *fidassi* della vostra promessa, voi lo sapete; quanto io v'*amassi*, non vi è ignoto; quanto poco *meritassi* la vostra dimenticanza, lo dica il vostro cuore per me.

Q. Let it finally be remarked, that the relative *che* requires the indicative when the subordinate proposition expresses any thing certain or positive, and the subjunctive when it relates to any thing uncertain or doubtful. Ex.

Bring me the book that pleases me.	*Ind.* Recami il libro che mi *piace*.
Bring me a book that may please me.	*Subj.* Recami un libro che mi *piaccia*.
I am looking for the road that leads to Florence.	*Ind.* Cerco la via che *mena* a Firenze.
I am seeking a road that may lead me to Florence.	*Subj.* Cerco una via che *meni* a Firenze.

However or *howsoever.*   { *Per quanto.* / *Per—che.*

Obs. R. *However* or *howsoever*, followed by an adjective, is rendered by *per quanto* invariably without *che*, or by *per* with *che*. In both cases the subjunctive is employed. Ex.

However learned you may be, there are many things which you do not know.	*Per quanto* dotto voi *siate* (or *per dotto che* voi *siate*), ignorate molte cose.
However happy she may be, she always thinks herself unhappy.	*Per quanto* fortunata ella *sia* (or *per fortunata ch'* ella *sia*), si crede sempre infelice.

Whatever, whatsoever. | *Per quanto.*

Obs. S. *Whatever* or *whatsoever*, followed by a substantive, is rendered by *per quanto* without *che*, but it agrees with the substantive, and is followed by the subjunctive. Ex.

Whatever endeavours he may make, he will never attain his aim.	*Per quanti* sforzi egli *faccia*, non arriverà mai al suo fine.
Whatever riches they may possess, they will never be contented.	*Per quante* ricchezze *possedano*, non saranno mai contenti.

Whoever, whosoever.   { *Chi che sia* (or *chichessia*). / *Chiunque.*

Of whomsoever you may speak, avoid slander.	Chi che sia la persona di cui parlate, evitate la maldicenza.

SEVENTIETH LESSON.

Whosoever may come, will be welcome.	Chiunque venga sarà ben venuto.
Whoever the stranger may be that you will see, receive him well.	Chi che sia lo straniero ch' Ella vedrà, l' accolga bene.
Whomsoever you may give this book to, recommend him to read it attentively.	A chiunque diate questo libro raccomandate di leggerlo attentamente.
I have seen nothing that could be blamed in his conduct.	Non ho veduto niente che si possa biasimare nella sua condotta.
I know nobody who is so good as you are.	Non conosco nessuno che sia così buono come Lei, or Voi. Non conosco nessuno che sia tanto buono quanto Lei, or Voi.
There is nobody who does not know it.	Non v' è chi non sappia ciò.

Whoever, whosoever. *Whatever, whatsoever.*	*Qualunque.*
Whoever may be your enemies, you have not to fear them so long as you act according to justice.	Qualunque siano i di Lei nemici non ha da temerli tanto che si conduce secondo la giustizia.
Whatever his intentions may be, I shall always behave towards him in the same manner.	Qualunque siano le sue intenzioni, mi condurrò sempre nella stessa maniera contro di lui (or verso di lui).

EXERCISES.

215.

Would you have money if your father were here?—I should have some if he were here.—Would you have been pleased if I had had some books?—I should have been much pleased if you had had some.—Would you have praised my little brother if he had been good?—If he had been good I should certainly (*sicuramente*) not only have praised, but also loved, honoured (*onorare*), and rewarded him.—Should we be praised if we did our exercises?—If you did them without a fault (*senza errore*), you would be praised and rewarded.—Would not my brother have been punished if he had done his exercises?—He would not have been punished if he had done them.—Would my sister have been praised if she had not been skilful?—She would certainly (*certa-*

mente) not have been praised if she had not been very skilful, and if she had not worked from morning till evening.—Would you give me something if I were very good ?—If you were very good, and if you worked well, I would give you a fine book.—Would you have written to your sister if I had gone to Paris ?—I would have written to her, and sent her something handsome if you had gone thither.—Would you speak if I listened to you ? —I would speak if you listened to me, and if you would answer me.—Would you have spoken to my mother if you had seen her ?—I would have spoken to her, and have begged her (*pregare*) to send you a handsome gold watch (*un bell' oriuolo d'oro*) if I had seen her.

Would you copy your exercises if I copied mine ?—I would copy them if you copied yours.—Would your sister have transcribed her letter if I had transcribed mine ?—She would have transcribed it if you had transcribed yours.—Would she have set out if I had set out ?—I cannot tell you what she would have done if you had set out.

216.

One of the valets de chambre (*uno dei camerieri*) of Louis (*di Luigi*) the Fourteenth requested that prince, as he was going to bed (*mentre questi andava a letto*), to recommend (*di far raccomandare*) to the first president (*il presidente*) a law-suit (*una lite*) which he had against (*contro*) his father-in-law, and said, in urging him (*sollecitandolo*): " Alas (*Ah*), Sire (*Sire*), you have but to say one word." " Well (*Eh*)," said Louis the Fourteenth, " it is not that which embarrasses me (*non è questo che mi dia fastidio*) ; but tell me (*dimmi*), if thou wert in thy father-in-law's place (*in luogo di*—), and thy father-in-law in thine, wouldst thou be glad if I said that word ?"

If the men should come it would be necessary to give them something to drink.—If he could do this he would do that.—I have always flattered myself, my dear brother, that you loved me as much as I love you ; but I now see that I have been mistaken. I should like to (*vorrei*) know why you went a walking without me (*senza di me*).—I have heard, my dear sister, that you are angry with me (*in collera contro di me*), because I went a walking without you (*senza di voi*).—I assure you that, had I known that you were not ill, I should have come for you (*venire a cercare qualcuno*); but I inquired (*informarsi*) at (*dal*) your physician's about your health (*sulla vostra salute*), and he told me, that you had been keeping your bed (*che voi stavate a letto*) the last eight days (*da otto giorni*).

217.

What do you think of our king?—I say he is a great man, but I add, that though kings be ever so powerful (*potente*), they die as well as the meanest (*abbietto*) of their subjects.—Have you been pleased with my sisters?—I have; for however plain (*brutto*) they may be, they are still very amiable; and however learned (*dotto*) our neighbour's (*fem.*) daughters, they are still sometimes mistaken.—Is not their father rich?—However rich he may be, he may lose all in an instant.—Whoever the enemy may be whose malice (*la di cui malizia*) you dread (*temere*), you ought to rely (*riposarsi*) upon your innocence; but the laws (*la legge*) condemn (*condannare*) all criminals (*il reo*) whatever they may be.—Whatever your intentions (*l'intenzione*) my be, you should have acted differently (*differentemente*).—Whatever the reasons (*la ragione*) be which you may allege (*allegare*), they will not excuse your action, blamable in itself.—Whatever may happen to you in this world, never murmur (*mormorare*) against Divine Providence (*la divina providenza*); for whatever we may suffer we deserve.—Whatever I may do, you are never satisfied.—Whatever you may say, your sisters shall be punished, if they deserve it, and if they do not endeavour (*studiarsi*) to mend (*emendarsi*).—Who has taken my gold watch?—I do not know.—Do not believe that I have had it, or that Miss C. has had your silver snuff-box (*la tabacchiera*), for I saw both in the hands of your sister when we were playing at forfeits (*a' pegni*).—To-morrow I shall set out for Dover; but in a fortnight I shall be back again (*tornare*), and then I shall come to see you and your family.—Where is your sister at present?—She is at Paris, and my brother is at Berlin.—That little woman is said to be going to marry General (*il generale*) K., your friend; is it true?—I have not heard of it.—What news is there of our great army?—It is said to be lying (*stare**)

between the Weser (*il Veser*) and the Rhine (*il Reno*).—All that the courier (*il corriere*) told me seeming (*parere* *) very probable (*verisimile*), I went home immediately, wrote some letters, and departed for London.

SEVENTY-FIRST LESSON.

Lezione settantesima prima.

OF THE IMPERATIVE.

This mood is formed from the present of the subjunctive by changing, for the first conjugation, the termination *i* of the second person singular into *a*, and for the two other conjugations *a* into *i*. All other persons of the imperative are like the present of the subjunctive, except the second person plural, which is formed, even in most of the irregular verbs, from the second person plural of the indicative.

	Conjug.	*Subj.* 2nd pers. sing.	*Imperative.* 2nd pers. sing.
That thou mayest speak, speak thou.	1st.	Parli.	Parla.
That thou mayest believe, believe thou.	2nd.	Creda.	Credi.
That thou mayest hear, hear thou.	3rd.	Senta.	Senti.

THE OTHER PERSONS OF THE IMPERATIVE ARE:

Let him speak, let us speak, speak ye, let them speak. — Parli, parliamo, *parlate*, parlino.
Let him believe, let us believe, believe ye, let them believe. — Creda, crediamo, *credete*, credano.
Let him hear, let us hear, hear ye, let them hear. — Senta, sentiamo, *sentite*, sentano.

	2nd pers.	3rd pers.	1st p. pl.	2nd p. pl.	3rd p. pl.
Have thou, &c.	Abbi,	abbia.	Abbiamo,	abbiate,	abbiano.
Be thou, &c.	Sii (sia),	sia.	Siamo,	siate,	siano.

Obs. A. The second person singular of the imperative is rendered by the infinitive whenever it is preceded by the negative *non*. Ex.

SEVENTY-FIRST LESSON. 395

Do not do that.	Non far questo.
Do not say that.	Non dir questo.
Do not deny that.	Non negar questo.
Do not believe that.	Non credere ciò.[1]
Have patience.	Abbiate pazienza.
Be (thou) attentive.	Sii attento.
Go (ye) thither.	Andatevi (or andate là).

Obs. B. The pronouns *mi, ti, ci, vi, si, melo, celo, glielo, &c.*, are joined to the imperative (the same as to the infinitive, Lesson XVII., and to the present participle, Lesson LVII.). Ex.

Give me.	Datemi.
Give us some.	Datecene.
Give it me.	Datemelo.
Send it to him (to her).	Mandateglielo.
Lend it to me.	Prestatemelo.
Believe (thou) me.	Credimi.

Obs. C. When the imperative is in the third person singular or plural, or when it is negative, the pronouns are not joined to it. Ex.

Let him believe me.	Mi creda.
Let them believe us.	Ci credano.
Do (thou) not believe me.	Non mi credere.
Do (ye) not tell it me.	Non me lo dite.
Do (thou) not listen to him.	Non l' ascoltare.
Let him not give it him.	Non glielo dia.
Let us not believe her.	Non le crediamo.
Do (ye) not believe me.	Non mi credete.
Let them not believe him.	Non gli credano.
Have the goodness to reach me that dish.	Abbiate (abbia) la bontà di porgermi questo piatto.

To borrow.	*Chiedere (ricevere) in prestito.*
I will borrow some money of you.	Voglio chiederle danaro in prestito.
I will borrow that money of you.	Voglio chiederle in prestito questo danaro.
Borrow it of (or from) him.	Chiedeteglielo in prestito.
I borrow it from him.	Glielo chiedo.
Do not tell him or her.	Non glielo dite (dica).
Do not return it to them.	Non lo rendete (renda) loro.

---

[1] This manner of rendering the imperative is elliptical, for there is always the verb *devi*, thou oughtest or shouldst, understood, as if we said: *Non devi far questo*, thou shouldst not do that; *non devi dir questo, non devi creder ciò*, &c.

SEVENTY-FIRST LESSON.

Patience, impatience.	La pazienza, l' impazienza.
The neighbour, the snuff-box.	Il prossimo, la tabacchiera.

Be (ye) good.	Siate buoni.
Know (ye) it.	Sappiatelo.

Obey your masters, and never give them any trouble.	Obbedite ai vostri maestri e non date loro mai dispiacere.
Pay what you owe, comfort the afflicted, and do good to those that have offended you.	Pagate ciò che dovete, consolate gl' infelici e fate del bene a quelli che vi hanno offesi.
Love God and thy neighbour as thyself.	Amate Iddio ed il prossimo come voi stessi.

To obey.	*Ubbidire (ubbidisco).* *Obbedire* 3 *(obbedisco).*
To comfort.	*Consolare* 1.
To offend.	*Offendere* * (is conjugated like *prendere* *) 2.

Let us always love and practise virtue, and we shall be happy both in this life and in the next.	Amiamo e pratichiamo sempre la virtù, e saremo felici in questa vita e nell' altra.
To practise.	*Praticare* 1.
Let us see which of us can shoot best.	Vediamo chi di noi tirerà meglio.

To express.	*Esprimere* * 2 (past part. *espresso*; pret. def. *espressi*).
To express one's self.	*Esprimersi.*
To make one's self understood.	*Farsi capire.*
To have the habit.	*Aver l' abitudine. Essere solito.*

To accustom.	*Avvezzare* 1, or *assuefare* * (like *fare* *).
To accustom one's self to something.	*Avvezzarsi a qualche cosa.*
Children must be accustomed early to labour.	Bisogna avvezzar presto i fanciulli al lavoro.

To be accustomed to a thing.	*Esser avvezzato (assuefatto) a qualche cosa.*
I am accustomed to it.	Io son avvezzato (avvezzo, assuefatto).
I cannot express myself in Italian, for I am not in the habit of speaking.	Non posso esprimermi bene in Italiano, perchè non ho l' abitudine di parlare.

SEVENTY-FIRST LESSON.

You speak properly. | Ella parla (voi parlate) propriamente.

To talk (converse). | Parlare 1, discorrere (discorso, discorsi) 2.
To chatter. | Cicalare 1. / Chiacchierare 1, ciorlare 1.
To prate. | Cianciare 1.
A prattler. | Un cicalone, un ciarlone
A chatterer. | Un ciarlatore.
To practise. | Esercitare 1.
I practise speaking. | Mi esercito a parlare.

To permit, to allow. | Permettere * (like mettere *).
The permission. | Il permesso. / La permissione.
I permit you to go thither. | Vi permetto di andarvi.

Do good to the poor, have compassion on the unfortunate, and God will take care of the rest. | Fate del bene ai poveri ed abbiate compassione degl' infelici; Dio avrà cura del resto.

To do good to some one. | Far del bene a qualcuno
To have compassion on some one. | Aver compassione di qualcuno.
Compassion. | La compassione.
Pity. | La pietà.
The rest. | Il resto.

If he comes tell him that I am in the garden. | Se viene diteglì ch' io sono nel giardino.
Ask the merchant, whether he can let me have the horse at the price which I have offered him. | Domandate al mercante, se può darmi il cavallo al prezzo che gli ho offerto.

THE ACCENTS.

There are in Italian two accents:
    I. The grave (`), and
    II. The acute (´).

I. THE GRAVE ACCENT.

This is put, 1. On nouns in *tà* and *tà* Such nouns have the singular and plural alike, as:

Beauty, goodness, virtue, youth. | Beltà, bontà, virtù, gioventù.

---

* Many Italian nouns in *tà* derive from the Latin nouns in *tas*, as: *castità*, chastity; *maestà*, majesty. Such nouns in *a* that are unaccented, are variable

These nouns ended formerly in *ade, ate, ude, ute*, and are still used thus in poetry.

2. On the third person singular of the preterite definite of verbs whose first person ends in two vowels, as:

| He loved, he believed, he heard. | Amò, credè, sentì. |

From *amai*, I loved; *credei*, I believed; *sentii*, I heard.
But write without an accent: *Vinse*, he vanquished; *prese*, he took; *diede*, he gave, from: *vinsi*, I vanquished; *presi*, I took; *diedi*, I gave, &c.

3. On the first and third persons singular of every verb in the future, as:

I shall speak, he will speak.	Parlerò, parlerà.
I shall believe, he will believe.	Crederò, crederà.
I shall feel, he will feel.	Sentirò, sentirà.

4. To make a distinction between words alike in orthography, but different in signification, such as:

Là, *lì*, there, and *la*, the, her; *li*, he, they.
Dà, he gives, and *da* (the ablative), from.
Dì, day, and *di* (the genitive), of.
Sì (the affirmation), yes, so, and *si* (the pronoun), one's self.
È, he or she is (the verb), and *e* (conjunction), and.

5. There are some other words which also have the grave accent, such as:

Più, more.
Giù, below.
Costì and *costà*, there.
Così, thus.
Già, already.
Ciò, that which.

Obs. When a word, having the grave accent, is joined to another word, the consonant of the latter must be doubled, and the accent taken off, as:

Dì and *dà* joined to *mi* become *dimmi*, tell (thou) me; *dammi*, give (thou) me.
Farò and *lo*, become *farollo*, I will do it.
Più and *tosto* make *piuttosto*, &c.

II. THE ACUTE ACCENT (').

This is seldom used in Italian. Some authors employ it:

1. On the letter i of words ending in *io* or *ia*, whenever *io* or *ia* are pronounced in two distinct syllables, such as:

| Folly, gallery. | Pazzía, galleria. |
| Desire, adieu. | Desío, addío. |

2. On words which have a double signification to avoid an ambiguous meaning, as:

Ténere, to hold, and *tènere*, tender.
Áncora, again, and *àncora*, an anchor.
Néttare, nectar, and *nettàre*, to clean, &c.

in the plural, as: *una visita*, a visit; plural, *le visite*, the visits: *grazia*, grace; plur. *grazie*, graces: *sapienza*, wisdom; plur. *sapienze*: *un poeta*, a poet; plur. *poeti*, poets.

EXERCISES.

218.

Have patience, my dear friend, and be not sad; for sadness alters (*cambiare*) nothing, and impatience makes bad worse (*peggiorare il male*). Be not afraid of your creditors; be sure that they will do you no harm. They will wait, if you cannot pay them yet.—When will you pay me what you owe me?—As soon as I have money I will pay all that you have advanced (*anticipare*) for me. I have not forgotten it, for I think of it (*vi penso*) every day. I am your debtor (*il debitore*), and I shall never deny (*negare*) it.—What a beautiful inkstand you have there! pray lend it me.—What do you wish to do with it?—I will show it to my sister.—Take it, but take care of it, and do not break it.—Do not fear (*Non tema di niente*).—What do you want of my brother?—I want to borrow money of him.—Borrow some of somebody else (*ad un altro*).—If he will not lend me any, I will borrow some of somebody else.—You will do well.—Do not wish for (*desiderare*) what you cannot have, but be contented with what Providence (*providenza*) has given you, and consider (*considerare*) that there are many men who have not what you have.—Life being short (*breve*), let us endeavour to make it as agreeable (*gradevole*) as possible (*quanto possibile*). But let us also consider that the abuse (*l'abuso*) of pleasure (*dei piaceri*) makes it bitter (*amaro*).—Have you done your exercises?—I could not do them, because my brother was not at home.—You must not get your exercises done by your brother, but you must do them yourself.—What are you doing there?—I am reading the book which you lent me.—You are wrong in always reading it.—What am I to do?—Draw this landscape, and when you have drawn it, you shall decline some substantives with adjectives.

219.

What must we do in order to be happy?—Always love and practise virtue, and you will be happy both in this life and in the next.—Since (*giacchè*) we wish to be happy, let us do good to the poor, and let us have compassion with the unfortunate; let us obey our masters, and never give them any trouble; let us com-

SEVENTY-FIRST LESSON.

fort the unfortunate, love our neighbours as ourselves, and not hate those (*e non odiamo quelli*) that have offended us; in short (*in una parola*), let us always fulfil our duty, and God will take care of the rest.—My son, in order to be loved you must be laborious (*laborioso*) and good. Thou art accused (*ti accusano*) of having been idle and negligent (*negligente*) in thy affairs. Thou knowest, however (*però*), that thy brother has been punished for having been naughty. Being lately (*l'altro giorno*) in town, I received a letter from thy tutor, in which he strongly (*molto*) complained of thee. Do not weep (*piangere*); now go into thy room, learn thy lesson, and be a good boy (*savio*), otherwise (*altrimenti*) thou wilt get nothing for dinner (*da pranzo*).—I shall be so good, my dear father, that you will certainly (*certamente*) be satisfied with me.—Has the little boy kept his word (*tener parola*)?—Not quite (*Non del tutto*); for after having said that, he went into his room, took his books, sat down at the table (*si mise al tavola*), and fell asleep (*s'addormentò*).—" He is a very good boy when he sleeps," said his father, seeing him some time after.

Good morning, Miss N. Ah! here are you at last (*eccola alla fine*); I have been waiting for you with impatience.—You will pardon (*perdonare*) me, my dear, I could not come sooner.—Sit down (*si accommodi*), if you please (*La prego*). How is your mother?—She is better to-day than she was yesterday.—I am glad of it (*ne sono contenta*).—Were you at the ball yesterday?—I was there.—Were you much amused (*divertirsi*)?—Only so so (*mediocremente*).—At what o'clock did you return (*ritornare*) home?—At a quarter past eleven.

220

Have you been learning Italian long?—No, Sir, I have been learning it only these six months.—Is it possible! you speak tolerably well (*passabilmente bene*) for so short a time (*per si poco tempo*).—You jest (*scherzare*); I do not know much of it yet.—Indeed, you speak it well already.—I think (*credo*) you flatter me a little.—Not at all (*nulla affatto*); you speak it properly (*convenevolmente*).—In order to speak it properly one must know more of it than I know (*che non so io*). You know enough of it to make yourself understood.—I still make many faults.—That is nothing (*non fa nulla*); you must not be bashful (*timido*); besides (*d'altronde*), you have made no faults in all you have said just now.—I am still timid (*timido*) because I am afraid of being laughed at (*che si beffino di me*).—They would be (*bisognerebbe essere*) very unpolite to laugh at you. Who would be so unpolite as to laugh at you? Do you not know the proverb (*il proverbio*)?—What proverb?—He who wishes to speak well must begin (*deve cominciare*) by speaking badly (*dal parlar male*).—Do you understand all I am telling you?—I understand (*intendere*) and comprehend (*capire*) it very well; but I cannot yet express myself well in Italian, because I am not in the habit of speaking it.—That will come in time (*col tempo*).—I wish (*desiderare*) it with all my heart.

Do you sometimes see my brother?—I see him sometimes; when I met him the other day he complained of you. "If he had behaved better, and had been more economical (*economo*)," said he, "he would have no debts (*il debito*), and I would not have been angry with him."—I begged him to have compassion on you, telling him that you had not even money enough to buy bread.—"Tell him when you see him," replied he to me, "that notwithstanding his bad behaviour (*la condotta*) towards me, I pardon him. Tell him also," continued he, "that one must not laugh at those (*che non bisogna beffarsi di coloro*) to whom one is under obligations. Have the goodness to do this, and I shall be much obliged to you (*tenutissimo*)," added he in going away (*allontanandosi*).

SEVENTY-SECOND LESSON.

Lezione settantesima seconda.

To stand up.	† Star in piedi. Stare sù.
To remain up.	† Restar in piedi.
Will you permit me to go to the market?	Vuol Ella permettermi d'andare al mercato?

SEVENTY-SECOND LESSON.

To hasten, to make haste.	*Sbrigarsi* 1.
Make haste, and return soon.	Sbrigatevi e ritornate presto.
Go and tell him that I cannot come to-day.	Andate a dirgli che oggi non posso venire.

Obs. A. Always put *a* before the infinitive, preceded by a verb of motion. The conjunction *and*, which in English follows the verbs *go* and *come*, is not rendered.

He came and told us he could not come.	Venne a dirci che non poteva venire.
Go and see your friends.	Andate a vedere i vostri amici.

To weep, to cry.	*Piangere** ; p. part. *pianto* ; pret. def. *piansi.*
The least blow makes him cry.	Il menomo (il più piccolo) colpo lo fa piangere.

To frighten.	*Spaventare* 1, *atterrire* (*isco*).
To be frightened, to startle.	*Spaventarsi, atterrirsi.*
The least thing frightens him (her).	La più piccola (la minima) cosa lo (la) spaventa.
Be not frightened.	Non si spaventi. Non si atterrisca. Non vi atterrite.

To be frightened at something.	*Spaventarsi di qualche cosa.*
What are you frightened at?	Di che si spaventa (vi spaventate)?
At my expense.	Alle mie spese (or a mie spese).
At his, her expense.	Alle sue spese (or a sue spese).
At our expense.	Alle nostre spese (or a nostre spese).
At other people's expense.	All' altrui spese (or ad altrui spese).
That man lives at every body's expense.	Quest' uomo vive alle spese di tutti.

To depend.	*Dipendere da.*
That depends upon circumstances.	Questo dipende dalle circostanze.
That does not depend upon me.	Questo non dipende da me.
It depends upon him to do that.	Dipende da lui di far ciò.
O! yes, it depends upon him.	Oh! sì, dipende da lui.

To astonish, to surprise.	{ *Stupire* 3 (*isco*). { *Sorprendere* * 2.
To be astonished, to wonder.	*Stupirsi, maravigliarsi.*
To be surprised at something.	*Essere maravigliato (sorpreso) di qualche cosa.*
I am surprised at it.	Ne sono sorpreso (maravigliato).
An extraordinary thing happened, which surprised every body.	Accadde una cosa straordinaria che sorprese ogni persona.

SEVENTY-SECOND LESSON. 403

To take place.	Aver luogo. Avvenire *, Accadere. Sopraggiugnere * (sopraggiunto (sopraggiunsi).
Many things have passed which will surprise you.	Avvennero molte cose che La sorprenderanno.
Many days will pass before that.	Molti giorni passeranno prima di ciò.
A man came in who asked me how I was.	Entrò un uomo che mi domandò come io stessi.
Then, thus, consequently. Therefore.	Dunque, adunque. Ecco perchè.
The other day.	L' altro giorno.
Lately.	Ultimamente, poco fa. Non è gran tempo, non ha guari.
In a short time.	Fra poco.
In.	Fra (tra) in.

Obs. D. When speaking of time, *fra* expresses the epoch, and *in* the duration. Ex.

He will arrive in a week.	Egli arriverà *fra* otto giorni.
It took him a week to make this journey.	Ha fatto questo viaggio *in* otto giorni.
He will have finished his studies in three months.	Egli avrà fatto i suoi studii *fra* tre mesi.
He finished his studies in a year.	Ha finito i suoi studii *in* un anno.
He has applied himself particularly to geometry.	Ha fatto uno studio particolare della geometria.

He has a good many friends.	Ha molti amici.
You have a great deal of patience.	Ella ha molta pazienza.
They have a great deal of money.	Hanno molto danaro.
You have a great deal of courage.	Ella ha molto coraggio.
To make a present of something to some one.	Far regalo di qualche cosa a qualcuno.
Mr. Lambertini wrote to me lately, that his sisters would be here in a short time, and requested me to tell you so; you will then be able to see them, and to give them the books which you have bought. They hope that you will make them a present of them. Their brother has assured me that they esteem you, without knowing you personally.	Il Signor Lambertini mi scrisse l' altro giorno che le sue signore sorelle verrebbero qui fra poco, e mi pregò di dirglielo. Potrà dunque vederle o dar loro i libri che ha comprati. Sperano che ne farà loro regalo. Il loro fratello m' ha assicurato che La stimano senza conoscerla personalmente.

SEVENTY-SECOND LESSON.

To want amusement.	Annoiarsi 1.
To get or be tired.	
How could I get tired in your company?	Come potrei annoiarmi presso di Lei?
	Come potrei annoiarmi nella di Lei compagnia.
He gets tired every where.	S' annoia dappertutto.

Agreeable, pleasing.	Gradevole, piacevole.
To be welcome.	Esser il ben venuto (il ben arrivato).
	Esser la ben venuta (la ben arrivata).
Be welcome.	Siate il ben venuto (la ben venuta).
You are welcome every where.	Ella è dappertutto il ben venuto.

EXERCISES.

221.

Have you already seen my son?—I have not seen him yet; how is he?—He is very well; you will not be able to recognize him, for he has grown very tall (*si è fatto molto grande*) in a short time.—Why does that man give nothing to the poor (*ai poveri*)? —He is too avaricious (*avaro*); he does not wish to open his purse for fear of losing his money.—What sort of weather is it? —It is very warm; it is long (*è un pezzo*) since we had any rain: I believe we shall have a storm (*un temporale*).—It may be (*può darsi*).—The wind rises (*alzarsi*), it thunders already; do you hear it?—Yes, I hear it, but the storm is still far off (*molto lontano*).—Not so far as you think; see how it lightens.—Bless me (*Dio mio*)! what a shower (*che pioggia dirotta*)! If we go into some place (*in qualche sito*), we shall be sheltered (*al coperto*) from the storm.—Let us go into that cottage then (*dunque*); we shall be sheltered there from the wind and the rain.—Where shall we go to now?—Which road shall we take?—The shortest (*corto*) will be the best.—We have too much sun, and I am still very tired; let us sit down under the shade of that tree.—Who is that man who is sitting under the tree?—I do not know him. —It seems he (*pare ch' ei*) wishes to be alone (*solo*); for when we offer to approach him (*gli andiamo vicino*), he pretends to be asleep.—He is like your sister: she understands Italian very

SEVENTY-SECOND LESSON. 405

well (*benissimo*); but when I begin to speak to her, she pretends not to understand me.—You have promised me to speak to the captain; why have you not done so?—I have not seen him yet; but as soon as I see him, I shall speak to him.

222.

Will you drink a cup of tea?—I thank you; I do not like tea.—Would you drink coffee?—With pleasure (*volentieri*), but I have just drunk some.—Do you not get tired here?—How could I get tired in this agreeable (*gradita*) society?—As to me, I always want amusement (*mi annoio sempre*).—If you did as I do (*come soglio far io*), you would not want amusement; for I listen to all those who tell me any thing. In this manner I learn a thousand agreeable things, and I have no time to get tired; but you do nothing of that kind (*di tutto ciò*), that is the reason why you want amusement.—I would do every thing like (*come*) you, if I had no reason (*motivo*) to be sad.—Have you seen Mr. Lambertini?—I have seen him; he told me that his sisters would be here in a short time, and desired me (*pregare*) to tell you so. When they have arrived you may give them the gold rings (*l' anello*) which you have bought; they flatter themselves that you will make them a present of them, for they love you without knowing you personally.—Has my sister already written to you?—She has written to me; I am going to answer her. Shall I (*debbo io*) tell her that you are here?—Tell her; but do not tell her that I am waiting for her impatiently (*con impazienza*).—Why have you not brought your sister along with you?—Which?—The one you always bring, the youngest.—She did not wish to go out, because she has the tooth-ache.—I am very sorry for it, for she is a very good girl.—How old is she?—She is nearly fifteen years old.—She is very tall (*grandissima*) for her age (*l' età*). How old are you?—I am twenty-two.—Is it possible! I thought you were not yet twenty.

SEVENTY-THIRD LESSON.

Lezione settantesima terza.

He is too fond of me not to do it.	Mi ama troppo per non farlo.
I go away not to displease him (displease her).	Me ne vado per non dispiacergli (dispiacerle).
One must be a fool not to perceive that.	Bisogna essere sciocco per non accorgersi di questo (or Bisogna aver poco senno per non accorgersi di questo).

To cease.	*Cessare* 1.
To dare.	*Ardire (ardisco¹), osare.*
To be able.	Potere*.
To know (can).	Sapere*.
You continually ask me for money.	† Non cessate mai dal chiedermi danaro.
She does not cease complaining.	† Dessa non si sta dal lagnarsi.
I do not dare to ask you for it.	Non ardisco chiedergliela.
She does not dare to tell you so.	Essa non ardisce dirgliela.
I cannot go thither.	Non posso andarvi.
I cannot tell you.	† Non saprei dirle, *or* dirvi.
You cannot believe it.	† Non potrebbe crederlo.

Besides, moreover.	*In oltre, di più.*
Besides that.	*Oltre ciò,* or *oltre di ciò.*
Besides.	*Altronde.*
Besides what I have just told you.	Oltre ciò che Le (vi) ho detto or ora.
There is no means of finding money now.	Adesso non vi è mezzo di trovar danaro.

---

¹ Not to confound the verb *ardire*, to dare, with *ardere*, to burn, its present participle, first person plural of the present tense indicative, first and second persons plural of the present tense subjunctive, and first person plural of the imperative, are substituted by the verb *osare*, as: Present participle, *osando*, daring: first person plural indicative, *Noi osiamo,* or *noi abbiamo l' ardire,* we dare; first and second persons plural subjunctive, *Osiamo, osiate,* or *che noi abbiamo l' ardire, che voi abbiate l' ardire,* that we may dare, that you may dare; first person plural of the imperative, *Osiamo,* let us dare.

SEVENTY-THIRD LESSON.

To push.	Spingere* 2 (p. part. spinto; pret. def. spinsi).
Along.	{ Lungo il (or al). { Rasente il, accanto di.
Along the road.	Lungo la via (lunghesso il camino).
Along the street.	Lungo la strada.
Along the coast.	Lungo il lido.
Along the river.	{ Lungo il fiume. { Lunghesso il fiume.
All along.	Pel corso di.
All the year round.	Pel corso dell' anno.
To enable to.	† Mettere nel caso (in istato) di.
To be able to.	{ † Essere in istato (nel caso) di. { Essere capace.
To the right. On the right side or hand.	{ A destra. A mano destra. { A diritta.
To the left. On the left side or hand.	{ A sinistra. Dal lato manco. { A manca.
Could you not tell me which is the nearest way to the city-gate?	Non potrebbe dirmi qual è la via la più corta per arrivar alla porta della città?
Go to the bottom of this street, and when you are there, turn to the right, and you will find a cross-way, which you must take.	Segua tutta questa strada, e quando sarà all' estremità, giri a destra, troverà una capocroce, or un crocicchio che traverserà.
And then?	E poi?
You will then enter a broad street, which will bring you to a great square, where you will see a blind alley.	Poi entrerà in una strada discretamente larga, che La menerà sopra una gran piazza dove vedrà un angiporto.
You must leave the blind-alley on your left, and pass under the arcade that is near it.	Lascierà l' angiporto dal lato manco, o passerà sotto gli archi che sono accanto.
Then you must ask again.	In seguito domanderà.
An arcade.	Un arco.
The cross-way.	La capocroce.
The blind-alley.	L' angiporto.
The shore, the bank.	La spiaggia, il lido.
To get married, to enter into matrimony.	Maritarsi, ammogliarsi.

SEVENTY-THIRD LESSON.

To marry somebody.	Sposare qualcuno.
To marry (to give in marriage).	Maritare.
My cousin, having given his sister in marriage, married Miss Delbi.	Mio cugino avendo maritato sua sorella, sposò la signorina Delbi.
Is your cousin married?	Il di Lei signor cugino è egli ammogliato?
No, he is still a bachelor.	No, Signore, è ancor celibe.
To be a bachelor.	Essere celibe, or scapolo.
Embarrassed, puzzled, at a loss.	*Imbarazzato, impacciato*
An embarrassment, a puzzle.	Un imbarazzo, un imbroglio.
You embarrass (puzzle) me.	Ella m' imbarazza.
You puzzle (perplex) me.	Ella mi mette nell' imbarazzo.
The marriage.	Il matrimonio.
He asks my sister in marriage.	Domanda mia sorella in matrimonio.

The measure.	*La misura.*
To take measures.	Prendere delle misure.
I shall take other measures.	Prenderò altre misure.

Goodness! how rapidly time passes in your society.	Dio! quanto presto passa il tempo nella di Lei società (nella di Lei compagnia).
The compliment.	Il complimento.
You make me a compliment which I do not know how to answer.	Mi fa un complimento al quale non so che rispondere.

The fault.	*Il fallo, la colpa.*
It is not my fault.	Non è mia colpa.
Do not lay it to my charge.	{ Non me lo imputi. { Non imputatemelo.
To lay to one's charge.	*Imputare a qualcuno.*
Who can help it?	Di chi è la colpa?
Whose fault is it?	
I cannot help it.	{ Non so che farvi. { Non saprei che farvi.

The delay.	La dilazione, il ritardo, l' indugio.
He does it without delay.	Lo fa senza ritardo.
I must go (must be off).	{ Sto per ritararmi (or ora me ne andrò). { Sto per andarmene via.
Go away! Begone!	{ Fuggi! Scappi! { Andatevene! Se ne vada!

SEVENTY-THIRD LESSON. 409

To jest.
The jest, the joke.
Seriously, in good earnest.
You are jesting.
He cannot take a joke, is no joker.
To take a joke.

Buffonare, burlare, scherzare.
Lo scherzo, la burla.
Senza burle (sul serio).
{ Ella burla (scherza).
{ Ella si burla.
† Non regge alla cella.
† Reggere * alla cella (*retto, ressi*).

To beg some one's pardon.
To pardon.

Domandar scusa a qualcuno.
Perdonare, far grazia, scusare.

I beg your pardon.

{ Mi perdoni. La mi scusi. Le domando scusa.
{ Perdonatemi. Vi domando scusa.

Pardon me.

{ Vossignoria mi scusi.
{ Mi scusi. Scusatemi.

The pardon.

Il perdono, la scusa.

To advance.

Avanzare. Andare avanti (innanzi).

The watch goes too fast (gains).
That clock goes too fast (gains).

L' oriuolo avanza (va avanti).
Quest' orologio anticipa.

To retard.

Ritardare 1.

The watch goes too slow (loses).
My watch has stopped.

L' oriuolo ritarda.
{ Il mio oriuolo si è fermato.
{ Il mio oriuolo sta (*or* è) fermo.

To stop.

Fermarsi 1.

Where did we stop?
We left off at the fortieth lesson, page one hundred and thirty-six.

† Dove ne eravamo?
† Eravamo alla lezione quarantesima, pagina cento trenta sei.

To wind up a watch.
To regulate a watch.

Caricare un oriuolo.
Regolare un oriuolo (méttere a segno un oriuolo).

Your watch is twenty minutes too fast, and mine a quarter of an hour too slow.

Il di Lei oriuolo avanza venti minuti, e il mio ritarda un quarto d' ora.

18

SEVENTY-THIRD LESSON.

It will strike twelve.	Sta per suonare mezzo giorno. Mezzo giorno suonerà or ora.
Has it already struck twelve?	Son già suonate le dodici?
It has already struck three.	Le tre sonò già sonate.
To strike.	*Suonare* 1. *Battere* 2.

On condition, *or* provided.	A condizione, sotto condizione. Col patto.
I will lend you money, provided you will henceforth be more economical than you have hitherto been.	Vi presterò del danaro, a condizione che sarete d' or innanzi più economo che non siete stato sino adesso (*or* che non lo foste finora).
Hereafter, for the future, henceforth.	D' or innanzi, d' oggi in avanti, in avvenire, nell' avvenire.
The future.	L' avvenire (*mas.*), il futuro.
Economical.	Economo, economico, risparmiante.
To renounce gambling.	Rinunciare al giuoco. Abbandonare il giuoco.
To follow advice (counsel).	*Seguire un consiglio (un parere).*
You look so melancholy.	Ella ha l' aspetto così melanconico.
Adieu, farewell. God be with you, good bye.	Addio.
Till I see you again. I hope to see you again soon.	Al piacere di rivederla. A rivederla.

EXERCISES.

223.

Why does my sister make no progress?—She would make some if she were as assiduous as you.—You flatter me.—Not at all (*niente affatto*); I assure you that I should be highly satisfied (*contentissimo*), if all my pupils worked (*studiare*) like you.—Why do you not go out to-day?—I would go out, if it were fine weather.—Shall I have the pleasure of seeing you to-morrow?—If you wish it I will come.—Shall I still be here when you arrive (*al di Lei ritorno*)?—Will you have occasion (*occasione*) to go to town this evening?—I do not know, but I would go now, if I had an opportunity (*una buona occasione*).—You would not have so much pleasure, and you would not be so happy, if you had not friends

SEVENTY-THIRD LESSON. 411

and books.—Man (*l' uomo*) would not experience (*provare*) so much misery in his career (*la carriera*), and he would not be so unhappy, were he not so blind (*cieco*).—You would not have that insensibility (*questa insensibilità*) towards the (*pei*) poor, and you would not be so deaf (*sordo*) to their supplications (*alle loro preghiere*), if you had been yourself in misery for some time (*qualche tempo*).—You would not say that if you knew me well.—Why has your sister not done her exercises?—She would have done them if she had not been prevented.—If you worked more, and spoke oftener, you would speak better.—I assure you, Sir, that I should learn better, if I had more time.—I do not complain of you, but of your sister.—You would have no reason (*Non avrebbe luogo*) to complain of her, had she had time to do what you gave her to do.—Would you be sorry (*spiacere ad uno*) if your mother were to arrive to-day?—I should not be sorry for it.—Would your sister be sorry if she were rich?—She would not be sorry for it.—Where were you when your sister went out?—I was in my room.—She wished she had known it (*Ella vorrebbe averlo saputo*); for, had she known it, she would have called you in order to take you along with her to the opera.—They say that the house of our neighbour has been burnt down (*sia stata abbruciata*).—Did you know it?—I was quite ignorant of (*ignorare intieramente che*) his house being on fire (*il fuoco fosse alla sua casa*); for had I known it, I would have run to his assistance (*in suo aiuto*).—What has my brother told you?—He has told me that he would be the happiest man in the world (*del mondo*), if he knew the Italian language, the finest of all languages.

224.

I should like to know (*vorrei pur sapere*) why I cannot speak as well as you.—I will tell you: if you did as I do you would speak well. You would speak as well as I, if you were not bashful (*timido*). But if you had studied your lessons more carefully (*meglio*), you would not be afraid to speak; for, in order to speak well one must know, and it is very natural (*molto naturale*) that he who does not know well what he has learnt, should be (*subj.*) timid. You would not be so timid as you are, if you were sure to make no mistakes (*sbagli*).

I come to wish you a good morning.—You are very kind (*amabilissimo*).—Would you do me a favour?—Tell me (*Dicami*, or *mi dica*) what you want, for I would do any thing to oblige you (*per renderle servigio*).—I want five hundred crowns, and I beg you to lend them to me.—I will return them to you as soon as I have received my money.—You would oblige me much (*rendere qualcuno obbligato*), if you would render me this service.—I would do it with all my heart (*di tutto cuore*), if I could; but having lost all my money, it is impossible for me (*mi è impossibile*) to render you this service.—May I ask you for (*oserei domandarle*) a little water?—What do you want water for?—Because I wish (*perchè vorrei*) to wash my hands.—If you would also give me a towel to wipe my hands after having washed them, I should be much obliged to you (*Le sarei tenutissimo*.—Why have your brothers sold their old horse?—They would not have got rid of it, if they had not got a better.—Why did not your sister get a better carriage?—If she had got rid of her old carriage, she would have got a better.—Would you execute (*fare**) a commission for me?—With much pleasure.—If the merchant would be satisfied with the sum which I offered for the horse, I would buy it.—I am sure that he would be satisfied, if you would add (*aggiungervi*) a few crowns more.—If I was sure of that I would add a few crowns more.—Children (*ragazzi miei*)! have you done your task?—We must be ill (*bisognerebbe che fossimo ammalati*) not to do it.—Is this wine sufficient for you (*Le basta*—)?—It would be sufficient for me if I was not very thirsty.—If your sisters have done their tasks (*il lor dovere*), why do they hide themselves?—They would not hide themselves, if they did not fear to be seen by their (*dalla lor*) governess (*maestra*), who would scold them for having gone a walking without telling her (*senza dirle nulla*).

225.

What o'clock is it?—It is half-past one.—You say it is half-past one, and by my watch (*al mio oriuolo*) it is but half-past twelve.—It will soon strike two.—Pardon me, it has not struck one.—I assure you it is five-and-twenty minutes past one, for my watch goes very well.—Bless me! how rapidly time passes in your society.—You make me a compliment which I do not know

how to answer. Have you bought your watch in Paris?—I have
not bought it, my uncle has made me a present of it.—What has
that woman intrusted you with?—She has intrusted me with the
secret of a great count who is in great embarrassment about the
marriage (*a cagione del matrimonio*) of one of his daughters.—
Does any one ask her (*La domanda forse qualcuno*) in marriage?
—The man who asks her in marriage is a nobleman of the
neighbourhood (*la vicinanza*).—Is he rich?—No, he is a poor
devil (*il diavolo*) who has not a sou (*un quattrino*).—You say you
have no friends among your school-fellows (*il condiscepolo*); but
is it not your fault? You have spoken ill (*sparlare*) of them, and
they have not offended you. Believe me, he who has no friends
deserves to (*meritare di*) have none.

226.

A Dialogue (Dialogo) between a Tailor and his Journeyman
(*il garzone*).

Charles (*Carlo*), have you taken the clothes to the Count of
(*della*) Torre?—Yes, Sir, I have taken them to him.—What did
he say?—Nothing but (*se non*) that he had a great mind to give
me a box on the ear (*uno schiaffo*), because I had not brought
them sooner.—What did you answer him?—Sir, said I, I do not
understand (*non tollero*) that joke: pay me what you owe me;
and if you do not do so instantly, I shall take other measures.
Scarcely had I said that, when he put his hand to his sword (*che
mise mano alla spada*), and I ran away (*prendere* la fuga*).

SEVENTY-FOURTH LESSON.
Lezione settantesima quarta.

To last (*to wear well*).	Durare 1.
That cloth will wear well.	Questo panno durerà molto.
How long has that coat lasted you?	Quanto tempo Le ha durato quest' abito?

SEVENTY-FOURTH LESSON.

To my liking.	A mio grado (a mio genio, a mio modo).
To every body's liking.	A grado di tutti.
Nobody can do any thing to his liking.	Non gli va niente a genio. Non si può far nulla a suo grado (a modo suo).

A boarding-house. A boarding-school.	Una pensione.
To keep a boarding-house.	Tenere pensione, tenere a dozzina.
To board with any one, or any where.	Essere in pensione di, essere a dozzina. Mettersi in pensione a.

To exclaim.	Esclamare 1.
To make uneasy.	Inquietare 1.
To get or grow uneasy.	Inquietarsi.
To be uneasy.	Esser inquieto (fem. inquieta).
Why do you fret (are you uneasy)?	Perchè mai s' inquieta?
I do not fret (I am not uneasy).	Non m' inquieto.
That news makes me uneasy.	Questa nuova m' inquieta.
I am uneasy at not receiving any news.	Sono inquieto di non ricevere nuove.
She is uneasy about that affair.	È inquieta su questo affare.
Do not be uneasy.	Non s' inquieti.
Quiet.	Tranquillo, quieto.

To quiet.	Tranquillare 1.
Compose yourself.	Si tranquilli (tranquillatevi).

To alter, to change.	Cambiare 1.
That man has altered a great deal since I saw him.	Quest' uomo ha molto cambiato da che non l' ho veduto.

To be of use.	Servire 3.
Of what use is that to you?	† A che Le serve (vi serve) ciò?
That is of no use to me.	† Non mi serve a niente.
Of what use is that to your brother?	† A che serve ciò al di Lei fratello?
It is of no use to him.	† Non gli serve a niente.
Of what use is that stick to you?	† A che Le serve questo bastone?
I use it to beat my dogs.	† Mi serve per battere i miei cani.
Of what use is that horse to your brother?	† A che serve questo cavallo al di Lei fratello?

SEVENTY-FOURTH LESSON. 415

He uses it to carry his vegetables to the market. † Gli serve a portar i suoi legumi al mercato.
Of what use are these bottles to your landlord? † A che servono queste bottiglie al di Lei locandiere?
They serve him to put his wine in. † Gli servono per metterci il suo vino.

To stand instead, to be as.   Servire di.

I use my gun as a stick. † Il mio schioppo mi serve di bastone.
This hole serves him as a house. † Questo buco gli serve di casa.
He used his cravat as a nightcap. † La sua cravatta gli ha servito di berretta da notte (di cuffia da notte).

To avail.   Servire (di before inf.).

What avails it to you to cry? † A che Le serve di piangere?
It avails me nothing. † Non mi serve a nulla.

Opposite to.   Dirimpetto a, in faccia a. Contro a (di), di contro a.

Opposite that house. Dirimpetto a questa casa.
Opposite the garden. Dirimpetto al giardino.

Opposite the church. In faccia (dirimpetto, di contro) alla chiesa.
Opposite to me. Dirimpetto a me.
Right opposite. Proprio in faccia.
He lives opposite the castle. Abita in faccia al castello.
I live opposite the king's library. Abito in faccia alla biblioteca reale.
To get hold of.
To take possession of. } Impadronirsi di.
To witness.
To show. } Attestare 1, testimoniare 1, dimostrare 1.
To give evidence against some one. Testimoniare contro qualcuno.
He has shown a great deal of friendship to me. Mi ha dimostrato molta amicizia.
To turn some one into ridicule. Porre in ridicolo qualcuno
To become ridiculous. Divenir ridicolo.
To make one's self ridiculous. Rendersi ridicolo.

To be born.   Esser nato.

Where were you born? † Dove è Ella nata?
I was born in this country. † Sono nato in questo paese.
Where was your sister born? † Dove è nata la di Lei sorella?
She was born in the United States of North America. † È nata negli Stati-Uniti dell' America settentrionale.

Where were your brothers born?	† Ove son nati i di Lei fratelli?
They were born in Italy.	† Son nati in Italia.

The boarder.	Il pensionario, Dozzinante.
The pouch.	Il carniere.
A pillow.	Un guanciale, piumaccio.
Down.	La peluria.

EXERCISES.

227.

What are you astonished at?—I am astonished to find you still in bed.—If you knew how (*quanto*) sick I am, you would not be astonished.—Has it already struck twelve?—Yes, madam, it is already half-past twelve.—Is it so late? Is it possible?—That is not late, it is still early.—Does your watch go well?—No, Miss N., it is a quarter of an hour too fast.—And mine is half an hour too slow.—Perhaps it has stopped?—In fact, you are right.—Is it wound up?—It is wound up, and yet (*pure*) it does not go.—Do you hear? it is striking one o'clock (*suona l' ora*).—Then I will regulate my watch and go home.—Pray (*di grazia*) stay a little longer (*La resti ancor un poco*)!—I cannot, for we dine precisely at one o'clock.—Adieu, then, till I see you again.—What is the matter with you, my dear friend? Why do you look so melancholy?—Nothing ails me (*non ho niente*).—Are you in any trouble (*Avresti a caso qualche dispiacere*)?—I have nothing, and even less than nothing, for I have not a penny (*un quattrino*), and owe a great deal to my creditors: am I not very unhappy?—When a man is well and has friends he is not unhappy.—Dare I ask you a favour?—What do you wish?—Have the goodness to lend me fifty crowns.—I will lend them you with all my heart, but on condition that you will renounce gambling (*rinunziare al giuoco*), and be more economical than you have hitherto been.—I see now (*Ora vedo*), that you are my friend, and I love you too much not to follow your advice.—John (*Giovanni*)!—What is your pleasure, Sir?—Bring some wine.—Presently, Sir.—Menico!—Madam?—Make the fire (*del fuoco*).—The maidservant has made it already.—Bring me some paper, pens, and ink. Bring me also some sand (*della sabbia*) or blotting-paper (*della carta sugante o succhia*), sealing-wax (*della cera lacca*), and a light (*un lume*).—Go and tell my sister not to wait for me, and be back again (*di ritorno*) at twelve o'clock in order to carry my letters to the post (*la posta*).—Very well (*benissimo*), Madam.

228.

Sir, may I (*ardirò io*) ask where the Earl of B. lives?—He lives near the castle on the other side of the river.—Could you tell me which road I must (*debba*) take to go thither?—You must go (*segua*) along the shore, and you will come to a little street (*quando sarà all' estremità prenda una contradella*) on the right, which will lead you straight (*direttamente*) to his house. It is a fine house, you will find it easily.—I thank you, Sir.—Does Count N. live here?—Yes, Sir, walk in (*favorisca di entrare*), if you please.—Is the Count at home? I wish to have the honour (*l' onore*) to speak to him.—Yes, Sir, he is at home; whom shall I have the honour to announce (*annunziare*)?—I am from B., and my name is (*chiamarsi*) F.

Which is the shortest (*corto*) way to the arsenal (*l' arsenale*)?—Go down (*segua*) this street, and when you come to the bottom (*sarà all' estremità*), turn to the left, and take the cross-way (*troverà una—che traverserà*); you will then enter into a rather narrow (*stretto*) street, which will lead you to a great square (*la piazza*), where you will see a blind alley.—Through (*per*) which I must pass?—No, for there is no outlet (*l' uscita*). You must leave it on the right, and pass under the arcade which is near it.—And then?—And then you must inquire further.—I am very much obliged (*tenutissimo*) to you.—Do not mention it (*Non ne val la pena*).—Are you able to translate an English letter into Italian?—I am.—Who has taught you?—My Italian master has enabled me to do it. (See end of Lesson XXIV.)

SEVENTY-FIFTH LESSON.
Lezione settantesima quinta.

To lose sight of.	† *Perdere di vista.* † *Dileguarsi dagli occhi (dalla vista.)* † *Lasciare andare dallo sguardo (dagli sguardi, dal guardo).*
The sight.	La vista.
I wear spectacles because my sight is bad (or because I have a bad sight).	Porto degli occhiali, perchè ho cattiva vista.
I am near-sighted.	† Ho la vista corta.
The ship is so far off that we shall soon lose sight of it.	† Il bastimento è così lontano che si dileguerà quanto prima dalla nostra vista (dai nostri occhi, dal nostro sguardo).
I have lost sight of that.	† Non so più nulla di ciò.
As it is long since I was in England, I have lost sight of your brother.	† Siccome è molto tempo che non sono stato in Inghilterra, ho perduto di vista il di Lei fratello.
As it is long since I have read any Italian, I have lost sight of it.	† Come è lungo tempo che non ho letto l' italiano, l' ho dimenticato (non lo so più).

You *ought* or *should* do that.	*Dovrebbe* far ciò.

Obs. A. Ought and *should* are rendered into Italian by the conditionals of the verb *dovere*, to be obliged, to owe.

He *ought* not to speak thus to his father.	Egli non *dovrebbe* parlar così a suo padre.
We *ought* to go thither earlier.	*Dovremmo* andarvi più per tempo (più di buon' ora).
They *should* listen to what you say.	*Dovrebbero* ascoltare ciò che Ella dice.
You *should* pay more attention to what I say.	*Dovreste* far più attenzione (star più attento) a ciò che dico.
You *ought to have* done that.	*Avrebbe dovuto* far ciò.
He *should have* managed the thing better than he has done.	Egli *avrebbe dovuto* regolarsi meglio che non ha fatto.
You *should have* managed the thing differently.	*Avrebbe dovuto* prendersi in modo diverso (or *maneggiare la cosa*).

SEVENTY-FIFTH LESSON. 419

They *ought to have* managed the thing as I did.	† *Avrebbero dovuto* agire in tal faccenda come mi vi son preso io.
We *ought to have* managed it differently from what they did.	† *Avremmo dovuto* condurci in tal faccenda diversamente di quello che hanno fatto.
You have managed the thing badly.	Vi siete mal preso.

To bid or *to wish*.	*Augurare* 1.
I bid you good morning.	Le auguro il buon giorno (Lesson XXVI.).
I wish you a good morning.	
I wish you a good journey.	Le auguro un buon viaggio

To play a game at billiards.	Far una partita al bigliardo (Lesson LI.).
To play upon the flute.	Suonare il flauto (Lesson LI.).
A fall.	Una caduta.
To have a fall.	† Far una caduta.
A stay, a sojourn.	Un soggiorno.
To make a stay.	Far un soggiorno.
Do you intend to make a long stay in the town?	Pensa Ella far un lungo soggiorno nella città?
I do not intend to make a long stay in it.	Non penso farvi un lungo soggiorno

To propose (meaning *to intend*).	{ *Proporre* *Far proposito* } di.
I propose going on that journey.	Mi propongo di far questo viaggio.
I propose (intend) joining a hunting party.	Mi propongo d' andare ad una partita di caccia.

To suspect, to guess.	*Sospettare* 1.
I suspect what he has done.	Sospetto ciò che ha fatto.
He does not suspect what is going to happen to him.	Non sospetta ciò che or ora gli accadrà (gli arriverà).

To think of some one or *of something*.	*Pensare a qualcuno, o a qualche cosa*.
Of whom do you think?	A chi pensa Ella?
Of what do you think?	A che pensa Ella?

To turn upon. *To be the question.*	*Trattarsi di.*
It is the question it turns upon.	Si tratta di.
The question is not pleasure, but your improvement.	Non si tratta del vostro piacere, ma dei vostri progressi.

420 SEVENTY-FIFTH LESSON.

You play, Sir; but playing is not the thing, but studying.	Giuocate, Signore; ma non si tratta di giuocare, si tratta di studiare.
What is going on?	Di che si tratta?
The question is what we shall do to pass the time agreeably.	Si tratta di sapere ciò che faremo per passar il tempo piacevolmente.

On purpose.	*Apposta.* *A bella posta.*
I beg your pardon, I have not done it on purpose.	Le domando scusa, non l' ho fatto apposta (a bella posta).

To hold one's tongue. *To stop speaking, to be silent.*	*Tacere**; past part. *taciuto*; pret. def. *tacqui.*

Obs. B. Five irregular verbs have their *perfetto remoto* in *equi*, viz.

Infinitive.		*Pret. Def.*	*Past Part.*
To please,	Piacere*.	Piacqui,	piaciuto.
To be situated,	Giacere*.	Giacqui,	giaciuto.
To be silent,	Tacere*.	Tacqui,	taciuto.
To hurt,	Nuocere*.	Nocqui,	nociuto.
To be born,	Nascere*.	Nacqui,	nato.

Do you hold your tongue?	Tacete?
I hold my tongue.	Taccio.
He holds his tongue.	Tace.
We are silent.	Tacciamo.
They are silent.	Tacciono.
After speaking half an hour, he held his tongue.	Dopo aver parlato mezz' ora tacque.

EXERCISES.

229.

Why does your mother fret?—She frets at receiving no news from her son, who is with the army.—She need not be uneasy about him, for whenever he gets into a scrape he knows how to get out of it again. Last summer, when we were a hunting together (*insieme*), night grew upon us (*la notte ci sorprese*) at least ten leagues (*la lega*) from our country-seat (*la casa di campagna*).

—Well (*Ebbene*), where did you pass the night?—I was very uneasy at first (*da principio*), but your brother not in the least (*non—affatto*); on the contrary, he tranquillized me, so that I lost my uneasiness. We found at last a peasant's hut, where we passed the night. Here (*ivi*) I had an opportunity of seeing how clever your brother is. A few benches and a truss of straw (*un fastello di paglia*) served him to make a comfortable bed; he used a bottle as a candlestick, our pouches served us as a pillow, and our cravats as nightcaps. When we awoke in the morning we were as fresh and healthy (*sano*) as if we had slept on down and silk.

A candidate (*un candidato*) petitioned (*domandare a*) the king of Prussia for an employment (*un impiego*). This prince asked him where he was born. "I was born at Berlin," answered he. "Begone," said the monarch (*il monarca*) "all the men of Berlin (*il berlinese*) are good for nothing." "I beg your majesty's (*la maestà*) pardon," replied the candidate, "there are some good ones, and I know two." "Which are those two?" asked the king. "The first," replied the candidate, "is your majesty, and I am the second." The king could not help laughing (*non potè astenersi dal ridere*) at this answer (*la risposta*), and granted the request (*accordare una domanda*).

230.

A thief having one day entered a boarding-house stole three cloaks (*il mantello*). In going away he was met by one of the boarders who had a fine laced (*gallonato*) cloak. Seeing so many cloaks, he asked the man where he had taken them. The thief answered boldly (*freddamente*) that they belonged to three gentlemen of the house who had given them to be cleaned (*da pulire*). "Then you must also clean mine, for it is very much in need of it (*averne gran bisogno*)," said the boarder; "but," added he, "you must return it to me at three o'clock." "I shall not fail (*mancare*), Sir," answered the thief, as he carried off (*portando via*) the four cloaks with which he has not yet returned (*che non ha ancora riportati*).—You are singing (*cantare*), gentlemen, but it is not a time for (*non si tratta di*) singing: you ought to be silent, and to listen to what you are told.—We are at a loss.—

What are you at a loss about?—I am going to tell you: the question is with us how we shall pass our time agreeably (*lietamente*).—Play a game at billiards or at chess.—We have proposed joining a hunting-party; do you go with us (*è Ella dei nostri*)?—I cannot, for I have not done my task yet; and if I neglect it, my master will scold me.—Every one according to his liking; if you like staying at home better than going a hunting (*che non d'andare alla caccia*) we cannot hinder you.—Does Mr. B. go with us?—Perhaps.—I should not like to go with him, for he is too great a talker (*troppo ciarlone*), excepting that (*da quello in fuori*) he is an honest man.

What is the matter with you? you look angry.—I have reason to be (*aver motivo d' essere*) angry, for there is no means of getting money now.—Have you been to Mr. A's.—I have been to his house; but there is no possibility (*non c' è mezzo*) of borrowing from him.—I suspected (*pensare*) that he would not lend me any, that is the reason why I did not wish to ask him, and had you not told me to do so, I should not have subjected myself (*non mi sarei esposto*) to a refusal (*il rifiuto*).

FOURTH MONTH.

Quarto mese.

SEVENTY-SIXTH LESSON.

Lezione settantesima sesta.

Towards.	*Verso.*
He comes towards me.	Viene verso di me.
He has behaved very well towards me.	Si è condotto benissimo verso di me.
We must always behave well towards every body.	Bisogna condursi sempre bene verso di tutti.
The behaviour of others is but an echo of our own. If we behave well towards them, they will also behave well towards us; but if we use them ill, we must not expect better from them.	La condotta degli altri non è che un eco della nostra. Se ci conduciamo bene verso di loro, si condurranno pur bene verso di noi; ma se trattiamo male con essi, non dobbiamo aspettare meglio da loro.
To treat or to use somebody well.	† *Comportarsi* bene con † *Trattare (usare)* qualcuno.
To use somebody ill.	† *Comportarsi* male con † *Trattare (usare)* qualcuno.
As you have always used me well, I will not use you ill.	† Come Ella si è sempre comportata bene con me, non mi comporterò male con Lei.
As he has always used me well, I have always used him in the same manner.	† Come s'è sempre comportato bene meco, mi sono sempre comportato della stessa maniera con lui.
To delay (to tarry).	*Tardare* 1 (a before Inf.).
Do not be long before you return.	Non tardate a ritornare.
I shall not be long before I return.	Non tarderò a ritornare.

To long for or to.	(*Desiderare* 1.. † *Esser impaziente di* (*tardar* † † *Non veder l' ora di.*
I long to see my brother.	*Sono impaziente di vedere mio fratello.*
He longs to receive his money.	È *impaziente di ricevere il suo danaro.* (*Non vede l'ora di ricevere il suo danaro.*)
We long for dinner, because we are very hungry.	*Siamo impazienti di pranzare, perchè abbiamo molto fame.*
They long to sleep, because they are tired.	*Desiderano di dormire, perchè sono stanchi.*
Oh, how much I long that some one may join me here!	*Oh! quanto mi tarda ch' altri qui giunga!* (*pres. of the subj.*)

To be at one's ease. *To be comfortable.*	*Essere agiato (comodo).*
To be uncomfortable.	*Essere mal comodo.* *Non essere agiato.*
I am very much at my ease upon this chair.	*Sono molto comodo su questa sedia.*
You are uncomfortable upon your chair.	*Ella è mal comodo sulla di Lei sedia.*
What can that be?	† *Che può essere?*
We are uncomfortable in that boarding-house.	*Siamo mal comodi in questa pensione.*
That man is well off, for he has plenty of money.	*Quest' uomo è agiato, perchè ha molto danaro.*
That man is badly off, for he is poor.	*Quest' uomo non è agiato, perchè è povero.*

To make one's self comfortable.	† *Accomodarsi.*
Make yourself comfortable.	*La si accomodi.*
To be uncomfortable.	*Essere incomodo.*
To inconvenience one's self. *To put one's self out of the way.*	*Incomodarsi.*
Do not put yourself out of the way.	*Non La si incomodi.*
That man never inconveniences himself; he never does it for any body.	*Quest' uomo non s' incomoda mai; non s' incomoda mai per alcuno.*
Can you, without putting yourself to inconvenience, lend me your gun?	*Può Ella, senza incomodarsi, prestarmi il di Lei fucile?*

SEVENTY-SIXTH LESSON.   425

To make entreaties.	Far istanze.
To beg with entreaty.	Pregare con istanza.
I employed every kind of entreaty to engage him to it.	Ne l' ho sollecitato con tutte le istanze possibili.
To solicit, to press, to sue, to entreat.	Sollecitare 1.

Here and there.	Quà e là.
Now and then.	{ Di distanza in distanza. { Di tanto in tanto.
From time to time.	{ Di quando in quando. { Di tempo in tempo.
Indifferently (good or bad).	Bene o male.
I have made my composition tolerably well.	Bene o male ho fatto la mia composizione.

To postpone, to put off.	Rimettere * a, differire (isco).
Let us put that off until to-morrow.	Rimettiamo questo a domani.
Let us put off that lesson until another time.	Rimettiamo questa lezione ad un' altra volta.

To impart something to some one.	† Far parola di qualche cosa a qualcuno.
Have you imparted that to your father?	Ha Ella fatto parola di ciò al di Lei padre?
I have imparted it to him.	Gliene ho fatto parola.

In vain.	Invano.
In vain I looked all around, I saw neither man nor house: not the least sign of settlement.	Io avea bel guardare tutto all' intorno, io non vedeva nè uomini nè case: non la minima apparenza d' abitazione.
A dwelling, habitation, settlement.	Un' abitazione.
In vain I speak, for you do not listen to me.	Ho bel parlare, Ella non m' ascolta.
In vain I do my best, I cannot do any thing to his liking.	Ho bel fare quanto so di meglio, non posso far niente a suo grado.
You may say what you please, nobody will believe you.	Ha bel dire, nessuno Le crederà.
It is in vain that they earn money, they will never be rich.	Invano si guadagnan danaro, non saranno mai ricchi.
We search in vain; for what we have lost we cannot find.	Cerchiamo invano, non potrem mai trovare ciò ch' abbiamo perduto.

SEVENTY-SIXTH LESSON.

To salute.	Salutare 1.
I have the honour to bid you adieu.	Ho l' onore di salutarla.
Present my compliments to him (to her).	Gli (le), presento i miei complimenti.
Remember me to him (to her).	Gli (le) dica molte cose da mia parte.
Pray present my compliments to your sister.	La prego di far i miei complimenti alla di Lei signora sorella.
Remember me (present my compliments) to him (to her).	Gli (le) presenti (offra) le mie civiltà (i miei umili rispetti), (civiltà obsolete).
I shall not fail.	Non mancherò.
The present (the present time or tense).	Il presente.
The past.	Il passato.
The future.	L' avvenire, il futuro.
The loss of time.	La perdita di tempo.
Enjoy all the pleasures that virtue permits.	Goda (godete) di tutti i piaceri che la virtù permette.

EXERCISES.

231.

I suspected (*pensare*) that you would be thirsty, and that your sister would be hungry; that is the reason why I brought you here. I am sorry, however (*però*), not to see your mother.—Why do you not drink your coffee?—If I were not sleepy I would drink it.—Sometimes (*ora*) you are sleepy, sometimes cold, sometimes warm, and sometimes something else is the matter with you (*ed ora qualche altra cosa*). I believe that you think too much of the misfortune that has happened to your friend (*fem.*).—If I did not think about it, who would think about it?—Of whom does your brother think?—He thinks of me, for we always think of each other (*l' uno all' altro*) when we are not together (*insieme*).

I have seen six players (*il giuocatore*) to-day, who were all winning (*guadagnare*) at the same time (*nell' istesso tempo*).—That cannot be (*non si dà*); for a player can only win when another loses.—You would be right if I spoke of people that had played at cards or billiards; but I am speaking of flute and violin players (*di suonatori di flauto e di violino*).—Do you some times practise (*fare*) music (*della musica*)?—Very often, for I like it much.—What instrument do you play (*suonare*)?—I play the violin, and my sister plays the harpsichord.—My brother who plays the bass (*il contrabasso*) accompanies (*accompagnare*) us, and Miss Stolz sometimes applauds (*applaudire—isco*) us.—Does she not also play some musical instrument (*istrumento di musica*)?—She plays the harp (*l' arpa*), but she is too proud (*fiera*) to practise music with us.—A very poor town (*una città alquanto povera*) went to considerable expense (*far una spesa considerevole*) in feasts and illuminations (*in feste ed illuminazioni*) on the occasion of its prince passing through (*del passaggio del suo—*). The latter seemed (*ne parve*) himself astonished. "It has only done," said a courtier (*un cortigiano*), "what it owed (*il suo debito*) (to your majesty)."—"That is true," replied (*riprendere**) another, "but it owes all that it has done."

232.

Have you made your Italian composition?—I have made it.—Has your tutor been pleased with it?—He has not. In vain I do my best, I cannot do any thing to his liking.—You may say what you please, nobody will believe you.—Can you, without putting yourself to inconvenience, lend me five hundred livres?—As you have always used me well, I will use you in the same manner. I will lend you the money you want, but on condition that you will return it to me next week.—You may depend upon it (*poter farne capitale*).—How has my son behaved towards you?—He has behaved well towards me, for he behaves well towards every body. His father often told him :—"The behaviour of others is but an echo of our own. If we behave well towards them, they will also (*pur*) behave well towards us; but if we use them ill, we must not expect better from them."—May I see your brothers?—You will see them to-morrow. As they have just arrived from a long journey (*il viaggio*), they long for sleep, for they are very tired.—What did my sister say?—She said that she longed for dinner, because she was very hungry.—Are you comfortable in your boarding-house?—I am very comfortable there.—Have you imparted to your brother what I told you?

—As he was very tired, he longed for sleep; so that I have put off imparting it to him till to-morrow.

233.

I have the honour to wish you a good morning. How do you do ?—Very well at your service (*per servirla*).—And how are all at home (*E come stanno in casa*) ?—Tolerably well (*passabilmente*), thank God (*grazie a Dio*) ! My sister was a little indisposed (*indisposta*), but she is better (*ristabilita*); she told me to give you her best (*m' ha incaricato di molti—per Lei*) compliments.—I am glad (*contentissimo*) to hear that she is well. As to you, you are health (*la salute*) itself (*stessa*); you cannot look better (*ha la miglior cera del mondo*).—I have no time to be ill; my business (*i miei affari*) would not permit me.—Please to sit down (*La si accomodi*); here is a chair.—I will not detain (*distrarre*) you from your business; I know that a merchant's time is precious (*che il tempo è prezioso per un negoziante*).—I have nothing pressing (*pressante*) to do now, my courier is already dispatched (*il mio corriere è già spedito*).—I shall not stay any longer. I only wished in passing by (*passando di qui*) to inquire about your health.—You do me much honour.—It is very fine weather to-day.—If you allow me I shall have the pleasure of seeing you again (*rivedere*) this afternoon (*questo dopo pranzo*), and if you have time, we will take a little turn together.—With the greatest pleasure. In that case I shall wait for you.—I will come for you (*verrò a prenderla*) about (*verso*) seven o'clock.—Adieu, then, till I see you again.—I have the honour to bid you adieu.

SEVENTY-SEVENTH LESSON.

Lezione settantesima settima.

To mean.	Valere *. Pretendere *. Intendere *, significare 1.
What do you mean?	Che pretendete (intendete)?
I mean.	Pretendo (intendo).
What does that man mean?	Che vuol quell' uomo?
He means.	Vuole (pretende, intende).
What does that mean?	Che significa questo?
That does not mean any thing.	Non significa niente.
I do not know what that means.	Non so che ciò significa. (Non so cosa significhi questo).
To be particular.	† Riguardarvi da vicino.
I do not like to deal with that man, for he is too particular.	† Non tratto volentieri con quell' uomo, perchè vi riguarda troppo da vicino, (or perchè è troppo singolare).
To grow impatient, to fret.	† Impazientarsi di.
Do not fret about that.	Non v' impazientite di ciò. Non impazientatevi di ciò.
To sit up, to watch.	Vegliare 1.
I have sat up all night.	Ho vegliato tutta la notte.
To advise.	Consigliare 1.
The dress, the costume.	Il vestire.
An elegant dress.	Un vestire elegante.
His dress is decent (elegant).	Il suo vestire è decente (elegante).
To dress one's self.	Vestirsi 3.
That man always dresses well.	Quest' uomo si veste sempre bene.
To find fault with something.	Trovare a ridire a qualche cosa.
That man always finds fault with every thing he sees.	Quest' uomo trova sempre a ridire a tutto ciò che vede.
Do you find fault with that?	Trova Ella a ridire a questo?
I do not find fault with it.	Non vi trovo niente a ridire.

A trick.	Una beffa, una burla.
To play a trick.	Fare una burla.
To play a trick on some one.	Fare una burla a qualcuno.
To take a turn.	† Fare un giro (una passeggiata).
I have taken a turn round the garden.	† Ho fatto un giro nel giardino.
He has taken a couple of turns round the garden.	† Egli ha fatto due giri nel giardino.
To take a little turn.	† Far un piccol giro.
To travel through Europe.	† Fare il giro dell' Europa.

More (meaning *besides*).	*Di più.*
You have given me three books, but I want three besides.	Ella mi ha dato tre libri, ma me ne occorrono tre di più.
Less.	*Di meno.*
Three less.	Tre di meno.
Three too many.	Tre di troppo.
To want.	*Occorrere* * ; p. part. *occorso*; pret. def. *occorsi*.
I want.	Mi occorre.
I want three books.	Mi occorrono tre libri.

My reach.	La mia vista (capacità).
Within my reach.	Alla mia vista.
Out of my reach.	Fuori della mia vista (or capacità).
Those things are not within the reach of every body.	Queste cose non sono della capacità di tutti, or alla portata di tutti.
That is not within the reach of my sight.	Ciò è troppo lontano per la mia vista.
Within gun-shot.	A un tiro di fucile.
A gun-shot (meaning distance).	Un tiro di fucile.
Two gun-shots (" ").	Due tiri di fucile.
How many shots have you fired ?	Quante volte ha Ella tirato (Lesson XLVIII.) ?

I wonder why that man makes such a noise.	† Vorrei sapere perchè quest' uomo fa un tale strepito (un tal rumore).
So long as.	{ *Quanto.* { *Finchè, fin tanto che.*
So long as you behave well, people will love you.	Finchè (or fintanto che) vi comporterete bene, vi ameranno.

SEVENTY-SEVENTH LESSON.

To carry off.	*Portar via, rapire (isco).*
A mouthful.	Una boccata. Un boccone.
To overwhelm, to heap, to load.	*Colmare 1.*
To overwhelm one with joy.	Colmare qualcuno di gioia.
Generous.	Generoso.
Beneficent, charitable.	Benefico, caritatevole.
You have heaped benefits upon me.	Ella mi ha colmato di benefizii.
Sincere.	Sincero.
Sincerely.	Sinceramente.
An advantage.	Un vantaggio.
The disadvantage, prejudice.	Lo svantaggio.
I shall never say any thing to your disadvantage.	Non dirò mai niente a svantaggio di Lei.
To surrender.	*Rendersi.*
The enemies have surrendered.	I nemici si sono resi.
To prefer.	*Preferire* (isco) (past part. preferito; pret. def. preferii or prefersi).*
I prefer the useful to the agreeable.	Preferisco l'utile al gradevole.

Obs. All the infinitive moods of a verb used substantively are masculine.

The drinking.	Il bere (il bevere).
The eating.	Il mangiare.
To behold.	*Guardare 1. Riguardare 1.*
Behold those beautiful flowers with their colours so fresh and bright.	Guardate quei superbi fiori d'un colore cosi fresco e splendido vivo.
The colour.	Il colore, il colorito.
The lily.	Il giglio.
The forget-me-not.	Il camedrio.
The rose.	La rosa.
An emblem.	Un' emblema.
Fresh verdure is salutary to our eyes.	La verzura fresca fa del bene ai nostri occhi (or ci fa del bene agli occhi).

EXERCISES.

234.

The loss of time is an irreparable (*irreparabile*) loss. A single minute (*un sol minuto*) cannot be recovered (*riguadagnare*) for all the gold in the (*del*) world. It is then (*dunque*) of the greatest importance (*della massima importanza*) to employ well the time which consists (*consistere*) only of minutes which we must make good of (*che bisogna mettere a profitto*). We have but the present; the past is no longer any thing (*non è più nulla*), and the future is uncertain (*incerto*). A great many people (*una infinità d' uomini*) ruin themselves (*rovinarsi*) because they wish to indulge themselves too much (*per voler avvantaggiare*). If most men (*la maggior parte degli uomini*) knew how to content themselves (*contentarsi*) with what they have, they would be happy; but their greediness (*la loro avidità*) very often makes (*rendere**) them unhappy.—In order to be happy we must forget the past, not trouble ourselves about the (*non inquietarsi dell'*) future, and enjoy the present.—I was very much dejected (*afflittissimo*) when my cousin came to me. "What is the matter with you?" he asked me. "Oh (*Ah*)! my dear cousin," replied I, " in losing that money I have lost every thing." "Do not fret," said he to me, " for I have found your money."

235.

Why have you played a trick upon that man?—Because he finds fault with every thing he sees.—What does that mean, Sir? —That means that I do not like to deal with you, because you are too particular.—I wonder why your brother has not done his task.—It was too difficult. He sat up all night, and has not been able to do it, because it was out of his power (*capacità*).—As soon as Mr. Civiltà sees me he begins to speak English, in order to practise, and overwhelms me with politeness (*la finezza*), so that I often do not know what to answer. His brothers do the same (*ne fanno altrettanto*). However, they are very good people (*sono buonissime persone*); they are not only (*non solamente*) rich and amiable, but they are also generous and charitable (*benefici*). They love me sincerely, therefore I love them also (*io pure*), and consequently (*perciò*) shall never say any thing to their disadvantage (*lo svantaggio*). I should love them still more, if they did not make so much ceremony (*tante cerimonie*); but every one has his faults, and mine is to speak too much of their ceremonies.

230.

Have the enemies surrendered?—They have not surrendered, for they did not prefer life (*la vita*) to death (*la morte*). They had neither bread, nor meat, nor water, nor arms (*nè armi*), nor money; notwithstanding they determined to die rather (*hanno preferito morire*) than surrender.—Why are you so sad?—You do not know what makes me uneasy, my dear friend (fem.)—Tell me, for I assure you that I share (*dividere* in egual modo*) your sufferings (*la pena*) as well as your pleasures.—I am sure that you feel for me (*prendere* parte alle mie pene*), but I cannot tell you now (*in questo momento*) what makes me uneasy. I will, however (*pure*), tell you when an opportunity offers (*al presentarsi dell' occasione*). Let us speak of something else now. What do you think of the man who spoke to us yesterday at the concert?—He is a man of much understanding (*di molto senno*), and not at all wrapped up in his own merits (*e non è mica infatuato del suo merito*). But why do you ask me that?—To speak of something.—It is said: contentment surpasses (*contento val meglio*) riches; let us then always be content. Let us share (*dividere**) (with each other) what we have, and remain (*e restiamo*) our lifetime (*tutta la nostra vita*) inseparable (*inseparabile*) friends. You will always be welcome at my house, and I hope to be equally so (*io pure*) at yours. If I saw you happy, I should be equally so, and we should be more contented than the greatest princes. We shall be happy (*Saremo felici*) when we are perfectly (*perfettamente*) contented with what we have; and if we do our duty as we ought (*bene*), God will take care of the rest. The past being no longer any thing, let us not be uneasy about the future, and enjoy (repeat the imperative) the present. (See end of Lesson XXIV.)

SEVENTY-EIGHTH LESSON.
Lezione settantesima ottava.

A gold watch.	Un oriuolo d' oro.
A marble statue.	Una statua di marmo.
A deserving soldier.	Un soldato di merito.
A talented youth.	Un giovane di talento.
A silk gown.	Una vesta di seta.
A mahogany table.	Una tavola di mogano.
A brick house.	Una casa di mattoni.
A stone house.	Una casa di pietra.
A velvet bonnet.	Un cappello di velluto.
A silver tankard.	Un boccale d' argento.
A one-story house.	Una casa d' un sol piano.
A two-story house.	Una casa di due piani.
A three-story house.	Una casa di tre piani.

Obs. A. As we have seen (Lesson II.), the preposition *di* expresses the matter of which a thing is made; but to mark the use of a thing, the preposition *da* must be made use of. (See *Obs. C.* Lesson VIII.) Ex.

A kitchen-table.	Una tavola da cucina.
A nightcap.	Una berretta da notte.
A powder-box.	Una scatola da polvere.
A neck-handkerchief.	Un fazzoletto da collo.
A handkerchief (for the nose).	Un fazzoletto da naso.
Writing-paper.	Carta da scrivere.
A wine-glass.	Un bicchiere da vino.
A princely magnificence.	Una magnificenza da principe.
A gallant action.	Un' azione da cavaliere.
Gunpowder.	Polvere da cannone.
Fire-arms.	Armi da fuoco.
A windmill.	Un mulino a vento.
A coffee-mill.	Un mulinello da caffè.
A water-mill.	Un mulino ad acqua.
A steam-mill.	Un mulino a vapore.
A one-horse waggon.	Una carrozza ad un cavallo.
A four-horse carriage.	Una carrozza a quattro cavalli.
A two-wheeled waggon.	Una carrozza a due ruote.
A four-wheeled waggon.	Una carrozza a quattro ruote.
The garden-door.	La porta del giardino.

Waiter! bring something to drink, to eat, to sit upon.	Garzone! portate da bere, da mangiare, da sedere.

SEVENTY-EIGHTH LESSON.

A three-corner hat.	Un cappello a tre punte.

Obs. B. The preposition *a* is made use of when the determinating noun expresses *resemblance* or *shape*.

A fashionable coat.	Un abito *alla* moda.
A pendulum-clock.	Un orologio a pendolo.
An hour-glass.	Un orologio a polvere.
A sailing vessel.	Una nave a vela.
A rowing vessel.	Una nave a remi.

He entreated him with joined hands.	Lo pregò a mani giunte.
Thou wantedst to act according to thy wish.	Volesti fare a tuo modo.
To play at first sight.	Suonare a prima vista.
To drive with six horses.	Andare a sei cavalli.
They will come at the fixed time.	Verranno all' ora stabilita.
At twelve o'clock (mid-day).	A mezzo giorno (alle dodici).
At twelve o'clock at night (midnight).	A mezza notte.
He came in time.	Venne a tempo.
To play at a game.	Giuocare a un giuoco.

To exaggerate.	Esagerare 1 † Spingere tropp' oltre. † Andar all' eccesso.
That man exaggerates all that he says and does.	Quest' uomo esagera quanto dice e quanto fa.
That man exaggerates his generosity.	Quest' uomo spinge tropp' oltre la sua generosità.

To take the place of, to be instead of.	Servire di, tener luogo di.
That man is a father to me.	Quest' uomo mi tiene luogo di padre. Quest' uomo mi serve di padre, or mi fa da.
That umbrella serves him as a stick.	Quest' ombrello gli tiene luogo di bastone.

An inch.	Un pollice.
On a small scale.	In piccolo.
On a large scale.	In grande.
Thereabouts, nearly.	Presso a poco, a un di presso.
Alternately, turn by turn.	Alternativamente.

SEVENTY-EIGHTH LESSON.

To endeavour, to strive.	Sforzarsi, studiarsi 1.
To give one's self up to grief.	Abbandonarsi al dolore.
To melt.	Fondere*; past part. *fuso*; pret. def. *fusi*. Struggere*; p. part. *strutto*; pret. def. *strussi*.
To melt in tears.	† Struggersi in lagrime.

To give birth to (meaning to raise, to cause).	Far nascere.
To raise difficulties.	† Far nascere delle difficoltà.
To cause quarrels.	† Far nascere delle questioni.
To cause suspicions.	† Far nascere dei sospetti.
The behaviour of that man raised suspicions in my mind.	† La condotta di quest' uomo fece nascere dei sospetti nella mia mente, or mi fece nascere dei sospetti.

To shake.	Scuotere*; p. part. *scosso*; pret. def. *scossi*.
Shake that tree, and the fruit will fall down.	Scuotete (scuota) quest' albero e ne cadranno i frutti.

To be in want of, to be short of, to want.	Mancare di. Aver mancanza di.
That man is in want of every thing.	Quest' uomo manca di tutto.
I am in want of nothing.	Non manco di niente, or non mi manca niente.

A place at table, including knife, fork, and spoon.	Una posata.
A table for four persons.	Una tavola da quattro posate.
A table for ten persons.	Una tavola da dieci posate.
A writing-table or desk.	Una tavola da scrivere.
A dining-room.	Una sala da pranzo.
A sleeping or bed-room.	Una camera da letto.
A repeater.	Un oriuolo a ripetizione.
An oil-bottle.	Una bottiglia da olio.
A mustard-pot.	Una mostardiera.
A pitcher.	Un vaso da acqua.
Boiled meat for dinner.	† La pentola.
A fowling-piece.	Un fucile da caccia.
A milk-pot.	Un vaso da latte.
A fishing-line.	Una lenza.

To exact, to want of.	*Esigere* ; p. part. *esatto*.
What do you want of me?	Che esigete (esige) da me?
What did you exact of me?	Che vuole da me?
I exact nothing of you.	Non esigo niente da voi.
	Non voglio niente da Lei.

The rabbit-man.	L' uomo *dei* conigli.
The oyster-woman.	La donna *dalle* ostriche.

Dainties.	I buoni bocconi.
He is fond of dainties.	Gli piacciono (ama) i buoni bocconi.
At broad daylight.	Di giorno.
To sit down to dinner.	Mettersi a tavola.

EXERCISES.

237.

Behold, ladies (*Signore*), those beautiful flowers, with their colours so fresh and bright; they drink nothing but water. The white lily has the colour of innocence (*l' innocenza*); the violet indicates gentleness (*indica la dolcezza*); you may see it in Louisa's eyes (*negli occhi di Luigia*). The forget-me-not has the colour of heaven, our future dwelling, and the rose, the queen of flowers, is the emblem of beauty and of joy. You see (*Mirasi*) all that personified (*personificato*) in seeing the beautiful Amelia (*Amalia*).—How beautiful is the fresh verdure (*la verzura*)! It is salutary to our eyes, and has the colour of hope (*la speranza*), our most faithful (*fedele*) friend (fem.), who never deserts (*abbandonare*) us, not even in death (*alla morte*).—One word more, my dear friend.—What is your pleasure?—I forgot to tell you to present my compliments to your mother. Tell her, if you please, that I regret (*che mi rincresce*) not having been at home when she lately honoured me with her visit. I thank you for her, I shall not fail. Farewell then (*State bene*).

238.

Has your sister been out to-day?—She has been out to buy several things (*per far delle compre*).—What has she bought?—She has bought (*La si è comprata*) a silk gown, a velvet bonnet, and a lace veil (*un velo di merletti*).—What have you done with my silver tankard?—It is on the kitchen-table, together with the (*colla*) oil-bottle, the milk-pot, the pitcher, the mustard-pot, and the coffee-mill.—Do you ask for a wine-bottle?—No, I ask for a bottle of wine, and not (*e non mica*) for a wine-bottle.—If you will have the goodness to give me the key of the wine-cellar I shall go for one.—What does that man want of me?—He exacts nothing; but he will accept what you will give him, for he is in want of every thing.—I will tell you that I am not fond of him, for his behaviour raises suspicions in my mind. He exaggerates all that he says and does.—You are wrong in having such a bad opinion (*un' opinione*) of him, for he has been a father to you.—I know what I say. He has cheated me on a small and on a large scale, and whenever he calls he asks me for something. In this manner he has alternately asked me for all I had: my fowling-piece, my fishing-line, my repeater, and my golden candlesticks.—Do not give yourself up so much to grief, else (*altrimenti*) you will make me melt in tears.

Democritus (*Democrito*) and Heraclitus were two philosophers of a very different character (*d' un indole molto differente*): the first laughed at the follies (*la follia*) of men, and the other wept at them. They were both right, for the follies of men deserve to be laughed and wept at.

239.

Have you seen your niece?—Yes; she is a very good girl, who writes well, and speaks Italian still better; therefore she is loved and honoured by every body.—And her brother, what is he doing?—Do not speak to me of him; he is a naughty boy, who writes always badly, and who speaks Italian still worse: he is therefore (*perciò*) loved by nobody. He is very fond of dainties, but he does not like books. Sometimes he goes to bed at broad day-light, and pretends to be ill; but when we sit down to dinner (*si va a tavola*) he is generally better again.—He is to study physic (*la medicina*), but he has not the slightest inclination for it (*alcuna voglia*). He is almost always talking of his dogs, which he loves passionately (*appassionatamente*). His father is extremely sorry for it. The young simpleton (*l' imbecille*) said

lately to his sister, "I shall enlist as soon as a peace (*la pace*) is proclaimed (*pubblicare*)."
My dear father and my dear mother dined yesterday with some friends at the king of Spain (*all' insegna del re di Spagna*).—Why do you always speak English and never Italian?—Because I am too bashful.—You are joking; is an Englishman ever bashful?—I have a keen appetite (*grand' appetito*): give me something good to eat.—Have you any money?—No, Sir.—Then I have nothing to eat for you.—Will you not let me have some (*non mi dà Ella*) on credit? I pledge (*impegnare*) my honour.—That is too little.—What (*come*), Sir!

SEVENTY-NINTH LESSON.

Lezione settantesima nona.

Just a little, ever so little.	*Alquanto.* *Un poco, un pochetto, un pochino.* *Un tantino.*
Will you do me the favour of giving me a piece of bread?	Vuol farmi il piacere di darmi un pezzo di pane?
Do you wish a great deal?	Ne vuol molto?
No, just a little.	No, un pochetto.
To turn to account. *To make the best of.*	† *Far valere (trar profitto).*
This man does not know how to make the best of his talents.	† Quest' uomo non sa far valere i suoi talenti.
That man turns his money to account in trade.	† Quest' uomo fa valere il suo danaro nel commercio.
How do you employ your money?	† Come fa Ella valere il di Lei danaro?
I turn it to account in the stocks.	† Lo faccio valere nei fondi pubblici.
To boast, to brag.	† *Farsi valere.*
I do not like that man, because he boasts too much.	† Non mi piace quest' uomo, perchè si fa troppo valere, or perchè si vanta troppo.

SEVENTY-NINTH LESSON.

Notwithstanding that. For all that, although.	Ciò non di meno (nullameno). Nondimeno, nulladimeno.
That man is a little bit of a rogue, but notwithstanding he passes for an honest man.	Quest' uomo è alquanto briccone, ciò non dimeno passa per un galantuomo.
Although that man is not very well, he notwithstanding works a great deal.	Quantunque costui non stia bene non tralascia di lavorar molto.
Although that woman is not very pretty, still she is very amiable.	Benchè questa donna non sia molto leggiadra, non tralascia (not elegant) d' esser molto amabile (or pure la è molto amabile).
Although that man has not the least talent, yet for all that he boasts a great deal.	Quantunque costui non abbia alcun talento, non tralascia di farsi molto valere.
Although the tavern-keeper's wife is rather swarthy, yet for all that she turns the business to good account.	Benchè la moglie di quest' oste sia un tantino bruna, non tralascia di far valere l' osteria, or pure fa bene gli affari della sua osteria.
I received your letter on the fifth, on the sixth, on the seventh. On the eighth.	Ho ricevuto la di Lei lettera il cinque, il sei, il sette. L' otto.
To go back, to return.	Ritornare 1, tornare 1.
The top. The bottom. Up to the top.	L' alto, la cima. Il basso, il fondo. Fino in alto.
The eldest brother. The eldest sister. He is the eldest.	Il fratello primogenito. La sorella primogenita. È il primogenito (il maggiore).
To appear, to seem.	Parere *, sembrare 1.
I appear, &c. We appear, &c. Appeared.	Paio, pari, pare. Paiamo (pariamo), parete, paiono; past part. parso ; pret. def. parvi.
To keep, to maintain.	Mantenere *.
My keeping or maintenance. My keeping costs me six hundred livres a-year.	Il mio mantenimento. Il mio mantenimento mi costa sei cento lire l' anno (all' anno).
To drive in, to sink.	Andar a fondo. Affondare 1.
To converse with some one.	Conversare con qualcuno [1].
A conversation.	Una conversazione.

[1] *Conversare in un paese* means: *frequentarvi*, to go often to a country.

SEVENTY-NINTH LESSON. 441

To spare.	*Risparmiare* 1.
Spare your money.	Risparmiate il vostro danaro.

To get tired.	*Stancarsi* 1, *annoiarsi* 1.
To be tired.	Esser stanco, lasso, annoiato.
To handle.	*Maneggiare* 1.
To lean against.	*Appoggiarsi*.
Lean against me.	Appoggiatevi a me.
Lean against the wall.	Appoggiatevi contro il muro.
To aim at.	{ *Prender di mira*. { *Metter in mira*.
Short.	Corto, subito.
To stop short.	Fermarsi subito.

Virtue is amiable.	La virtù è amabile.
Vice is odious.	Il vizio è odioso.

Obs. A. Before substantives taken in a general sense, and in the whole extent of their signification, no article is made use of in English, but in Italian it cannot be dispensed with.

Men are mortal.	Gli uomini sono mortali.
Gold is precious.	L' oro è prezioso.
Corn is sold a crown a bushel.	Il grano si vende uno scudo lo (or allo) staio.
Beef costs four-pence a pound.	Il manzo costa quattro soldi la (or alla) libbra.
The horror of vice, and the love of virtue, are the delights of the wise man.	L' orrore del vizio e l' amore della virtù sono i diletti del savio.
England is a fine country.	L' Inghilterra è un bel paese.
Italy is the garden of Europe.	L' Italia è il giardino dell' Europa.
The dog is the friend and companion of man.	Il cane è l' amico ed il compagno dell' uomo.
Thessaly produces wine, oranges, lemons, olives, and all sorts of fruit.	La Tessaglia produce del vino, delle melarancie, dei cedri, delle ulive ed ogni sorta di frutti.
He ate the bread, meat, apples, and petty-patties; he drank the wine, beer, and cider.	Mangiò il pane, la carne, le mele ed i pasticcini; bevette il vino, la birra ed il cidro.
Beauty, gracefulness, and wit, are valuable endowments when heightened by modesty.	La bellezza, le grazie e l' ingegno sono vantaggi preziosissimi, quando la modestia lor dà rilievo (or risalto).

I shall go to Germany on my return from Italy.	Andrò in Alemagna al mio ritorno d'Italia.	
The balance of Europe.	L' equilibrio d' Europa.	
He lives in Spain.	Vive in Ispagna.	

OF PROPER NAMES.

They have generally no article in Italian, and are declined by means of prepositions, such preposition is called the indefinite article, viz.

N. } A.	Peter,	Rome.	N. } A.	Pietro,	Roma.
G.	of Peter,	of Rome.	G.	di Pietro,	di Roma.
D.	to Peter,	to Rome.	D.	a Pietro,	a Roma.
Abl.	from Peter,	from Rome.	Abl.	da Pietro,	da Roma.

The wife of Joseph or Joseph's wife.	La moglie di Giuseppe.
I said so to Theresa.	Lo dissi a Teresa.
I have received this book from Alexander.	Ho ricevuto questo libro da Alessandro.
He is from Vienna.	Egli è di Vienna.
He goes to Venice.	Va a Venezia.
He departs from London.	Parte da Londra.

Obs. B. The article, however, is made use of in the following instances:

a) When the name is preceded by an adjective, as:

The brave Cæsar.	Il valoroso Cesare.
The divine Raphael.	Il divino Rafaello (*or* Raffaelie).

b) Some proper names of men and gods take the article in the plural when they stand as appellative nouns, as:

The Ciceros.	I Ciceroni.
The gods of the ancient Romans.	Gli dei degli antichi Romani.

Also in the singular, when they are used to mark another person, as:

The Solon of France.	Il Solone della Francia.

c) When known personages, particularly learned or renowned men, are mentioned by their family-names, as:

Tasso.	Il Tasso.
Petrarca.	Il Petrarca.
Fiammetta.	La Fiammetta.

Obs. C. When a whole part of the world is mentioned, the article is generally made use of, as:

Europe is more peopled than Africa.	L' Europa è più popolata dell' Africa.
The States of America.	Gli Stati dell' America.
Italy is on three sides surrounded by the sea.	L' Italia è da tre parti circondata dal mare.

SEVENTY-NINTH LESSON.

Obs. D. Some countries and islands have always the article, such as:

Tyrol, Switzerland, Moldavia.	Il Tirolo, la Svizzera, la Moldavia.
Morea, Crimea, China.	La Morea, la Crimea, la China.
Japan, Peru, India.	Il Giappone, il Perù, la India.
Brazil, Virginia, Sicily.	Il Brasile, la Virginia, la Sicilia.
Sardinia, Corsica, Ireland.	La Sardegna, la Corsica, l' Irlanda.
Iceland, Capri.	L' Islanda, la Capraia.

And a few others.

Obs. E. The names of countries which are called after their capitals have never the article, as:

Naples, Venice, Geneva.	Napoli, Venezia, Genova[*], &c.

Obs. F. The names of the seas, rivers, and mountains, have always the article, as:

The Atlantic ocean, the Danube, the Po.	L' Atlantico, il Danubio, il Po, &c.

EXERCISES.

240.

Will you relate (*raccontare*) something to me ?—What do you wish me to relate to you ?—A little anecdote, if you like.—A little boy one day at table (*a tavola*) asked for some meat; his father said that it was not polite to ask for any, and that he should wait until some was given to him (*che gliene desero*). The poor little boy seeing every one eat, and that nothing was given to him, said to his father: "My dear father, give me a little salt, if you please." "What will you do with it ?" asked the father. "I wish to eat it with the meat which you will give me," replied (*replicare*) the child. Every body admired (*ammirare*) the little boy's wit; and his father, perceiving that he had nothing, gave him meat without his asking for it (*senza ch' egli ne domandasse*). —Who was that little boy that asked for meat at table ?—He was the son of one of my friends.—Why did he ask for some meat ? —He asked for some because he had a good appetite.—Why did his father not give him some immediately ?—Because he had forgotten it.—Was the little boy wrong in asking for some ?—He was wrong, for he ought to have waited.—Why did he ask his

---

[*] Also the names of the following islands have no article: Cipro, Corfù, Creta, Cerigo, Candia, Maiorca, Minorca, Malta, Ischia, Procida, Lipari, Rodi, Scio, and a few others.

father for some salt?—He asked for some salt, that (*affinchè*) his father might perceive that he had no meat, and that he might give him some (*e gliene desse*).

Do you wish me to relate to you another anecdote?—You will greatly oblige me.—Some one, purchasing some goods of a shopkeeper (*il mercante*), said to him: "You ask too much; you should not sell so dear to me as to another, because I am a friend (*sono amico di casa*)." The merchant replied, "Sir, we must gain something by (*coi*) our friends, for our enemies will never come to the shop."

241.

Where shall you go next year?—I shall go to England, for it is a fine kingdom (*il regno*), where I intend spending the summer on my (*al mio*) return from France.)—Whither shall you go in the winter?—I shall go to Italy, and thence (*di là*) to the West Indies; but before that I must go to Holland to take leave of my friends.—What country do these people inhabit (*abitare*)?—They inhabit the south (*il mezzo giorno*) of Europe; their countries are called Italy, Spain, and Portugal, and they themselves (*ed essi medesimi*) are Italians, Spaniards, and Portuguese; but the people called Russians, Swedes, and Poles, inhabit the north (*il Settentrione*) of Europe; and the names of their countries are Russia, Sweden, and Poland (*Polonia*). France and Italy are separated (*separare*) by the Alps (*le Alpi*), and France and Spain by the Pyrenees (*i Pirenei*).—Though the Mahometans (*il Maomettano*) are forbidden the use of wine (*proibire qualche cosa ad uno*), yet for all that some of them drink it.—Has your brother eaten any thing this morning?—He has eaten a great deal; though he said he had no appetite, yet for all that he ate all the meat, bread, and vegetables (*e tutti i legumi*), and drank all the wine, beer, and cider.—Are the eggs (*le uova* plur. of *l' uovo*) dear at present?—They are sold at six livres a hundred.—Do you like grapes (*le uve* or *l' uva*)?—I do not only like grapes, but also plums (*use prugna*), almonds, nuts, and all sorts of fruit (*di frutti*).—Though modesty, candour, and an amiable disposition (*l' amabilità*) are valuable endowments, yet for all that there are some ladies that are neither modest, nor candid (*candido*), nor amiable.—The fear of death, and the love of life, being natural to men (*nell' uomo*), they ought to shun (*fuggire*) vice (*il vizio*), and adhere to (*attenersi a*) virtue.

EIGHTIETH LESSON.

Lezione ottantesima.

To give occasion to.	*Dar motivo di.*
Do not give him cause to complain.	Non dategli (non gli dia) motivo di lagnarsi.
To leave it to one.	*Rimettersi al giudizio d' alcuno.*
I leave it to you.	Mi rimetto al di Lei giudizio.
A good bargain.	Un buon mercato.
To stick, or to abide by a thing.	† Tenersi a. Stare a.
I abide by the offer you have made me.	† Mi tengo (or sto) all' offerta ch' Ella mi ha fatta.
I do not doubt but you are my friend.	Non dubito ch' Ella non sia mio amico.

Obs. A. The verb *dubitare*, negatively used, requires *non* before the subjunctive.

I do not doubt but he will do it.	Non dubito che non lo faccia.
To suffer, to bear.	*Soffrire* 3. *Sopportare* 1.
They were exposed to the whole fire of the place.	Erano esposti a tutto il fuoco della piazza.
To examine one artfully, or to draw a secret from one.	† *Sorprendere il segreto di qualcuno.*
I examined him artfully, and by that means I have made myself acquainted with all his affairs.	Ho sorpreso il suo segreto, e così mi son messo al fatto di tutti i suoi affari.

To bear, to put up with.	Sottoporsi * (conjugated like porre * (ponere), Lessons LXV. and LXXIV.).
You will be obliged to put up with all he wishes.	Le sarà forza (Ella sarà costretta) di sottoporsi a tutto ciò ch' egli vorrà.

Thick.	Denso, spesso, folto.
A thick cloud.	Un nuvolo denso (or una nuvola densa).
A thick beard.	Una barba folta.
A burst.	Uno scroscio.
A burst of laughter.	Uno scroscio di risa.
To burst out laughing.	† Dar uno scroscio di risa.
	† Far uno scroscio di risa.
To burst out.	Scrosciare 1.
To burst out a laughing.	Scoppiare dalle risa.
Splendour, brightness.	Lo splendore.
To make a great show.	Far pompa.
To light.	Illuminare 1.
The noise, the crack.	Lo strepito, lo scoppio.

To suffer one's self to be beaten.	Lasciarsi battere.
To let or to suffer one's self to fall.	Lasciarsi cadere.
To suffer one's self to be insulted.	Lasciarsi oltraggiare.
To suffer one's self to die.	Lasciarsi morire.
To let one's self be struck.	Lasciarsi percuotere.
To send back, to send away	Rimandare 1.
To extol, to praise up.	Vantare 1.
To boast, to praise one's self.	Vantarsi 1.

Go thither.	Andatevi.
Let us go thither.	Andiamvi.

Obs. B. The letter o of the first and third persons plural of the Imperative is omitted before the adverb of place, *ci, vi*.

Let them go thither.	Vadanvi.
	Ch' eglino vi vadano.
Go thou.	Va.
Go (thou) thither.	Vacci.
Go (thou) away.	Vattene.
Let him go thither.	Ch' esso ci vada.
Go away, begone.	Andatevene.
Let us begone.	Andiamcene.
Let him go away, let him begone.	Ch' egli se ne vada.

EIGHTIETH LESSON.

Give me.	Datemi.
Give it to me.	Datemelo.
Give it him.	Dateglielo.
Give him some.	Dategliene.
Get paid.	Fatevi pagare.
Let us set out.	Partiamo.
Let us breakfast.	Facciamo colazione.
Let him give it me.	Ch' egli me lo dia.
Let him be here at twelve o'clock.	Ch' egli sia qui a mezzo giorno.
Let him send it me.	Ch' egli me lo mandi.
He may believe it.	Ch' egli lo creda.
Make an end of it.	Finite.
Let us finish.	Finiamo.
Let him finish.	Ch' egli finisca.
Let him take it.	Ch' egli lo prenda.
Let her say so.	Ch' essa lo dica.

The starling.
Lo stornello, lo storno.

If I were to question you as I used to do at the beginning of our lessons, what would you answer?
Se vi presentassi adesso delle questioni come ve ne presentai al principiare delle nostre lezioni (come prima lo aveva l' abitudine di farlo), che rispondereste?

We found these questions at first rather ridiculous, but, full of confidence in your method, we answered as well as the small quantity of words and rules we then possessed allowed us.
Abbiamo trovato a prima vista tali questioni alquanto ridicole; ma pieni di confidenza nel di Lei metodo, vi abbiamo risposto per quanto ce lo permetteva il picciol corredo di parole e di regole che avevamo allora.

We were not long in finding out that those questions were calculated to ground us in the rules, and to exercise us in conversation, by the contradictory answers we were obliged to make.
Non abbiamo tardato ad accorgerci che tali questioni miravano o tendevano ad inculcarci i principii ed esercitarci alla conversazione colle risposte contradditorie che eravamo costretti di farci.

We can now almost keep up a conversation in Italian.
Adesso possiamo presso a poco sostenere una conversazione in Italiano.

This phrase does not seem to us logically correct.
Questa frase non ci pare logicamente corretta.

We should be ungrateful, if we allowed such an opportunity to escape without expressing our liveliest gratitude to you.
Saremmo ingrati, se lasciassimo sfuggire una così bella occasione senza dimostrarle la più viva gratitudine.

In all cases, at all events. In ogni caso.
The native. Il nativo.
The insurmountable difficulty. La difficoltà insuperabile.

EXERCISES.

242.

A young prince (*un principino*), seven years old, was admired by every body for his wit (*a cagione del suo spirito*); being once in the society of an old officer (*l' uffiziale*), the latter observed, in speaking of the young prince, that when children discovered so much genius (*aver molto spirito*) in their early years, they generally grew very stupid (*ne hanno ordinariamente pochissimo*) when they came to maturity (*quando sono avvanzati in età*). "If that is the case," said the young prince, who had heard it, "then you must have been remarkable for your genius (*aver moltissimo spirito*) when you were a child (*nella sua infanzia*)."

An Englishman, on first visiting (*al primo giugnere in*) France, met with (*s'avvenne—in*) a very young child in the streets of Calais, who spoke the French language with fluency and elegance (*correntemente e con eleganza*).—"Good Heaven (*gran Dio*)! is it possible," exclaimed he, "that even children here speak the French language with purity (*la purezza*)?"

Let us seek (*ricercare*) the friendship of the good, and avoid (*evitare*) the society of the wicked (*dei cattivi*); for bad company corrupts (*le cattive società corrompono*) good manners (*i buoni costumi*).—What sort of weather is it to-day?—It snows continually, as it snowed yesterday, and, according to all appearances, will also snow to-morrow.—Let it snow; I should like it to snow still more, for I am always very well when it is very cold.—And I am always very well when it is neither warm nor cold.—It is too windy to-day, and we should do better if we stayed at home. —Whatever weather it may be, I must go out; for I promised to be with my sister at a quarter past eleven, and I must keep my word (*tenere* parola*).

243.

Will you drink a cup of coffee?—I thank you, I do not like coffee.—Then you will drink a glass of wine?—I have just drunk some.—Let us take a walk.—Willingly (*con molto piacere*); but where shall we go to?—Come with me into the garden of my aunt; we shall find there very agreeable society.—I believe it;

but the question is (*resta a sapere*) whether this agreeable society will admit me (*mi corrà*).—You are welcome every where.— What ails you (*che avete*), my friend? How do you like that wine?—I like it very well (*squisito*); but I have drunk enough of it (*bastantemente*).—Drink once more.—No, too much is unwholesome (*ogni eccesso è nocivo*); I know my constitution (*il temperamento*).—Do not fall. What is the matter with you?—I do not know; but my head is giddy (*mi gira la testa*); I think I am fainting (*cadere in deliquio*, or *svenire*).—I think so also (*io pure*), for you look almost like a dead person (*un morto*).—What countryman are you?—I am an Englishman.—You speak Italian so well that I took you for an Italian by birth (*un Italiano di nazione*).—You are jesting.—Pardon me; I do not jest at all.— How long have you been in Italy?—A few days.—In earnest (*davvero*)?—You doubt it, perhaps, because I speak Italian; I knew it before I came to Italy.—How did you learn it so well?— I did like the prudent starling.

Tell me, why are you always on bad terms (*essere sempre in dissensione*) with your wife? and why do you engage in unprofitable trades (*occuparsi di mestieri inutili*)? It costs so much trouble (*si dura tanta pena*) to get (*ad ottenere*) a situation (*un impiego*); and you have a good one, and neglect it. Do you not think of (*pensare a*) the future?—Now allow me to speak also (*alla mia volta*). All you have just said seems reasonable; but it is not my fault, if I have lost my reputation (*la riputazione*); it is that of my wife: she has sold my finest clothes, my rings (*l' anello*), and my gold watch. I have a host of (*esser carico di*) debts, and I do not know what to do.—I will not excuse (*scolpare*) your wife; but I know that you have also (*pure*) contributed (*contribuire*) to your ruin (*la perdita*). Women are generally good when they are left so (*quando si lasciano buone*).

244.
DIALOGUE.

The Master.—If I were now to ask you such questions as I did in the beginning of our lessons, viz. (*tali che*): Have you the hat which my brother has?—Am I hungry? Has he the tree of my brother's garden? &c., what would you answer?

The Pupils.—We are obliged (*essere costretto*) to confess that we found these questions at first rather ridiculous; but, full of confidence in your method, we answered as well as the small quantity of words and rules we then possessed allowed us. We were, in fact, not long in finding out that these questions were calculated to ground us in the rules, and to exercise us in conversation, by the contradictory answers we were obliged to make. But now that we can almost keep up a conversation in the beautiful language which you teach us, we should answer: It is impossible that we should have the same hat which your brother has, for two persons cannot have one and the same thing. To the second question we should answer, that it is impossible for us to know whether you are hungry or not. As to the last, we should say: that there is more than one tree in a garden; and in asking us whether he has the tree of the garden, the phrase does not seem to us logically correct. At all events we should be ungrateful (*ingrato*) if we allowed such an opportunity to escape without expressing (*dimostrare*) our liveliest gratitude to you for the trouble you have taken. In arranging those wise combinations (*la combinazione*) you have succeeded in grounding us almost imperceptibly (*impercettibilmente*) in the rules, and exercising us in the conversation of a language which, taught in any other way, presents to foreigners, and even to natives, almost insurmountable difficulties. (See end of Lesson XXIV.)

EIGHTY-FIRST LESSON.

Lezione ottantesima prima

It lacks (wants) a quarter.	† Ci vuole un quarto.
	† Manca un quarto.
It wants (lacks) a half.	¹ Ci vuol la metà.
	† Manca la metà.
How much does it want?	Quanto ci vuole?
It does not want much.	Non ci vuol molto.

EIGHTY-FIRST LESSON. 451

It wants but a trifle.
It wants but an inch of my being as tall as you.
It lacked a great deal of my being as rich as you.
    The half.
    The third part.
    The fourth part.
You think you have returned me all; a great deal is wanting.
The younger is not so good as the elder by far.
Our merchants are far from giving us an idea of the virtue mentioned by our missionaries: they may be consulted on the depredations of the mandarins.
He is nearly as tall as his brother.

A discourse, impeded or embarrassed by nothing, goes on and flows from itself, and sometimes proceeds with such rapidity that it is only with difficulty that the mind of the speaker follows the words.

{ Ci manca poco.
{ Non ci manca se non poco.
Ci vuole un pollice perch' io sia della sua statura.
Ci mancava molto perch' io fossi ricco quanto Lei.
La metà, il mezzo.
Il terzo.
Il quarto.
Ella crede forse (voi credete forse) avermi tutto reso ; ci manca molto.
Il cadetto è molto meno savio del primogenito.
I nostri negozianti son ben lontani dal fornirci l' idea di quella virtù donde ci parlano i nostri missionarii: si può consultarli sui ladronecci dei mandarini.
Gli manca ben poco ad esser grande come suo fratello.

Un discorso chiaro e sciolto procede e fluisce da sé stesso e talvolta così rapidamente ch' egli è solo con difficoltà che il pensiero dell' oratore può tenergli dietro.

In a foolish manner, at random. | *Sconsideratamente, disavvedutamente.*

He speaks at random like a crazy man. | Parla sconsideratamente come un pazzo.

    To resort to violence.
    A fact.
    It is a fact.
    Else, or else.
    To make fun of.
To contradict, to give one the lie.
Should he say so, I would give him the lie.
His actions belie his words.

    To scratch.

† Venirne alle vie di fatto (agli atti di violenza).
Un fatto.
È un fatto.
Se non, altrimenti.
Beffarsi, burlarsi di.
Smentire qualcuno.
Se dicesse questo lo smentirei.

Le sue azioni smentiscono le sue parole.

    Graffiare 1.

EIGHTY-FIRST LESSON.

To escape.	*Scappare, scampare* 1.
I fell from the top of the tree to the bottom, but I did not hurt myself much.	Sono caduto dalla cima dell' albero (al basso) e non mi son fatto molto male.
I escaped with a scratch.	L' ho scappata con una graffiatura.
The thief has been taken, but he will escape with a few months' imprisonment.	Il ladro è stato preso, ma scamperà con alcuni mesi di prigione, or ma se la passerà con.

By dint of.	† *Pel gran (a forza di).*
By dint of labour.	† Pel gran lavoro.
By too much weeping.	† Pel gran piangere.
You will cry your eyes out.	† Pel gran piangere che fa, perderà gli occhi.
I obtained of him that favour by dint of entreaty.	† Ottenni da lui questo favore pel gran pregare (a forza di pregare).

That excepted.	*Da quello in fuori. Eccettuato questo.*
That fault excepted, he is a good man.	Da questo in fuori (eccettuato questo) è un buon uomo.

To vie with each other.	† *A gara, a prova (l' uno dell' altro).* † *A concorrenza.*
Those men are trying to rival each other.	† Questi uomini lavorano a gara.

Clean.	Netto, pulito.
Clean linen.	Della biancheria pulita. Della biancheria di bucato.

The more—as.	*Tanto più—che.*
The less—as.	*Tanto meno—che.*
I am the more discontented with his conduct, as he is under many obligations to me.	Sono tanto più malcontento della sua condotta ch' egli è molto obbligato verso di me (egli mi ha molte obbligazioni).
I am the less pleased with his conduct, as I had more right to his friendship.	Sono tanto meno soddisfatto della sua condotta ch' io aveva più diritti alla sua amicizia di qualunque altro.

I wish that.	† *Vorrei che.*
I wish that house belonged to me.	† Vorrei che questa casa fosse mia.

EIGHTY-FIRST LESSON. 453

To muse, to think.	*Meditare* 1, *star pensieroso* (or *sopra pensiero*).
I thought a long time on that affair.	Ho meditato molto tempo su questo affare (ho pensato molto tempo su questo affare).

To be naked.	*Esser nudo (ignudo).*
To have the head uncovered.	Aver la testa scoperta.
To have the feet uncovered.	Aver i piedi scalzi.
To be barefooted.	Essere piè scalzi.
To be bareheaded.	Essere a capo scoperto.
To ride barebacked.	Cavalcare a bardosso (or a schiena nuda).

To have like to, or to think to have.	*Mancare* 1, *star per.*
I had like to have lost my money.	Stetti per perdere il mio danaro. Poco mancò ch' io non perdessi il mio danaro.
I thought I had lost my life.	Credei perdere la vita.
We had like to have cut our fingers.	Poco mancò che non ci tagliassimo le dita.
He was very near falling.	Stette quasi per cadere.
He was within a hair's breadth of being killed.	Poco mancò che non fosse ucciso. Poco ci volle ch' egli non fosse ucciso. Credè (pensò) essere ucciso.
He had like to have died.	Credè (credette) morire.

At, on, or upon your heels.	Alle vostre spalle.
The enemy is at our heels.	Il nemico c' insegue alle spalle.

To strike (in speaking of lightning).	*Cascare* 1, *cadere*
The lightning has struck.	Il fulmine cadde.
The lightning struck the ship.	Il fulmine cadde sul bastimento.
While my brother was on the open sea, a violent storm rose unexpectedly; the lightning struck the ship, which is set on fire, and the whole crew jumped into the sea to save themselves by swimming.	Trovandosi mio fratello in alto mare, sopravvenne fiera tempesta; il fulmine cadde sul bastimento che mise in fuoco, e tutto l' equipaggio si gettò al mare per salvarsi a nuoto.
He was struck with fright when he saw that the fire was gaining on all sides.	Fu preso da spavento vedendo che il fuoco imperversava da ogni lato.
He did not know what to do.	Non sapeva a che appigliarsi.
He hesitated no longer.	Non istette più in forse.

EIGHTY-FIRST LESSON.

I have not heard of him yet.	Non ho ancor avuto sue nuove.
An angel.	Un angelo.
A master-piece.	Un capo d' opera.
Master-pieces.	Capi d' opera.

Obs. Of a word compounded by means of a preposition, expressed or understood, the first word only takes the mark of the plural.

Four o'clock flowers.	Gelsomini di notte.

His *or* her physiognomy.	La sua fisonomia.
His *or* her shape.	Le sue forme, la sua statura *o* figura.
The expression.	L' espressione.
The look.	L' aspetto, la ciera.
Contentment.	Il contento.
Respect.	Il rispetto.
Admiration.	L' ammirazione.
Grace, charm.	Le grazie.
Delightfully.	A maraviglia.
Fascinating.	Attraente, lusinghiero.
Thin (slender).	Svelto, asciutto, smilzo, magro.
Uncommonly well.	Superiormente bene.
His *or* her look inspires respect and admiration.	Il suo aspetto inspira deferenza ed ammirazione.

EXERCISES.

245.

Will you be my guest (*mangiare con qualcuno*)?—I thank you; a friend of mine has invited me to dinner: he has ordered (*fare apparecchiare*) my favourite dish (*un cibo favorito*).—What is it? —It is a dish of milk (*dei latticinii*).—As to me, I do not like milk-meat: there is nothing like (*niente di meglio che*) a good piece of roast beef or veal.—What has become of your younger brother?—He has suffered shipwreck (*far naufragio*) in going to America.—You must give me an account of that (*La mi racconti quest' avvenimento*).—Very willingly (*volontierissimo*).—Being on the open sea, a great storm arose. The lightning struck the ship and set it on fire. The crew jumped into the sea to save themselves by swimming. My brother knew not what to do, having never learnt to swim. He reflected in vain; he found no means to save his life. He was struck with fright when he saw that the fire was gaining on all sides. He hesitated no longer, and

jumped into the sea. Well (*su via*) what has become of him?—
I do not know, having not heard of him yet.—But who told you
all that?—My nephew, who was there, and who saved himself.
—As you are talking of your nephew (*a proposito del—*) where
is he at present?—He is in Italy.—Is it long since you heard of
him?—I have received a letter from him to-day.—What does he
write to you?—He writes to me that he is going to marry a
young woman who brings him a hundred thousand crowns.—Is
she pretty?—Handsome as an angel; she is a master-piece of
nature. Her physiognomy is mild and full of expression; her
eyes are the finest in the (*del*) world, and her mouth is charming
(*e la sua bocca è leggiadra*). She is neither too tall nor too short;
her shape is slender; all her actions are full of grace, and her
manners are engaging. Her looks inspire respect and admiration. She has also a great deal of wit; she speaks several languages, dances uncommonly well, and sings delightfully. My
nephew finds but one defect in her (*le trova che un difetto*).—And
what is that defect?—She is affected (*aver delle pretensioni*).—
There is nothing perfect in the (*al*) world.—How happy you are!
you are rich, you have a good wife, pretty children, a fine house,
and all you wish.—Not all, my friend.—What do you desire
more?—Contentment (*la contentezza*); for you know that he only
is happy who is contented (*che può dirsi contento*).

EIGHTY-SECOND LESSON.

Lezione ottantesima seconda.

To unriddle, to disentangle. To find out.	Sviluppare 1, sciogliere * (sciolto, sciolsi) 1. Distrigare 1, distinguere * 2 (p. part. distinto, pret. def. distinsi).
To disentangle the hair. To unriddle difficulties. I have not been able to find out the sense of that phrase.	Pettinare i capelli. Sciogliere difficoltà. Non ho potuto distinguere il senso di questa frase.

A quarrel.	Una querela, una rissa.
To have differences (a quarrel) with somebody.	Aver delle quistioni con qualcuno.

To take good care, to shun, to beware.	*Guardarsi da.*
I will take care not to do it.	Mi guarderò bene dal farlo.
Mind you do not lend that man money.	Guardatevi dal prestare danaro a costui.
He takes care not to answer the question which I asked him.	Si guarda bene dal rispondere alla questione che gli ho fatta.
To ask a question.	Far una questione (or una domanda).
If you take it into your head to do that, I will punish you.	Se vi avvisate di farlo, vi punirò.
To take into one's head.	Avvisarsi (mettersi in capo).

To become, to fit well.	*Star bene, convenire*, affarsi.*
Does that become me?	Mi sta bene questo?
That does not become you.	Non vi (Le) sta bene.
It does not become you to do that.	Non vi (Le) conviene di far ciò.
That fits you wonderfully well.	Questo Le (vi) sta a maraviglia.
Her head-dress did not become her.	La sua acconciatura di capo le stava male.
It does not become you to reproach me with it.	Non vi sta bene di rinfacciarmelo.

To reproach.	*Rinfacciare* 1.

To follow from it.	*Seguire, succedere**; p. part. *successo*; pret. def. *successi*.
It follows from it that you should not do that.	Ne segue che non dovreste (dovrebbe) far ciò.
How is it that you have come so late?	Come mai è Ella (siete) venuta (venuto) così tardi?
I do not know how it is.	Non so come.
How is it that he had not his gun?	Come mai non aveva il suo fucile?
I do not know how it happened.	Non so come.

To fast.	*Digiunare, far astinenza.*
To be fasting.	Essere a digiuno.
To give notice to, to let any body know.	Avvertire (avvisare) qualcuno di qualche cosa.
To warn some one of something.	
Give notice to that man of his father's return.	Avvertite (avvisate) costui del ritorno di suo padre.

EIGHTY-SECOND LESSON. 457

To clear, to elucidate, to clear up.	Schiarire 3 (isco). Rischiarare 1.
The weather is clearing up.	Il tempo si rischiara.

To refresh.	Rinfrescare 1.
Refresh yourself, and return to me immediately.	Rinfrescatevi e ritornate subito.
To whiten, to bleach.	Imbiancare 1.
To blacken.	Annerire (isco), abbrunare.
To turn pale, to grow pale.	Impallidire (isco).
To grow old.	Invecchiare 1.
To grow young.	Ringiovinire (isco).
That makes one look young again.	† Questo ringiovinisce il volto.
To blush, to redden.	Arrossire (isco).

To make merry.	*Rallegrare* 1, *divertire* 3.
To make one's self merry.	Rallegrarsi, divertirsi.
He makes merry at my expense.	Si diverte alle mie spese.

To feign, to dissemble, to pretend.	*Fingere**; past part. *finto*; pret. def. *finsi*.
He knows the art of dissembling.	Possiede l' arte di fingere.
To possess.	*Possedere** (is conjugated like *sedere**, Lesson LI.).

To procrastinate, to go slowly.	† *Mandar le cose in lungo.*
I do not like to transact business with that man, for he always goes very slowly about it.	Non mi piace far affari con costui, perchè manda sempre le cose in lungo.

A proof.	Una prova.
It is a proof.	È una prova.

To stray, to get lost, to lose one's way, to lose one's self.	*Smarrirsi.*
Through.	A traverso. Per mezzo. Da banda a banda. Da parte a parte.
The cannon-ball went through the wall.	La palla di cannone è passata a traverso la muraglia.
I ran him through the body.	Gli ho passato la mia spada da parte a parte.

EIGHTY-SECOND LESSON.

APOSTROPHE AND ELISION.

The apostrophe is used,—

1. After the articles *lo, la, li, gli*, and their oblique cases, when they meet before words beginning with a vowel, or when they are abbreviated, as:

The soul, the honour.	L' anima, l' onore.
Of the books, to the fathers.	Dè libri, a' padri, &c.

Obs. A. The articles *lo, la*, are never abridged in the plural, unless the noun following *lo* begins with an *i* [1]. Ex.

The friends, the coats.	Gli amici, gli abiti.
The loves, the honours.	Gli amori, gli onori.
The shades, the inventions.	Le ombre, le invenzioni.
The eminences, the executions.	Le eminenze, le esecuzioni.

But write.

The geniuses, the English, the instruments.	Gl' ingegni, gl' Inglesi, gl' istrumenti.

Obs. B. Whenever the prepositions: *con*, with; *in*, in; *su*, upon; *per*, for, by, meet with the definite articles, *il, lo, la*, they are contracted: thus *nel* is said instead of *in il, nello*, instead of *in lo*, &c. According to this contraction we may and write:

	SINGULAR.		PLURAL	
	Masculine.	*Feminine.*	*Masculine.*	*Feminine*
In the.	Nel, nello	" Nella.	Nei or ne', negli.	Nelle.
With the.	Col, collo	" Colla.	Col or co', con gli or cogli.	Colle.
Upon the.	Sul, sullo	" Sulla.	Su' or sui, sugli.	Sulle.
For the.	Pel, pello	" Pella.	Palli, pei or pe', per gli.	Pelle [2].

EXAMPLES.

In the garden, in the spirit, in the room.	Nel giardino, nello spirito, nella camera.
In the gardens, in the spirits, in the rooms.	Ne' giardini, negli spiriti, nelle camere, &c.

2. In the article *il* the letter *i* is sometimes cut off, and an apostrophe put in its stead, after a word ending with a vowel, but not the vowel of that word. This, however, is more frequently the case in poetry than in prose. Ex.

The whole country.	Tutto 'l paese.
Let him tell me his name.	Mi dica 'l suo nome.

3. *Mi, ti, ci, vi, ne, se, si, di*, receive the apostrophe before a vowel. Ex.

You understand me.	Voi m' intendete.
He understands it.	Ei l' intende.
He will mistake.	S' ingannerà.
If he likes.	S' egli vuole.

---

[1] Words ending in *gli* and *ci* are never abridged, unless the following word begins with *i*, as: *quegl' intervalli*, those intervals; *dolc' inganni*, sweet illusions. But write *quegli amici*, those friends, and not *quegl' amici*.

[2] The contractions contained in this last line are less generally made use of.

EIGHTY-SECOND LESSON.   459

Obs. C. Ci, however, is never abridged before *a, o, u,* to avoid harshness. Ex.

We want.	Ci abbisogna.
We are in want of.	Ci occorre.
They unite us.	Ci uniscono.

4. The words *uno, bello, grande, santo, quello, buono,* are often abridged before masculine nouns beginning with a consonant or a vowel, but never before feminine nouns (except when beginning with a vowel), or before *s* followed by a consonant. (See *Obs. G., H., I.,* Lesson X.) Ex.

A book, a fine book, a large horse.	Un libro, un bel libro, un gran cavallo.
Saint Peter, that soldier, good bread.	San Pietro, quel soldato, buon pane.
A friend, a fine man, great genius.	Un amico, un bell' uomo, grand' ingegno.
Holy Anthony, that love, good orator.	Sant' Antonio, quell' amore, buon oratore.
Large boat, great army.	Gran barca, grand' armata.

5. Words in the singular, having one (not two) of the liquid consonants, *l, m, n, r,* before their final vowel, may lose this, unless before words beginning with *s,* followed by a consonant. The vowels after *m* and *n* are not so often dropped as those after *l* and *r,* except in verbs, where the vowel after *m* is frequently dropped. Ex.

The rising sun.	Il sol nascente (*instead of* sole nascente).
Your welfare.	Il ben vostro (*instead of* bene vostro).
The serene sky.	Il ciel sereno (*instead of* cielo sereno).
Full senate.	Pien Senato (*instead of* pieno senato).
Light wind.	Leggier vento (*instead of* leggiero vento).
Let us wait.	Attendiam (*instead of* attendiamo).
Let us go.	Andiam (*instead of* andiamo).
Let us feign.	Fingiam (*instead of* fingiamo), &c.

Obs. D. Cannot be abridged:—(a) The words, *chiaro,* clear; *raro,* rare; *nero,* black; *oscuro,* dark; and some others. (b) The first person singular of the present of the indicative, as: *Io perdono,* I pardon; *io mi consolo,* I console myself, &c., except *sono,* first person singular and third person plural of the auxiliary *essere.* Ex.

I am ready.	Io son pronto (*for* io sono pronto).
They are come.	Eglino son venuti (*for* eglino sono venuti).

6. Infinitives, when joined to *mi, ti, ci, vi, si, ne, lo, la, le, li, gli,* or any other word, drop their final *e.* Ex.

To see him.	Per vederlo (*for* per vedere lo).
To feel one's self.	Sentirsi (*for* sentire si).
To repent.	Pentirsi (*for* pentire si).

Obs. E. Words having the grave accent are never abridged, as: *dirà*, I shall say; *farò*, I will make; *felicità*, happiness, &c., except *che*, with its compounds: *perchè*, why? *benchè*, although; *sicchè*, therefore, so that, &c., which are sometimes abridged. Ex.

| Because he was. | Perch' era. |
| Though he might go. | Bench' andasse, &c. |

AUGMENTATIONS.

1. When words beginning with *s* followed by a consonant are preceded by one of the prepositions *in*, *con*, *per*, or by the negative *non*, the letter *i* is prefixed to them for the sake of euphony. (See *Obs. F.* Lesson LV.) Ex.

In the street.	In istrada (*for* in strada).
In a state (able).	In istato (*for* in stato).
With terror.	Con ispavento (*for* con spavento).
With study.	Con istudio (*for* con studio).
By mistake.	Per isbaglio (*for* per sbaglio).
Do not jest.	Non ischerzate (*for* non scherzate).
Not to stay.	Non istare (*for* non stare).

2. The preposition *a*, and the conjunctions *e*, *o*, *nè* are changed into *ad*, *ed*, *od*, *ned*, before a vowel; *od* and *ned*, however, are less frequently made use of than *ad* and *ed*. Ex.

To Anthony.	Ad Antonio.
You and I.	Voi ed io.
We and he.	Noi ed egli.
Neither thou nor she.	Nè tu ned essa.

EXERCISES.

246.

The Emperor Charles the Fifth being one day out a hunting, lost his way in the forest, and having come to a house entered it to refresh himself. There were in it four men, who pretended to sleep. One of them rose, and approaching the Emperor, told him he had dreamt he should take his watch, and took it. Then another rose, and said he had dreamt that his *surtout* fitted him wonderfully, and took it. The third took his purse. At last the fourth came up, and said he hoped he would not take it ill if he searched him, and in doing it perceived around the emperor's neck a small gold chain to which a whistle was attached which he wished to rob him of. But the Emperor said: " My good friend, before depriving me of (*spogliare qualcuno di qualche cosa*) this trinket (*il gioiello*), I must teach you its virtue." Saying this, he whistled. His attendants (*i suoi uffiziali*), who were seeking him, hastened to the house, and were thunderstruck (*soprafatti dallo stupore*) to behold his majesty in such a state. But the Emperor, seeing himself out of danger (*fuor di pericolo*), said (*li prevenne dicendo*): "These men (*Ecco degli uomini che*) have dreamt all that they liked. I wish in my turn also to dream." And after having mused a few moments, he said: "I have dreamt that you all four deserve to be hanged:" which was no sooner spoken than executed before the house.

A certain king making one day his entrance into a town at two o'clock in the afternoon (*dopo mezzo giorno*), the senate sent some deputies (*un deputato*) to compliment him. The one who was to speak (*portar la parola*) began thus (*in questi termini*): "Alexander the Great, the great Alexander," and stopped short (*e tosto s' arrestò*).—The king, who was very hungry (*aver molta fame*), said : " Ah! my friend, Alexander the Great had dined, and I am still fasting." Having said this, he proceeded to (*proseguire verso*) the *hôtel de ville* (*il palazzo della città*), where a magnificent dinner had been prepared for him.

247.

A good old man (*un vecchierello*), being very ill, sent for his wife, who was still very young, and said to her : " My dear, you see that my last hour is approaching, and that I am compelled to leave you. If, therefore, you wish me to die in peace you must do me a favour (*una grazia*). You are still young, and will, without doubt, marry again (*rimaritarsi*): knowing this, I request of you not to wed (*prendere*) M. Lewis (*Luigi*); for I confess that I have always been very jealous of him, and am so still. I should, therefore, die in despair (*disperato*) if you do not promise me that." The wife answered: " My dear husband (*mio caro marito*), I entreat you, let not this hinder you from dying peaceably ; for I assure you that, if even I wished to wed him I could not do so, being already promised to another."

It was customary with Frederick (*Federico*) the Great, whenever a new soldier appeared in his guards, to ask him three questions; viz. "How old are you? How long have you been in my service? Are you satisfied with your pay and treatment?" It happened that a young soldier, born in France, who had served in his own country, desired to enlist in the Prussian service. His figure caused him immediately to be accepted; but he was totally ignorant of the German dialect; and his captain giving him notice that the king would question him in that tongue the first time he should see him, cautioned him, at the same time, to learn by heart the three answers that he was to make to the king. Accordingly he learnt them by the next day; and as soon as he appeared in the ranks Frederick came up to interrogate him: but he happened to begin upon him by the second question, and asked him, "How long have you been in my service?" "Twenty-one years," answered the soldier. The king, struck with his youth, which plainly indicated that he had not borne a musket so long as that, said to him, much astonished: "How old are you?" "One year, an't please your majesty (*con buona grazia della Maestà Vostra*)." Frederick, more astonished still, cried, "You or I must certainly be bereft of our senses." The soldier, who took this for the third question, replied firmly (*con molto sangue freddo*): "Both, an't please your majesty (*quando piaccia a Vostra Maestà*)."

EIGHTY-THIRD LESSON.

Lezione ottantesima terza.

To double.	Addoppiare 1.
	Doppiare 1, raddoppiare 1.
The double.	Il doppio.
Your share, your part.	La vostra parte.
That merchant asks twice as much as he ought.	Questo mercante domanda il doppio.
You must bargain with him; he will give it you for the half.	Bisogna mercanteggiare con lui; glielo darà per la metà prezzo.
You have twice your share.	Ella ha due volte tanto.
You have three times your share.	Ella ha tre volte tanto.

To renew.	Rinnovare, rinnovellare 1.
To stun.	Stordire (isco).
Wild, giddy.	Stordito.
To shake somebody's hand.	Stringere la mano a qualcuno.
Open, frank, real.	Franco, aperto, schietto.

I tell you yes.	† Vi dico di sì.
I tell you no.	† Vi dico di no.
I told him yes.	† Gli dissi di sì.
I told him no.	† Gli dissi di no.

To lay up, to put by.	Serrare 1, riporre * (posto, posi). Chiudere, rinchiudere * (chiuso, chiusi).
Put your money by.	Chiuda (chiudete) il di Lei (il vostro) danaro.
As soon as I read my book I put it by.	Appena ho letto il mio libro, lo ripongo.
I do not care much about going to the play to-night.	Non mi do molta briga d' andare allo spettacolo questa sera. Non mi curo molto d' andare allo spettacolo questa sera.

To care.	Darsi briga, curarsi.
To satisfy one's self with a thing.	Saziarsi 1.
I have been eating an hour, and I cannot satisfy my hunger.	È un' ora che mangio e non posso saziarmi. Mangio da un' ora e non posso saziarmi.

To be satisfied.	Essere sazio.
To quench one's thirst.	Dissetarsi 1.
I have been drinking this half hour, but I cannot quench my thirst.	È una mezz' ora che bevo, ma non posso dissetarmi.
To have one's thirst quenched.	Esser dissetato.

To thirst for, to be thirsty or dry.	Esser assetato, aver gran sete.
He is a blood-thirsty fellow.	È un uomo assetato di sangue. È un uomo attibondo di sangue.
On both sides, on every side.	Da un canto e dall' altro. D' ambo i lati.
On all sides.	Da tutti i lati.

EIGHTY-THIRD LESSON.

Allow me, my lady, to introduce to you Mr. G., an old friend of our family.	Permetta, Signora, ch' io Le presenti il Signor di G. come un vecchio amico della nostra famiglia.
I am delighted to become acquainted with you.	Sono contentissima, Signore, (mi è gratissimo, Signore) di far la di Lei conoscenza.
I shall do all in my power to deserve your good opinion.	Farò tutto ciò che sarà in mio potere per rendermi degno della di Lei buona grazia.
Allow me to introduce to you Mr. B. whose brother has rendered such eminent services to your cousin.	Signore, permettano ch' io Lor presenti il Signor di B. il cui fratello ha reso così eminenti servigi al Loro cugino.
How happy we are to see you at our house!	Ah, Signore, quanto siamo contente di riceverla in casa nostra!
It is the finest country in Europe.	È il più bel paese dell' Europa.
Candia is one of the most agreeable islands in the Mediterranean.	Candia è una delle isole più amene del Mediterraneo.
He lives in his retreat like a real philosopher.	Vive nel suo ritiro come un vero filosofo (da vero filosofo).
You live like a king.	Vivete (Ella vive) da re.
He acts like a madman.	Si comporta come un furioso.
To behave like a blunderbuss.	Condursi come uno stordito.
Who knocks as if he were master where I am?	Chi picchia da padrone ove son io?
Good morning.	Buon giorno. Ben levato.
You are out very early.	Così di buon' ora in piedi.
I wish you a good morning.	Le auguro il buon giorno.
You rose early (in good time, late).	Vossignoria (Ella) s' è levata a buon' ora (per tempo, tardi).
Had you a good night's rest?	Ha Ella dormito (riposato) bene?
Good evening.	Buona sera (felice sera).
Good night.	Buona notte (felice notte).
I wish you a good night's rest.	Riposi bene. Dorma bene.
I wish you a good appetite.	Le auguro un buon appetito.
I wish you the same.	Parimenti.
May it do you good.	Buon pro Le faccia.
A happy new year.	Buon capo d' anno.
A happy journey.	Buon viaggio.
I wish you good luck.	Le auguro (Le desidero) un prospero successo.
God bless you.	Il ciel La benedica.
God preserve you.	Dio la guardi.
When shall I have the pleasure of seeing you again?	Quando avrò il piacere di rivederla?
Soon. In a short time.	Presto. Fra poco (tempo).
Adieu! till we meet again.	Addio, Signore! a rivederci.

EIGHTY-THIRD LESSON.

Your most humble servant.	Umilissimo servo. M' inchino a Lei. Le sono schiavo.
Your most obedient servant.	Servo divoto. Divotissimo servo. I miei rispetti. Padron riverito.
I am entirely yours.	Son tutto suo.
Adieu.	La riverisco.
How is your Lordship?	Come sta Vossignoria Illustrissima?
How do you do?	Come va? Come se la passa?
Well, at your service.	Bene, per servirla (per ubbidirla).
I am glad of it.	Ne godo. Me ne rallegro. Me ne consolo.

How is your health?	Come sta V. S. (Ella) di salute?
I am well, very well, tolerably, so so, unwell.	Sto bene, ottimamente, passabilmente, mediocremente, male.
Not too well. So so.	Non troppo bene. Così così.
You do not look very well.	Ella non ha troppo buona ciera.
What is the matter with you?	Che cosa ha?
I am a little indisposed.	Sono un poco indisposto (a).
I am sorry for it.	Me ne dispiace. Me ne rincresce.

Welcome, Sir.	Ben venuta, Vossignoria.
I am happy to see you.	Mi rallegro di vederla.
It seems a century since I had the pleasure of seeing you.	Mi pare cent' anni che non ho avuto il piacer di vederla.
It is a good while since I had the pleasure of seeing you.	È già lungo tempo (è già un bel pezzo) che non ebbi il piacere di vederla.
Give this gentleman a chair.	Date una sedia (date da sedere) a questo Signore.
Please to sit down.	Si serva. S' accomodi, La prego. La supplico, resti servita.
Sit down. Be seated.	Si metta a sedere. Resti a sedere.
Sit by my side.	Segga accanto a me.
Take a chair.	Prenda una sedia.
I thank you, I prefer to stand.	La ringrazio, voglio restare in piedi.
Do not trouble yourself.	Non s' incomodi, La prego.
Do as if you were at home.	Faccia conto d' essere a casa sua.
Do not make any compliments.	Non fate cerimonie (complimenti).
I will not trouble you any longer.	Non voglio recarle incomodo più a lungo. Voglio levarle l' incomodo.
Do you wish to leave already?	Or mai se ne vuol andare? Se ne vuolegli andare?
Stay a little longer.	Si trattenga ancora un poco.
I must beg you to excuse me this time.	Per questa volta convien (bisogna) che La preghi di dispensarmene.

20*

Are you in such a hurry?	Ha poi tanta premura?
You are in a great hurry, Sir.	Ha molta fretta, Signore.
I must go.	Bisogna ch' io me ne vada.
I have pressing business.	Ho degli affari di premura.
I speak frankly.	Io parlo schietto, senza suggezione.
I hope then to have the honour another time.	Spero dunque d' aver l' onore un' altra volta.
Favour me oftener (with your visits).	Mi favorisca più spesso.
Farewell.	Si conservi.
Till we meet again.	A buon rivederci.

It is the prerogative of great men to conquer envy; merit gives it birth and merit destroys it.	Vincer l' invidia è privilegio dei grandi uomini; il merito la fa nascere, il merito la fa morire.

EXERCISES.

248.

A man had two sons, one of whom liked to sleep very late in the morning (*tutta la mattina*), and the other was very industrious, and always rose very early. The latter (*costui*), having one day gone out very early found a purse well filled with money. He ran to his brother to inform him (*a fargli parte*) of his good luck (*la buona fortuna*), and said to him: "See, Luigi, what is got (*guadagnarsi*), by (*a*) rising early."—"Faith (*in fede mia*)!" answered his brother, "if the person to whom it belongs had not risen earlier than I, he would not have lost it."

A lazy young fellow being asked what made him lie (*stare*) in bed so long—"I am busied (*essere occupato*)," said he, "in hearing counsel every morning. Industry (*il lavoro*) advises me to get up; sloth (*la pigrizia*) to lie still; and so they give me twenty reasons pro and con (*pro e contro*). It is my part (*tocca a me*) to hear what is said on both sides; and by the time the cause (*la causa*) is over (*intesa*) dinner is ready."

A beautiful story is related of a great lady, who, being (*si racconta un bel tratto d'—*) asked where her husband was, when he lay concealed (*essere nascosto*) for having been deeply concerned in a conspiracy (*per essere stato complice d' una conspirazione,*) resolutely (*coraggiosamente*) answered, she had hid him. This confession drew her before the king, who told her that nothing but her discovering where her lord was concealed could save her from the torture (*che non poteva evitare la tortura quando non iscoprisse il ritiro del suo sposo*). "And will that do (*bastare*)?" said the lady. "Yes," said the king, "I give you my word for it." "Then," says she, "I have hid him in my heart, where you will find him." Which surprising answer (*questa risposta ammirabile*) charmed her enemies.

249.

Cornelia, the illustrious (*illustre*), mother of the Gracchi (*dei Gracchi*), after the death of her husband, who left her with twelve children, applied herself (*consacrossi*) to the care of her family, with a wisdom (*con tal saviezza*) and prudence (*la prudenza*) that acquired for her (*che si acquistò*) universal esteem (*la stima universale*). Only three out of (*fra*) the twelve lived to the years of maturity (*l' età matura*); one daughter, Sempronia, whom she married to the second Scipio Africanus (*Scipione l' Africano*); and two sons, Tiberius (*Tiberio*) and Caius (*Caio*), whom she brought up (*educare*) with so much care, that, though they were generally acknowledged (*benchè si sapesse generalmente*) to have been born with the most happy dispositions (*la disposizione*), it was judged that they were still more indebted (*pure si ritenevano debitori—più*) to education than nature. The answer she gave (*fare**) a Campanian lady (*una dama della Campania*) concerning them (*su di essi*) is very famous (*celeberrima*), and includes in it (*rinchiudere**) great instruction for ladies and mothers.

That lady, who was very rich, and fond of pomp and show (*essere appassionato pel fasto e lo splendore*), having displayed (*esporre**) her diamonds (*il diamante*), pearls (*la perla*), and richest jewels (*il monile*), earnestly desired Cornelia to let her see her jewels also. Cornelia dexterously (*destramente*) turned the conversation to another subject to wait the return of her sons, who were gone to the public schools. When they returned (*Arrivati che furono*), and entered their mother's apartment, she said to the Campanian lady, pointing to them (*mostrandoli*): "These are my jewels, and the only ornaments (*l' unico ornamento*) I prize (*apprezzare*)." And such ornaments, which are the strength (*la* *forza*) and support (*il sostegno*) of society, add a brighter lustre (*un più gran lustro*) to the fair (*la bellezza*) than all the jewels of the East (*dell' Oriente*).

EIGHTY-FOURTH LESSON.
Lezione ottantesima quarta.

CONSTRUCTION, OR SYNTAX.

1. The regular construction has this principle for basis, that the governing word or part of speech has always its place before the governed.

According to this principle, the subject or nominative, with all the words that determine it, takes the first place in the sentence; then follows the verb, then the objective case (accusative), with all its determinations, then the indirect object (genitive, dative, or ablative), with its determinations; at last the modifications, showing the different circumstances of place, time, &c. Ex.

I shall surely send to-morrow the most faithful of my servants to you, in order to return you the manuscripts with which you have intrusted me not long ago; and I write this note to you, that you may let me know the hour at which my servant will find you at home.	Manderò domani senza fallo il più fedele dei miei servitori da Lei, per restituirle i manoscritti affidatimi da qualche tempo; e Le scrivo questa cartolina, or biglietino, acciochè mi faccia sapere l' ora alla quale il mio servo La troverà in casa.
I have the honour to return you the Italian book which you had the goodness to lend me. I have read it with much pleasure, and am very much obliged to you for it.	Ho! l' onore di rimandarle il libro Italiano che Ella ebbe la bontà di prestarmi. L' ho letto con molto piacere, e glie ne sono tenutissimo.

2. As for the irregular construction or inversion, which the Italians, in imitation of the Latins, use very freely, it is impossible to lay down any fixed rules; it depends entirely on the particular stress the person who writes or speaks wishes to lay on certain words, which he then puts at the head of the sentence. The following sentence, which may be rendered in Italian in seven different ways, may stand as an instance:

I submit to you.
{
Rendo me a voi.
A voi rendo me.
Mi rendo a voi.
Rendomi a voi.
A voi mi rendo.
Vi rendo me. (Not elegant).
Rendomivi.
}

EIGHTY-FOURTH LESSON.

3. Inversions, however, when used properly, contribute uncommonly to elegance, beauty, and harmony of language. This may be exemplified in the following beautifully constructed expression of Boccaccio, which *if constructed regularly*, would lose all its harmony, beauty, and interest.

O dearest heart, all my duties towards thee are fulfilled; I have nothing else to do, but to go with my soul to keep thee company.	O molto amato cuore, ogni mio officio verso te è fornito, nè più altro mi resta a fare, se non di venire con la mia anima a fare la tua compagnia.[1]

EXPLETIVES AND LICENSES.

1. EXPLETIVES, which the Italians call *ripieno*, i. e. full, filled, are employed for the purpose of giving more emphasis, fulness, harmony, and elegance, to the sentence. The principal are:

BELLO.

I have paid a hundred crowns.	Ho pagato cento *begli* scudi.
Your suit of clothes is finished.	Il di Lei vestito è *bell* e fatto.

BENE.

I asked him, if he had the courage to send him away, and he answered, yes.	Gli domandai, se gli bastasse l'animo di cacciarlo via: ed egli rispose, si *bene*.

GIÀ.

I do not think that you will take it ill.	Non credo *già* che l' avrete a (*or* per) male.
I should not like him to go.	Non vorrei *già* ch' egli partisse.

MAI.

He is always repeating the same things.	Torna *mai* sempre a dire l' istesso cosa.
Always.	*Mai* sempre.

NON.

He is more learned than I thought.	Egli è più dotto ch' io *non* credeva.
Learning is of greater value than riches.	La dottrina è di più gran prezzo che *non* la richezze.

POI.

What he told me is not true.	Non è *poi* vero quanto mi disse.

PURE.

They are now disposed to come.	Ora sono *pur* disposti a venire.

Obs. A. This expletive is often used to strengthen the imperative. Ex.

---

[1] Re-establish the regular construction, all the beauty, harmony, and lively interest which is felt in reading it, disappears: "O cuore amato molto, ogni mio officio è fornito verso te, nè mi resta più altro a fare, se non di venire a farti compagnia con la mia anima."

EIGHTY-FOURTH LESSON.

Say (i. e. you have only to say).	Dite pure.
Go (i. e. you may go).	Andate pure.
Give (i. e. you may give).	Date pure.

VIA.

Are you willing to do it? do it.	Volete farlo? via fatelo.
Let us make peace.	Via facciamo la pace.

MI, TI, CI, VI, SI, NE.

I thought you were an Italian.	Io mi credeva che voi foste Italiano.
I wish thou wouldst stay with us this evening.	Desidero che tu con noi ti rimanga questa sera.
She left.	Essa se ne partì.
I do not know whether you know that man.	Non so se voi vi conosciate quest'uomo.
He leads a gay life.	Egli se la passa assai lietamente.

II. As to the licenses, they are very numerous in Italian, and are chiefly permitted and made use of in poetry, viz.

a) The letter v is sometimes left out, chiefly in the imperfect of the indicative, as:

    Avea, potea, finia, dee, deono, bee, bea, &c. for
    Aveva, poteva, finiva, deve, devono, beve, beva, &c.

b) The letters g and gg are sometimes substituted for other letters, as:

    Seggio, veggio, caggio, veggendo, cheggio, veglio, spreglio, &c., for
    Siedo, vedo, cado, vedendo, chiedo, vecchio, specchio, &c.

c) The third person plural of the preterite definite of the indicative, ending in *arono*, is often abridged into *aro*, chiefly in poetry, as:

    Amaro, legaro, andaro, for
    Amarono, legarono, andarono.

d) The syllable *at* is often rejected in poetry in the past participle, as:

    Colmo, adorno, chino, domo, oso, for:
    Colmato, adornato, chinato, domato, osato, &c.

e) The letter o is often added in poetry to the preterite definite of verbs ending in *ire*, as:

    Rapio, finio, empio, uscio, for
    Rapì, finì, empì, uscì.

f) The articles *dello*, *della*, *degli*, *dei*, *delle*, are by the poets often written.
    De lo, de la, de gli, de li, de le.

Obs. B. A great number of figurative, as well as Latin words, are also used by the Italian poets, which are hardly ever used in prose; thus you will find:

Air, sword.	Aer for aria; brando for spada.
Poem, food.	Carme for verso; esca for cibo.
Ship, carriage.	Legno for vascello or carrozza.
Eyes, hand.	Lumi for occhi; palma for mano.
Bell.	Squilla for campana.
Ever.	Unqua, unquanche, unquanco, for mai.
Poet, men, heroes, &c.	Vate for poeta; viri for uomini, &c.

Obs. C. No abridgment takes place:

a) In the last word of a sentence, chiefly in prose.

b) In the words which have an accent on their last syllable, except *che* with its compounds, as: *benchè*, *perchè*, *poichè*, &c.

c) In words ending in *a* before a consonant, except the adverbs, *allora*, *talora*, *ancora*, &c., and the word *suora*, sister, when used as an adjective. Say *alcuna persona*, *nessuna pena*, and not *alcun persona*, *nessun pena*.

d) In words terminating in a diphthong, as: *occhio*, *specchio*, *cambio*, &c.

EXERCISES.

250.

POLITENESS (*Creanza*).

When the Earl of Stair was at the court of Louis the Fourteenth, his manners, address, and conversation, gained much on the esteem and friendship of that monarch. One day, in a circle of his courtiers, talking of the advantage of good breeding and easy manners, the king offered to lay a wager he would name an English nobleman that should excel in those particulars any Frenchman of his court. The wager was jocularly accepted, and his majesty was to choose his own time and place for the experiment.

To avoid suspicion, the king let the subject drop for some months, till the courtiers thought (*onde far credere*) he had forgotten it; he then chose the following stratagem: he appointed Lord Stair, and two of the most polished noblemen of his court, to take an airing with him after the breaking up of the levee (*all' uscire del grand lever*); the king accordingly came down the great staircase at Versailles, attended by those three lords, and coming up to the side of the coach, instead of going in first as usual, he pointed to the French lords to enter; they, unaccustomed to the ceremony, shrunk back, and submissively declined the honour; he then pointed to Lord Stair, who made his bow, and sprang into the coach; the king, and the French lords followed.

When they were seated, the king exclaimed: "Well, gentlemen, I believe you will acknowledge I have won my wager." "How so, Sire?" "Why," continued the king, "when I desired you both to go into the coach, you declined it; but this polite foreigner (pointing to Lord Stair) no sooner received the commands of a king, though not his sovereign, than he instantly obeyed."

The courtiers hung down their heads in confusion, and acknowledged the justice of his majesty's claim.

251.

MILDNESS.

The mildness of Sir Isaac Newton's temper through the course of his life commanded admiration from all who knew him; but in no instance perhaps more than the following. Sir Isaac had a favourite little dog, which he called Diamond; and being one day called out of his study into the next room, Diamond was left behind. When Sir Isaac returned, having been absent but a few minutes, he had the mortification to find that Diamond, having thrown down a lighted candle among some papers, the nearly finished labour of many years was in flames, and almost consumed to ashes. This loss, as Sir Isaac Newton was then very far advanced in years, was irretrievable; yet, without once striking the dog, he only rebuked him with this exclamation: "O, Diamond! Diamond! thou little knowest the mischief thou hast done."

Zeuxis (*Zeuxi*) entered into a contest of art with Parrhasius (*Parrasio*). The former painted grapes so truly, that birds came and pecked at them. The latter delineated a curtain so exactly, that Zeuxis coming in said: "Take away the curtain that we may see this piece." And finding his error, said: "Parrhasius, thou hast conquered: I only deceived birds, thou an artist."

Zeuxis painted a boy carrying grapes; the birds came again and pecked. Some applauding, Zeuxis flew to the picture in a passion, saying: "My boy must be (*bisogna dire che—è*) very ill painted."

The inhabitants of a great town offered to Marshal de Turenne one hundred thousand crowns upon condition that he should take another road, and not march his troops their way. He answered them: "As your town is not on the road I intend to march, I cannot accept the money you offer me."

A corporal of the life-guards of Frederick the Great, who had a great deal of vanity, but at the same time was a brave fellow, wore a watch-chain, to which he affixed a musket-bullet instead of a watch, which he was unable to buy. The king, being inclined one day to rally him, said: "Apropos, corporal, you must have been very frugal to buy a watch: it is six o'clock by mine; tell me what it is by yours?" The soldier, who guessed the king's intention, instantly drew out the bullet from his fob, and said: "My watch neither marks five nor six o'clock; but it tells me every moment, that it is my duty to die for your majesty." "Here, my friend," said the king, quite affected, "take this watch, that you may be able to tell the hour also." And he gave him his watch, which was adorned with brilliants.

252.

My dear friend (*carissima amica*),—As we have next Tuesday several persons to dinner whose acquaintance, I am sure, you would be delighted to make, I request you to add by your presence to the pleasure, and by your brilliant and cultivated mind to the mirth of our assembly. I hope you will accept my invitation, and awaiting your answer I send you a thousand compliments.

Dearest friend (*amatissima amica*),—I accept the more readily your very kind invitation for Tuesday next, as my disappointment at seeing so little of you latterly has been very great. I thank you for your kind remembrance, and send you a thousand kisses.

EIGHTY-FIFTH LESSON.

Lezione ottantesima quinta.

TREATISE OF THE ITALIAN VERBS.

I. CONJUGATION OF THE AUXILIARY VERBS,

Essere, to be, and *Avere*, to have.

Present of the Infinitive (Infinito Presente).

| Avere, to have. | Essere, to be. |

EIGHTY-FIFTH LESSON.

Past of the Infinitive (Infinito Passato).

Avere avuto, to have had. | Essere stato, to have been.

Present Participle (Participio Presente).

Avendo,[1] having. | Essendo, being.

Past Participle (Participio Passato).

Masc. Avuto; *fem.* avuta. | *Masc.* Stato; *fem.* stata.
Plur. Avuti; *fem.* avute. | *Plur.* Stati; *fem.* state.

INDICATIVE (Indicativo).

Present (Presente).

Io ho (ò, see Lesson VII, Note 1),	I have.	Io sono,	I am.
Tu hai (ài),	thou hast.	Tu sei (se'),	thou art.
Egli (esso) } ha, (à)	he has.	Egli (esso) } è,	he is.
Ella (essa) }	she has.	Ella (essa) }	she is.
Noi abbiamo,	we have.	Noi siamo,	we are.
Voi avete,	you have.	Voi siete,	you are.
Eglino (essi) } hanno	they have.	Eglino (essi) } sono,	they are.[2]
Elleno (esse) } (ànno),		Elleno (esse) }	

Imperfect (Imperfetto).

Aveva (avea),	I had.	Io era,	I was.
Avevi,	thou hadst.	Tu eri,	thou wast.
Aveva (avea),	he had.	Egli era,	he was.
Avevamo,	we had.	Noi eravamo,	we were.
Avevate,	you had.	Voi eravate,	you were.
Avevano (aveano),	they had.	Essi erano,	they were.

Preterite Definite (Passato Rimoto).

Ebbi,	I had.	Fui,	I was.
Avesti,	thou hadst.	Fosti,	thou wast.
Ebbe,	he had.	Fu (poet. fue),	he was.
Avemmo,	we had.	Fummo,	we were.
Aveste,	you had.	Foste,	you were.
Ebbero,	they had.	Furono (poet. furo),	they were.

Preterperfect (Passato Prossimo).

Ho	}	I have	Sono } stato;	I have }
Hai		thou hast	Sei } fem. stata,	thou hast }
Ha	} avuto, had.	he has	È }	he has } been.
Abbiamo		we have	Siamo. }	we have }
Avete		you have	Siete. } stati;	you have }
Hanno.	}	they have	Sono } fem. state,	they have }

---

[1] There is another present participle, which is seldom used as such, viz. *avente*, having (See Lesson LVII.).

[2] The personal pronouns: *io*, I; *tu*, thou; *egli*, he; *ella*, she, &c., are not indispensable in the Italian conjugation. You may as well say: *sono, sei, è; avrò, avrai, avrà*, as: *io, sono, tu sei, egli è; io avrò, tu avrai, egli avrà*. But when there is a particular stress to be put on the person, or when an ambiguous meaning is to be avoided, the pronouns must be expressed. Ex. *Noi siamo ingannati, e non voi*, We are deceived, not you.

EIGHTY-FIFTH LESSON. 475

Pluperfect (Trapassato).

	I had had, &c.		I had been, &c.
Aveva		Era	
Avevi		Eri	stato;
Aveva	avuto.	Era	fem. stata.
Avevamo		Eravamo	
Avevate		Eravate	stati;
Avevano		Erano	fem. state.

Preterite Anterior (Passato Rimoto Composto).

	I had had, &c.		I had had, &c.
Ebbi		Fui	
Avesti		Fosti	stato;
Ebbe	avuto.	Fu	fem. stata.
Avemmo		Fummo	
Aveste		Foste	stati;
Ebbero		Furono	fem. state.

Future (Futuro Imperfetto).

Avrò,	I shall have,	Sarò,	I shall be.
Avrai,	thou wilt have,	Sarai,	thou wilt be.
Avrà,	he will have.	Sarà,	he will be.
Avremo,	we shall have.	Saremo,	we shall be.
Avrete,	you will have.	Sarete,	you will be.
Avranno,	they will have.	Saranno,	they will be.

Future Past (Futuro Perfetto).

Avrò	I shall have had.	Sarò	stato;	I shall have been.
Avrai	thou wilt have had,	Sarai	fem.	
Avrà,	&c.	Sarà	stata.	thou wilt have
Avremo	avuto,	Saremo	stati;	been, &c.
Avrete		Sarete	fem.	
Avranno		Saranno	state.	

Conditional Present (Condizionale Presente).

Avrei,	I should have.	Sarei,	I should be.
Avresti,	thou wouldst have.	Saresti,	thou wouldst be.
Avrebbe (poet. avria),	he would have.	Sarebbe (poet. saria, fora).	he would be.
Avremmo,	we should have.	Saremmo,	we should be.
Avreste,	you would have.	Sareste,	you would be.
Avrebbero (poet. avriano).	they would have.	Sarebbero, (poet. sariano, sariono, sorano.)	they would be.

Past Conditional (Condizionale Passato).

Avrei		I should have had	Sarei	stato;	I should have been.
Avresti			Saresti	fem.	
Avrebbe		thou wouldst	Sarebbe	stata.	thou wouldst
Avremmo	avuto.	have had,	Saremmo	stati;	have been,
Avreste		&c.	Sareste	fem.	&c.
Avrebbero			Sarebbero	state.	

EIGHTY-FIFTH LESSON.

Present of the Subjunctive (Congiuntivo Presente).

Che io abbia,	that I may have.	Che io sia,	that I may be.
" tu abbia (abbi),	that thou mayest have.	" tu sia (sii),	that thou mayest be.
" egli abbia,	that he may have.	" egli sia,	that he may be.
" noi abbiamo,	that we may have.	" noi siamo,	that we may be.
" voi abbiate,	that you may have.	" voi siate,	that you may be.
" essi abbiano,	that they may have.	" essi siano,	that they may be.

Imperfect of the Subjunctive (Imperfetto del Congiuntivo).

S' io avessi,	If I had.	S' io fossi,	If I were.
Se tu avessi,	if thou hadst.	Se tu fossi,	if thou wert.
S' egli avesse,	if he had,	S' egli fosse,	if he were,
Se noi avessimo,	&c.	Se noi fossimo,	&c.
Se voi aveste,		Se voi foste.	
S' essi avessero.		S' essi fossero.	

Perfect of the Subjunctive (Passato Prossimo del Congiuntivo).

That I may have had, &c.   That I may have been, &c.

Ch' io abbia		Ch' io sia
Che tu abbia (abbi)		Che tu sia (sii) } stato ; *fem.* stata.
Ch' egli abbia	} avuto.	Ch' egli sia
Che noi abbiamo		Che noi siamo
Che voi abbiate		Che voi siate } stati ; *fem.* state.
Ch' essi abbiano		Ch' essi siano

Pluperfect of the Subjunctive (Trapassato del Congiuntivo).

If I had had, &c.   If I had been, &c.

S' io avessi		S' io fossi
Se tu avessi		Se tu fossi } stato ; *fem.* stata.
S' egli avesse	} avuto.	S' egli fosse
Se noi avessimo		Se noi fossimo
Se voi aveste		Se voi foste } stati ; *fem.* state.
S' eglino avessero		S' essi fossero

IMPERATIVE (Imperativo).
(No first person singular.)

Abbi,	Have (thou).	Sii (sia)[2],	Be (thou).
Abbia,	let him (her) have.	Sia,	let him (her) be.
Abbiamo,	let us have.	Siamo,	let us be.
Abbiate,	have (ye).	Siate,	be (ye).
Abbiano,	let them have.	Siano,	let them be.

OBSERVATIONS.

A. There is, is in Italian rendered by *essere*, preceded by *ci* or *vi.* Ex.

[2] The second person singular of the imperative is rendered by the infinitive when it is negative. Ex. *Non amare,* be thou not ; *non avere,* have thou not (Lesson LXXI.).

EIGHTY-FIFTH LESSON. 477

There is a great quantity.	C' è (v' è) una gran quantità.
There are people.	Ci sono (vi sono) delle persone.
There was once a wise Grecian.	C' era una volta un savio Greco.
There were nations.	V' erano de' popoli.
There has been a singer.	C' è stata una cantatrice.
There were princes.	Ci sono stati de' principi.
Is there any physician here?	C' è (v' è) or avvi (evvi) qui un qualche medico?

B. Instead of *esservi*, *avervi* could in some cases be used, and may stand in the singular, though the substantive be in the plural. Ex.

There are princes.	V' ha (instead of v' hanno) de' principi.
There are many things.	V' ha molte cose.
There are many poor people.	V' ha (or havvi) molta gente povera.

C. If *of it* or *of them* is understood, it is rendered by *ne*. Ex.

There is no more of it.	Non ce n' è più.
There are many of them.	Ce ne sono molti.
There were only two (of them).	Non ve n' erano che due.
There are no physicians here.	Medici qui non ce ne sono.
I do not think that there are any.	Non credo che ve n' abbia.

D. Sometimes it may be rendered by *si dà* or *si danno*. Ex.

There is nothing worse in the world.	Non si dà al mondo cosa peggiore.
There are some who pretend.	Si danno di quelli che sostengono.

E. The adverbs *ci*, *vi*, are left out when time is spoken of. Ex.

It is a month. It is two years.	È un mese. Sono due anni.
A few months ago.	Pochi mesi sono (or pochi mesi fa).
It is a long while since I saw her.	È un bel pezzo, che non l' ho veduta.
This happened two months ago.	Ciò accadde due mesi fa.

F. *Avere* and *essere* are followed by the preposition *da* before the infinitive, when they are employed in the signification of *must* or *shall*. Ex.

You shall do it thus.	Avete da farlo così (instead of dovete farlo così).
He shall know.	Egli ha da sapere.
We must all die.	Abbiamo tutti da morire.
It is to be feared.	È da temersi.
He is not to be excused.	Egli non è da scusare.

G. In other instances *a* precedes the infinitive. Ex.

I should like to ask a favour of you.	Avrei a pregarla d' un favore.
She went to see her.	Ella fu a ritrovarla.

II. CONJUGATION OF THE REGULAR VERBS.

Present of the Infinitive (Infinitivo Presente).

Parlare, to speak.	Credere, to believe.	Nutrire, to nourish.

Past of the Infinitive (Infinitivo Passato).

Aver parlato, to have spoken.	Aver creduto, to have believed.	Aver nutrito, to have nourished.

EIGHTY-FIFTH LESSON.

Present Participle (Participio Presente).

| Parlando (parlante¹) speaking. | Credendo (credente), believing. | Nutrendo (nutrente), nourishing. |

Past Participle (Participio Passato).

| Parlato, spoken. | Creduto, believed. | Nutrito, nourished. |

INDICATIVE (Indicativo).

Present (Presente).

I speak, &c.	I believe, &c.	I nourish, &c.
Parl-o.	Cred-o.	Nutr-o, (isco).
— i.	— i.	— i, (isci).
— a.	— e.	— e, (isce).
— iamo.	— iamo.	— iamo.
— ate.	— ete.	— ite.
— ano.	— ono.	— ono, (iscono).

Imperfect (Imperfetto).

I spoke, &c.	I believed, &c.	I nourished, &c.
Parl-ava.	Cred-eva (ea).	Nutr-iva (ia).
— avi.	— evi.	— ivi.
— ava.	— eva (ea).	— iva (ia).
— avamo.	— evamo.	— ivamo.
— avate.	— evate.	— ivate.
— avano.	— evano (eano).	— ivano.

Præterite Definite (Passato Rimoto).

I spoke, or did speak, &c.	I believed, or did believe, &c.	I nourished, or did nourish, &c.
Parl-ai.	Cred-ei, (etti).	Nutr-ii.
— asti.	— esti.	— isti.
— ò.	— è, (ette).	— ì.
— ammo.	— emmo.	— immo.
— aste.	— este.	— iste.
— arono.	— erono, (ettero).	— irono.

Præterperfect (Passato Prossimo).

I have spoken, &c.	I have believed, &c.	I have nourished, &c.
Ho Hai Ha Abbiamo Avete Hanno } parlato,	creduto,	nutrito.

¹ There is this difference between the two present participles, that the first in *ando, endo* applies to a person *while* speaking, believing, &c.; and the second in *ante, ente* to a person *who* speaks, believes, &c. (See Lesson LVII.)

EIGHTY-FIFTH LESSON. 479

Pluperfect (Trapassato).

I had spoken, &c.	I had believed, &c.	I had nourished, &c.
Aveva Avevi Aveva Avevamo Avevate Avevano } parlato,	creduto,	nutrito.

Preterite Anterior (Passato Rimoto composto).

I had spoken, &c.	I had believed, &c.	I had nourished, &c.
Ebbi Avesti Ebbe Avemmo Aveste Ebbero } parlato,	creduto,	nutrito.

Future (Futuro Imperfetto).

I shall speak, &c.	I shall believe, &c.	I shall or will nourish, &c.
Parl-erò. — erai. — erà. — eremo. — erete. — eranno.	Cred-erò. — erai. — erà. — eremo. — erete. — eranno.	Nutr-irò. — irai. — irà. — iremo. — irete. — iranno.

Future Past (Futuro Perfetto).

I shall have spoken, &c.	I shall have believed, &c.	I shall have nourished, &c.
Avrò Avrai Avrà Avremo Avrete Avranno } parlato,	creduto.	nutrito.

Conditional Present (Condizionale Presente).

I should or would speak, &c.	I should or would believe, &c.	I should or would nourish, &c.
Parl-erei. — eresti. — erebbe. — eremmo. — ereste. — erebbero	Cred-erei. — eresti. — erebbe. — eremmo. — ereste. — erebbero	Nutr-irei. — iresti. — irebbe. — iremmo. — ireste. — irebbero

Conditional Past (Condizionale Passato).

I should or would have spoken, &c.	I should or would have believed, &c.	I should or would have nourished, &c.
Avrei Avresti Avrebbe Avremmo } parlato, Avreste Avrebbero	creduto,	nutrito.

Present of the Subjunctive (Congiuntivo Presente).

That I may speak, &c.	That I may believe, &c.	That I may nourish, &c.
Ch' io parl-i.	cred-a.	nutr-a (isca).
— i.	— a.	— a (isca).
— i.	— a.	— a (isca)
— iamo.	— iamo.	— iamo.
— iate.	— iate.	— iate.
— ino.	— ano.	— ano (iscano).

Imperfect of the Subjunctive (Imperfetto del Congiuntivo).

If I spoke, &c.	If I believed, &c.	If I nourished, &c.
S' io parl-assi.	cred-essi.	nutr-issi.
— assi.	— essi.	— issi.
— asse.	— esse.	— isse.
— assimo.	— essimo.	— issimo.
— aste.	— este.	— iste.
— assero.	— essero.	— issero.

Preterperfect of the Subjunctive (Passato Prossimo del Congiuntivo).

That I may have spoken, &c.	That I may have believed, &c.	That I may have nourished, &c.
Ch' io abbia Che tu abbia Ch' egli abbia Che noi abbiamo } par- Che voi abbiate lato, Ch' essi abbiano.	creduto,	nutrito.

Pluperfect of the Subjunctive (Trapassato del Congiuntivo).

If I had spoken, &c.	If I had believed, &c.	If I had nourished, &c.
S' io avessi Se tu avessi S' egli avesse Se noi avessimo } parla- Se voi aveste to, S' essi avessero	creduto,	nutrito.

EIGHTY-FIFTH LESSON. 461

IMPERATIVE (Imperativo).

Speak (thou), see note 3, p. 476, &c.	Believe (thou), &c.	Nourish (thou), &c.
Parl-a.	Cred-i.	Nutr-i. (*isci*.)
— i.	— a.	— a. (*isca*.)
— iamo.	— iamo.	— iamo.
— ate.	— ete.	— ite.
— ino.	— ano.	— ano. (*iscano*.)

III. CONJUGATION OF THE PASSIVE VOICE.

Obs. To form the passive voice the Italians use to place before the past participle of the active verb the auxiliary *essere*, but often also, and more elegantly, one of the verbs, *venire*, to come; *andare*, to go; *restare*, to rest; *rimanere*, to remain; *stare*, to stop, stay, to express with more emphasis a continuance of action.⁸ (See Lesson XLII. and XLIX.)

Present of the Infinitive (Infinito Presente).
Essere amato *or* amata, to be loved.

Past of the Infinitive (Infinito Passato).
Essere stato amato *or* stata amata, to have been loved.

Present Participle (Participio Presente).
Essendo amato, amata, amati, amate, being loved.

Past Participle (Participio Passato).
Stato amato, stata amata, stati amati, state amate, been loved.

INDICATIVE (Indicativo).

Present (Presente).

Io sono	*or*	vengo	amato,	*fem.* a,	I am loved.
Tu sei	"	vieni	amato,	" a,	thou art loved.
Egli è	"	viene	amato,		he is loved.
Ella è	"	viene	amata,		she is loved.
Noi siamo	"	veniamo	amati,	" e,	we are loved.
Voi siete	"	venite	amati,	" e,	you are loved.
Essi sono	"	vengono	amati, }	. .	they are loved.
Esse sono	"	vengono	amate,		

⁸ EXAMPLES:

Vien lodato da tutti,	He is praised by every body.
Venne accusata,	She was accused.
Verranno biasimate,	They will be blamed.
Questa voce va posta prima,	This word must be placed at the head.
Ne restai (or rimasi) maraviglioto (instead of ne fui maravigliato),	I was quite surprised at it.
Essa non ne restò (fu) persuasa,	She was not convinced of it.
I cavalli stanno (sono) attaccati alla carrozza,	The horses are put to the carriage.

21

EIGHTY-FIFTH LESSON.

Imperfect (Imperfetto).

Io era	or	veniva	amato, *fem.* a,		I was loved.	
Tu eri	"	venivi	amato,	" a,	thou wert loved.	
Egli era	"	veniva	amato,		he was loved.	
Ella era	"	veniva	amata,		she was loved.	
Noi eravamo	"	venivamo	amati,	" e,	we were	}
Voi eravate	"	venivate	amati,	" e,	you were	} loved.
Essi erano	"	venivano	amati,	}	. . they were	}
Esse erano	"	venivano	amate,			

Preterite definite (Passato Rimoto).

Io fui	or	venni	amato, *fem.* a,		I was	}
Tu fosti	"	venisti	amato,	" a,	thou wert	}
Egli fu	"	venne	amato,		he was	}
Ella fu	"	venne	amata,		she was	} loved.
Noi fummo	"	venimmo	amati,	" e,	we were	}
Voi foste	"	veniste	amati,	" e,	you were	}
Essi furono	"	vennero	amati,	}	. . . they were	}
Esse furono	"	vennero	amate,			

Preterperfect (Passato Prossimo).

Io sono stato amato } I have been loved, &c.
Io sono stata amata }

Noi siamo stati amati } we have been loved, &c.
Noi siamo state amate }

Pluperfect (Trapassato).

Io era stato amato, &c.   I had been loved, &c.

Obs. The *Preterite Anterior* of the passive voice: *io fui stato* with a past participle, is not used in Italian.

Future (Futuro).

Io sarò or verrò amato or a, &c.   I shall be loved, &c.

Future Past (Futuro Perfetto).

Io sarò stato amato, &c.   I shall have been loved, &c.

Conditional present (Condizionale presente).

Io sarei	or	verrei	amato	or amata, I should be	}
Tu saresti	"	verresti	amato	" amata, thou wouldst be	} loved, &c.
Egli sarebbe	"	verrebbe	amato,	he would be	}
Ella sarebbe		verrebbe	amata, &c.	she should be	}

Conditional Past (Condizionale Passato).

Io sarei stato amato, &c.   I should have been loved.

EIGHTY-FIFTH LESSON.

Present of the Subjunctive (Congiuntivo Presente).

Che io sia	or venga	amato or amata,	that I may be	
— tu sia	" venga	amato " amata,	that thou mayst be	
— egli sia	" venga	amato "	that he may be	
— ella sia	" venga	amata "	that she may be	loved.
— noi siamo	" veniamo amati " amate,		that we may be	
— voi siate	" veniate amati " amate,		that you may be	
— essi siano	" vengano amati }		that they may be	
— esse siano	" vengano amate }			

Imperfect of the Subjunctive (Imperfetto del Congiuntivo).

Se io fossi	or venissi	amato or amata,		
— tu fossi	" venissi	amato " amata,		
— egli fosse	" venisse	amato,		
— ella fosse	" venisse	amata,		
— noi fossimo	" venissimo amati	" amate,	If I were loved, &c.	
— voi foste	" veniste	amati " amate,		
— essi fossero	" venissero amati,			
— esse fossero	" venissero amate,			

Perfect of the Subjunctive (Passato Prossimo del Congiuntivo).

Ch' io sia stato amato,
Ch' io sia stata amata, &c. } That I may have been loved, &c.
Che noi siamo stati amati,
Che noi siamo state amate, &c.

Pluperfect of the Subjunctive (Trapassato del Congiuntivo).
Se io fossi stato amato, &c. If I had been loved, &c.

IV. MODEL OF THE CONJUGATION OF A REFLECTIVE VERB GOVERNING THE ACCUSATIVE (See Lessons XLIII. and XLIV.).

Infinitive Present (Infinito Presente).
Difendersi, to defend one's self.

Infinitive Past (Infinito Passato).
Essersi difeso, to have defended one's self.

Present Participle (Participio Presente).
Difendentesi*, defending one's self.

---

* The participle, joined to the different pronouns, would be thus:

Present.			*Perfect*.		
Difendendomi,	defending	myself.	Essendomi		having defended myself.
Difendendoti,	"	thyself.	Essendoti	difeso-a.	having defended thyself.
Difendendosi,	"	himself or herself.	Essendosi		having defended himself or herself.
Difendendoci,	"	ourselves.	Essendoci		having defended ourselves.
Difendendovi,	"	yourselves.	Essendovi	difesi-e.	having defended yourselves.
Difendendosi,	"	themselves.	Essendosi		having defended themselves.

EIGHTY-FIFTH LESSON.

Participle Past (Participio Passato).

Difesomi,
Difesoti, } defended one's self.
Difesisi,
Difesoci,

INDICATIVE (Indicativo).

Present (Presente).

Io mi difendo,	I defend myself.
Tu ti difendi,	thou defendest thyself.
Egli } si difende,	{ he defends himself.
Ella }	{ she defends herself.
Noi ci difendiamo,	we defend ourselves.
Voi vi difendete,	you defend yourselves.
Essi } si difendono,	they defend themselves.
Esse }	

Imperfect (Imperfetto).

I defended myself, &c.

Mi difendeva.	Ci difendevamo.
Ti difendevi.	Vi difendevate.
Si difendeva.	Si difendevano.

Preterite Definite (Passato Rimoto).

I defended myself, &c.

Mi difesi.	Ci difendemmo.
Ti difendesti,	Vi difendeste.
Si difese.	Si difesero.

Preterperfect (Passato Prossimo).

I have defended myself, &c.

Mi sono }	Ci siamo }
Ti sei } difeso; *fem.* difesa⁷.	Vi siete } difesi; *fem.* difese.
Si è }	Si sono }

Pluperfect (Trapassato).

I had defended myself, &c.

Mi era }	Ci eravamo }
Ti era } difeso; *fem.* difesa.	Vi eravate } difesi; *fem.* difese.
Si era }	Si erano }

Preterite Anterior (Passato Rimoto composto).

I had defended myself, &c.

Mi fui }	Ci fummo }
Ti fosti } difeso; *fem.* difesa.	Vi foste } difesi; *fem.* difese.
Si fu }	Si furono }

---

[7] The reflective verbs in Italian being considered as passive, take in their compound tenses the auxiliary *essere*, which agrees in gender and number with the person.

EIGHTY-FIFTH LESSON.

Future Present (Futuro Imperfetto).
I shall defend myself, &c.

Mi difenderò.   Ci difenderemo.
Ti difenderai.   Vi difenderete.
Si difenderà.   Si difenderanno.

Future Past (Futuro Perfetto).
I shall have defended myself, &c.

Mi sarò   ⎫   Ci saremo   ⎫
Ti sarai   ⎬ difeso ; *fem.* difesa.   Vi sarete   ⎬ difesi ; *fem.* difese.
Si sarà   ⎭   Si saranno   ⎭

Conditional Present (Condizionale Presente).
I should defend myself, &c.

Mi difenderei.   Ci difenderemmo.
Ti difenderesti.   Vi difendereste.
Si difenderebbe.   Si difenderebbero.

Conditional Past (Condizionale Passato).
I should have defended myself, &c.

Mi sarei   ⎫   Ci saremmo   ⎫
Ti saresti ⎬ difeso ; *fem.* difesa.   Vi sareste   ⎬ difesi ; *fem.* difese.
Si sarebbe ⎭   Si sarebbero ⎭

Present of the subjunctive (Congiuntivo Presente).
That I may defend myself, &c.

Che io mi difenda.   Che noi ci difendiamo.
— tu ti difenda.   — voi vi difendiate.
— egli ⎫   — essi ⎫
— ella ⎬ si difende.   — esse ⎬ si difendano.

Imperfect of the Subjunctive (Imperfetto del Congiuntivo).
If I defended myself, &c.

Se mi difendessi.   Se ci difendessimo.
— ti difendessi.   — vi difendeste.
— si difendesse.   — si difendessero.

Preterperfect of the Subjunctive (Passato Prossimo del Congiuntivo).
That I may have defended myself, &c.

Che mi sia ⎫   Che ci siamo ⎫
— ti sia   ⎬ difeso ; *fem.* difesa.   — vi siate   ⎬ difesi ; *fem.* difese.
— si sia   ⎭   — si siano   ⎭

Pluperfect of the Subjunctive (Trapassato del Congiuntivo).
If I had defended myself, &c.

Se mi fossi ⎫   Se ci fossimo ⎫
— ti fossi   ⎬ difeso ; *fem.* difesa.   — vi foste   ⎬ difesi ; *fem.* difese.
— si fosse   ⎭   — si fossero ⎭

IMPERATIVE (Imperativo).

Difenditi,   Defend thyself.
Non ti difendere,   do not defend thyself.
Si difenda egli,   let him defend himself.

Difendiamoci,   let us defend ourselves.
Difendetevi,   defend yourselves.
Si difendano essi,   let them defend themselves.

V. MODEL OF THE CONJUGATION OF A REFLECTIVE VERB GOVERNING THE DATIVE (See Lesson LIV.).

Infinitive Present (Infinito Presente).
Procurarselo, to get, procure it.

Infinitive Past (Infinito Passato).
Esserselo procurato, to have got it.

Present Participle (Participio Presente).
Procurandoselo, getting it.

Participle Past (Participio Passato).
Procuratoselo, got it.

INDICATIVE (Indicativo).

Present (Presente).
I get it, &c.

Io me lo procuro.   Noi ce lo procuriamo.
Tu te lo procuri.   Voi ve lo procurate.
Egli / Ella } se lo procura.   Essi / Esse } se lo procurano.

Imperfect (Imperfetto).
I got it, &c.   Io me lo procurava, &c.

Preterite Definite (Passato Rimoto).
I got it, &c.   Io me lo procurai, &c.

Preterperfect (Passato Prossimo).
I have got it, &c.

Io me lo sono ⎫   Noi ce lo siamo ⎫
Tu te lo sei ⎬ procurato.   Voi ve lo siete ⎬ procurato.
Egli / Ella } se lo è ⎭   Essi / Esse } se lo sono ⎭

Pluperfect (Trapassato).
I had procured it, &c.   Me lo era procurato, &c.

Preterite Anterior (Passato Rimoto composto).
I had procured it, &c.   Me lo fui procurato, &c.

Future Present (Futuro Imperfetto).
I shall procure it, &c.   Me lo procurerò, &c.

Future Past (Futuro Perfetto).
I shall have procured it, &c.   Me lo sarò procurato, &c.

EIGHTY-FIFTH LESSON.

Conditional Present (Condizionale Presente).

I should procure it, &c. | Io me lo procurerei, &c.

Conditional Past (Condizionale Passato).

I should have procured it, &c. | Me lo sarei procurato, &c.

Present of the Subjunctive (Congiuntivo Presente).

That I may procure it, &c.

Che io me lo procuri. | Che noi ce lo procuriamo.
— tu te lo procuri. | — voi ve lo procuriate.
— egli } se lo procuri. | — essi } se lo procurino.
— ella } | — esse }

Imperfect of the Subjunctive (Imperfetto del Congiuntivo).

If I procured it, &c. | S' io me lo procurassi, &c.

Preterperfect of the Subjunctive (Passato Prossimo del Congiuntivo).

That I may have procured it, &c.

Che io me lo sia } | Che noi ce lo siamo }
— tu te lo sia } procurato. | — voi ve lo siate } procurato.
— egli } se lo sia } | — essi } se lo siano }
— ella } | — esse }

Pluperfect of the Subjunctive (Trapassato del Congiuntivo).

If I had procured it, &c. | S' io me lo fossi procurato, &c.

IMPERATIVE (*Imperativo*).

Procuratelo, | Procure (thou) it.
Non telo procurare, | do (thou) not procure it.
Se lo procuri egli, | let him procure it.
Procuriamocelo, | let us procure it.
Procuratevelo, | procure (ye) it.
Se lo procurino essi, | let them procure it.

OBSERVATIONS ON THE CONJUGATION OF THE REGULAR VERBS.

A. The final *e* of the infinitives in *are*, *ere*, and *ire*, may be dropt before a vowel as well as before a consonant (except before *s* followed by a consonant), without an apostrophe being put in its stead. Ex.

Egli vuol *far* questo. | He wishes to do this.
Voglio *legger* questo libro. | I wish to read this book.
Non *dormir* punto. | Not to sleep at all.

B. The dropping of the final vowel may also take place before a consonant in those persons of the verbs which end in *no*, and have the accent on the last syllable but one. Ex.

EIGHTY-FIFTH LESSON.

Siam liberi (*instead of* siamo).   We are free.
Eravam contenti (*instead of* eravamo).   We were satisfied.
Sarem lodati (*instead of* saremo).   We shall be praised.
Amiam sinceramente (*instead of* amiamo).   We love sincerely.

But when the accent rests on the last syllable but two the last vowel cannot be dropped. We could not say:

Fossim, *for* fossimo colpevoli.   Were we guilty.
Avessim, *for* avessimo veduto.   Had we seen.
Amassim, *for* amàssimo tutti.   Did we love all.

C. The abbreviation may further take place in all the third persons plural that have *no* or *ro* for their ending, as:

Aman, they love; senton, they feel; *instead of* amano, sentono.
Amavan, they loved; amaron, they loved; *instead of* amavano, amarono.
Amasser, did they love; potrebbe, they could; avrebber, they would have; *instead of* amassero, potrebbero, avrebbero.

D. The third person plural of the *perfetto rimoto* is often abridged in more than one manner, as:

Instead of andarono, they went; *you will find:* andaron, andaro, andâr.
" " furono, they were; " " furon, furo, fur.

E. The third person singular of the present tense of verbs in *ere* often loses the final *e* when it is preceded by *l*, *r*, or *n*, as:

Si suol dire, they use to say,   *Instead of* suole.
Si duol di questo, they are sorry for it,   " " duole.
Ciò val molto, this is worth much,   " " vale.
Vuol fare, he will do,   " " vuole.

Also,

Par, 3rd pers. sing. of parere, to appear,   Instead of pare.
Pon, " " porre (ponere), to put,   " " pone.
Tien, " " tenere, to hold,   " " tiene.
Vien, " " venire, to come,   " " viene.
Riman, " " rimanere, to remain,   " " rimane.
Son, 1st pers. sing. and 3rd pers. plur. of *essere* to be,   sono.

I. ON THE VERBS IN *are*.

1. Verbs whose infinitives end in *care* or *gare* insert an *h* as often as *g* or *c* meets with *e* or *i*. Ex.

Present.—Cerco, I seek; cerchi (not cerci), thou seekest; cerchiamo, we seek, &c.

Future.—Cercherò, I shall seek; cercherai, thou wilt seek; cercherà, he will seek; cercheremo, we shall seek, &c.

Present Subj.—Ch' io cerchi, that I may seek, &c.; cerchiamo, that we may seek; cerchiate, that you may seek; cerchino, that they may seek.

2. When the infinitive ends in *ciare*, *giare*, *gliare*, and *sciare*, the letter *i* must be left out as often as it meets with *i* or *e*. Ex.

EIGHTY-FIFTH LESSON.   489

To threaten, to eat, to advise, to leave.	*Minacciare, mangiare, consigliare, lasciare.*
Thou threatenest, eatest, advisest, leavest.	*Tu minacci, mangi, consigli, lasci.*
I shall threaten, eat, advise, leave.	*Io minaccerò, mangerò, consiglierò, lascerò.*
I should threaten, eat, advise, leave.	*Io minaccerei, mangerei, consiglierei, lascerei.*

3. But in verbs whose first person singular of the present tense indicative has the accent upon the letter *i*, the second person singular must be written with ii. Ex.

I send, I spy.	*Invio, spio.*
Thou sendest, thou spiest.	*Tu invii, tu spii.*

II. ON THE VERBS IN *ere*.

1. The greatest irregularity in the verbs in *ere* takes place in the *perfetto rimoto*, and the past participle. Very few verbs in *ere* have in this tense the regular ending in *ei*, and even those that have it, may take also the irregular ending in *etti*, as may be seen above in the conjugation of *credere*, which has *credei* and *credetti*[8].

2. To know, therefore, the perfetto rimoto of those verbs which have not the regular ending *ei*, it is only necessary to know the first person singular. That once known, the third person singular is formed from it by changing *i* into *e*; and from this again the third person plural is formed by joining to it *ro*. The remaining three persons are always formed regularly. Ex.

To please. Preterite definite: I pleased.	*Piacere.* Perf. rimoto: *piacqui.*
He pleased, they pleased.	3rd pers. sing. *piacque;* 3rd. pers. plur. *piacquero.*
Thou pleasedst, we pleased.	2nd pers. sing. *piacesti;* 1st pers. plur. *piacemmo.*
You pleased.	2nd pers. plur. *piaceste.*
To write. Pret. def. I wrote.	*Scrivere.* Perf. Rimoto: *scrissi.*
He wrote, they wrote.	3rd pers. sing. *scrisse;* 3rd pers. plur. *scrissero.*
Thou wrotest, we wrote.	2nd pers. sing. *scrivesti;* 1st pers. plur. *scrivemmo.*
You wrote.	2nd pers. plur. *scriveste.*

3. *a)* Of the verbs in *ere* the following have the double form in the *perfetto rimoto*, i. e. the regular in *ei*, and the irregular in *etti*.

---

[8] Here the pronunciation renders the letter *i* again necessary.
[9] In Tuscany the ending in *etti* seems to be preferred.

21*

EIGHTY-FIFTH LESSON.

Infinitive.	Perfetto Rimoto.		Participio Passato.
	1st form.	2nd form.	
Assistere, to assist,	assistei,	assistetti,	assistito.
Desistere, to desist.			
Esistere, to exist.			
Insistere, to insist.			
Resistere, to resist.			
Sussistere, to subsist.			
Battere, to beat,	battei,	battetti[10],	battuto.
Combattere, to fight.			
Compiere, to accomplish,	compiei,	compietti,	compiuto.
Empiere, to fill.			
Credere, to believe,	credei,	credetti,	creduto.
Esigere, to exact,	esigei,	esigetti,	esatto.
Fendere, to split,	fendei,	fendetti,	fenduto (fesso).
Fremere, to roar, to shudder,	fremei,	fremetti,	fremuto.
Gemere, to groan,	gemei,	gemetti,	gemuto.
Mietere, to mow,	mietei,	mietetti,	mietuto.
Pendere, to hang,	pendei,	pendetti,	penduto.
Perdere, to lose,	perdei,	perdetti,	perduto.
Premere, to press,	premei,	premetti,	premuto.
Ricevere, to receive,	ricevei,	ricevetti,	ricevuto.
Serpere, to creep,	serpei,	serpetti,	serputo.
Solvere, to dissolve,	solvei,	solvetti,	soluto.
Splendere, to shine,	splendei,	splendetti,	splenduto.
Stridere, to creak,	stridei,	stridetti,	striduto.
Vendere, to sell,	vendei,	vendetti,	venduto.

The following with the accent on the last syllable but one have also the perfetto rimoto in *ei* and *etti*:

Cadere, to fall,	cadei,	cadetti,	caduto.
Dovere, to owe,	dovei,	dovetti,	dovuto.
Godere, to enjoy,	godei,	godetti,	goduto.
Potere, to be able (can),	potei,	potetti,	potuto.
Sedere, to sit,	sedei,	sedetti,	seduto.
Temere, to fear,	temei,	temetti,	temuto.

Obs. Some have, besides the two mentioned forms in *ei* and *etti*, a third form in *si*. Of these three forms sometimes the one, sometimes the other, is employed. They are the following:

Assolvere, to absolve,	assolvei,	assolvetti and assolsi,	{ assoluto, { assolto.
Risolvere, to resolve.			
Chiudere, to shut,	chiudei,	chiudetti and chiusi,	chiuso.

---

[10] The ending in *etti* is generally, for the sake of euphony, avoided in verbs having in their radicals one or two *t*'s. N. B. The greatest part in *etti* are now quite obsolete.

EIGHTY-FIFTH LESSON. 491

Infinitive.	Perfetto Rimoto.		Part. Pass.
	1st form.	2nd form.	
Cadere, to yield,	cadei,	cadetti and caddi,	caduto, casco.
Concedere, to grant.			
Lucere, to shine,	lucei,	lucetti and lussi,	luciuto.
Perdere, to lose,	perdei,	perdetti and persi,	perduto, perso.
Persuadere, to persuade,	persuadei,	persuadetti and persuasi,	persuaso.
Dissuadere, to dissuade, dissuadei, &c.			
Presumere, to presume,	presumei,	presumetti and presunsi,	presunto.
Rendere, to render,	rendei,	rendetti and resi,	renduto, reso.
Spendere, to spend,	spendei,	spendetti and spesi,	speso.
Bevere } to drink, Bere }	bevei,	beveitti and bevvi,	bevuto.

b) The following five, and their compounds, have the *perfetto rimoto* in *cqui*:

Piacere, to please,	piacqui,	piaciuto.
Giacere, to lie, to be situate,	giacqui,	giaciuto.
Tacere, to be silent,	tacqui,	taciuto.
Nuocere, to hurt,	nocqui,	nociuto.
Nascere, to be born,	nacqui,	nato.

c) The following three in *bbi*:—

Avere, to have,	ebbi,	avuto.
Conoscere, to know,	conobbi,	conosciuto.
Crescere, to grow,	crebbi,	cresciuto.

d) The following two in *ddi*:—

Cadere, to fall,	caddi,	caduto.
Vedere, to see,	{ vidi, veddi, (antiquated) }	visto.

e) The following two in *ppi*:—

Rompere, to break,	ruppi,	rotto.
Sapere, to know,	seppi,	saputo.

f) The following two in *vi*:—

Bere or bevere, to drink,	bevvi,	bevuto.
Parere, to appear,	parvi,	parato, parso.

g) The following two in *li* and *nI*:—

Volere, to be willing, to wish,	volli,	voluto.
Tenere, to hold,	tenni,	tenuto.

EIGHTY-FIFTH LESSON.

h) All the other verbs in *ere* have the *perfetto rimoto* in *si* or *ssi*, and the past participle in *so*, *to*, or *sto*. The following is an alphabetical list of them.

Obs. Derivative and compound verbs follow the same conjugation as their simple. It is further to be observed that the monosyllabical particles *a*, *o*, *da*, *fra*, *ra*, *so*, *su*, double the following consonant, when it is not *s impura* (i. e. *s* followed by a consonant), as : *accorrere*, to run up; *apporre*, to oppose ; *dabbene*, honest; *frammettere*, to put between; *raggiungere*, to rejoin ; *socchiudere*, to shut up; *suddividere*, to subdivide, &c.

Infinitivo.	Prima persona dell' Indicativo Presente.	Perfetto rimoto.	Participio passato.
Accendere, to light,	accendo,	accesi,	acceso.
Riaccendere, to re-kindle (See above Obs.).			
Accorgersi, to perceive,	accorgo,	accorsi,	accorto.
Scorgere, to notice (See the above Obs.).			
Affliggere,[1] to afflict,	affliggo,	afflissi,	afflitto.
Appendere, to hang up,	appendo,	appesi,	appeso.
Sospendere, to delay (See the above Obs.).			
Ardere, to burn,	ardo,	arsi,	arso.
Ascondere, to conceal,	ascondo,	ascosi,	ascoso, ascosto.
Nascondere, to hide (See the above Obs.).			
Assolvere, to absolve,	assolvo,	assolsi,	assolto.
Risolvere, to resolve (See the above Obs.).			
Assorbere, to absorb,	assorbo,	assorsi,	assorto.
Assumere, to assume,	assumo,	assunsi,	assunto.
Presumere, to presume (See the above Obs.).			
Riassumere, to re-assume (See the same).			
Chiedere, to ask,	chiedo,	chiesi,	chiesto.
Richiedere, to demand (See the above Obs.).			
Chiudere, to shut,	chiudo,	chiusi,	chiuso.
Concludere (or Conchiudere), to infer,			
Escludere, to exclude,			
Includere (or Inchiudere), to inclose,			
Racchiudere, to enclose,		(See the above Obs.)	
Richiudere, to include,			
Rinchiudere,			
Schiudere, to open, to exclude,			
Socchiudere, to shut up,			
Cingere or Cignere, to gird,	cingo, cigno,	cinsi,	cinto.

---

[1] Verbs having a vowel before *gere*, double the letter *g*, as : *leggere*, to read ; *leggo*, I read ; *leggi*, thou readest ; *legge*, he reads ; *leggiamo*, we read ; *leggete*, you read ; *leggono*, they read, &c. There is further to be remarked that verbs ending in *ggere*, *vere*, and *arre*, as : *affliggere*, to afflict ; *scrivere*, to write ; *trarre*, to draw, double in the *perfetto rimoto* the latter *s*, and have in the past participle *tt*, e. g. *afflissi*, *scrissi*, *trassi*; *afflitto*, *scritto*, *tratto*.

EIGHTY-FIFTH LESSON.

Infinitivo.	Prima persona dell' Indicativo presente.	Perfetto rimoto.	Participio passato.
Accingersi or accignersi, to prepare one's self (See the above Obs.).			
Cogliere,[a] or Corre, } to gather,	coglio, colgo,	colsi,	colto.
Accogliere or accorre, to receive, Raccogliere or raccorre, to collect, to pick up,	} (See the above Obs.).		
Commettere, to connect,	commetto,	commessi,	commesso.
Correre, to run,	corro,	corsi,	corso.
Accorrere, to run up, Concorrere, to concur, Discorrere, to discourse, Incorrere, to incur, Percorrere, to run over, Ricorrere, to have recourse,	} (See the above Obs.).		
Cuocere, to boil, to cook,	cuoco,	cossi,	cotto.
Deludere, to delude,	deludo,	delusi,	deluso.
Alludere, to allude, Illudere, to delude,	} (See the above Obs.)		
Difendere, to defend,	difendo,	difesi,	difeso.
Offendere, to offend (See the above Obs.).			
Discutere, to examine,	discuto,	discussi,	discusso.
Distinguere, to distinguish,	distingo,	distinsi,	distinto.
Estinguere, to extinguish (See the above Obs.).			
Dividere, to divide,	divido,	divisi,	diviso.
Suddividere, to subdivide (See the above Obs.).			
Dolere, to ache,	dolgo, doglio,	dolsi,	doluto.
Erigere, to erect,	erigo,	eressi,	eretto.
Espellere, to expel,	espello,	espulsi,	espulso.
Impellere, to impel (See the above Obs.).			
Esprimere, to express,	esprimo,	espressi,	espresso.
Opprimere, to oppress, Comprimere, to compress, Deprimere, to depress, Imprimere, to impress, Sopprimere, to suppress,	} (See the above Obs.)		
Figgere, to fix.	figgo,	fissi,	fisso, fitto.
Affiggere, to post up, Crocifiggere (or crocifiggere), to crucify, Prefiggere, to prefix, Sconfiggere, to conquer, Trafiggere, to pierce,	} (See Obs. above.)		

[a] Verbs in *gliere* change this ending in the *perfetto rimoto* into *lsi*, and in the past participle into *lto*, e. g. *sciogliere*, to untie—*sciolsi, sciolto ; togliere*, to lay hold of—*tolsi, tolto, &c.*

Infinitive.	Prima persona dell' Indicativo presente.	Perfetto rimoto.	Participio passato.
Fingere, to feign,	fingo,	finsi,	finto.
Fondere, to melt,	fondo,	fusi,	fuso.
Confondere, to confound,			
Diffondere, to pour out,			
Infondere, to infuse,	(See Obs. above.)		
Rifondere, to restore,			
Trasfondere, to pour from one vessel to another,			
Frangere, to break,	frango,	fransi,	franto.
Infrangere, to break to pieces,	(See Obs. above.)		
Rifrangere, to reflect,			
Friggere, to fry,	friggo,	frissi,	fritto.
Giongere, or Giugnere, } to arrive,	giungo,	giunsi,	giunto.
Aggiungere, to add,			
Congiungere, to join,			
Disgiungere, to disjoin,			
Raggiungere, to rejoin,	(See Obs. above.)		
Soggiungere, to add, reply,			
Sopraggiungere, Sovraggiungere, } to happen,			
Incidere, to make an incision,	incido,	incisi,	inciso.
Circoncidere, to circumcise,			
Decidere, to decide,	(See Obs. above.)		
Recidere, to cut,			
Intridere, to knead,	intrido,	intrisi,	intriso.
Leggere, to read,	leggo,	lessi,	letto.
Eleggere, to elect,	(See Obs. above.)		
Rileggere, to read over again,			
Mergere, to plunge,	mergo,	mersi.	merso.
Immergere, to immerge,	(See the above Obs.)		
Sommergere, to submerge,			
Mettere, to put,	metto,	misi,	messo.
Ammettere, to admit,			
Commettere, to commit,			
Compromettere, to compromise,			
Dimettere, to discontinue,			
Dismettere, to dismiss,			
Frammettere, Inframmettere, } to insert,			
Intromettere, to let in,	(See Obs. above.)		
Ommettere, to omit,			
Permettere, to permit,			
Premettere, to put before,			
Promettere, to promise,			
Rimettere, to remit,			
Scommettere, to lay a wager,			

EIGHTY-FIFTH LESSON.

Infinitivo.	Prima persona dell' Indicativo presente.	Perfetto rimoto.	Participio passato.
Mettere, to put,	metto,	misi,	messo.
Smettere, to dismiss,			
Sommettere, } to submit,	(See Obs. above.)		
Sottomettere, }			
Trasmettere, to transmit,			
Mordere, to bite,	mordo,	morsi,	morso.
Mungere and } to milk,	{ mungo, }	munsi,	munto.
Mugnere. }	{ mugno, }		
Muovere, to move,	muovo,	mossi,	mosso.
Commuovere, to disturb,			
Dismuovere, to stir up,			
Promuovere, to promote,	(See Obs. above.)		
Rimuovere, to remove,			
Smuovere, to pervert,			
Negligere, to neglect,	negligo,	neglessi,	negletto.
Opprimere, to oppress,	opprimo,	oppressi,	oppresso.
Percuotere, to strike,	percuoto,	percossi,	percosso.
Scuotere, to shake, } (See Obs. above).			
Riscuotere, to exact, }			
Piangere, to weep,	piango,	piansi,	pianto.
Pingere and Pignere, to paint,	pingo,	pinsi,	pinto.
Dipingere, to depict (See Obs. above).			
Porgere, to reach,—	porgo,	porsi,	porto.
Prendere, to take,	prendo,	presi,	preso.
Apprendere, to learn, to hear,			
Comprendere, to comprehend,			
Intraprendere, to undertake,	(See Obs. above.)		
Riprendere, to retake,			
Sorprendere, to surprise,			
Proteggere, to protect,	proteggo,	protessi,	protetto.
Pungere, to sting,	pungo,	punsi,	punto.
Radere, to shear,	rado,	rasi,	raso.
Redimere, to redeem,	redimo,	redensi,	redento.
Reggere, to reign, to govern,	reggo,	ressi,	retto.
Correggere, to correct,			
Ricorreggere, to correct again,	(See Obs. above.)		
Dirigere, to direct,			
Erigere, to erect,			
Ridere, to laugh,	rido,	risi,	riso.
Deridere, to deride (See Obs. above).			
Rimanere, to remain,	rimango,	rimasi,	{ rimasto, rimaso.
Rispondere, to answer.	rispondo,	risposi,	risposto.
Corrispondere, to agree with (See Obs. above).			
Rodere, to gnaw,	rodo,	rosi,	roso.
Corrodere, to fret (See Obs. above).			

Infinitive.	Prima persona dell' Indicativo presente.	Perfetto rimoto.	Participio passato.
Scegliere or Scerre, to choose,	scelgo, sceglio,	scelsi,	scelto.
Prescegliere, to select (See Obs. above).			
Scendere, to descend,	scendo,	scesi,	sceso.
Ascendere, to ascend, Condiscendere, to condescend, Discendere, to descend, Trascendere, to exceed.	(See the above Obs.)		
Sciogliere, or Sciorre, to untie,	sciolgo, scioglio,	sciolsi,	sciolto.
Disciogliere or disciorre, to dissolve (See Obs. above).			
Scrivere, to write,	scrivo,	scrissi,	scritto.
Ascrivere, to ascribe, Descrivere, to describe, Inscrivere, to inscribe, Prescrivere, to prescribe, Rescrivere, to transcribe, Soprascrivere, to superscribe, Sottoscrivere, to subscribe, Trascrivere, to copy,	(See Obs. above.)		
Sorgere or Surgere, to rise,	sorgo, surgo,	sorsi, sursi,	sorto.
Risorgere, to resist, Insorgere, to rise against,	(See Obs. above.)		
Spargere, to spread,	spargo,	sparsi,	sparso.
Spendere, to spend,	spendo,	spesi,	speso.
Spergere, to waste,	spergo,	spersi,	sperso.
Aspergere, to sprinkle, Cospergere, to besprinkle, Dispergere, to disperse,	(See Obs. above.)		
Spingere or Spignere, to push,	spingo,	spinsi,	spinto.
Respingere, Rispignere, to repulse, Sospingere, Sospignere, to push away,	(See Obs. above.)		
Stringere or Strignere, to squeeze,	stringo,	strinsi,	stretto.
Astringere, Costringere, to force, Restringere, Ristringere, to restrain,	(See Obs. above.)		
Struggere, to dissolve,	struggo,	strussi,	strutto.
Distruggere, to destroy (See Obs. above).			
Svellere, to pull out,	svello, svelgo,	svelsi,	svelto.

EIGHTY-FIFTH LESSON.

Infinitivo.	Prima persona dell' Indicativo presente.	Perfetto rimoto.	Participio passato.
Tendere, to tend,	tendo,	tesi,	teso.
Attendere, to wait, Contendere, to contend, Estendere, to stretch, Intendere, to understand, Pretendere, to pretend, Soprintendere, to superintend, Sottintendere, to understand,	(See above Obs.)		
Tergere, to wipe,	tergo,	tersi,	terso.
Tingere or Tignere, } to dye, colour,	tingo,	tinsi,	tinto.
Intingere, to steep, Attingere, to reach, Ritingere, to die again,	(See Obs. above.)		
Togliere or Torre, } to seize,	tolgo, toglio, }	tolsi,	tolto.
Distogliere or distorre, to divert from, Ritogliere or ritorre, to retake,	(See Obs. above.)		
Torcere, to twist,	torco,	torsi,	torto.
Contorcere, to wring, Ritorcere, to twist again,	(See Obs. above.)		
Valere, to be worth,	valgo,	valsi,	{ valso, valuto.
Prevalere, to prevail (See Obs. above).			
Uccidere, to kill,	uccido,	uccisi,	ucciso.
Ancidere (poetical), to kill (See Obs. above).			
Ungere, to anoint,	ungo,	unsi,	unto.
Vincere, to vanquish,	vinco,	vinsi,	vinto.
Convincere, to convince (See Obs. above.)			
Vivere, to live,	vivo,	vissi,	{ vivuto, vissuto.
Rivivere, to revive, Sopravvivere, to survive,	(See Obs. above.)		
Volgere, to turn,	volgo,	volsi,	volto.
Avvolgere, Ravvolgere, Rinvolgere, } to wrap up, Sconvolgere, to invert, Stravolgere, Travolgere, } to overturn,	(See Obs. above.)		

OBSERVATIONS.

A. Verbs ending in *ucere*, *gliere*, *nere*, *acre*, are contracted in the infinitive, so that they have two infinitives, i. e. the ancient Latin, as: *adducere*, to adduce; *cogliere*, to gather; *ponere*, to put; *trarre* (and *traggere*), to draw; and the modern contracted infinitive, as: *addurre, corre, porre, trarre*. The second contracted infinitive is generally used; from it are formed the future and the present conditional, as: *addurrò, corrò, porrò, trarrò*, and *addurrei, correi, porrei, trarrei*. All the other tenses are formed from the ancient infinitive, as from *conducere*, Pres. *conduco, conduci, conduce*, &c. Imperfect: *conducevo*, &c. Imperf. subj. *conducessi*, &c.

In the following verbs the infinitive is contracted, and the contraction maintained for the future and present conditional:—

Infinitivo.	Presente.	Perfetto rimoto.	Participio passato.	Futuro.
Addurre, to adduce, *instead of* adducere,	adduco,	addussi,	addotto,	addurrò
Condurre, *instead of* conducere, to conduct.				
Dedurre, " " deducere, to deduce.				
Introdurre, " " introducere, to introduce.				
Produrre, " " producere, to produce.				
Ricondurre, " " riconducere, to reconduct.				
Ridurre, " " riducere, to reduce.				
Riprodurre, " " riproducere, to reproduce.				
Sedurre, " " seducere, to seduce.				
Tradurre, " " traducere, to translate.				
Bere, to drink, instead of bevere,	bevo,	bevvi,	bevuto,	berrò.
Porre, to put, instead of ponere,	pongo,	posi,	posto,	porrò.

And so all those compounded from it, as:

Anteporre, to prefer.
Apporre, to impute.
Comporre, to compound.
Contrapporre, to oppose.
Deporre, to depose.
Disporre, to dispose.
Esporre, to expose.
Frapporre, to interpose.

Imporre, to impose.
Opporre, to oppose.
Posporre, to postpone.
Preporre, to prefer.
Proporre, to propose.
Soprapporre, to put upon.
Sottoporre, to subdue.
Supporre, to suppose.

| Trarre, to draw, instead of traere. | traggo, | trassi, | tratto, | trarrò. |

And so:

Astrarre, to abstract.
Attrarre, to attract.
Contrarre, to contract.

Detrarre, to detract.
Estrarre, to extract.
Sottrarre, to deliver.

| Corre[1] or cogliere, to gather, | colgo, coglio, | colsi, | colto, | corrò or coglierò. |
| Scerre or scegliere, to choose, | scelgo, scelgo, | scelsi, | scelto, | scerrò or sceglierò. |

---

[1] In the verbs in *gliere* the contracted form is generally preferred in poetry.

EIGHTY-FIFTH LESSON.

Infinitivo.		Presente.	Perfetto rimoto.	Participio passato.	Futuro.
Sciorre or sciogliere,	to untie,	sciolga, scioglio,	sciolsi,	sciolto,	sciorrò or scioglierò.
Torre or togliere,	to take,	tolga, toglio,	tolsi,	tolto,	torrò or toglierò.

Obs. B. Besides these, there are those verbs in *ere* that have (like *avere*) the accent on the last syllable but one; they are not contracted in the infinitive, but in the future and conditional, where they reject the letter *e* of the last syllable but one, as:

	Futuro.	Condizionale.
Avere, to have.	Avrò,	avrei.
Dovere, to owe.	Dovrò,	dovrei.
Potere, to be able (can).	Potrò,	potrei.
Sapere, to know.	Saprò,	saprei.
Vedere, to see.	Vedrò,	vedrei.
Parere, to appear.	Parrò,	parrei.

Obs. C. But when the verbs in *ere* (with the accent on the last syllable but one), end in *nere* and *lere*, the letter *n* or *l* is in the contraction changed into *r*, as:

	Futuro.	Condizionale.
Rimanere, to remain.	Rimarrò,	rimarrei.
Tenere, to hold.	Terrò,	terrei.
Dolere, to hurt.	Dorrò,	dorrei.
Valere, to be worth.	Varrò,	varrei.
Volere, to be willing.	Vorrò,	vorrei.

CONJUGATION OF A VERB WITH TWO INFINITIVES.

Present of the Infinitive.
Addurre, to allege; formerly *adducere*.

Present Participle.
Adducendo, alleging.

Past of the Infinitive.
Avere addotto, to have alleged.

Past Participle.
Addotto, alleged.

Present of the Indicative.
I allege, &c.

Adduc-o,	Adduc-iamo,
Adduc-i,	Adduc-ete,
Adduc-e.	Adduc-ono.

Imperfect.
I alleged, &c.

Adduc-eva,	Adduc-evamo,
Adduc-evi,	Adduc-evate,
Adduc-eva.	Adduc-evano.

Passato Rimoto.
I alleged, &c.

Addussi,	Adduc-emmo,
Adduc-esti,	Adduc-este,
Addusse,	Addussero.

Preterperfect.
Ho addotto, &c.   I have alleged, &c.
Pluperfect.
Aveva addotto, &c.   I had alleged, &c.
Preterite Anterior (Passato Rimoto Composto).
Ebbi addotto, &c.   I had alleged, &c.
Future Present or Simple.
I shall allege, &c.

Addurr-ò,	Addurr-emo,
Addurr-ai,	Addurr-ete,
Addurr-à,	Addurr-anno.

Future Past. (Futuro Perfetto).
Avrò addotto, &c.   I shall have alleged, &c.

Conditional Present.
I should allege, &c.

Addurr-ei,	Addurr-emmo,
Addurr-esti,	Addurr-este,
Addurr-ebbe.	Addurr-ebbero.

Past Conditional.
Avrei addotto, &c.   I should have alleged, &c.

Present of the Subjunctive.
That I may allege, &c.

Adduc-a,	Adduc-iamo,
Adduc-a,	Adduc-iate,
Adduc-a.	Adduc-ano.

Imperfect of the Subjunctive.
If I alleged, &c.

Adduc-essi,	Adduc-essimo,
Adduc-essi,	Adduc-este,
Adduc-esse.	Adduc-essero.

Preterperfect of the Subjunctive.
Che abbia addotto, &c.   That I may have alleged, &c.

Pluperfect of the Subjunctive.
S' io avessi addotto, &c.   If I had alleged, &c.

Imperative.

Adduc-i, allege (thou).	Adduc-iamo, let us allege.
Non addurre, do not allege.	Adduc-ete, allege (ye).
Adduc-a, let him allege.	Adduc-ano, let them allege.

III. ON THE VERBS IN ire.

Of the verbs in *ire* only the following are entirely regular:

Infinitivo.	*Presente.*	*Perfetto rimoto.*	*Participio passato.*
Aprire, to open,	apro,	aprii (apersi),	aperto.
Bollire, to boil,	bollo,	bollii,	bollito.
Convertire, to convert,	converto,	convertii,	convertito.
Coprire, to cover,	copro,	coprii (copersi),	coperto.
Cucire, to sew,	cucio,	cucii,	cucito.
Dormire, to sleep,	dormo,	dormii,	dormito.
Fuggire, to flee,	fuggo,	fuggii,	fuggito.
Partire, to depart,	parto,	partii,	partito.
Pentirsi, to repent,	mi pento,	mi pentii,	pentito.
Seguire, to follow,	seguo,	seguii,	seguito.
Sentire, to feel,	sento,	sentii,	sentito.
Servire, to serve,	servo,	servii,	servito.
Soffrire, to suffer,	soffro,	soffrii (soffersi),	sofferto.
Sortire, to choose,	sorto,	sortii,	sortito.
Vestire, to clothe,	vesto,	vestii,	vestito.

The remaining verbs in *ire* differ from the above regular form in so much that they end in the present tense in *isco*. This irregularity also takes place in the present of the subjunctive and imperative, as has been shown heretofore in the conjugation of *nutrire* (p. 477).

There is, however, still some doubt existing with respect to the first and second persons plural of these verbs; for in conversation, as well as in some Italian authors, *finischiamo, nutrischiamo*, &c., as well as: *finiamo, nutriamo*, are employed. Modern authors, however, seem to incline for the regular form in the first and second persons plural (as in *nutrire*, p. 477), except, notwithstanding, where a double meaning is to be avoided; as in the verbs: *ardire*, to dare; *atterrire*, to frighten; *marcire*, to rot; *smaltire*, to digest; &c. where *ardiamo, atterriamo, marciamo, smaltiamo*, are avoided, not to mistake them for the first person plural of *ardere*, to burn; *atterrare*, to throw down; *marciare*, to march; *smaltare*, to enamel.

The following verbs and their compounds terminate almost always in *isco*. Those marked with a cross (†) have also the regular form, as: *abborrire—abborriamo, abborro*; but the form in *isco* is preferred in conversation, the other in poetry and the didactic style.

Infinitivo.	*Presente.*	*Perfetto rimoto.*	*Participio passato.*
Abolire, to abolish,	abolisco,	abolii,	abolito.
†Abborrire, to abhor,	abborrisco,	abborrii,	abborrito.
Arricchire, to enrich,	arricchisco,	arricchii,	arricchito.
Arrossire, to blush,	arrossisco,	arrossii,	arrossito.
Bandire, to banish,	bandisco,	bandii,	bandito.
Capire, to understand,	capisco,	capii,	capito.
Colpire, to strike,	colpisco,	colpii,	colpito.
Compatire, to pity,	compatisco,	compatii,	compatito.
Concepire, to conceive,	concepisco,	concepii,	concepito.
Digerire, to digest,	digerisco,	digerii,	digerito.

EIGHTY-FIFTH LESSON.

Infinitive.	Presente.	Perfetto rimoto.	Participio passato.
Eseguire, to execute,	eseguisco,	eseguii,	eseguito.
Fiorire, to blossom,	fiorisco,	fiorii,	fiorito.
Gradire, to approve,	gradisco,	gradii,	gradito.
†Impazzire, to grow mad,	impazzisco,	impazzii,	impazzito.
Incrudelire, to grow cruel,	incrudelisco,	incrudelii,	incrudelito,
†Languire, to languish,	languisco,	languii,	languito.
Patire, to suffer,	patisco,	patii,	patito.
Perire, to perish,	perisco,	perii,	perito.
Spedire, to dispatch,	spedisco,	spedii,	spedito.
Tradire, to betray,	tradisco,	tradii,	tradito.
Ubbidire, to obey,	ubbidisco,	ubbidii,	ubbidito
Unire, to unite,	unisco,	unii,	unito.

Obs. The verbs *aprire*, to open; *coprire*, to cover; *ricoprire*, to cover again; *scoprire*, to uncover; *offrire*, to offer; as also *differire*, to differ; *profferire*, to utter; *soffrire*, to suffer; have a double *perfetto rimoto*, viz. the regular, as: *aprii*, *offerii*, &c., and an irregular, as *apersi*, *offersi*, &c. Ex.

| I opened, thou openedst, he opened, | Aprii or apersi, apristi, aprì or aperse. |
| We, you, they opened, | Aprimmo, apriste, aprirono, or apersero. |

Obs. A. **Influire** (also *influere*), to influence, has in the perfetto rimoto only *influssi*.

Obs. B. The verb *apparire*, to appear, and its compound *comparire*, to appear, have in the perfetto rimoto, besides the regular form in *ii*, another in *vi*,[a] as:

| I appeared, thou appearedst, he appeared. | Apparii *and* apparvi, apparisti, apparì *or* apparve. |
| We, you, they appeared. | Apparimmo, appariste, apparirono *and* apparvero. |

Obs. C. Of the verbs in *ire* the following three are contracted in the future and conditional:

To die,	*morire*,	future	*morrò*,	conditional	*morrei*.
To ascend,	*salire*,	"	*sarrò*,	"	*sarrei* (poetical).
(in prose)			*salirò*,	"	*salirei*.
To come,	*venire*,		*verrò*,	"	*verrei*.

Obs. D. The only one of the verbs in *ire* that has a contracted infinitive is *dire*, formerly *dicere*, to say.

I. IRREGULAR VERBS IN *are*.

There are only four irregular verbs of the first conjugation, viz.—

Andare, to go; *fare* (formerly *facere*), to make, to do; *dare*, to give; *stare*, to stand.

---

[a] This double form in the *perfetto rimoto* is to be attributed to the double infinitive of the verbs; for we find also *apparere*, *comparere*, though the latter be not used.

N. B. The Italian language is very rich in the verbs in *isco*.

EIGHTY-FIFTH LESSON.

They are conjugated in the following manner:

Infinitive Present.

Andare, to go.	Fare, to do.	Dare, to give.	Stare, to stand.

Infinitive Past.

Essere andato, to have gone.	Aver fatto, to have done.	Aver dato, to have given.	Essere stato, to have stood.

Participle Present.

Andando, going.	Facendo, doing.	Dando, giving.	Stando, standing.

Participle Past.

Andato, gone.	Fatto, done.	Dato, given.	Stato, stood.

Present Indicative.

I go, &c.	I do, &c.	I give, &c.	I stand, &c.
Vado (or vo),	Faccio (or fo),	Do,	Sto,
vai,	fai,	dai,	stai,
va,	fà (face),	dà,	sta,
andiamo,	facciamo,	diamo,	stiamo,
andate,	fate,	date,	state,
vanno,	fanno.	danno.	stanno.

Imperfect.

I went, &c.	I did, &c.	I gave, &c.	I stood, &c.
And-ava,	Fac-eva (fea),	Da-va,	Sta-va,
and-avi,	fac-evi,	da-vi,	sta-vi,
and-ava,	fac-eva (fea),	da-va,	sta-va,
and-avamo,	fac-evamo,	da-vamo,	sta-vamo,
and-avate,	fac-evate,	da-vate,	sta-vate,
and-avano.	fac-evano.	da-vano.	sta-vano.

Preterite Definite (Passato Rimoto).

I went, did go, &c.	I did, did do, &c.	I gave, did give, &c.	I stood, did stand, &c.
And-ai,	Feci (fei),	Diedi (detti),	Stetti,
and-asti,	fac-esti,	desti,	stesti,
and-ò,	fece (fè', feo),	diede (diè, dette),	stette,
and-ammo,	fac-emmo,	demmo,	stemmo,
and-aste,	fac-este,	deste,	steste,
and-arono.	fecero (fenno, ferono).	diedero (diarono, dettero).	stettero.

Preterperfect (Passato Prossimo).

I have gone, &c.	I have done (made), &c.	I have given, &c.	I have stood, &c.
Sono andato, &c.	Ho fatto, &c.	Ho dato, &c.	Sono stato, &c.

Pluperfect.

I had gone, &c.	I had done (made), &c.	I had given, &c.	I had stood, &c.
Era andato, &c.	Aveva fatto, &c.	Aveva dato, &c.	Era stato, &c.

EIGHTY-FIFTH LESSON.

Preterite Anterior (Passato Rimoto Composto).

I had gone, &c.	I had done, &c.	I had given, &c.	I had stood, &c.
Fui andato, &c.	Ebbi fatto, &c.	Ebbi dato, &c.	Fui stato, &c.

Future.

I shall go, &c.	I shall do or make, &c.	I shall or will give, &c.	I shall or will stand, &c.
And-rò,	Fa-rò,	Da-rò,	Sta-rò,
and-rai,	fa-rai,	da-rai,	sta-rai,
and-rà,	fa-rà,	da-rà,	sta-rà,
and-remo,	fa-remo,	da-remo,	sta-remo,
and-rete,	fa-rete,	da-rete,	sta-rete,
and-ranno.	fa-ranno.	da-ranno.	sta-ranno.

Future Past.

I shall have gone, &c.	I shall have done, &c.	I shall have given, &c.	I shall have stood, &c.
Sarò andato, andata, &c.	Avrò fatto, &c.	Avrò dato, &c.	Sarò stato, stata, &c.

Conditional Present.

I should go, &c.	I should do, &c.	I should give, &c.	I should stand, &c.
And-rei,	Fa-rei,	Da-rei,	Sta-rei,
and-resti,	fa-resti,	da-resti,	sta-resti,
and-rebbe,	fa-rebbe (ia),	da-rebbe,	sta-rebbe,
and-remmo,	fa-remmo,	da-remmo,	sta-remmo,
and-reste,	fa-reste,	da-reste,	sta-reste,
and-rebbero.	fa-rebbero (iano).	da-rebbero.	sta-rebbero.

Conditional Past.

I should have gone, &c.	I should have done, &c.	I should have given, &c.	I should have stood, &c.
Sarei andato, andata, &c.	Avrei fatto, &c.	Avrei dato, &c.	Sarei stato, stata, &c.

Present of the Subjunctive.

That I may go, &c.	do or make, &c.	give, &c.	stand, &c.
Che io vada,	faccia,	dia,	stia,
che tu vada,	faccia,	dia,	stia,
ch'egli vada,	faccia,	dia,	stia,
che noi andiamo,	facciamo,	diamo,	stiamo,
che voi andiate,	facciate,	diate,	stiate,
che essi vadano.	facciano.	diano (dieno).	stiano (stieno).

Imperfect of the Subjunctive.

If I went, &c.	made, &c.	gave, &c.	stood, &c.
Se io and-assi,	fac-essi,	d-essi,	st-essi,
so tu and-assi,	fac-essi,	d-essi,	st-essi,
s'egli and-asse,	fac-esse,	d-esse,	st-esse,
se noi and-assimo,	fac-essimo,	d-essimo,	st-essimo,
se voi and-aste,	fac-este,	d-este,	st-este,
s'eglino and-assero.	fac-essero.	d-essero.	st-essero.

EIGHTY-FIFTH LESSON.

Perfect of the Subjunctive.

That I may have gone, &c.	may have done, &c.	may have given, &c.	may have stood, &c.
Che io sia andato, andata, &c.	abbia fatto, &c.	abbia dato, &c.	sia stato, stata, &c.

Pluperfect of the Subjunctive.

If I had gone, &c.	had gone, &c.	had given, &c.	had stood, &c.
Se fossi andato, andata, &c.	avessi fatto, &c.	avessi dato, &c.	fossi stato, stata, &c.

Imperative.

Va, go (thou),	Fa, do (thou),	Dà, give (thou),	Sta, stand (thou),
non andare, go (thou) not,	non fare, do (thou) not,	non dare, give thou (not),	non istare, do (thou) not stand,
vada, let him go,	faccia, let him do,	dia, let him give,	stia, let him stand,
andiamo, let us go,	facciamo, let us do,	diamo, let us give,	stiamo, let us stand,
andate, go (ye),	fate, do (ye),	date, give (ye),	state, stand (ye),
vadano, let them go.	facciano, let them do.	diano, let them give.	stiano, let them stand.

Obs. A. Verbs compounded of *dare* and *stare*, such as: *secondare*, to assist; *circondare*, to encompass;—*accostare*, to approach; *contrastare*, to resist; *ostare*, to oppose; *costare*, to cost; *restare*, to rest, are regular; except, *ridare*, to give again, which is conjugated like *dare*, to give; and *soprastare* or *sovrastare*, to superintend, to threaten, which is conjugated like *stare*, to stand.

Obs. B. Verbs compounded of *fare*, as: *disfare*, to undo; *rifare*, to repair; *soddisfare*, to satisfy; *sopraffare*, to overpower, &c. are always irregular like *fare*, to do.

II. IRREGULAR VERBS IN *ere*.

Preliminary Observations.—If the learner has studied well all that we said on the irregularity of the Italian verbs, he has in the following irregular verbs only to make himself acquainted with the present of the indicative and subjunctive, and in order to know this he has only to remark the following:—

When an irregular verb has in the first person singular of the present tense other consonants than those of the infinitive, as—in *potere*, where it has *posso* instead of *poto*, it retains those consonants also in the first and third persons plural, as: *possiamo*, we can; *possono*, they can, and in all the persons of the present of the subjunctive, as: *possa*, I may be able; *possi*, thou mayest be able; *possa*, he may be able; *possiamo*, *possiate*, *possono*. The imperfect of the indicative and that of the subjunctive are always regularly formed from the infinitive. Ex. Inf. *pot-ere*; Imperf. Ind. *pot-eva*; Imperf. subj. *pot-essi*, &c.

EIGHTY-FIFTH LESSON.

1. IRREGULAR VERBS HAVING THE ACCENT ON THE LAST SYLLABLE BUT ONE.

I.

Inf. pres. Potére, to be able (can).
Inf. past. Aver potuto, to have been able.

Pres. part. Potendo, being able.
Past part. Potuto, been able.

Present indic.
Posso, I can, &c.
Puoi.
Può (*puote*).
Possiamo.
Potete.
Possono (*ponno*).

Present subj.
Ch' io possa, that I may be able, &c.
Che tu possa (*possi*).
Ch' egli possa.
Che noi possiamo.
Che voi possiate.
Ch' eglino possano.

Imperf. Poteva, &c. I could, &c.
Perfetto rimot. Potei (*potetti*), potesti, potè, potemmo, poteste, poterono (*potettero*), I could, &c.
Imperf. subj. Se potessi, &c. If I could, &c.
Futuro. Potrò, potrai, &c. I shall be able, &c.
Cond. pres. Potrei (*potria*), potresti, &c. I should be able, &c.

2.

Inf. pres. Dovére, to be obliged (must).
Inf. past. Aver dovuto, to have been obliged.

Pres. part. Dovendo, being obliged.
Past part. Dovuto, been obliged.

Present ind.
Devo (*debbo, deggio*), I must, &c.
Devi (*dei*).
Deve (*debbe, dee*).
Dobbiamo (*deggiamo*).
Dovete.
Devono (*debbono, deggiono*).

Pres. subj.
Ch' io debba (*deggia*), that I may be obliged, &c.
Che tu debba (*deggia*).
Ch' egli debba (*deggia*).
Che noi dobbiamo (*deggiamo*).
Che voi dobbiate (*deggiate*).
Ch' eglino debbano (*deggiano*).

Imperf. Doveva, &c. I was obliged, &c.
Perf. rim. Dovei (*dovetti*), dovesti, dovè (*dovette*), dovemmo, doveste, dovettero, I was obliged, &c.
Imperf. subj. Dovessi, &c. If I were obliged, &c.
Futuro. Dovrò, dovrai, &c. I shall be obliged, &c.
Cond. pres. Dovrei, &c. I should be obliged, &c.

3.

Inf. pres. Volére, to be willing.
Inf. past. Aver voluto, to have been willing.

Pres. part. Volendo, being willing.
Past part. Voluto, been willing.

Pres. ind. Voglio (*vo'*), vuoi, vuole, vogliamo, volete, vogliono, I am willing, &c.

EIGHTY-FIFTH LESSON.

Pres. subj. Che io voglia, tu voglia, egli voglia, vogliamo, vogliate, vogliano, that I may be willing, &c.⁵
Imperf. Voleva, &c. I was willing, &c.
Perf. rim. Volli, volesti, volle, volemmo, voleste, vollero, I was willing, &c.
Imperf. subj. Se volessi, &c., if I were willing, &c.
Future. Vorrò, vorrai, &c. I shall be willing, &c.
Cond. pres. Vorrei, vorresti, &c. I should be willing, &c.

4.

Inf. pres. Solére, to be accustomed. | *Pres. part.* Solendo, being accustomed.
Inf. past. Essere solito, to have been accustomed. | *Past part.* Solito, been accustomed.
Pres. ind. Soglio, suoli, suole, sogliamo, solete, sogliono, I am accustomed, &c.
Pres. subj. Ch' io soglia, che tu soglia, ch' egli soglia, sogliamo, sogliate, sogliano, that I may be accustomed, &c.
Imperf. Soleva, solevi, soleva, &c. I was accustomed, &c.
Imperf. subj. Se io solessi, tu solessi, egli solesse, &c. If I was accustomed, &c.
Obs. This verb is defective, and the tenses wanting are generally made up by means of the past participle with *essere*, as: io sono, io era, io fui, io sarò solito, &c.

5.

Inf. pres. Sapére, to know. | *Pres. part.* Sapendo, knowing.
Inf. past. Aver saputo, to have known. | *Past part.* Saputo, known.
Pres. indic. So, sai, sa, sappiamo, sapete, sanno, I know, &c.
Pres. subj. Ch' io sappia, tu sappia, egli sappia, noi sappiamo, voi sappiate, essi sappiano, that I may know, &c.
Imperf. Sapeva, sapevi, &c. I knew, &c.
Perf. rim. Seppi, sapesti, seppe, sapemmo, sapeste, seppero, I knew, &c.
Imperf. subj. Se io sapessi, tu sapessi, egli sapesse, &c. If I knew, &c.
Future. Saprò, saprai, &c. I shall know, &c.
Cond. pres. Saprei, sapresti, saprebbe, &c. I should know, &c.
Imperative. Sappi, sappia, sappiamo, sappiate, sappiano, know thou, &c.

6.

Inf. pres. Vedére, to see. | *Pres. part.* Vedendo (*veggendo*), seeing.
Inf. past. Aver veduto, to have seen. | *Past part.* Veduto (*visto*), seen.

---

⁵ The irregular verbs in *Ére* (with the accent on the last syllable but one), as *valére; dolére*, to grieve; *valére*, to be worth, and their compounds, take in the first person *g*, which is retained in the persons mentioned in the Preliminary Observations (p. 505). In *dolére* and *valére g* may precede or follow the letter *i*, except in the first and second persons plural, where the soft sound, *dogliamo, dogliate*, is preferred to the hard, *dolghiamo, dolghiate*.

EIGHTY-FIFTH LESSON.

Pres. ind. Vedo (veggo, veggio), vedi, vede, vediamo (veggiamo), vedete, vedono (veggono, veggiono), I see, &c.
Pres. subj. Ch' io, tu, egli veda (vegga, veggia), noi vediamo (veggiamo), &c., that I may see, &c.*
Imperf. Io vedeva, tu vedevi, &c. I saw, &c.
Perf. rim. Vidi, vedesti, vide, vedemmo, vedeste, videro, I saw, &c.
Imperf. subj. Se io vedessi, tu vedessi, &c. If I saw, &c.
Future. Vedrò, vedrai, &c. I shall see, &c.
Cond. pres. Vedrei, vedresti, vedrebbe, &c. I should see, &c.
Imperative. Vedi, veda (vegga), vediamo (veggiamo), vedete, vedano (veggano), see thou, &c.

7.

Inf. pres. Sedére, to sit.
Inf. past. Aver (or essere) seduto, to have sat.
Pres. part. Sedendo (seggendo), sitting.
Past part. Seduto.

Pres. ind. Siedo (segga, seggio), siedi, siede, sediamo (seggiamo), sedete, siedono (seggono, seggiono), I sit, &c.
Pres. subj. Ch' io, tu, egli sieda (segga, seggia), sediamo (seggiamo), sediate (seggiate), siedano (seggano, seggiano), that I may sit, &c.
Imp. Sedeva, sedevi, &c. I sat, &c.
Perf. rim. Sedei (sedetti), sedesti, sedè (sedette), sedemmo, sedeste, sederono (sedettero), I sat.
Imperf. subj. Se io sedessi, tu sedessi, &c. If I sat.
Future. Sederò (poet. sedrò), &c. I shall sit, &c.
Cond. pres. Sederei, &c. I should sit, &c.
Imperative. Siedi, sieda (segga), sediamo (seggiamo), sedete, siedano (seggano), sit thou, &c.

8.

Inf. pres. Parére, to appear.
Inf. past. Aver paruto (parso), to have appeared.
Pres. part. Parendo, appearing.
Past part. Paruto (parso), appeared.

Pres. ind. Paio, pari, pare, paiamo (pariamo), parete, paiono, I appear, &c.
Pres. subj. Ch' io paia, tu paia, egli paia, pariamo, pariate, paiano, that I may appear, &c.
Imperf. Pareva, parevi, &c. I appeared, &c.
Perf. rim. Parvi, paresti, parve, paremmo, pareste, parvero, I appeared, &c.
Imperf. subj. Se paressi, &c. If I appeared, &c.
Future. Parrò, parrai, parrà, &c. I shall appear, &c.
Cond. pres. Parrei, parresti, &c. I should appear, &c.

---

* Verbs in *dere* (with the accent on the last syllable but one) may in the first person of the present take instead of *d* the letter *g*, which is doubled between two vowels, and pronounced either hard, as in *go*, or soft, as the English *j*. Only there is to be observed, that, as here above (note *), in the first and second persons plural, the soft sound, as *veggiamo, veggiate*, is to be preferred to the hard: *vegghiamo, vegghiate*.

EIGHTY-FIFTH LESSON. 509

9.

Inf. pres. Dolére (see note §, p. 507), | *Pres. part.* Dolendo, grieving.
to grieve.
Inf. past. Essere doluto, to have | *Past part.* Doluto, grieved.
grieved.

Pres. ind. Doglio (*dolgo*) duoli, duole, dogliamo (*dolghiamo*), dolete, dogliono (*dolgono*), I grieve, &c.
Pres. subj. Ch' io' tu, egli doglia (*dolga*), dogliamo (*dolghiamo*), dogliate (*dolghiate*), dogliano (*dolgano*), that I may grieve, &c.
Imperf. Doleva, dolevi, &c. I grieved, &c.
Perf. rim. Dolsi, dolesti, dulse, dolemmo, doleste, dolsero, I grieved, &c.
Imperf. subj. Se dolessi, &c. If I grieved, &c.
Future. Dorrò, dorrai, &c. I shall grieve, &c.
Cond. pres. Dorrei, dorresti, &c. I should grieve, &c.

10.

Inf. pres. Valére (see note §, p. 507), | *Pres. part.* Valendo, being worth.
to be worth.
Inf. past. Aver valuto, to have been | *Past part.* Valuto (*valso*), been worth.
worth.

Pres. ind. Vaglio (*valgo*), vali, vale, vagliamo (*valghiamo*), valete, vagliono (*valgono*), I am worth, &c.
Pres. subj. Ch' io, tu, egli vaglia (*valga*), vagliamo (*valghiamo*), vagliate, vagliano (*valgano*), that I may be worth, &c.
Imperf. Valeva, valevi, &c. I was worth, &c.
Perf. rim. Valsi, valesti, valse, valemmo, valeste, valsero, I was worth, &c.
Imperf. subj. Se io valessi, &c. If I was worth, &c.
Future. Varrò, varrai, varrà, &c. I shall be worth, &c.
Cond. pres. Varrei, varresti, &c. I should be worth, &c.
Imperative. Vali, vaglia, vagliamo, valete, vagliano, be thou worth, &c.

11.

Inf. pres. Cadére (see note §, p. 508), | *Pres. part.* Cadendo, falling.
to fall.
Inf. past. Essere caduto, to have | *Past part.* Caduto, fallen.
fallen.

Pres. ind. Cado (*caggio*, poet.), cadi, cade, cadiamo (*caggiamo*), cadete, cadono (*caggiono*), I fall, &c.
Pres. subj. Ch' io, tu, egli cada (*caggia*), cadiamo (*caggiamo*), &c., that I may fall, &c.
Imperf. Cadeva, cadevi, &c. I fell, &c.
Perf. rim. Caddi, cadesti, cadde, cademmo, cadeste, caddero, I fell, &c.
It also has: cadei or cadetti, &c.
Imperf. subj. Se lo cadessi, &c. If I fell, &c.
Future. Cadrò, cadrai, cadrà, cadremo, cadrete, cadranno (better than caderò), &c. I shall fall, &c.
Cond. pres. Cadrei, cadresti, &c. I should fall.

EIGHTY-FIFTH LESSON.

12.

Inf. pres. Tenére, to hold. | *Pres. part.* Tenendo, holding.
Inf. past. Aver tenuto, to have held. | *Past part.* Tenuto, held.

Pres. ind. Tengo, tieni, tiene, teniamo (tenghiamo), tenete, tengono, I hold, &c.
Pres. subj. Ch' io, tu, egli, tenga, teniamo (tenghiamo), teniate (tenghiate), tengano, that I may hold, &c.[7]
Imperf. Teneva, tenevi, &c. I held, &c.
Perf. rim. Tenni, tenesti, tenne, tenemmo, teneste, tennero, I held, &c.
Imperf. subj. Se io tenessi, &c. If I held, &c.
Future. Terrò, terrai, terrà, terremo, terrete, terranno, I shall hold, &c.
Cond. pres. Terrei, terresti, terrebbe, &c. I should hold, &c.
Imperative. Tieni, tenga, teniamo, tenete, tengano, hold thou, &c.

13.

Inf. pres. Rimanére (see note 7,) to remain. | *Pres. part.* Rimanendo, remaining.
Inf. past. Esser rimasto (rimaso), to have remained. | *Past part.* Rimasto or rimaso, remained.

Pres. ind. Rimango, rimani, rimane, rimaniamo (rimanghiamo), rimanete, rimangono, I remained, &c.
Pres. subj. Ch' io, tu, egli rimanga, noi rimaniamo (rimanghiamo), voi rimaniate (rimanghiate), essi rimangano, that I may remain, &c.
Imperf. Rimaneva, &c. I remained, &c.
Perf. rim. Rimasi, rimanesti, rimase, rimanemmo, rimaneste, rimasero, I remained, &c.
Imperf. subj. Se io rimanessi, &c. If I remained, &c.
Future. Rimarrò, rimarrai, &c. I shall remain, &c.
Cond. pres. Rimarrei, rimarresti, rimarrebbe, &c. I should remain, &c.
Imperative. Rimani, rimanga, rimaniamo, rimanete, rimangano, remain thou, &c.

14.

Inf. pres. Piacére, to please. | *Pres. part.* Piacendo, pleasing.
Inf. past. Aver piaciuto, to have pleased. | *Past part.* Piaciuto, pleased.

Pres. ind. Piaccio, piaci, piace, piacciamo, piacete, piacciono, I please, &c.
Pres. subj. Ch' io, tu, egli piaccia, piacciamo, piacciate, piacciano, that I may please, &c.
Imperf. Piaceva, piacevi, &c. I pleased, &c.
Perf. rim. Piacqui, piacesti, piacque, piacemmo, piaceste, piacquero, I pleased, &c.
Imperf. subj. Se io piacessi, &c. If I pleased, &c.
Future. Piacerò, piacerai, &c. I shall please, &c.
Cond. pres. Piacerei, &c. I should please, &c.

---

[7] Verbs in *nére* (with the accent on the last syllable but one), as *tenére*, to hold; *rimanére* (also *venire*, to come), may take in the first person of the present tense after n the letter g, which is retained in the persons mentioned in the Preliminary Observations. In the first and second persons plural, *teniamo*, *veniamo*, *teniate*, *veniate*, are preferred to *tenghiamo*, *venghiamo*, *tenghiate*, *venghiate*.

EIGHTY-FIFTH LESSON.   511

Obs. In the same manner are conjugated *tacére*, to be silent, and *giacére*, to lie (be situate). The letter *c* is always doubled when it is followed by two vowels, except in the past participle.

II. IRREGULAR VERBS, HAVING THE ACCENT ON THE LAST SYLLABLE BUT TWO.

15.

Inf. pres. Porre (formerly ponere), to put. | *Pres. part.* Ponendo, putting.
Inf. past. Aver posto, to have put. | *Past part.* Posto, put.
Pres. ind. Pongo, poni, pone, poniamo (*ponghiamo*), ponete, pongono, I put, &c.
Pres. subj. Ch' io, tu, egli ponga, poniamo (*ponghiamo*), poniate (*ponghiate*), pongano, that I may put, &c.
Imperf. Poneva, ponevi, poneva, &c. I did put, &c.
Perf. rim. Posi, ponesti, pose, ponemmo, poneste, posero, I did put, &c.
Imperf. subj. S' io ponessi, &c. If I put, &c.
Future. Porrò, porrai, &c. I shall put, &c.
Cond. pres. Io porrei, tu porresti, egli porrebbe, &c. I should put, &c.
Imperative. Poni, ponga, poniamo, ponete, pongano, put thou, &c.

Obs. In the same manner are conjugated all its compounds, as : *comporre*, to compound ; *preporre*, to prefer, &c. (See Obs. 492, and Obs. A. 493.)

16.

Inf. pres. Dire (formerly dicere), to say. | *Pres. part.* Dicendo, saying.
Inf. past. Aver detto, to have said. | *Past part.* Detto, said.
Pres. indic. Dico, dici, dice, diciamo, dite, dicono, I say, &c.
Pres. subj. Ch' io, tu, egli dica, diciamo, diciate, dicano, that I may say, &c.
Imperf. Diceva, dicevi, &c. I said, &c.
Perf. rim. Dissi, dicesti, disse, dicemmo, diceste, dissero, I said, &c.
Imperf. subj. Se lo dicessi, &c. If I said, &c.
Future. Dirò, dirai, &c. I shall say, &c.
Cond. pres. Direi, diresti, &c. I should say, &c.
Imperative. Di', dica, diciamo, dite, dicano, say thou, &c.

17.

Inf. pres. Bevere or bere, to drink. | *Pres. part.* Bevendo, drinking.
Inf. past. Aver bevuto, to have drunk. | *Past part.* Bevuto, drunk.
Pres. ind. Bevo, bevi, beve, beviamo, bevete, bevono, I drink, &c.
Pres. subj. Ch' io, tu, egli beva, beviamo, beviate, bevano, that I may drink, &c.
Imperf. Beveva (bevea), bevevi, &c. I drank, &c.
Perf. rim. Bevetti (bevvi), bevesti, bevette (bevve), bevemmo, beveste, bevettero (bevvero)[1], I drank, &c.
Imperf. subj. Se lo bevessi, &c. If I drank, &c.
Future. Berò, berai, berà (better than beverò), &c. I shall drink, &c.
Cond. pres. Berei, beresti, &c. I should drink, &c.
Imperative. Bevi, beva, beviamo, bevete, bevano, drink thou, &c.

---

[1] The perf. rim. *babbi, babbe, babbero*, is used in poetry.

18.

Inf. pres. Spegnere, to extinguish. | *Pres. part.* Spegnendo, extinguishing.
Inf. past. Avere spento, to have extinguished. | *Past part.* Spento, extinguished.

Pres. ind. Spegno (*spengo*), spegni, spegne, spegniamo (*spenghiamo*), spegnete, spegnono (*spengono*), I extinguish, &c.

Pres. subj. Ch' io, tu, egli spegna (*spenga*), spegniamo (*spenghiamo*), spegniate (*spenghiate*), spegnano (*spengano*), that I may extinguish, &c.

Imperf. Spegneva, &c. I extinguished, &c.

Perf. rim. Spensi, spegnesti, spense, spegnemmo, spegneste, spensero, I extinguished, &c.

Imperf. subj. Se io spegnessi, &c. If I extinguished, &c.

Future. Spegnerò, spegnerai, &c. I shall extinguish, &c.

Cond. pres. Spegnerei, spegneresti, &c. I should extinguish, &c.

Imperative. Spegni, spenga, spegniamo, spegnete, spengano, extinguish thou, &c.

Obs. In the same manner are conjugated: *cingere*, to gird; *spingere*, to push; *stringere*, to squeeze; *tingere*, to dye (colour); and their compounds.

19.

Inf. pres. Scegliere (or *scerre*), to choose. | *Pres. part.* Scegliendo, choosing.
Inf. past. Aver scelto, to have chosen. | *Past part.* Scelto, chosen.

Pres. ind. Scegilo (*scelgo*), scegli, sceglie, scegliamo, scegliete, scelgono (*scelgono*), I choose.

Pres. subj. Ch' io, tu, egli scelga (*scelga*), scegliamo, scegliate, scelgano (*scelgano*), that I may choose, &c.

Imperf. Sceglieva, &c. I chose, &c.

Perf. rim. Scelsi, scegliesti, scelse, scegliemmo, sceglieste, scelsero, I chose, &c.

Imperf. subj. Se io scegliessi, &c. If I chose, &c.

Future. Sceglierò (and *scerrò,*) &c. I shall choose, &c.

Cond. pres. Sceglierei and *scerrei*, &c. I should choose, &c.

Imperative. Scegli, scelga, scegliamo, scegliete, scelgano, choose thou, &c.

Obs. In the same manner are conjugated: *sciogliere* or *sciorre*, to untie; *togliere* or *torre*, to take away; *cogliere* or *corre*, to gather, and their compounds, as: *distorre*, to remove; *raccorre*, to pick up; *disciorre*, to dissolve, &c.

20.

Inf. pres. Trarre, *formerly* traere, to draw. | *Pres. part.* Traendo, drawing.
Inf. past. Aver tratto, to have drawn. | *Past part.* Tratto, drawn.

Pres. indic. Traggo, trai (*traggi*), trae (*tragge*), traiamo (*traggiamo*), traete, traggono, I draw, &c.

Pres. subj. Ch' io, tu, egli tragga, traiamo (*traggiamo*), traiate (*traggiate*), traggano, that I may draw, &c.

Imperf. Traeva, traevi, &c. I drew, &c.

Perf. rim. Trassi, traesti, trasse, traemmo, traeste, trassero, I drew, &c.

Imperf. subj. Se io traessi, &c. If I drew, &c.

Future. Trarrò, trarrai, trarrà, &c.   I shall draw, &c.
Cond. pres. Trarrei, trarresti, trarrebbe, &c.   I should draw, &c.
Imperative. Trai, tragga, traiamo (*traggiamo*), traete, traggano, draw thou, &c.

Obs. In the same manner are conjugated: *attrarre*, to attract; *contrarre*, to contract; *detrarre*, to detract.

III. IRREGULAR VERBS IN *ire*.

21.

Inf. pres. Apparire, to appear suddenly. | *Pres. part.* Apparendo, appearing.
Inf. past. Essere apparito or apparso, to have appeared. | *Past part.* Apparito *and* apparso, appeared.

Pres. indic. Apparisco (*appaio*), apparisci (*appari*), apparisce (*appare*), appariamo, apparite, appariscono (*appaiono*), I appear, &c.
Pres. subj. Ch' io, tu, egli apparisca (*appaia*), appariamo, appariate, appariscano (*appaiano*), that I may appear, &c.
Imperf. Appariva, apparivi, &c.   I appeared, &c.
Perf. rim. Apparii (*apparvi*), apparisti, apparì (*apparve*), apparimmo, appariste apparirono (*apparvero*), I appeared, &c.
Imperf. subj. Se io apparissi, &c.   If I appeared, &c.
Future. Apparirò, &c.   I shall appear, &c.
Cond. pres. Apparirei, &c.   I should appear, &c.
Imperative. Apparisci, apparisca, appariamo, apparite, appariscano, appear thou, &c.

Obs. In the same manner are conjugated its compounds: *comparire*, to appear; *trasparire*, to be transparent; *sparire*, to disappear, &c.

22.

Inf. pres. Venire, to come. | *Pres. part.* Venendo, (*also* vegnente), coming.
Inf. past. Essere venuto, to have come. | *Past part.* Venuto, come.

Pres. ind. Vengo, vieni, viene, veniamo (*venghiamo*), venite, vengono, I come, &c.
Pres. subj. Ch' io, tu, egli venga, veniamo (*venghiamo*), veniate (*venghiate*), vengano, that I may come, &c.
Imperf. Veniva, venivi, &c.   I came, &c.
Perf. rim. Venni, venisti, venne, venimmo, veniste, vennero, I came, &c.
Imperf. subj. Se io venissi, &c.   If I came, &c.
Future. Verrò, verrai, verrà, verremo, verrete, verranno, I shall come, &c.
Cond. pres. Verrei, verresti, verrebbe, &c.   I should come, &c.
Imperative. Vieni, venga, veniamo, venite, vengano, come thou, &c.

23.

Inf. pres. Morire, to die (expire). | *Pres. part.* Morendo, dying.
Inf. past. Essere morto, to have died. | *Past part.* Morto, died.

Pres. ind. Muoio (*muoro*), muori, muore, moriamo (*muoiamo*), morite, muoiono (*muorono*), I die, &c.

EIGHTY-FIFTH LESSON.

Pres. subj. Ch' io, tu, egli muoia, moriamo (muoiamo), moriate (muoiate), muoiano, that I may die, &c.
Imperf. Moriva, &c. I died, &c.
Perf. rim. Morii, moristi, &c. I died, &c.
Imperf. subj. Se io morissi, &c. If I died, &c.
Future. Morrò (morirò), morrai, morrà, morremo, morrete, morranno, I shall die, &c.
Cond. pres. Morrei (morirei), morresti, &c. I should die, &c.
Imperative. Muori, muoia, muoiamo, morite, muoiano, die thou, &c.

24.

Inf. pres. Salire, to ascend.   *Pres. part.* Salendo, ascending.
Inf. past. Essere salito, to have ascended.   *Past part.* Salito, ascended.
Pres. ind. Salgo (saglio, salisco), sali (salisci), sale (salisce), sagliamo (salghiamo), salite, salgono (sagliono, saliscono), I ascend, &c.
Pres. subj. Ch' io, tu, egli salga (saglia, salisca), sagliamo (salghiamo), sagliate (salghiate), salgano (sagliano, saliscano), that I may ascend, &c.
Imperf. Saliva, &c. I ascended, &c.
Perf. rim. Salii, &c. I ascended, &c.
Imperf. subj. Se io salissi, &c. If I ascended, &c.
Future. Salirò, &c. I shall ascend, &c.
Cond. pres. Salirei, &c. I should ascend, &c.
Imperative. Sali, salga, sagliamo, salite, salgano, ascend thou, &c.

25.

Inf. pres. Udire, to hear.   *Pres. part.* Udendo, hearing.
Inf. past. Aver udito, to have heard.   *Past part.* Udito, heard.
Pres. ind. Odo, odi, ode, udiamo, udite, odono, I hear, &c.
Pres. subj. Ch' io, tu, egli oda, udiamo, udiate, odano, that I may hear, &c.
Imperative. Odi, oda, udiamo, udite, odano, hear thou, &c.
    Obs. The remaining tenses are regular.

26.

Inf. pres. Uscire, also escire, to go out.   *Pres. part.* Uscendo (escendo), going out.
Inf. past. Essere uscito (escito) to have gone out.   *Past part.* Uscito (escito), gone out.
Pres. ind. Esco, esci, esce, usciamo (esciamo), uscite (escite), escono, I go out, &c.
Pres. subj. Ch' io, tu, egli esca, usciamo (esciamo), usciate (esciate), escano, that I may go out, &c.
Imperative. Esci, esca, usciamo, uscite, escano, go thou out, &c.
    Obs. The remaining tenses are regular.

    Obs. Some verbs are only irregular in the *perfetto rimoto* and past participle,

EIGHTY-FIFTH LESSON.   515

Inf.	*Perf. rim.*	*Past part.*
Aprire, to open.	April *and* sperai.	Aperto.
Coprire, to cover.	Copril *and* coperal.	Coperto.
Offerire, to offer.	Offerii *and* offeral.	Offerto.
Influire, to influence.	Influii *and* influssi. (obs.)	Influito. / Influsso.
Dire, to say.	Dissi.	Detto.

DEFECTIVE VERBS (*Verbi difettivi*).

They are so called, because they are not used in all tenses and persons, but only in those which are met with in good authors. They are the following:

Inf. pres. Gire, to go (only used in poetry). | *Past. part.* Gito, gone.
Pres. indic. Gite, ye go.
Imperf. Giva (gia), I, thou, he went; givamo, we went; givate, you went; givano (giano), they went.
Perf. rim. Gisti, thou wentest; gì (gìo), he went; gimmo, we went; giste, you went; girono, they went.
Imperf. subj. Se io gissi, tu gissi, egli gisse, gissimo, giste, gissero, if I went, &c.
Future. Girò, I shall go; girai, thou wilt go; girà, he will go; giremo, girete, giranno, we, you, they will go.
Cond. pres. Girei, giresti, girebbe, giremmo, gireste, girebbero, I should go &c.
Imperative. Gite, go ye.

Inf. pres. Ire, to go. | *Past. part.* Ito, gone.
Pres. ind. Ite, ye go. | *Imperf.* Iva, he went.
Future. Iremo, we shall go; Irete, you will go; Iranno, they will go.
Imperative. Ite, go ye.

Inf. pres. Riedere, to return. | *Pres. part.* Riedendo, returning.
Pres. ind. Riedo, I return; riedi, thou returnest; riede, he returns.
Imperf. Riedeva, I returned, &c.
Imperative. Riedi, return thou; rieda, let him return; riedano, let them return.

Inf. pres. Olire, to smell.
Imperf. Oliva, I smelt; olivi, thou smeltest; oliva, he smelt; olivano, they smelt.

Inf. pres. Calére, to care.	*Past part.* Caluto, cared.
Pres. ind. Mi cale, I care.	*Imperf.* Mi caleva, } I cared.
Pres. subj. Che mi caglia, that I may care.	*Perf. rim.* Mi calsi, }
Imperf. subj. Se mi calesse, if I cared.	*Cond. pres.* Mi calerebbe *or* carrebbe, I would care.

Licére *or* lecére, to be permitted,
This verb has only lice and lece, it is permitted. Past part. lecito and licito permitted. Even its infinitive is never used.

EIGHTY-FIFTH LESSON.

EXERCISE.

253.

THE FOUR LANGUAGES.

A TALE.

We have all read in the Holy Scriptures the miracle of the tongues of fire which descended from heaven upon the disciples of Christ, and immediately communicated to those men, who were complete strangers to all human learning, the knowledge of the several idioms they required in order to preach the gospel to the world.

What a miracle then did for the apostles, let us now do for ourselves by our own labour: for the study of languages is certainly a most useful study; it enables us to hold communication with all nations; It renders the whole world, as it were, our home.

Such was the opinion of young Edmund de Grancey's parents, who, some fifty years ago, possessed one of the finest estates in Dauphiné. Though unacquainted with foreign languages themselves, they were nevertheless sensible of the importance they might be of to their son. "No man on earth," would the Baron de Grancey frequently say, "knows what may be his future destiny. I therefore wish, should Edmund have occasion to travel, that he may never find himself a stranger in any country. I remember well how much I was embarrassed for want of knowing the German when I was a prisoner in Prussia during the seven years' war."

Endowed with a happy facility, Edmund made rapid progress under the able masters that were called in to instruct him. At the age of twelve, he was already able to read the charming fables of Lessing in German, the History of England by Hume, the beautiful lyric tragedies of Metastasio, that Italian poet whose language is so harmonious. He could already express himself with tolerable accuracy in these three idioms; and, not to mention his maternal tongue, which he knew very well, he could write a letter, almost without a mistake, in Italian, German, and English.

Meantime the revolution broke out. The Baron de Grancey, whose fortune had always been employed in doing good, never suspected that the political tempest could at all concern him; but the event soon proved that he was labouring under a fatal illusion. He received information that sentence of proscription had been pronounced against him, and orders issued for his being thrown into prison. The baron was therefore obliged to fly with his wife and son, and to gain with all speed the frontiers of Piedmont. The fatal news reached him at a moment when he was visiting a farm at some distance from his castle; so that he could only carry with him the little money he had on his person, which amounted to about twenty-five louis. They had not even the consolation of bidding adieu to their native abode.

At Edmund's age, we feel a lively pleasure in hurrying for the first time along the public roads; we look with amazement at the new objects that present themselves on every side; after having gone a few leagues, we think we have reached the utmost extremities of the earth. Edmund would, however, have enjoyed this pleasure with greater relish had it not been accompanied with the exile of his family.

The Baron and Baroness de Grancey had at first betaken themselves to Turin. After having received a supply of money which their friends had contrived to send them from France, they left that city in order to go and settle at Rome, until better times. But in order to do this, it was necessary to traverse a great part of Italy. As their resources were but scanty, the exiles took the ordinary conveyances from one town to another; a means of travelling which is neither elegant nor expeditious, but which is accompanied with but little expense. During this journey, as well as on every other occasion since their arrival in Italy, Edmund served as interpreter to his parents. It was an interesting spectacle to see this child of thirteen thus repaying his father and mother for the education he had received from them. — Edmund frequently heard those around him saying: "Do you see that French lady and gentleman, with their son? They have reason to congratulate themselves on having such a child. Poor exiles! they do not understand a word of our language; without him they would be much embarrassed — it is really admirable!" This importance, which events had given him, was far from rendering Edmund proud; but he congratulated himself every moment on his having studied the Italian with so much attention, and to such purpose.

The sort of car in which our emigrants were journeying, contained, besides two other travellers, a composer of music, who was going to Florence in order to get an opera represented; he was a good-natured juvenile *maestro*, and equally skilled in the culinary as in the musical art: the other was an abbé, who, though an excellent man and very pious to boot, loved music to the full as much as his neighbour the *maestro*. The coachman kept singing on his box, endeavouring from time to time to mend the sluggish pace of his horses: it was, as you may observe, a sort of musical caravan. The sun was about to disappear from the horizon, and the *maestro*, who had received from nature a vigorous appetite, was beginning to long for supper, when the travellers perceived the wished-for inn where they were to sup and pass the night. It was already so full that the master and mistress found great difficulty in answering all their guests. The arrival of the coach increased their difficulties. The *maestro* in particular called loudly for supper; but finding that they were not preparing it quick enough to answer his impatience, he took possession of the stove, threw off his coat, tucked up his sleeves, and set about preparing himself the classic *macaroni*.

Madame de Grancey, who till lately had lived so comfortably in her own castle, served by numerous domestics, surrounded by all the accommodations which usually accompany riches and security, had more difficulty than her husband in bringing her mind to so sudden and so complete a change. But as she did not want courage, she soon became resigned, and sat down with a good grace to the homely supper of the inn. The most conspicuous dish was the macaroni prepared by the musician, who received on that occasion almost as many compliments as he had ever done for the best of his operas.

When the repast was finished, a still greater difficulty awaited the host; this was to find beds for so many guests: the first comers had bespoke all the rooms in the house; the *maestro* and the abbé installed themselves the best way they could in the travellers' room; so that the French emigrants were obliged to take up their lodgings for the night in a small building attached to the inn, where some sorry beds had been hastily prepared, the matresses of which contained more straw than wool.

The room, in which the baron with his wife and son were lodged, was separated from the neighbouring one by a very thin partition. Scarcely had our travellers gone to bed when they heard some talking in the next room. They distinguished the voices of two men conversing together; but M. and Madame de Grancey, fatigued by their journey, and besides not understanding what was said, soon fell asleep. Edmund, on the contrary, lost not a word; and some expressions he heard uttered by those in the neighbouring room sufficiently arrested his attention to keep him awake.

.... " Don't speak too loud, Jacomo," said one of them to his companion.

" Poh !" replied the other, " what does it signify ? the French travellers whom we have for neighbours don't understand a word of Italian; of that I am quite certain; for, finding myself in the court with the old gentleman and his wife, I asked them, merely by way of conversation, where they came from; they made me a sign that they did not understand me. Set your mind at ease, then, Battista; we may talk over our intended expedition with perfect freedom."

Edmund remained in bed quite motionless, and listened with an attentive ear. He had guessed the intentions of these men from the very first. He took care, however, not to give way to any feeling of terror. Instead of crying out, and calling for assistance, he commanded himself with a coolness above his years, being aware of the signal service he might render, not only to his parents, but to all that were in the inn. A noise of pots and bottles, which accompanied their conversation, announced that they had had recourse to the glass in order to heighten their courage; in proportion as they drank, their voices became louder and their expressions less guarded.

" Hah !" replied one of them, " to-morrow morning, by break of day, the coach sets off again; before reaching the next village there is a bend in the road quite close upon the wood: we could not have a better place for taking our stand.—But should they defend themselves?...."—"Poh! they have no arms,...... besides, though they had, they will be taken by surprise—our pistols are double charged; we shall send in two or three shots amongst them, which will settle the business.—And then all will be ours!.... what a glorious windfall!"

The two robbers ceased speaking; one of them lay down and fell asleep; the other began to walk about the room. Edmund returned thanks to God that he had been able to understand the conversation of these two wretches, and supplicated his aid in this important crisis. He then groped his way to his father's bedside and awoke him—"Father," said he, in a low voice, "in that room close by, there are two robbers; they are to await our coach in order to rob and murder us."—"What! child, are you sure of that?"—"Yes, yes, father, I am quite certain of it; not a word of what they said has escaped me; they did not know that I understood Italian, so that they spoke without any disguise. It is at a turn of the road, near some wood that they are to lie in wait for us."

M. de Grancey thought for a moment, in order to consider what plan it would be necessary to adopt; then, without awaking his wife, who might have been seized with terror, he got up.—"Come with me, my dear child," said he; "you have saved us all; come, and make as little noise as possible."

The baron and his son directed their steps towards the inn, and knocked at the door: the host, after having opened it, asked what they wanted by coming and disturbing people in the middle of the night. Edmund, who performed the part of interpreter, told him all he had heard.—"Good God, sir!" cried the host, terrified at the idea of having robbers in his house, "I could wager that these are the very individuals who plundered one of my cousins, some three weeks ago."—"Is there not," asked M. de Grancey, "a troop of horse in the neighbourhood?"—"Yes, sir, about two miles from this."—"Well, then, cause some one to mount on horseback, or rather ride yourself full speed, in order to give notice to the armed force."

Some minutes after, the innkeeper galloped off for the nearest town, and M. de Grancey returned with Edmund to his apartment, both of them observing the strictest silence. About an hour after, they heard their neighbours go down stairs. The two robbers met the landlord in the court just as he returned from his journey; and, having discharged their bill, they set off.

Dawn at last appeared; the coachman ordered the travellers to get ready. He was just going to put the horses to, when the tramp of horse was heard upon the road; on looking in that direction, they saw four dragoons, who were conducting two men with their hands bound, both of whom were wounded. In these two prisoners they recognized Jacomo and Battista. Before reaching their place of ambush, they had fallen into the midst of the armed force which had been previously posted there. The soldiers immediately seized them, and discovered in their persons two robbers whom they had long been in search of, but had hitherto been unable to find.

The travellers had all learned from the landlord the name of their deliverer. Madame de Grancey embraced her son with great emotion: the good abbé called him a new Daniel: the *maestro* struck up, in honour of the little French boy, a song of triumph, which he took from his new opera. In the midst of all these congratulations, Edmund thought only of the happiness he felt in having saved his father and mother.

Some days after, the emigrant family entered the states of the Church, where every step gives rise to recollections of former greatness; at last they descried, while yet at a great distance, the cupola of St. Peter's, which announced to them their approach to the ancient capital of the world.

During his stay at Rome, Edmund laboured with renewed zeal in order to perfect himself in the knowledge of English and German. His grammars and dictionaries, works which in our youth frequently appear to us so dull and so dry, pleased him more than books of the most amusing nature; for he recollected how much he was indebted to that sort of study.

It was while he was thus employed that an old companion of M. de Grancey, who had taken refuge in Dresden, wrote in order to induce him to come and settle in that city, giving him hopes that he would be able to procure for him an honourable employment.

M. de Grancey decided upon going: his resources were diminishing; his estates in France had been confiscated, and the future gave no signs of any favourable change. Having collected all his remaining property, he left Rome, and set out on his journey to Saxony. The exiles every where met with the most cordial reception; for there is nowhere to be found a better or more hospitable people than the Germans. But, for want of knowing the idiom of those that were speaking around them, M. and Madame de Grancey would again have found themselves in the utmost embarrassment, had it not been for their Edmund, their dear interpreter.

From his very first entrance into Germany, he could make himself perfectly understood. Constant practice soon rendered him quite familiar with the language of Goethe and Schiller, which is reckoned so difficult. He, too, when he first began to study it, was a little frightened at the strangeness of its Gothic characters, and the apparent harshness of its words, which are, however, very agreeable in the mouth of one who knows how to pronounce them; but he now perceived that the belief of its *impossibility*, which then alarmed him, was altogether groundless.

At his arrival in Dresden, M. de Grancey experienced a cruel disappointment; that person high in office, upon whom his friend had counted, was no longer in place; the friend himself had been sent to another town in Saxony; so that, after many useless endeavours, M. de Grancey was obliged to give up all hope of success. This was a terrible blow for the poor exiles: their resources were now quite exhausted by their long journey; and of the town in which they found themselves they knew not a single individual. The health of Madame de Grancey began to give way under so many fatigues; and M. de Grancey, who would have submitted with courage even to manual labour, now felt the first symptoms of a painful disease. By little and little the exiled family had sold for their subsistence the few jewels that fortune had left them; the cross of Saint Louis, which M. de Grancey had gained by a heroic action, was the only article of value which he wished to preserve to the last. When walking with his lady, more than one head was uncovered on seeing the noble decoration which sparkled on the threadbare coat of the French emigrant. Edmund saw but too well the situation of his parents; more than once he had surprised his mother with tears in her eyes; his inability to assist that mother, that father whom he loved so dearly, overwhelmed him with grief; he was constantly trying to find out some means of being useful to them, and this state of continual anxiety rendered him sad and thoughtful. Meantime the poverty of the exiles was increasing every day.

Things had come to this extremity, when one evening, Edmund, who had been allowed by his parents to take a turn through the town, entered as thoughtful but less sad than usual. He seemed to be absorbed by some important idea which every now and then presented some rays of hope. When he embraced the baron, he said to him, with a tone of greater animation than usual: "O father, if I could but be useful to you!"

Next morning he went out earlier than usual, and directed his steps towards one of the principal streets of Dresden, in which was the shop of Mr. Petrus Meyer, a bookseller well known in the town. Edmund entered the shop, which contained an immense collection of works in all known languages. He asked if he could speak to the master of the house. A clerk having received permission, introduced him into the private room of Mr. Petrus Meyer. He was a man of about fifty, rather stout, wrapt in a large dressing-gown, with a cloth cap on his head, and seated before a table covered with ledgers. In one hand he held a pen with which he was writing, and in the other an enormous pipe, which surrounded him with a dense atmosphere of smoke.

Through the midst of that cloud Mr. Petrus cast his eyes upon the youth, and was immediately struck with his fine features, and the modest confidence with which he presented himself. Edmund had stopped near the door, with his hat off; the bookseller having taken the pipe from his mouth:

"Well, child," said he to him in the language of the country, "what is it you want?"

"Sir," replied Edmund, "you will, I hope, excuse me for calling upon you, though I have not the honour of either knowing or being known to you."

"Certainly, certainly ... you are a foreigner, I presume; are you a Frenchman?"

"Why, I am. Ah, sir, do you find my German bad? Have I made any mistakes?"

"Not at all, my child .... only a slight accent .... how old are you?"

"Fourteen...."

"There are few so young who can speak a foreign language so well as you do ours."

"Oh, how happy I am to hear you say that!"

"Why so?"

"Because, sir, as I was passing yesterday before your house, an idea struck me; I said to myself: Perhaps they may want some one who can translate into German books written in French, or else to draw up some letters of commerce .... and I have taken the liberty to come and speak to you about it, sir."

Edmund's face, and the manner in which he expressed himself, quite captivated Mr. Meyer's attention.

"Who are you, then, my child? Are you alone in Dresden?"

"No, sir, I am here with my father and mother; my father is called the Baron de Grancey, knight of Saint Louis, and a gentleman from the province of Dauphiné; he is an emigrant: we were once rich; but are so no longer. I am sure that my parents are in difficulty; and I wish, young as I am, to gain some money for them. You can make inquiry about us of Madame Krantz, at the sign of the *Golden Eagle*, where we lodge."

"You are a noble youth, and God will bless you," said Mr. Petrus Meyer, taking Edmund by the hand with an emotion which belied his habitual phlegm: "yes .... I will give you employment."

"Oh, sir," cried Edmund, embracing him with ardour, "and will you really give me employment? Could I but gain any thing, however little, I would be so obliged to you for it."

"Well, well, ... return to-morrow, don't forget, do you hear me, don't forget ...."

After repeated thanks, Edmund left him, so delighted, that in returning to the *Golden Eagle*, he bounded rather than walked. He arrived quite out of breath, ran up stairs, and entering, embraced his father and mother repeatedly, shedding tears of joy, of which they could not comprehend the cause.

EIGHTY-FIFTH LESSON.

"My dear parents," said he, "now I can labour, now I can be of some use to you."

"You, child, in what way?"

"Yes, father, yes, mother; thanks to the German which you caused me to learn, I shall gain some money for you; I have found here a bookseller, an excellent man, who has promised to employ me . . . . oh, how happy, how happy I am!"

Next day Edmund did not fail to call on Mr. Meyer: that bookseller dictated to him several letters on commercial business, which Edmund turned into French as fast as he heard them. Besides this, he gave him an elementary French work to translate, which he wished to publish in German. For these different labours, he allowed him a salary of one hundred florins a month: this was quite sufficient to place his parents above want, and even to enable them to save something. You may guess what was Edmund's delight: scarcely a day passed on which he did not exclaim with transport: "How fortunate it is that I learnt German!"

At the end of ten months, this means of subsistence was overturned. Mr. Meyer fell ill and died, lamented by all his friends, and particularly by Edmund, who looked upon him as a second father. His commercial house was dissolved. So that with him the exiles lost the only resource which enabled them to subsist; and Edmund could not find another. What was now to be done? What was to become of them? Madame de Grancey was tormented by an insupportable malady; this was the continual, the ardent desire of visiting France, or at least of getting near to it; that sort of slow fever, in short, which is called the *home sickness*. Their native land was shut against the exiles; they could not even think of settling near its frontiers, which were at that time the theatre of war between France and the allied powers. Madame de Grancey sometimes thought that if she could but live in England, in that country so near to their native land, she should find herself better. Her imagination, acting upon her already enfeebled body, rendered this belief with her what might truly be called a *fixed idea*.

The baron yielded to the desires of his wife; they set off, embarked at Hamburgh, and soon arrived in London. They had been but a few days in that capital when one morning Edmund and his father were passing through a populous quarter of the town, where there were in particular a great number of sailors. At that time there was a certain degree of agitation among the people. The war between France and England was then at the hottest. Spies sent by the French republic were said to be at that time in London. This rumour, commented upon and exaggerated by the common people and sailors, produced a general excitement. It appears that on that day, a man, pointed out as a French spy, had been pursued, but in vain, by the infuriated populace. M. de Grancey and his son knew nothing of this circumstance. They soon, however, remarked that the multitude were looking at them and pointing to them with a threatening air. They quickened their pace, but the crowd increased around them until their path was completely stopped. The word, "A spy! spy!" rang in their ears: four men started out from the multitude, and advanced towards the baron with the intention of striking him. Some one had thought that he recognized in him that French spy who had been pursued in vain. This was quite enough to excite the blind fury of the populace against M. de Grancey, who could neither understand nor speak their language. Had he been alone, it would probably have ended fatally with him; fortunately, however, he was accompanied by his son. At the terrible word "spy," Edmund, who understood well what it meant, threw himself before his father. "What do you want?" cried he.—"To throw the French spy into the Thames," was the reply from hundreds of voices. Edmund, transported by almost supernatural energy, covered his father's body by holding him closely embraced. He then began in English to harangue the furious populace. This he did with such energy, such logic, as nothing but imminent peril could have inspired. He told them who his father was, and where he lived. The people stopped, and became uncertain. Some constables with truncheons, which are the ensigns of those appointed to maintain order, had time to reach the scene of tumult; they then extricated M. de Grancey, and he and his son at last got home in safety. This time it was, when his mother was not present, for fear of alarming her, that Edmund said, as he embraced his father: "Oh! how I thank you for causing me to learn English!"

But the trials of our exiles came at last to a close. A milder rule was established in France, and his friends had at last been able to get the name of M. de Grancey erased from the list of emigrants. He received this happy information about a month after his last adventure. They wrote to him at the same time that he would recover a great part of his property which had not been sold. We may imagine the joy of the whole family. They were at last about to revisit their native country, after so many sufferings and disappointments. The exiles returned all three to France, the soil of which they trod with rapture. The baron and baroness were never weary of telling again and again, how their son had been their interpreter, their supporter, their deliverer!—Edmund did not grow vain on that account, but we have been assured that, at an after period, when married, and the father of a family, in his turn, whenever his children became disheartened by the difficulties they met with in the study of languages, he took pleasure in relating his history to them in order to renew their courage.

INDEX.

LIST OF TABLES

CONTAINED IN THIS VOLUME.

DECLENSION of the definite article in the singular masculine, 1; when the word begins with *s* followed by a consonant (or *z*), 2; when the word begins with a vowel, 3; in the plural, 26; when the word begins with *s*, followed by a consonant, or with a vowel, 27; in the singular and plural feminine, 279; contraction of the definite article masculine, 210; feminine, 279.
DECLENSION of the indefinite article masculine, 42; feminine, 286; of the partitive article masculine, 37; feminine, 286.
DECLENSION of the personal pronouns, 80; of the demonstrative pronouns, questo (cotesto), quello, 22.
DECLENSION of the interrogative pronouns, 62.
CONJUGATION of the auxiliaries *Avere* and *Essere*, 423; of the regular verbs, 477; of the passive voice, 481; of a reflective verb governing the accusative, 484; of a reflective verb governing the dative, 486; of a verb with two infinitives, 499; of the irregular verbs in *are*, 502; of the irregular verbs in *ere*, 505; of the irregular verbs in *ire*, 513; of the defective verbs, 515.

A.

A, to, 111, 125, 173. Obs. B. 435.
ACCENTS. The grave accent (`), 397; the acute accent (´), 398.
ADJECTIVE agrees with its noun or pronoun in number, Obs. A. B. 92. Feminine adjectives, and their formation from masculine adjectives, C. D. 285, 286. Abridgment of the adjectives, *uno, buono, bello, grande, santo, quello,* Obs. G. H. I. 34, 35. 459. Comparison of adjectives, Obs. A. B. 128. Adjectives that are irregular in the formation of the comparatives and superlatives, Obs. F. 129; Obs. G. 129.
ADVERBS *of quantity,* 58, 59, 60, 128, 180, 192, 295. Adverbs *of place,* 69, 72, 78, 95, 153, 154, 160, 164, 173.
227, 239, 244, 407. Adverbs *of quality and manner,* 365, 404, 420, 430, 436, 439, 450, 451. Adverbs *of number,* 142, 371. Adverbs *of time,* 82, 96, 105, 121, 132, 133, 138, 142, 164, 165, 168, 200, 227, 410. Comparative adverbs, 59, 60, 121. Comparison of adverbs, 130. Formation of superlative adverbs, Obs. II. ibid.
ADVICE to professors, Note 1, 1; to pupils, Note 7, 4.
AFFINITY between the Latin, Italian, and French languages, Note 4, 6.
APOSTROPHE, 458.
ARTICLE (definite): its declension in the singular masculine, when the word begins with any consonant, except *s* followed by another consonant, 1; when the word begins with *s* fol-

INDEX.   529

lowed by a consonant (or with s), 2; when the word begins with a vowel, Obs. A. 3; in the plural when the word begins with a consonant, except *s* followed by a consonant, 26; when the word begins with *s* followed by a consonant, or with a vowel, 27; feminine, 279; contraction of the definite article with certain prepositions, masculine, 210; feminine, 279. In Italian the definite article precedes the possessive pronoun, except when it is immediately followed by a noun of quality or kindred, Obs. B. 3; Rule, 12.—*Indefinite article*: its declension masculine, 42; feminine, 286.—*Partitive article*: masculine, singular and plural, 27, 28; feminine, singular and plural, 286.—Use of the article before proper names, 442.

AUGMENTATIONS, 460.
AUGMENTATIVES, 32.

AVERE, to have; avuto, had, 137, 141. To be, rendered by avere, 8, 9. Aver bisogno, to be in want of, 96, 97. Aver paura, vergogna, torto, ragione, tempo, coraggio, desiderio or voglia, to be afraid, ashamed, wrong, right, to have time, courage, a mind, a wish, 62. Aver bello, in vain, 425. Conjugation of avere, 473 et seqq.

B.

BE (to), translated by avere:* Are you hungry? Ha Ella fame? Avete fame? 8. I am thirsty, ho sete; I am sleepy, ho sonno, 8. I am afraid, ho paura; I am warm, ho caldo; I am cold, ho freddo, 10. Are you ashamed? Ha Ella vergogna? Avete vergogna? I am wrong, ho torto; You are right, Ella ha ragione, Avete ragione, 15.

DELLO, fine, handsome, or beautiful. Before a consonant (not before *s*, followed by a consonant,) bel is used, Note 9, 5.
BUONO, good, Note 1, 5.

C.

COLUI, il quale (or che), quello, il quale (or che), him who. Plur. Coloro,

i quali (or che), quelli, i quali (or che), those who. When ought colui, coloro, and when quello, quelli, to be employed? Obs. 190.

CONDITIONAL tenses; their formation, and when they are employed, 387 et seqq.

CONJUNCTIONS which govern the subjunctive, Remarks, 378 et seqq. Conjunctions expressing certainty require the indicative, Rem. E. 379 et seqq. Conjunctions with the preterite anterior, 399.

CONSTRUCTION, or Syntax, 468.

D.

DA, from, Obs. C. 23; Obs. C. 85; Notes 1, 2, 68. 191, 192, 244. 255. 353. 368; Obs. A. 434.
DI, of, Obs. A. G. Di, to, 62. Di qua della via, on this side of the road; di là della via, on that side of the road, 174. Dirimpetto, opposite to, 415. Obs. A. 414; Obs. 454.

DIMINUTIVES, 32.

E.

ELISION, 458 et seqq.
ELLA, she. See Way of Addressing a person in Italian.
ESSERE*, to be, stato, fem. stata, been, Obs. 137. Essere impaziente di (tardare), to long for; essere agiato (comodo), to be comfortable; essere mal comodo, non essere agiato, to be uncomfortable, 424. Conjugation of essere, 473.

EXPLETIVES, 462.

F.

FUTURE, its formation; firm or simple future, Rule, 220. Obs. A. 221. Compound or past future; its formation, 300. The future is used in Italian when the present is employed in English, Obs. 308. The conditional conjunction se, if, may in Italian be followed by the future, Obs. 369.

23

H.

Hour, ora. *What o'clock is it?* and similar expressions, 96.

I.

IL (definite article, masculine singular, when the word begins with a consonant, except *s* followed by another consonant), the, L

INPERATIVE: its formation, and when it must be employed, Obs. A. 394. Obs. B. C. 395, 446, 447. The personal pronouns and the relative *se* are joined to the imperative, Obs. B. C. 395.

IMPERFECT (the) of the Indicative: its formation, Note 1, 314: when it must be employed, Obs. 314. Imperfect of the Subjunctive: its formation, Obs. A. 385; when it must be employed, Rem. II. 3d5 et seqq.

IN, in, 68, 69. 85, 89. Obs. A. 133.

IN LUOGO DI, *invece di*, instead of, followed in Italian by the infinitive, 110.

INFINITIVE: means to distinguish the Infinitive of each conjugation, 63. The personal pronouns and the relative *se* are joined to the infinitive, Obs. 64. The infinitive, preceded by the preposition *di*, 63, Obs. 110, 125; by the preposition *a*, 111. Obs. A. 133; by *per*, 76. The Infinitive without a preposition, Obs. B. 134.

L.

LA, she. See Way of Addressing a person in Italian.

LICENCES, 469, 470, 471.

LEGNO (il), the wood, and *la legna*, the wood for fuel, Note 3, 5.

LEI, you. See Way of Addressing a person in Italian.

Lo (definite article, masculine singular, when the word begins with *s* followed by a consonant, or with *z*), the, 2. Before a vowel the same article is changed into *l'*, Obs. A. 3. When the word beginning with *s* followed by a consonant, or with *z*, is preceded by another word, the article is no more *lo*, but *il*, Obs. C. 3. *Le* (pronoun), li, 5.

M.

MINE, *il mio*; of mine, *del mio*; from mine, *dal mio*, 11.

N.

NE, some of it, of it, some of them, of them. Place of the relative *ne* with regard to the personal pronouns, Obs. A. 74. Obs. B. 79; in conjunction with the infinitive, Obs. 64; with the present participle, Obs. C. 300; in conjunction with the imperative, Obs. B. C. 395. *Ne*, from it, from there, thence, 164.

NEITHER—nor. *non*—*nè*, *nè*, 13.

No, no, 5. *Non*, not, ibid. *Non*—*nè*, *nè*, neither—nor, 13. *Non*—*niente*, *non*—*nulla* (or simply *nulla*, before a verb), nothing or not any thing. Obs. A. 8. 14. *Non*—*niente di buono*, nothing good, Obs. B. 9.

No, no; not, *non*, 5. Nothing, or not any thing, *non*—*niente*, *non*—*nulla* (or simply *nulla* before the verb), Obs. A. 8. 14. Nothing, or not any thing good, *niente di buono*, Obs. B. 9.

NUMBERS (Cardinal), 41. 47. 51. The cardinal numbers are employed when speaking of the days of the month, 51. Ordinal numbers, 51, 52. Distributive numbers, *primieramente*, *in primo luogo*, firstly; *secondariamente*, *in secondo luogo*, &c. 371. The English ordinal number rendered in Italian by the cardinal: I received your letter on the fifth, on the sixth, &c. *Ho ricevuto la di Lei lettera il cinque, il sei*, &c. 440.

O.

OF, *di*, Obs. A. 6.

OF the, *del* (before a consonant), *dello* (before *s*, followed by a consonant), *dell'* (before a vowel), 10.

On purpose, *apposta a bella posta*, 420.

Or, *o*, 11.

P.

PARTICIPLE past; its formation, Notes 1, 2, 3. Obs. 137, 138. It agrees with its object in number, ☞ 141. ☞ 239. Obs. E. 247. ☞ 304. It serves to form the passive voice, 196. ☞ 239.

PARTICIPLE present; its formation and use, 299. The personal pronouns and the relative *ne* are joined to the present participle, Obs. C. 300.

PASSATO RIMOTO (or *remoto*) the preterite definite; its formation, Note 1, Obs. A. 318; Notes 2, 3, 4, Obs. B. 319. When it is employed, 320.

PER, to (in order to), 76. *Per lo spazio di*, during, 165. *Per timore (per tima)*, for fear of, 369. *Pel corso di*, all along, 407. *Per mezzo*, through, 457.

PLURAL: its formation in nouns and adjectives, Rule, 26, & *seqq*., Obs. and Rules, 279, & *seqq*.

PLUPERFECT (the) of the Indicative; its formation and its use, Obs. D. 320, 321. Pluperfect of the Subjunctive: its formation, Obs. B. 385; its use, 388.

PREPOSITIONS, which in Italian are followed by the infinitive, whilst in English they are followed by the present participle, ☞ 184, Obs. C. 276. The English preposition *for* with the verbs *to ask, domandare, chiedere; to pay, pagare*, is not rendered in Italian, ☞ 185. Use of the preposition A, 111, 124, 173. Obs. B. 435: of the preposition DA, Obs. C. 23. Obs C. 85, Notes 1, 2, 69, 181, 192, 197, 244, 245, 353, 368. Obs. A. 434: of the preposition DI, Obs. A. 6, 63. Obs. A. 434. Obs. 454: of the preposition IN, 64, 69, 85, 89. Obs. A. 133: of the preposition PER, to (meaning *in order to*), 76; (meaning *during*), 165; (meaning *for fear of*), 369; (meaning *all along*), 407; (meaning *through*), 457. The infinitive without a preposition, Obs. B. 114.

PRESENT (the) tense Indicative: its formation, Note 1, 100. Obs. A. 101. There is no distinction in Italian between *I love, do love, am loving*, Obs. B. 102. Verbs whose infinitive ends in *care* or *gare* insert an *h* as often as *g* or *c* meets with *i* or *e*, Obs. C. 103. 489. Present of the Subjunctive: its formation, 377. When it must be employed, *Rem*. A. B. C. 378, *et seqq*.

PRETERITE (the) definite. See *Passato rimoto* (or *remoto*). Preterite anterior: its formation and its use, 321, 322.

PRETERPERFECT of the Indicative: its formation and use, 146. Preterperfect of the Subjunctive: its formation and its use, Obs. B. 385 *et seqq*.

PRIMA *di, innanzi di (che), avanti di*, before, 125.

PRONOUN: Personal pronouns, 80, 281. Order of the personal pronouns in the sentence, 78. Place of the relative *ne* with regard to the personal pronoun, 79. Joining of the personal pronouns and the relative *ne* to the infinitive (See Infinitive); to the present participle (See Participle); to the imperative (See Imperative). The personal pronouns are joined to *ecco*, Obs. A. 325. Absolute possessive pronouns, 29, 30, 92, 284. In Italian the article precedes the possessive pronouns, whether conjunctive or absolute, Obs. B. 3, 29, 30, 92, 229, 273, 284, 292. Obs. 348. In Italian the qualifications of *Signore*, Mr., *Signora*, Mrs., *Signorina*, Miss, usually follow the possessive pronouns, Obs. B. 273. Demonstrative pronouns, 10, 16. Obs. A. 22. Obs. B. 23, 29, 33, 34, 147, 285, 287. Determinative pronouns, 33, 109, 110. Interrogative pronouns, 3, 9, 16, 18, 29, 83, 97, 181, 229, 285, 347, 348. Relative pronouns, 23, 33, 41, 109, 190, 216, 217, 218, 297. Indefinite pronouns, Obs. 20, 50, 56, 58, 59, 60. Obs. C. 148. Use of the indefinite pronoun *si*, they, the people, any one, or one, 169, 170. Indefinite pronouns requiring the subjunctive, Obs. P. R. 390. Obs. S. 391. Pronouns of reflective verbs, Obs. A. 203. The reflective pronouns *myself, thyself*, &c

rendered by *io stesso* or *io medesimo, tu stesso*, or *tu medesimo*, &c., 356. Pronouns of address, *tu, Ella, Lei, Vossignoria*, and when they are used, 90 *et seqq*.

Q.

QUALCHE *cosa* (*alcuna cosa*), something or any thing, 7. *Qualche cosa di buono*, something, or any thing good, Obs. B. 9.

QUALE? or CHE? (interrogative pronoun), which or what. When is *quale* and when *che* (plural *quali che*) to be employed? Obs. D. 3. Note 6, 4.

QUEL, *quello, quell'*, that, Obs. 10. *Quello*, that, or the one, *ibid*.

QUESTO (*cotesto*), this one ; *quello*, that one. When must *questo*, when *cotesto*, and when *quello* be used? Obs. B. 22.

S.

SE, if, 193 ; requires the imperfect of the subjunctive, 325. *Se* may be followed by the future, Obs. B. 269.

SI, they, the people, any one, or one, 169, 170.

SIGNORE, Sir. When ought this word to be written with an *e* at the end, and when not? Note 3, 2.

SOMETHING or any thing, *qualche cosa*, or *alcuna cosa*, 7. Something, or any thing good, *qualche cosa di buono*, Obs. B. 9.

SUBJUNCTIVE, 272 *et seqq.*, 384 *et seqq.* See PRESENT, IMPERFECT, &c.

SUBSTANTIVE: formation of the plural, 26 *et seqq.*, 280 *et seqq.* Gender of substantives, Notes and Obs. 28, 29, 280 *et seqq.* Substantives having a distinct form for individuals of the female sex, Obs. 293, 294.

SUO, his. See Way of Addressing a person in Italian.

SUPPRESSION OF VOWELS. When two words finish with the same vowel, that of the first word is generally suppressed, Note 1, 5. No vowel is suppressed before *s* followed by a consonant, *ibid.* See Elision.

T.

THAT, *quel, quello, quell'*; use of each of these pronouns, Obs. 10. That or the one, *quello, ibid*.

THE, definite article, *il, lo, la, i, gli, le*, 1, 2. See ARTICLE.

THERE or thither, *vi* or *ci*, 72, 73. *There is, c'è vi è* (*vi ha avvi*). *There are, ci sono* or *vi sono*, 160. 227.

Tu, thou. See Way of Addressing a person in Italian.

V.

VERBS: the three conjugations, 66. Verbs requiring the preposition *di* before the infinitive, 63. Obs. 110, 125. Verbs requiring the preposition *a* (*ad*), and those requiring the preposition *in*, 110. Obs. A. 122. Verbs requiring the preposition *per*, 76. Verbs which do not require a preposition before the infinitive, Obs. B. 134. Treatise of the Italian verbs, 113 *et seqq*. Compound and derivative verbs are conjugated like their primitives, Obs. 158. Auxiliary verbs (see AVERE*, ESSERE*). Verbs which require *essere* for their auxiliary, 203. Obs. F. 303. The past participle of such verbs must agree in gender and number with the nominative of the verb *essere*, ☞ 304. Active verbs, 146. Their conjugation, 177 *et seqq*. Neuter verbs, 152. Passive verbs, 196, ☞ 239. Their conjugation, 482 *et seqq*. Reflective verbs, 203, 204. Their conjugation, 483 *et seqq*., 486 *et seqq*. Impersonal verbs, 191, 199, 215. Way of rendering in Italian the English interrogatives *do* and *am*, 124. Irregular verbs: in *are*, 502 *et seqq*. ; in *ere*, 505 *et seqq*. ; in *ire*, 513 *et seqq*. Defective verbs, 515.

Voi, you. See Way of Addressing a person in Italian.

VOSSIGNORIA (V. S.), your worship, *Vossignoria Illustrissima*, your lordship. See Way of Addressing a person in Italian.

VOSTRA ALTEZZA, your Highness.
—— ECCELLENZA, your Excellency.
—— MAESTÀ, your Majesty. See Way of Addressing a person in Italian.

W.

WATCH: to wind up, to regulate the watch, and similar expressions, 409.
WAY (to ask one's), 407.
—— of Addressing a person in Italian, Note 2, 1, 2. Note 2, 20 et seqq.

WHAT ! *che ? che cosa ? cosa ?* 2.
WHICH or WHAT ! *quale* or *che* (plural *quali*, *che*) ? When is *quale*, and when *che*, to be employed ? Obs. D. 3, Note 6, 4.

Y.

YOURS, *il vostro, il suo, il di Lei;* of yours, *del vostro, del suo, del di Lei;* from yours, *dal vostro, dal suo, dal di Lei,* 11.

THE END

COMPANION TO OLLENDORFF'S ITALIAN GRAMMAR.

D. Appleton & Co. publish

CRESTOMAZIA ITALIANA:

A COLLECTION OF

SELECTED PIECES IN ITALIAN PROSE,

DESIGNED AS A

CLASS READING-BOOK FOR BEGINNERS

IN THE STUDY OF

THE ITALIAN LANGUAGE.

By E. FELIX FORESTI, LL. D.,

PROFESSOR OF THE ITALIAN LANGUAGE AND LITERATURE IN COLUMBIA COLLEGE AND IN THE UNIVERSITY OF THE CITY OF NEW-YORK.

One neat volume, 12mo.

PREFACE.—This volume is intended as a reading-book for those who are commencing the study of the Italian language; and the Grecism of its title—CRESTOMAZIA ITALIANA—sufficiently indicates that it contains a selection of pleasing and useful pieces of Italian prose, taken from the best writers.

In its compilation, the aim has been more particularly to engage the mind and enlist the feelings of the student; for to read without sympathy, is to acquire a distaste for learning—to march without making progress. For this reason, principally, preference has been given to modern authors, most of whom are still living. It is not meant, by so doing, to dispute the universally acknowledged merit of the ancient Italian writers registered in the classic catalogue approved by the despotical dictatorship of the Academy of the Crusca. They are unquestionably masters in purity of language and style; but the subjects upon which they wrote are not the best calculated to inspire with sympathy and interest the young—especially the young American—mind. On the contrary, modern authors, influenced by the existing principles relative to social improvement, and by a philosophical criticism far superior to that of the ancients, wrote in Italy, as elsewhere, with more depth of thought, freshness and vigour of style, and in a tone and spirit more in accordance with the opinions and taste of the present time; and it is quite probable their writings will be more relished by the readers of to-day.

The selections contained in this volume have been made from the works of eminent men, whose fame rests upon an authority of far more weight and power than that of the Crusca—the united public voice of their native country.

The Italian, owing to the freedom of its construction, is not so grammatically simple as the French; it is, besides, exceedingly rich in idioms: to facilitate, therefore, the progress of the student, in the rendering of the most difficult idiomatic forms or phrases, a glossary has been subjoined to each particular selection.

ACCOMPANIMENT TO OLLENDORFF'S GERMAN GRAMMAR.

D. Appleton & Co. Publish

A PROGRESSIVE GERMAN READER,

PREPARED WITH REFERENCE TO

OLLENDORFF'S GERMAN GRAMMAR,

WITH COPIOUS NOTES AND A VOCABULARY.

BY G. J. ADLER,

Professor of the German Language and Literature in the University of the City of N. Y.

One neat Volume, 12mo.

The favorable reception which Ollendorff's German Grammar has received from the American public, has induced the Publishers and the Editor to comply with the very general demand for a *German Reader*.

Complaints, more or less loud, have been made both by teacher and learner, against most of the Readers heretofore offered to the public in this country, as well as in England and Germany. Books of this kind now in the market, may be reduced to two classes: 1st. *Selections from the German Classics, or Elegant Extracts*, corresponding somewhat to our English Readers. Of these, two deserve special notice, viz. GEORGE MUELL'S PROSE ANTHOLOGY, (Carlsruhe and London, 1839,) and in this country, FOLLEN'S GERMAN READER. The objections to the former are, that it contains no poetry, and hence lacks an essential element of an introduction to German Literature, and presents too little variety to the learner; it has, moreover, no vocabulary, and the most difficult passages are often left unnoticed in the annotations. The latter is, as it regards the variety and the good taste exhibited in its matter, far superior to any other similar work, and has for many years been almost the only Reader in use among us. To learners not classically educated, however, (and to many that are,) the pieces near the beginning are by far too difficult, and the assistance too scanty. The arrangement is not progressive, so that pieces over the end of the book are much easier than many in the beginning or middle.

2d. The second class of Readers are such as profess to *facilitate* the business of reading. They are generally based on the *Hamiltonian* method, i. e., the pieces are accompanied with translations, either *interlinear* and *literal*, or *free* and *opposite*. The difficulty with the books of this class is, that they leave the learner where they found him, unable by himself to account for the grammatical construction of a sentence; and when he lays aside the book to take up another, he finds that it is one thing to read by the aid of a translation and quite another to read understandingly. The principal books of this class are Zimmer's *German Teacher*, (Heidelberg and London, 1839,) *Gand's Literary Companion*, (Frankfort, 1841,) better in its selections than the first, and *Bokum's German Reader*, (Philadelphia.)

The plan of this German Reader is as follows, viz.:

1. The pieces are both prose and poetry, selected from the best authors, and are so arranged as to present sufficient variety to keep alive the interest of the scholar.

2. It is progressive in its nature, the pieces being at first very short and easy, and increasing in difficulty and length as the learner advances.

3. At the bottom of the page constant references to the Grammar are made, the difficult passages are explained and rendered. To encourage the first attempt of the learner as much as possible, the twenty-one pieces of the first section are analyzed, and all the necessary words given at the bottom of the page. The notes, which at first are very abundant, diminish as the learner advances.

4. It contains *five* sections. The *first* contains easy pieces, chiefly in prose, with all the words necessary for translating them; the *second*, short pieces in prose and poetry alternately, with copious notes and renderings; the *third*, short popular tales of GRIMM and others; the *fourth*, select ballads and other poems from BUERGER, GOETHE, SCHILLER, UHLAND, SCHWAB, CHAMISSO, &c. ; the *fifth*, prose extracts from the first classics.

5 At the end is added a VOCABULARY of all the words occurring in the book.

CLASSICAL & SCHOOL BOOKS.

ARNOLD.—A FIRST AND SECOND LATIN BOOK
And Practical Grammar. By Thomas K. Arnold, A.M. Revised and carefully Corrected, by J. A. Spencer, A.M. One volume, 12mo., neatly bound, 75 cents.

☞ If preferred, the First Latin Book, or the Second Latin Book and Grammar, can be had separately. Price 50 cents each.

The chief object of this work (which is founded on the principles of imitation and frequent repetition) is to enable the pupil to do exercises from the first day of his beginning his accidence.

ARNOLD.—LATIN PROSE COMPOSITION:
A Practical Introduction to Latin Prose Composition. By Thomas K. Arnold, A.M. Revised and Corrected by J. A. Spencer, A.M. One volume, 12mo., neatly bound, $1.00.

This work is also founded on the principles of imitation and frequent repetition. It is at once a Syntax, a Vocabulary, and an Exercise Book; and considerable attention has been paid to the subject of Synonymes.

ARNOLD.—A FIRST AND SECOND GREEK BOOK;
With Easy Exercises and Vocabulary. By Thomas K. Arnold, A.M. Revised and Corrected by J. A. Spencer, A.M. 12mo.

ARNOLD.—GREEK PROSE COMPOSITION:
A Practical Introduction to Greek Prose Composition. By Thomas K. Arnold, A.M. Revised and Corrected by J. A. Spencer, A.M. One volume, 12mo.

This work consists of a Greek Syntax, founded on Buttmann's, and Easy Sentences translated into Greek, after given Examples, and with given Words.

ARNOLD.—A GREEK READING BOOK;
Including a Complete Treatise on the Greek Particles. By Thomas K. Arnold, A.M. Revised by J. A. Spencer, A.M. One volume, 12mo.

ARNOLD.—CORNELIUS NEPOS;
With Practical Questions and Answers, and an Imitative Exercise on each Chapter. By Thomas K. Arnold, A.M. Revised, with Additional Notes, by Prof. Johnson, Professor of the Latin Language in the University of the City of New-York. One neat volume, 12mo.

"ARNOLD'S GREEK AND LATIN SERIES.—The publication of this valuable collection of classical school books may be regarded as the presage of better things in respect to the mode of teaching and acquiring languages. Heretofore boys have been condemned to the drudgery of going over Latin and Greek Grammar without the remotest conception of the value of what they were learning, and every day becoming more and more disgusted with the dry and unmeaning task; but now, by Mr. Arnold's admirable method—substantially the same with that of Ollendorff—the moment they take up the study of Latin or Greek, they begin to learn sentences, to acquire ideas, to see how the Romans and Greeks expressed themselves, how their mode of expression differed from ours, and by degrees they lay up a stock of knowledge which is utterly astonishing to those who have dragged on month after month in the old-fashioned, dry, and tedious way of learning languages.

"Mr. Arnold, in fact, has had the good sense to adopt the system of nature. A child learns his own language by imitating what he hears, and constantly repeating it till it is fastened in the memory; till the same way Mr. A. puts the pupil immediately to work at Exercises in Latin and Greek, involving the elementary principles of the language—words are supplied—the mode of putting them together is told the pupil—he is shown how the ancients expressed their ideas; and then, by repeating these things again and again—*iterum iterumque*—the docile pupil has them indelibly impressed upon his memory and rooted in his understanding.

"The American editor is a thorough classical scholar, and has been a practical teacher for years in this city. He has devoted the utmost care to a complete revision of Mr. Arnold's works, has corrected several errors of inadvertence or otherwise, has rearranged and improved various matters in the early volumes of the series, and has attended most diligently to the accurate printing and mechanical execution of the whole. We anticipate most confidently the speedy adoption of these works in our schools and colleges."—*Cour. & Enq.*

☞ Arnold's Series of Classical Works has attained a circulation almost unparalleled in England, having introduced into nearly all the great Public Schools and leading Educational Institutions. They are also very highly recommended by some of the best American Scholars, for introduction into the Classical Schools of the United States. They are already used in the University of the City of New-York, Rutgers' Female Institute, N. Y.; Union College, Schenectady; Mt. St. Mary's College, Md.; Yale College, New-Haven; and numerous large schools throughout the Union.

Appletons' Catalogue of Valuable Publications.

CLASSICAL & SCHOOL BOOKS—Continued

ARNOLD.—LECTURES ON MODERN HISTORY.
By Thomas Arnold, D.D. With an Introduction and Notes, by Prof. Henry Reed. One volume 12mo., $1.25.

☞ This volume has already been adopted as a text-book in the University of Pennsylvania and Union College, Schenectady.

ADLER.—A NEW GERMAN READER;
With Reference to Ollendorff's German Grammar. By G. J. Adler, Prof. of th German Language and Lit. in the University of the City of New-York. (In Press.

GRAHAM.—ENGLISH SYNONYMES;
Classified and Explained, with Practical Exercises. By G. T. Graham, author of "Helps to English Grammar," etc. Edited, with illustrative authorities, by Henry Reed, Prof. of Eng. Lit. in the University of Pennsylvania. One volume, 12mo.

"It is impossible not to praise both the design and execution of this work. It fills a chasm in our scholastic literature. Previous to this publication, we had but three works of the kind, whether for young or old students, (Trusler, Taylor, Crabb,) and not one of them is practical enough for elementary purposes."—*London Athenæum.*

GESENIUS.—HEBREW GRAMMAR, BY RODIGER.
Gesenius's Hebrew Grammar. Enlarged and Improved by E. Rödiger, Prof. of Oriental Literature in the University of Halle. Translated by Benj. Davies, Doct. in Philosophy of the University of Leipsic; with a Hebrew Reading Book, prepared by the translator, carefully reprinted from the fourteenth edition, (just published in London, by Bagster.) Complete in one handsome 8vo. volume.

"The excellence of Gesenius's Grammar is universally acknowledged. Its adaptation, both in matter and method, to meet the wants of Hebrew students, is triumphantly established by the fact that no fewer than thirteen editions have been sold. The new edition, from which this translation has been made, was prepared by Prof. Rödiger, and appeared in 1845. Among living Philologists, there are but few names in higher repute than Rödiger's. His edition of the Grammar may therefore be supposed to contain some real improvements, as well as changes and additions and this presumption is fully borne out by a comparison with the thirteenth edition, which was itself improved by the author's last revision. The addition of the Reading Book, as an introduction to the translating of Hebrew, will prove (the exception begun) of material service to the student in mastering the Grammar and acquiring the language."—*Ext. from Translator's Pref*

GUIZOT.—GENERAL HISTORY OF CIVILIZATION
In Europe, from the fall of the Roman Empire to the French Revolution. Translated from the French of M. Guizot, Professor of History to la Faculte des Lettres of Paris, and Minister of Public Instruction. Third American edition, with Notes by C. S. Henry, D. D. One volume, 12mo., $1,00.

"M. Guizot, in his instructive Lectures, has given us an epitome of modern history, distinguished by all the merit which, in another department, renders Blackstone a subject of such peculiar and unbounded praise—a work closely condensed, including nothing useless, omitting nothing essential; written with grace, and conceived and arranged with consummate ability."—*Boston Trans.*

KEIGHTLEY.—THE MYTHOLOGY OF GREECE
And Italy; designed for the use of Schools. By Thomas Keightley. Numerous wood-cut illustrations. One volume, 18mo., half bound, 44 cents.

"This is a neat little volume, and well adapted to the purpose for which it was prepared. It presents, in a very compendious and convenient form, every thing relating to the subject, of importance to the young student."—*L. I. Star.*

MICHELET.—HISTORY OF THE ROMAN REPUBLIC.
By M. Michelet, Professor of History in the College of France, author of "The History of France," etc. One vol., 12mo.

"I have looked over Michelet's Roman History in the original, with the admiration which all the works of that great master must inspire. It is in many respects admirably adapted to the purposes of instruction in our higher seminaries of learning, &c. "ALONZO POTTER. "*Union College.*"

MANDEVILLE.—NEW ENGLISH READER:
A Course of Reading for Common Schools and the Lower Classes of Academies, on a Scientific plan; being in part an abridgement of the author's "Elements of Reading and Oratory." By H. Mandeville, Prof. of Moral Philosophy and Belles Lettres in Hamilton College, N. Y. One volume, 12mo.

Appletons' Catalogue of Valuable Publications.

CLASSICAL & SCHOOL BOOKS—Continued.

OLLENDORFF.—NEW GERMAN GRAMMAR.

A New Method of Learning to Read, Write, and Speak the German Language. By H. G. Ollendorff. Reprinted from the Frankfort edition; to which is added a Systematic Outline of the different Parts of Speech, their Inflection and Use, with full Paradigms, and a complete list of the Irregular Verbs. By G. J. Adler, Prof. of the German Language in the University of the City of New York. 12mo, $1.50.

"Ollendorff's New Method of Learning to Read, Write, and Speak the German Language, has had an extensive circulation in England, and its demand in this country also has constantly been increasing of late. Nor is its popularity undeserved; for it supplies a deficiency which has been long and deeply felt by all those who have engaged in either teaching or learning the German.

"The German has hitherto been treated too much like a dead language; and hence many, disgusted with the cumbrous terminology and crabbed rules which in the very outset met their eye, have given up the acquisition of the language in despair. Ollendorff has completely remedied this evil. Beginning with the simplest phrases, he gradually introduces every principle of Grammar; and he does it by interblending the rules with such copious exercises and idiomatic expressions, that, by a few months' diligent application, and under the guidance of a skilful instructor, any one may acquire every thing that is essential to enable him to read, to write, and to converse in the language." ☞ A Key to the above, in a separate volume, uniform; price 75 cents.

OLLENDORFF.—NEW FRENCH GRAMMAR.

A New Method of Learning to Read, Write, and Speak the French Language. By H. G. Ollendorff. With an Appendix, containing the Cardinal and Ordinal Numbers, and full Paradigms of the Regular and Irregular, Auxiliary, Reflective, and Impersonal Verbs, by J. L. Jewett. One volume, 12mo, $1.50.

"The plan pursued in teaching the French is substantially the same with that developed in the German Method. Avoiding the exclusively didactic character of the older treatises on the one hand, and the tedious prolixity of detail which encumbers modern systems on the other, Ollendorff combines and thoroughly teaches at once both the theory and practice of the language. The student who pursues his method will therefore be relieved from the apprehension of either forgetting his rules before practice has grounded him in their principles, or of learning sentences by rote which he cannot analyze. Speaking and writing French, which in other systems is delayed until the learner is presumed to be master of Etymology and Syntax, and consequently is seldom acquired, by this method is commenced with the first lesson, continued throughout, and made the efficient means of acquiring, almost imperceptibly, a thorough knowledge of grammar; and this without diverting the learner's attention for a moment from the language itself, with which he is naturally most desirous of becoming familiar.

The text of Ollendorff, carefully revised and corrected, is given in the present edition without abridgment. To this the American editor has added an Appendix, containing the cardinal and Ordinal Numbers, and full conjugation of all the Verbs. The work is thus rendered complete, and the necessity of consulting other treatises is wholly obviated."

☞ A Key to the above, in a separate volume, uniform; 75 cents.

OLLENDORFF.—NEW ITALIAN GRAMMAR.

A New Method of Learning to Read, Write, and Speak the Italian Language. By H. G. Ollendorff. With Additions and Corrections, by Felix Foresti, Prof. of the Italian Language in the University of the City of N. Y. One vol., 12mo. (In Press.)

M. Ollendorff's System, applied to the study of the Italian Language, possesses all the advantages of his method of learning the German and French, and will undoubtedly, as its merits be come known, take the place of all other Grammars.

☞ A Key to the above, in a separate volume, uniform.

REID.—A DICTIONARY OF THE ENGLISH LANGUAGE;

Containing the Pronunciation, Etymology, and Explanation of all Words authorized by eminent writers; to which are added a Vocabulary of the Roots of English Words, and an accented list of Greek, Latin, and Scripture Proper Names. By Alexander Reid, A. M., Rector of the Circus School, Edinburgh. With a Critical Preface by Henry Reed, Prof. of Eng. Lit. In the Univ. of Pa. 12mo, near 600 p, $1.

The attention of Professors, Students, Tutors, and Heads of Families is solicited to this volume. Notwithstanding its compact size and distinctness of type, it comprises forty thousand words. In addition to the correct orthoepy, this manual of words contains four valuable improvements:—

I. The primitive word is given, and then follow the immediate derivatives in alphabetical order, with the part of speech appended.

II. After the primitive word is inserted the original term whence it is formed, with the name of the language from which it is derived.

III. There is subjoined a Vocabulary of the Roots of English words, by which the accuracy of each of them is instantly discoverable.

IV. An accented List, to the number of fifteen thousand, of Greek, Latin, and Scripture Pro

CLASSICAL & SCHOOL BOOKS—Continued.

SURRENNE.—THE STANDARD PRONOUNCING DICTIONARY OF THE FRENCH AND ENGLISH LANGUAGES, in two parts. Part one, French and English; part two, English and French; the first part comprehending words in common use—terms connected with Science—terms belonging to the Fine Arts—4000 Historical names—4000 Geographical names—11,000 terms lately published, with the pronunciation of every word according to the French Academy, and the most eminent Lexicographers and Grammarians; together with 750 Critical Remarks, in which the various methods of pronouncing employed by different authors are investigated and compared with each other. The second part, containing a copious Vocabulary of English words and expressions, with the pronunciations according to Walker. The whole preceded by a practical and comprehensive system of French pronunciation. By Gabriel Surrenne, F.A.S.E., French Teacher in Edinburgh, Corresponding Member of the French Grammatical Society of Paris. One volume, 12mo., nearly 900 pages, neatly bound—$1,50.

"This work must have been one of very great labor, as it is evidently of deep research. We have given it a careful examination, and are perfectly safe in saying, we have never before seen any thing of the kind at all to compare with it. Our space will not permit us give more than this general testimony to its value. Long as the title is, and much as it promises, our examination of the work proves that all the premises are fulfilled, and we think that no student of the French language should, for a moment, hesitate to possess himself of it. Nor, indeed, will it be found less useful to the accomplished French scholar, who will find in it a fund of information which can go where he met with in any one book. Such a work has for a long time been greatly needed, and Mr. Surrenne has supplied the deficiency in a masterly style. We repeat, therefore, our well-digested opinion, that no one in search of a knowledge of the niceties of the French language, should be without it."—*National Magazine for May*, 1846.

TAYLOR.—A MANUAL OF ANCIENT AND MODERN HISTORY; comprising, I. Ancient History, containing the Political History, Geographical Position, and Social State of the Principal Nations of Antiquity, carefully digested from the Ancient Writers, and illustrated by the discoveries of Modern Scholars and Travellers.
II. Modern History, containing the Rise and Progress of the principal European Nations, their Political History, and the Changes in their Social Condition; with a History of the Colonies founded by Europeans. By W. Cooke Taylor, LL. D., of Trinity College, Dublin. Revised, with additions on American History, by C. S. Henry, D.D., Professor of History in the University of N. Y. One handsome vol., 8vo., of 800 pages, $2,25. ☞ For convenience as a class-book, the Ancient or Modern portion can be had in separate volumes.

This Manual of History is fast superseding all other compends, and is already adopted as a text-book in Harvard, Columbia, Yale, New-York, Pennsylvania, and Brown Universities, and several leading Academies.

WARNER.—RUDIMENTAL LESSONS IN MUSIC.
Containing the Primary Instruction requisite for all Beginners in the Art, whether Vocal or Instrumental. By James F. Warner, translator of "Weber's Theory of Musical Composition," "Kübler's Anleitung zum Gesang-Unterrichte," [Boston Academy's Manual,] &c., &c. One vol., 18mo., cloth, 50 cents.

"We do not know how we can do a more substantial service to teachers and scholars in music vocal or instrumental, than by urging them to adopt this volume as a class book. It is full and complete on every topic connected with the subject, clear in its arrangement, and concise in expression. The illustrations are numerous and ingenious, and must prove very valuable aids to the learner, in comprehending the subject, as well as to the teacher in imparting instruction."—*Tribune*

WARNER.—FIRST STEPS IN SINGING.
The Primary Note Reader, or First Steps in Singing at Sight. By James F. Warner. 12mo., 25 cents.

This volume of musical exercises is designed as a supplement to the author's "Rudimental Lessons in Music." The two works, taken together, are intended to furnish the beginner in vocal music, with a complete set of books adapted to his purpose.

WRIGHT.—PRIMARY LESSONS:
In which a Single Letter is first Taught, with its power; then another Letter is Taught in the same manner, and the two combined into a Word—an application of the letters being made in words as fast as they are learned. The words thus learned are arranged into easy sentences, so that the learner is immediately initiated into Reading Lessons. By Albert D. Wright, author of "Analytical Orthography," "Phonological Chart, &c.

www.ingramcontent.com/pod-product-compliance
Lightning Source LLC
Chambersburg PA
CBHW031942290426
44108CB00011B/643